Certification Study Companion Series

The Apress Certification Study Companion Series offers guidance and hands-on practice to support technical and business professionals who are studying for an exam in the pursuit of an industry certification. Professionals worldwide seek to achieve certifications in order to advance in a career role, reinforce knowledge in a specific discipline, or to apply for or change jobs. This series focuses on the most widely taken certification exams in a given field. It is designed to be user friendly, tracking to topics as they appear in a given exam and work alongside other certification material as professionals prepare for their exam.

More information about this series at https://link.springer.com/bookseries/17100.

LPIC-3 Virtualization and Containerization Study Guide

Certification Companion for the LPIC-3 305 Exam

Antonio Vazquez

Apress®

LPIC-3 Virtualization and Containerization Study Guide: Certification Companion for the LPIC-3 305 Exam

Antonio Vazquez
Madrid, Spain

ISBN-13 (pbk): 979-8-8688-1079-4 ISBN-13 (electronic): 979-8-8688-1080-0
https://doi.org/10.1007/979-8-8688-1080-0

Copyright © 2024 by Antonio Vazquez

This work is subject to copyright. All rights are reserved by the Publisher, whether the whole or part of the material is concerned, specifically the rights of translation, reprinting, reuse of illustrations, recitation, broadcasting, reproduction on microfilms or in any other physical way, and transmission or information storage and retrieval, electronic adaptation, computer software, or by similar or dissimilar methodology now known or hereafter developed.

Trademarked names, logos, and images may appear in this book. Rather than use a trademark symbol with every occurrence of a trademarked name, logo, or image we use the names, logos, and images only in an editorial fashion and to the benefit of the trademark owner, with no intention of infringement of the trademark.

The use in this publication of trade names, trademarks, service marks, and similar terms, even if they are not identified as such, is not to be taken as an expression of opinion as to whether or not they are subject to proprietary rights.

While the advice and information in this book are believed to be true and accurate at the date of publication, neither the authors nor the editors nor the publisher can accept any legal responsibility for any errors or omissions that may be made. The publisher makes no warranty, express or implied, with respect to the material contained herein.

>Managing Director, Apress Media LLC: Welmoed Spahr
>Acquisitions Editor: James Robinson-Prior
>Development Editor: James Markham
>Coordinating Editor: Gryffin Winkler

Cover designed by eStudioCalamar

Distributed to the book trade worldwide by Apress Media, LLC, 1 New York Plaza, New York, NY 10004, U.S.A. Phone 1-800-SPRINGER, fax (201) 348-4505, e-mail orders-ny@springer-sbm.com, or visit www.springeronline.com. Apress Media, LLC is a California LLC and the sole member (owner) is Springer Science + Business Media Finance Inc (SSBM Finance Inc). SSBM Finance Inc is a **Delaware** corporation.

For information on translations, please e-mail booktranslations@springernature.com; for reprint, paperback, or audio rights, please e-mail bookpermissions@springernature.com.

Apress titles may be purchased in bulk for academic, corporate, or promotional use. eBook versions and licenses are also available for most titles. For more information, reference our Print and eBook Bulk Sales web page at http://www.apress.com/bulk-sales.

Any source code or other supplementary material referenced by the author in this book is available to readers on GitHub (https://github.com/Apress). For more detailed information, please visit https://www.apress.com/gp/services/source-code.

If disposing of this product, please recycle the paper

This book is dedicated to my wonderful family.

Table of Contents

About the Author xix

About the Technical Reviewer xxi

Acknowledgments xxiii

Introduction xxv

Chapter 1: Virtualization Concepts and Theory 1

Introduction 1

Emulation 2

    Game Console Emulators 3

    Terminal Emulators...4

    Printer Emulators...5

    Network Emulators...6

    System Emulators 6

Simulation 7

Virtualization 7

Types of Virtualization 10

Pros and Cons of Virtualization 11

Migration of Physical to Virtual Machines 12

    VMware Converter 12

    virt-p2v 12

TABLE OF CONTENTS

    openQRM 13

    Clonezilla 13

Migrating Virtual Machines Between Systems 14

Summary 14

Chapter 2: QEMU 15

Introduction to QEMU 16

    Installation on Ubuntu 16

Full System Emulation in QEMU 17

    Emulating an x86 System 18

    Emulating an ARM System 29

    Emulating a SPARC System 34

User Mode Emulation in QEMU 41

QEMU with KVM 45

QEMU Networking 47

    User Networking 48

    Networking by Using TUN/TAP Devices 62

    Creating a Bridge for External Access 68

QEMU Guest Agent 70

QEMU Monitor 76

Other Useful QEMU Options 88

Summary 91

Chapter 3: Xen 93

Xen Architecture 93

Installation and Configuration of Xen 94

    Installing Xen 95

    Configuring Xen 97

    Creating a Logical Volume to Store the Virtual Machines 98

TABLE OF CONTENTS

Creating Virtual Machines 100
    Installing a Virtual Machine by Editing a Configuration File 100
XenStore 130
GRUB Start Options 132
Managing Xen with xl/xm/XAPI 135
Xen Troubleshooting 144
Summary 145

Chapter 4: libvirt Virtual Machine Management 147

Introduction to libvirt 148
Installing libvirt 148
virt-manager 149
    Installing and Managing a Virtual Machine with virt-manager 159
Accessing libvirt from Our Own Programs 177
    Accessing libvirt from a C Program 177
    Accessing libvirt from a Python Program 180
    Migrating a Virtual Machine to Another Host 182
Managing Snapshots 193
Storage Pools and Volumes 197
Networking 201
Monitoring 212
virsh 214
libvirt Configuration Files 219
    libvirt.conf 219
    libvirtd.conf 220
    qemu.conf 222
    virtlogd.conf 223
    virtlockd.conf 223

ix

TABLE OF CONTENTS

dnsmasq 223

radvd 225

Summary 226

Chapter 5: Virtual Machine Disk Image Management 227

Virtual Disk Image Formats 228

    Raw Images 228

    qcow and qcow2 229

    VMDK 230

Managing Disk Images with qemu-img 230

    Getting Information with qemu-img 230

    Creating Disk Image Files with qemu-img 232

    Creating Overlays with qemu-img 233

    Converting Between Different Disk Formats 235

    Basic Usage of VirtualBox to Check the Image Disk File 236

Mounting Partitions and Accessing Files Contained in Virtual Disks 241

    Troubleshooting libguestfs 244

    guestmount/guestunmount 248

    virt-cat 251

    virt-copy-in 254

    virt-copy-out 255

    virt-diff 256

    virt-inspector 257

    virt-filesystems 258

    virt-rescue 259

    virt-df 262

    virt-resize 263

    virt-sparsify 267

virt-p2v	269
virt-v2v	277
virt-sysprep	282
Open Virtualization Format	285
Summary	290

Chapter 6: Proxmox and Open vSwitch 291

Introduction to Proxmox	291
systemd-machined	309
Open vSwitch	313
Summary	318

Chapter 7: Container Virtualization Concepts 319

System Containers and Application Containers	320
Kernel Namespaces	320
Mount Namespaces	323
Process Namespaces	327
User Namespaces	328
Combining Several Namespaces to Craft Our First "Container"	329
Network Namespaces	333
chroot	336
Control Groups	341
Linux Capabilities	345
Security and Containers	353
SELinux	353
AppArmor	359
seccomp	362
Summary	362

TABLE OF CONTENTS

Chapter 8: Linux Containers (LXC) **363**

LXC 363

    Installing LXC 364

    Configuring LXC 365

    LXC in RedHat/Rocky/CentOS 386

    Security in LXC 399

    Other LXC Commands 404

LXD 407

    Creating Our First Container on LXD 412

    Managing Server and Container Configuration 416

    Networking in LXD 419

    Storage in LXD 424

    LXD Profiles 427

    Limiting the Use of Resources on LXD 432

Summary 433

Chapter 9: Docker **435**

Introduction to Docker 435

Installing Docker 436

Docker Images 438

Docker Containers 440

Docker Architecture 445

Docker Volumes 450

    Bind Mounts 453

    Named Volumes 455

    tmpfs Volumes 458

    Sharing Volumes Between Containers 458

    Using Remote Volumes 460

    Deleting and Pruning Volumes 463

xii

Docker Networking 464
    Creating a New Network 467
    Mapping Ports 470
Customizing Our Own Containers 471
    Exporting a Container to an Image 471
    Using a Dockerfile to Create a Container 475
Logging in Docker 482
Saving and Restoring Containers 487
Creating a Local Registry 492
Customizing Security Options 496
Summary 498

Chapter 10: Container Orchestration Platforms 499

Container Orchestration 499
docker compose 500
    Installing docker compose 500
    Creating a Service with docker compose 502
    Creating a Multi-container Service 506
docker swarm 510
    docker swarm Architecture 510
    Initializing a docker swarm Cluster 511
    Adding Additional Nodes to the Swarm Cluster 513
    Deploying Services in docker swarm 515
    Overlay Networks 519
    Constraints 520
    Creating a Global Service 522
    Docker Secrets 523
    Stacks 524

TABLE OF CONTENTS

Kubernetes 527
- Kubernetes Architecture 527
- Installing minikube 529
- Pods 531
- First Steps with minikube 532
- Deploying a Pod in Kubernetes 539
- Replicasets 540
- Deployments 542
- Other Kubernetes-Related Items 546

Helm 546
OpenShift 553
Rancher 557
Summary 563

Chapter 11: podman and Other Container-Related Tools 565

Introduction 565
Open Container Initiative 566
podman 566
- Installing podman 566
- podman Images 567
- podman Containers 569

buildah 571
skopeo 573
FreeBSD Jails 575
rkt 577
OpenVZ 583
Summary 588

xiv

TABLE OF CONTENTS

Chapter 12: Cloud Management Tools 589

Introduction to Cloud Computing 589

OpenStack 592

    First Steps with OpenStack 593

Terraform 613

    Installing Terraform 613

    Terraform Providers 616

    Deploying Our Docker Infrastructure with Terraform 622

Public Clouds 635

    Amazon Web Services 636

    Microsoft Azure 637

    Google Cloud 637

Summary 638

Chapter 13: Packer 641

Introduction to Packer 641

Installing Packer 641

Packer Integrations (Plug-ins) 644

    Installing a Packer Plug-In 645

Building an Image 646

    Building a VirtualBox Image 646

    Building an LXC Image 651

    Automating the Installation of Ubuntu to Generate an
Image with Packer 659

Provisioning with Packer and Integration with vagrant 671

Summary 676

xv

TABLE OF CONTENTS

Chapter 14: cloud-init 677

Introduction to cloud-init 677

Configuring a Local QEMU Instance 678

Instance Metadata Services (IMDS) 686

Datasources 686

    Config Drive 686

Configuring a LXD Container Instance 687

Managing Filesystems with cloud-init 689

Installing Software Packages 692

Summary 694

Chapter 15: vagrant 695

vagrant Architecture 695

Installing vagrant 696

Deploying Our First Virtual Environment with vagrant 701

    Initializing vagrant 702

    vagrant Files 703

    Running a Vagrantfile 704

Working with Different vagrant Environments 707

    Installing Additional vagrant Boxes 709

    Checking the Status of the vagrant Deployments 711

    Searching for vagrant Boxes 712

    Provisioning with vagrant 713

    Port Redirection 717

    Customizing Network Settings 721

Shared Folders in vagrant 724
Managing the State of the VM from vagrant 726
Deploying Multiple Virtual Machines from a Single Vagrantfile 728
Summary 734

Index 735

About the Author

Antonio Vazquez is a Senior Linux System Administrator with over 20 years of experience in the IT field. As an avid champion of FOSS, he has been using Linux for decades, holding many professional certifications including the LPIC-3 certification, RHCE, and many SUSE certifications as well as non-Linux-related topics including cloud and security. Currently, he works for a leader in the aerospace sector, managing the Linux/UNIX infrastructure.

Antonio is also an LPI-approved trainer who teaches students to get LPI certified and also writes books in his spare time.

About the Technical Reviewer

Raul Arias is a professional specialized in systems administration, IT infrastructure, and cloud solutions, with over 20 years of experience in the technology sector. Throughout his career, he has worked with some of the most important companies in the industry, serving in both technical and consulting roles. With extensive training in technologies such as VMware, Citrix, Nutanix, and Microsoft, he has gained comprehensive expertise in the implementation, management, and migration of complex IT environments.

Raul's career stands out for his deep technical knowledge, his ability to manage complex IT environments, and his commitment to continuous improvement through certification and education. He currently continues to contribute his expertise in technological consulting, helping companies implement efficient and secure solutions in the digital era.

Acknowledgments

I'd like to express my gratitude to the people at Apress/Springer Nature; it's always a pleasure working with you. I would also like to thank the Linux Professional Institute for their great job, as well as those who are involved in one way or another in the open source community.

Introduction

It's been about five years since I wrote my book on LPIC-3 300. At that time, I had the feeling that there were too few resources available to study for any of the LPIC-3 certifications. Today, I think that the situation has improved slightly, but I still feel the available resources are scarce. With this book, I attempt to help those studying for the LPIC-3 305 to better understand and develop the skills needed to pass the exam and, more importantly, to put them at work in the real world.

LPI certifications are vendor neutral; however, for practical reasons, I needed to use Ubuntu 22 as the main operating system throughout the book. This choice is due to the fact that Ubuntu is one of the main players in the Linux world, together with Red Hat, SUSE, and others. Despite having used mainly Ubuntu, most of the content you see in this book can be applied to the most popular Linux distributions as well.

The topics covered in the book are based on the official objectives defined by LPI. Always trying to prioritize those topics with a higher weight in the exam. The order of the book is also closely related to the official objectives with small variations for didactic purposes.

If you have any suggestions, opinions, questions, or criticisms about this book, you can contact me via LinkedIn at https://www.linkedin.com/in/antoniojosevazquez/.

CHAPTER 1

Virtualization Concepts and Theory

In this chapter, we'll cover the following concepts:

- Virtualization terminology
- Pros and cons of virtualization
- Variations of hypervisors and virtual machine monitors
- Migration of physical to virtual machines
- Migration of virtual machines between host systems

We will also be introduced to the following terms and utilities: hypervisor, Hardware Virtual Machine (HVM), paravirtualization (PV), emulation and simulation, CPU flags, */proc/cpuinfo*, and migration.

Introduction

When thinking of virtualization, people usually refer to the process of running a virtual (rather than actual) version of a machine. The concept of virtualization, however, can be applied not only to machines but also to storage devices, networks, etc. By using the term "virtualization" with a broad and generic meaning, we can "virtualize" machines in many

CHAPTER 1 VIRTUALIZATION CONCEPTS AND THEORY

different ways, by using software emulation, hardware virtualization, containers, etc. During the course of the book, we'll study the main concepts and we'll see practical examples.

Emulation

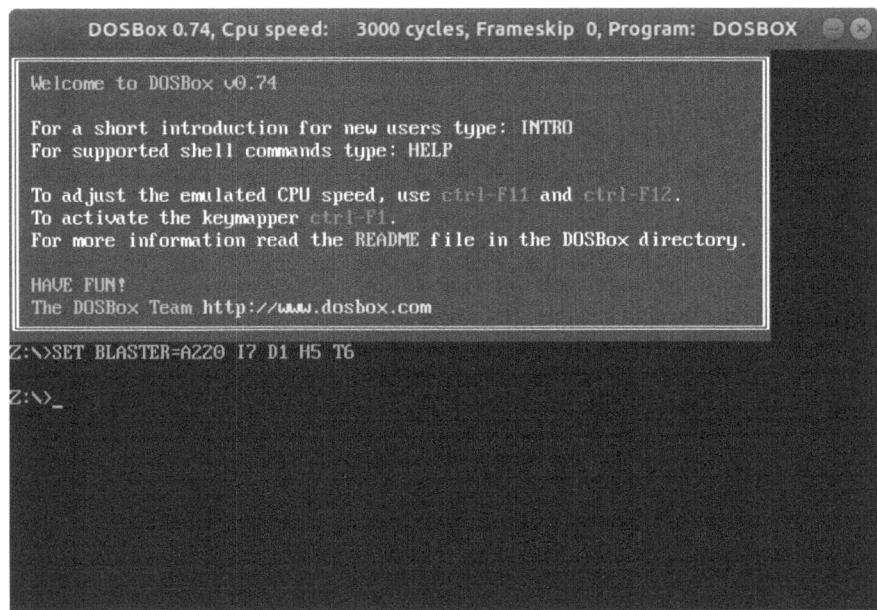

Figure 1-1. *DOSBox*

We can create a "virtual" machine by using software to emulate another system. This has been done, for instance, to emulate classical Z80-based personal computers like Spectrum, Amstrad, Commodore, etc. A well-known emulator is MAME (Multiple Arcade Machine Emulator), used to emulate classical arcade machines. DOSBox (Figure 1-1) is another example of emulator, often used to play old DOS-based games and other programs. Finally, we can mention QEMU (Quick Emulator), which we'll study in detail in Chapter 2.

CHAPTER 1 VIRTUALIZATION CONCEPTS AND THEORY

All these programs use software to emulate the behavior of every hardware component in the original machine. Let's see more in detail what emulation is.

We can define an emulator as a piece of hardware or software that enables a computer system to behave like another. Quite often emulators just emulate a hardware architecture; if some particular firmware or operating system is required, it needs to be provided or emulated as well. Maybe you're familiar with some computer emulator that requires the user to provide some ROM file to work. There are several types of emulator depending on what they're used for. We'll enumerate some of them.

Game Console Emulators

This is the first type of emulator we talked about earlier. There are many emulators for different platforms, for instance, Fuse for Spectrum, Caprice for Amstrad, Retro Virtual Machine for Spectrum and Amstrad (Figure 1-2), PPSSPP for PlayStation Portable, PCSXR for PlayStation 1, and so on.

CHAPTER 1 VIRTUALIZATION CONCEPTS AND THEORY

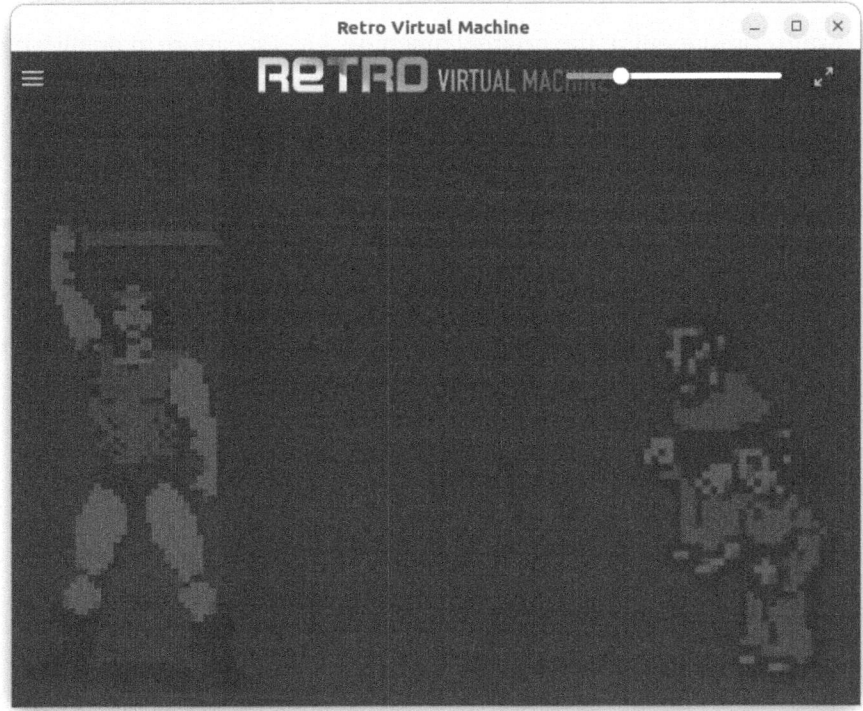

Figure 1-2. *Retro Virtual Machine*

Terminal Emulators

In the old times, it was quite normal having one big mainframe computer and several "dumb" terminals. These terminals consisted only of a keyboard and monitor and connected to the mainframe, which was in charge of performing the actual computing. Nowadays, modern-day computers use terminal emulators to connect remotely to other systems. You're probably familiar with programs like PuTTY (Figure 1-3), a multiplatform terminal emulator.

CHAPTER 1   VIRTUALIZATION CONCEPTS AND THEORY

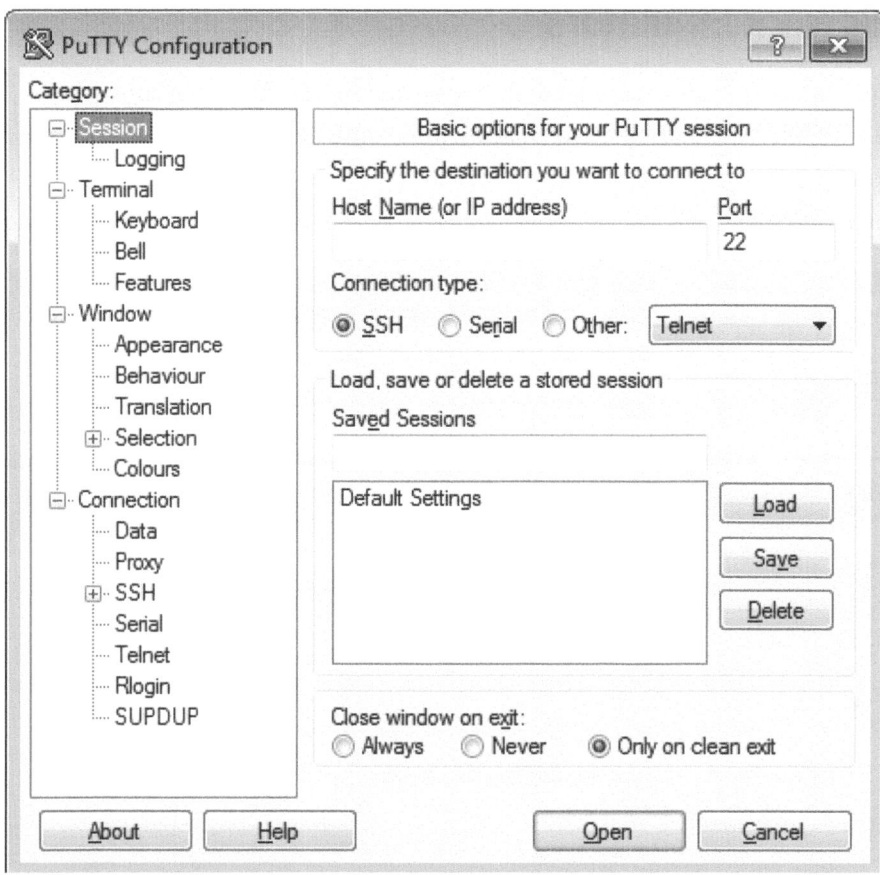

Figure 1-3. *PuTTY*

Printer Emulators

When an application wants to print a document, the application will need to send the proper information to the printer using a *Page Description Language* (PDL). Two of the most used PDLs are Postscript and PCL. The *Printer Command Language* (PCL) was developed by Hewlett Packard. Many printers from different manufacturers use emulation to support PCL language.

CHAPTER 1   VIRTUALIZATION CONCEPTS AND THEORY

Network Emulators

Network emulators are designed to test the performance of applications in a real network. They allow to test routers and switches' configurations. Some of the most well known are GNS3 (Figure 1-4) and Cisco Packet Tracer.

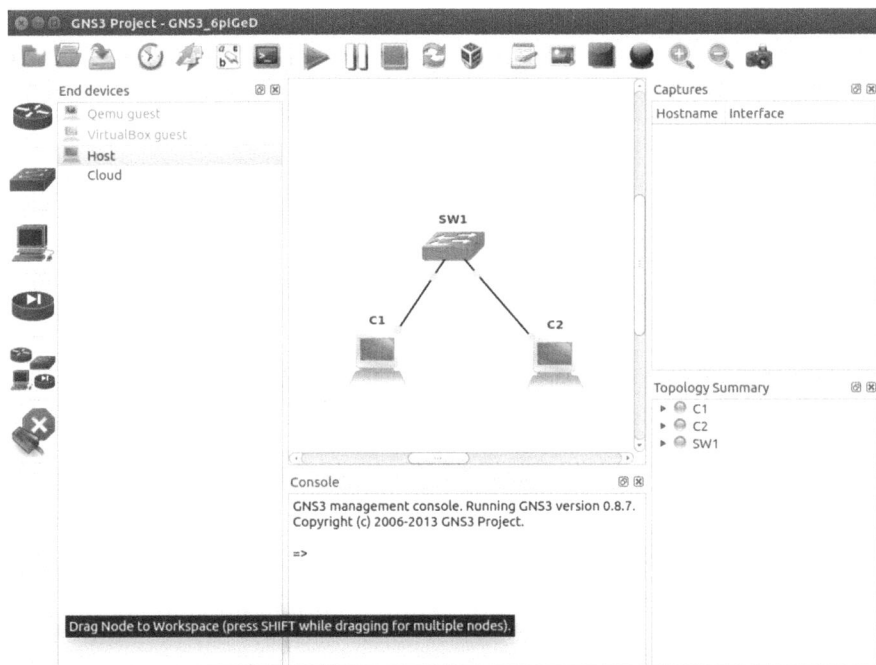

Figure 1-4. GNS3

System Emulators

There are also programs that emulate full systems like QEMU, which we'll discuss in detail in the next chapter, and PearPC. PearPC emulates PowerPC systems on x86 hosts.

Simulation

A concept very similar to **emulation** is **simulation**; although in some cases these two terms are used interchangeably, there are some differences. In a simulator, the main goal is to make the simulator behave as close to the original as possible.

For instance, an emulator could mimic the way another system works but at a higher level, not going into much detail on the low level. On the other hand, a simulator should try to mimic the way the original system works at all levels.

There is also another difference, an emulator is designed with the main goal of providing the same functionality of the original system, but not so on working in the same way as the original system. That is, emulators usually can execute any program designed for the original system. However, as we mentioned before, simulators are more interested in mimicking the way the original system works and less interested in providing the functionality. For that reason, quite often programs designed for the original system perform worse in a simulator or even don't work at all.

Virtualization

As we said before, initially "virtual" machines were implemented only by the use of software, but soon Intel and AMD included in their processors new extensions called Intel VT-x and AMD-V, respectively. This hardware-assisted virtualization offers a better performance than a software-only solution. In a Linux system, we can check the */proc/cpuinfo* file to see the characteristics of the processor: speed, model, CPU flags, etc. If the processor supports hardware-assisted virtualization, the corresponding flag will be present.

CHAPTER 1 VIRTUALIZATION CONCEPTS AND THEORY

If we have an Intel CPU, we'll look for the vmx flag.

antonio@antonio-HP:~$ grep vmx /proc/cpuinfo

.
.
.

flags   : .... vmx ....

And if we have an AMD CPU, it is the svm flag we should search for.

antonio@antonio-Aspire-A315-23:~$ grep svm /proc/cpuinfo

.
.
.

flags   : .... svm ....

We could get more or less the same information with the **lscpu** command.

```
antonio@antonio-HP:~$ lscpu
Architecture:         x86_64
.
.
.
Virtualization:       VT-x
.
.
.
Flags:                .......vmx.......
antonio@antonio-HP:~$

antonio@antonio-Aspire-A315-23:~$ lscpu
Architecture:         x86_64
```

```
CPU op-mode(s):        32-bit, 64-bit
 .
 .
 .
Virtualization:        AMD-V
 .
 .
 .
Flags:                 .......svm.......
antonio@antonio-Aspire-A315-23:~$
```

When a system has a CPU with these flags enabled, it can easily execute virtual machines. The piece of software that hosts the virtual machines is called the **hypervisor**. Sometimes, instead of the term hypervisor, the term **virtual machine monitor** is used. In this case, we can properly talk about "virtualization."

The hypervisor manages the virtual machines, assigning the resources they need to operate normally. There are two different types of hypervisors:

- Type I hypervisor, also known as "bare-metal" hypervisor: In this case, the hypervisor runs directly on the system hardware. Examples of this type of hypervisor are VMware ESXi, Microsoft Hyper-V, or Xen.

- Type II hypervisor: These hypervisors run as an application on the operating system. A few examples are VMware Workstation, Oracle VirtualBox (Figure 1-5), or Microsoft Virtual PC.

CHAPTER 1   VIRTUALIZATION CONCEPTS AND THEORY

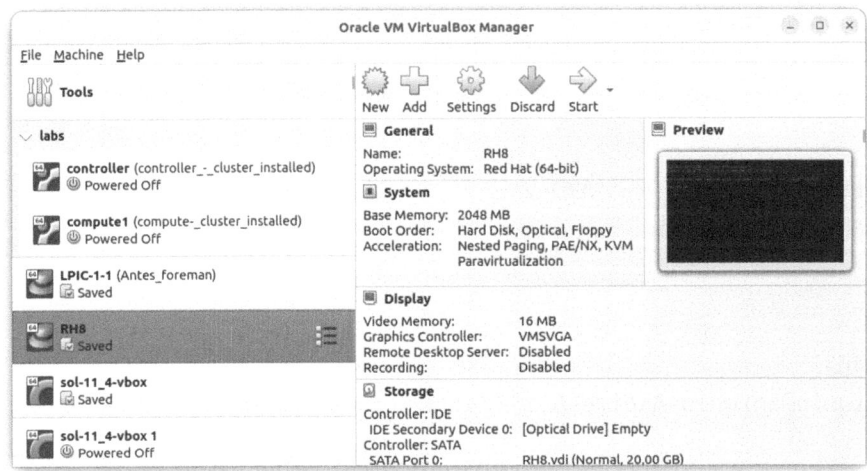

Figure 1-5. *Oracle VirtualBox*

Types of Virtualization

We have seen previously that we can talk about "virtualization" in a broad sense, which includes software emulation and simulation. But we should only talk properly about "virtualization" when hardware virtualization is present.

From this starting point, we can differentiate many types of virtualization depending on the criteria used. Initially we can enumerate these two types of virtualization:

- Full virtualization: The hypervisor recreates almost every component of the original system, making it possible for the guest OS to run unmodified.

- Paravirtualization: Access to hardware resources is offered through a special interface. This is more efficient because the hypervisor doesn't need to perform many high-cost operations needed in full

10

virtualization. However, the guest operating system needs to be modified so that it can be executed in a paravirtualized environment.

There are also other solutions that combine characteristics of full virtualization and paravirtualization, like PVHVM or PVH. As this is an introductory, we won't go into much detail, but we'll see these other virtualization types in Chapter 3.

When using paravirtualization, we'll talk about paravirtualized virtual machines. And when using full virtualization, we'll talk about Hardware Virtual Machines, or HVM.

We should also mention here another concept, **OS-level virtualization**. In this case, the kernel allows multiple user space instances to exist completely isolated. These instances are usually named **containers** in Linux environments, although different terms are also used for the same concept in other operating systems, like jails in FreeBSD or zones in Solaris.

Pros and Cons of Virtualization

Using virtualization has many advantages. We can enumerate the following:

- Cost efficiency: The hardware is much more efficiently used; we no longer need a dedicated physical server for every logical server.

- Easier administration: By using virtualization, we can use snapshots to revert back changes when needed; we can also automate many tasks by using orchestration.

- Efficient use of energy: By using less hardware, less energy is needed, which in turn reduces costs.

Unfortunately, there are also a few drawbacks that we need to know about when considering virtualization:

- Not all software and/or hardware can be easily virtualized.
- Hardware access is indirect and consequently less efficient.

Migration of Physical to Virtual Machines

Virtualizing an existing physical machine, we can benefit from the advantages of virtualization. Simplifying back up and restore operations. This procedure is often referred to as Physical to Virtual migration or P2V for short. There are different tools we can use for P2V. We'll enumerate just a few of them.

VMware Converter

One of the most used tools to perform P2V migrations nowadays is VMware stand-alone converter. This is a commercial tool very easy to use.

virt-p2v

virt-p2v converts a physical machine into a virtual machine managed by KVM. Later in this book, we'll study KVM and this tool with some more detail and see an example.

openQRM

openQRM is a management platform for heterogeneous data center infrastructures with many interesting capabilities, among them P2V and V2V conversions.

Clonezilla

Another possibility, although not as easy as those we've seen previously, is to clone the disk of the server we plan to virtualize. A very good tool that we can use for this purpose is Clonezilla (Figure 1-6). Later we should convert the disk image file to a format recognized by the hypervisor we use. We can see a complete example at their official website.

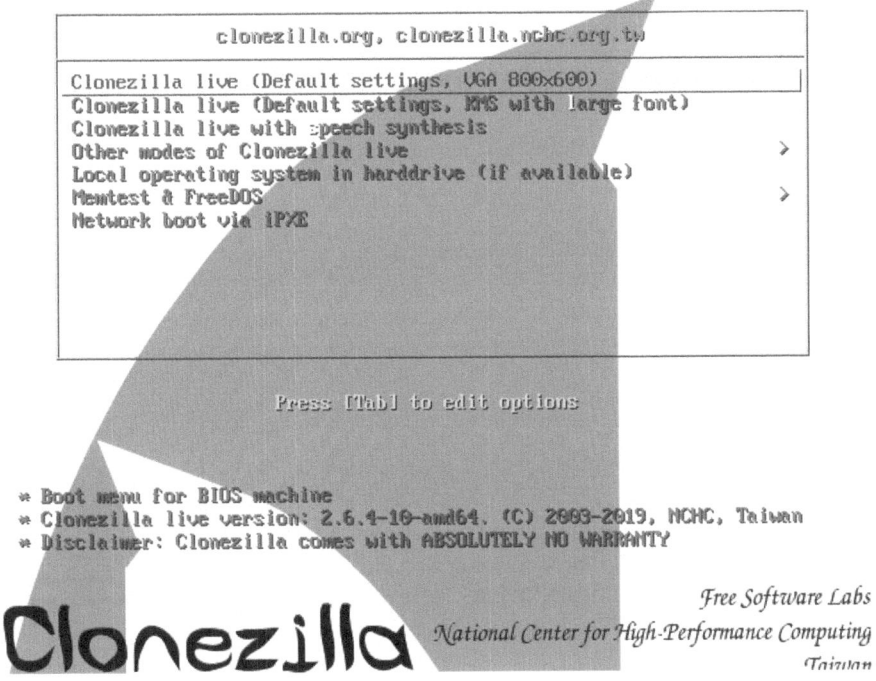

Figure 1-6. Booting Clonezilla Live

CHAPTER 1 VIRTUALIZATION CONCEPTS AND THEORY

Migrating Virtual Machines Between Systems

In addition to converting physical machines into virtual machines, sometimes we might need to migrate virtual machines from a certain hypervisor to another; this is called V2V for short. We'll see in the upcoming chapters several practical examples.

Summary

In this brief chapter, we've studied some theoretical concepts that will help us to better understand the upcoming sections of this book.

CHAPTER 2

QEMU

In this chapter, we'll see a brief introduction to some of the characteristics of QEMU, a great emulation software that can also be used in addition to a hypervisor to provide hardware virtualization. But QEMU has also much more to offer.

In this chapter, we'll cover the following concepts:

- Understand the architecture of QEMU, including KVM, networking, and storage
- Start QEMU instances from the command line
- Manage snapshots using the QEMU monitor
- Install the QEMU Guest Agent and VirtIO device drivers
- Troubleshoot QEMU installations, including networking and storage
- Awareness of important QEMU configuration parameters

We will also be introduced to the following terms and utilities: kernel modules (kvm, kvm-intel, and kvm-amd), */dev/kvm*, QEMU monitor, QEMU, qemu-system-x86, ip, brctl, and tunctl.

CHAPTER 2   QEMU

Introduction to QEMU

QEMU (Quick Emulator) is an open source emulator and virtualizer. This great tool can perform full system emulation and user mode emulation and even run KVM or Xen virtual machines with near-native performance. We'll see these points in detail later.

Installation on Ubuntu

The installation of QEMU is very easy. We can search for the QEMU packages with apt.

antonio@antonio-Laptop:~$ apt search qemu

And we'll see a lot of related packages. We just said before that QEMU can work in two modes: full system emulation and user mode emulation. In the listing of QEMU-related packages, we can see the following items:

qemu-system-x86/jammy-updates,now 1:6.2+dfsg-2ubuntu6.19 amd64 [installed]
  QEMU full system emulation binaries (x86)
qemu-system-arm/jammy-updates,now 1:6.2+dfsg-2ubuntu6.19 amd64 [installed,automatic]
  QEMU full system emulation binaries (arm)

As the name implies, these two packages will allow us to emulate x86 and arm systems, respectively. In this same listing, we can also find this line:

qemu-user/jammy-updates,now 1:6.2+dfsg-2ubuntu6.19 amd64 [installed]
  QEMU user mode emulation binaries

This is the package used for user mode emulation. In my case, the packages appear as "installed" because I installed them previously. The installation procedure is the usual in Ubuntu.

```
antonio@antonio-Laptop:~$ sudo apt install qemu-system-x86
.
.
.
antonio@antonio-Laptop:~$ sudo apt install qemu-user
```

Full System Emulation in QEMU

As we mentioned before, QEMU can emulate a full system, including a processor and various peripherals. QEMU can emulate not only the x86 architecture but also many others such as arm, PowerPC, s390, or SPARC. After installing the right software package for the architecture we want to emulate, we can see there are a lot of **qemu-system-xxx** commands:

```
antonio@antonio-Laptop:~$ qemu-system-[TAB][TAB]
qemu-system-aarch64         qemu-system-ppc64
qemu-system-alpha           qemu-system-ppc64le
qemu-system-arm             qemu-system-riscv32
qemu-system-avr             qemu-system-riscv64
qemu-system-cris            qemu-system-rx
qemu-system-hppa            qemu-system-s390x
qemu-system-i386            qemu-system-sh4
qemu-system-m68k            qemu-system-sh4eb
qemu-system-microblaze      qemu-system-sparc
qemu-system-microblazeel    qemu-system-sparc64
qemu-system-mips            qemu-system-tricore
qemu-system-mips64          qemu-system-x86_64
```

```
qemu-system-mips64el      qemu-system-x86_64-microvm
qemu-system-mipsel        qemu-system-x86_64-spice
qemu-system-nios2         qemu-system-xtensa
qemu-system-or1k          qemu-system-xtensaeb
qemu-system-ppc
```

We'll see a couple of examples in which we will emulate an x86 and a SPARC system.

Emulating an x86 System

We'll work in this case in an Ubuntu 22 workstation, but the procedure is similar in other Linux distributions. We already installed the software so we're ready to start working with it.

The main command to launch the emulation is **qemu-system-*(architecture-type)***, for example, **qemu-system-x86_64**. If we take a look at the help (qemu-system-x86_64 help), we'll see a brief description of all the options available. This list can be overwhelmingly exhaustive at first, so we'll see step by step the most important ones. We start by launching the command without any parameters, so that the default values are applied.

```
antonio@antonio-Laptop:~$ qemu-system-x86_64
```

We'll see immediately a new window (Figure 2-1).

CHAPTER 2 QEMU

```
Booting from DVD/CD...
Boot failed: Could not read from CDROM (code 0003)
Booting from ROM...
iPXE (PCI 00:03.0) starting execution...ok
iPXE initialising devices...ok


iPXE 1.21.1+git-20220113.fbbdc3926-0ubuntu1 -- Open Source Network Boot Firmware
-- https://ipxe.org
Features: DNS HTTP HTTPS iSCSI NFS TFTP VLAN AoE ELF MBOOT PXE bzImage Menu PXEX
T
net0: 52:54:00:12:34:56 using 82540em on 0000:00:03.0 (Ethernet) [open]
  [Link:up, TX:0 TXE:0 RX:0 RXE:0]
Configuring (net0 52:54:00:12:34:56)...... ok
net0: 10.0.2.15/255.255.255.0 gw 10.0.2.2
net0: fec0::5054:ff:fe12:3456/64 gw fe80::2
net0: fe80::5054:ff:fe12:3456/64
Nothing to boot: No such file or directory (https://ipxe.org/2d03e13b)
No more network devices

No bootable device.
```

Figure 2-1. *QEMU VM with no BOOT device*

We see a clear message that says that there is no boot device. In this example, we'll tell QEMU to boot from a Debian 10 ISO file that we downloaded previously from the official Debian website. If we check the command help, we'll see these two relevant entries:

antonio@antonio-Laptop:~$ qemu-system-x86_64 --help
QEMU emulator version 6.2.0 (Debian 1:6.2+dfsg-2ubuntu6.19)

.

.

.

-boot [order=drives][,once=drives][,menu=on|off]
      [,splash=sp_name][,splash-time=sp_time][,reboot-
      timeout=rb_time][,strict=on|off]
                'drives': floppy (a), hard disk (c), CD-ROM
                (d), network (n)
                'sp_name': the file's name that would be passed
                to bios as logo picture, if menu=on

19

CHAPTER 2 QEMU

```
               'sp_time': the period that splash picture last
               if menu=on, unit is ms
               'rb_timeout': the timeout before guest reboot
               when boot failed, unit is ms
```
-
-
-

```
-cdrom file    use 'file' as IDE cdrom image (cdrom is
ide1 master)
```
-
-
-

We see how easy it is to use an ISO file as a virtual CDROM. The **-boot** parameter has many options to choose from, but for now, we only need to specify the boot device, in our case the CDROM, that is, the "-d" option. We launch the command again with the new options.

```
antonio@antonio-Laptop:~$ qemu-system-x86_64 -cdrom
antonio/isos/debian-12.5.0-amd64-DVD-1.iso -boot d
```

This time we'll see the installation menu (Figure 2-2). However, if we choose to perform a graphical installation, the program hangs with a black window without showing any error message. To try and get more information about what's going on, we'll close the window and relaunch **QEMU**, but this time we'll select the "Install" option to perform a text install.

CHAPTER 2 QEMU

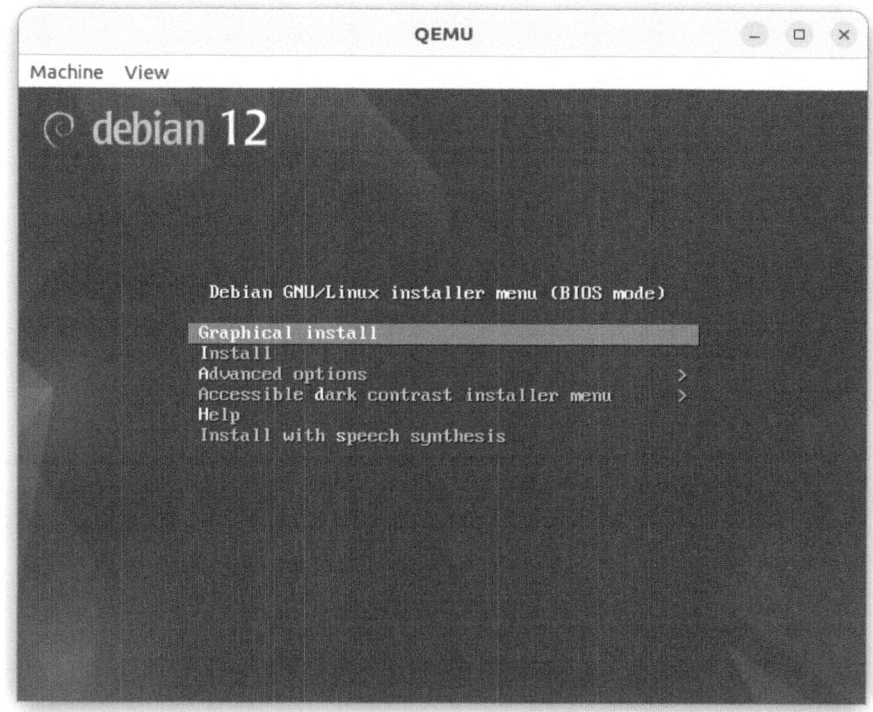

Figure 2-2. *Installation menu*

This time we'll see an error when creating the initramfs file (Figure 2-3).

21

CHAPTER 2　QEMU

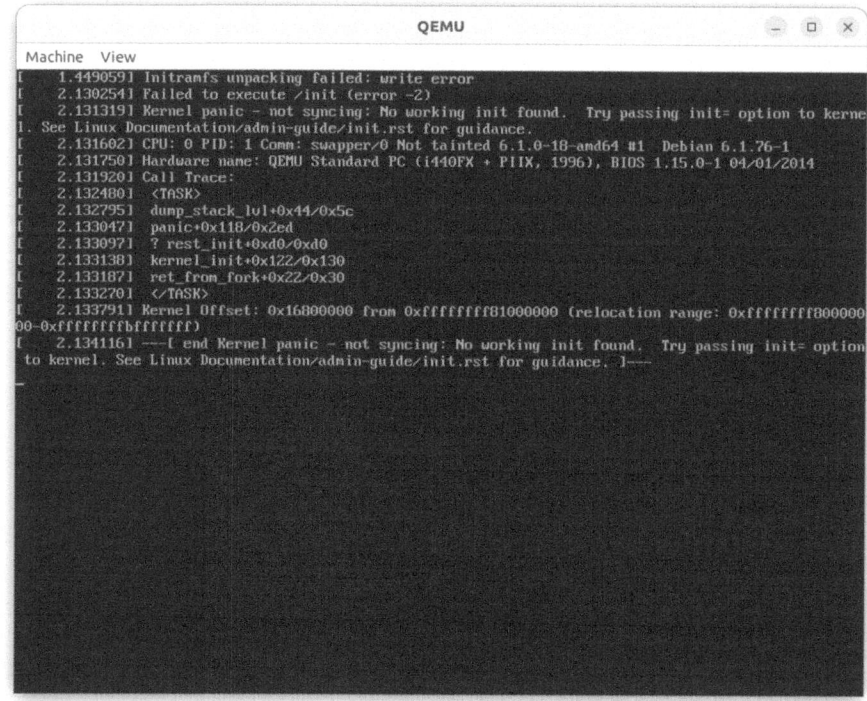

Figure 2-3. *Error when creating the initramfs file*

The initramfs file is an in-memory filesystem used during the Linux startup procedure. As it uses RAM memory, the first thing we need to do is to check the amount of RAM available when we launch **QEMU**. We can do it by using the QEMU monitor; this is something that we'll see in more detail later in this same chapter, but for now, we can access it by pressing CTRL+ALT and then SHIFT and 2 (Figure 2-4).

CHAPTER 2 QEMU

Figure 2-4. *QEMU monitor*

Later we'll review some interesting features of the QEMU monitor; for now, we'll use it to check the amount of memory available for the virtual machine with the **info memory_size_summary** command (Figure 2-5).

23

CHAPTER 2   QEMU

Figure 2-5. *RAM memory available with the QEMU monitor*

The number we see on the screen is the amount of memory in bytes, 134217728 in this case, which is 134217728/(1024*1024)=128 MiB. In this day and age, this value is extremely low, so we're going to increase that value when launching QEMU again.

We'll take a new look at the contextual help, and we'll see this option:

```
-m [size=]megs[,slots=n,maxmem=size]
            configure guest RAM
            size: initial amount of guest memory
            slots: number of hotplug slots (default: none)
            maxmem: maximum amount of guest memory
            (default: none)
```

24

CHAPTER 2   QEMU

So we'll use the -m parameter to launch QEMU again, this time with 2 MiB RAM.

antonio@antonio-Laptop:~$ qemu-system-x86_64 -m 2048 -cdrom \
antonio/isos/debian-12.5.0-amd64-DVD-1.iso -boot d

In this occasion, after selecting "Graphical install", we can see that the installation program actually starts (Figure 2-6).

Figure 2-6. *Graphical install*

We'll choose our language and then click "Continue" to resume the installation. We'll select the appropriate settings, country, keyboard layout, etc. We're not going to describe here the full installation procedure as you've probably already installed several Linux systems.

CHAPTER 2   QEMU

At some point, we'll get to a new screen, in which we're informed that no disk drive was detected (Figure 2-7). This is perfectly normal, as we haven't specified any hard disk drive when launching QEMU. We'll cancel the installation at this point.

Figure 2-7. *No disk drive detected*

We need to define the disk that will be used by the QEMU virtual machine. If we check again the help of the **qemu-system-x86_64** command, we'll see this in the first lines:

```
antonio@antonio-Laptop:~$ qemu-system-x86_64 --help
QEMU emulator version 6.2.0 (Debian 1:6.2+dfsg-2ubuntu6.19)
```

```
Copyright (c) 2003-2021 Fabrice Bellard and the QEMU Project
developers
usage: qemu-system-x86_64 [options] [disk_image]

'disk_image' is a raw hard disk image for IDE hard disk 0
·
·
·
```

We need to pass the name of a disk image to the command, and this disk image will be assigned to the IDE hard disk 0. Of course this can be customized with advanced options, but for now, it fits our needs. Now we just need to create the disk image.

Disk images in QEMU are created with the **qemu-img** command. Again, if we check the command help, we'll see a long list of options. This command includes many subcommands. Later in this book, we'll study this tool in more detail. Right now we only need to create a new disk image, so this is the subcommand that we need to look at:

```
antonio@antonio-Laptop:~$ qemu-img --help
qemu-img version 6.2.0 (Debian 1:6.2+dfsg-2ubuntu6.19)
Copyright (c) 2003-2021 Fabrice Bellard and the QEMU Project
developers
usage: qemu-img [standard options] command [command options]
QEMU disk image utility
·
·
·
  create [--object objectdef] [-q] [-f fmt] [-b backing_file]
  [-F backing_fmt] [-u] [-o options] filename [size]
·
·
·
```

We'll create a 10 GB image, and we'll use the qcow2 format (-f parameter), as recommended in the official documentation.

```
antonio@antonio-Laptop:~$ mkdir QEMU_VMs
antonio@antonio-Laptop:~$ cd QEMU_VMs/
antonio@antonio-Laptop:~/QEMU_VMs$ qemu-img create -f qcow2 debian.qcow2 10G
Formatting 'debian.qcow2', fmt=qcow2 cluster_size=65536 extended_l2=off compression_type=zlib size=10737418240 lazy_refcounts=off refcount_bits=16
antonio@antonio-Laptop:~/QEMU_VMs
```

We can finally relaunch QEMU with all the needed parameters to finish the installation of the operating system.

```
antonio@antonio-Laptop:~/QEMU_VMs$ qemu-system-x86_64
\> -m 2048 \
> -cdrom ../antonio/isos/debian-12.5.0-amd64-DVD-1.iso
\> -boot d debian.qcow2
```

We'll select "Graphical install" and complete the installation process as we'd do on any physical system. The process can take some time as the default emulation is significantly slower than native performance. When the installation finishes, we can launch QEMU again and boot from the disk this time:

```
antonio@antonio-Laptop:~/QEMU_VMs$ qemu-system-x86_64 -m 2048
\> -boot c debian.qcow2
```

And we'll see the login screen of our newly installed server (Figure 2-8).

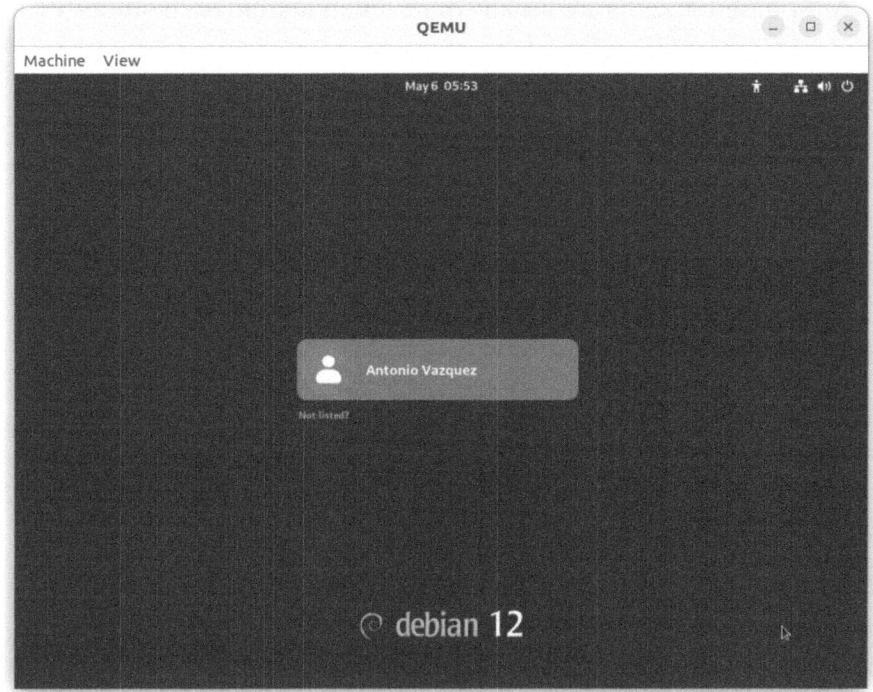

Figure 2-8. Debian 12 graphical login

Emulating an ARM System

As we said before, QEMU can emulate different architectures. In this example, we'll emulate an ARM system. This architecture is used in several light and portable devices like mobile phones and single board computers such as the Raspberry Pi.

To emulate an ARM system, first of all, we'll install the **qemu-system-arm** package.

```
antonio@antonio-Laptop:~$ sudo apt install qemu-system-arm
```

CHAPTER 2 QEMU

ARM-based systems are usually quite different from each other, much more than systems based on x86 architectures. So installing a complete OS in a QEMU instance emulating an ARM system would be possible, but complicated and slow. Fortunately QEMU offers the possibility of using "direct kernel loading," that is, launching the kernel directly from the command line by using a kernel file previously downloaded instead of having to emulate all the boot process from the virtual disk.

To do this, we need an appropriate kernel. Luckily somebody has already done this, and we can simply download it from the Debian site.

```
antonio@antonio-Laptop:~/QEMU_VMs$ wget https://people.debian.
org/~aurel32/qemu/armel/vmlinuz-2.6.32-5-versatile
--2024-05-06 22:46:49--  https://people.debian.org/~aurel32/
qemu/armel/vmlinuz-2.6.32-5-versatile
Resolving people.debian.org (people.debian.org)...
209.87.16.67, 2607:f8f0:614:1::1274:67
Connecting to people.debian.org (people.debian.
org)|209.87.16.67|:443... connected.
HTTP request sent, awaiting response... 200 OK
Length: 1248532 (1,2M)
Saving to: 'vmlinuz-2.6.32-5-versatile'

vmlinuz-2.6.32-5-versatile
100%[========>]   1,19M   438KB/s    in 2,8s

2024-05-06 22:46:53 (438 KB/s) - 'vmlinuz-2.6.32-5-versatile'
saved [1248532/1248532]
```

We'll also download the corresponding **initrd** file.

```
antonio@antonio-Laptop:~/QEMU_VMs$ wget https://people.debian.
org/~aurel32/qemu/armel/initrd.img-2.6.32-5-versatile
--2024-05-06 22:59:42--  https://people.debian.org/~aurel32/
qemu/armel/initrd.img-2.6.32-5-versatile
```

CHAPTER 2   QEMU

```
Resolving people.debian.org (people.debian.org)...
209.87.16.67, 2607:f8f0:614:1::1274:67
Connecting to people.debian.org (people.debian.org)
|209.87.16.67|:443... connected.
HTTP request sent, awaiting response... 200 OK
Length: 2500152 (2,4M)
Saving to: 'initrd.img-2.6.32-5-versatile'

initrd.img-2.6.32-5-versatile
100%[============>]   2,38M   605KB/s    in 4,0s

2024-05-06 22:59:48 (605 KB/s) - 'initrd.img-2.6.32-5-
versatile' saved [2500152/2500152]
```

Finally, we download the disk image.

```
antonio@antonio-Laptop:~/QEMU_VMs$ wget https://people.debian.
org/~aurel32/qemu/armel/debian_squeeze_armel_standard.qcow2
--2024-05-07 05:50:30--  https://people.debian.org/~aurel32/
qemu/armel/debian_squeeze_armel_standard.qcow2
Resolving people.debian.org (people.debian.org)...
209.87.16.67, 2607:f8f0:614:1::1274:67
Connecting to people.debian.org (people.debian.org)
|209.87.16.67|:443... connected.
HTTP request sent, awaiting response... 200 OK
Length: 236730880 (226M)
Saving to: 'debian_squeeze_armel_standard.qcow2'

debian_squeeze_armel_standard.qc
100%[========================>] 225,76M  17,0MB/s    in 22s

2024-05-07 05:50:54 (10,4 MB/s) - 'debian_squeeze_armel_
standard.qcow2' saved [236730880/236730880]
```

31

CHAPTER 2 QEMU

We launch now our ARM-based Debian.

antonio@antonio-Laptop:~/QEMU_VMs$ qemu-system-arm -M versatilepb -kernel vmlinuz-2.6.32-5-versatile -initrd initrd.img-2.6.32-5-versatile debian_squeeze_armel_standard.qcow2 -append "root=/dev/sda1"

We'll review briefly the parameters used. We specify the machine type "-M versatilepb". We can obtain a list of the emulated machines with the **qemu-system-arm -machine help** command.

```
antonio@antonio-Laptop:~/QEMU_VMs$ qemu-system-arm
-machine help
Supported machines are:
akita                Sharp SL-C1000 (Akita) PDA (PXA270)
.
.
.
raspi0               Raspberry Pi Zero (revision 1.2)
raspi1ap             Raspberry Pi A+ (revision 1.1)
raspi2b              Raspberry Pi 2B (revision 1.1)
.
.
.
versatileab          ARM Versatile/AB (ARM926EJ-S)
versatilepb          ARM Versatile/PB (ARM926EJ-S)
.
.
.
```

We also pass the location of the kernel file (-kernel option) and the initrd file (-initrd option). Finally, we specify the name of the disk file and the kernel command line used (-append option).

When the system boots, we'll see the login screen (Figure 2-9). The default credentials are "root/root". We can interact with our system in the same way as if we were working on an x86-based Debian (Figure 2-10).

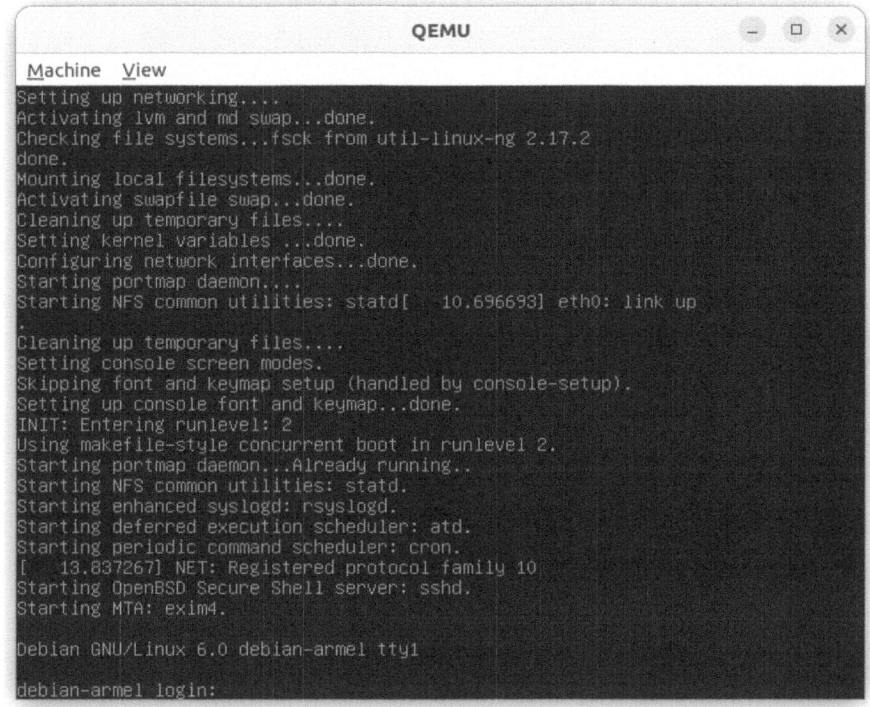

***Figure 2-9.** Emulating an ARM system (I)*

CHAPTER 2 QEMU

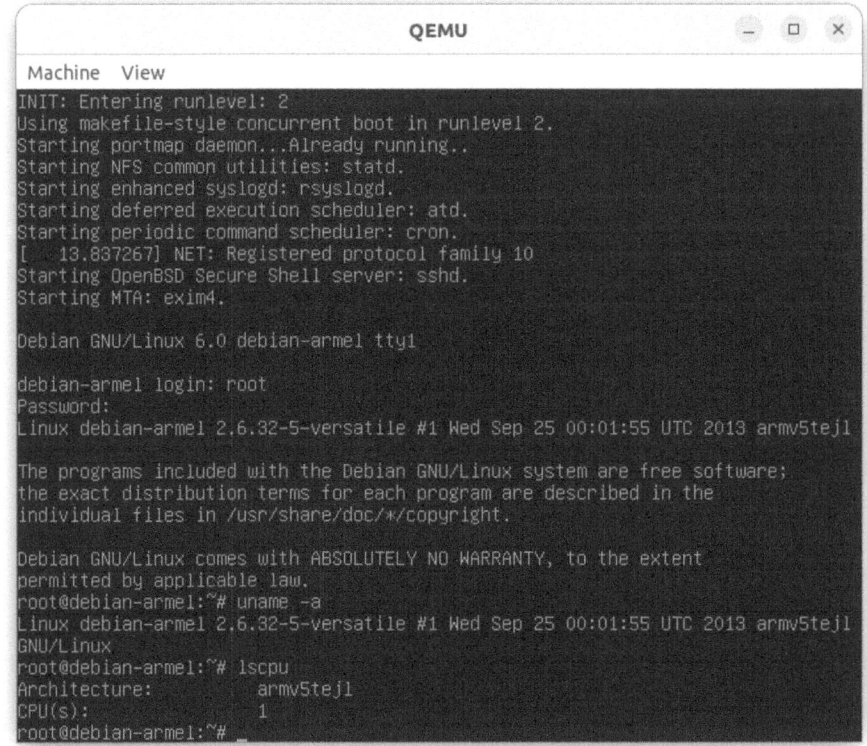

Figure 2-10. Emulating an ARM system (II)

Emulating a SPARC System

SPARC (Scalable Processor ARChitecture) was developed by Sun Microsystems. It is used mainly as the hardware platform for Solaris servers, but it supports other operating systems as well, such as Linux and FreeBSD.

Similarly to what we did before, we need to install the corresponding package.

antonio@antonio-Laptop:~$ sudo apt install qemu-system-sparc

CHAPTER 2 QEMU

After installing the package, we have two commands available: **qemu-system-sparc** and **qemu-system-sparc64**. As we did when we emulated an ARM device, we can list the machines that can be emulated.

```
antonio@antonio-Laptop:~$ qemu-system-sparc -M help
Supported machines are:
LX                   Sun4m platform, SPARCstation LX
SPARCClassic         Sun4m platform, SPARCClassic
SPARCbook            Sun4m platform, SPARCbook
SS-10                Sun4m platform, SPARCstation 10
SS-20                Sun4m platform, SPARCstation 20
SS-4                 Sun4m platform, SPARCstation 4
SS-5                 Sun4m platform, SPARCstation 5 (default)
SS-600MP             Sun4m platform, SPARCserver 600MP
Voyager              Sun4m platform, SPARCstation Voyager
leon3_generic        Leon-3 generic
none                 empty machine
antonio@antonio-Laptop:~$ qemu-system-sparc64 -M help
Supported machines are:
niagara              Sun4v platform, Niagara
none                 empty machine
sun4u                Sun4u platform (default)
sun4v                Sun4v platform
```

We can get an overview of how to emulate a SPARC system on the wiki page. In the first example, we see this:

```
qemu-system-sparc \
  -drive file=hd.qcow2,if=scsi,bus=0,unit=0,media=disk \
  -drive file=cdrom.iso,format=raw,if=scsi,bus=0,unit=2,
  media=cdrom,readonly=on \
  -boot d
```

35

CHAPTER 2 QEMU

We see some new options and others that we saw previously. We're launching QEMU specifying a CDROM and a hard disk. We did the same thing when we emulated an x86_64 system, but this time the syntax is different. The **-device** parameter is very versatile, and we can use it to specify many more options, such as the file used, the interface, the bus, and so on. In this example, we're using it to define a hard disk and a CDROM drive, but we can use this same parameter to define all sorts of devices like network cards. Finally, we see the **-boot** option that we already know.

We'll create a qcow2 file that will be the hard disk used by QEMU. As we already know, we can use **qemu-img** to create this file.

```
antonio@antonio-Laptop:~/QEMU_VMs$ qemu-img create \
> -f qcow2 sparchd.qcow2 10
Formatting 'sparchd.qcow2', fmt=qcow2 cluster_size=65536 extended_l2=off compression_type=zlib size=10 lazy_refcounts=off refcount_bits=16
```

If we have an installation CD image, we can launch QEMU to emulate a SPARC system like this:

```
antonio@antonio-Laptop:~/QEMU_VMs$ qemu-system-sparc \
> -drive file=sparchd.qcow2,if=scsi,bus=0,unit=0,media=disk \
> -drive file=CD.iso,format=raw,if=scsi,bus=0,unit=2,media=cdrom,readonly=on \
> -boot d
```

After a couple of minutes, we'll see an installation screen (Figure 2-11).

CHAPTER 2 QEMU

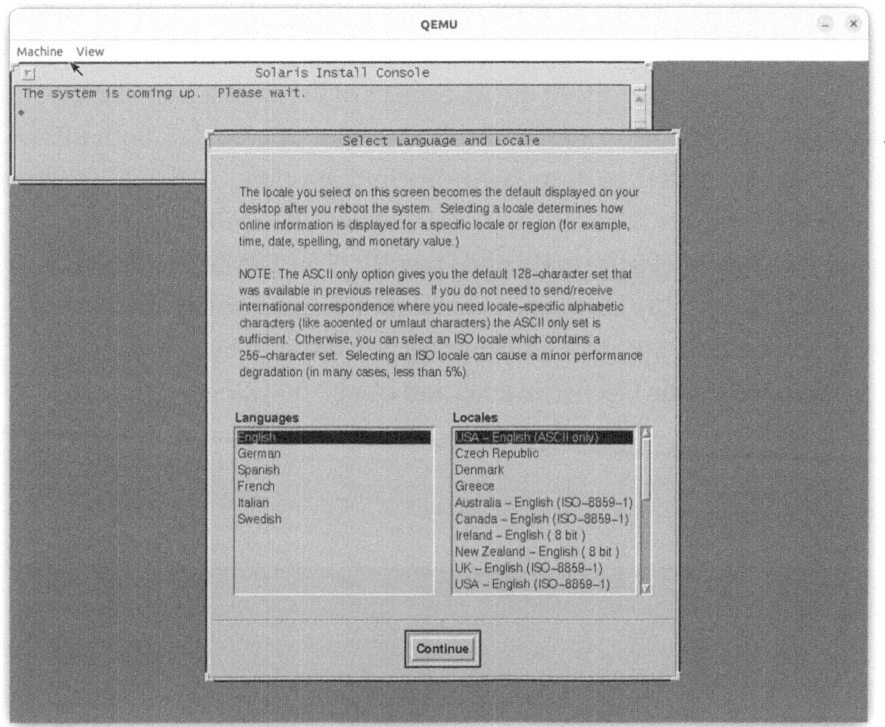

Figure 2-11. *Installing a Solaris box*

We won't install the OS now because it's not the purpose of this book, but you can see a complete example of how to emulate an old SPARC workstation here.

We can also emulate more advanced SPARC processors like UltraSPARC T1 (codename niagara). If we remember, one of the machine types that is supported by **qemu-system-sparc64** is niagara. Let's try to launch a new QEMU instance with this machine type.

antonio@antonio-Laptop:~/QEMU_VMs$ qemu-system-sparc64 -M niagara
Could not open option rom 'nvram1': No such file or directory
qemu-system-sparc64: Unable to load a firmware for -M niagara

37

CHAPTER 2   QEMU

As we can see, we get an error message because QEMU couldn't load a firmware for this machine. As you know, x86-based systems have a BIOS/UEFI that takes care of one of the first stages of the system boot. SPARC-based systems also use a similar firmware called OpenBOOT. Both BIOS/UEFI and OpenBOOT perform hardware initialization.

QEMU uses free firmware implementations like SeaBIOS for x86 emulated systems (Figure 2-12) and OpenBIOS for SPARC emulated systems (Figure 2-13). However, to emulate a niagara system, we'll need another specific firmware. This firmware was released by Sun under the GNU General Public License in 2005 and can be downloaded from this Oracle site.

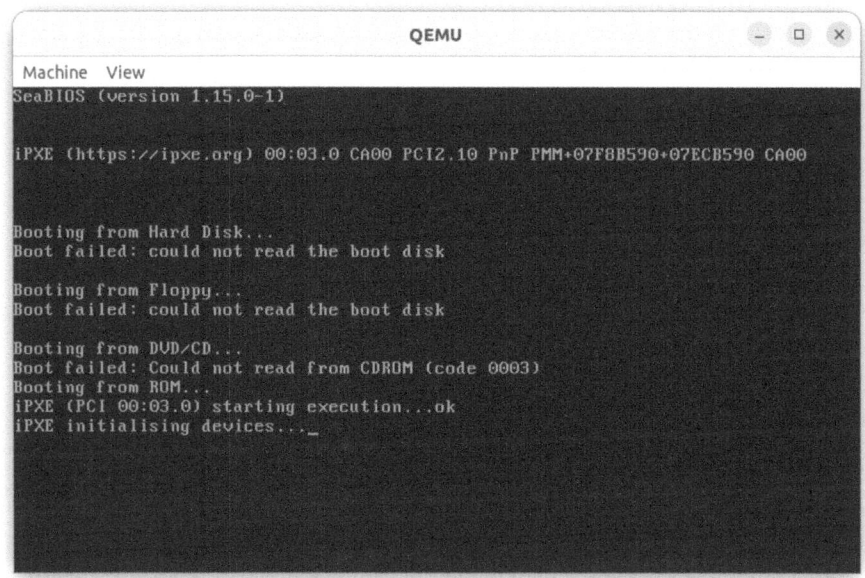

Figure 2-12. SeaBIOS

CHAPTER 2   QEMU

Figure 2-13. *OpenBIOS*

After downloading OpenSPARC, we uncompress the package.

antonio@antonio-Laptop:~/QEMU_VMs$ bunzip2 OpenSPARCT1_Arch.1.5.tar.bz2

And we extract the tar archive.

antonio@antonio-Laptop:~/QEMU_VMs$ tar -xvf OpenSPARCT1_Arch.1.5.tar

39

CHAPTER 2   QEMU

A new S10image folder will be created. Inside this folder we have the files we need to emulate a niagara SPARC system; we'll launch a new QEMU instance like this:

```
antonio@antonio-Laptop:~/QEMU_VMs$ qemu-system-sparc64 -M niagara -L S10image/ -nographic -m 256 -drive if=pflash,readonly=on,file=S10image/disk.s10hw2
```

We pass the location of the firmware with the **-L** parameter. When using the **-nographic** option, we completely disable any graphic output so that QEMU behaves like a command-line application. We also use the **-device** option, which we already know, to define a flash device that hosts a Solaris 10 image.

After executing, QEMU will show the "ok prompt," something that most Solaris admins are familiar with.

```
cpu Probing I/O buses
```

```
Sun Fire T2000, No Keyboard
Copyright 2005 Sun Microsystems, Inc.  All rights reserved.
OpenBoot 4.20.0, 256 MB memory available, Serial #1122867.
[mo23723 obp4.20.0 #0]
Ethernet address 0:80:3:de:ad:3, Host ID: 80112233.
```

```
ok
```

This is not a Solaris book, so we won't describe the characteristics of the OpenBOOT environment and the commands associated. But we can, for example, list the devices.

```
ok show-disks
a) /virtual-devices@100/disk@0
q) NO SELECTION
Enter Selection, q to quit: q
ok
```

We can also boot the OS.

```
ok boot
Boot device: vdisk   File and args:
Loading ufs-file-system package 1.4 04 Aug 1995 13:02:54.
FCode UFS Reader 1.12 00/07/17 15:48:16.
Loading: /platform/SUNW,Sun-Fire-T2000/ufsboot
Loading: /platform/sun4v/ufsboot
SunOS Release 5.10 Version Generic_118822-23 64-bit
Copyright 1983-2005 Sun Microsystems, Inc.  All rights reserved.
Use is subject to license terms.
Hostname: unknown

unknown console login: root
Last login: Wed Feb  8 09:01:28 on console
Sun Microsystems Inc.    SunOS 5.10      Generic January 2005
#
```

When we're done, we can exit QEMU with Ctrl+a x. There are many other platforms that can be emulated with QEMU, PowerPC, alpha, etc. But we won't explain all of them. I think that what we've seen so far is enough to see the potential of this tool as a full system emulator.

User Mode Emulation in QEMU

We've already seen QEMU working as a full system emulator; let's see now user mode emulation.

QEMU can run single Linux programs that were compiled for a different architecture. To use this mode, we need to install the **qemu-user** package.

```
antonio@antonio-HP-Laptop-15s-fq1xxx:~$ sudo apt install
qemu-user
```

CHAPTER 2 QEMU

Now let's suppose we have a Linux system in a different architecture, for example, an ARM-based SBC such as the well-known Raspberry Pi. We could easily compile a simple program and run it locally in the Raspberry Pi.

This would be the source code file *hello.c*.

```
pi@raspberrypi:~$ cat hello.c
#include <stdio.h>

int main(int argc)
{
    printf("Hello World! I am a raspberry");

    return 0;
}
```
We compile the source code file to generate an executable binary file
```
pi@raspberrypi:~$ gcc hello.c -o hello
```
And we execute it
```
pi@raspberrypi:~$ ./hello
Hello World! I am a raspberry
```

By using the **file** command, we see that the binary file is a 32-bit ELF executable for ARM.

```
pi@raspberrypi:~$ file hello
hello: ELF 32-bit LSB executable, ARM, version 1 (SYSV), dynamically linked (uses shared libs), for GNU/Linux 2.6.26, BuildID[sha1]=0x2e095d28174261a8daf9aaf047c82cd24b847727, not stripped
```

We can copy that file to an x86-based Linux machine. And we can also execute it thanks to QEMU. According to the official documentation, the way to execute a binary file of a different architecture is by launching the appropriate QEMU command, **qemu-arm** in this case.

```
antonio@antonio-Laptop:~/QEMU_tests$ scp pi@192.168.1.250:/
home/pi/hello .
pi@192.168.1.250's password:
hello                                100% 5462     855.8KB/s   00:00
antonio@antonio-Laptop:~/QEMU_tests$ file hello
hello: ELF 32-bit LSB executable, ARM, EABI5 version 1 (SYSV),
dynamically linked, interpreter /lib/ld-linux-armhf.so.3, for
GNU/Linux 2.6.26, BuildID[sha1]=285d092ea8614217f0aaf9dad22
cc8472777844b, not stripped
antonio@antonio-Laptop:~/QEMU_tests$ qemu-arm hello
qemu-arm: Could not open '/lib/ld-linux-armhf.so.3': No such
file or directory
```

We get an error message because the executable file was dynamically linked and our x86 system doesn't have the dynamic libraries for the ARM architecture. We could download a copy of the needed libraries or we could generate a static binary instead. As the second option is simpler, this is what we'll do.

```
pi@raspberrypi:~$ gcc hello.c -static -o hello2
```

And we copy the executable file to our x86 system.

```
antonio@antonio-Laptop:~/QEMU_tests$ scp pi@192.168.1.250:/
home/pi/hello2 .
pi@192.168.1.250's password:
hello2                               100%  565KB 619.2KB/s   00:00
```

And now we can execute successfully our minimalistic program.

```
antonio@antonio-Laptop:~/QEMU_tests$ qemu-arm hello2
Hello World! I am a raspberry
```

CHAPTER 2 QEMU

In addition to using the **qemu-arm** command, we can also execute it as we'd do with any other native binary. This is possible because, by default, the binary format handlers for this qemu-user package are registered with the kernel.

```
antonio@antonio-Laptop:~/QEMU_tests$ ./hello2
Hello World! I am a raspberry
```

Of course we can also invert the process and execute x86_64 binary files in our ARM-based Raspberry Pi. We'll begin by compiling a simple program. We'll generate a statically linked binary this time.

```
antonio@antonio-Laptop:~/QEMU_tests$ cat hello_x86_64.c
#include <stdio.h>

int main(int argc)
{
    printf("Hello World! I am a x86_64 PC");

    return 0;
}
antonio@antonio-Laptop:~/QEMU_tests$ gcc hello_x86_64.c \
> -static -o hello_x86_64_static
```

And we copy the binary file to our Raspberry Pi.

```
antonio@antonio-Laptop:~/QEMU_tests$ scp hello_x86_64_static
pi@192.168.1.53:/home/pi
pi@192.168.1.53's password:
hello_x86_64_static              100%   879KB    1.9MB/s   00:00
```

If we try to execute this binary file in the Raspberry Pi before installing the QEMU user module, we'll get this descriptive error:

```
pi@raspberrypi:~ $ ./hello_x86_64_static
-bash: ./hello_x86_64_static: cannot execute binary file: Exec format error
```

So we'll install the **qemu-user** package.

```
pi@raspberrypi:~ $ sudo apt install qemu-user
```

And from now on, we can execute the program, either by using the **qemu-x86_64** command:

```
pi@raspberrypi:~ $ qemu-x86_64 ./hello_x86_64_static
Hello World! I am a x86_64_PC
```

or by executing directly the binary:

```
pi@raspberrypi:~ $ ./hello_x86_64_static
Hello World! I am a x86_64_PC
```

QEMU with KVM

QEMU can also work with a hypervisor like KVM and Xen. In this case, QEMU is in charge of emulating hardware, but the execution of the guest is performed by the hypervisor. In the rest of the chapter, we'll see how KVM and QEMU work together. And in the next chapter, we'll study Xen.

Kernel-based virtual machine (KVM) is a Linux kernel module that makes it possible for the Linux kernel to work as a hypervisor. Beginning with kernel version 2.6.20 it is included in the official kernel mainline. It relies on processors with hardware virtualization extensions, such as Intel VT or AMD-V. In order to take advantage of it, we must check that our CPU actually supports that feature. As we saw in Chapter 1, this is done by searching for the corresponding CPU flag, **vmx** for Intel-based processors and **svm** for AMD-based processors.

```
antonio@antonio-Laptop:~$ grep -E '(vmx|svm)' /proc/cpuinfo
flags      : ....... vmx .......
```

CHAPTER 2   QEMU

KVM complements perfectly QEMU, making it possible for QEMU to take advantage of the processor virtualization extensions. KVM is included in modern distributions so we don't need to install the module itself, but we'll check that the module is actually loaded.

```
antonio@antonio-Laptop:~$ lsmod | grep kvm
kvm_intel              487424  0
kvm                   1409024  1 kvm_intel
irqbypass               12288  1 kvm

antonio@antonio-Aspire-A315-23:~/QEMU_VMs$ lsmod | grep kvm
kvm_amd                 98304  0
ccp                     86016  1 kvm_amd
kvm                    655360  1 kvm_amd
```

To enable KVM acceleration when launching QEMU, we just need to specify either the **–accel kvm** parameter or the formerly used **-enable-kvm** parameter.

```
antonio@antonio-Laptop:~/QEMU_VMs$ qemu-system-x86_64 -m 1024 -boot c --accel kvm debian.qcow2
```

We might get this error message:

```
Could not access KVM kernel module: Permission denied
qemu-system-x86_64: failed to initialize KVM: Permission denied
```

As normal users don't have access to */dev/kvm*, we either run QEMU with root privileges or grant permissions on */dev/kvm* to the current user.

After successfully launching QEMU with KVM, we'll immediately notice that the performance is much better.

QEMU Networking

A server without networking would be pretty much useless these days, so when working with QEMU virtual machines, we need to take this into account as well. The QEMU wiki has a lot of useful information that we'll try to summarize here.

To have an operational network in the VM, we need a network backend. This network backend defines how the emulated network interface interacts with the host's network. Currently there are four different network backends that can be used with QEMU:

- User networking: This is the default backend; we'll see it in the upcoming section.

- TAP networking: This is probably the best option when we need to further customize the network configuration beyond the functionality provided by user networking. We will also study this backend in more detail later in this chapter.

- VDE: This backend uses the Virtual Distributed Ethernet, which provides virtual software-defined network interface cards (NIC). Although this backend is a perfectly valid solution, it is usually not the preferred option, as TAP networking provides the same functionality and it is easier to set up.

- Socket networking: It's used to create a network of guests that can see each other. Due to its simplicity and limited usefulness, it's rarely used, being TAP networking the preferred choice.

User Networking

By default, without specifying any networking-related option, QEMU will use "user networking," also called SLIRP. In this case, the guest system will be assigned an IP address in the 10.0.2.0/24 network. The IP address 10.0.2.2 will be used as the default gateway, and 10.0.2.3 will serve as a DNS server. Optionally we could also launch a Samba server. This is represented in Figure 2-14, taken from the QEMU wiki.

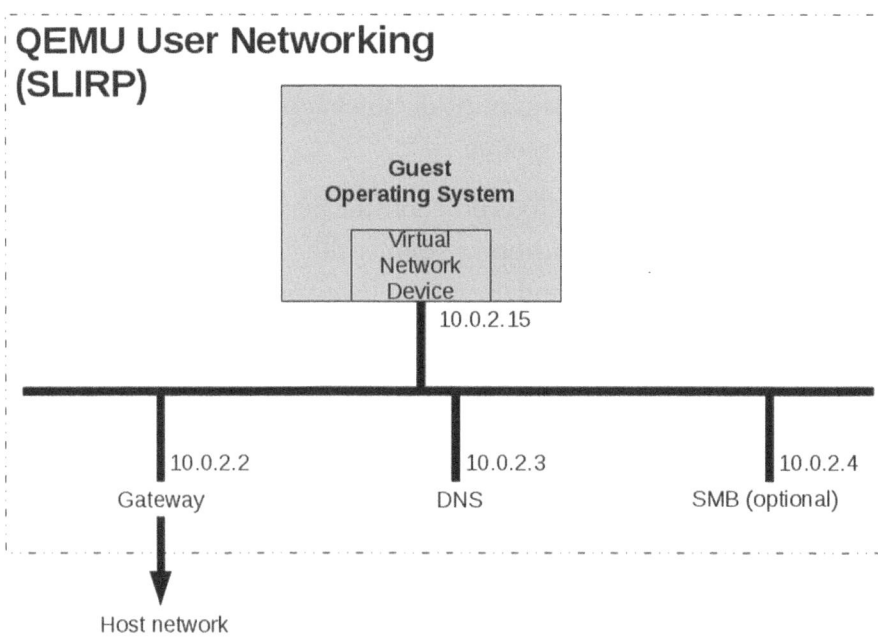

Figure 2-14. QEMU user networking (image under GNU Free Doc License)

From the guest, we can check this from the command line (Figures 2-15 and 2-16).

CHAPTER 2   QEMU

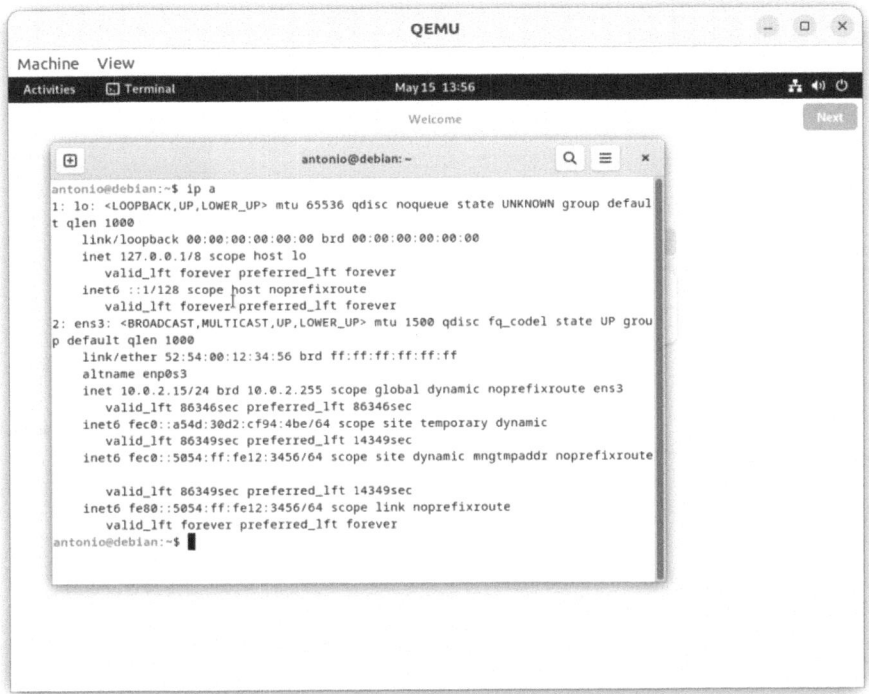

Figure 2-15. *User networking default IP configuration*

CHAPTER 2   QEMU

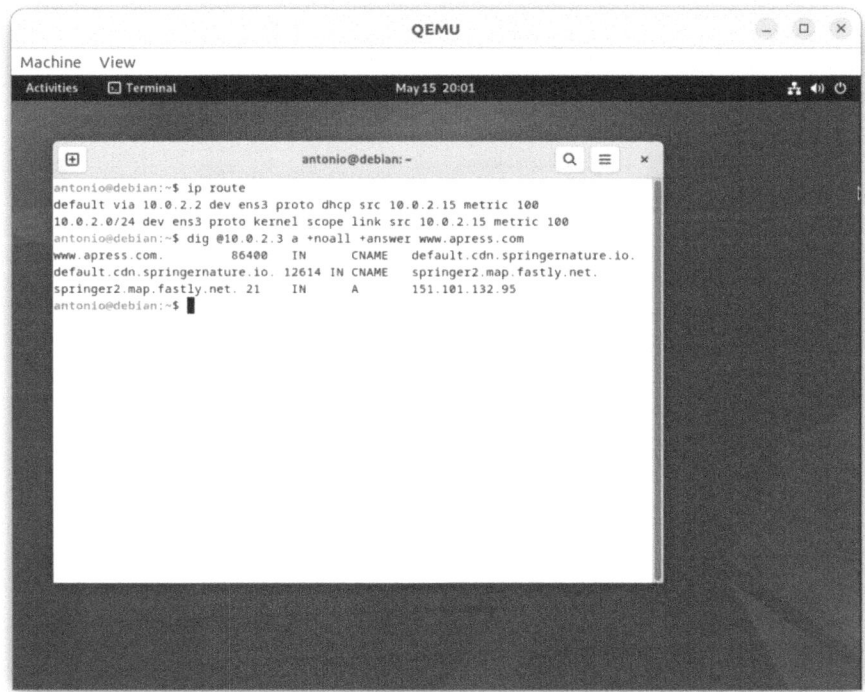

Figure 2-16. *QEMU user networking. DNS server and default gateway*

The default gateway will be located by default at the 10.0.2.2 IP address (Figure 2-16). We can use this address to access services running in the host. For instance, let's assume we are running an http server on the host.

antonio@antonio-Laptop:~/QEMU_VMs$ python3 -m http.server 8888
Serving HTTP on 0.0.0.0 port 8888 (http://0.0.0.0:8888/) ...

In this case, we can access the http server from the QEMU VM by launching a web browser and pointing it to the 10.0.2.2 IP address and the 8888 port (Figure 2-17).

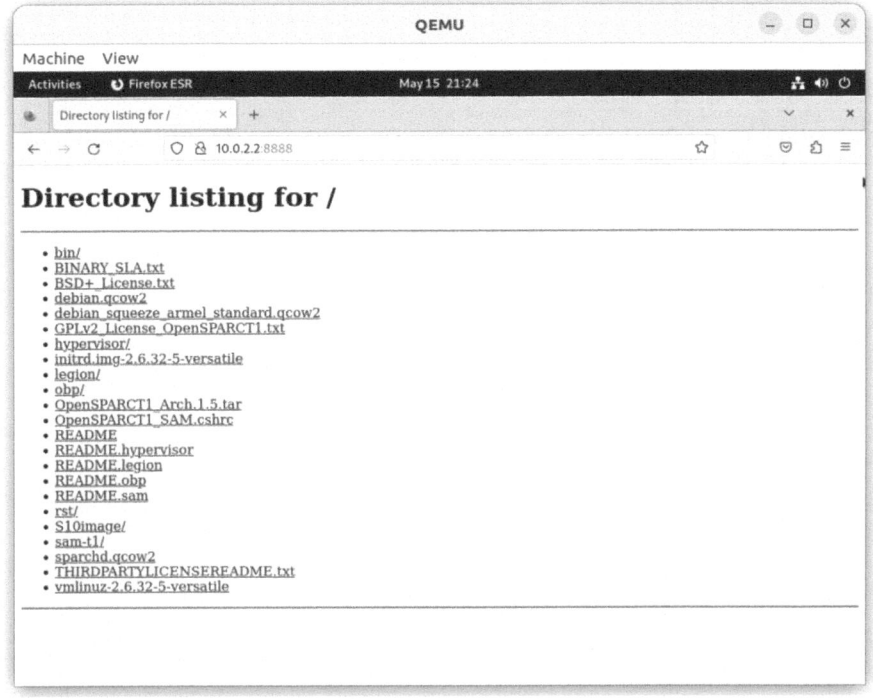

Figure 2-17. *Accessing the host web server from the guest system*

This automatic network configuration can be all we need in certain situations, but sometimes we'll need to customize the network settings. We'll see the parameters we need to define the network settings. To start with, we'll open the QEMU monitor, as we saw before in this chapter (pressing CTRL+ALT and then SHIFT and "2"). And we'll type "info network" (Figure 2-18).

CHAPTER 2   QEMU

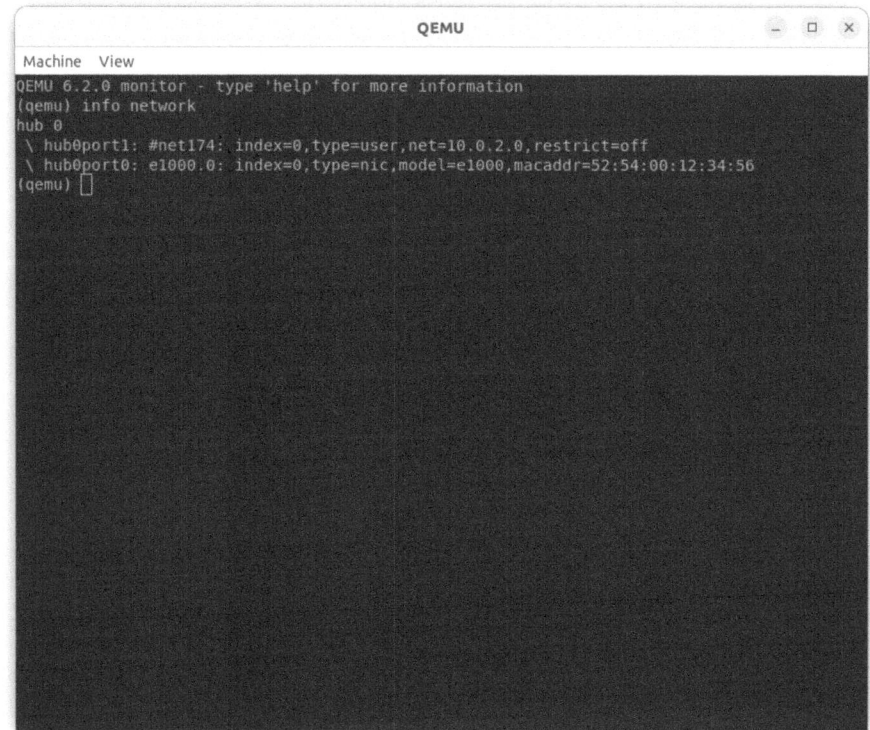

Figure 2-18. Network configuration in the QEMU monitor

We can see clearly the IP address as well as many other settings that will help us understand how to define the networking in QEMU.

If we list the options of the command qemu-system-x86_64, we'll see among many others this option:

antonio@antonio-Laptop:~/QEMU_VMs$ qemu-system-x86_64 –help

·
·
·

-nic none   use it alone to have zero network devices
                 (the default is to
                 provided a 'user' network connection)

-
-
-

We can launch QEMU with the "**-net none**" option if we don't want to have any network device. The help text says clearly that by default a 'user' network connection is provided. This type of connection used to be specified with the "**-net nic -net user**" option, but this syntax is deprecated. If we consult the QEMU wiki or the man pages, we'll see that now the preferred syntax is to use the "**-netdev**" option.

Let's launch QEMU with the same default configuration. But this time we'll explicitly use the network-related parameters in the command line. This will help us to better understand how to set up more advanced network settings in QEMU. As we said, we need to use the "**-netdev**" parameter.

If we check the man page of **qemu-system-x86_64** and search for the "**-netdev**" option, we'll see this line:

```
-netdev user,id=id[,option][,option][,...]
Configure user mode host network backend which requires no
administrator privilege to run.
```

We use "user" to tell that we want to use a "user network," and we must assign an id. This id will be used to associate the backend we just defined with a device, a network device to be exact.

If we look at the man page again and search for the "-nic" option, which configures the network backend and the network device in one go, we'll see an example:

```
qemu-system-x86_64 -netdev user,id=n1,ipv6=off -device e1000,ne
tdev=n1,mac=52:54:98:76:54:32
qemu-system-x86_64 -nic user,ipv6=off,model=e1000,m
ac=52:54:98:76:54:32
```

CHAPTER 2   QEMU

We can list the different network device models with the "-device list" option. We'll see the different models for "USB devices," "network devices," "storage devices," and so on. These are some of the network device models supported by QEMU.

antonio@antonio-Laptop:~/QEMU_VMs$ qemu-system-x86_64 -device help

.

.

.

Network devices:
name "e1000", bus PCI, alias "e1000-82540em", desc "Intel Gigabit Ethernet"

.

.

.

name "pcnet", bus PCI

.

.

name "rtl8139", bus PCI

.

.

name "vmxnet3", bus PCI, desc "VMWare Paravirtualized Ethernet v3"

Depending on the device model, we can use a series of options; we can list these options with the qemu-system-x86_64 -device model,help. By comparing the e1000 and the rtl8139 devices, we'll see some minor differences.

antonio@antonio-Laptop:~/QEMU_VMs$ qemu-system-x86_64 -device e1000,help
e1000 options:

CHAPTER 2 QEMU

```
  acpi-index=<uint32>     - (default: 0)
  addr=<int32>            - Slot and optional function number,
                            example: 06.0 or 06 (default: -1)
  autonegotiation=<bool>  - on/off (default: true)
  bootindex=<int32>
  extra_mac_registers=<bool> - on/off (default: true)
  failover_pair_id=<str>
  init-vet=<bool>         - on/off (default: true)
  mac=<str>               - Ethernet 6-byte MAC Address,
                            example: 52:54:00:12:34:56
  migrate_tso_props=<bool> - on/off (default: true)
  mitigation=<bool>       - on/off (default: true)
  multifunction=<bool>    - on/off (default: false)
  netdev=<str>            - ID of a netdev to use as a backend
  rombar=<uint32>         - (default: 1)
  romfile=<str>
  romsize=<uint32>        - (default: 4294967295)
  x-pcie-extcap-init=<bool> - on/off (default: true)
  x-pcie-lnksta-dllla=<bool> - on/off (default: true)
antonio@antonio-Laptop:~/QEMU_VMs$ qemu-system-x86_64 -device
rtl8139,help
rtl8139 options:
  acpi-index=<uint32>     - (default: 0)
  addr=<int32>            - Slot and optional function number,
                            example: 06.0 or 06 (default: -1)
  bootindex=<int32>
  failover_pair_id=<str>
  mac=<str>               - Ethernet 6-byte MAC Address,
                            example: 52:54:00:12:34:56
  multifunction=<bool>    - on/off (default: false)
  netdev=<str>            - ID of a netdev to use as a backend
```

CHAPTER 2   QEMU

```
    rombar=<uint32>         -  (default: 1)
    romfile=<str>
    romsize=<uint32>        -  (default: 4294967295)
    x-pcie-extcap-init=<bool> - on/off (default: true)
    x-pcie-lnksta-dllla=<bool> - on/off (default: true)
```

Now that we understand the parameters needed, let's launch qemu-system-x86_64 again.

```
antonio@antonio-HP-Laptop-15s-fq1xxx:~/QEMU_VMs$ qemu-system-x86_64 -m 2048 \
> -accel kvm -netdev user,id=my_network \
> -device e1000,netdev=my_network debian.qcow2
```

The system will boot up normally. If we open the QEMU monitor again and type "info network", we'll see the information in Figure 2-19.

Figure 2-19. QEMU monitor network settings

We'll stop the VM and launch a new QEMU instance. But this time we'll customize some parameters.

antonio@antonio-Laptop:~/QEMU_VMs$ qemu-system-x86_64 -m 2048 -accel kvm -netdev user,id=my_network2,net=192.168.7 4.0/24,dhcpstart=192.168.74.17 -device rtl8139,netdev=my_ network2,mac=52:54:00:77:77:77 debian.qcow2

We have added a couple of options to the **-netdev** parameter: **net,** to use a specific network address instead of the default, and **dhcpstart**, to use the built-in DHCP server included in QEMU, specifying the first available IP address too. We also used a different network device model (rtl8139), and we added the **mac** option to define the MAC address to use.

CHAPTER 2   QEMU

After booting up the VM, we open the QEMU monitor again, and we see the network settings with "info network". As expected, we get the information we provided on the command line (Figure 2-20).

Figure 2-20. QEMU monitor customized network settings

And if we execute "ip a" in the console, we'll see that the IP address is the first available IP defined in the DHCP scope (Figure 2-21).

58

CHAPTER 2   QEMU

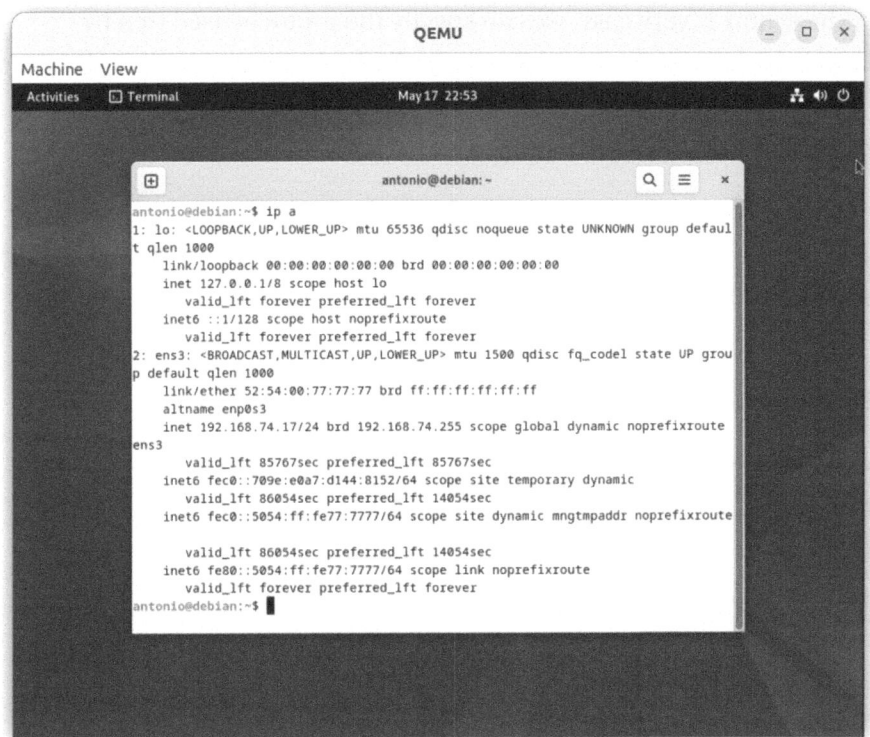

Figure 2-21. *IP address*

QEMU Port Forwarding

When using user networking, we can also forward ports from the host to the virtual machine, so that every connection to a certain port in the host will be forwarded to the VM. For example, we can forward every connection to the host port 10022 to the VM port 22.

If we look again at the man page, in the options available in user networking, we'll see the following line:

hostfwd=[tcp|udp]:[hostaddr]:hostport-[guestaddr]:guestport

CHAPTER 2   QEMU

The syntax is very easy; we can specify the protocol used (tcp by default), the host address and port, as well as the guest address and port. As we said before, in our example, we'll redirect all connections to TCP port 10022 in any address of the host to TCP port 22 in the guest.

```
antonio@antonio-Laptop:~/QEMU_VMs$ qemu-system-x86_64 -m 2048
-accel kvm -netdev user,id=my_network,hostfwd=tcp::10022-:22
-device e1000,netdev=my_network debian.qcow2
```

If we check the listening port in the host, we'll see that the QEMU binary is the one that is actually listening.

```
antonio@antonio-Laptop:~/QEMU_VMs$ lsof -i :10022
COMMAND     PID    USER   FD   TYPE DEVICE SIZE/OFF NODE NAME
qemu-syst 102743 antonio   16u  IPv4 2215091      0t0  TCP
*:10022 (LISTEN)
```

Now we can easily connect with ssh to the virtual machine.

```
antonio@antonio-Laptop:~/QEMU_VMs$ ssh -p 10022 antonio@localhost
The authenticity of host '[localhost]:10022 ([127.0.0.1]:10022)' can't be established.
ED25519 key fingerprint is SHA256:jAO5MUsqGOYePF3fs+ReUFOPYITJpPW6FzEtkDQ3vOo.
This key is not known by any other names
Are you sure you want to continue connecting (yes/no/[fingerprint])? yes
Warning: Permanently added '[localhost]:10022' (ED25519) to the list of known hosts.
antonio@localhost's password:
Linux debian 6.1.0-18-amd64 #1 SMP PREEMPT_DYNAMIC Debian 6.1.76-1 (2024-02-01) x86_64
```

The programs included with the Debian GNU/Linux system are free software;
the exact distribution terms for each program are described in the
individual files in /usr/share/doc/*/copyright.

Debian GNU/Linux comes with ABSOLUTELY NO WARRANTY, to the extent
permitted by applicable law.
antonio@debian:~$ ip address show
1: lo: <LOOPBACK,UP,LOWER_UP> mtu 65536 qdisc noqueue state UNKNOWN group default qlen 1000
    link/loopback 00:00:00:00:00:00 brd 00:00:00:00:00:00
    inet 127.0.0.1/8 scope host lo
       valid_lft forever preferred_lft forever
    inet6 ::1/128 scope host noprefixroute
       valid_lft forever preferred_lft forever
2: ens3: <BROADCAST,MULTICAST,UP,LOWER_UP> mtu 1500 qdisc fq_codel state UP group default qlen 1000
    link/ether 52:54:00:12:34:56 brd ff:ff:ff:ff:ff:ff
    altname enp0s3
    inet 10.0.2.15/24 brd 10.0.2.255 scope global dynamic noprefixroute ens3
       valid_lft 86213sec preferred_lft 86213sec
    inet6 fec0::2555:6d54:86f7:8239/64 scope site temporary dynamic
       valid_lft 86216sec preferred_lft 14216sec
    inet6 fec0::5054:ff:fe12:3456/64 scope site dynamic mngtmpaddr noprefixroute
       valid_lft 86216sec preferred_lft 14216sec
    inet6 fe80::5054:ff:fe12:3456/64 scope link noprefixroute
       valid_lft forever preferred_lft forever
antonio@debian:~$

CHAPTER 2 QEMU

Networking by Using TUN/TAP Devices

Using the default user networking mode can be enough for certain purposes, but it has many limitations. To overcome those limitations, we can use TUN/TAP devices. TUN/TAP devices are kernel-based virtual network devices entirely supported in software. TUN devices work at the network layer, whereas TAP devices work at the data link layer.

In order to create a TUN/TAP device, we'll need the **tunctl** command, which is included in the uml-utilities package.

```
antonio@antonio-Laptop:~$ apt search tunctl
Sorting... Done
Full Text Search... Done
uml-utilities/jammy 20070815.4-1 amd64
  User-mode Linux (utility programs)

antonio@antonio-Laptop:~$ sudo apt install uml-utilities
```

Once installedthe package, we can use the **tunctl** command. We can use it to create a persistent TUN/TAP device owned by user antonio.

```
antonio@antonio-Laptop:~$ tunctl -u antonio
TUNSETIFF: Operation not permitted
antonio@antonio-Laptop:~$ sudo tunctl -u antonio
Set 'tap0' persistent and owned by uid 1000
antonio@antonio-Laptop:~/QEMU_VMs$ ip link show dev tap0
13: tap0: <BROADCAST,MULTICAST> mtu 1500 qdisc noop state DOWN mode DEFAULT group default qlen 1000
    link/ether 06:20:7a:ac:29:38 brd ff:ff:ff:ff:ff:ff
```

We are now ready to use the tap device with QEMU; in order to do that, we need to specify the netdev and dev parameters, as we saw before when we talked about user networking. If we take a look again at the man page of qemu-system-x86_64, we'll see the following line regarding TAP networking:

```
-netdev tap,id=id[,fd=h][,ifname=name][,script=file]
[,downscript=dfile][,br=bridge][,helper=helper]
Configure a host TAP network backend with ID id.
```

The syntax is very similar to what we have already seen when studying user network. The main difference is that we must use "-netdev tap" instead of "-netdev user". Next we'll see a practical example, but first we'll delete the tap0 interface we created manually because when using TAP networking, QEMU itself takes care of creating the TAP interfaces.

```
antonio@antonio-Laptop:~/QEMU_VMs$ sudo tunctl -d tap0
Set 'tap0' nonpersistent
```

We'll clarify all these concepts with an example. We launch a QEMU instance with the following options:

```
antonio@antonio-Laptop:~/QEMU_VMs$ qemu-system-x86_64 -accel
kvm -m 2048 -netdev tap,id=tap_network -device virtio-
net,netdev=tap_network debian.qcow2
qemu-system-x86_64: -netdev tap,id=tap_network: could not
configure /dev/net/tun: Operation not permitted
```

We see QEMU tried to create the TUN/TAP device, but it couldn't because we need sudo permissions to achieve that. We'll launch the instance again with sudo.

```
antonio@antonio-HP-Laptop-15s-fq1xxx:~/QEMU_VMs$ sudo qemu-
system-x86_64 -accel kvm -m 2048 -netdev tap,id=tap_network
-device virtio-net,netdev=tap_network debian.qcow2
W: /etc/qemu-ifup: no bridge for guest interface found
```

CHAPTER 2 QEMU

This time the VM will boot. The options used are basically the same as those we used with user network, but using TAP network instead. Besides we use this time a different device, virtio-net, a paravirtualized (Chapter 1) device. Right after launching the instance, we see a warning about a missing bridge that we can ignore for now.

Once the system is booted, we'll see a "Connection failed" message (Figure 2-22).

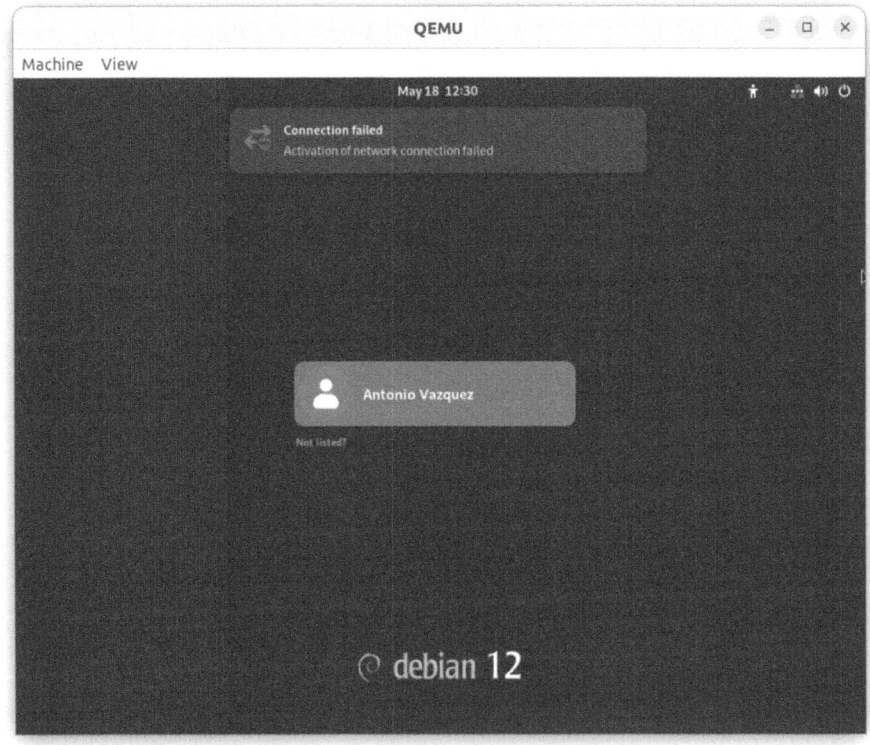

Figure 2-22. *QEMU instance using TAP network*

As we have done several times before, we can also use the QEMU monitor to get more information about the network (Figure 2-23).

CHAPTER 2 QEMU

```
                            QEMU                    _  □  ×
Machine  View
QEMU 6.2.0 monitor - type 'help' for more information
(qemu) info network
virtio-net-pci.0: index=0,type=nic,model=virtio-net-pci,macaddr=52:54:00:12:34:56
 \ tap_network: index=0,type=tap,ifname=tap0,script=/etc/qemu-ifup,downscript=/etc/qe
mu-ifdown
(qemu) ▊
```

Figure 2-23. *QEMU monitor. Networking info*

We can also check the network configuration from the console. We'll see that the ip interface exists in the guest (Figure 2-24).

CHAPTER 2   QEMU

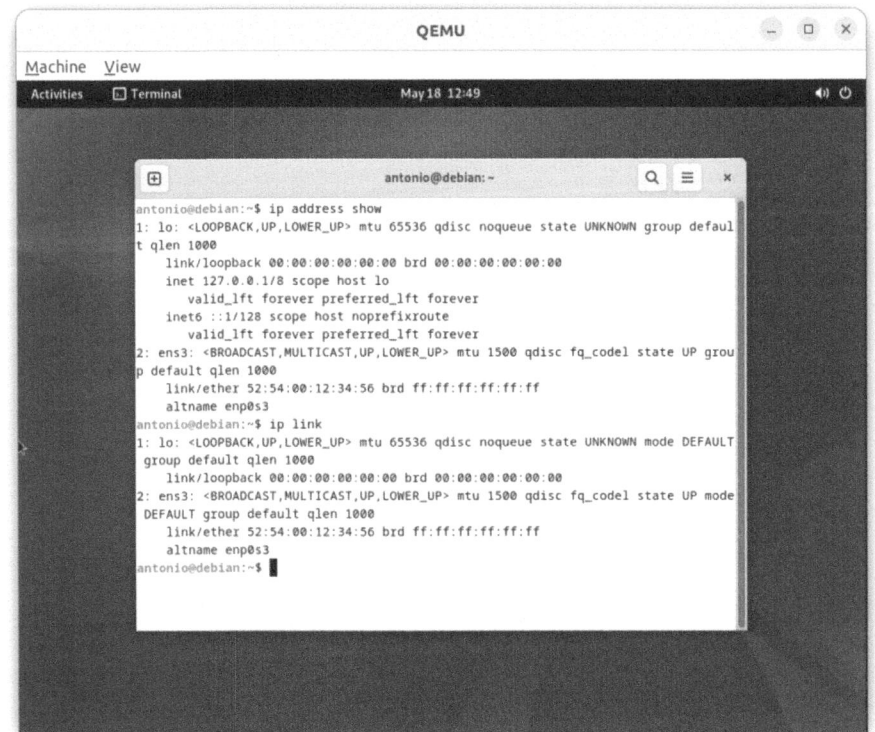

Figure 2-24. *IP settings*

In the host, we can see that QEMU has created successfully the tap interface.

antonio@antonio-Laptop:~/QEMU_VMs$ ip address show dev tap0
14: tap0: <BROADCAST,MULTICAST,UP,LOWER_UP> mtu 1500 qdisc fq_codel state UNKNOWN group default qlen 1000
    link/ether 06:20:7a:ac:29:38 brd ff:ff:ff:ff:ff:ff
    inet6 fe80::420:7aff:feac:2938/64 scope link
       valid_lft forever preferred_lft forever
antonio@antonio-Laptop:~/QEMU_VMs$ ip link show dev tap0
14: tap0: <BROADCAST,MULTICAST,UP,LOWER_UP> mtu 1500 qdisc fq_codel state UNKNOWN mode DEFAULT group default qlen 1000
    link/ether 06:20:7a:ac:29:38 brd ff:ff:ff:ff:ff:ff

The interfaces exist in both sides of the connection, but they don't have any IP address assigned. We'll set an IP address for each interface. We'll begin in the host side.

```
antonio@antonio-Laptop:~/QEMU_VMs$ sudo ip address add
10.7.7.1/24 dev tap0
antonio@antonio-Laptop:~/QEMU_VMs$ ip address show dev tap0
14: tap0: <BROADCAST,MULTICAST,UP,LOWER_UP> mtu 1500 qdisc
fq_codel state UNKNOWN group default qlen 1000
    link/ether 06:20:7a:ac:29:38 brd ff:ff:ff:ff:ff:ff
    inet 10.7.7.1/24 scope global tap0
       valid_lft forever preferred_lft forever
    inet6 fe80::420:7aff:feac:2938/64 scope link
       valid_lft forever preferred_lft forever
```

And we do the same thing on the guest.

```
antonio@debian:~$ su - root
Password:
root@debian:~# ip address add 10.7.7.2/24 dev ens3
root@debian:~# ip address show dev ens3
2: ens3: <BROADCAST,MULTICAST,UP,LOWER_UP> mtu 1500 qdisc
fq_codel state UP group default qlen 1000
    link/ether 52:54:00:12:34:56 brd ff:ff:ff:ff:ff:ff
    altname enp0s3
    inet 10.7.7.2/24 scope global ens3
       valid_lft forever preferred_lft forever
```

We must also make sure that the interfaces are active in both sides with the "**ip link show**" command; if that's not the case, we'll activate them.

```
antonio@antonio-Laptop:~/QEMU_VMs$ sudo ip link set tap0 up

root@debian:~# ip link set ens3 up
```

CHAPTER 2   QEMU

After that, we should be able to ping the interfaces.

```
root@debian:~# ping -c 1 10.7.7.1
PING 10.7.7.1 (10.7.7.1) 56(84) bytes of data.
64 bytes from 10.7.7.1: icmp_seq=1 ttl=64 time=0.147 ms

--- 10.7.7.1 ping statistics ---
1 packets transmitted, 1 received, 0% packet loss, time 0ms
rtt min/avg/max/mdev = 0.147/0.147/0.147/0.000 ms

antonio@antonio-Laptop:~/QEMU_VMs$ ping -c 1 10.7.7.2
PING 10.7.7.2 (10.7.7.2) 56(84) bytes of data.
64 bytes from 10.7.7.2: icmp_seq=1 ttl=64 time=0.448 ms

--- 10.7.7.2 ping statistics ---
1 packets transmitted, 1 received, 0% packet loss, time 0ms
rtt min/avg/max/mdev = 0.448/0.448/0.448/0.000 ms
```

If for any reason the ping command does not work, we must review the procedure and check that both sides of the connection have the IP address correctly assigned, that both interfaces are up, and that there are no typos in the address.

The communication between the host and the guest is now analogous to the communication between two devices in the same network; we can ping each host, scan the ports, access any available service, etc.

Creating a Bridge for External Access

We have seen in the previous section how to set up a TAP network. But in this case, the communication is limited to the host. The guest VM won't be able to reach any network device external to the host in which it is running.

In order to be able to access the external network, we'll create a bridge in our host, connecting the tap interface previously created with a physical interface in the host. To do it, we'll use the **brctl** command, which is included in the bridge-utils package. So, first of all, we need to install this package.

CHAPTER 2   QEMU

```
antonio@antonio-Laptop:~$ apt-file find brctl
bash-completion: /usr/share/bash-completion/completions/brctl
bridge-utils: /sbin/brctl
```
.
.
.
```
antonio@antonio-Laptop:~$ sudo apt install bridge-utils
```

Once **brctl** is installed, we create a bridge.

```
antonio@antonio-Laptop:~$ sudo brctl addbr my_bridge0
```

We add the tap interface to the bridge.

```
antonio@antonio-Laptop:~/QEMU_VMs$ sudo brctl addif my_
bridge0 tap0
```

And we also add the host's Ethernet interface to the other end of the bridge.

```
antonio@antonio-Laptop:~/QEMU_VMs$ sudo brctl addif my_bridge0
enx28ee520617e2
```

We make sure that the bridge interface is up; if that's not the case, we'll activate it.

```
antonio@antonio-Laptop:~/QEMU_VMs$ ip link show my_bridge0
15: my_bridge0: <BROADCAST,MULTICAST> mtu 1500 qdisc noop state DOWN mode DEFAULT group default qlen 1000
    link/ether 66:2d:06:dc:de:8e brd ff:ff:ff:ff:ff:ff
antonio@antonio-Laptop:~/QEMU_VMs$ sudo ip link set my_bridge0 up
```

```
antonio@antonio-Laptop:~/QEMU_VMs$ ip link show my_bridge0
15: my_bridge0: <BROADCAST,MULTICAST,UP,LOWER_UP> mtu 1500
qdisc noqueue state UP mode DEFAULT group default qlen 1000
    link/ether 66:2d:06:dc:de:8e brd ff:ff:ff:ff:ff:ff
```

Now we just need to set up an IP address on the guest system that is in the same range used in our network.

```
antonio@debian:~$ su - root
Password:
root@debian:~# ip address add 192.168.1.3/24 dev ens3
```

From now on, we can access any device on the same network, and the guest is also accessible from the network. If we set up the default gateway, we can also access external networks.

QEMU Guest Agent

In order to improve the overall performance of any QEMU-based virtual machine, we can install the QEMU System Agent. It provides a service (agent) that runs inside the guest and communicates with the host using a virtio-serial channel *org.qemu.guest_agent.0*. This allows to perform a series of functions in the guest from the host.

As we already have installed a Debian server with QEMU, we can search for the QEMU system agent package on the guest system.

```
antonio@debian:~$ apt search qemu-guest-agent
Sorting... Done
Full Text Search... Done
qemu-guest-agent/unknown,now 1:7.2+dfsg-7+deb12u5 amd64
[installed]
  Guest-side qemu-system agent
```

CHAPTER 2 QEMU

This software will allow us to perform many operations like querying and setting system time, initiating gust shutdown, performing guest filesystem sync operations, and so on. We'll install it the usual way.

```
antonio@debian:~$ su - root
Password:
root@debian:~# apt install qemu-guest-agent
```

After installing it, we check the status of the associated service.

```
root@debian:~# systemctl status qemu-guest-agent.service
○ qemu-guest-agent.service - QEMU Guest Agent
     Loaded: loaded (/lib/systemd/system/qemu-guest-agent.
     service; static)
     Active: inactive (dead)
root@debian:~#
```

As the service is currently stopped, we'll try to start it.

```
root@debian:~# systemctl start qemu-guest-agent.service
A dependency job for qemu-guest-agent.service failed. See
'journalctl -xe' for details.
```

The system tries to start the service, but it fails and returns an error message. As suggested, we check the system journal.

```
root@debian:~# journalctl -xe
```

After browsing the journal, we'll see a few lines similar to these:

```
 The unit run-credentials-systemd\x2dtmpfiles\x2dclean.service.
mount has successfully entered the 'dead' state.
May 18 15:51:07 debian systemd[1]: Expecting device dev-virtio\
x2dports-org.qemu.guest_agent.0.device - /dev/virtio-ports/
org.qemu.>
```

71

CHAPTER 2 QEMU

       Subject: A start job for unit dev-virtio\x2dports-org.qemu.guest_agent.0.device has begun execution
       Defined-By: systemd
       Support: https://www.debian.org/support

       A start job for unit dev-virtio\x2dports-org.qemu.guest_agent.0.device has begun execution.

       The job identifier is 1860.
May 18 15:52:37 debian systemd[1]: dev-virtio\x2dports-org.qemu.guest_agent.0.device: Job dev-virtio\x2dports-org.qemu.guest_agent.>
May 18 15:52:37 debian systemd[1]: Timed out waiting for device dev-virtio\x2dports-org.qemu.guest_agent.0.device - /dev/virtio-por>
       Subject: A start job for unit dev-virtio\x2dports-org.qemu.guest_agent.0.device has failed
       Defined-By: systemd
       Support: https://www.debian.org/support

       A start job for unit dev-virtio\x2dports-org.qemu.guest_agent.0.device has finished with a failure.

       The job identifier is 1860 and the job result is timeout.
May 18 15:52:37 debian systemd[1]: Dependency failed for qemu-guest-agent.service - QEMU Guest Agent.

It's not always easy finding the right information in the system journal; in our case, the line we must pay special attention to is this one:

Timed out waiting for device dev-virtio\x2dports-org.qemu.guest_agent.0.device - /dev/virtio-ports/org.qemu.guest_agent.0.

CHAPTER 2   QEMU

As implied by the error message, this device doesn't exist.

```
root@debian:~# ls /dev/virtio-ports/org.qemu.guest_agent.0
ls: cannot access '/dev/virtio-ports/org.qemu.guest_agent.0':
No such file or directory
```

We need to define the virtio-serial device when launching QEMU. We can see the detailed information in the QEMU wiki. According to it, we must include these options when launching QEMU:

```
-chardev socket,path=/tmp/qga.sock,server=on,wait=off,id=qga0
-device virtio-serial
-device virtserialport,chardev=qga0,name=org.qemu.guest_agent.0
```

As we said when defining the QEMU Guest Agent, it communicates with the host using a virtio-serial channel *org.qemu.guest_agent.0*. In the above lines, we see that we're defining a virtio-serial device with that exact name, which is backed by a character device. Let's launch QEMU again with all these options.

```
antonio@antonio-Laptop:~/QEMU_VMs$ sudo qemu-system-x86_64 -accel kvm -m 2048 -netdev user,id=my_network,hostfwd=tcp::10022-:22 -device e1000,netdev=my_network -chardev socket,path=/tmp/qga.sock,server=on,wait=off,id=qga0 -device virtio-serial -device virtserialport,chardev=qga0,name=org.qemu.guest_agent.0 debian.qcow2
```

Now we'll check again the status of the QEMU Guest Agent service.

- qemu-guest-agent.service - QEMU Guest Agent
     Loaded: loaded (/lib/systemd/system/qemu-guest-agent.service; static)
     Active: active (running) since Sat 2024-05-18 16:58:46 CEST; 3min 19s ago

Chapter 2   QEMU

```
  Main PID: 415 (qemu-ga)
     Tasks: 2 (limit: 2291)
    Memory: 1.3M
       CPU: 232ms
    CGroup: /system.slice/qemu-guest-agent.service
            └─415 /usr/sbin/qemu-ga
```

As we can see, this time the service is up and running.

Before trying to perform a simple test on the QEMU Guest Agent, we'll learn a bit about how this agent works. The QEMU Guest Agent uses the QEMU machine protocol (QMP) to communicate and interact. We can test it by launching any QEMU instance with the following option:

```
-qmp tcp:localhost:4444,server,wait=off
```

This option redirects the monitor to the TCP port 4444, so that we can interact with it using a tool like **telnet**. From the host, we can now telnet local port 4444, and we'll see this:

```
antonio@antonio-Laptop:~/QEMU_VMs$ telnet localhost 4444
Trying 127.0.0.1...
Connected to localhost.
Escape character is '^]'.
{"QMP": {"version": {"qemu": {"micro": 0, "minor": 2,
"major": 6}, "package": "Debian 1:6.2+dfsg-2ubuntu6.19"},
"capabilities": ["oob"]}}
```

In the open telnet connection, we can type the following:

```
{ "execute": "qmp_capabilities" }
```

If all goes well we'll see this line:

```
{"return": {}}
```

Now QMP is in command mode, and we can issue commands. We can list the commands available with this instruction:

`{ "execute": "query-commands" }`

It will return a very long list, which we see abridged here.

`{"return": [{"name": "device_add"}, {"name": "query-pci"}, {"name": "query-acpi-ospm-status"},…`

Now that we understand a bit better how QMP works, we'll test the QEMU Guest Agent. To better interact with the agent, we'll install **socat**. Socat will make it easier to communicate with a byte stream.

```
antonio@antonio-Laptop:~$ apt search socat
Sorting... Done
Full Text Search... Done
socat/jammy 1.7.4.1-3ubuntu4 amd64
  multipurpose relay for bidirectional data transfer

antonio@antonio-Laptop:~$ sudo apt install socat
```

Next we use **socat** to connect the standard input/output to the socket used by QEMU agent user.

`antonio@antonio-Laptop:~$ sudo socat STDIO UNIX:/tmp/qga.sock`

Now we're ready to type the commands. First, we make sure that the channel is synchronized.

`{"execute":"guest-sync", "arguments":{"id":1234}}`

If we receive this response, everything is fine.

`{"return": 1234}`

We can also ping the agent.

{"execute":"guest-ping"}
{"return": {}}

And we can get info about the supported commands.

{"execute": "guest-info"}
{"return": {"version": "7.2.9", "supported_commands": [{"enabled": true, "name": "guest-get-cpustats", "success-response": true}, {"enabled": true, "name": "guest-get-diskstats", "success-response": true}, {"enabled": true, "name": "guest-ssh-remove-authorized-keys", "success-response": true

.

.

.

We can get statistics about the CPU usage, or get information about the logged-in users in the guest system.

{"execute": "guest-get-cpustats"}
{"return": [{"cpu": 0, "guestnice": 0, "idle": 1845870, "steal": 130, "iowait": 560, "system": 8170, "guest": 0, "nice": 430, "irq": 0, "type": "linux", "user": 7820, "softirq": 20}]}

{"execute": "guest-get-users"}
{"return": [{"login-time": 1716047181.1631711, "user": "antonio"}]}

QEMU Monitor

When working with QEMU, we have access to a special console that we can use to monitor different aspects of the VM; this console is called QEMU monitor. We can access it by keeping pressed down the "mouse grab" key

CHAPTER 2   QEMU

combination, which is by default CTRL+ALT, and then pressing the SHIFT key and "2". To switch back to the normal OS console, we repeat the same process but pressing the SHIFT key and "1" instead of "2". We have already seen many examples when studying the networking options before in the book. Now we'll see many other useful tasks that we can perform on the QEMU monitor.

From the QEMU monitor, we can perform many tasks; maybe the first command that we type should be "info", which provides a list of commands that we can use (Figure 2-25).

```
                                QEMU
Machine  View
info qtree    -- show device tree
info ramblock -- Display system ramblock information
info rdma     -- show RDMA state
info registers [-a] -- show the cpu registers (-a: all - show register info for all
 cpus)
info replay   -- show record/replay information
info rocker name -- Show rocker switch
info rocker-of-dpa-flows name [tbl_id] -- Show rocker OF-DPA flow tables
info rocker-of-dpa-groups name [type] -- Show rocker OF-DPA groups
info rocker-ports name -- Show rocker ports
info roms     -- show roms
info sev      -- show SEV information
info sgx      -- show intel SGX information
info snapshots -- show the currently saved VM snapshots
info spice    -- show the spice server status
info status   -- show the current VM status (running|paused)
info sync-profile [-m] [-n] [max] -- show synchronization profiling info, up to max
 entries (default: 10), sorted by total wait time. (-m: sort by mean wait time; -n:
 do not coalesce objects with the same call site)
info tlb      -- show virtual to physical memory mappings
info tpm      -- show the TPM device
info trace-events [name] [vcpu] -- show available trace-events & their state (name:
 event name pattern; vcpu: vCPU to query, default is any)
info usb      -- show guest USB devices
info usbhost  -- show host USB devices
info usernet  -- show user network stack connection states
info uuid     -- show the current VM UUID
info version  -- show the version of QEMU
info vm-generation-id -- Show Virtual Machine Generation ID
info vnc      -- show the vnc server status
(qemu)
```

Figure 2-25. QEMU monitor. Getting info

CHAPTER 2   QEMU

We can get information about the disk devices with "info block" (Figure 2-26).

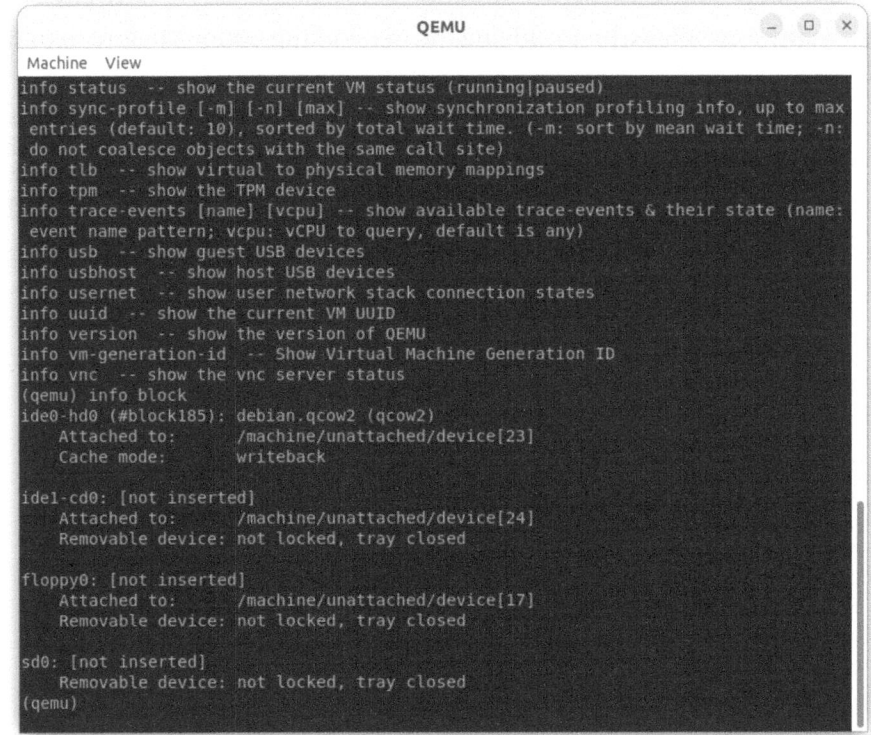

Figure 2-26. QEMU monitor. Getting disk devices information

In the output, we see that no CD/DVD is attached right now. We can insert a CD/DVD using the command **change ide1-cd0** *path_to_iso* (Figure 2-27).

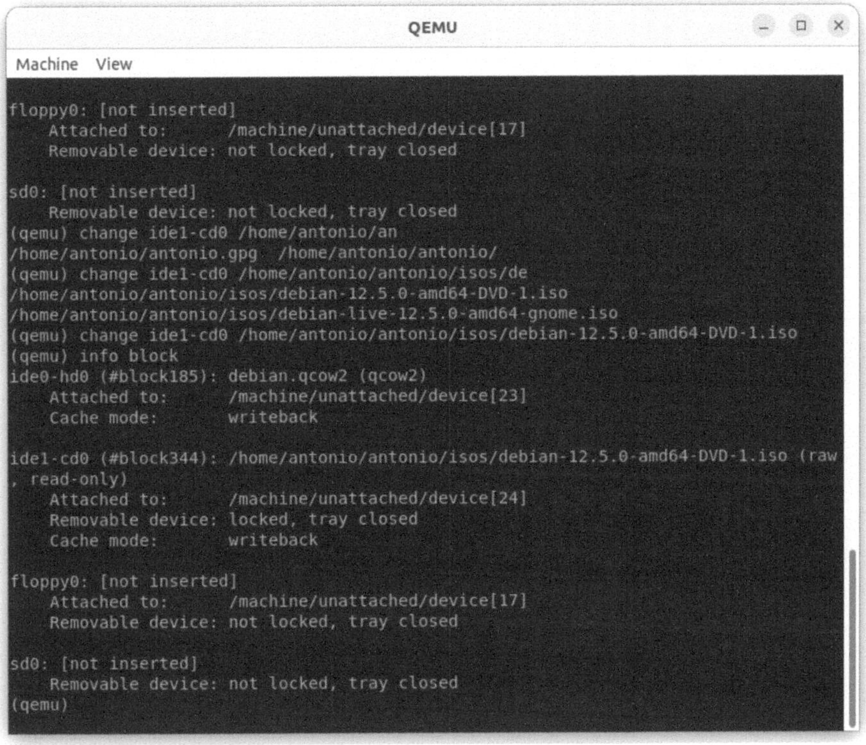

Figure 2-27. QEMU monitor. Inserting a CD/DVD

CHAPTER 2   QEMU

If we switch from the QEMU monitor to the server console (CTRL+ALT) and SHIFT+1, we'll see that we have a CD/DVD inserted (Figure 2-28).

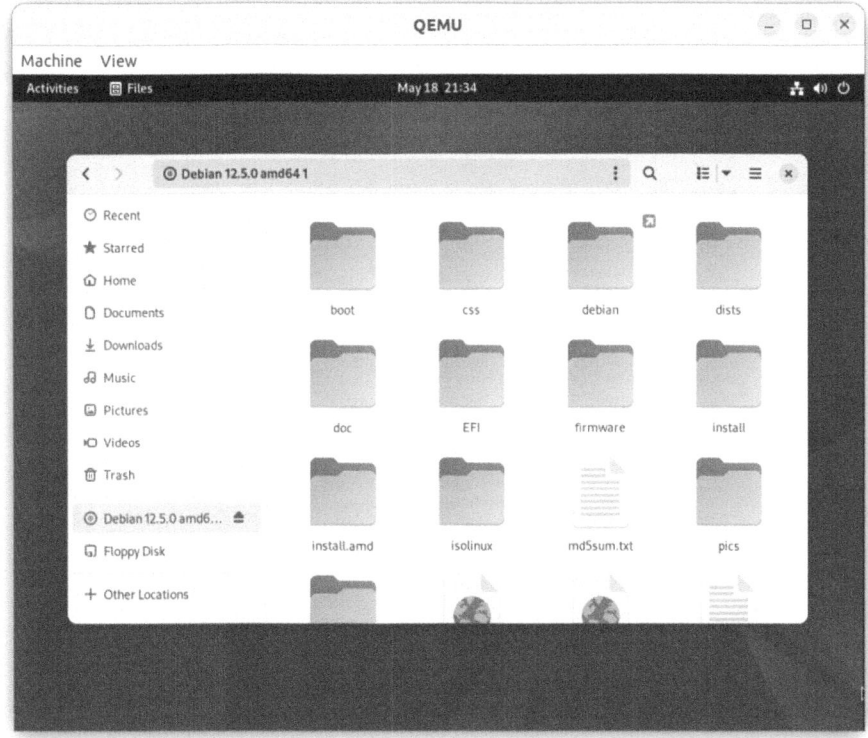

Figure 2-28. *Accessing the CD/DVD from the File Manager*

CHAPTER 2 QEMU

A command that can be useful sometimes is getting a screenshot of the VM. We can do it with the screendump command (Figure 2-29).

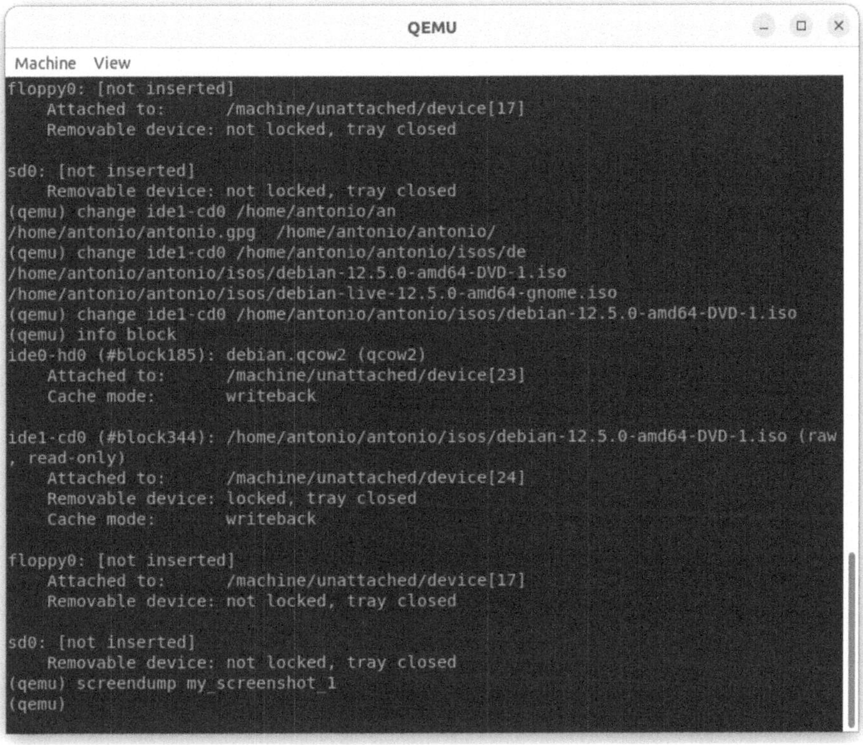

```
                              QEMU                          _  □  ×
 Machine  View
floppy0: [not inserted]
    Attached to:     /machine/unattached/device[17]
    Removable device: not locked, tray closed

sd0: [not inserted]
    Removable device: not locked, tray closed
(qemu) change ide1-cd0 /home/antonio/an
/home/antonio/antonio.gpg  /home/antonio/antonio/
(qemu) change ide1-cd0 /home/antonio/antonio/isos/de
/home/antonio/antonio/isos/debian-12.5.0-amd64-DVD-1.iso
/home/antonio/antonio/isos/debian-live-12.5.0-amd64-gnome.iso
(qemu) change ide1-cd0 /home/antonio/antonio/isos/debian-12.5.0-amd64-DVD-1.iso
(qemu) info block
ide0-hd0 (#block185): debian.qcow2 (qcow2)
    Attached to:     /machine/unattached/device[23]
    Cache mode:      writeback

ide1-cd0 (#block344): /home/antonio/antonio/isos/debian-12.5.0-amd64-DVD-1.iso (raw
, read-only)
    Attached to:     /machine/unattached/device[24]
    Removable device: locked, tray closed
    Cache mode:      writeback

floppy0: [not inserted]
    Attached to:     /machine/unattached/device[17]
    Removable device: not locked, tray closed

sd0: [not inserted]
    Removable device: not locked, tray closed
(qemu) screendump my_screenshot_1
(qemu)
```

Figure 2-29. QEMU monitor. Getting a screenshot

CHAPTER 2 QEMU

We can access the newly created screenshot from the host by using the File Manager and opening the path QEMU was launched from (Figure 2-30).

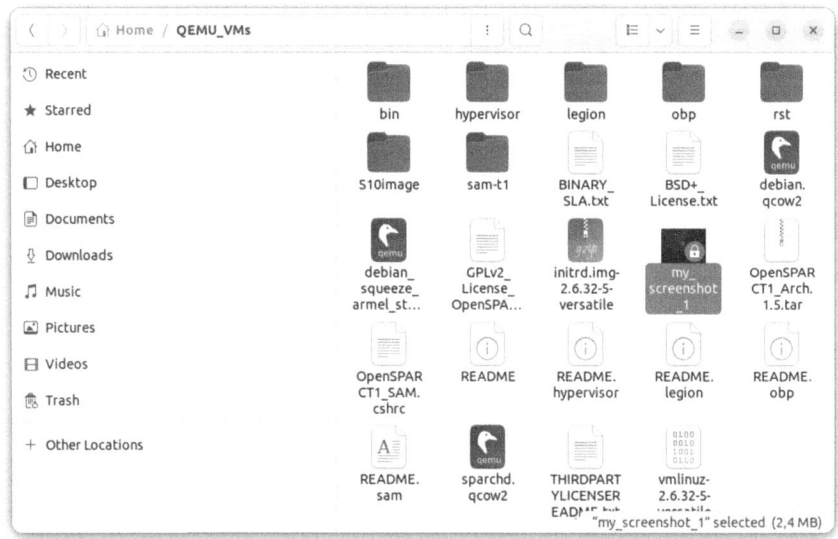

Figure 2-30. Screenshot generated from the QEMU monitor

Another very important feature is the ability to create snapshots. This is very practical when we need to apply software updates, or perform major changes in a system, and we want to make sure that we can roll back to a known state if any problem arises.

To test snapshot creation and restoration, we'll begin by creating a simple text document in our guest.

```
antonio@debian:~$ mkdir documents
antonio@debian:~$ cd documents/
antonio@debian:~/documents$ echo "This is a very important document" > important_doc.txt
antonio@debian:~/documents$ ls
important_doc.txt
```

CHAPTER 2 QEMU

And now we create a snapshot with the **savevm** command (Figure 2-31).

```
                              QEMU                        _  □  x
 Machine  View
      Attached to:       /machine/unattached/device[17]
      Removable device: not locked, tray closed

 sd0: [not inserted]
      Removable device: not locked, tray closed
 (qemu) change ide1-cd0 /home/antonio/an
 /home/antonio/antonio.gpg  /home/antonio/antonio/
 (qemu) change ide1-cd0 /home/antonio/antonio/isos/de
 /home/antonio/antonio/isos/debian-12.5.0-amd64-DVD-1.iso
 /home/antonio/antonio/isos/debian-live-12.5.0-amd64-gnome.iso
 (qemu) change ide1-cd0 /home/antonio/antonio/isos/debian-12.5.0-amd64-DVD-1.iso
 (qemu) info block
 ide0-hd0 (#block185): debian.qcow2 (qcow2)
      Attached to:       /machine/unattached/device[23]
      Cache mode:        writeback

 ide1-cd0 (#block344): /home/antonio/antonio/isos/debian-12.5.0-amd64-DVD-1.iso (raw
 , read-only)
      Attached to:       /machine/unattached/device[24]
      Removable device: locked, tray closed
      Cache mode:        writeback

 floppy0: [not inserted]
      Attached to:       /machine/unattached/device[17]
      Removable device: not locked, tray closed

 sd0: [not inserted]
      Removable device: not locked, tray closed
 (qemu) screendump my_screenshot_1
 (qemu) savevm my_snapshot_1
 (qemu)
```

Figure 2-31. *QEMU monitor. Creating a snapshot*

We'll delete now the document we just created.

antonio@debian:~/documents$ cat important_doc.txt
This is a very important document
antonio@debian:~/documents$ rm important_doc.txt
antonio@debian:~/documents$ cat important_doc.txt
cat: important_doc.txt: No such file or directory

CHAPTER 2 QEMU

If we want to revert our system to a previous state, we need to check whether we have any snapshot available. In this case, we know we have a snapshot available, but if we didn't know, we'd need to use the **info snapshots** command (Figure 2-32).

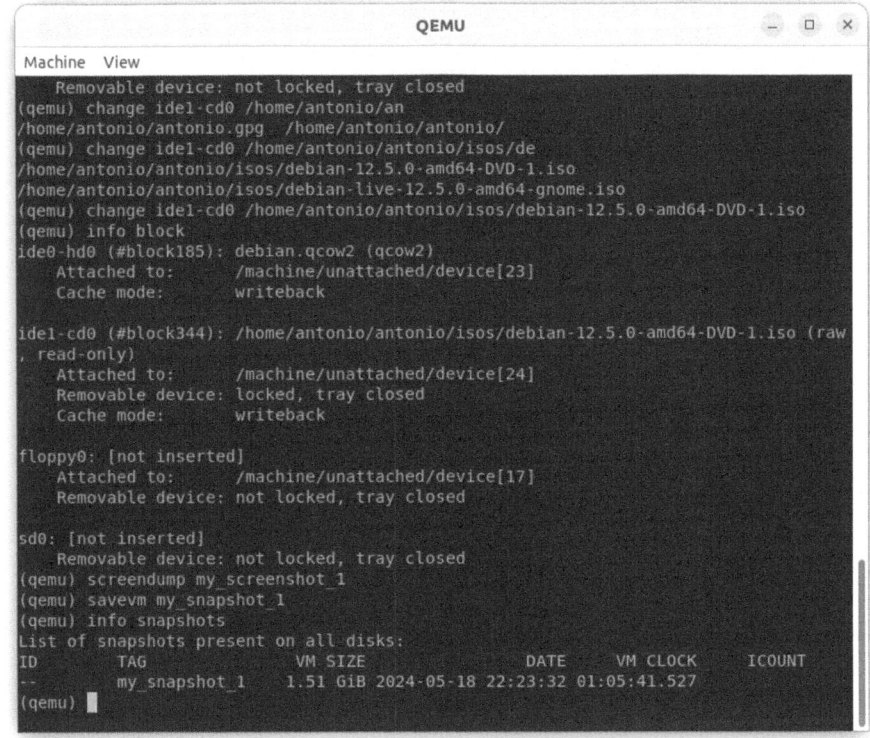

Figure 2-32. QEMU monitor. Getting the list of snapshots

CHAPTER 2   QEMU

As we have a snapshot available, we can restore it with "**loadvm**" (Figure 2-33).

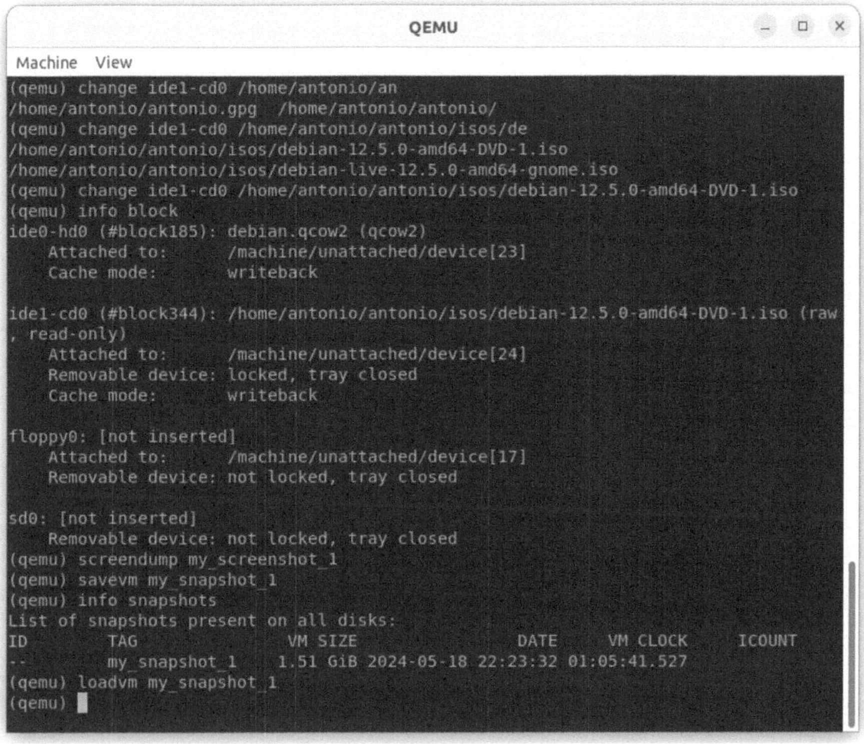

Figure 2-33. QEMU monitor. Restoring a snapshot

CHAPTER 2 QEMU

Finally, if we don't need a snapshot anymore, we can delete it with "delvm" (Figure 2-34).

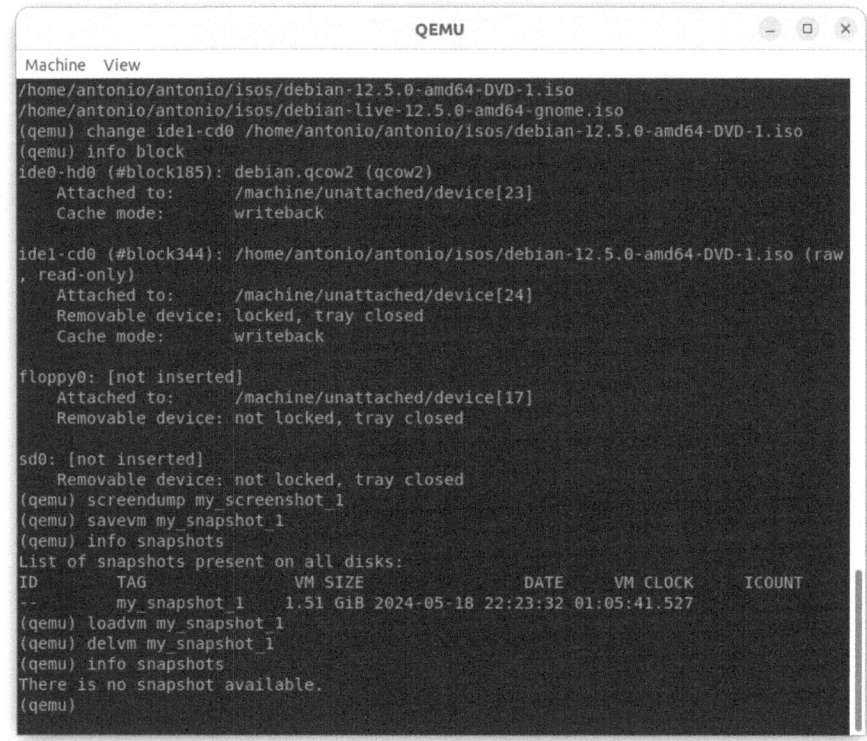

Figure 2-34. QEMU monitor. Deleting a snapshot

CHAPTER 2 QEMU

Besides getting information about the network, we can also obtain information about the CPU, the memory installed, etc. We can also obtain information about KVM acceleration or the network connections (Figure 2-35).

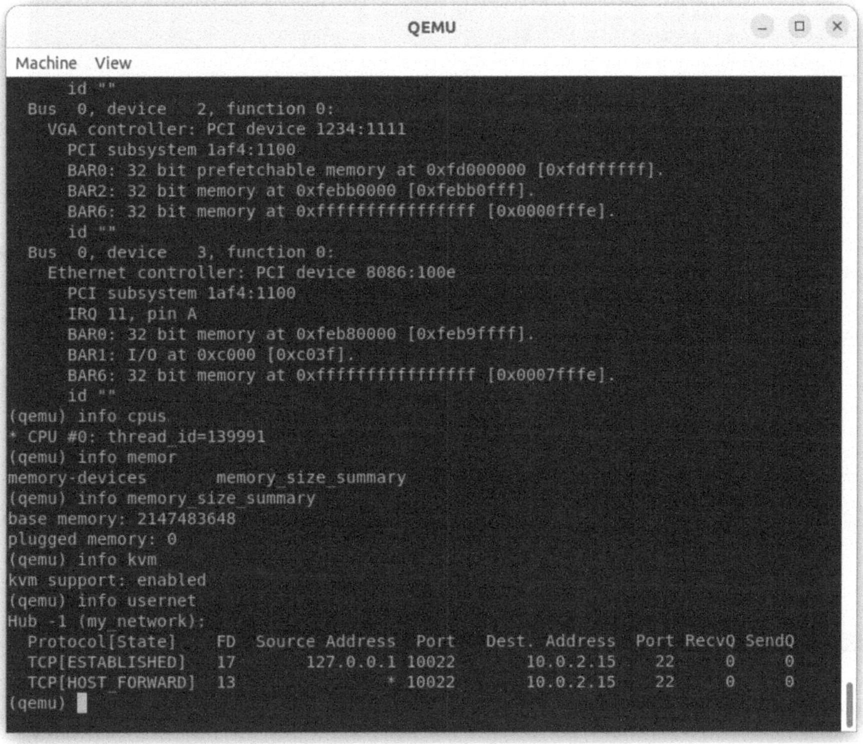

Figure 2-35. QEMU monitor. Getting information from the system

From the QEMU monitor, we can also shut down or reset the system with **system_powerdown** or **system_reset**, respectively (Figure 2-36).

Figure 2-36. QEMU monitor. Shutting down the system

Other Useful QEMU Options

We have seen many options that we can use with QEMU; of course not all of them as that would require a whole book (or several books). Here we'll see a few more options we haven't seen so far which can be also very useful.

When studying networking, we saw we could emulate different devices: e1000, rtl8139, paravirtualized devices, etc. The same thing applies to CPU; we can emulate many CPU models. We can obtain the full list with **qemu-system-x86_64 -cpu help**.

```
antonio@antonio-Laptop:~/QEMU_VMs$ qemu-system-x86_64 -cpu help
Available CPUs:
x86 486                    (alias configured by machine type)
x86 486-v1
x86 Broadwell              (alias configured by machine type)
x86 Broadwell-IBRS         (alias of Broadwell-v3)
.
.
.
```

In addition to the CPU model, we can also specify the number of CPUs with the **-smp** option.

About the disk options, so far we have launched the QEMU instances by passing the name of the file that contains the virtual disk image we generated previously with **qemu-img** without any additional parameters. If you remember, when we studied the QEMU monitor and checked the information of the disk devices, we saw that the disk was an IDE device, but we can specify an SCSI device, a flash disk, etc.

Finally, I would like to comment that when launching QEMU instances, a new graphical window pops up. This is because the default **-display** option is **sdl**, and unless we explicitly say otherwise, this will be the display used. Apart from **sdl**, we can use other options like **vnc** or **nographic**. In fact, when we used QEMU to emulate a SPARC system, we used this last option.

CHAPTER 2   QEMU

As a practical example, we're going to launch a new QEMU instance with some of these options.

antonio@antonio-Laptop:~/QEMU_VMs$ sudo qemu-system-x86_64 -accel kvm -m 2048 -netdev user,id=my_network,hostfwd=tcp::10022-:22 -device e1000,netdev=my_network -cpu core2duo -smp cpus=2 -display vnc=0.0.0.0:0 -drive file=debian.qcow2,if=virtio

Now we won't see any graphical window popping up. But we can connect with ssh and check some of the customized characteristics we just defined when launching the QEMU instance.

```
antonio@debian:~$ lscpu
Architecture:          x86_64
  CPU op-mode(s):      32-bit, 64-bit
  Address sizes:       40 bits physical, 48 bits virtual
  Byte Order:          Little Endian
CPU(s):                2
  On-line CPU(s) list: 0,1
Vendor ID:             GenuineIntel
  Model name:          Intel(R) Core(TM)2 Duo
CPU     T7700   @ 2.40GHz
```

We can clearly see same CPU model we specified, and we also realize that we have two CPUs. If we check the disk, we'll see that it is identified as */dev/vda*, because we explicitly said that we'd be using paravirtualization (virtio option in -drive).

```
antonio@debian:~$ su - root
Password:
root@debian:~# fdisk -l
```

```
Disk /dev/vda: 10 GiB, 10737418240 bytes, 20971520 sectors
```
.
.
.

Finally, we can connect to the server console with any VNC client (Figure 2-37).

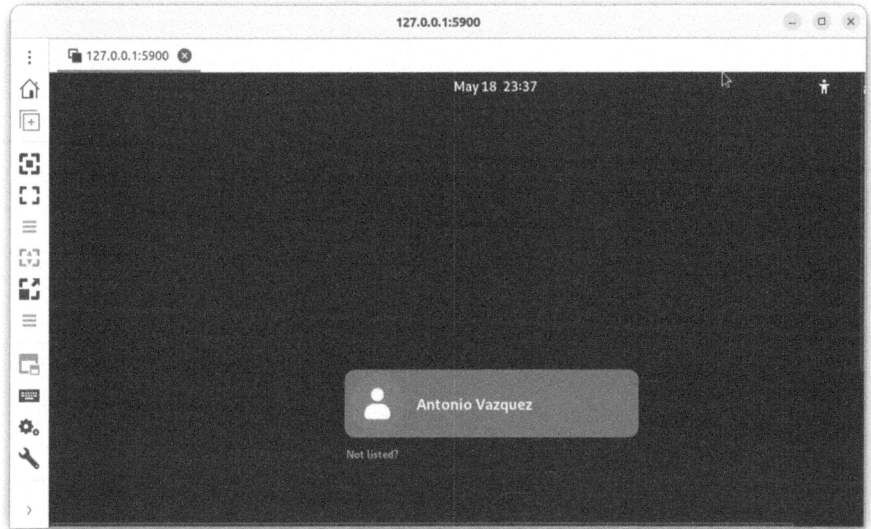

Figure 2-37. *Accessing the server console with VNC*

Summary

In this chapter, we have become familiar with a fantastic open source tool, QEMU. This program can not only perform full system emulation, either hardware or software based, but can also perform user mode emulation. In addition, it works perfectly well in association with KVM or Xen, which makes it an amazing program for anybody interested in emulation and/or virtualization.

CHAPTER 2 QEMU

In the chapter, we emulated different architectures like ARM and SPARC. We executed binaries compiled for different processors and experienced about the different options we have available to set up the network. We also learned how useful the QEMU monitor can be and experienced launching QEMU with different parameters.

CHAPTER 3

Xen

In this chapter, we'll cover the following concepts:

- Xen architecture, networking, and storage
- Xen configuration
- Xen utilities
- Troubleshooting Xen installations
- Basic knowledge of XAPI
- Awareness of XenStore
- Awareness of Xen Boot Parameters
- Awareness of the xm/xl utility

Xen Architecture

Xen is a type 1 hypervisor that allows to execute different operating systems on the same machine. It was originally developed at the University of Cambridge, and it is now maintained by the Linux Foundation. We can take a look at its architecture in Figure 3-1.

CHAPTER 3 XEN

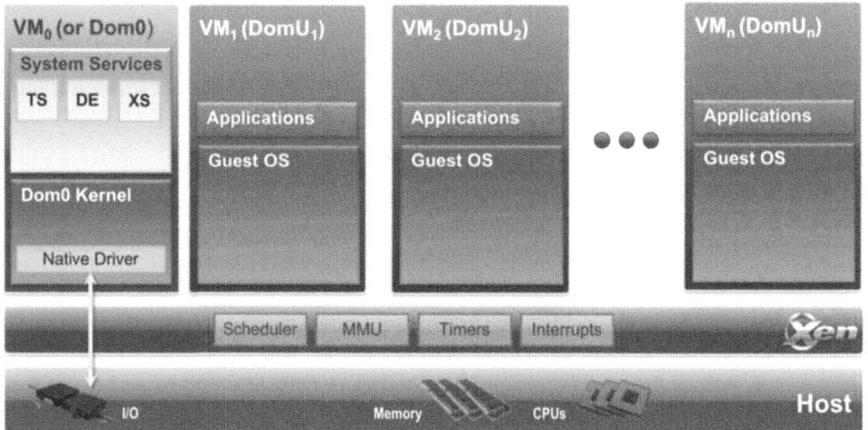

Figure 3-1. Xen architecture, from the Xen wiki page used under Creative Commons License

The hypervisor executes directly on the host, and we have a Control Domain (Domain 0) that has the ability to communicate with the hypervisor and tell it to start and stop the unprivileged domains, called $domU_x$. In addition, the Control Domain also has the needed drivers to access the hardware. In this chapter, we'll use the terms "unprivileged domain" and "virtual machine" interchangeably.

Installation and Configuration of Xen

The installation of Xen is not very complicated, but it is not as straightforward as the use of KVM either. We'll need to install a customized kernel to use Xen. We'll see this procedure in detail in the following sections.

Installing Xen

Xen can be downloaded from the Xen project web page and manually installed, but there are also precompiled versions available for the main Linux distributions. We'll install Xen on an Ubuntu 20 server. We should make sure that the future Xen server has enough resources to host the virtual machines; otherwise, we might run into situations in which the hypervisor seems to execute but when creating and managing virtual machines, we might get strange errors that are not always easy to troubleshoot. In our case, we'll be using a 2 CPU server with 4 GB RAM and about 20 GB of space disk available for the VMs.

Installing on Ubuntu 20

If we perform a search of Xen-related packages, we'll see a package similar to this one:

```
antonio@ubuntu:~$ apt search xen-hypervisor-4.11-amd64
Sorting... Done
Full Text Search... Done
xen-hypervisor-4.11-amd64/focal-updates,focal-security
4.11.3+24-g14b62ab3e5-1ubuntu2.3 amd64
  Xen Hypervisor on AMD64
```

To install Xen, we need to install this package.

```
antonio@ubuntu:~$ sudo apt install xen-hypervisor-4.11-amd64
```

After installing Xen, the Grub boot loader is modified accordingly to load the kernel with Xen support.

It is also a good idea to install the Xen tools, which will be very helpful to manage our Xen environment.

```
antonio@ubuntu:~$ sudo apt install xen-tools
```

If we now restart the Ubuntu server, the kernel with Xen will be loaded automatically. However, if we want to make sure of it and have the option to choose which kernel to boot from, we should make some changes to our system. We can see grub default settings in the */etc/default/grub* file. In the first lines, we'll see something like this:

```
antonio@ubuntu:~$ cat /etc/default/grub
# If you change this file, run 'update-grub' afterwards
  to update
# /boot/grub/grub.cfg.
# For full documentation of the options in this file, see:
#   info -f grub -n 'Simple configuration'
GRUB_DEFAULT=0
GRUB_TIMEOUT_STYLE=hidden
GRUB_TIMEOUT=0
GRUB_DISTRIBUTOR='lsb_release -i -s 2> /dev/null || echo Debian'
GRUB_CMDLINE_LINUX_DEFAULT="quiet"
GRUB_CMDLINE_LINUX="find_preseed=/preseed.cfg auto noprompt priority=critical locale=en_US"
```

To see the grub menu when the system boots, we need to change the value of the GRUB_TIMEOUT_STYLE parameter, and we also need to edit the GRUB_TIMEOUT parameter to set the number of seconds that the menu will be shown before booting the default kernel.

```
GRUB_TIMEOUT_STYLE=menu
GRUB_TIMEOUT=5
```

After modifying the file, we'll execute the **update-grub** command to apply the changes to the current configuration.

```
antonio@ubuntu:~$ sudo update-grub
```

CHAPTER 3   XEN

From now on, every time we boot the system, we'll see the grub menu (Figure 3-2).

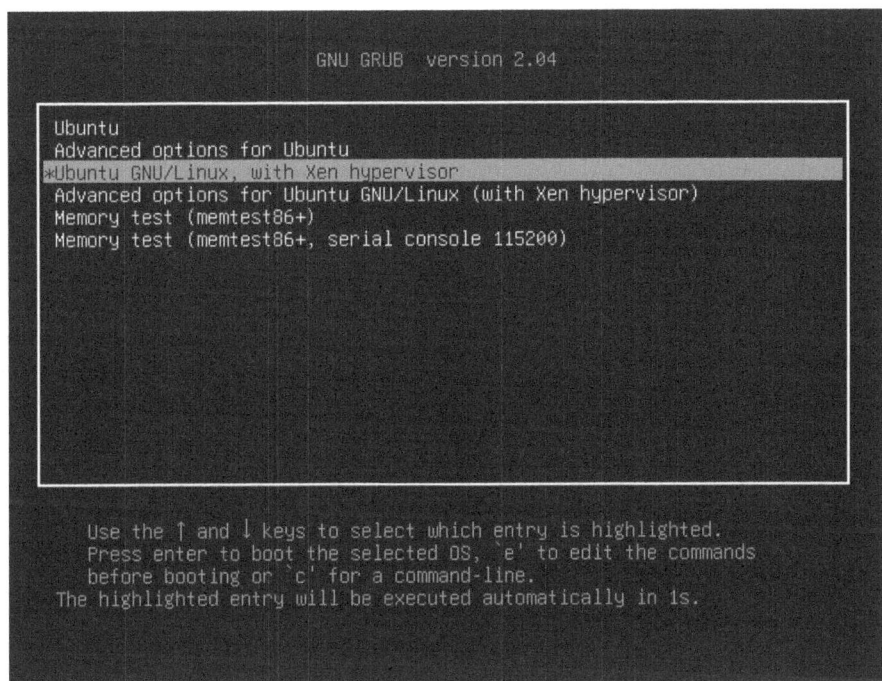

Figure 3-2. Ubuntu grub menu

Configuring Xen

Once we boot the Xen host with the appropriate kernel, we can use many tools to check that everything is working. For instance, we can use the **xen list** command.

```
antonio@ubuntu:~$ sudo xen list
[sudo] password for antonio:
Name                          ID   Mem   VCPUs    State    Time(s)
Domain-0                      0    3916  2        r-----   98.7
```

97

CHAPTER 3 XEN

Or we can get the same information with **xl list**.

```
antonio@ubuntu:~$ sudo xl list
Name                            ID   Mem VCPUs      State   Time(s)
Domain-0                         0  3916     2      r-----    100.3
```

Another command we can use to list the VMs/domains currently executing is **xentop**.

```
antonio@ubuntu:~$ sudo xentop
xentop - 11:19:47   Xen 4.11.4-pre
1 domains: 1 running, 0 blocked, 0 paused, 0 crashed, 0 dying,
0 shutdown
Mem: 4193720k total, 3134908k used, 1058812k free    CPUs: 2
@ 2099MHz
      NAME  STATE   CPU(sec) CPU(%)     MEM(k) MEM(%)
MAXMEM(k) MAXMEM(%) VCPUS NETS NETTX(k) NETRX(k) VBDS
VBD_OO   VBD_RD   VBD
_WR  VBD_RSECT  VBD_WSECT SSID
  Domain-0 -----r       13921  128.1    3083376   73.5
no limit         n/a     2    0         0         0
     0         0    0
     0         0         0    0
```

In all the cases, we'll see that right now we only have the privileged domain running. In the next sections, we'll begin to create some additional VMs/unprivileged domains.

Creating a Logical Volume to Store the Virtual Machines

Even though it is not necessary, it is, however, a good idea to keep the VMs and their related files in a dedicated storage location, such as a logical volume. In our example, we'll create a new logical volume for this purpose.

Assuming we already have added a new disk with enough capacity, we'll create the corresponding physical volume. The procedure is about the same in any Linux server. We'll see how to do it in Ubuntu.

```
antonio@ubuntu:~$ sudo pvcreate /dev/sdb
  Physical volume "/dev/sdb" successfully created.
```

And then we create the Volume Group.

```
antonio@ubuntu:~$ sudo vgcreate VM_VG /dev/sdb
  Volume group "VM_VG" successfully created
```

Finally, we create the corresponding Logical Volume.

```
antonio@ubuntu:~$ sudo lvcreate -n VM_LV -l 100%free VM_VG
  Logical volume "VM_LV" created.
```

We format the Logical Volume we just created and we mount it.

```
antonio@ubuntu:~$ sudo mkfs.ext4 /dev/mapper/VM_VG-VM_LV
[sudo] password for antonio:
mke2fs 1.44.1 (24-Mar-2018)
Creating filesystem with 5241856 4k blocks and 1310720 inodes
Filesystem UUID: 5e7fa6b6-1362-4eb5-a645-487dd02ae7f4
Superblock backups stored on blocks:
    32768, 98304, 163840, 229376, 294912, 819200, 884736,
    1605632, 2654208, 4096000

Allocating group tables: done
Writing inode tables: done
Creating journal (32768 blocks): done
Writing superblocks and filesystem accounting information: done

antonio@ubuntu:~$ sudo mkdir /XEN_VMS
antonio@ubuntu:~$ sudo mount /dev/mapper/VM_VG-VM_LV /XEN_VMS/
antonio@ubuntu:~$ sudo chown antonio /XEN_VMS
```

CHAPTER 3   XEN

In addition to having a dedicated Logical Volume for our virtual machines, it would also be a good idea to have another LV to store the installation ISO images.

Finally, we edit the */etc/fstab* file, so that the filesystem is automatically mounted when the system boots.

Creating Virtual Machines

We can create a new virtual machine using different tools. In the next chapter, when we study libvirt, we'll see many utilities like **virsh** or **virt-manager**, which can be very convenient when creating virtual machines in Xen (and also in other hypervisors). For now, we'll create the VMs manually by creating the corresponding configuration file.

Installing a Virtual Machine by Editing a Configuration File

In Xen, every virtual machine will need to have an associated text file. In the */etc/xen/* folder, we can find different example files. The content of the folder differs depending on the Linux distribution we are working with, but the example files are similar. For instance, in Ubuntu, we have a couple of example files about a paravirtualized Linux and a fully virtualized (hvm) Linux.

Here we see some of the main lines of the paravirtualized Linux configuration file.

```
antonio@ubuntu:~$ cat /etc/xen/xlexample.pvlinux
#============================================================
# Example PV Linux guest configuration
#============================================================
#
```

```
# This is a fairly minimal example of what is required for a
# Paravirtualised Linux guest. For a more complete guide see
xl.cfg(5)

# Guest name
name = "example.pvlinux"

.
.
.
# Kernel image to boot
kernel = "/boot/vmlinuz"

# Ramdisk (optional)
#ramdisk = "/boot/initrd.gz"

# Kernel command line options
extra = "root=/dev/xvda1"

# Initial memory allocation (MB)
memory = 128

.
.
.
# Number of VCPUS
vcpus = 2

# Network devices
# A list of 'vifspec' entries as described in
# docs/misc/xl-network-configuration.markdown
vif = [ '' ]

# Disk Devices
# A list of 'diskspec' entries as described in
# docs/misc/xl-disk-configuration.txt
disk = [ '/dev/vg/guest-volume,raw,xvda,rw' ]
```

CHAPTER 3 XEN

As for the fully virtualized Linux, we can see pretty much the same options with a few key differences.

```
antonio@ubuntu:~$ cat /etc/xen/xlexample.hvm
#============================================================
# Example HVM guest configuration
#============================================================
#
# This is a fairly minimal example of what is required for an
# HVM guest. For a more complete guide see xl.cfg(5)

# This configures an HVM rather than PV guest
type = "hvm"

# Guest name
name = "example.hvm"
·
·
·
# Initial memory allocation (MB)
memory = 128
·
·
·
# Number of VCPUS
vcpus = 2

# Network devices
# A list of 'vifspec' entries as described in
# docs/misc/xl-network-configuration.markdown
vif = [ '' ]
```

```
# Disk Devices
# A list of 'diskspec' entries as described in
# docs/misc/xl-disk-configuration.txt
disk = [ '/dev/vg/guest-volume,raw,xvda,rw' ]

# Guest VGA console configuration, either SDL or VNC
sdl = 1
#vnc = 1
```

Let's take a look at some of the main options.

- Type: This parameter is used to specify whether the domain created will be fully virtualized or paravirtualized. Possible values are "**pv**" for paravirtualized domains and "**hvm**" for fully virtualized domains with emulated BIOS, disk, and network peripherals. There is also an intermediate option, "**pvh**", a lightweight hvm without many of the emulated devices we find on "normal" hvm guests. If we do not specify the type parameter, it is assumed that we're defining a paravirtualized domain.

- Name: This is the name of the domain; it must be unique in a host.

- Kernel: Specifies the path of the kernel image, accessible to the host. This option is used when using direct kernel boot.

- Ramdisk: Specifies the path of the disk image, accessible to the host. As the "kernel" option, this one is also used in direct kernel boot.

CHAPTER 3   XEN

- Extra: This is an extra parameter appended to the kernel command line.

- Memory: Used to set the amount of memory in megabytes.

- Vcpus: This parameter sets the number of virtual CPUs.

- Vif: Specifies the network interfaces.

- Disk: As the name implies, it specifies the disks that are provided to the guest.

- SDL: When enabled, the display is presented via an X window using Simple DirectMedia Layer.

- Vnc: This parameter allows to access the display through the VNC protocol.

Now that we have some knowledge about the main options in a configuration file, we'll apply this knowledge to create our first Xen-based VM.

Installing Alpine Linux As a Paravirtualized Unprivileged Domain

We'll install our first VM on Xen. For that, we'll choose a lightweight Linux distribution named Alpine. We'll download the needed files from the Alpine Linux website (Figure 3-3).

CHAPTER 3 XEN

Figure 3-3.   Alpine Linux

We'll go to "Downloads" and then to "Virtual" (Figure 3-4), and we'll download the ISO file for the x86_64 architecture.

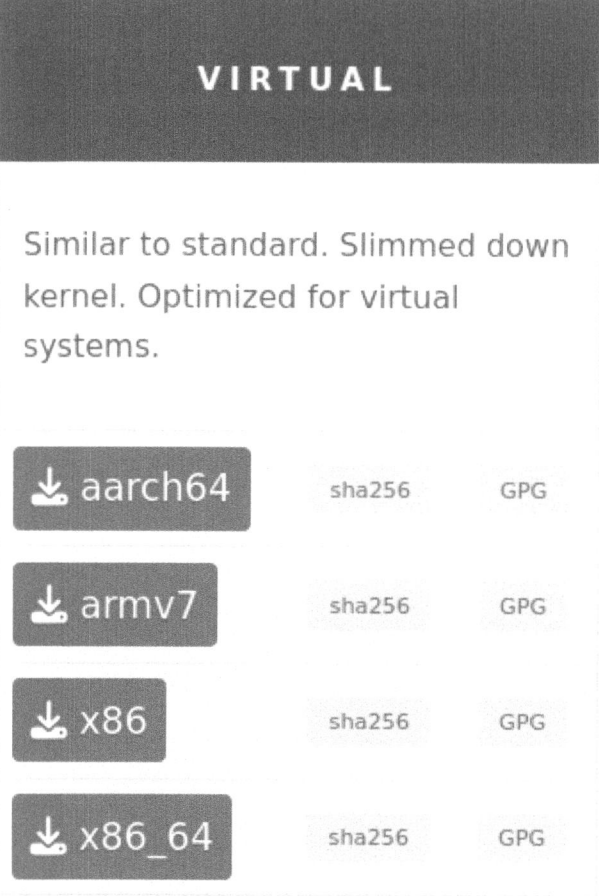

Figure 3-4. Alpine ISO files optimized for virtualized environments

```
antonio@ubuntu:/XEN_VMS$ wget https://dl-cdn.alpinelinux.org/
alpine/v3.20/releases/x86_64/alpine-virt-3.20.0-x86_64.iso
```

Initial Customization of the Example Configuration File

Now we'll take one of the example files we mentioned previously, and we'll edit it accordingly to create our first VM. In this first example, we'll use a paravirtualized VM/domain.

```
antonio@ubuntu:/XEN_VMS$ cp /etc/xen/xlexample.pvlinux
alpine.pvlinux
```

We'll edit a few lines of the configuration file we just copied. At the beginning of the file, we'll see this line:

```
# Guest name
name = "example.pvlinux"
```

We'll change it to add a more appropriate name.

```
name = "alpine.pvlinux"
```

Then we'll see an entry for the kernel to load.

```
# Kernel image to boot
kernel = "/boot/vmlinuz"
```

We'll use the kernel file inside the ISO file we just downloaded, so we'll need to mount it first.

```
antonio@ubuntu:/XEN_VMS$ sudo mount -o loop alpine-
virt-3.20.0-x86_64.iso /mnt/
mount: /mnt: WARNING: device write-protected, mounted
read-only.
```

Inside the */boot* directory, we'll find the kernel file.

```
antonio@ubuntu:/XEN_VMS$ ls /mnt/boot/
System.map-6.6.31-0-virt  config-6.6.31-0-virt  dtbs-virt
grub  initramfs-virt  modloop-virt  syslinux  vmlinuz-virt
```

So we'll edit the corresponding parameter in the *alpine.pvlinux* file.

```
# Kernel image to boot
kernel = "/mnt/boot/vmlinuz-virt"
```

CHAPTER 3 XEN

Right after the kernel option, we'll see the ramdisk entry, which is commented out by default.

```
# Ramdisk (optional)
#ramdisk = "/boot/initrd.gz"
```

After mounting the ISO file, we could see the ramdisk file in the same directory as the kernel file. We'll edit this entry in the file as well.

```
# Ramdisk (optional)
ramdisk = "/mnt/boot/initramfs-virt"
```

The initial memory allocation is just 128 MB.

```
# Initial memory allocation (MB)
memory = 128
```

Alpine Linux is very light, so this amount of memory is probably enough, but we'll increase it a little bit.

```
# Initial memory allocation (MB)
memory = 512
```

By default, two virtual CPUs are created for the VM.

```
# Number of VCPUS
vcpus = 2
```

We'll change this value to 1.

```
# Number of VCPUS
vcpus = 1
```

Finally, at the bottom of the file, we'll see the definition of the disk or disks associated with the VM.

```
# Disk Devices
# A list of `diskspec' entries as described in
# docs/misc/xl-disk-configuration.txt
disk = [ '/dev/vg/guest-volume,raw,xvda,rw' ]
```

In the default value, a logical volume is used as the disk for the VM, but it is also possible to use a file, as we'll see now. We'll use **dd** to create a 1 GiB disk file.

```
antonio@ubuntu:/XEN_VMS$ dd if=/dev/zero of=alpine.hd bs=1M count=1024
1024+0 records in
1024+0 records out
1073741824 bytes (1.1 GB, 1.0 GiB) copied, 2.02189 s, 531 MB/s
```

And we'll edit the "disk" entry to use the newly created file as the disk for the VM.

```
# Disk Devices
# A list of 'diskspec' entries as described in
# docs/misc/xl-disk-configuration.txt
disk = [ 'alpine.hd,raw,xvda,rw' ]
```

The final *alpine.pvlinux* file will look like this:

```
antonio@ubuntu:/XEN_VMS$ cat alpine.pvlinux
# =============================================================
# Example PV Linux guest configuration
# =============================================================
#
# This is a fairly minimal example of what is required for a
# Paravirtualised Linux guest. For a more complete guide see
  xl.cfg(5)
```

```
# Guest name
name = "alpine.pvlinux"

# 128-bit UUID for the domain as a hexadecimal number.
# Use "uuidgen" to generate one if required.
# The default behavior is to generate a new UUID each time the
  guest is started.
#uuid = "XXXXXXXX-XXXX-XXXX-XXXX-XXXXXXXXXXXX"

# Kernel image to boot
kernel = "/mnt/boot/vmlinuz-virt"

# Ramdisk (optional)
ramdisk = "/mnt/boot/initramfs-virt"

# Kernel command line options
extra = "root=/dev/xvda1"

# Initial memory allocation (MB)
memory = 512

# Maximum memory (MB)
# If this is greater than `memory' then the slack will start
  ballooned
# (this assumes guest kernel support for ballooning)
#maxmem = 512

# Number of VCPUS
vcpus = 1

# Network devices
# A list of 'vifspec' entries as described in
# docs/misc/xl-network-configuration.markdown
vif = [ '' ]
```

```
# Disk Devices
# A list of `diskspec' entries as described in
# docs/misc/xl-disk-configuration.txt
disk = [ 'alpine.hd,raw,xvda,rw' ]
```

Now we are ready to create the VM.

antonio@ubuntu:/XEN_VMS$ sudo xl create -f alpine.pvlinux

But we'll get this error:

```
Parsing config from alpine.pvlinux
libxl: error: libxl_exec.c:117:libxl_report_child_exitstatus:
/etc/xen/scripts/vif-bridge online [6063] exited with error
status 1
libxl: error: libxl_device.c:1286:device_hotplug_child_death_
cb: script: Could not find bridge device xenbr0
libxl: error: libxl_create.c:1519:domcreate_attach_devices:
Domain 7:unable to add vif devices
libxl: error: libxl_exec.c:117:libxl_report_child_exitstatus:
/etc/xen/scripts/vif-bridge offline [6094] exited with error
status 1
libxl: error: libxl_device.c:1286:device_hotplug_child_death_
cb: script: Could not find bridge device xenbr0
libxl: error: libxl_domain.c:1034:libxl__destroy_domid: Domain
7:Non-existant domain
libxl: error: libxl_domain.c:993:domain_destroy_callback:
Domain 7:Unable to destroy guest
libxl: error: libxl_domain.c:920:domain_destroy_cb: Domain
7:Destruction of domain failed
```

CHAPTER 3 XEN

When creating a Xen VM, a series of scripts are executed. We see here that the */etc/xen/scripts/vif-bridge* script failed because it couldn't find the xenbr0 device. Even though we haven't defined any network interface in the configuration file, Xen by default searches for a bridge named xenbr0.

Creating a Bridge

We'll see more details later, but for now, we'll just create a bridge with that same name and no interfaces attached, just to skip that error.

```
antonio@ubuntu:/XEN_VMS$ sudo brctl addbr xenbr0
```

And we try to create the VM again.

```
antonio@ubuntu:/XEN_VMS$ sudo xl create -f alpine.pvlinux
Parsing config from alpine.pvlinux
```

In this case, we don't see any errors, so we assume that Xen is creating the VM. We can list the VMs with **xl**.

```
antonio@ubuntu:/XEN_VMS$ sudo xl list
Name                         ID   Mem  VCPUs  State    Time(s)
Domain-0                      0   3011    2   r-----    476.8
alpine.pvlinux                9    512    1   -b----      1.3
```

We see the virtual machine/domain alpine.pvlinux, but its state is not "r" (running), but "b" (blocked). This could indicate a problem, or maybe it's just due to the fact that the system has gone to sleep because it has nothing else to do. In any of these cases, it's useful to connect to the console of the virtual machine to see what is actually happening.

```
antonio@ubuntu:/XEN_VMS$ sudo xl console alpine.pvlinux
```

We'll see something like this:

.
.
.
```
[    0.711629] Loading boot drivers: ok.
ok.
[    0.714930] Mounting root...
 * Mounting root: [    1.100682] block xvda: the capability
   attribute has been deprecated.
mount: mounting /dev/xvda1 on /sysroot failed: Invalid argument
[    1.240716] Mounting root: failed.
failed.
initramfs emergency recovery shell launched. Type 'exit' to
continue boot
sh: can't access tty; job control turned off
~ #
```

We see that the system didn't boot correctly; let's detach the server console by pressing CTRL+5 and recap what we have seen so far.

The virtual machine tried to mount */dev/xvda1*, because this is specified in this line of the alpine.pvlinux file:

```
# Kernel command line options
extra = "root=/dev/xvda1"
```

Here we're telling that the root filesystem is in the first partition of the disk */dev/xvda*. And in the disk definition, we see this:

```
disk = [ 'alpine.hd,raw,xvda,rw' ]
```

The disk is defined in the *alpine.hd* file we just created, but this file is completely empty; it has no partitions and no filesystems. The fact that the system can't boot is normal behavior.

Defining a CDROM Drive

What we'll do now is to install the OS from the ISO file we just downloaded. To do it, we need to define a CDROM device and boot the VM from the CDROM.

First of all, we'll see in more detail how we defined the disk for our VM. The first entry is the name of the file we created. The second entry, raw in this case, is the format of the disk. We have already seen when we spoke about QEMU that the disk files can have different formats like qcow2, raw, etc. In this case, we created a disk in raw format, that is, without a format. The third entry is the name of the device, xvda in this example as we're using paravirtualization. Finally, the fourth entry sets the access mode of the device, read/write in this case.

To know how to define a CDROM device, we can see the man page for xl.cfg.

antonio@ubuntu:/XEN_VMS$ man xl.cfg

In the page, we'll see this brief description:

disk=["DISK_SPEC_STRING", "DISK_SPEC_STRING", ...]
    Specifies the disks (both emulated disks and Xen
    virtual block devices) which are to be provided
    to the guest, and what objects on the host they
    should map to. See xl-disk-configuration(5) for more
    details.

To gather more information, we'll open the man page for xl-disk-configuration. In the first lines, we'll see an example of how to define a CDROM device using different formats.

antonio@ubuntu:/XEN_VMS$ man xl-disk-configuration

-
-
-

CHAPTER 3 XEN

```
/root/image.iso,,hdc,cdrom
/root/image.iso,,hdc,,cdrom
/root/image.iso,raw,hdc,devtype=cdrom
format=raw, vdev=hdc, access=ro, devtype=cdrom,
target=/root/image.iso
raw:/root/image.iso,hdc:cdrom,ro    (deprecated,
see below)
```

We'll use the fourth format, as it is possibly the most intuitive, but you're free to use any of them. We'll edit the disk entry in the *alpine. pvlinux* file to add the information for the CDROM definition; we'll also adapt the disk definition so that both lines use the same format.

```
disk = [
        'format=raw, vdev=xvda, access=rw, target=alpine.hd',
        'format=raw, vdev=xvdc, access=r, devtype=cdrom,
        target=alpine-virt-3.20.0-x86_64.iso'
]
```

And we'll comment out the "extra" option.

```
# Kernel command line options
#extra = "root=/dev/xvda1"
```

We'll shutdown the VM we had created previously.

```
antonio@ubuntu:/XEN_VMS$ sudo xl shutdown alpine.pvlinux
```

And we create the VM again with the new options. We'll use the "-c" option to connect automatically to the VM console.

```
antonio@ubuntu:/XEN_VMS$ sudo xl create -c -f alpine.pvlinux
Parsing config from alpine.pvlinux
[    0.000000] Linux version 6.6.31-0-virt (buildozer@
build-3-20-x86_64) (gcc (Alpine 13.2.1_git20240309) 13.2.1
```

CHAPTER 3   XEN

20240309, GNU ld (GNU Binutils) 2.42) #1-Alpine SMP PREEMPT_
DYNAMIC Fri, 17 May 2024 11:04:37 +0000
[0.000000] Command line:
[0.000000] ACPI in unprivileged domain disabled
[0.000000] Released 0 page(s)
[0.000000] BIOS-provided physical RAM map:
.
.
.
 * Starting busybox syslog ... [ok]
 * Starting firstboot ... [ok]

Welcome to Alpine Linux 3.20
Kernel 6.6.31-0-virt on an x86_64 (/dev/hvc0)

localhost login:

The system booted from CD, and we're faced with a login prompt. We can log in as "root" without a password.

localhost login: root
Welcome to Alpine!

The Alpine Wiki contains a large amount of how-to guides and general information about administrating Alpine systems. See <https://wiki.alpinelinux.org/>.

You can setup the system with the command: setup-alpine

You may change this message by editing /etc/motd.

localhost:~#

We can start the installation procedure by executing the command setup-alpine. The installation procedure is quite easy to follow, but when trying to contact a mirror, it will fail, as currently our Xen VM doesn't have Internet connectivity.

```
localhost:~# setup-alpine

 ALPINE LINUX INSTALL
 ----------------------
 Hostname
 ----------
 Enter system hostname (fully qualified form, e.g. 'foo.example.
 org') [localhost] my-alpine
 .
 .
 .
 wget: bad address 'mirrors.alpinelinux.org'
```

Configuring Networking

We had created a bridge named xenbr0, but we didn't add any interfaces to it, so the domain/virtual machine has no connectivity. We'll need to configure the bridge properly.

First, we add a connected interface to our bridge.

```
antonio@ubuntu:~$ sudo ip brctl addif xenbr0 ens33
```

And then we make sure that the bridge is up.

```
antonio@ubuntu:~$ sudo ip link set xenbr0 up
```

Now we get back to the *alpine.pvlinux* file. We'll see these lines regarding the network interface:

```
# Network devices
# A list of 'vifspec' entries as described in
# docs/misc/xl-network-configuration.markdown
vif = [ '' ]
```

We can specify several options regarding the virtual network interface, such as the MAC address, the IP address, the bridge used, etc. We can take a look at the xl-network-configuration man page to see some examples. In our case, we'll just specify the bridge name. We'll configure the IP later.

```
# Network devices
# A list of 'vifspec' entries as described in
# docs/misc/xl-network-configuration.markdown
vif = [ bridge=xenbr0' ]
```

And we'll start again the VM with the new settings.

```
antonio@ubuntu:~$ sudo xl create -c -f alpine.pvlinux
```

In the VM/domain, we'll see that we already have an Ethernet interface.

```
localhost:~# ip a
1: lo: <LOOPBACK> mtu 65536 qdisc noop state DOWN qlen 1000
    link/loopback 00:00:00:00:00:00 brd 00:00:00:00:00:00
2: eth0: <BROADCAST,MULTICAST> mtu 1500 qdisc noop state DOWN
    qlen 1000
     link/ether 00:16:3e:3c:d5:68 brd ff:ff:ff:ff:ff:ff
```

And in the host, we can see that a new virtual interface has been created and added to the xenbr0 bridge, allowing the communication between the host and the guest.

CHAPTER 3 XEN

```
antonio@ubuntu:~$ ip link
1: lo: <LOOPBACK,UP,LOWER_UP> mtu 65536 qdisc noqueue state
   UNKNOWN mode DEFAULT group default qlen 1000
   link/loopback 00:00:00:00:00:00 brd 00:00:00:00:00:00
2: ens33: <BROADCAST,MULTICAST,UP,LOWER_UP> mtu 1500 qdisc
   fq_codel master xenbr0 state UP mode DEFAULT group default
   qlen 1000
   link/ether 00:0c:29:c4:d1:d0 brd ff:ff:ff:ff:ff:ff
   altname enp2s1
3: xenbr0: <BROADCAST,MULTICAST,UP,LOWER_UP> mtu 1500 qdisc
   noqueue state UP mode DEFAULT group default qlen 1000
   link/ether 00:0c:29:c4:d1:d0 brd ff:ff:ff:ff:ff:ff
4: vif3.0: <NO-CARRIER,BROADCAST,MULTICAST,UP> mtu 1500 qdisc mq
   master xenbr0 state DOWN mode DEFAULT group default qlen 1000
   link/ether fe:ff:ff:ff:ff:ff brd ff:ff:ff:ff:ff:ff

antonio@ubuntu:~$ brctl show
bridge name     bridge id               STP enabled     interfaces
xenbr0          8000.000c29c4d1d0       no              ens33
                                                        vif3.0
```

We only have to add an IP to the interface on the guest and activate the interface.

```
localhost:~# ip address add 192.168.1.60/24 dev eth0
```

Now we can ping the host from the guest and vice versa.

```
localhost:~# ip link set eth0 up
localhost:~# ping 192.168.1.51
PING 192.168.1.51 (192.168.1.51): 56 data bytes
64 bytes from 192.168.1.51: seq=0 ttl=64 time=1.236 ms
```

Now that we have connectivity, we could install the OS with setup-alpine. But we'll get to that in the next example.

CHAPTER 3   XEN

Using a Logical Volume As the Disk of the VM

So far, we have used a file as a hard disk for our VM/domain, but we can also use a LV for that. To do it, we'll create a LV on the host. We had already created a LV as a good practice to store our virtual machines; we'll follow the same procedure to create a new LV in which to install a Xen domain/virtual machine. We repeat the same steps, and this time we create a LV named XENLV, included in a VG named XENVG.

```
antonio@ubuntu:~$ sudo lvs XENVG
  LV    VG    Attr       LSize Pool Origin Data% Meta% Move
  Log Cpy%Sync Convert
  XENLV XENVG -wi-a----- 2,00g
```

To use a LV instead of a file as the disk of our virtual machine, we need to open the *alpine.pvlinux* file and edit the "disk" entry. This is the current value of this entry:

```
disk = [
        'format=raw, vdev=xvda, access=rw, target=alpine.hd',
        'format=raw, vdev=xvdc, access=r, devtype=cdrom,
        target=alpine-virt-3.20.0-x86_64.iso'
]
```

We need to edit the entry for the hard disk, changing the target. After editing, it should look like this:

```
disk = [
        'format=raw, vdev=xvda, access=rw, target=/dev/
        XENVG/XENLV',
        'format=raw, vdev=xvdc, access=r, devtype=cdrom,
        target=alpine-virt-3.20.0-x86_64.iso'
]
```

CHAPTER 3   XEN

We save the changes and recreate the VM again. We'll shutdown any previously running instances if necessary.

```
antonio@ubuntu:/XEN_VMS$ sudo xl create -c -f alpine.pvlinux
.
.
.
Welcome to Alpine Linux 3.17
Kernel 5.15.79-0-virt on an x86_64 (/dev/hvc0)

localhost login: root
Welcome to Alpine!

The Alpine Wiki contains a large amount of how-to guides and
general information about administrating Alpine systems.
See <https://wiki.alpinelinux.org/>.

You can setup the system with the command: setup-alpine

You may change this message by editing /etc/motd.

localhost:~#
```

We launch **setup-alpine** to start the OS installation.

```
localhost:~# setup-alpine
.
.
.
Available interfaces are: eth0.
Enter '?' for help on bridges, bonding and vlans.
Which one do you want to initialize? (or '?' or 'done') [eth0]
Ip address for eth0? (or 'dhcp', 'none', '?') [dhcp]
Do you want to do any manual network configuration? (y/n) [n]
udhcpc: started, v1.35.0
udhcpc: broadcasting discover
```

121

CHAPTER 3 XEN

```
udhcpc: broadcasting select for 10.0.3.16, server 10.0.3.2
udhcpc: lease of 10.0.3.16 obtained from 10.0.3.2, lease
time 86400
```
.
.
.

After setting up the network, we need to select the time zone; we select a proxy if necessary and choose a mirror.

.
```
Enter mirror number (1-81) or URL to add (or r/f/e/done) [1]
Added mirror dl-cdn.alpinelinux.org
Updating repository indexes... done.
```
.

We now select the disk where we'll install the OS.

.
```
Available disks are:
  xvda     (2.1 GB  )
Which disk(s) would you like to use? (or '?' for help or
'none') [none] xvda
The following disk is selected:
  xvda     (2.1 GB  )
How would you like to use it? ('sys', 'data', 'crypt', 'lvm' or
'?' for help) [?] sys
WARNING: The following disk(s) will be erased:
  xvda     (2.1 GB  )
```
.
```
Creating file systems...
Installing system on /dev/xvda3:
```

```
/mnt/boot is device /dev/xvda1
100% ■■■■■■■■■■■■■■■■■■■■■■■■■■■■■■■■■■■■■■
■■■■■■■■■■==> initramfs: creating /boot/initramfs-virt
/boot is device /dev/xvda1

Installation is complete. Please reboot.
alpine:~#
```

The installation is complete. Before rebooting, we need to change some parameters in the *alpine.pvlinux* file, so we'll shut down the VM.

```
antonio@ubuntu:/XEN_VMS$ sudo xl shutdown alpine.pvlinux
```

The first thing we'll do is to suppress the disk entry for the CDROM, leaving only the entry for the hard disk.

```
disk = [
    'format=raw, vdev=xvda, access=rw, target=/dev/XENVG/XENLV',
]
```

We also have to change the parameters for the kernel and the ramdisk file. We used previously those of the ISO file; now we'll use the files installed in the VM disk.

We unmount the ISO file.

```
antonio@ubuntu:/XEN_VMS$ sudo umount /mnt
```

And we mount the LV in which we installed the system. We can't mount directly the system partition inside the LV, so we'll need to associate it with a loop device first.

```
antonio@ubuntu:/XEN_VMS$ sudo losetup -Pf /dev/XENVG/XENLV
antonio@ubuntu:/XEN_VMS$ sudo ls -ld /dev/XENVG/XENLV
```

CHAPTER 3   XEN

```
lrwxrwxrwx 1 root root 7 jun  9 14:23 /dev/XENVG/XENLV
-> ../dm-0
antonio@ubuntu:/XEN_VMS$ sudo losetup -a | grep dm-0
/dev/loop0: [0006]:18381 (/dev/dm-0)
```

If we open the loop device, we'll see the partitions.

```
antonio@ubuntu:/XEN_VMS$ sudo fdisk /dev/loop0

Welcome to fdisk (util-linux 2.36.2).
.
.
.
Device         Boot  Start   End      Sectors Size Id Type
/dev/loop0p1 *       2048    616447   614400  300M 83 Linux
/dev/loop0p2         616448  1550335  933888  456M 82 Linux swap
                                                      / Solaris
/dev/loop0p3         1550336 4194303  2643968 1,3G 83 Linux

Command (m for help): q
```

And now we can mount the boot partition locally in the host.

```
antonio@ubuntu:/XEN_VMS$ sudo mount /dev/loop0p3 /mnt
antonio@ubuntu:/XEN_VMS$ sudo mount /dev/loop0p1 /mnt
antonio@ubuntu:/XEN_VMS$ sudo ls /mnt
boot           extlinux.conf    ldlinux.c32    libcom32.
c32    lost+found   menu.c32           vesamenu.c32
config-virt    initramfs-virt   ldlinux.sys    libutil.c32    mboot.
c32    System.map-virt  vmlinuz-virt
```

We review the alpine.pvlinux file to make sure that we're pointing to the correct kernel and ramdisk files.

```
# Kernel image to boot
kernel = "/mnt/boot/vmlinuz-virt"

# Ramdisk (optional)
ramdisk = "/mnt/boot/initramfs-virt"
```

Finally, we also need to update the "extra" parameter to include the kernel command-line options needed to properly boot the system.

```
extra = "root=/dev/xvda3 rootfstype=ext4"
```

The alpine.pvlinux file should look more or less like this right now:

```
# Guest name
name = "alpine.pvlinux"

# 128-bit UUID for the domain as a hexadecimal number.
# Use "uuidgen" to generate one if required.
# The default behavior is to generate a new UUID each time the
  guest is started.
#uuid = "XXXXXXXX-XXXX-XXXX-XXXX-XXXXXXXXXXXX"

# Kernel image to boot
kernel = "/mnt/boot/vmlinuz-virt"

# Ramdisk (optional)
ramdisk = "/mnt/boot/initramfs-virt"

# Kernel command line options
extra = "root=/dev/xvda3 rootfstype=ext4"

# Initial memory allocation (MB)
memory = 512

# Maximum memory (MB)
# If this is greater than `memory' then the slack will start
  ballooned
```

CHAPTER 3 XEN

```
# (this assumes guest kernel support for ballooning)
#maxmem = 512

# Number of VCPUS
vcpus = 1

# Network devices
# A list of 'vifspec' entries as described in
# docs/misc/xl-network-configuration.markdown
vif = [ 'bridge=xenbr0' ]

# Disk Devices
# A list of 'diskspec' entries as described in
# docs/misc/xl-disk-configuration.txt
disk = [
    'format=raw, vdev=xvda, access=rw, target=/dev/XENVG/XENLV',
]
```

And we launch again the VM/domain.

```
antonio@ubuntu:/XEN_VMS$ sudo xl create -c -f alpine.pvlinux
Parsing config from alpine.pvlinux
.
.
.
[    0.787245] Mounting root...
 * Mounting root: [    1.558391] EXT4-fs (xvda3): mounted
filesystem with ordered data mode. Opts: (null). Quota
mode: none.
[    1.558630] Mounting root: ok.
ok.
.
.
.
```

```
Welcome to Alpine Linux 3.17
Kernel 5.15.160-0-virt on an x86_64 (/dev/hvc0)

alpine login:
```

We log in with the password set during the installation, and we're ready to start working with the new system.

```
alpine:~# df -h
Filesystem              Size      Used  Available Use% Mounted on
devtmpfs                10.0M     0     10.0M     0%   /dev
shm                     113.0M    0     113.0M    0%   /dev/shm
/dev/xvda3              1.2G      54.1M 1.1G      5%   /
tmpfs                   45.2M     64.0K 45.2M     0%   /run
/dev/xvda1              271.1M    17.9M 234.2M    7%   /boot
tmpfs                   113.0M    0     113.0M    0%   /tmp
```

Working with a Hardware Virtualized Machine

We'll see now an example of a fully virtualized machine, also referred in Xen as a hardware virtualized machine (HVM). As many of the options are the same for both paravirtualized and fully virtualized domains, we'll try to keep this example as simple as possible. We'll use the following configuration file:

```
#============================================================
# Example HVM guest configuration
#============================================================
#
# This is a fairly minimal example of what is required for an
# HVM guest. For a more complete guide see xl.cfg(5)

# This configures an HVM rather than PV guest
type = "hvm"
```

```
# Guest name
name = "alpine.hvm"

# Initial memory allocation (MB)
memory = 256

# Number of VCPUS
vcpus = 1

# Network devices
# A list of 'vifspec' entries as described in
# docs/misc/xl-network-configuration.markdown
vif = [ 'bridge=xenbr0' ]

# Disk Devices
# A list of `diskspec' entries as described in
# docs/misc/xl-disk-configuration.txt
disk = [ 'format=qcow2, vdev=xvda, access=rw, target=alpine_disk.qcow' ]

# Guest VGA console configuration, either SDL or VNC
#sdl = 1
vnc = 1
```

At the beginning, we tell Xen that we'll use a fully virtualized machine. We do that with the "type=hvm" parameter. When we worked with paravirtualization, we didn't need to add the "type=pv" because this is the default value.

Another option we hadn't seen so far is the VGA console configuration. We can use this section to tell Xen to provide a graphical console as a graphical window (option sdl) or as a VNC instance (option vnc). In our case, we'll use vnc to connect to the virtual machine.

CHAPTER 3 XEN

We create the virtual machine/domain in the same way we did with the paravirtualized domain.

```
antonio@ubuntu:/XEN_VMS$ sudo xl create -f alpine.hvm
Parsing config from alpine.hvm
```

After a few seconds, we'll see the VM already executing.

```
antonio@ubuntu:/XEN_VMS$ sudo xl list
Name                          ID  Mem  VCPUs State   Time(s)
Domain-0                      0   1226 1     r-----  31.5
alpine.hvm                    3   120  1     ------  10.6
```

To access the console, we can use any vnc client, such as Tiger VNC viewer (Figure 3-5).

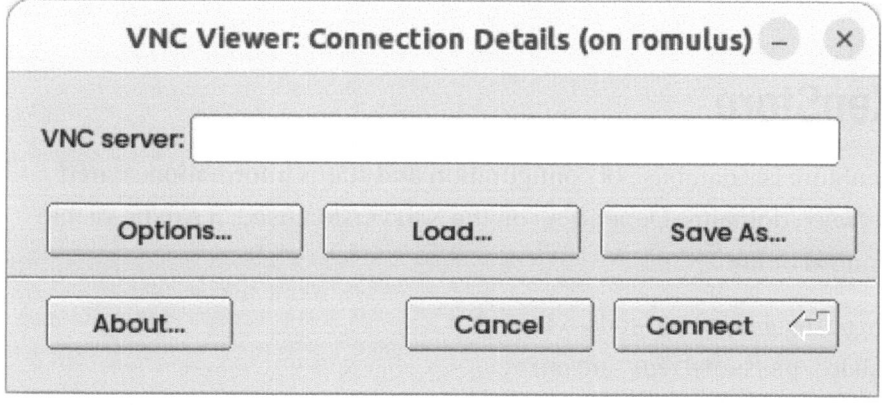

Figure 3-5. *VNC viewer*

And we'll access the server console (Figure 3-6).

CHAPTER 3   XEN

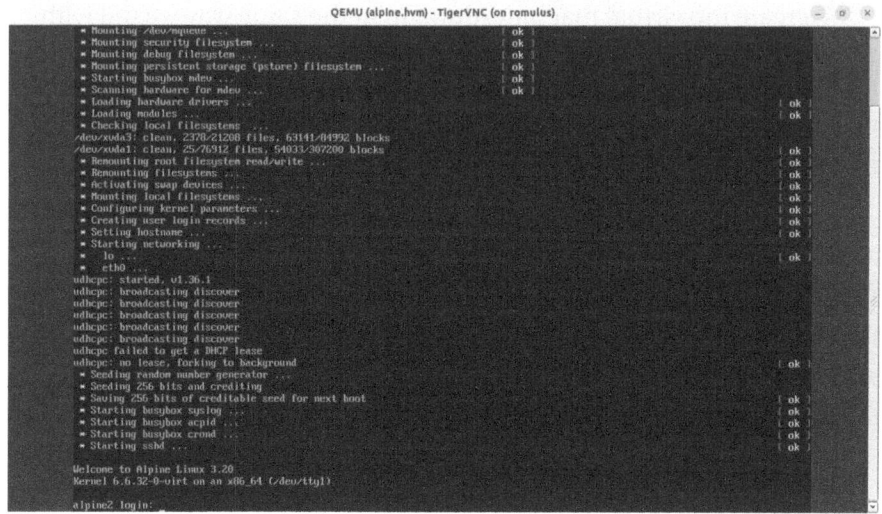

Figure 3-6. *Server console accessed through VNC*

XenStore

XenStore is a database of configuration and status information shared between domains. Depending on the Xen version used, it can be visible using **xl** or not.

```
antonio@ubuntu:~$ sudo xl list
[sudo] password for antonio:
Name                    ID  Mem  VCPUs  State   Time(s)
Domain-0                0   3527 2      r-----  95.3

romulus:/home/antonio/XEN # xl list
Name                    ID  Mem  VCPUs  State   Time(s)
Domain-0                0   1226 1      r-----  1027.7
Xenstore                1   31   1      -b----  0.6
alpine.hvm              3   120  1      -b----  1034.1
```

130

CHAPTER 3 XEN

XenStore is usually managed by Dom0, but we can also perform basic operations on it. For instance, we can use **xenstore-ls** to dump all the information contained in the XenStore database.

```
romulus:/home/antonio/XEN # xenstore-ls
tool = ""
 xenstored = ""
  domid = "1"
local = ""
 domain = ""
 .
 .
 .
vm = ""
 1175b42d-a0c0-4bc4-915d-f62512d44284 = ""
  name = "alpine.hvm"
  uuid = "1175b42d-a0c0-4bc4-915d-f62512d44284"
 .
 .
 .
```

We can also query the xenstore database to get information about a given virtual machine; first, we list the identifiers of every running virtual machine.

```
romulus:/home/antonio/XEN # xenstore list /vm
1175b42d-a0c0-4bc4-915d-f62512d44284
```

And then, we can obtain data such as the VM name or the start time.

```
romulus:/home/antonio/XEN # xenstore list /vm/1175b42d-
a0c0-4bc4-915d-f62512d44284
name
uuid
```

CHAPTER 3   XEN

```
rtc
image
start_time
romulus:/home/antonio/XEN # xenstore read /vm/1175b42d-
a0c0-4bc4-915d-f62512d44284/name
alpine.hvm
```

GRUB Start Options

As we have seen at the beginning of this chapter, Xen is a Linux kernel optimized to be used as a hypervisor. Many relevant options for the normal functioning of the hypervisor can be customized in GRUB.

In Ubuntu, when installing Xen, a new file */etc/default/grub.d/xen.cfg* is created. In this file, we can see many variables that can be set to pass options to the hypervisor. Let's take a look at the first lines of this file:

```
antonio@ubuntu:/XEN_VMS$ cat /etc/default/grub.d/xen.cfg
# When running update-grub with the Xen hypervisor installed, there are
# some additional variables that can be used to pass options to the
# hypervisor or the dom0 kernel.
#
# The configuration in here makes it possible to have different options set
# for the linux kernel when booting with or without Xen.

echo "Including Xen overrides from /etc/default/grub.d/xen.cfg"
```

CHAPTER 3 XEN

```
###################################################################
# Xen Hypervisor Command Line Options
#
# The first two options are used to generate arguments for the
  hypervisor.
# Commonly used options are:
#
# dom0_mem=<size> (for arm)
# dom0_mem=<size>,max:<size> (for x86)
#    Sets the amount of memory dom0 uses to a fixed size. All
     other memory
#    will be usable for domUs. For x86, this prevents
     ballooning actions
#    from happening to take away memory from the dom0 or return
     it back. For
#    arm, setting this option is required. E.g. (for x86) dom0_
     mem=4G,max:4G
#
# dom0_max_vcpus=<min>-<max>
#    Limits the amount of physical cpus that dom0 is using, so
     it will not
```
-
-
-

We can see that the dom0_mem variable sets the amount of memory used by Dom0. This value is usually dynamically assigned by the system, but if we want to assign a fixed value, we can do that by editing the corresponding GRUB entry (Figure 3-7).

CHAPTER 3 XEN

```
                    GNU GRUB  version 2.04

9-68807ae3401e
        fi
        echo         'Loading Xen 4.14.5_08-150300.3.40 ...'
        if [ "$grub_platform" = "pc" -o "$grub_platform" = "" ]; then
            xen_rm_opts=
        else
            xen_rm_opts="no-real-mode edd=off"
        fi
        multiboot2      /boot/xen-4.14.5_08-150300.3.40.gz placeholder\
  vga=gfx-1024x768x16 ${xen_rm_opts} dom0_mem=512_
        echo         'Loading Linux 5.3.18-59.10-default ...'
        module2         /boot/vmlinuz-5.3.18-59.10-default placeholder ro\
ot=UUID=8dd5816c-06ff-4ef1-9409-68807ae3401e  ${extra_cmdline} splash=si\
lent mitigations=auto quiet
        echo         'Loading initial ramdisk ...'


   Minimum Emacs-like screen editing is supported. TAB lists
   completions. Press Ctrl-x or F10 to boot, Ctrl-c or F2 for a
   command-line or ESC to discard edits and return to the GRUB
   menu.
```

Figure 3-7. *Setting the amount of memory used by Dom0 on GRUB*

In this example, the amount of memory set is too small and Dom0 cannot boot (Figure 3-8), but this is OK as we only wanted to show an example on how to pass this parameter to the hypervisor.

```
(XEN) Xen kernel: 64-bit, lsb, compat32
(XEN) Dom0 kernel: 64-bit, PAE, lsb, paddr 0x1000000 -> 0x4000000
(XEN)
(XEN) ******************************************
(XEN) Panic on CPU 0:
(XEN) Domain 0 allocation is too small for kernel image
(XEN) xxxxxxxxxxxxxxxxxxxxxxxxxxxxxxxxxxxxxxxxxx
(XEN)
(XEN) Reboot in five seconds...
```

Figure 3-8. *Dom0 memory allocation too small*

Of course, there are many more parameters that can be passed to the kernel adding the corresponding options in GRUB, like dom0_max_vcpus, console, etc.

Managing Xen with xl/xm/XAPI

So far we have used **xl** to manage Xen, but this is not the only choice we have. In the early days of Xen, **xend** was the toolstack used to manage the Xen hypervisor. The client tool **xm** interacted with xend to perform the needed operations.

Later, with Xen 4.1, a new toolstack, **libxenlight**, was developed. Its use was preferred over that of **xend/xm**. The client tool used with libxenlight is **xl**, of which we have already seen many examples in this chapter.

For some time, both toolstacks were available to manage Xen, although the use of xend/xm was considered deprecated. But since Xen 4.5, it has been completely removed. Its use was quite similar to that of xl. If we work with a Xen version prior to 4.5, we might still use xm, as in this example:

```
SUSE:~ # xm
Usage: xm <subcommand> [args]

Control, list, and manipulate Xen guest instances.

Common 'xm' commands:

   console            Attach to <Domain>'s console.
   vncviewer          Attach to <Domain>'s VNC server.
   create             Create a domain based on <ConfigFile>.
   .
   .
   .
```

If we want to list the virtual machines, we can do it very similarly to what we did before with **xl**.

```
SUSE:~ # xm list
Name                       ID   Mem  VCPUs State    Time(s)
Domain-0                   0    912  1     r-----   22.3
```

CHAPTER 3   XEN

As we said before, its use is completely deprecated and it has been completely removed in newer versions, so we won't get into much detail.

About **xl**, we have already seen several examples, but we'll try to get into a bit more of detail here. There is a configuration file at */etc/xen/xl.conf*, with some default values.

```
romulus:~ # cat /etc/xen/xl.conf
## Global XL config file ##

# Set domain-id policy. "xen" means that the hypervisor will
  choose the
# id of a new domain. "random" means that a random value will
  be chosen.
#domid_policy="xen"

# Control whether dom0 is ballooned down when xen doesn't
  have enough
# free memory to create a domain.  "auto" means only
  balloon if dom0
# starts with all the host's memory.
autoballoon="off"
```

.
.
.

We have already seen many useful subcommands associated with **xl**, such as create or shutdown. We can get a full list of supported subcommands by typing **xl** without any arguments.

```
romulus:~ # xl
Usage xl [-vfN] <subcommand> [args]

xl full list of subcommands:

  create               Create a domain from config file <filename>
```

CHAPTER 3 XEN

  config-update   Update a running domain's saved
configuration, used when rebuilding the domain after reboot.
WARNING: xl now has better capability to manage domain
configuration, avoid using this command when possible
  list   List information about all/some domains
·
·
·

It's not possible to see an example of every subcommand, but we'll see an interesting option to save and restore virtual machines. To do that, we'll use the subcommand "save".

```
romulus:/home/antonio/XEN # xl list
Name                         ID  Mem   VCPUs  State   Time(s)
Domain-0                     0   1226  1      r-----  352.1
Xenstore                     1   31    1      -b----  0.3
alpine.pvlinux               4   256   1      -b----  3.2
romulus:/home/antonio/XEN # xl save alpine.pvlinux alpine.BK
Saving to alpine.BK new xl format (info 0x3/0x0/1167)
xc: error: SUSEINFO: domid 4: 85bf7e31-ef42-4ed4-b519-
bc17f0bcc48c save start, 65536 pages allocated
xc: info: Saving domain 4, type x86 PV
xc: error: SUSEINFO: domid 4: 525824 bytes + 65536 pages in
0.477550453 sec, 536 MiB/sec
xc: Frames: 65536/65536   100%
xc: End of stream: 0/0    0%
xc: error: SUSEINFO: domid 4: save done
```

After creating the backup, we could copy it to an external storage location so that it would be available for restoration if needed.

```
romulus:/home/antonio/XEN # scp alpine.BK
root@192.168.1.34:/XEN
```

CHAPTER 3   XEN

When we perform a backup using xl save, the virtual machine we're saving is automatically shut down. We'll start it again to perform a simple test before restoring it.

```
romulus:/home/antonio/XEN # xl create -f alpine.pvlinux
```

We'll connect to the console and we'll delete a file.

```
romulus:/home/antonio/XEN # xl console alpine.pvlinux
.
.
.
alpine:~# rm /etc/os-release
alpine:~# cat /etc/os-release
cat: can't open '/etc/os-release': No such file or directory
```

Now we'll restore the virtual machine.

```
romulus:/home/antonio/XEN # xl restore alpine.BK
Loading new save file alpine.BK (new xl fmt info 0x3/0x0/1167)
 Savefile contains xl domain config in JSON format
Parsing config from <saved>
xc: info: Found x86 PV domain from Xen 4.14
xc: error: SUSEINFO: domid 5: 85bf7e31-ef42-4ed4-b519-bc17f0
    bcc48c restore start
xc: info: Restoring domain
xc: info: Restore successful
xc: error: SUSEINFO: domid 5: restore done
xc: info: XenStore: mfn 0x6e0a8, dom 1, evt 1
xc: info: Console: mfn 0x6e0a7, dom 0, evt 2
```

CHAPTER 3   XEN

And we'll check that the file has been recovered.

```
romulus:/home/antonio/XEN # xl console alpine.pvlinux
.
.
.
alpine:~# cat /etc/os-release
NAME="Alpine Linux"
ID=alpine
VERSION_ID=3.17.7
PRETTY_NAME="Alpine Linux v3.17"
HOME_URL="https://alpinelinux.org/"
BUG_REPORT_URL="https://gitlab.alpinelinux.org/alpine/
aports/-/issues"
alpine:~#
```

Another useful subcommand is "**xl migrate**", which we can use to migrate Xen virtual machines between two hypervisors. Of course, we need to make sure that both hypervisors are compatible.

Apart from **xm** and **xl**, it is also possible to use an API specifically developed to manage Xen, the Xen API or XAPI. The truth is that XAPI is very rarely used to manage the Xen servers running on Linux distributions like Ubuntu or SUSE. In these cases, the use of libvirt is preferred. In the next chapter, we'll see in detail how the use of libvirt eases the management of Xen and KVM. However, XAPI is the recommended way to manage Xenserver. Xenserver is a commercial product based on Xen (Figure 3-9).

CHAPTER 3 XEN

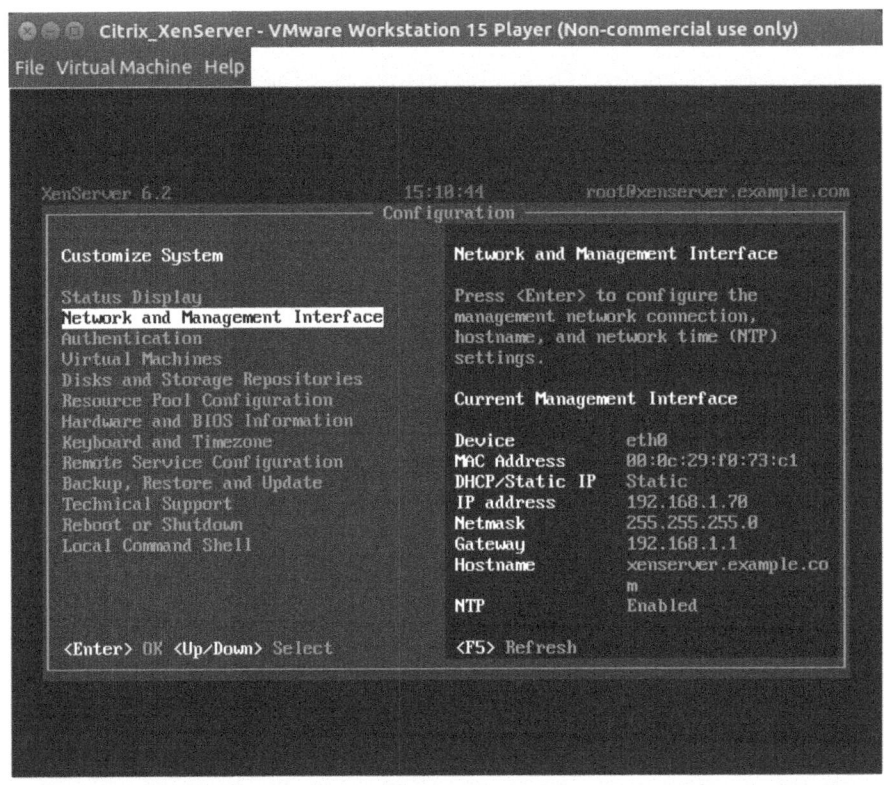

Figure 3-9. Xenserver

In a similar way to what we have seen with **xm** and **xl**, we can also use a command-line client to interact with XAPI, the **xe** command. With the help option, we can see a full list of subcommands.

```
[root@xenserver ~]# xe help
Usage: xe <command> [-s server] [-pw passwd] [-p port] [-u user] [-pwf password-file]
 [command specific arguments]

To get help on a specific command: xe help <command>
To get a full listing of commands: xe help --all
```

CHAPTER 3 XEN

```
Common command list
-------------------
    cd-list, diagnostic-vm-status, network-list, snapshot-clone
    snapshot-copy, snapshot-disk-list, snapshot-export-
    to-template
    snapshot-reset-powerstate, snapshot-revert, snapshot-
    uninstall, sr-list
    template-export, template-uninstall, vm-cd-add, vm-cd-eject
    vm-cd-insert, vm-cd-list, vm-cd-remove, vm-checkpoint,
    vm-clone vm-compute-maximum-memory, vm-copy, vm-disk-add,
    vm-disk-list vm-disk-remove, vm-export, vm-import,
    vm-install, vm-list, vm-migrate vm-pause, vm-reboot,
    vm-reset-powerstate, vm-resume, vm-shutdown vm-snapshot,
    vm-snapshot-with-quiesce, vm-start, vm-suspend
    vm-uninstall, vm-unpause, vm-vif-list
[root@xenserver ~]#
```

We can list the virtual machines this way:

```
[root@xenserver ~]# xe vm-list
uuid ( RO)             : 7591587f-f715-48d3-aeaf-5ca9a19adad7
    name-label ( RW): Control domain on host: xenserver.
    example.com
    power-state ( RO): running

uuid ( RO)             : 3ebcca37-da7c-9d56-4dec-e40b1a268e0d
    name-label ( RW): Windows 7 (32-bit) (1)
    power-state ( RO): halted
```

CHAPTER 3   XEN

We can see that one virtual machine is halted. We can started with "**xe vm-start**". If we're not sure about the syntax, we can check the contextual help.

```
[root@xenserver ~]# xe help vm-start
command name          : vm-start
      reqd params     :
      optional params : force, on, paused, <vm-selectors>
      description     : Start the selected VM(s). Where
                        pooling is enabled, the host on
                        which to start can be specified
                        with the 'on' parameter that takes
                        a uuid. The optional parameter
                        '--force' will bypass any hardware-
                        compatibility warnings. The simplest
                        way to select the VM on which the
                        operation is to be performed is by
                        supplying the argument 'vm=<name or
                        uuid>'. VMs can also be specified
                        by filtering the full list of VMs on
                        the values of fields. For example,
                        specifying 'power-state=halted' will
                        select all VMs whose power-state
                        field is equal to 'halted'. Where
                        multiple VMs are matching, the option
                        '--multiple' must be specified to
                        perform the operation. The full list
                        of fields that can be matched can
                        be obtained by the command 'xe vm-
                        list params=all'. If no parameters to
                        select VMs are given, the operation
                        will be performed on all Vms.
```

CHAPTER 3 XEN

Finally, we can start the virtual machine and check its state again.

```
[root@xenserver ~]# xe vm-start vm=3ebcca37-da7c-9d56-4dec-
e40b1a268e0d
[root@xenserver ~]# xe vm-list
uuid ( RO)              : 7591587f-f715-48d3-aeaf-5ca9a19adad7
    name-label ( RW): Control domain on host: xenserver.
                      example.com
    power-state ( RO): running

uuid ( RO)              : 3ebcca37-da7c-9d56-4dec-e40b1a268e0d
    name-label ( RW): Windows 7 (32-bit) (1)
    power-state ( RO): running
```

In addition to the use of xe, we can also develop our own programs in C, Python, and other languages using XAPI to manage Xenserver. This is exactly what the OpenXenManager program does (Figure 3-10).

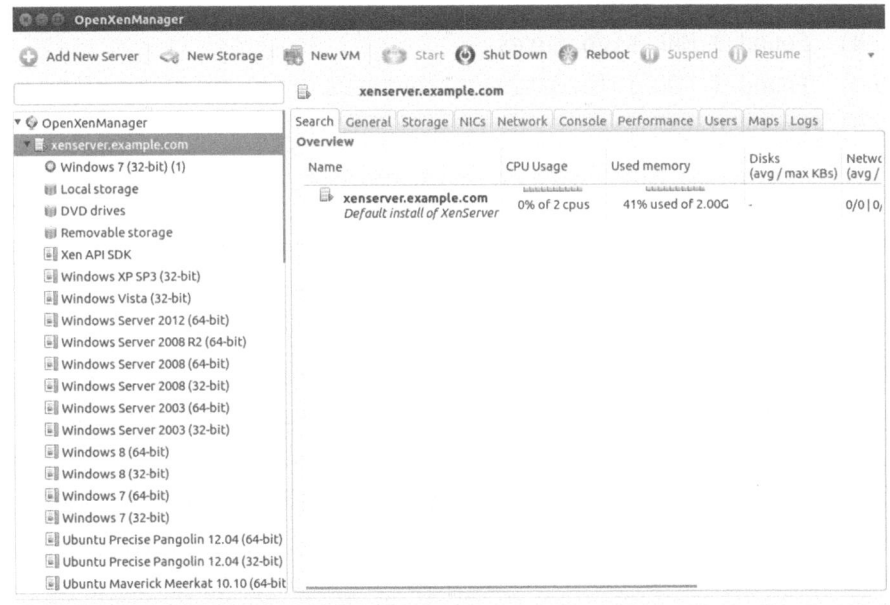

***Figure 3-10.** OpenXenManager*

143

CHAPTER 3   XEN

Xen Troubleshooting

One of the first commands we should execute when troubleshooting Xen is **xl dmesg**.

```
antonio@ubuntu:/XEN_VMS$ sudo xl dmesg
(XEN) parameter "placeholder" unknown!
(XEN) Xen version 4.11.4-pre (Ubuntu 4.11.3+24-g14b62ab3e5-1ub
untu2.3) (ubuntu-devel-discuss@lists.ubuntu.com) (gcc (Ubuntu
9.4.0-1ubuntu1~20.04.1) 9.4.0) debug=n  Tue Aug 23 12:11:30
UTC 2022
(XEN) Bootloader: GRUB 2.04-1ubuntu26.2
(XEN) Command line: placeholder
(XEN) Xen image load base address: 0xbf400000
(XEN) Video information:
(XEN)  VGA is text mode 80x25, font 8x16
(XEN) Disc information:
(XEN)  Found 1 MBR signatures
(XEN)  Found 1 EDD information structures
(XEN) Xen-e820 RAM map:
```

With this command, we could see error messages like the following, in which we tried to create a HVM guest not having the hardware virtualization extensions active:

.

.

(XEN) hvm.c:543:d0 Attempt to create a HVM guest on a non-VT/AMDV platform.

.

.

It is also a good idea to check the log files located at */var/log/xen/*.

```
antonio@ubuntu:/XEN_VMS$ ls -lrth /var/log/xen/
.
.
.
-rw-r--r-- 1 root root 5,2K jun 15 01:22 xen-boot.log
-rw-r--r-- 1 root root  194 jun 15 12:55 xl-alpine.
pvlinux.log.2
-rw-r--r-- 1 root root  281 jun 15 13:12 xl-alpine.
pvlinux.log.1
-rw-r--r-- 1 root root   62 jun 15 13:13 xl-alpine.pvlinux.log
```

Summary

In this chapter, we have seen what is probably, together with KVM, the most used hypervisor in Linux environments. We have seen its basic architecture and how to create virtual machines from configuration files. Now you're probably familiar with the most common parameters used in the cfg files associated to each virtual machine/unprivileged domain.

We performed basic administration tasks such as starting a domain or shutting it down and defining disks and CD drives. We also made the domain available in the network. We have seen examples of the two main virtualization options we have available in Xen: paravirtualization and hardware virtualized machines.

We also briefly reviewed the role of XenStore and how to edit the boot loader to customize how Xen works. We also studied the use of xl/xm and XAPI to manage Xen domains and how to perform some basic troubleshooting.

Later, when we study libvirt, we'll see that there are more friendly ways to manage virtual machines.

CHAPTER 4

libvirt Virtual Machine Management

In this chapter, we'll cover the following concepts:

- Understand the architecture of libvirt
- Manage libvirt connections and nodes
- Create and manage QEMU and Xen domains, including snapshots
- Manage and analyze resource consumption of domains
- Create and manage storage pools and volumes
- Create and manage virtual networks
- Migrate domains between nodes
- Understand how libvirt interacts with Xen and QEMU
- Understand how libvirt interacts with network services such as dnsmasq and radvd
- Understand libvirt XML configuration files
- Awareness of virtlogd and virtlockd

CHAPTER 4   LIBVIRT VIRTUAL MACHINE MANAGEMENT

Introduction to libvirt

libvirt is an API for the management of virtualization platforms. Currently it supports Xen, KVM, QEMU, LXC, and many more. This API can be accessed from C, Python, Java, and more languages (Figure 4-1).

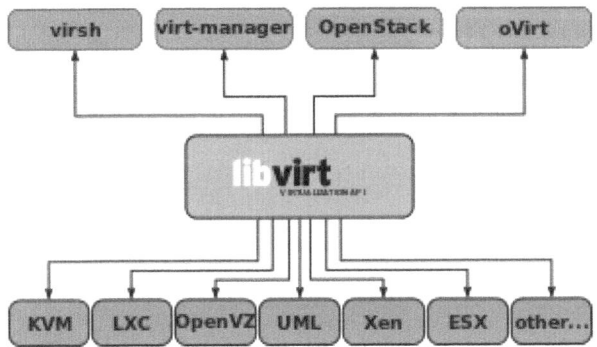

Figure 4-1.   libvirt API, image taken from Wikipedia under Creative Commons License. Attribution: Shmuel Csaba Otto Traian

Installing libvirt

To benefit from the ease of use of libvirt, the first thing we need to do is installing it. We'll search for a package named libvirt.

antonio@antonio-Laptop:~$ apt search libvirt

·
·

libvirt-daemon/jammy-updates,jammy-security,now
8.0.0-1ubuntu7.10 amd64 [installed,automatic]
  Virtualization daemon

·
·

CHAPTER 4   LIBVIRT VIRTUAL MACHINE MANAGEMENT

We can see there are many packages related to libvirt. We'll begin by installing the *libvirt-daemon* package.

```
antonio@antonio-Laptop:~$ sudo apt install libvirt-daemon
```

Later we'll use the command **virsh**, included in the *libvirt-clients* package. We'll install this package as well.

```
antonio@antonio-Laptop:~$ sudo apt install libvirt-clients
```

virt-manager

Another interesting tool based in libvirt is **virt-manager**; this is a graphical application that makes the creation and management of virtual machines much more user friendly.

We install **virt-manager** if it is not already installed.

```
antonio@antonio-Laptop:~$ sudo apt install virt-manager
```

We launch **virt-manager** and a new window will open. By default, the program will try to connect to the local Xen hypervisor (Figure 4-2). If there is no local Xen hypervisor running, we could get the error message shown in Figure 4-3.

CHAPTER 4   LIBVIRT VIRTUAL MACHINE MANAGEMENT

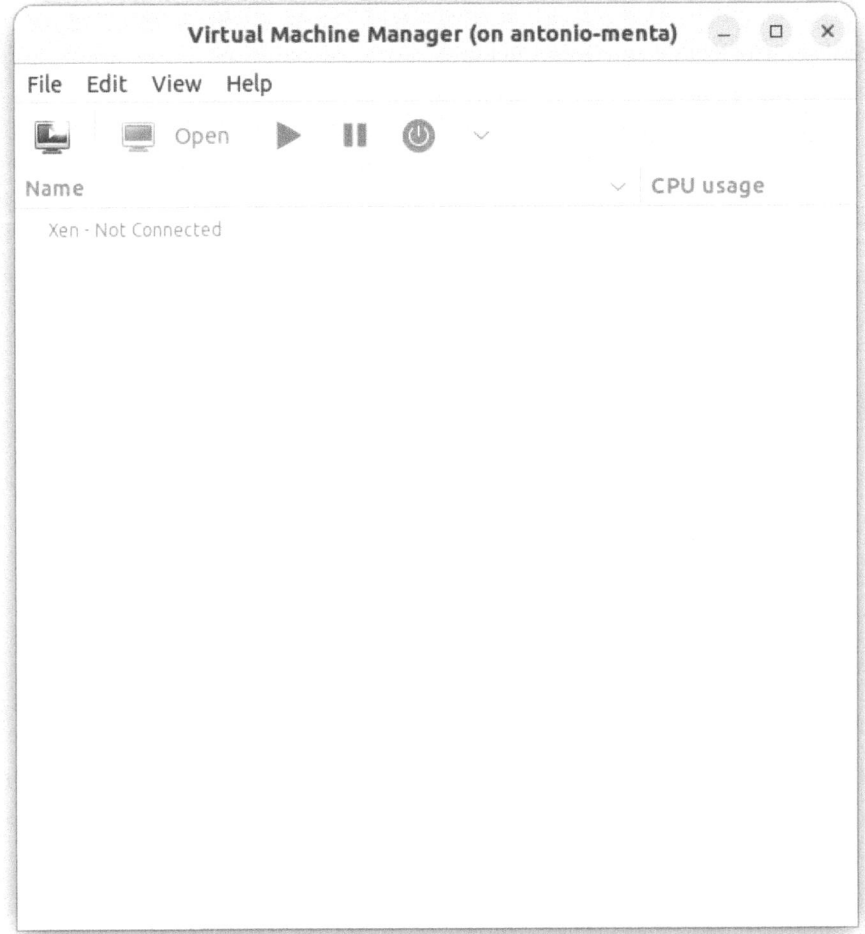

Figure 4-2. virt-manager trying to connect to a local Xen server

CHAPTER 4   LIBVIRT VIRTUAL MACHINE MANAGEMENT

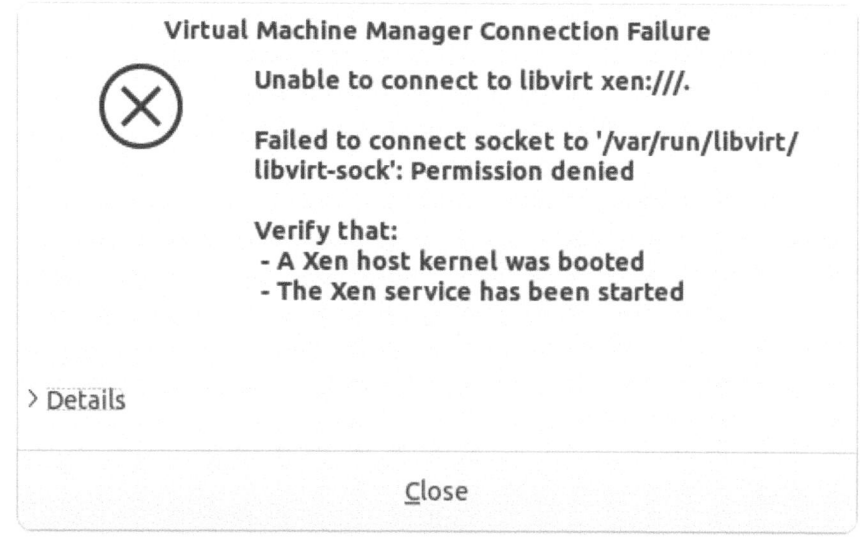

Figure 4-3. Error connecting to a local Xen server

virt-manager can also be used to manage remote hypervisors. For instance, we can connect to one of the remote Xen hypervisors we worked with in the previous chapter. We need to click "File" ➤ "Add connection..."; a new window will pop up (Figure 4-4).

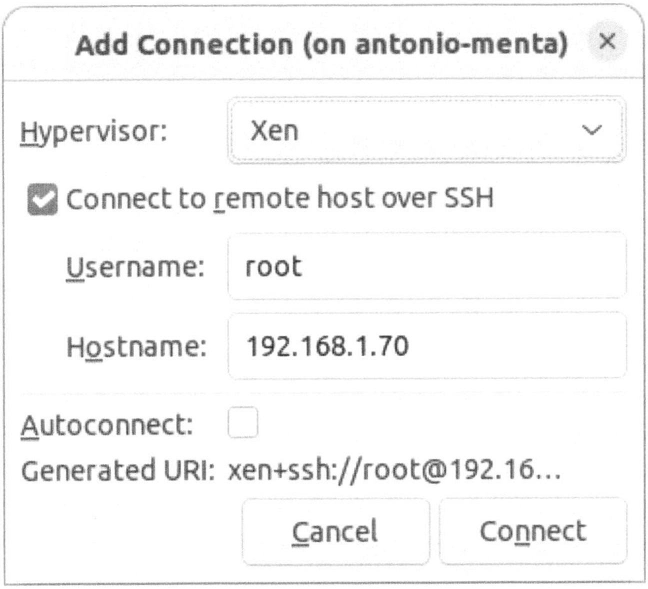

CHAPTER 4   LIBVIRT VIRTUAL MACHINE MANAGEMENT

Figure 4-4. Connecting to a remote Xen server

If we haven't set up ssh key-based authentication and we don't have the ssh askpass installed, we'll get an error message when virt-manager tries to connect to the remote hypervisor (Figure 4-5).

CHAPTER 4 LIBVIRT VIRTUAL MACHINE MANAGEMENT

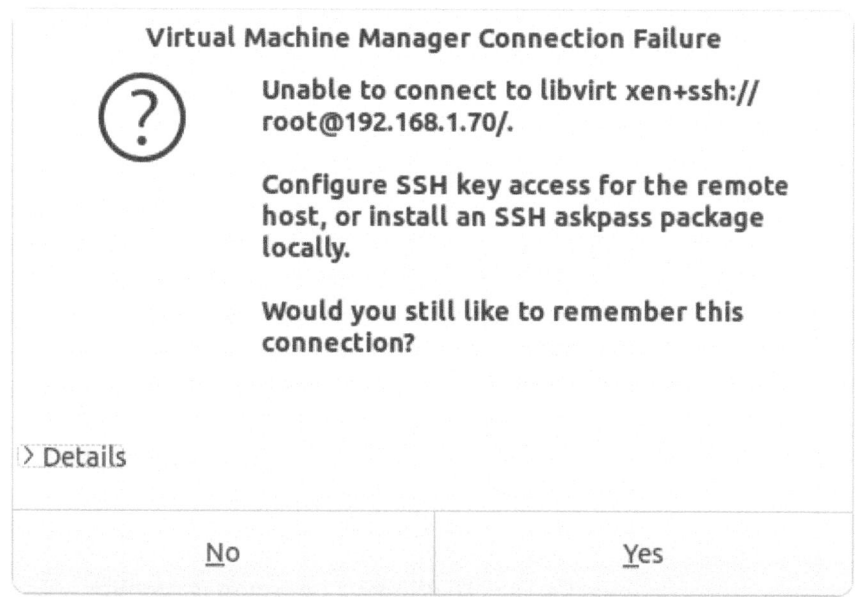

Figure 4-5. Error trying to connect to the remote hypervisor

If we prefer to be asked for the password when connecting to the remote Xen system, we need to install the ssh-askpass package.

antonio@antonio-Laptop:~$ apt search askpass

.
.
.

ssh-askpass/jammy,now 1:1.2.4.1-13 amd64
  under X, asks user for a passphrase for ssh-add

antonio@antonio-HP-Laptop-15s-fq1xxx:~$ sudo apt install ssh-askpass

CHAPTER 4 LIBVIRT VIRTUAL MACHINE MANAGEMENT

Now we're ready to connect to the remote Xen server. But we must also make sure that libvirt is also installed (and running) on the target server; otherwise, we'll get the error shown in Figure 4-6.

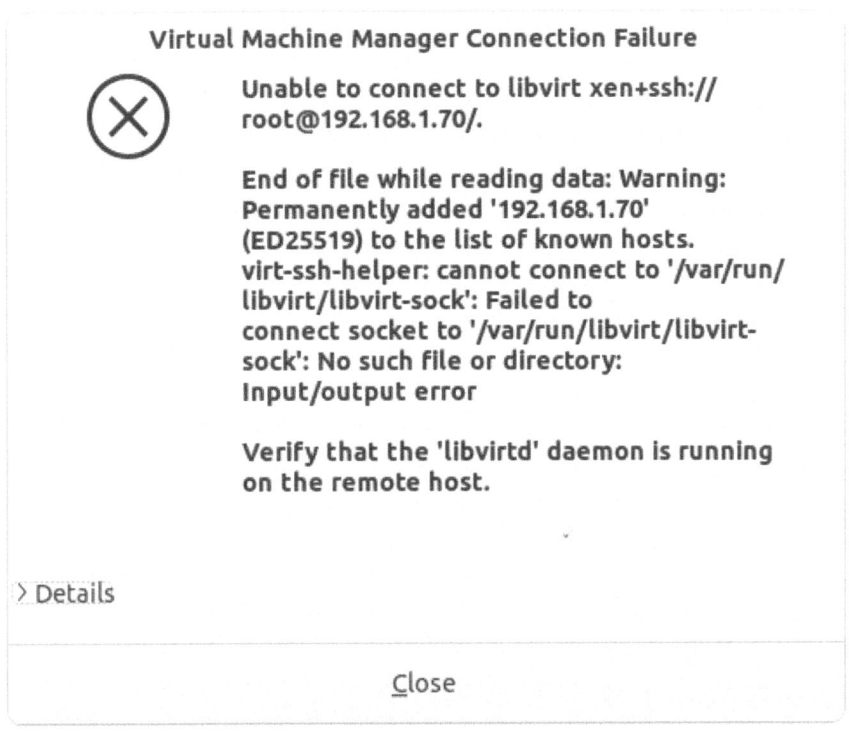

Figure 4-6. libvirt not running on the remote server

Finally, we will be able to connect (Figure 4-7).

CHAPTER 4   LIBVIRT VIRTUAL MACHINE MANAGEMENT

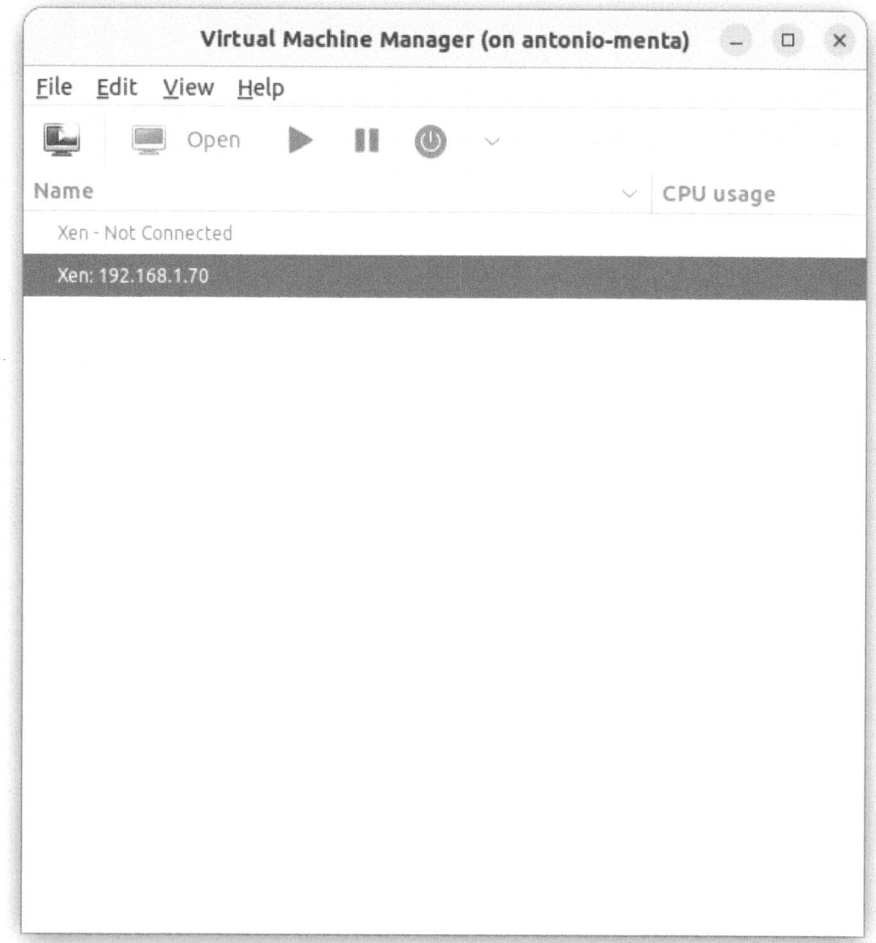

Figure 4-7. *virt-manager connected to a remote Xen hypervisor*

In addition to Xen, virt-manager can also be used to manage many other hypervisors and also containers. For instance, we can use virt-manager to connect to our local system, in which we installed QEMU previously (Figure 4-8).

CHAPTER 4   LIBVIRT VIRTUAL MACHINE MANAGEMENT

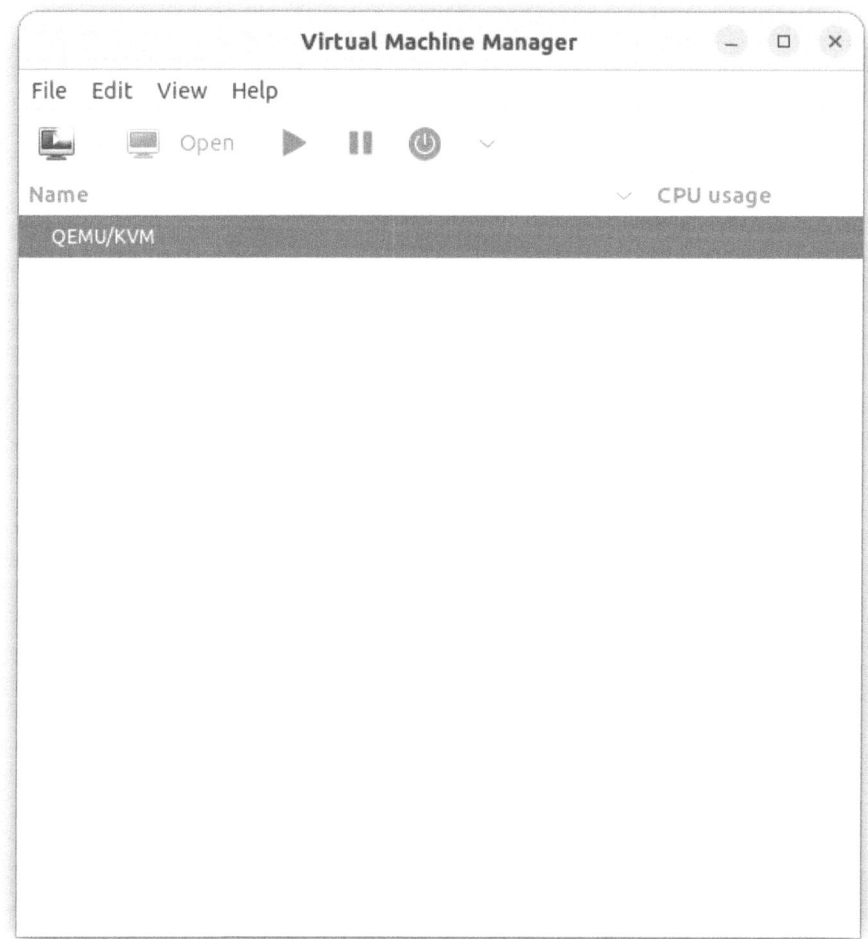

Figure 4-8. *virt-manager connected to the local QEMU/KVM hypervisor*

We haven't studied LXC so far, but we can also use virt-manager to manage Linux containers. At this point, we're not going to dive into container creation; we'll do that later in the book, but we'll see how we can set up virt-manager to manage containers as well as virtual machines. Later, when we study LXC, we'll see some examples of the use of **virt-manager** and containers.

CHAPTER 4   LIBVIRT VIRTUAL MACHINE MANAGEMENT

First, we need to open **virt-manager** and click "File" ➤ "New Connection". Then, on the "Hypervisor" field, we select "Libvirt-LXC" (Figure 4-9).

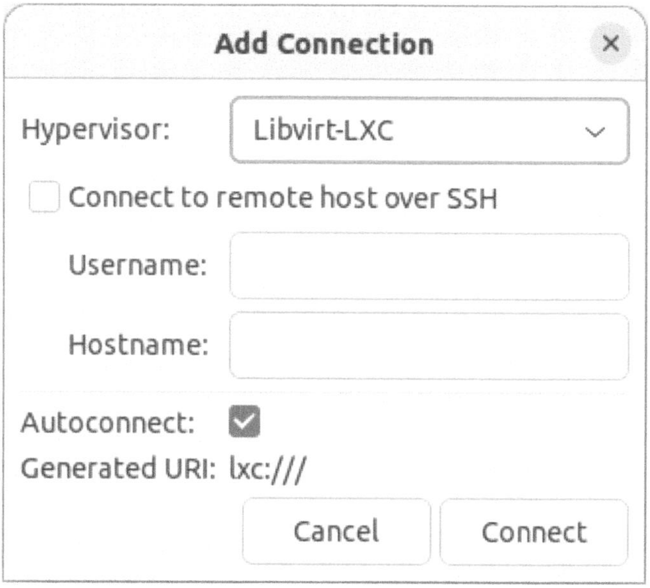

Figure 4-9. Using virt-manager to manage LXC

For the connection to be successful, we need to install the corresponding libvirt connection driver for LXC. Otherwise, we'll get the error message shown in Figure 4-10.

CHAPTER 4   LIBVIRT VIRTUAL MACHINE MANAGEMENT

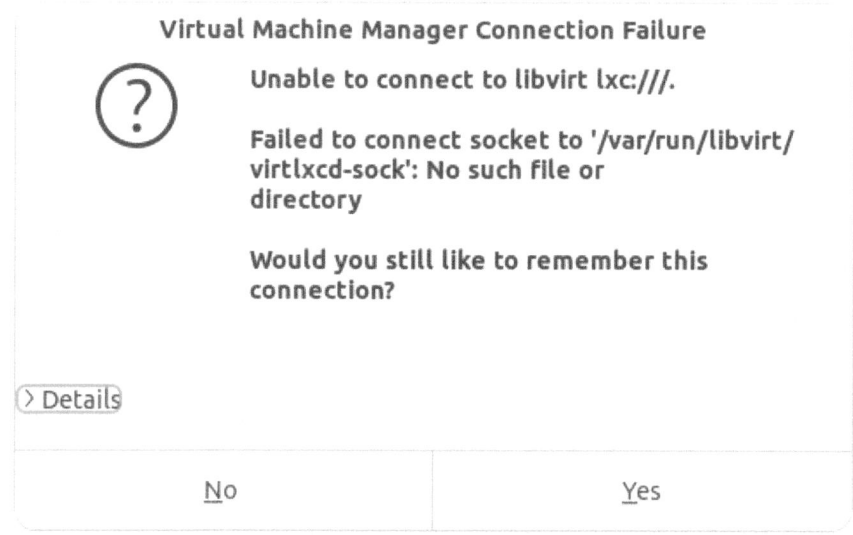

Figure 4-10. Error when trying to manage LXC from virt-manager

We'll install the required driver in the host system.

antonio@antonio-Laptop:~$ sudo apt install libvirt-daemon-driver-lxc

After that, we'll restart the **libvirtd** service.

antonio@antonio-Laptop:~$ sudo systemctl restart libvirtd

And we're ready to manage LXC as well as QEMU/KVM virtual machines with **virt-manager** (Figure 4-11).

CHAPTER 4   LIBVIRT VIRTUAL MACHINE MANAGEMENT

Figure 4-11. *virt-manager connected to QEMU/KVM and LXC*

Installing and Managing a Virtual Machine with virt-manager

In the previous chapters about QEMU and Xen, we have already created virtual machines. Tools like **virt-manager** and **virsh**, which we'll see later, greatly simplify the creation and management of virtual machines.

CHAPTER 4   LIBVIRT VIRTUAL MACHINE MANAGEMENT

We'll begin by connecting to our local QEMU/KVM hypervisor and clicking on the first icon on the left, "Create a new Virtual Machine". Then we'll see a new window with several options (Figure 4-12).

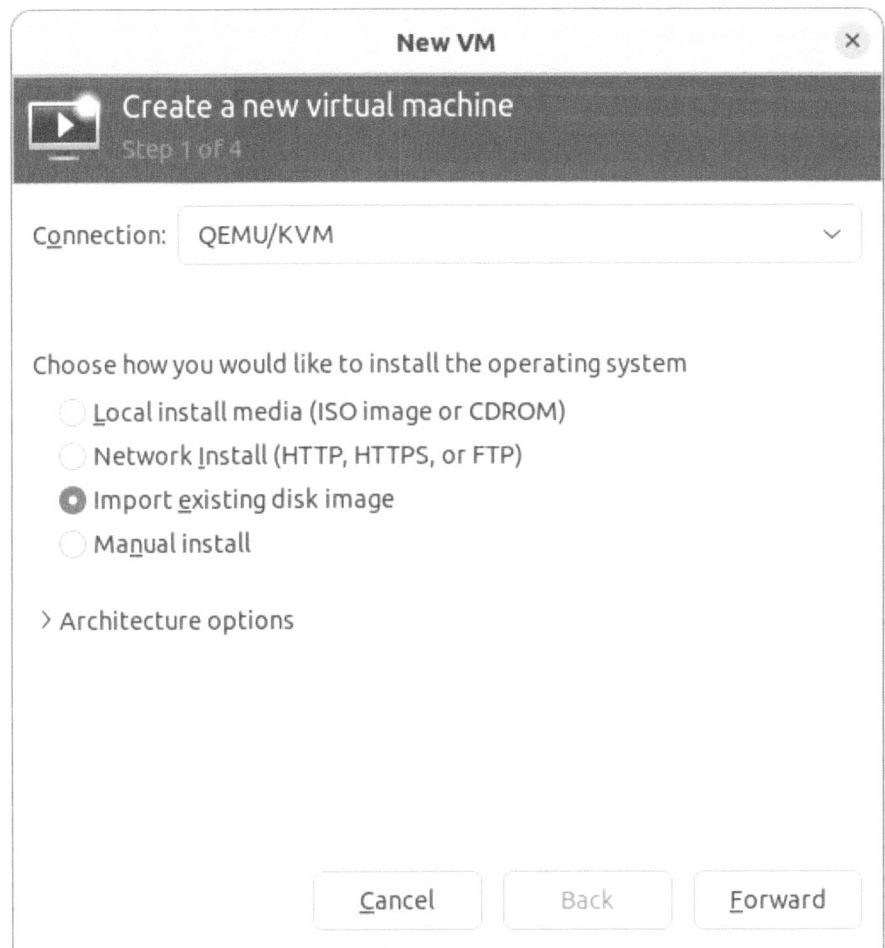

Figure 4-12. Creating a new QEMU/KVM virtual machine

We can install a new server manually from an ISO file, using a network installation server or importing a disk image. We can also select the architecture of the VM; the default value is x86_64, but we can select any of the architectures supported by QEMU.

CHAPTER 4 LIBVIRT VIRTUAL MACHINE MANAGEMENT

Importing an Existing Virtual Machine into virt-manager

As we already installed manually a virtual machine in QEMU, we'll import this disk image in virt-manager. We select the "Import existing disk image" option and click the "Forward" button.

In the next screen, we need to specify the storage path (Figure 4-13).

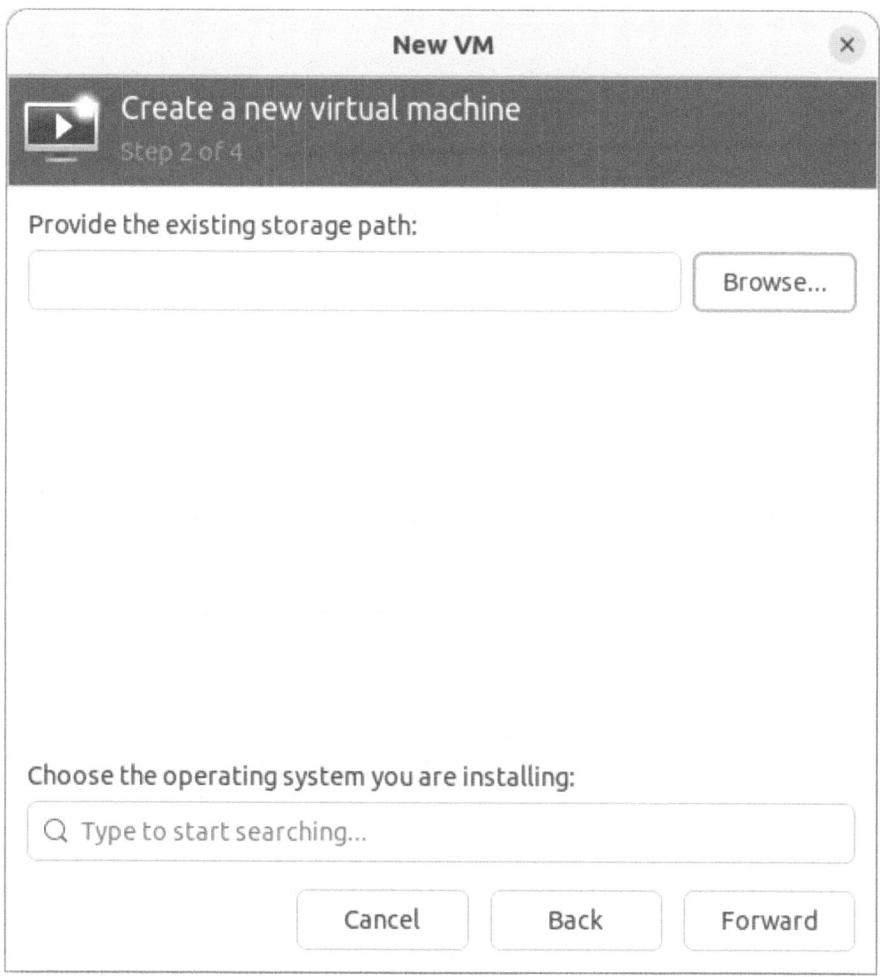

Figure 4-13. Providing the storage path

CHAPTER 4   LIBVIRT VIRTUAL MACHINE MANAGEMENT

When clicking the "Browse" button, we access the "storage volume" windows (Figure 4-14). A storage volume in libvirt is an abstraction used to define an available storage space. By default, a single storage volume of the type dir exists in the path */var/lib/libvirt/images*.

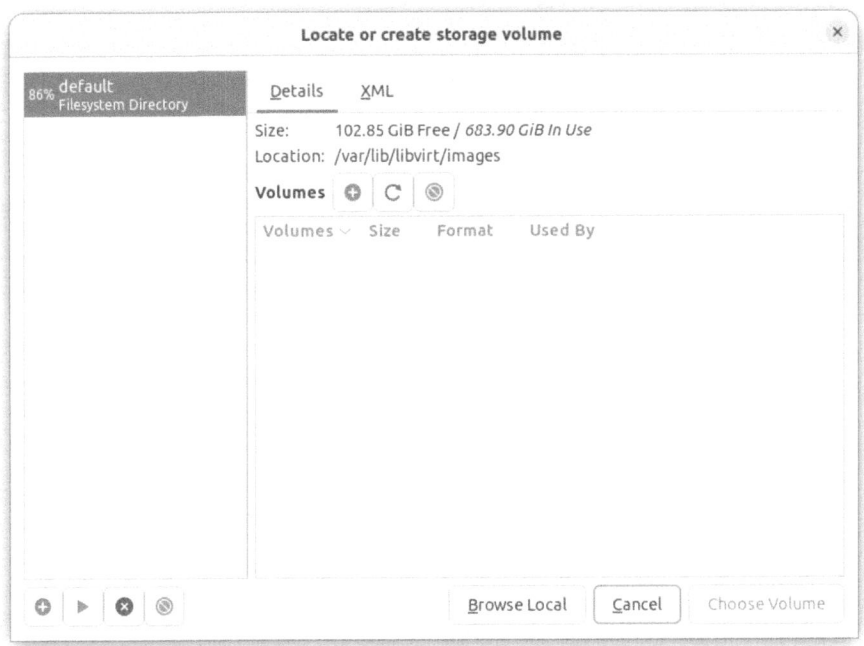

***Figure 4-14.** Default storage volume*

To import the QEMU virtual machine we created in Chapter 2, we need to create a new storage volume from the folder in which the disk file is located. We'll click on the "+" sign to create a new storage volume of the type dir, and we'll point it to the folder in which the QEMU virtual machine is located (Figure 4-15).

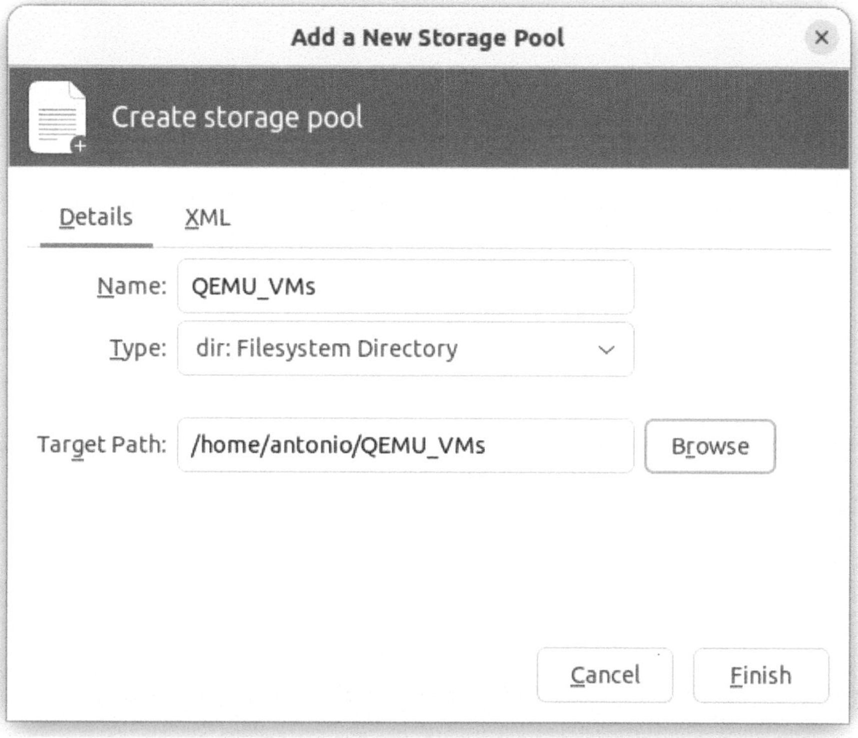

CHAPTER 4 LIBVIRT VIRTUAL MACHINE MANAGEMENT

Figure 4-15. Adding a new storage volume

Once the new storage volume is created and activated, we can see all the files present (Figure 4-16).

CHAPTER 4   LIBVIRT VIRTUAL MACHINE MANAGEMENT

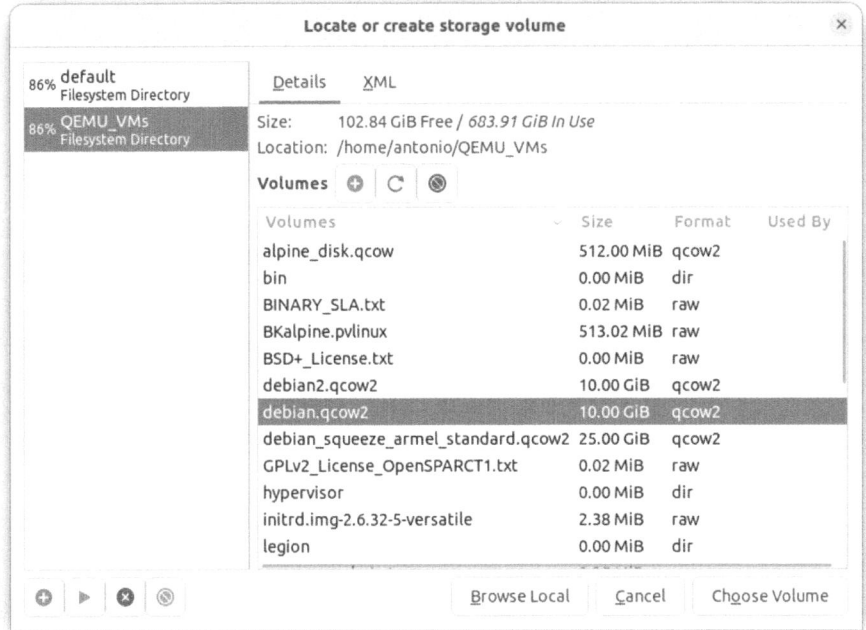

Figure 4-16. *New storage volume created*

Now we can finally select the disk file that we want to import, and we'll get back to the "New VM" window. We'll choose the OS of the disk that we're importing too (Figure 4-17).

164

CHAPTER 4   LIBVIRT VIRTUAL MACHINE MANAGEMENT

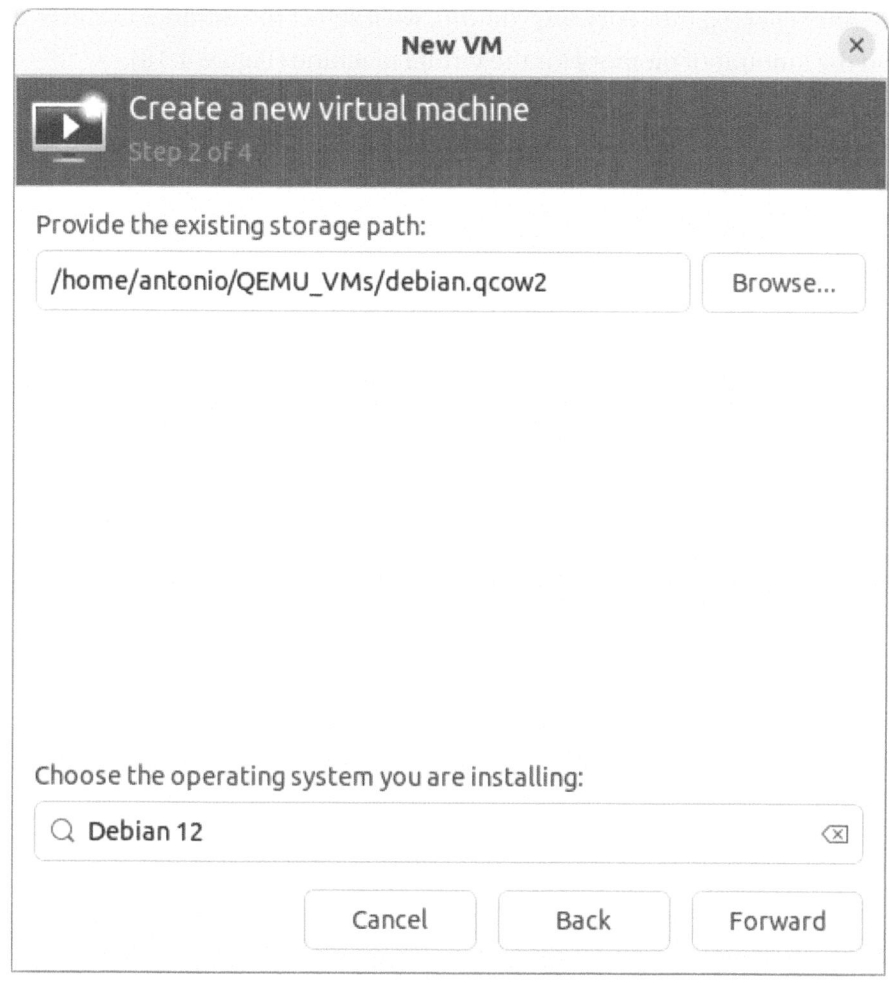

Figure 4-17. Importing a virtual machine into virt-manager. Step 2

CHAPTER 4   LIBVIRT VIRTUAL MACHINE MANAGEMENT

After clicking the "Forward" button, we'll select the number of CPUs and the amount of memory for the virtual machine (Figure 4-18).

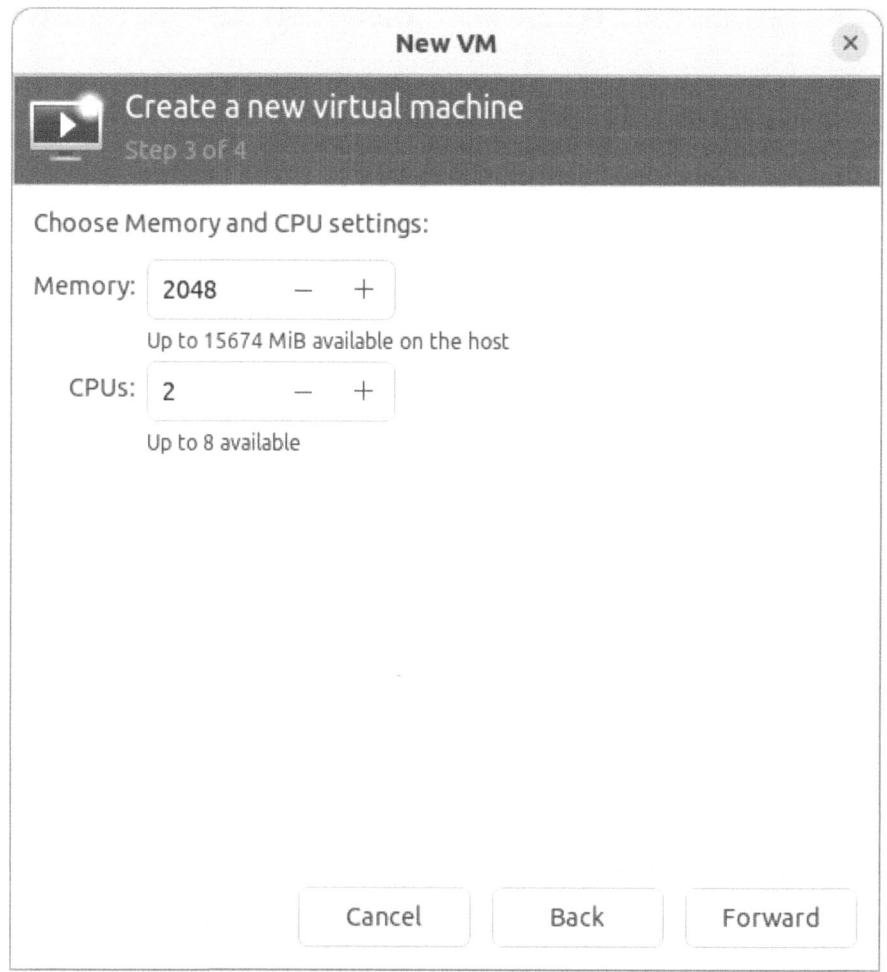

Figure 4-18. Importing a virtual machine into virt-manager. Step 3

In the last step, we assign a name to the virtual machine (Figure 4-19). We can see a brief summary of the settings applied to the machine. We can edit some of these settings, but for now, we'll leave them unchanged. We click the "Finish" button and we'll see the machine booting (Figure 4-20).

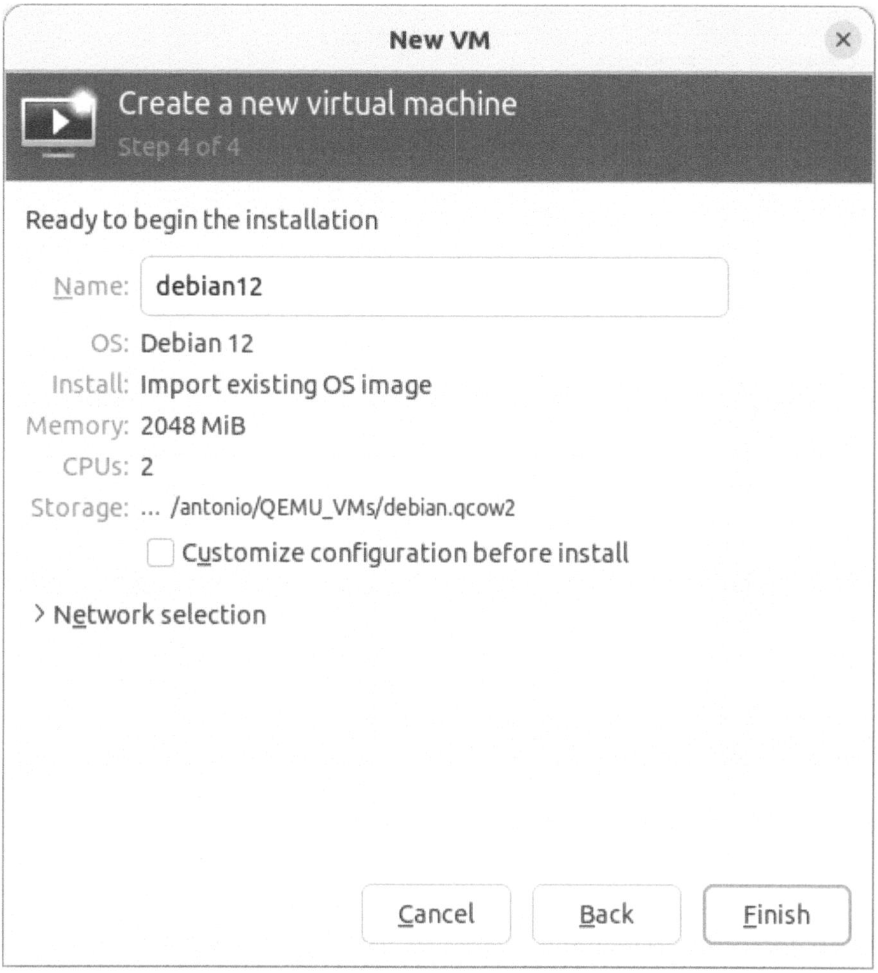

CHAPTER 4   LIBVIRT VIRTUAL MACHINE MANAGEMENT

Figure 4-19. Importing a virtual machine into virt-manager. Step 4

CHAPTER 4   LIBVIRT VIRTUAL MACHINE MANAGEMENT

Figure 4-20. Booting up the virtual machine

From the **virt-manager** console, we can work on the virtual machine as we'd do in any physical server. We can also click on the "show virtual hardware details" (Figure 4-21) to get information about the virtual machine, such as performance, CPUs, memory, networking, etc.

CHAPTER 4   LIBVIRT VIRTUAL MACHINE MANAGEMENT

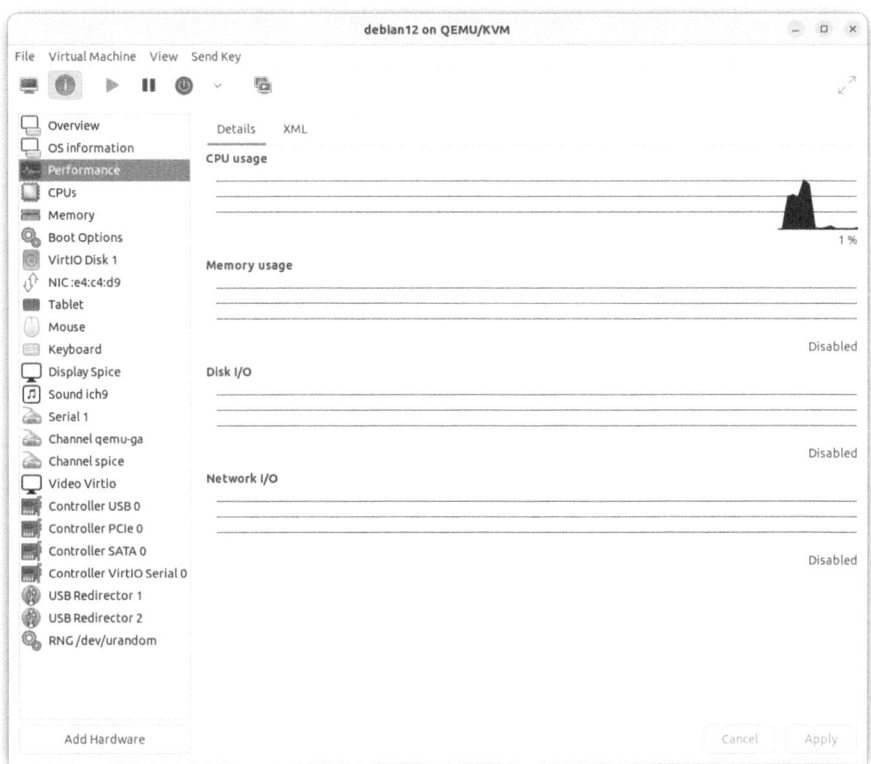

Figure 4-21. *Virtual machine details*

When we're done, we can shut down the machine either from the console itself or by using the power button in **virt-manager**. If we decide to use the power button, we can shut down the virtual machine gracefully or we can force it to shut down if the system is unresponsive.

Creating a Fresh New Virtual Machine in virt-manager

In addition to importing already-existing virtual machines, we can also install a new virtual machine. We won't repeat the whole process because it is quite similar to what we did previously in this same book, but we'll see the first steps.

CHAPTER 4   LIBVIRT VIRTUAL MACHINE MANAGEMENT

As we did before, when importing an existing VM, we connect to our local QEMU/KVM hypervisor and click "Create a new Virtual Machine", and we select the option (Figure 4-22).

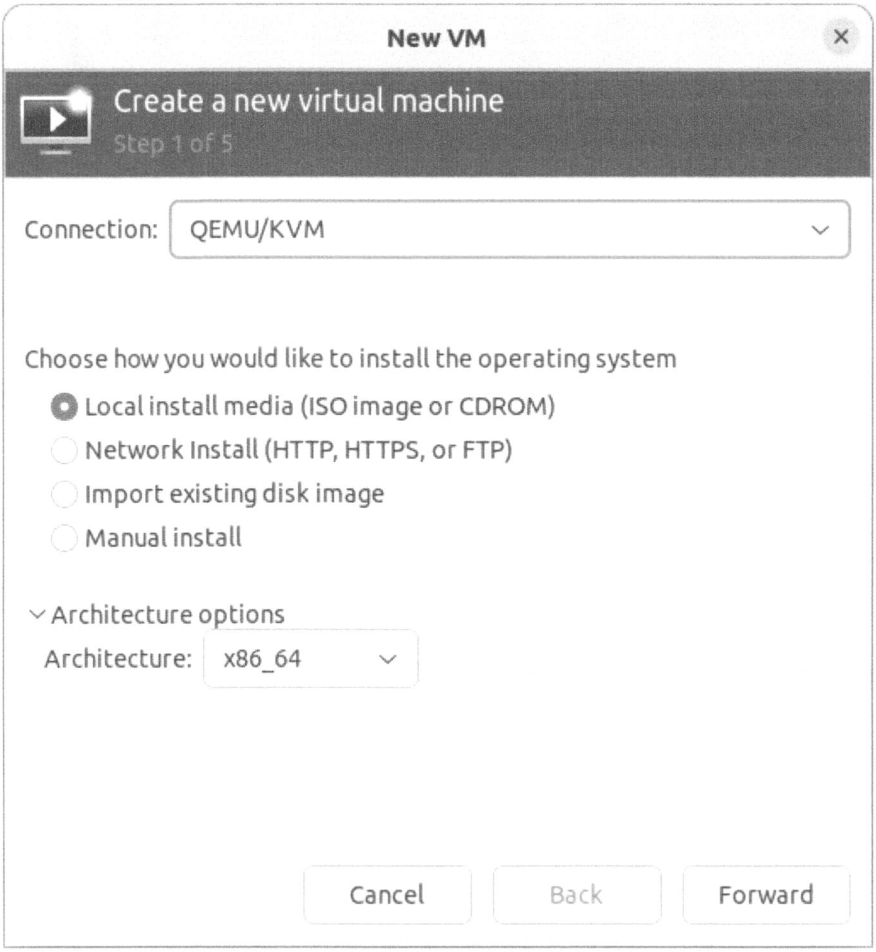

Figure 4-22. Creating a new VM in virt-manager installing from local media

CHAPTER 4 LIBVIRT VIRTUAL MACHINE MANAGEMENT

In the next screen, we need to specify the path to the install media (Figure 4-23). We click the "Browse" button.

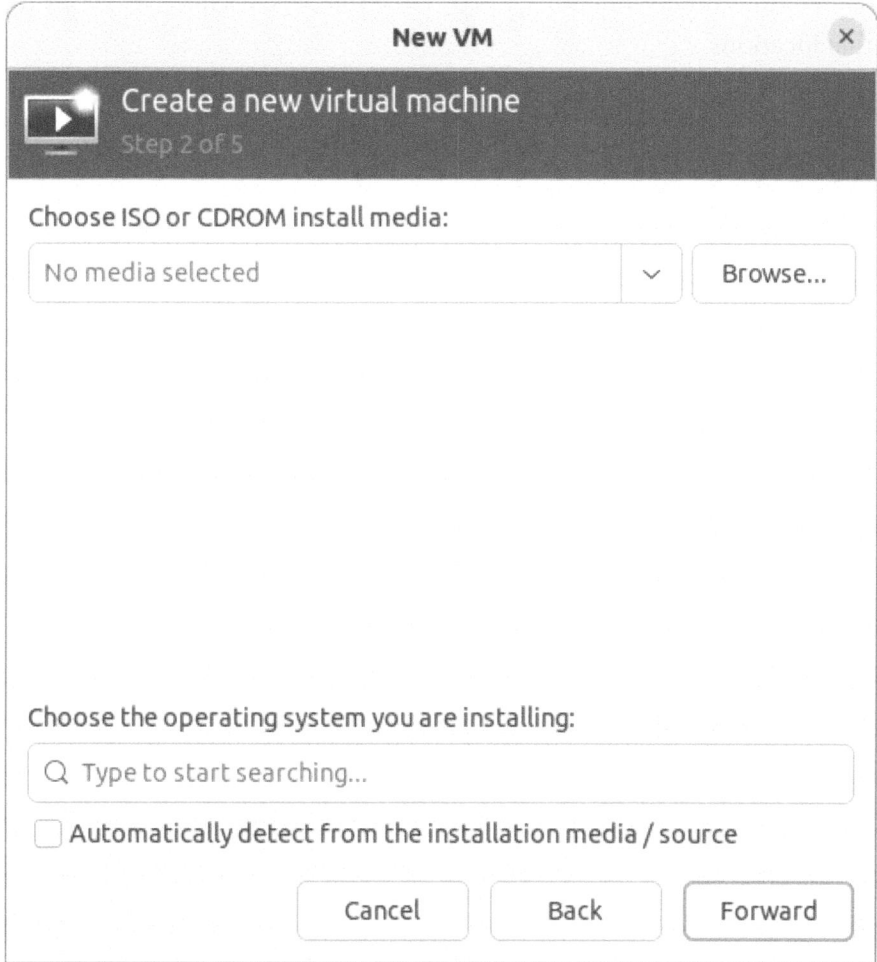

Figure 4-23. *Locating the install media*

CHAPTER 4   LIBVIRT VIRTUAL MACHINE MANAGEMENT

We'll search for the ISO installation file in the storage volumes already defined (Figure 4-24). In our case, we assume that the ISO file is already located in the */home/antonio/QEMU_VMs/* folder; if it's not, we'll copy it to that location.

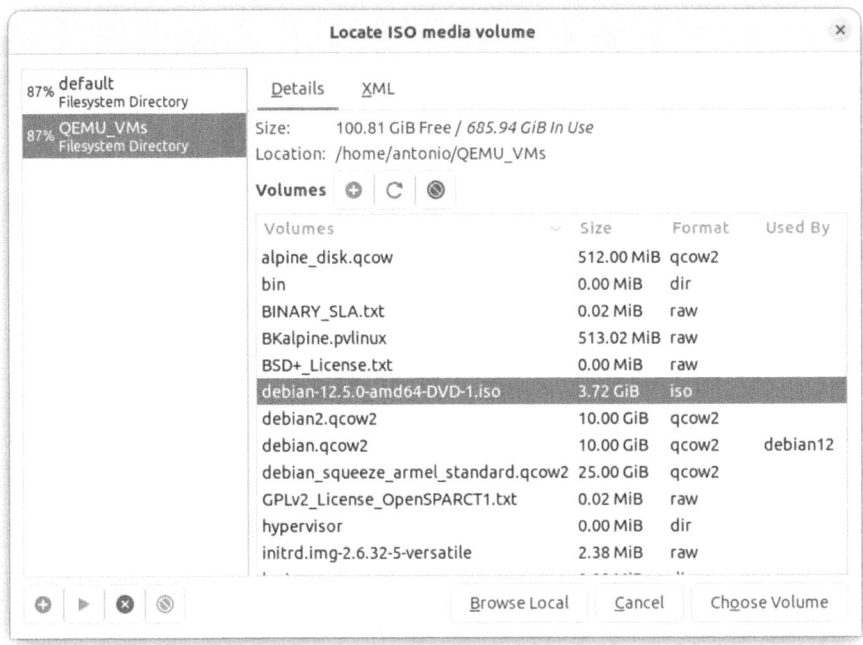

Figure 4-24. *Selecting the ISO file*

We click the ISO file and select the operating system, Debian 12 in this example (Figure 4-25).

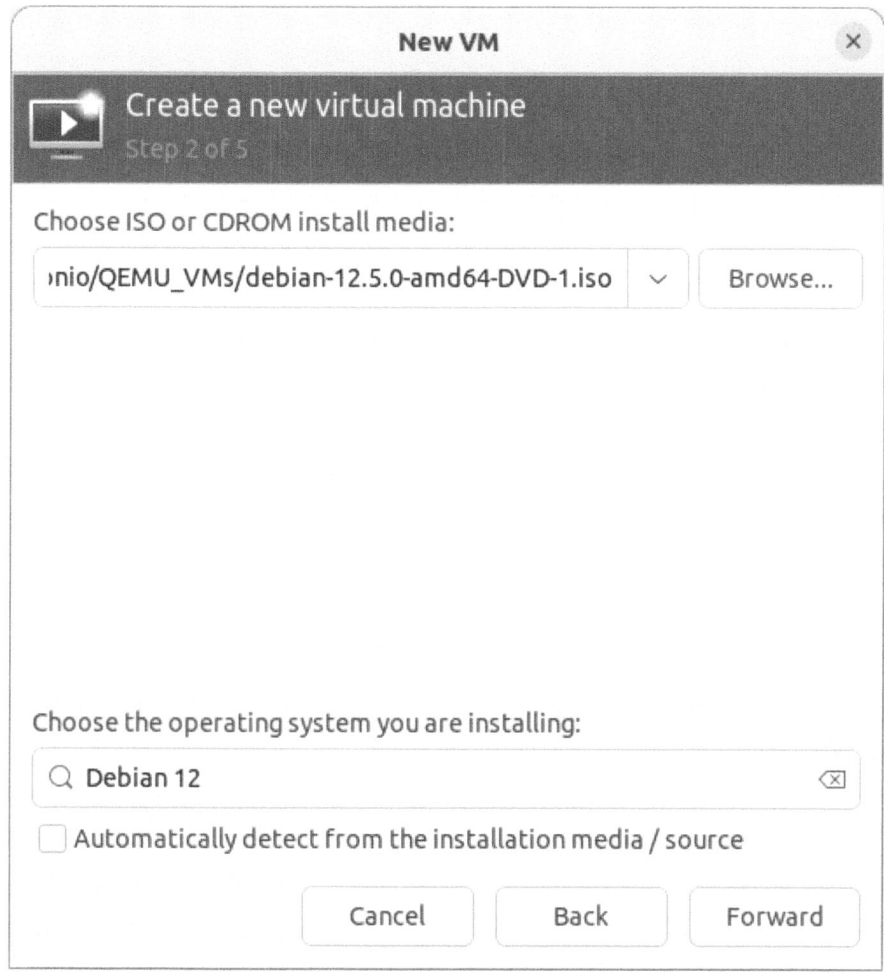

Figure 4-25. *Creating a new VM from the installation media*

CHAPTER 4 LIBVIRT VIRTUAL MACHINE MANAGEMENT

We choose the number of CPUs and memory assigned, as well as the disk storage (Figures 4-26 and 4-27).

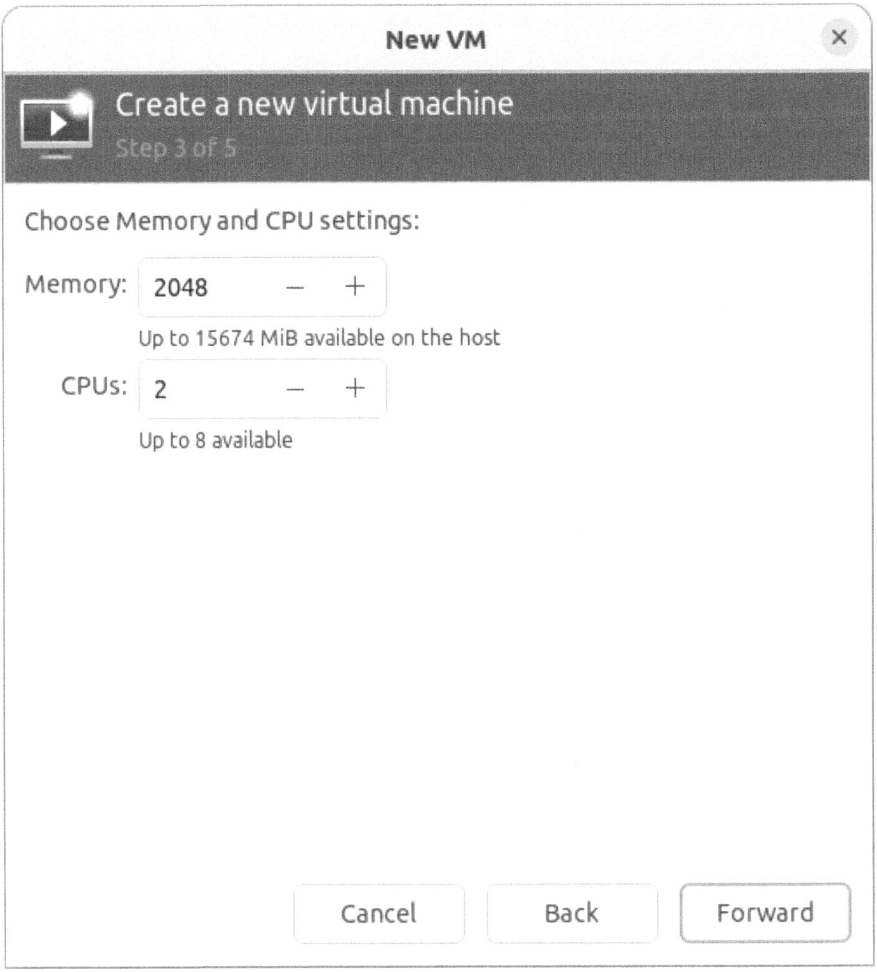

Figure 4-26. Choosing CPU and memory settings

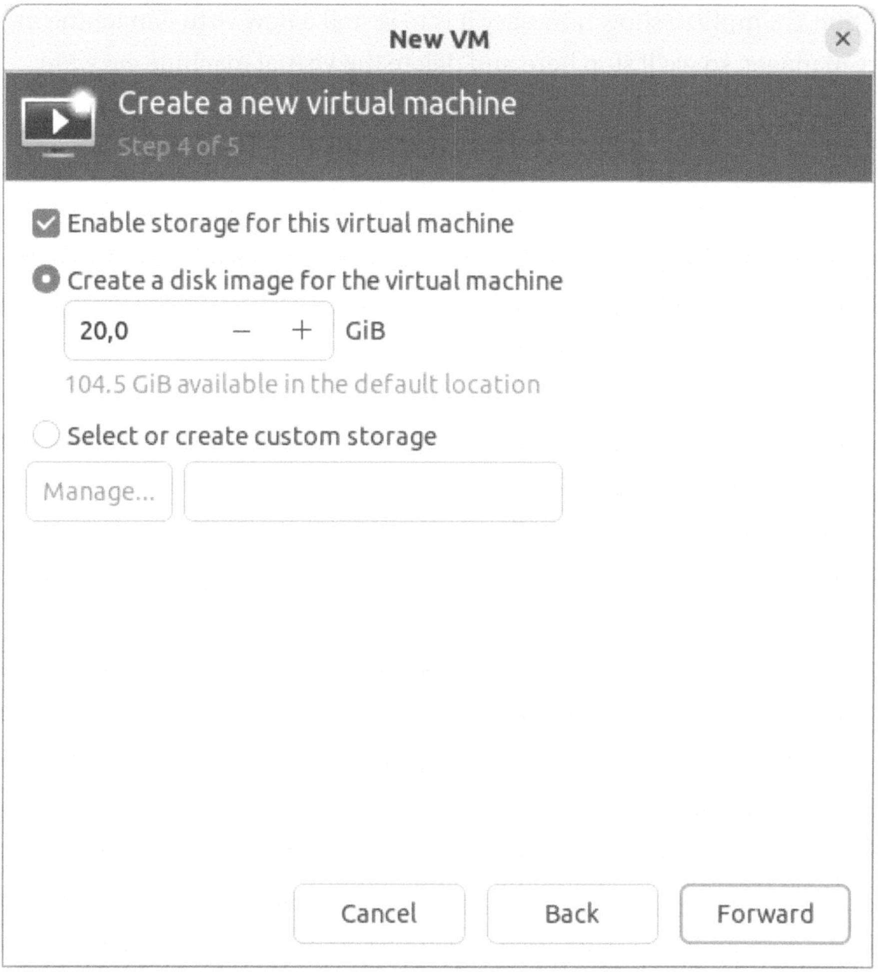

CHAPTER 4   LIBVIRT VIRTUAL MACHINE MANAGEMENT

Figure 4-27. Assigning the disk space to the new VM

After that, we get to the last window of the VM creation. We assign a name to our new VM, and we can see a brief summary of the settings (Figure 4-28). After clicking the "Finish" button, the virtual machine will boot from the virtual CD and start the installation process (Figure 4-29). As we said before, we won't complete the installation as the purpose of this

CHAPTER 4   LIBVIRT VIRTUAL MACHINE MANAGEMENT

section is simply to show how easy it is to install a new virtual machine in virt-manager, so we'll stop here and delete the virtual machine we were installing.

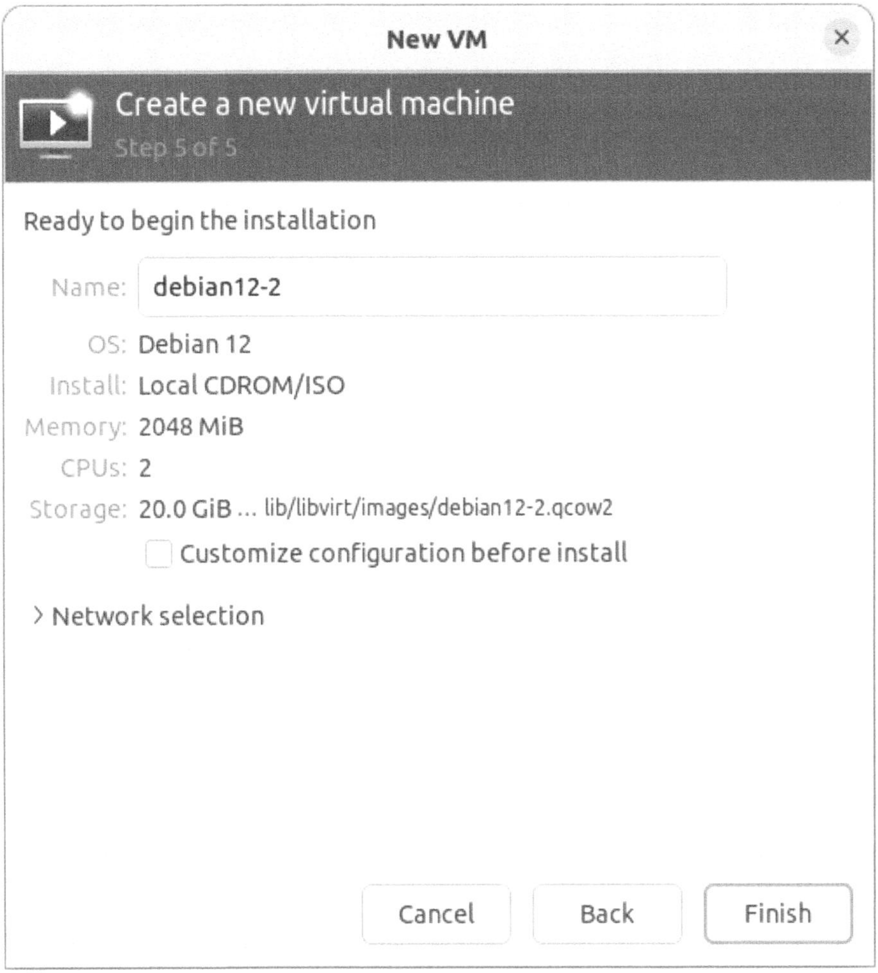

Figure 4-28. VM settings summary

CHAPTER 4   LIBVIRT VIRTUAL MACHINE MANAGEMENT

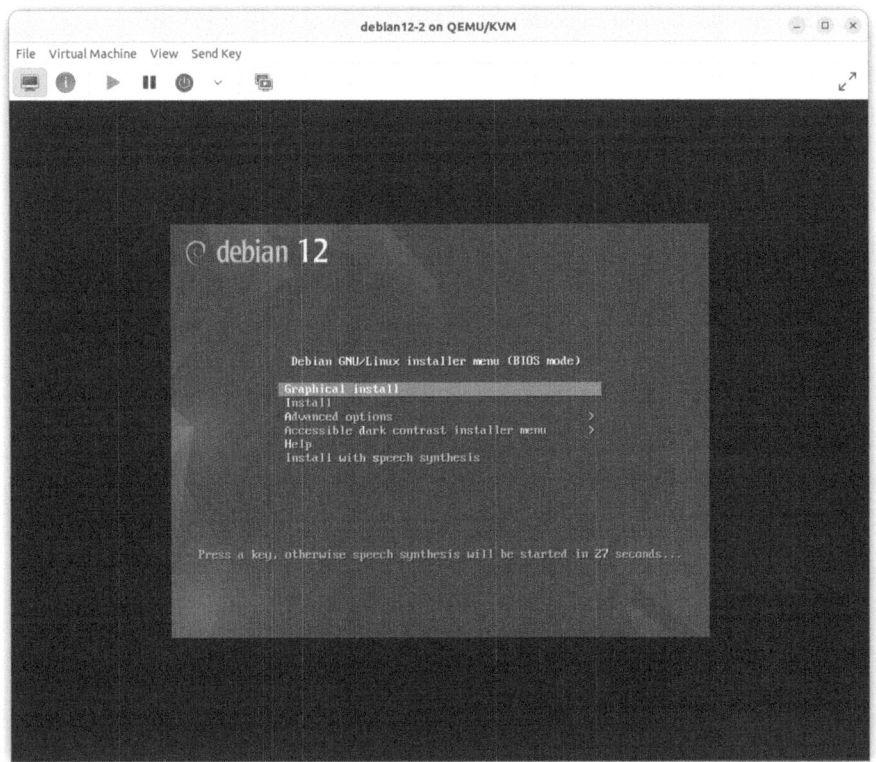

Figure 4-29. Beginning the installation

Accessing libvirt from Our Own Programs

As we mentioned before, we can access this API from many languages. We'll see a few simple examples.

Accessing libvirt from a C Program

In order to create a C program able to interact with libvirt, we need to install first the libvirt-dev package.

antonio@antonio-HP:~$ sudo apt install libvirt-dev

CHAPTER 4 LIBVIRT VIRTUAL MACHINE MANAGEMENT

After installing the package, we'll get a bunch of header files.

```
antonio@antonio-HP:~$ ls /usr/include/libvirt/
libvirt-admin.h            libvirt-host.h         libvirt-qemu.h
libvirt-common.h           libvirt-interface.h    libvirt-secret.h
libvirt-domain.h           libvirt-lxc.h          libvirt-storage.h
libvirt-domain-snapshot.h  libvirt-network.h      libvirt-stream.h
libvirt-event.h            libvirt-nodedev.h      virterror.h
libvirt.h                  libvirt-nwfilter.h
```

This is not supposed to be a book about libvirt programming, so we won't get into much detail, but we'll show an easy example to see how to manage our virtual machines from our C programs using the libvirt API.

In the beginning of this chapter, we installed the **libvirt-clients** package, which includes the virsh command. We're not going to study **virsh** now; we'll do that later. But we'll execute it to obtain some information about the virtual machines that libvirtd is currently aware of.

We'll begin by listing all the domains/virtual machines.

```
antonio@antonio-Laptop:~$ virsh list --all
 Id   Name       State
----------------------------
 -    debian12   shut off
```

The VM we imported in virt-manager is currently shut down. We'll start it because we need to know the domain ID for our example.

```
antonio@antonio-Laptop:~$ virsh start debian12
Domain 'debian12' started

antonio@antonio-HP-Laptop-15s-fq1xxx:~$ virsh list --all
 Id   Name       State
----------------------------
 2    debian12   running
```

CHAPTER 4 LIBVIRT VIRTUAL MACHINE MANAGEMENT

In my case, the domain ID is "2", but in your case, you might get a different value. Let's proceed to code our little example in C. We'll see the source code and we'll explain it later.

```
antonio@antonio-Laptop:~/antonio/programming/c/libvirt$
cat uno.c
#include <stdio.h>
#include "libvirt/libvirt.h"

int main(int argc, char **argv) {
        virConnectPtr c;
        virDomainPtr d;
        char *name;

        c = virConnectOpen(NULL);
        d = virDomainLookupByID(c, 2);
        name = virDomainGetName(d);

        printf("name of domain %d is %s\n", 2, name);
        return 0;
}
```

First, we include in our program the *libvirt* library, as well as the *stdio* library. Then we declare a couple of variables c and d, which are respectively pointers to a *virConnect* struct and a *virDomain* struct. We open a connection to the hypervisor with the *virConnectOpen* function. As we didn't specify which hypervisor to connect to, but used the parameter "NULL", the function will try every hypervisor until one successfully opens.

Once we have a connection established, we search for the domain with the ID 2, as we previously saw, by using the function *virDomainLookupByID*, and we get its associated name with *virDomainGetName*. Finally, we print the result on the screen.

179

If we compile the program and execute it, we'll see the name of the VM with the ID 2.

```
antonio@antonio-Laptop:~/antonio/programming/c/libvirt$ gcc uno.c -lvirt -o uno
antonio@antonio-Laptop:~/antonio/programming/c/libvirt$ ./uno
name of domain 2 is debian12
```

Accessing libvirt from a Python Program

We mentioned in the beginning of the chapter that the libvirt API can be accessed by using many program languages. We already have seen how to access it from a C program, and now we'll do the same thing from a Python program.

To use the API, we'll have to install the *python3-libvirt* package in Ubuntu Linux.

```
antonio@antonio-Laptop:~$ sudo apt install python3-libvirt
```

We can now create our own Python programs to interact with libvirt. As an example, we'll use the Python interpreter interactively to see how easy it is to integrate libvirt in our Python programs. We'll assume that our virtual machine named "debian 12" is already running; if it's not, we'll start it either with **virt-manager** or **virsh**. After that, we start the Python interpreter.

```
antonio@antonio-Laptop:~$ python3
Python 3.10.12 (main, Nov 20 2023, 15:14:05) [GCC 11.4.0] on linux
Type "help", "copyright", "credits" or "license" for more information.
>>>
```

We need to import the libvirt Python module we installed previously.

```
>>> import libvirt
```

We can now connect to libvirtd.

```
>>> conn = libvirt.open()
```

We didn't use any parameter, so we'll connect to the first available hypervisor. We can see the hypervisor we're connected to with this command:

```
>>> conn.getURI()
'qemu:///system'
```

We'll do something simple such as obtaining the domain IDs.

```
>>> conn.listDomainsID()
[5]
```

We see that currently we only have a domain ID, which is 5 in this case. In your case, it could be any other value. We'll search the domain associated to this ID. And we'll assign this pointer value to a variable named domid.

```
>>> conn.lookupByID(5)
<libvirt.virDomain object at 0x7765cfe38670>
>>> domid = conn.lookupByID(5)
```

Now, we can perform several operations. We'll see just a few examples, such as getting the domain name, showing the VM configuration as an XML file, or getting the type of virtual machine.

```
>>> libvirt.virDomain.name(domi)
'debian12'
>>> libvirt.virDomain.XMLDesc(domid)
```

```
'<domain type=\'kvm\' id=\'5\'>\n  <name>debian12</
name>\n  <uuid>05959a22-b9e4-4d99-a3ae-16f946880ff1</
uuid>\n  <metadata>\n    <libosinfo:libosinfo
.
.
.
>>> libvirt.virDomain.OSType(domid)
'hvm'
```

To finish this brief demonstration on how to interact with libvirt from Python, we see how to connect to a different hypervisor or container runtime. Previously we opened a connection to LXC from virt-manager. Now we'll do the same thing from Python.

```
>>> conn2 = libvirt.open('lxc:///')
```

As we haven't studied containers so far – we'll do that later – we don't have any containers in our host. However, the example is perfectly valid to show how libvirt can be accessed from Python.

```
>>> conn2.listDomainsID()
[]
```

Migrating a Virtual Machine to Another Host

We have seen previously how to connect **virt-manager** to a remote host. Thanks to this, we can migrate a virtual machine between different hosts. We'll create a new connection to a remote host the usual way by clicking "File" ➤ "Add connection" and we'll fill in the needed parameters (Figure 4-30).

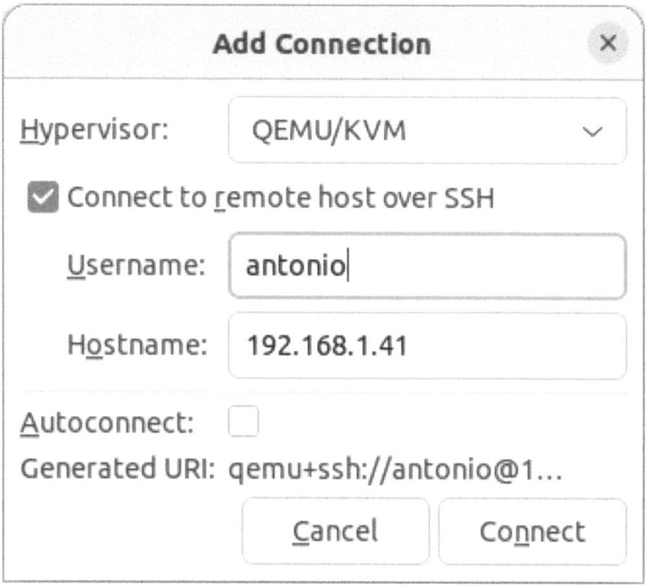

CHAPTER 4 LIBVIRT VIRTUAL MACHINE MANAGEMENT

Figure 4-30. Connecting to a remote QEMU/KVM host

Once the connection is successfully established, we'll see the list of the virtual machines in the remote hypervisor (Figure 4-31).

CHAPTER 4　LIBVIRT VIRTUAL MACHINE MANAGEMENT

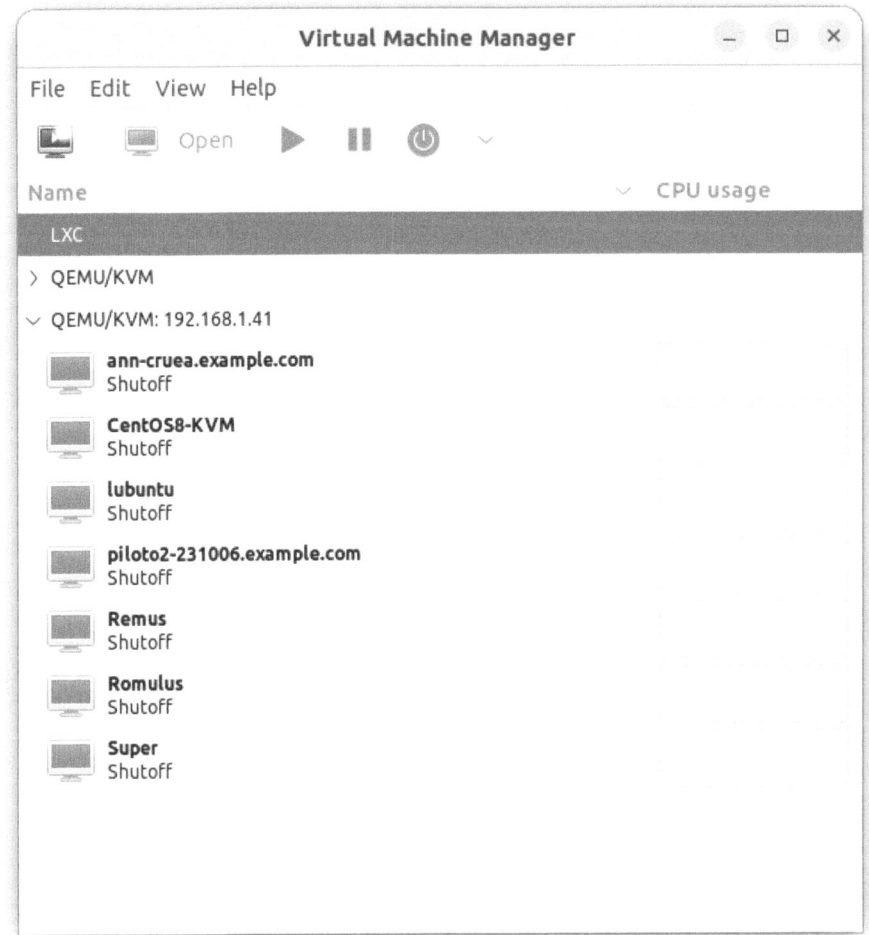

Figure 4-31. Virtual machines in the remote QEMU/KVM hypervisor

If we want to migrate the VM "debian12" currently running on our local host, we'll select it (Figure 4-32) and right-click the migrate option. In the next window, we'll see a summary of the operation (Figure 4-33), the source and destination host, etc.

CHAPTER 4   LIBVIRT VIRTUAL MACHINE MANAGEMENT

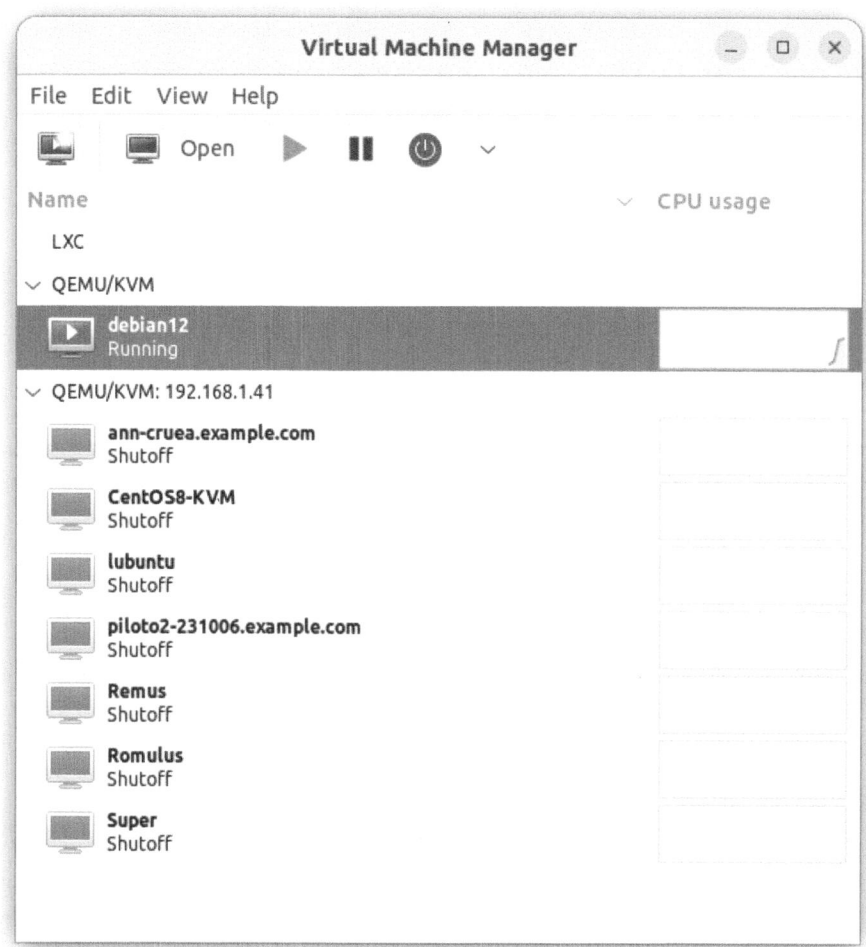

Figure 4-32. *Migrating a VM from the local host to a remote host*

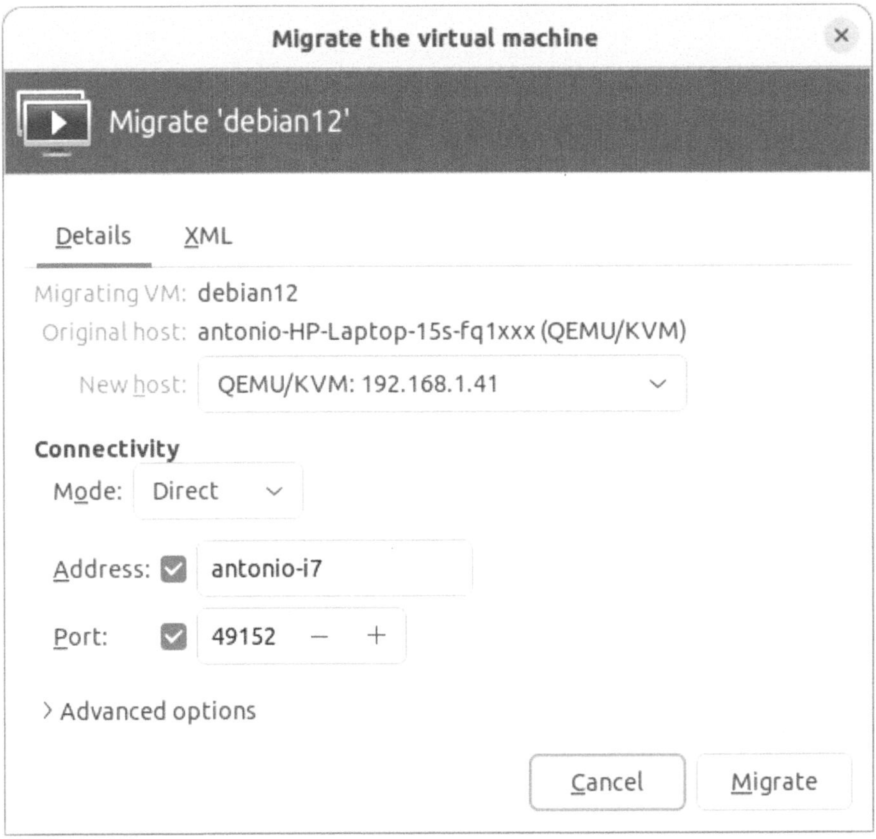

CHAPTER 4   LIBVIRT VIRTUAL MACHINE MANAGEMENT

Figure 4-33.   VM migration summary

However, when we click the "Migrate" button, we'll get the error shown in Figure 4-34.

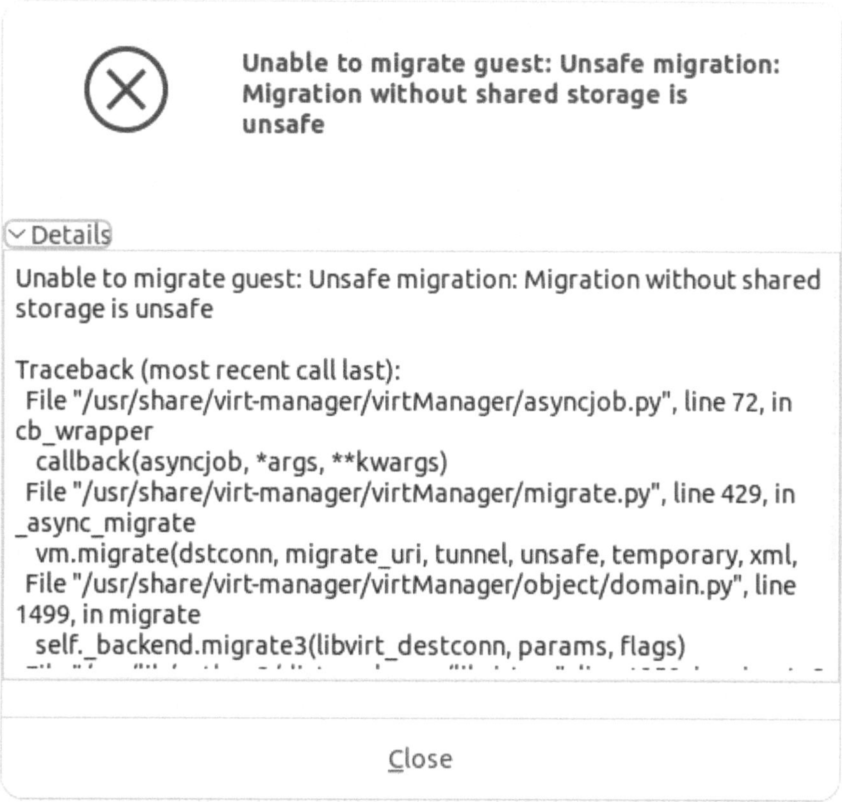

CHAPTER 4 LIBVIRT VIRTUAL MACHINE MANAGEMENT

Unable to migrate guest: Unsafe migration: Migration without shared storage is unsafe

⌄ Details

Unable to migrate guest: Unsafe migration: Migration without shared storage is unsafe

Traceback (most recent call last):
 File "/usr/share/virt-manager/virtManager/asyncjob.py", line 72, in cb_wrapper
   callback(asyncjob, *args, **kwargs)
 File "/usr/share/virt-manager/virtManager/migrate.py", line 429, in _async_migrate
   vm.migrate(dstconn, migrate_uri, tunnel, unsafe, temporary, xml,
 File "/usr/share/virt-manager/virtManager/object/domain.py", line 1499, in migrate
   self._backend.migrate3(libvirt_destconn, params, flags)

Close

Figure 4-34. Migration error

We got an error because currently the storage pool in which the disk file is located is a directory local to the QEMU/KVM host. That is considered insecure and by default is not allowed. Later we'll see briefly that we can create many different storage pools, some of which are shared.

For now, we'll see how to perform the migration modifying the default Advanced options so that unsafe migration is allowed. We'll repeat the procedure, but this time we'll migrate a VM from the remote host to the local host. We'll select the "lubuntu" VM (Figure 4-35) and right-click on the "migrate" option. This time we'll edit the Advanced options and activate the "Allow unsafe" option (Figure 4-36).

CHAPTER 4   LIBVIRT VIRTUAL MACHINE MANAGEMENT

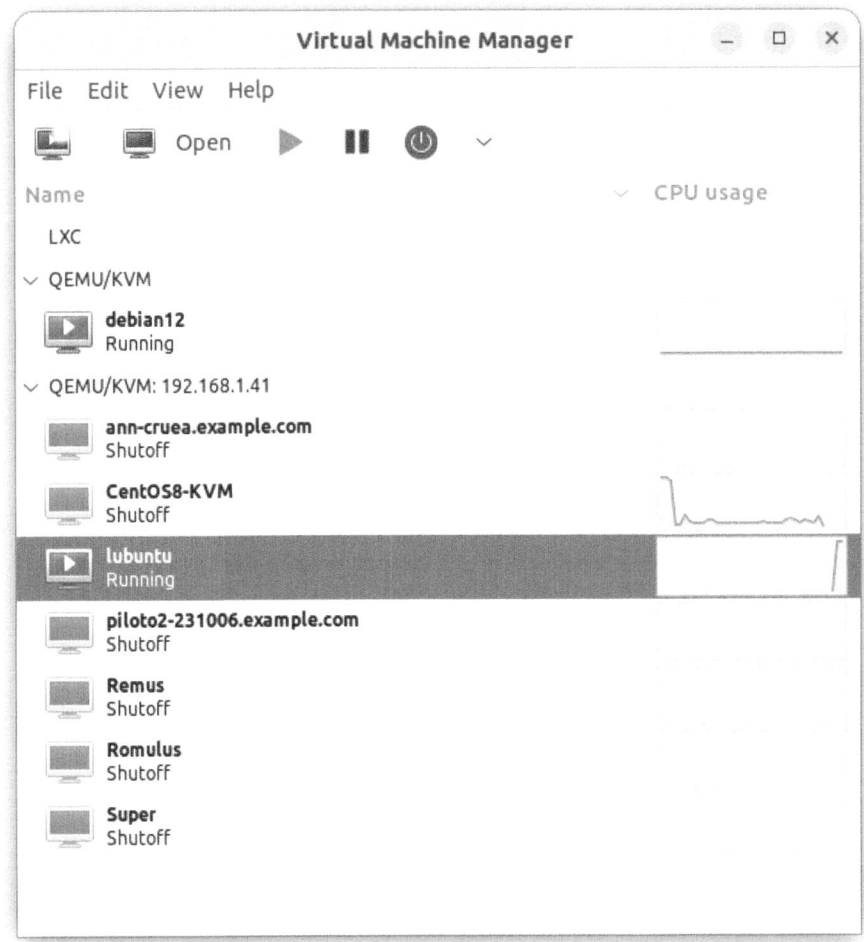

Figure 4-35. *Migrating a VM*

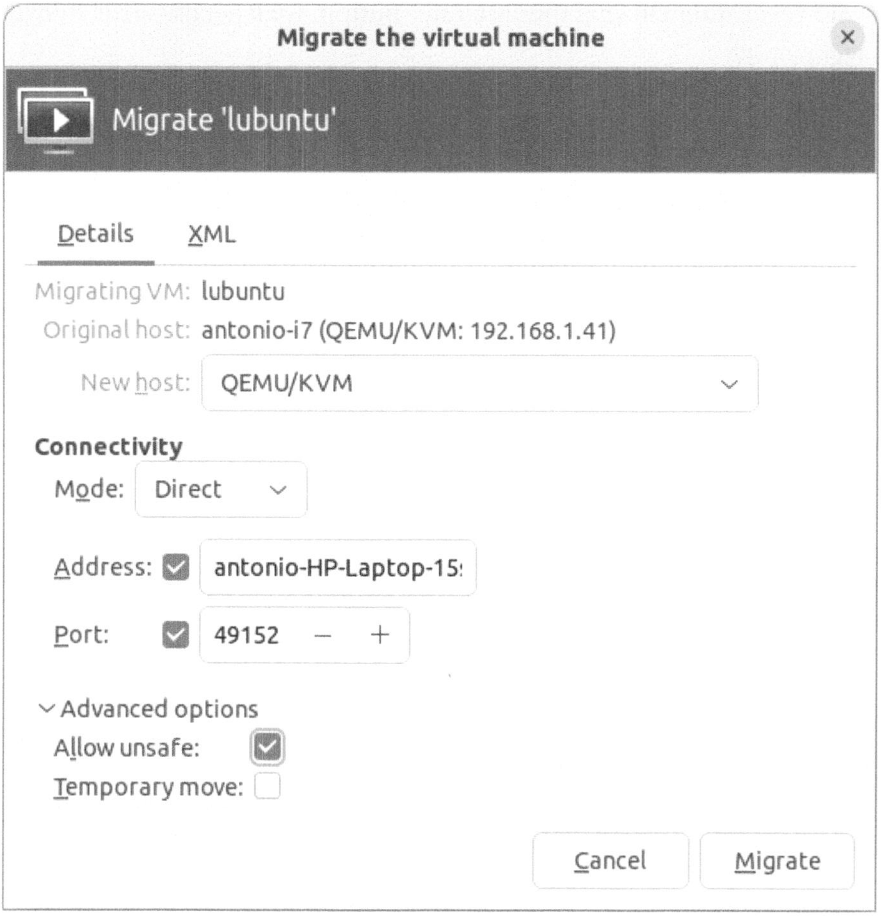

CHAPTER 4   LIBVIRT VIRTUAL MACHINE MANAGEMENT

Figure 4-36. Allowing unsafe migration

CHAPTER 4 LIBVIRT VIRTUAL MACHINE MANAGEMENT

However, after clicking the "Migrate" button, we'll get the error shown in Figure 4-37.

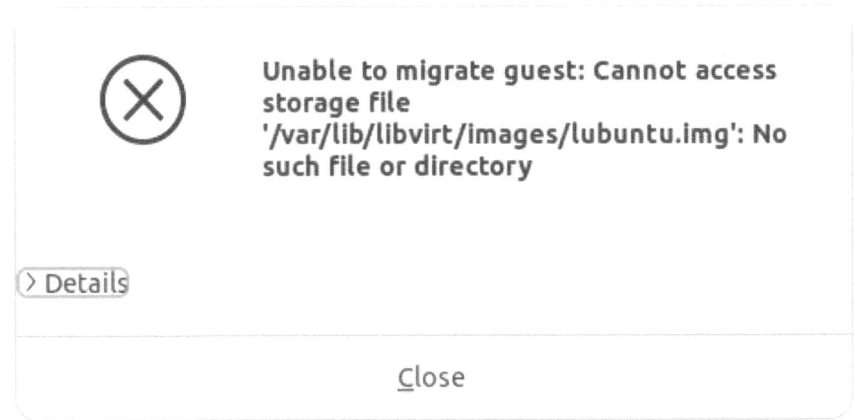

Figure 4-37. Error migrating the VM. Unable to access the storage file

This error is completely normal; the disk file currently only exists on the remote host, not on the local host. So when the migration process tries to access the storage file in the destination host, it returns this error. To fix this, we'll copy the disk file from the remote host to the local host with **scp** or any other tool.

antonio@antonio-Laptop:~$ sudo scp antonio@192.168.1.41:/var/lib/libvirt/images/lubuntu.img   /var/lib/libvirt/images/

Once the file has been copied, we'll try to migrate again. This time the procedure starts to execute (Figure 4-38).

CHAPTER 4   LIBVIRT VIRTUAL MACHINE MANAGEMENT

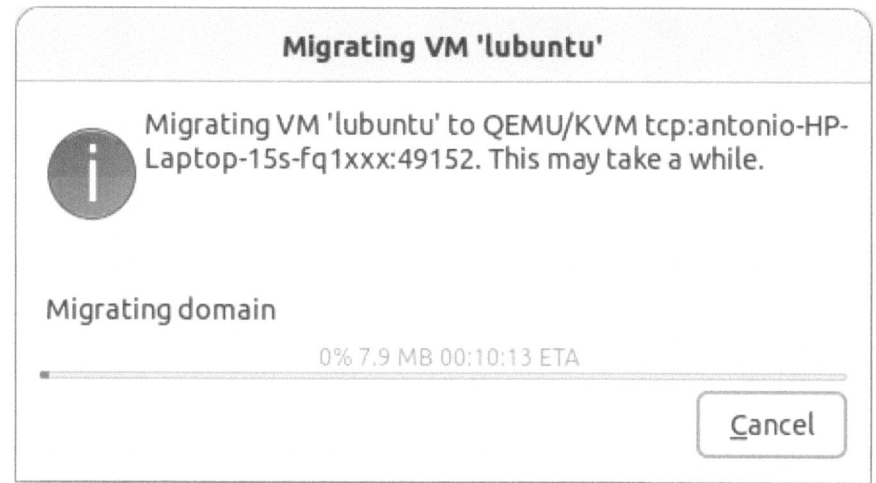

Figure 4-38. Migrating a VM

The migration can take a while, but after it is complete, we can see the VM running on the local QEMU/KVM host (Figure 4-39). And we can access the server console and manage it (Figure 4-40).

191

CHAPTER 4   LIBVIRT VIRTUAL MACHINE MANAGEMENT

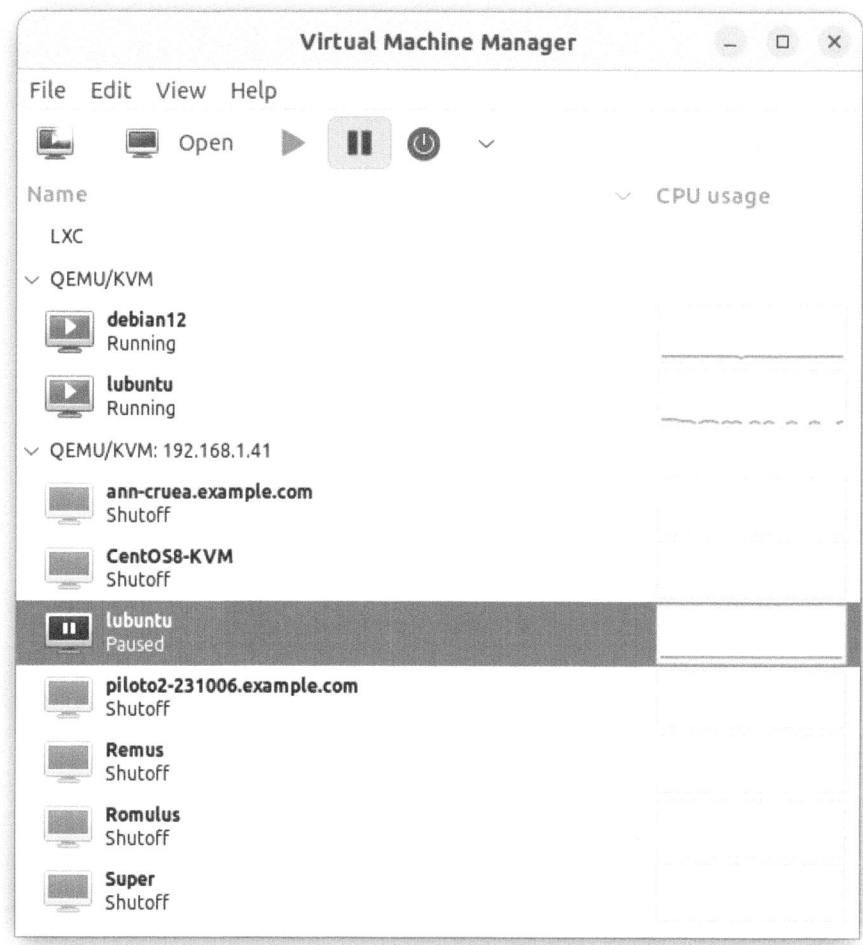

Figure 4-39. *Migration completed*

CHAPTER 4 LIBVIRT VIRTUAL MACHINE MANAGEMENT

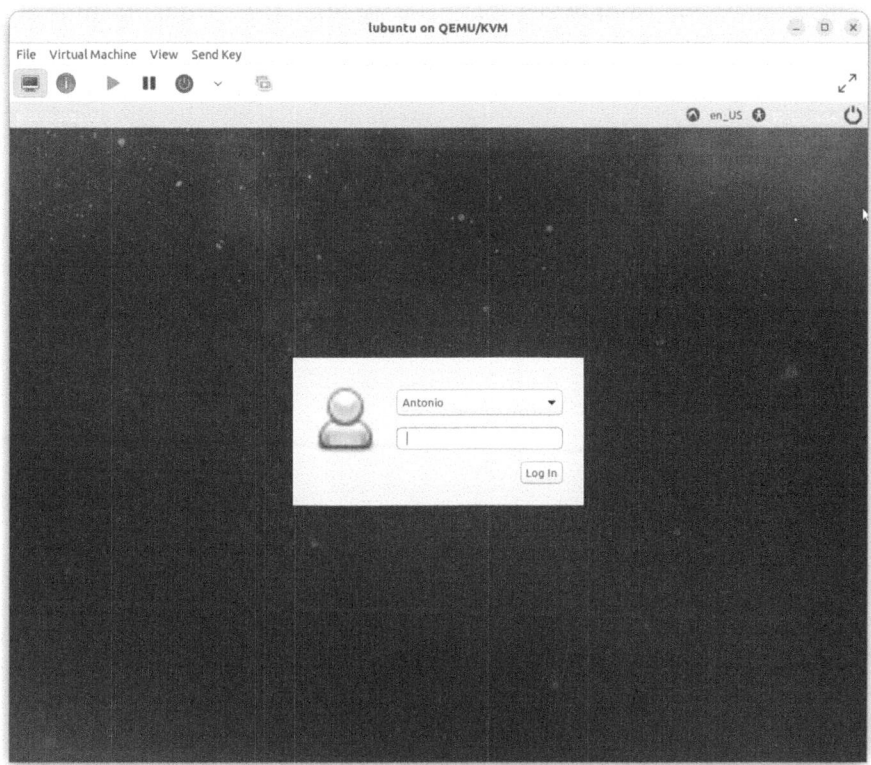

Figure 4-40. Accessing the console of the migrated VM

Managing Snapshots

We have already seen that we can create snapshots in QEMU by using QEMU monitor; we can also create snapshots in Xen domains using the **xl** command. But now we'll see we can do this same thing in a much easier way from **virt-manager**.

CHAPTER 4   LIBVIRT VIRTUAL MACHINE MANAGEMENT

To create a snapshot in virt-manager, we open the virtual machine and click on the last icon, "Manage VM snapshots" (Figure 4-41).

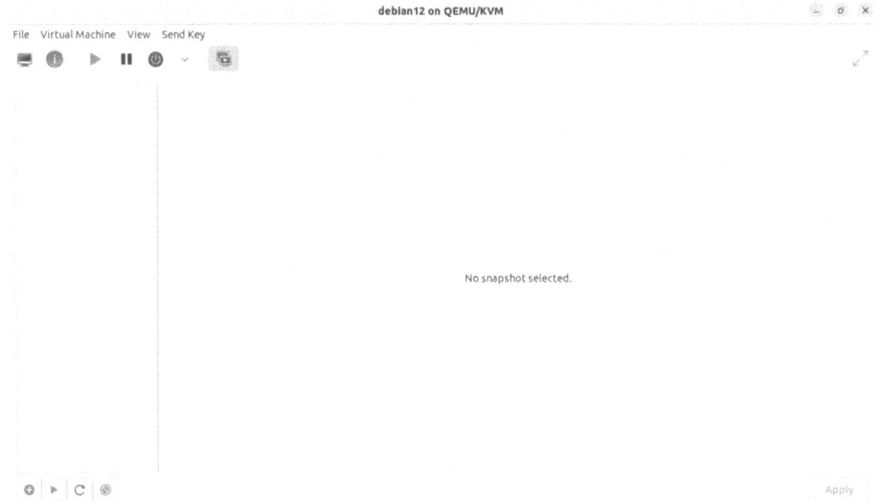

Figure 4-41. Managing VM snapshots

We'll click on the "+" icon to create a new snapshot (Figure 4-42).

CHAPTER 4   LIBVIRT VIRTUAL MACHINE MANAGEMENT

Figure 4-42. *Creating a snapshot in virt-manager*

CHAPTER 4   LIBVIRT VIRTUAL MACHINE MANAGEMENT

If we want to restore the snapshot, we select it (Figure 4-43) and click the "play" button (run selected snapshot). We confirm that we want to restore the snapshot discarding the current changes (Figure 4-44).

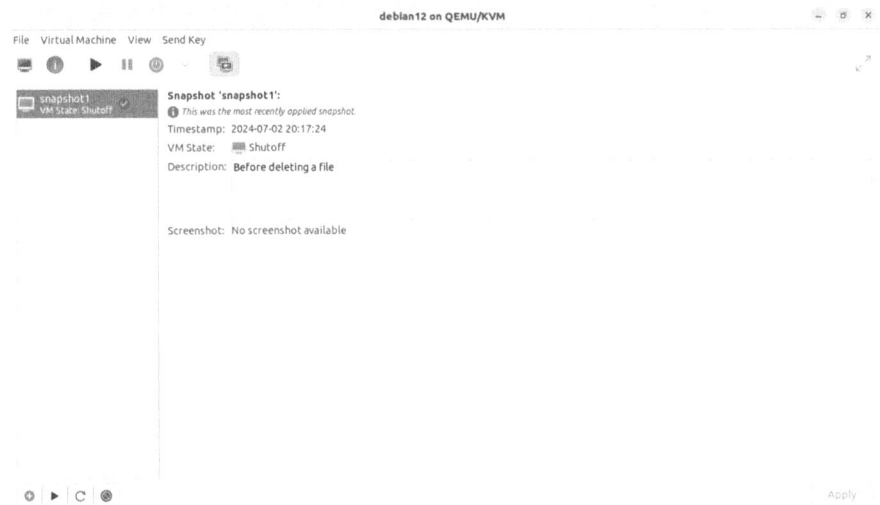

Figure 4-43. Restoring a snapshot

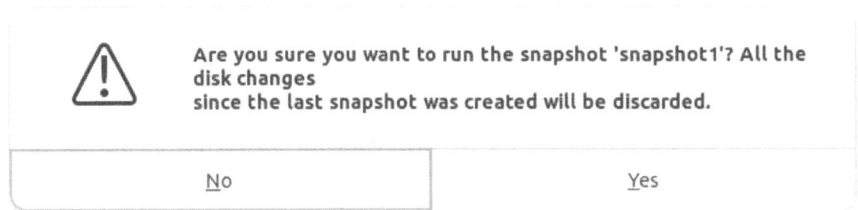

Figure 4-44. Confirming that we want to restore the snapshot

Finally, when we no longer need the snapshot, we can delete it by clicking on the "delete snapshot" icon.

Storage Pools and Volumes

Every VM machine needs to store its data somewhere; this is where storage pools and storage volumes come into play. The storage pool is a certain amount of storage set aside by the administrator to be used by the virtual machines. The storage pool is divided into storage volumes.

For example, when we used a local directory as the storage pool, every file inside that local directory was a storage volume. These volumes are assigned to the virtual machines as block devices.

In libvirt, we can create the following storage pools:

- dir: Filesystem Directory
- disk: Physical Disk Device
- fs: Preformatted Block Device
- gluster: Gluster Filesystem
- iscsi: iSCSI Target
- logical: LVM Volume Group
- mpath: Multipath Device Emulator
- netfs: Network Exported Directory
- rbd: RADOS Block Device/Ceph
- scsi: SCSI Host Adapter
- sheepdog: Sheepdog Filesystem
- zfs: ZFS Pool

As we can see, there are many different types of storage pools. We won't see each and every one of them, but we'll see a couple of examples.

We have already seen the dir type so we'll see two different types of storage pool. We'll begin by creating an NFS share in a server, and then we'll create a storage pool of the type netfs. We've seen already how to

CHAPTER 4   LIBVIRT VIRTUAL MACHINE MANAGEMENT

create a storage volume when we created our first virtual machine in virt-manager. We'll repeat the procedure, but this time we'll select the type netfs (Figure 4-45).

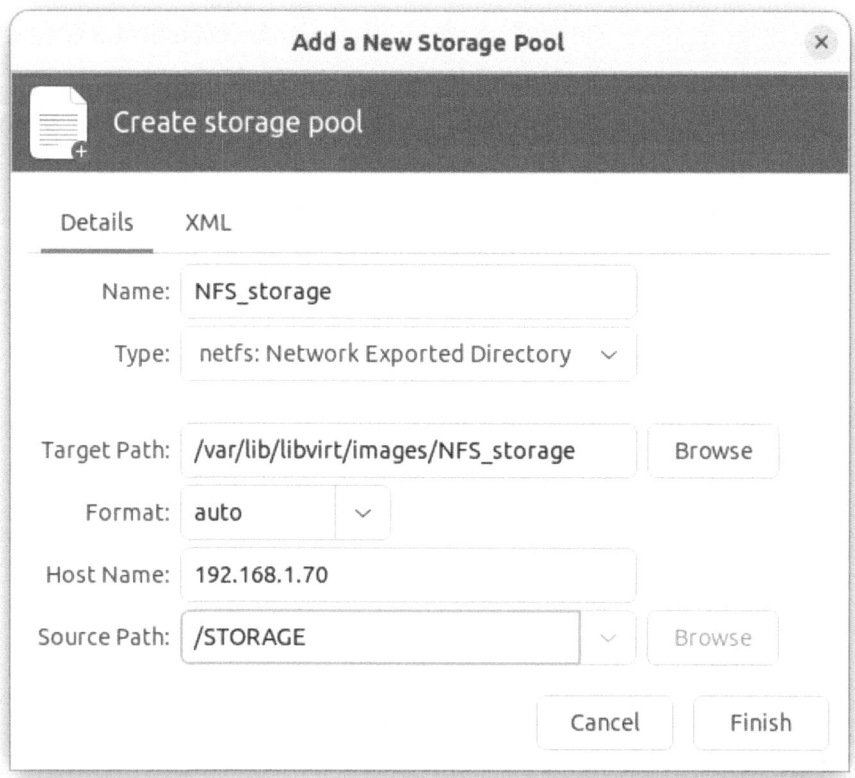

Figure 4-45. *Creating a storage pool of the type netfs*

CHAPTER 4 LIBVIRT VIRTUAL MACHINE MANAGEMENT

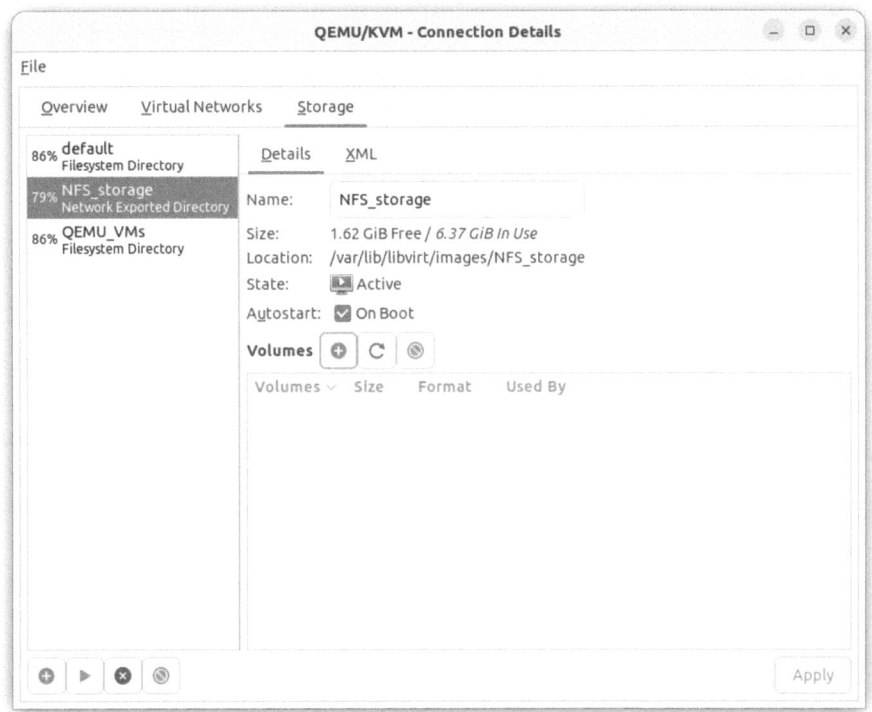

***Figure 4-46.** Network exported storage pool*

Once created, we can access it in the same way as the dir type storage volume previously created (Figure 4-46). The way to work is basically the same for both types; each file in the NFS share will be a storage volume, just like we have seen in the dir type.

If we want to create a storage pool of the type "logical", the procedure is quite similar. We create a new storage pool, and this time we choose the type "logical" and select a volume group that needs to exist in our host (Figure 4-47).

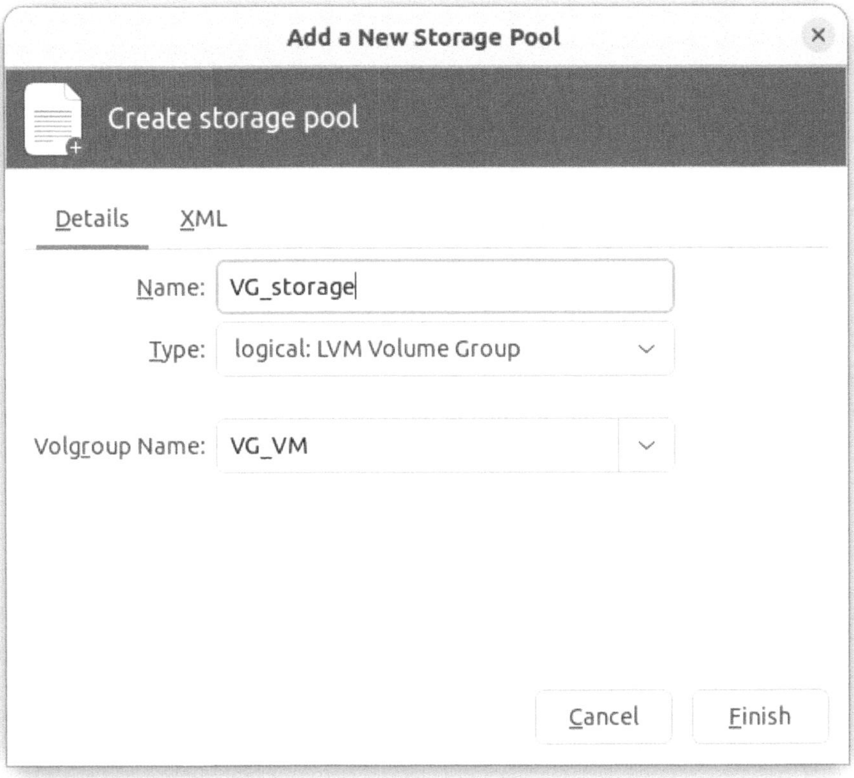

CHAPTER 4   LIBVIRT VIRTUAL MACHINE MANAGEMENT

Figure 4-47. Creating a storage pool of the type "logical"

Similarly to what we've seen in the previous types of storage pools created, the storage pool is divided into storage volumes. So if we install a new virtual machine and decide to store that virtual machine in the newly created logical storage pool, we'll see later that a new file (a storage volume) is created (Figure 4-48).

CHAPTER 4   LIBVIRT VIRTUAL MACHINE MANAGEMENT

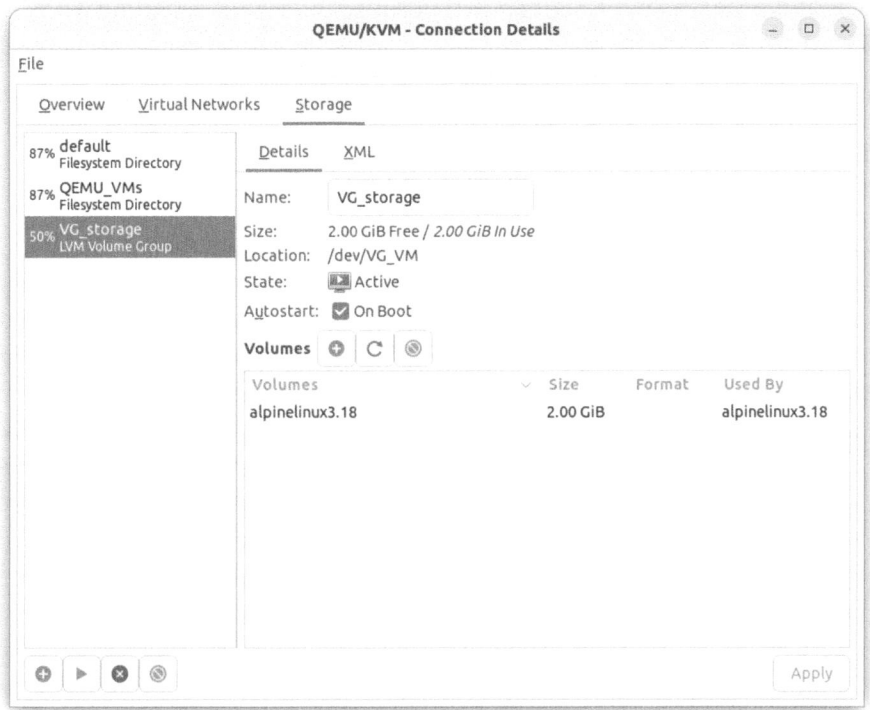

Figure 4-48. *Storage pool with a newly created storage volume*

Networking

When installing libvirt, a new interface virbr0 is created. This is a bridge used by default by libvirt to establish the communication between the virtual machines and the host and, in some cases, the external network. We can list this interface in the host.

```
antonio@antonio-Laptop:~$ ip link show virbr0
3: virbr0: <NO-CARRIER,BROADCAST,MULTICAST,UP> mtu 1500 qdisc
noqueue state DOWN mode DEFAULT group default qlen 1000
    link/ether 52:54:00:35:f1:14 brd ff:ff:ff:ff:ff:ff
```

201

CHAPTER 4 LIBVIRT VIRTUAL MACHINE MANAGEMENT

In this case, the interface is down because the virtual machine we created previously with **virt-manager** is currently down. If we start it, we'll see that the status of the interface changes to "up".

```
antonio@antonio-Laptop:~$ ip link show virbr0
3: virbr0: <BROADCAST,MULTICAST,UP,LOWER_UP> mtu 1500 qdisc
noqueue state UP mode DEFAULT group default qlen 1000
    link/ether 52:54:00:35:f1:14 brd ff:ff:ff:ff:ff:ff
```

We can see the network settings by opening the virtual machine from virt-manager and selecting the "Show virtual hardware details" option (Figure 4-49).

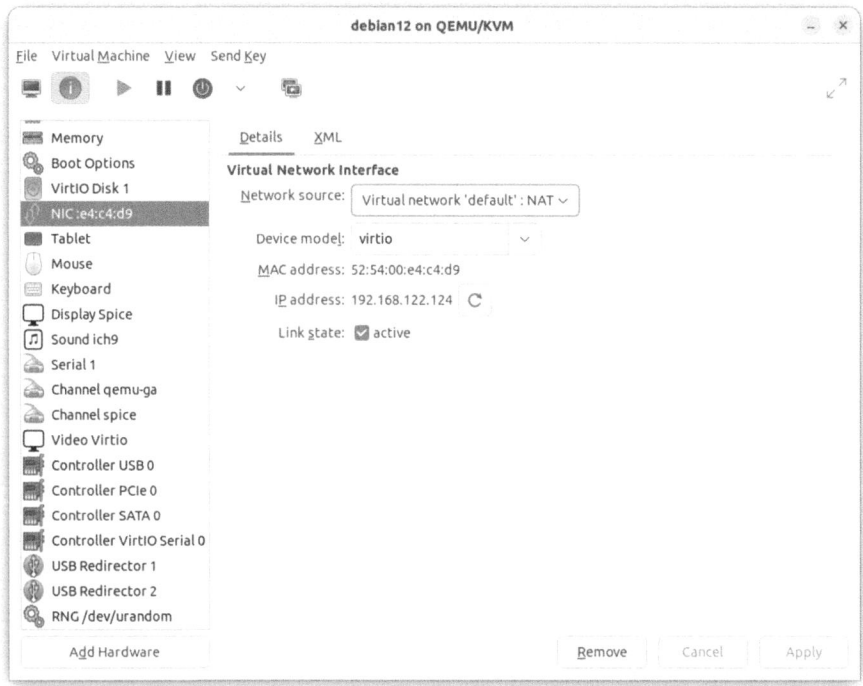

Figure 4-49. *Virtual machine network settings*

CHAPTER 4 LIBVIRT VIRTUAL MACHINE MANAGEMENT

In this example, we can see that the NIC of the VM is connected to the network "Virtual Network default", and it is using NAT (Network Address Translation). We can also see the IP address assigned to the VM through DHCP.

If we take a look at the "Virtual Networks" section of the current hypervisor (Figure 4-50), we'll see that currently we only have one virtual network defined. We can see the range of addresses that are assigned to the clients through DHCP, as well as the fact that the network is using NAT.

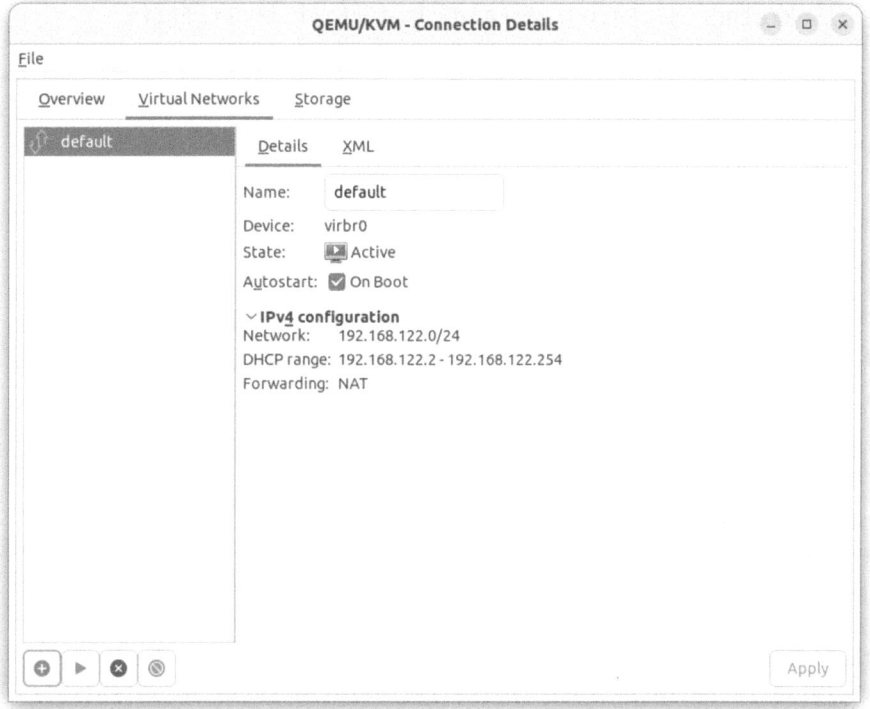

Figure 4-50. *Virtual networks*

Now that we have an overall idea of networking in libvirt, let's see a bit more of detail about it.

CHAPTER 4   LIBVIRT VIRTUAL MACHINE MANAGEMENT

We've seen that right after installing libvirt, a new network interface named **virbr0** is created. By default, all virtual machines created using libvirt will be connected to this interface. We have seen this in the case of our "Debian 12" virtual machine. If we check the network settings from the virtual machine itself, we'll see this:

```
antonio@debian:~$ ip address show enp1s0
2: enp1s0: <BROADCAST,MULTICAST,UP,LOWER_UP> mtu 1500 qdisc fq_codel state UP group default qlen 1000
    link/ether 52:54:00:e4:c4:d9 brd ff:ff:ff:ff:ff:ff
    inet 192.168.122.124/24 brd 192.168.122.255 scope global dynamic noprefixroute enp1s0
       valid_lft 2671sec preferred_lft 2671sec
    inet6 fe80::5054:ff:fee4:c4d9/64 scope link noprefixroute
       valid_lft forever preferred_lft forever
antonio@debian:~$ ip route
default via 192.168.122.1 dev enp1s0 proto dhcp src 192.168.122.124 metric 100
192.168.122.0/24 dev enp1s0 proto kernel scope link src 192.168.122.124 metric 100
```

We can see that it got its IP address and gateway address through DHCP. Of course the IP address of the gateway is that of the virbr0 network interface.

```
antonio@antonio-Laptop:~$ ip address show virbr0
3: virbr0: <BROADCAST,MULTICAST,UP,LOWER_UP> mtu 1500 qdisc noqueue state UP group default qlen 1000
    link/ether 52:54:00:35:f1:14 brd ff:ff:ff:ff:ff:ff
    inet 192.168.122.1/24 brd 192.168.122.255 scope global virbr0
       valid_lft forever preferred_lft forever
```

CHAPTER 4   LIBVIRT VIRTUAL MACHINE MANAGEMENT

Both DHCP and DNS services are provided by **libvirt** using **dnsmasq**. This is a light DNS/DHCP server. This software can work independently but in libvirt is fully integrated and can be managed using the usual libvirt tools.

The default network uses NAT (Network Address Translation); that is, when communicating with the outside world, the host IP is used instead of the guest IP. We'll see an example. Let's suppose we want to access a web server from our "Debian 12" virtual machine.

```
antonio@debian:~$ wget http://192.168.1.250
```

In the web server logs, we will find an entry similar to this one:

```
192.168.1.20 - - [06/Jul/2024:12:24:45 +0200] "GET / HTTP/1.1" 200 2562 "-" "Wget/1.21.3"
```

We can see that the IP registered is that of the host, not that of the guest. This is accomplished by modifying the properties of the Linux firewall. Describing exactly how NAT works is well beyond the scope of this book, but we'll see an example of the firewall configuration in the host.

```
antonio@antonio-Laptop:~$ sudo iptables -t nat -L
.
.
.
Chain LIBVIRT_PRT (1 references)
target     prot opt source               destination
RETURN     all  --  192.168.122.0/24     base-address.mcast.net/24
RETURN     all  --  192.168.122.0/24     255.255.255.255
MASQUERADE tcp  --  192.168.122.0/24     !192.168.122.0/24     masq ports: 1024-65535
MASQUERADE udp  --  192.168.122.0/24     !192.168.122.0/24     masq ports: 1024-65535
MASQUERADE all  --  192.168.122.0/24     !192.168.122.0/24
```

This default network configuration is most of the time everything we need to work, but there are many other options available. We'll see a couple of them.

We'll start by creating a routed network. We create a new virtual network, but this time we choose the "Routed" mode. We can also edit the DHCP settings if we want to, but the default values are OK for this example. We also assign a descriptive name to this new virtual network (Figure 4-51).

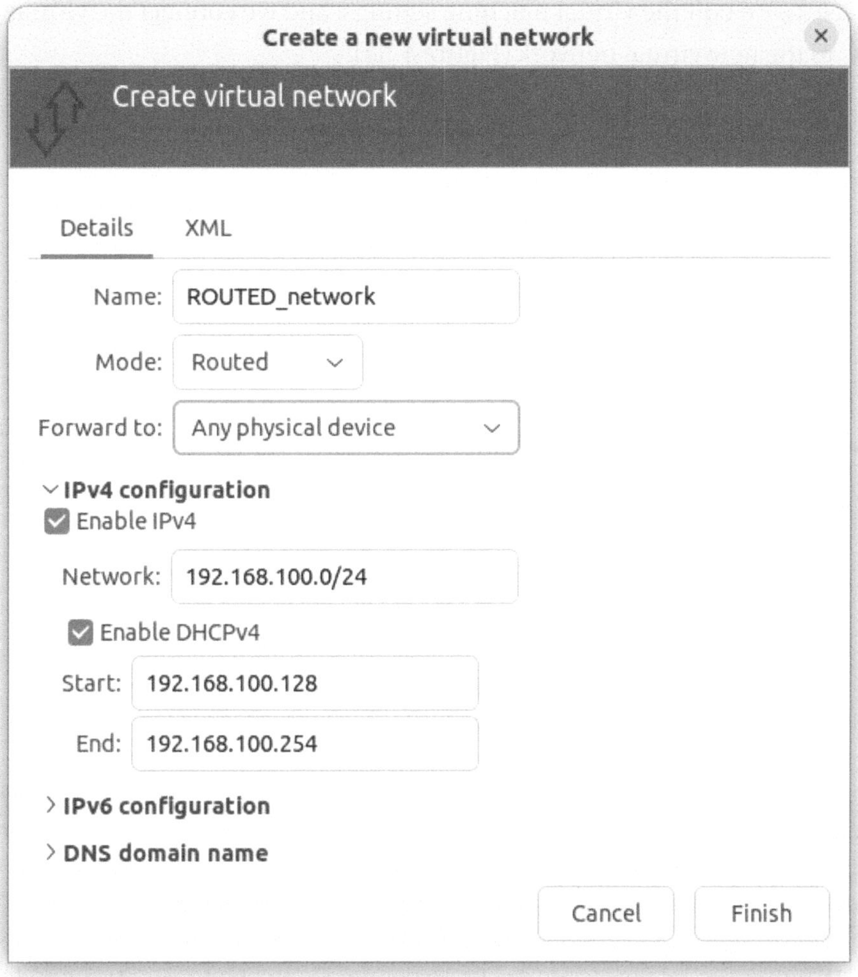

Figure 4-51. Creating a routed virtual network

CHAPTER 4 LIBVIRT VIRTUAL MACHINE MANAGEMENT

Next, we edit the virtual machine settings, and we connect the virtual NIC to the new virtual network (Figure 4-52).

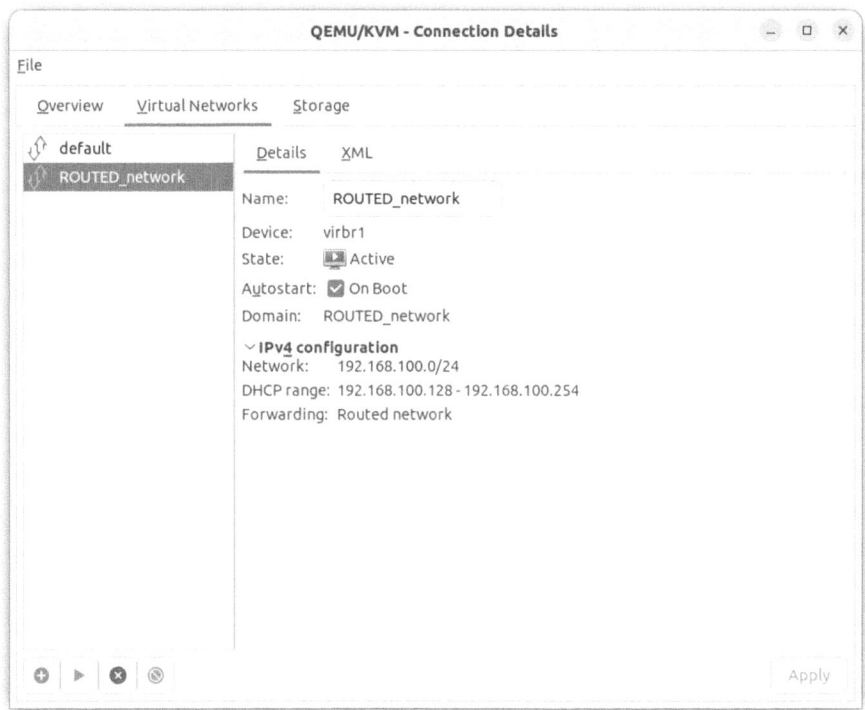

Figure 4-52. Connecting the Debian 12 virtual machine to the new virtual network

We might need to refresh the IP settings from the VM console, to make sure that the new settings are active.

Right after creating the network, a new network interface appears in the host.

```
antonio@antonio-Laptop:~$ ip address show virbr1
45: virbr1: <BROADCAST,MULTICAST,UP,LOWER_UP> mtu 1500 qdisc noqueue state UP group default qlen 1000
    link/ether 52:54:00:9a:49:a6 brd ff:ff:ff:ff:ff:ff
```

208

CHAPTER 4   LIBVIRT VIRTUAL MACHINE MANAGEMENT

```
   inet 192.168.100.1/24 brd 192.168.100.255 scope
global virbr1
      valid_lft forever preferred_lft forever
```

Now we can connect again from the host to the guest, but if we try to access the same web server from the local network, we won't be able.

```
antonio@debian:~$ wget    http://192.168.1.250
--2024-07-06 12:47:50--   http://192.168.1.250/
Connecting to 192.168.1.250:80...
```

This behavior is perfectly normal. The default virtual network was using NAT, so when the web server received an HTTP request, the source address was that of the libvirt host, and the web server knows how to handle that. However, now we're using a routed network, so there is no NAT and the real IP from the guest is used. When the web server from the local network receives a request from 192.168.100.149, it doesn't know how to send the information back. It tries to use the default gateway, but the default network doesn't know that IP either and the TCP packet is finally discarded.

To solve this situation, we need to edit the routing tables in our network. The simplest way to do it in this example is by editing the routing table in the web server computer so that every packet addressed to the 192.168.100.0/24 network is forwarded to the libvirt host computer.

```
root@raspberrypi:/var/log/apache2# ip route add
192.168.100.0/24 via 192.168.1.20 dev eth0
```

Now we can repeat the test; this time we'll be able to access the web server from the local network.

```
antonio@debian:~$ wget    http://192.168.1.250
--2024-07-06 13:02:52--   http://192.168.1.250/
Connecting to 192.168.1.250:80... connected.
```

And in the Apache logs, we'll see that the recorded IP address is that of the guest.

```
192.168.100.149 - - [06/Jul/2024:13:02:52 +0200] "GET / HTTP/1.1" 200 2562 "-" "Wget/1.21.3"
```

Another interesting virtual network type is "Isolated". In this case, the libvirt guest can communicate with each other and with the host, but not with the outside world. The way to create it is exactly similar to what we saw before with the routed mode. In this case, however, we specify the "Isolated" mode and assign a network that is currently not in use (Figure 4-53).

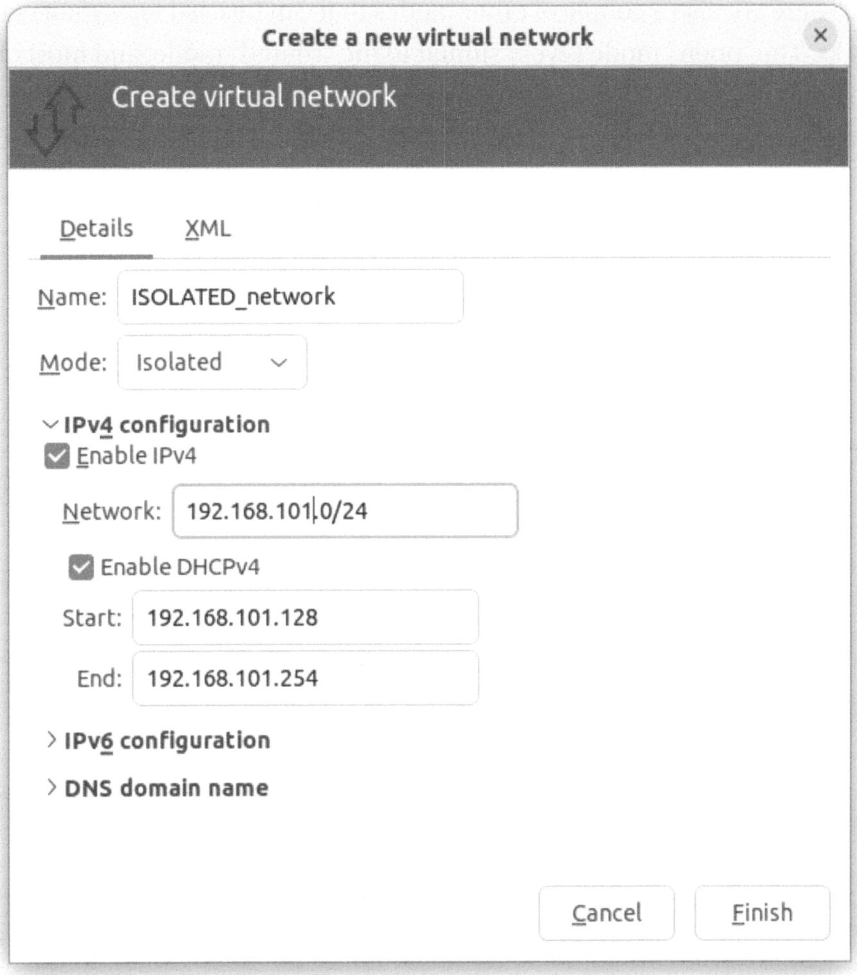

CHAPTER 4   LIBVIRT VIRTUAL MACHINE MANAGEMENT

Figure 4-53. *Creating an isolated virtual networking*

The way to work with this isolated virtual network is exactly the same as what we have seen so far; we just need to edit the virtual machine settings and connect the NIC to this new network. As we said before, with this network, we can only communicate internally with the host and with other guests, not with the outside world.

CHAPTER 4   LIBVIRT VIRTUAL MACHINE MANAGEMENT

There are also a couple of other modes that can be used for virtual networks. The "open" mode is very similar to the "routed" mode, and most of the time they provide basically the same functionality. Finally, the "SR-IOV pool" type is very specific and allows different virtual machines to share a single hardware interface.

Monitoring

When we first introduced **virt-manager**, we mentioned very briefly that it can also be used to monitor the use of resources like CPU, memory, and so on. However, by default, only the CPU is monitored (Figure 4-54).

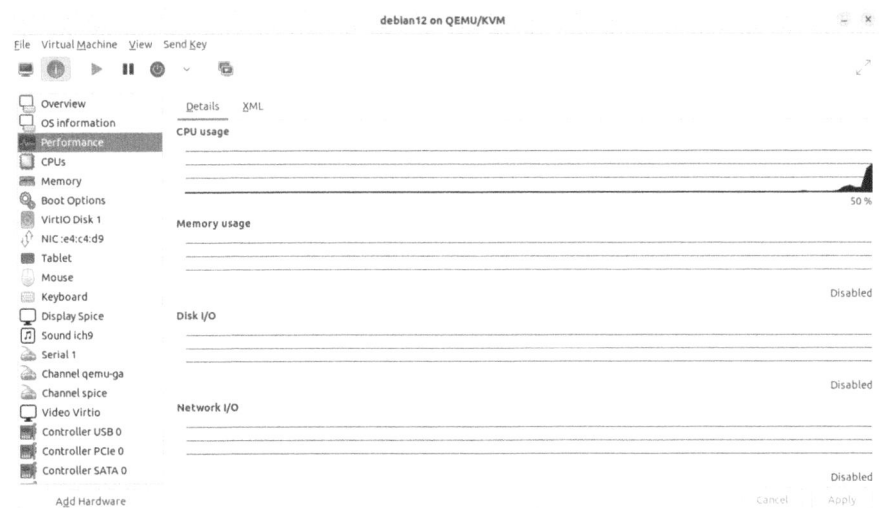

Figure 4-54. Monitoring the CPU

CHAPTER 4 LIBVIRT VIRTUAL MACHINE MANAGEMENT

To monitor memory, disk, and network usage, we need to edit the preferences by clicking "Edit" ➤ "Preferences" on the main window of virt-manager. In the new window, we click on the "Polling" tab and select all the check boxes (Figure 4-55).

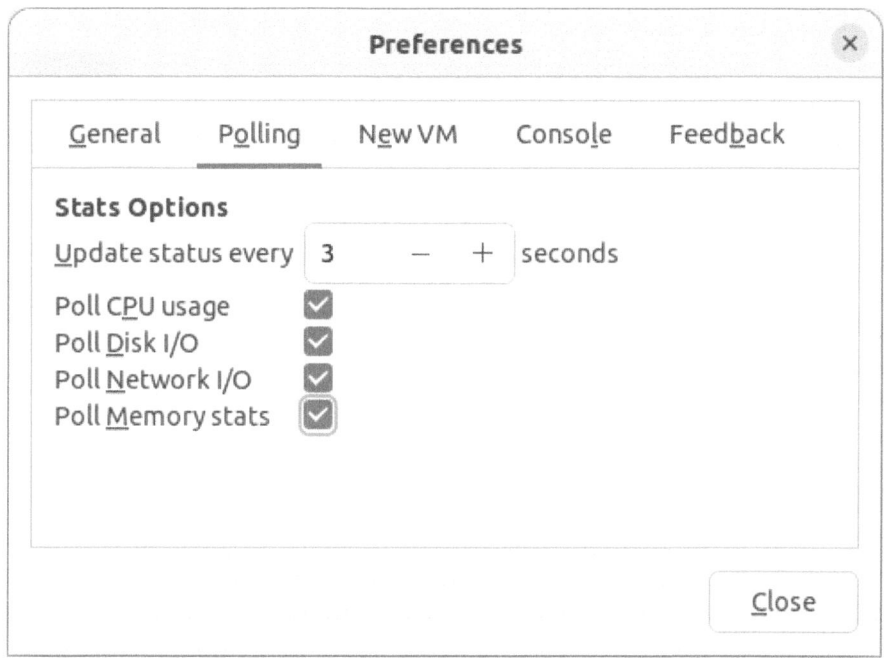

Figure 4-55. *Editing the polling preferences*

After saving the changes, we can see performance data for memory, disk, and network interfaces, not only for the CPU (Figure 4-56).

CHAPTER 4   LIBVIRT VIRTUAL MACHINE MANAGEMENT

Figure 4-56. *Guest performance*

virsh

We have already seen a few examples about how to use the **libvirt** API from **virt-manager** and even a couple of simple examples in which we used our own programs. Even though **virt-manager** is a very convenient tool, sometimes it is preferable to use a command-line tool like **virsh**, which can be used in scripts more easily.

We can execute **virsh** with the proper parameters in the command line or we can use it interactively through the **virsh** shell.

```
antonio@antonio-Laptop:~$ virsh
Welcome to virsh, the virtualization interactive terminal.

Type:  'help' for help with commands
       'quit' to quit

virsh #
```

CHAPTER 4   LIBVIRT VIRTUAL MACHINE MANAGEMENT

Usually virsh will connect automatically to the local hypervisor, but we can specify the URI to connect to explicitly.

```
antonio@antonio-Laptop:~$ virsh connect qemu:///system
```

If we type "help" either from the **virsh** shell or as a subcommand, we'll see a long list of parameters that can be used.

```
virsh # help
Grouped commands:

 Domain Management (help keyword 'domain'):
    attach-device                  attach device from an XML file
    attach-disk                    attach disk device
    attach-interface               attach network interface
    autostart                      autostart a domain
```

.
.
.

We can list the virtual machines currently running with "virsh list".

```
antonio@antonio-Laptop:~$ virsh list
 Id   Name       State
---------------------------
 4    debian12   running
```

If the virtual machine is not running, it won't appear in the previous listing, but we could see it with the "--all" parameter.

```
antonio@antonio-Laptop:~$ virsh list --all
 Id   Name       State
---------------------------
 4    debian12   running
```

CHAPTER 4   LIBVIRT VIRTUAL MACHINE MANAGEMENT

We can edit any virtual machine/domain .

```
antonio@antonio-Laptop:~$ virsh edit debian12
```

Now the XML file associated with the virtual machine will be opened in the default editor.

```
  GNU nano 6.2                                 /tmp/virsh86SMQ2.xml
<domain type='kvm'>
  <name>debian12</name>
  <uuid>05959a22-b9e4-4d99-a3ae-16f946880ff1</uuid>
  <metadata>
    <libosinfo:libosinfo xmlns:libosinfo="http://libosinfo.org/
    xmlns/libvirt/domain/1.0">
      <libosinfo:os id="http://debian.org/debian/12"/>
    </libosinfo:libosinfo>
  </metadata>
  <memory unit='KiB'>2097152</memory>
.
.
.
```

Apart from editing the virtual machine/domain, we can obtain a summary of the configuration.

```
antonio@antonio-Laptop:~$ virsh dominfo debian12
Id:             4
Name:           debian12
UUID:           05959a22-b9e4-4d99-a3ae-16f946880ff1
OS Type:        hvm
State:          running
CPU(s):         2
CPU time:       231,2s
Max memory:     2097152 KiB
```

```
Used memory:     2097152 KiB
Persistent:      yes
Autostart:       disable
Managed save:    no
Security model: apparmor
Security DOI:    0
Security label: libvirt-05959a22-b9e4-4d99-a3ae-16f946880ff1 (enforcing)
```

It is also possible to manage the snapshots of a virtual machine/domain using virsh.

```
antonio@antonio-Laptop:~$ virsh snapshot-list --domain debian12
 Name   Creation Time   State
--------------------------------
```

We can also use virsh to list the defined networks, create, or delete them.

```
antonio@antonio-Laptop:~$ virsh net-list
 Name              State    Autostart   Persistent
----------------------------------------------------------
 default           active   yes         yes
 ISOLATED_network  active   yes         yes
 ROUTED_network    active   yes         yes
```

And we can see the details of a certain network.

```
antonio@antonio-Laptop:~$ virsh net-info default
Name:        default
UUID:        e4e9c8b1-7913-4744-b8b2-205ce8ce6068
Active:      yes
Persistent:  yes
Autostart:   yes
Bridge:      virbr0
```

CHAPTER 4　LIBVIRT VIRTUAL MACHINE MANAGEMENT

We can also list the storage pool and volumes and also create them or destroy them.

```
antonio@antonio-Laptop:~$ virsh pool-list
 Name        State     Autostart
---------------------------------
 default     active    yes
 QEMU_VMs    active    yes

antonio@antonio-Laptop:~$ virsh vol-list --pool QEMU_VMs
 Name                          Path
-----------------------------------------------------------------
 alpine-virt-3.20.0-x86_64.iso  /home/antonio/
                                QEMU_VMs/alpine-
                                virt-3.20.0-x86_64.iso
 alpine_disk.qcow               /home/antonio/QEMU_VMs/
                                alpine_disk.qcow
 bin                            /home/antonio/QEMU_VMs/bin
 BINARY_SLA.txt                 /home/antonio/QEMU_Vms/
                                BINARY_SLA.txt
 .
 .
 .
```

Of course we can start, pause, and stop the virtual machines with **virsh** as well.

```
antonio@antonio-Laptop:~$ virsh shutdown debian12
Domain 'debian12' is being shutdown
antonio@antonio-Laptop:~$ virsh list --all
 Id   Name       State
----------------------------
 -    debian12   shut off
```

libvirt Configuration Files

We can see many configuration files in the */etc/libvirt* folder. These files modified the behavior of both the libvirt clients as well as the **libvirtd** service itself.

libvirt.conf

One of these files is libvirt.conf. This file is very concise as we can see here.

```
antonio@antonio-Laptop:~$ cat /etc/libvirt/libvirt.conf
#
# This can be used to setup URI aliases for frequently
# used connection URIs. Aliases may contain only the
# characters   a-Z, 0-9, _, -.
#
# Following the '=' may be any valid libvirt connection
# URI, including arbitrary parameters

#uri_aliases = [
#   "hail=qemu+ssh://root@hail.cloud.example.com/system",
#   "sleet=qemu+ssh://root@sleet.cloud.example.com/system",
#]

#
# These can be used in cases when no URI is supplied by the
  application
# (@uri_default also prevents probing of the hypervisor driver).
#
#uri_default = "qemu:///system"
```

CHAPTER 4 LIBVIRT VIRTUAL MACHINE MANAGEMENT

We can see a couple of variables that can be defined here. One of them is **uri_aliases**, an array of aliases to connect to different systems. The full URI to connect to a system can be a bit complicated to remember, for instance, when we used virt-manager to connect to a remote Xen host, the URI was something like this: *xen+ssh://root@192.168.1.70/*. We could define an easier-to-remember alias so that every time we need to connect to it, we just type the alias instead of the full URI.

The other variable defined in this file is **uri_default**. When we connected to libvirt from Python, we didn't specify any URI, so we connected to the default one. If this var is not manually set in the *libvirt.conf* file, the default value will be the local QEMU/KVM hypervisor.

libvirtd.conf

Contrary to what we saw on the *libvirt.conf* file, the *libvirtd.conf* file is very long and has many options that can be customized to alter how the **libvirtd** service works.

Due to its size, we want to show it here, but we can mention a few parameters that can be edited to better suit our needs. We can, for instance, issue certificates and define the location of these certificates in the *libvirtd.conf* file. This way we can also configure the use of TLS in libvirtd.

The relevant section of the file to configure the certificates is this one:

```
# TLS x509 certificate configuration
#

# Use of TLS requires that x509 certificates be issued.
  The default locations
# for the certificate files is as follows:
#
```

CHAPTER 4   LIBVIRT VIRTUAL MACHINE MANAGEMENT

```
#    /etc/pki/CA/cacert.pem - The CA master certificate
#    /etc/pki/libvirt/servercert.pem - The server certificate
     signed by cacert.pem
#    /etc/pki/libvirt/private/serverkey.pem - The server
     private key
#
# It is possible to override the default locations by altering
  the 'key_file',
# 'cert_file', and 'ca_file' values and uncommenting
  them below.
#
# NB, overriding the default of one location requires
  uncommenting and
# possibly additionally overriding the other settings.
#

# Override the default server key file path
#
#key_file = "/etc/pki/libvirt/private/serverkey.pem"

# Override the default server certificate file path
#
#cert_file = "/etc/pki/libvirt/servercert.pem"

# Override the default CA certificate path
#
#ca_file = "/etc/pki/CA/cacert.pem"

# Specify a certificate revocation list.
#
# Defaults to not using a CRL, uncomment to enable it
#crl_file = "/etc/pki/CA/crl.pem"
```

CHAPTER 4 LIBVIRT VIRTUAL MACHINE MANAGEMENT

We can also configure auditing in the following section.

```
################################################################
#
# Auditing
#
# This setting allows usage of the auditing subsystem to be
  altered:
#
#   audit_level == 0  -> disable all auditing
#   audit_level == 1  -> enable auditing, only if enabled on
    host (default)
#   audit_level == 2  -> enable auditing, and exit if
    disabled on host
#
#audit_level = 2
#
# If set to 1, then audit messages will also be sent
# via libvirt logging infrastructure. Defaults to 0
#
#audit_logging = 1
```

There are many more options that can be edited, but we won't cover them here. The file is well documented so you can have a look at it if you're particularly interested in customizing a certain feature.

qemu.conf

Another interesting file is *qemu.conf*. We have seen that **libvirt** can connect to different systems, QEMU/KVM hypervisors, Xen hypervisors, etc. To do it, it needs the corresponding driver. In the particular case of QEMU/KVM,

CHAPTER 4 LIBVIRT VIRTUAL MACHINE MANAGEMENT

this driver can be customized by editing this file. We're not going to describe this file, but we can customize things such as the use of vnc or SPICE to connect to the server.

We also have other similar files to customize the use of the different drivers used by libvirt to connect to the different systems.

virtlogd.conf

The **virtlogd** service manages the logs of the virtual machine consoles. The */etc/libvirt/virtlogd.conf* file is used to customize logging-related parameters such as the log level, log output, and so on. Usually we won't need to edit it.

virtlockd.conf

Another **libvirt** service is **virtlockd**. This service manages locks when virtual machines need to access their resources, such as their disks. The configuration file for this service is */etc/libvirt/virtlockd.conf* and is very similar to the previous file we've seen. The file is used mainly to customize the logging for this service. Most of the time we don't need to edit it.

dnsmasq

libvirt integrates the use of other network services like **dnsmasq**. We already saw it briefly when describing how networking works in libvirtd. **dnsmasq** is a software that works as a DNS and DHCP server. It is very light and very easy to configure.

CHAPTER 4   LIBVIRT VIRTUAL MACHINE MANAGEMENT

If we list the processes in a computer running **libvirt**, we'll see something similar to this:

```
antonio@antonio-Laptop:~$ ps -ef | grep dnsmasq
libvirt+    1878       1  0 jul01 ?        00:00:00 /usr/sbin/dnsmasq --conf-file=/var/lib/libvirt/dnsmasq/default.conf --leasefile-ro --dhcp-script=/usr/lib/libvirt/libvirt_leaseshelper
root        1879    1878  0 jul01 ?        00:00:00 /usr/sbin/dnsmasq --conf-file=/var/lib/libvirt/dnsmasq/default.conf --leasefile-ro –dhcp-script=/usr/lib/libvirt/libvirt_leaseshelper
```

And if we open the configuration file */var/lib/libvirt/dnsmasq/default.conf*, we'll see how easy it is to configure this server.

```
antonio@antonio-HP-Laptop-15s-fq1xxx:~$ sudo cat /var/lib/libvirt/dnsmasq/default.conf
##WARNING: THIS IS AN AUTO-GENERATED FILE. CHANGES TO IT ARE
  LIKELY TO BE
##OVERWRITTEN AND LOST.  Changes to this configuration should
  be made using:
##     virsh net-edit default
## or other application using the libvirt API.
##
## dnsmasq conf file created by libvirt
strict-order
user=libvirt-dnsmasq
pid-file=/run/libvirt/network/default.pid
except-interface=lo
bind-dynamic
```

CHAPTER 4 LIBVIRT VIRTUAL MACHINE MANAGEMENT

```
interface=virbr0
dhcp-range=192.168.122.2,192.168.122.254,255.255.255.0
dhcp-no-override
dhcp-authoritative
dhcp-lease-max=253
dhcp-hostsfile=/var/lib/libvirt/dnsmasq/default.hostsfile
addn-hosts=/var/lib/libvirt/dnsmasq/default.addnhosts
```

As the file itself implies, we should not edit this file directly, but using **virsh** or **virt-manager** instead. But it can give us a good idea of how this service works.

radvd

In all the examples so far, we have used IPv4. These IPv4 settings were provided by dnsmasq. We could use IPv6 settings for the virtual machines as well. IPv6 has more autoconfiguration features than IPv4 because the IPv6 clients can obtain their IPv6 address automatically from an IPv6-capable router. This router should be able to manage ICMP Router solicitation messages and answer with ICMP Router advertisement messages. In Linux systems, the software needed to do that is the **radvd** package.

This **radvd** service is not very often used, as sometimes we don't need IPv6. Besides, **dnsmasq** can also serve IPv6 addresses through DHCP instead of relying on the autoconfiguration features of the protocol. In any case, we must be aware that it is also possible to see it in use in the network.

Summary

In this chapter, we have seen a much more friendly way to manage our virtual machines. We studied **libvirt** architecture and how it provides a common API to manage different hypervisors. This API can be directly accessed with our own programs, but it is definitely more convenient using tools like **virt-manager** or **virsh**.

We've used it to interact with **QEMU/KVM** as well as **Xen** hypervisors. We've created and manage snapshots. And we've seen the performance information that **libvirt** provides.

We've seen that we have many choices when deciding what type of storage to use, from local folders to network file systems. We've also created and used different virtual networks, and we've seen how external services like **dnsmasq** and **radvd** interact with **libvirt**.

We could also easily migrate a virtual machine from one hypervisor to another using **virt-manager**, though we could have used **virsh** as well.

CHAPTER 5

Virtual Machine Disk Image Management

In this chapter, we'll cover the following concepts:

- Understand features of various virtual disk image formats, such as raw images, qcow2, and VMDK

- Manage virtual machine disk images using qemu-img

- Mount partitions and access files contained in virtual machine disk images using libguestfish

- Copy physical disk content to a virtual machine disk image

- Migrate disk content between various virtual machine disk image formats

- Awareness of Open Virtualization Format (OVF)

- Awareness of VirtualBox

We will also be introduced to the following terms and utilities: **qemu-img, guestfish, guestmount, guestunmount, virt-cat, virt-copy-in, virt-copy-out, virt-diff, virt-inspector, virt-filesystems, virt-rescue, virt-df, virt-resize, virt-sparsify, virt-p2v, virt-p2v-make-disk, virt-v2v,** and **virt-sysprep**.

CHAPTER 5   VIRTUAL MACHINE DISK IMAGE MANAGEMENT

Virtual Disk Image Formats

A disk image file is a file that contains the structure as well as the content of a storage device: a hard disk, a DVD drive, floppy disk, etc. We're talking about a single disk image, but to be more precise, we should note that a disk image can be stored in one or more physical files.

There are several disk image formats, of which we'll enumerate here briefly a few:

- Raw disk images: These are complete dumps bit to bit of the original disk/device. They don't hold any additional data beyond the disk content.

- qcow images: It is a format used by QEMU. It uses "copy on write" to optimize storage.

- VMDK: Format developed originally by VMware and released as an open format later.

Raw Images

Raw images are those that keep an exact copy bit by bit of a device. These images include not only the actual data but also any control field that might be present in the original device.

Raw images are used for instance in computer forensics to get an exact copy of the original device. Many computer forensic tools can create raw disk images from a physical device. We can use the well-known **dd** command included in almost all Linux distributions to obtain a raw disk image. It lacks some of the most advanced features we can find in some computer forensic tools, but I will fit perfectly our needs for didactic purposes.

CHAPTER 5　VIRTUAL MACHINE DISK IMAGE MANAGEMENT

As an example, we'll create a raw disk image of a partition from a USB disk.

```
antonio@antonio-Laptop:~/VMDISKS$ sudo dd if=/dev/sda1 of=USBpart.img
3926495+0 records in
3926495+0 records out
2010365440 bytes (2,0 GB, 1,9 GiB) copied, 32,8104 s, 61,3 MB/s
```

Now we can use the **qemu-img** command, which we saw briefly when we studied QEMU, to get some information about the disk file we just created.

```
antonio@antonio-Laptop:~/VMDISKS$ qemu-img info USBpart.img
image: USBpart.img
file format: raw
virtual size: 1.87 GiB (2010365440 bytes)
disk size: 1.87 GiB
```

As we can see, **qemu-img** clearly identifies the disk file format as raw.

qcow and qcow2

QEMU copy on write (qcow) is a disk image format used by QEMU, which we already studied in Chapter 2. It uses a "copy on write" approach, which means that data is only copied in the disk when it is actually needed. This is a much more efficient approach than that of raw images, and thus, the files are much smaller in size.

There are currently several versions of this format available: 1, 2, and 3. Obviously the first version is qcow1, but it is rarely used today. The newer qcow2 format was almost completely different from the first version, and it is widely used today. The newest version, qcow3, is basically an extension of qcow2.

VMDK

Virtual Machine Disk (VMDK) is a disk image format initially developed by VMware but released later as an open format. Nowadays it is supported not only by VMware products but also by third-party products like QEMU or VirtualBox. It can use advanced features like copy on write, thin or thick provisioning, and so on.

Managing Disk Images with qemu-img

One particularly useful utility to work with disk images is **qemu-img**. We already used it in Chapter 2, when creating a QEMU virtual machine. But this tool offers many more possibilities. We already have this tool installed in our system, but if we need to install it in a different system, we'll have to install the qemu-utils package.

antonio@antonio-Laptop:~/VMDISKS$ sudo apt install qemu-utils

Getting Information with qemu-img

We have seen already some examples of use. We can use qemu-img to get some basic information about the disk image file we created when we studied QEMU.

antonio@antonio-Laptop:~/QEMU_VMs$ qemu-img info debian.qcow2
image: debian.qcow2
file format: qcow2
virtual size: 10 GiB (10737418240 bytes)
disk size: 7.98 GiB
cluster_size: 65536
Format specific information:
    compat: 1.1

CHAPTER 5   VIRTUAL MACHINE DISK IMAGE MANAGEMENT

```
    compression type: zlib
    lazy refcounts: false
    refcount bits: 16
    corrupt: false
    extended l2: false
```

We can see a lot of interesting information, about virtual and real size, compression type, and so on. In this case, we didn't have any snapshots, but if we have snapshots associated with the disk, we'll see them as well, as in the following example:

```
antonio@antonio-Aspire-A315-23:~/QEMU_VMs$ qemu-img info
debian.qcow2
image: debian.qcow2
file format: qcow2
virtual size: 10G (10737418240 bytes)
disk size: 5.4G
cluster_size: 65536
Snapshot list:
ID    TAG              VM SIZE              DATE         VM CLOCK
1     210115debian     912M 2021-01-15 23:29:32    00:13:25.513
Format specific information:
    compat: 1.1
    lazy refcounts: false
    refcount bits: 16
    corrupt: false
```

We can use **qemu-img** to check other file disk formats than qcow2, as we can see in the next example:

```
antonio@antonio-Laptop:~$ qemu-img info VirtualBox\ VMs/Rocky/
Rocky.vdi
image: VirtualBox VMs/Rocky/Rocky.vdi
```

231

CHAPTER 5 VIRTUAL MACHINE DISK IMAGE MANAGEMENT

```
file format: vdi
virtual size: 40 GiB (42949672960 bytes)
disk size: 14.6 GiB
cluster_size: 1048576
```

Creating Disk Image Files with qemu-img

We can also use **img-create** to create disk images as we saw in Chapter 2. Let's create three different disk images: a raw disk image, a qcow2 image, and a VMDK disk image.

```
antonio@antonio-Laptop:~/VMDISKS$ qemu-img create -f raw rawdisk.img 1G
Formatting 'rawdisk.img', fmt=raw size=1073741824

antonio@antonio-Laptop:~/VMDISKS$ qemu-img create -f qcow2 qcow2disk.qcow2 1G
Formatting 'qcow2disk.qcow2', fmt=qcow2 cluster_size=65536 extended_l2=off compression_type=zlib size=1073741824 lazy_refcounts=off refcount_bits=16

antonio@antonio-Laptop:~/VMDISKS$ qemu-img create -f vmdk vmdkdisk.vmdk 1G
Formatting 'vmdkdisk.vmdk', fmt=vmdk size=1073741824 compat6=off hwversion=undefined
```

If we list these files, we'll see the first differences.

```
antonio@antonio-Laptop:~/VMDISKS$ ls -lh
total 212K
-rw-r--r-- 1 antonio antonio 193K jul  8 15:05 qcow2disk.qcow2
-rw-r--r-- 1 antonio antonio 1,0G jul  8 15:03 rawdisk.img
-rw-r--r-- 1 antonio antonio 192K jul  8 15:05 vmdkdisk.vmdk
```

CHAPTER 5   VIRTUAL MACHINE DISK IMAGE MANAGEMENT

As expected, the raw disk is taking up all the 1 GB space, but the qcow2 and the VMDK disks use a much more efficient approach and their real size is much smaller than the logical size. We can also get some more information with the **file** command.

```
antonio@antonio-Laptop:~/VMDISKS$ file *
qcow2disk.qcow2: QEMU QCOW2 Image (v3), 1073741824 bytes
rawdisk.img:     data
vmdkdisk.vmdk:   VMware4 disk image
```

Creating Overlays with qemu-img

Overlay images are backed by another image.

To see it more clearly, we're going to create an overlay using the original disk of the Debian 12 virtual machine we created previously.

```
antonio@antonio-Laptop:~/QEMU_VMs$ qemu-img create -f qcow2 -b
debian.qcow2 -F qcow2 debianoverlay
Formatting 'debianoverlay', fmt=qcow2 cluster_size=65536
extended_l2=off compression_type=zlib size=10737418240
backing_file=debian.qcow2 backing_fmt=qcow2 lazy_refcounts=off
refcount_bits=16
```

If we use **qemu-img** to get information about the disk file we just created, we can clearly see its backing file.

```
antonio@antonio-HP-Laptop-15s-fq1xxx:~/QEMU_VMs$ qemu-img info
debianoverlay
image: debianoverlay
file format: qcow2
virtual size: 10 GiB (10737418240 bytes)
disk size: 196 KiB
cluster_size: 65536
backing file: debian.qcow2
```

233

```
backing file format: qcow2
Format specific information:
    compat: 1.1
    compression type: zlib
    lazy refcounts: false
    refcount bits: 16
    corrupt: false
    extended l2: false
```

We can have different overlays backed by the same image file: one with all the updates, another one without updates, etc. One with development tools, another with production tools.

If we check the size of the overlay image previously created, we'll see it is very small in size.

```
antonio@antonio-Laptop:~/QEMU_VMs$ ls -lh debianoverlay
-rw-r--r-- 1 antonio antonio 193K jul  9 11:41 debianoverlay
```

As long as we keep working with the virtual machine associated to the overlay image, the file size will increase. Let's start a QEMU virtual machine backed by that overlay image.

```
antonio@antonio-Laptop:~/QEMU_VMs$ qemu-system-x86_64 -m 2048
-accel kvm debianoverlay
```

Once the VM is up and running, we can perform some basic operations like downloading files. In this case, we'll download the Linux kernel source code, located at https://kernel.org (Figure 5-1).

CHAPTER 5   VIRTUAL MACHINE DISK IMAGE MANAGEMENT

Figure 5-1. *Downloading some files*

When we're done working with the virtual machine, we can check the size of the overlay image again. As we can see, it is significantly bigger.

antonio@antonio-Laptop:~/QEMU_VMs$ ls -lh debianoverlay
-rw-r--r-- 1 antonio antonio 268M jul 9 19:48 debianoverlay

Converting Between Different Disk Formats

Another very interesting feature of **qemu-img** is the ability to convert a disk file to a different format.

CHAPTER 5   VIRTUAL MACHINE DISK IMAGE MANAGEMENT

As an example, we'll convert our qcow2 image file already created to a VMDK format disk file.

```
antonio@antonio-Laptop:~/QEMU_VMs$ qemu-img convert -f qcow2 debian.qcow2 -O vmdk debian.vmdk
```

The procedure is really fast. We can use qemu-img again to check the new disk image file.

```
antonio@antonio-Laptop:~/QEMU_VMs$ qemu-img info debian.vmdk
image: debian.vmdk
file format: vmdk
virtual size: 10 GiB (10737418240 bytes)
disk size: 6.12 GiB
cluster_size: 65536
Format specific information:
    cid: 268441838
    parent cid: 4294967295
    create type: monolithicSparse
    extents:
        [0]:
            virtual size: 10737418240
            filename: debian.vmdk
            cluster size: 65536
            format:
```

Basic Usage of VirtualBox to Check the Image Disk File

The file seems to be OK. To actually test it, we can use **VirtualBox**. We haven't studied VirtualBox yet. As it is included in the official exam objectives, we'll see it very briefly here.

CHAPTER 5   VIRTUAL MACHINE DISK IMAGE MANAGEMENT

VirtualBox is a type II hypervisor; that is, it is an application that runs on the computer, such as any other application like LibreOffice Writer, Firefox, etc. It is very easy to install; we won't see how to install because it is not required for the exam, but it is very easy and you won't have any trouble.

Once it is installed, we can launch it and we'll see something similar to Figure 5-2, with the only difference that right after a fresh install, there will be no virtual machines created on **VirtualBox**.

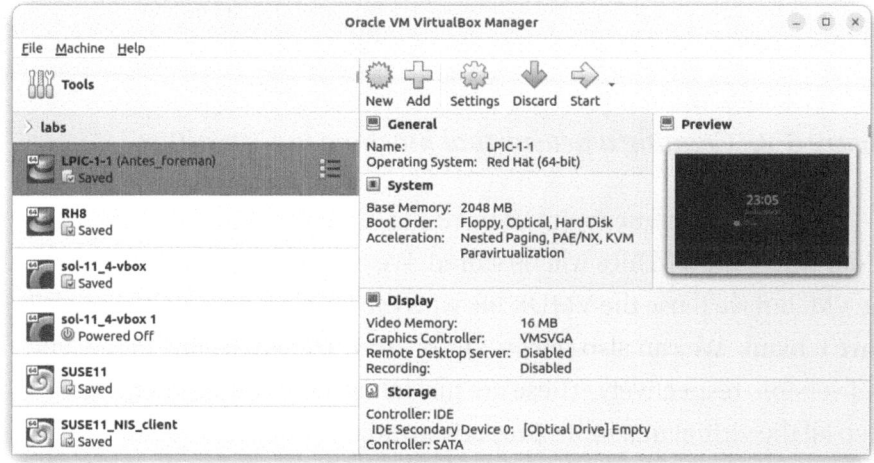

Figure 5-2. *VirtualBox*

We'll use the VMDK disk file previously converted from the *debian.qcow2* file to create our new virtual machine in VirtualBox. We click on the "New" icon to create a new virtual machine (Figure 5-3).

CHAPTER 5   VIRTUAL MACHINE DISK IMAGE MANAGEMENT

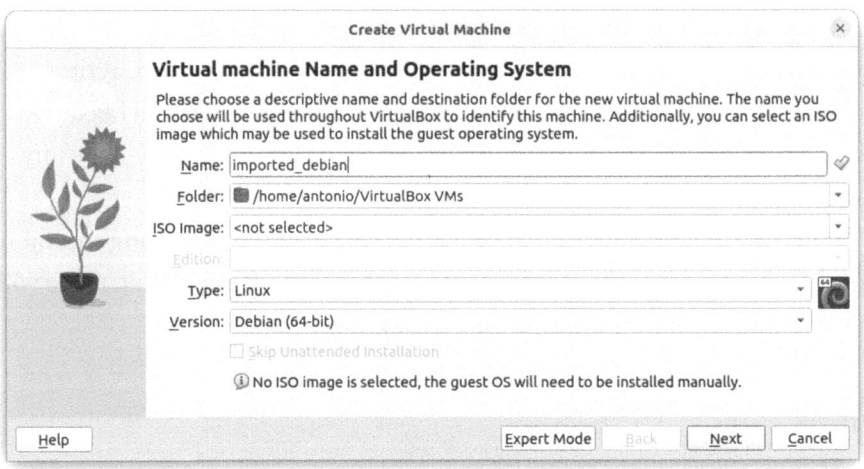

Figure 5-3. Creating a new virtual machine in VirtualBox

We'll assign a name to the VM. We can leave the default value for the folder where the VM files will be stored. We can choose an ISO file to install the VM, but we'll use the VMDK file with the OS already installed so we'll leave it blank. We can also select "Linux" and "Debian 64 bit" in the type and version, respectively. These are just labels, but they will help us to keep all the virtual machines properly arranged. We click "Next".

In the next screen (Figure 5-4), we can edit the hardware specifications. One CPU and 2 GB of RAM should be more than enough for our testing purposes. We click "Next" again.

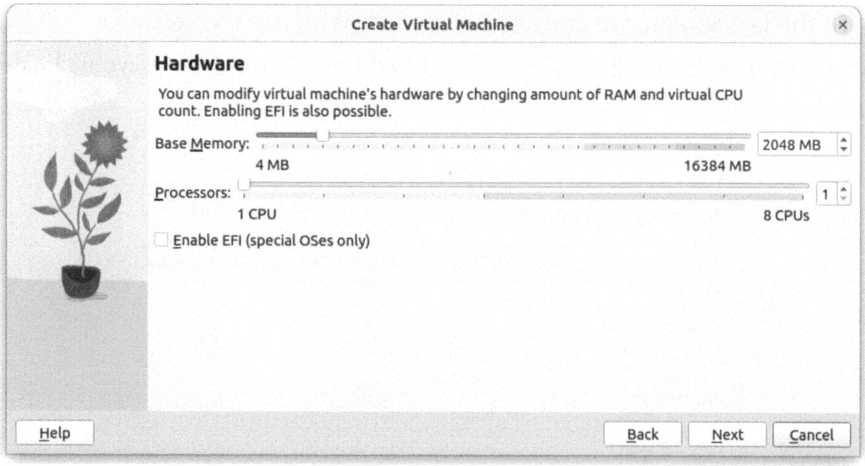

CHAPTER 5 VIRTUAL MACHINE DISK IMAGE MANAGEMENT

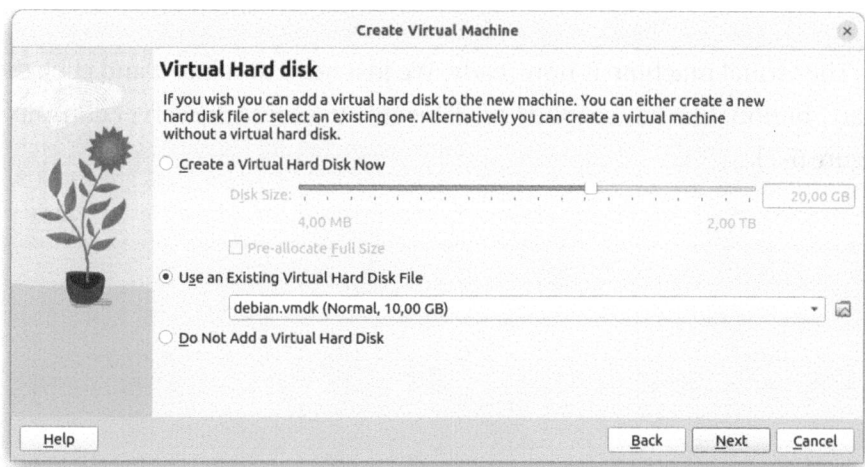

Figure 5-4. Hardware specifications

In the next screen, we could create a new disk, but we'll choose to use an existing disk instead (Figure 5-5). And we click "Next".

Figure 5-5. Using an existing virtual disk

239

CHAPTER 5 VIRTUAL MACHINE DISK IMAGE MANAGEMENT

In the last screen, we can see a summary with the VM settings previously assigned (Figure 5-6). If we need to edit something, we'll click "Back" to change it; otherwise, we click "Finish".

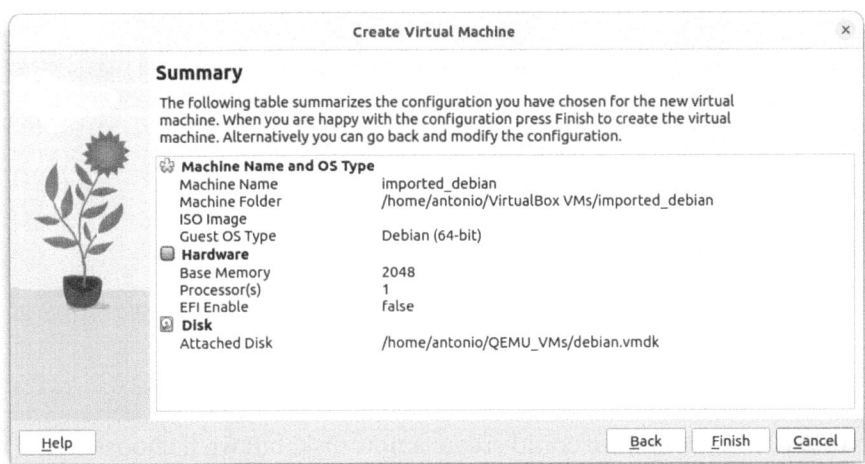

Figure 5-6. *Virtual machine settings summary*

The virtual machine is now ready. We just need to select it and click the "Start" button. In a few seconds, we'll be able to access the server console (Figure 5-7).

CHAPTER 5   VIRTUAL MACHINE DISK IMAGE MANAGEMENT

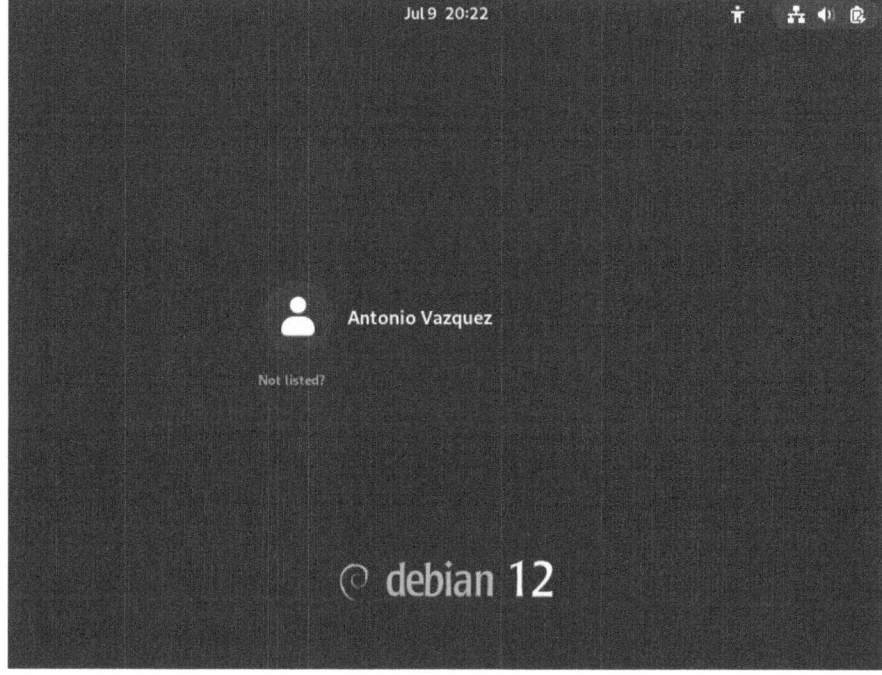

Figure 5-7. *Virtual machine console*

Mounting Partitions and Accessing Files Contained in Virtual Disks

There is a C library named *libguestfs*, which can be used to access and modify files in virtual disk images. The needed packages to install this library and its utilities are usually included in the repositories of the main Linux distributions. In our case, we'll install these tools in Ubuntu.

antonio@antonio-Laptop:~/QEMU_VMs$ sudo apt install libguestfs-tools

CHAPTER 5 VIRTUAL MACHINE DISK IMAGE MANAGEMENT

Once the installation is complete, we can use the tools included. One of these tools is **guestfish**. It can be executed in an interactive way.

```
antonio@antonio-Laptop:~/QEMU_VMs$ guestfish

Welcome to guestfish, the guest filesystem shell for
editing virtual machine filesystems and disk images.

Type: 'help' for help on commands
      'man' to read the manual
      'quit' to quit the shell

><fs>
```

By typing "help" on the command line, we get a brief description of the main commands.

```
><fs> help
Add disk images to examine using the '-a' or '-d' options, or
the 'add'
command.
Or create a new disk image using '-N', or the 'alloc' or
'sparse' commands.
Once you have done this, use the 'run' command.

For more information about a command, use 'help cmd'.

To read the manual, type 'man'.

><fs>
```

As we can see, we need to add a disk image with the "**add**" subcommand and execute "**run**".

```
><fs> add debian.qcow2
><fs> run
```

CHAPTER 5 VIRTUAL MACHINE DISK IMAGE MANAGEMENT

```
libguestfs: warning: current user is not a member of the KVM
group (group ID 129). This user cannot access /dev/kvm, so
libguestfs may run very slowly. It is recommended that you
'chmod 0666 /dev/kvm' or add the current user to the KVM group
(you might need to log out and log in again).
libguestfs: error: /usr/bin/supermin exited with error
status 1.
To see full error messages you may need to enable debugging.
Do:
  export LIBGUESTFS_DEBUG=1 LIBGUESTFS_TRACE=1
and run the command again. For further information, read:
  http://libguestfs.org/guestfs-faq.1.html#debugging-libguestfs
You can also run 'libguestfs-test-tool' and post the
*complete* output
into a bug report or message to the libguestfs mailing list.
><fs>
><fs> exit
```

In this case, we get an error because we are executing **guestfish** as a standard user and this user does not have permissions to access */dev/kvm*. To circumvent this, we can add our current user to the kvm group or execute **guestfish** as root.

```
antonio@antonio-Laptop:~/QEMU_VMs$ sudo guestfish
[sudo] password for antonio:

Welcome to guestfish, the guest filesystem shell for
editing virtual machine filesystems and disk images.

Type: 'help' for help on commands
      'man' to read the manual
      'quit' to quit the shell
```

243

CHAPTER 5   VIRTUAL MACHINE DISK IMAGE MANAGEMENT

```
><fs>
><fs> add debian.qcow2
><fs> run
 100%
⟦▓▓▓▓▓▓▓▓▓▓▓▓▓▓▓▓▓▓▓▓▓▓▓▓▓▓▓▓▓▓▓▓▓▓▓▓▓▓▓▓▓▓▓▓▓▓▓▓▓▓▓▓⟧
▓▓▓▓▓▓▓▓▓▓▓▓▓▓▓▓▓▓▓▓▓▓▓▓▓▓▓▓▓▓▓▓▓▓▓▓▓▓▓▓▓▓▓▓▓▓⟧ 00:00
><fs>
```

Troubleshooting libguestfs

In this case, we could execute "run" without any issue, but it is possible that we get an error; let's see an easy example.

```
><fs> add debian.qcow2
><fs> run
libguestfs: error: appliance closed the connection
unexpectedly.
This usually means the libguestfs appliance crashed.
Do:
  export LIBGUESTFS_DEBUG=1 LIBGUESTFS_TRACE=1
and run the command again.  For further information, read:
  http://libguestfs.org/guestfs-faq.1.html#debugging-libguestfs
 •
 •
 •
```

In this example, we get a new error. Luckily, the tool itself provides us with some valuable information to troubleshoot this incident. So we'll enable debugging by exporting the two environment variables mentioned before.

CHAPTER 5   VIRTUAL MACHINE DISK IMAGE MANAGEMENT

```
antonio@antonio-Aspire-A315-23:~/QEMU_VMs$ sudo su root
root@antonio-Aspire-A315-23:/home/antonio/QEMU_VMs# export
LIBGUESTFS_DEBUG=1 LIBGUESTFS_TRACE=1
root@antonio-Aspire-A315-23:/home/antonio/QEMU_VMs# guestfish
libguestfs: trace: set_verbose true
libguestfs: trace: set_verbose = 0
.
.
.
Welcome to guestfish, the guest filesystem shell for
editing virtual machine filesystems and disk images.

Type: 'help' for help on commands
      'man' to read the manual
      'quit' to quit the shell

><fs> add debian.qcow2
libguestfs: trace: add_drive "debian.qcow2"
libguestfs: trace: add_drive = 0
><fs> run
libguestfs: trace: launch
libguestfs: trace: get_tmpdir
libguestfs: trace: get_tmpdir = "/tmp"
.
.
.
ioctl(KVM_CREATE_VM) failed: 16 Device or resource busy
qemu-system-x86_64: failed to initialize KVM: Device or
resource busy
qemu-system-x86_64: Back to tcg accelerator
qemu-system-x86_64: CPU model 'host' requires KVM
libguestfs: error: appliance closed the connection
```

CHAPTER 5   VIRTUAL MACHINE DISK IMAGE MANAGEMENT

```
unexpectedly, see earlier error messages
.
.
.
```

As expected, we get a lot of information, and at one point, we can see the message "failed to initialize KVM: Device or resource busy". The reason we were getting this message is because we were executing an instance of VirtualBox, which was using KVM. After shutting down this VirtualBox instance, we can execute **guestfish** again.

```
antonio@antonio-Aspire-A315-23:~/QEMU_VMs$ sudo guestfish
[sudo] password for antonio:

Welcome to guestfish, the guest filesystem shell for
editing virtual machine filesystems and disk images.

Type: 'help' for help on commands
      'man' to read the manual
      'quit' to quit the shell

><fs> add debian.qcow2
><fs> run
 100% [▓▓▓▓▓▓▓▓▓▓▓▓▓▓▓▓▓▓▓▓▓▓▓▓▓▓▓▓▓▓▓▓▓▓▓▓▓▓▓▓▓▓▓▓] 00:00
><fs>
```

After successfully executing "run", we can work on the disk image, mounting it and accessing the contents of the files. If at any point we're not sure about what command to use, we can type "help".

```
><fs> help
Find out what filesystems are available using 'list-
filesystems' and then
```

CHAPTER 5 VIRTUAL MACHINE DISK IMAGE MANAGEMENT

```
mount them to examine or modify the contents using
'mount-ro' or
'mount'.

For more information about a command, use 'help cmd'.

To read the manual, type 'man'.

><fs>
```

As suggested, we'll list the filesystems in the disk file.

```
><fs> list-filesystems
/dev/sda1: ext2
/dev/debian-vg/root: ext4
/dev/debian-vg/swap_1: swap
><fs>
```

We successfully managed to get a list of the filesystems contained in the virtual disk file. With this information, we can mount one of these filesystems in **guestfish** and see its contents.

```
><fs> mount-ro /dev/debian-vg/root /
><fs> ls /
.cache
bin
boot
dev
etc
home
initrd.img
initrd.img.old
lib
lib64
lost+found
```

CHAPTER 5 VIRTUAL MACHINE DISK IMAGE MANAGEMENT

```
media
mnt
opt
proc
root
run
sbin
srv
sys
tmp
usr
var
vmlinuz
vmlinuz.old
><fs>
```

We can also read (and modify) any file. When we finish our work, we type "exit".

```
><fs> cat /etc/hostname
debian

><fs> exit
```

guestmount/guestunmount

Apart from accessing files from inside the **guestfish** shell, we can also mount the filesystems contained in the virtual disk file directly in the host. To do it, we can use the **guestmount** command. We can use list the main options with the --help option.

```
antonio@antonio-Laptop:~$ guestmount --help
guestmount: FUSE module for libguestfs
```

CHAPTER 5   VIRTUAL MACHINE DISK IMAGE MANAGEMENT

```
guestmount lets you mount a virtual machine filesystem
Copyright (C) 2009-2020 Red Hat Inc.
Usage:
  guestmount [--options] mountpoint
Options:
  -a|--add image        Add image
  --blocksize[=512|4096]
                        Set sector size of the disk for
                        -a option
  -c|--connect uri      Specify libvirt URI for -d option
  --dir-cache-timeout   Set readdir cache timeout
                        (default 5 sec)
  -d|--domain guest     Add disks from libvirt guest
.
.
.
```

Most of the tools included in the **libguestfs** suite have similar options, so we'll describe briefly the main ones.

We can use "-a" to add a disk image and work with that file, or we can use "-d" to work with the disk associated to a libvirt domain. We can also use "-v" (verbose) to get more information about what the tool is actually doing.

In our example, we'll add (-a) the disk image *debian.qcow2* and mount (-i) its filesystem(s) automatically. To make sure we don't make any undesired modifications, we'll mount it in read-only mode (--ro). We could specify the file system to mount, but in this example, we'll let the tool itself to try and guess it.

```
antonio@antonio-Laptop:~/QEMU_VMs$ sudo guestmount -a debian.qcow2 -i --ro /mnt/mydata
```

CHAPTER 5   VIRTUAL MACHINE DISK IMAGE MANAGEMENT

If we list the */mnt/mydata* folder, we'll see that the filesystem was mounted correctly.

```
antonio@antonio-Laptop:~/QEMU_VMs$ sudo ls /mnt/mydata
bin   dev   home            initrd.img.
old   lib64  media   opt   root   sbin   sys   usr   vmlinuz
boot  etc   initrd.img  lib          lost+found   mnt    proc run
srv   tmp   var   vmlinuz.old
```

We can also see the contents of any file.

```
antonio@antonio-HP-Laptop-15s-fq1xxx:~/QEMU_VMs$ sudo cat /mnt/mydata/etc/hosts
127.0.0.1 localhost
127.0.1.1 debian.mydomain debian

# The following lines are desirable for IPv6 capable hosts
::1     localhost ip6-localhost ip6-loopback
ff02::1 ip6-allnodes
ff02::2 ip6-allrouters
```

Once we're done, we can unmount the filesystem with **guestunmount**.

```
antonio@antonio-Laptop:~/QEMU_VMs$ sudo guestunmount /mnt/mydata
```

We've used a disk image file in our example, but as we said before, we can also use the same tool by connecting to a libvirt domain. We'll begin by listing the currently defined domains. For that, we can use **virsh**.

```
antonio@antonio-Laptop:~/QEMU_VMs$ virsh list --all
 Id    Name        State
----------------------------
 -     debian12    shut off
```

250

CHAPTER 5   VIRTUAL MACHINE DISK IMAGE MANAGEMENT

We have a shutdown domain; we'll start it.

```
antonio@antonio-HP-Laptop-15s-fq1xxx:~/QEMU_VMs$ virsh start debian12
Domain 'debian12' started
```

We check that the domain is up and running.

```
antonio@antonio-HP-Laptop-15s-fq1xxx:~/QEMU_VMs$ virsh list
 Id   Name       State
---------------------------
 1    debian12   running
```

Now we connect to the domain and mount the filesystem locally. As it is a running domain, we'll use the "read only" option to avoid data corruption.

```
antonio@antonio-HP-Laptop-15s-fq1xxx:~/QEMU_VMs$ sudo guestmount -d debian12 -i --ro /mnt/mydata/
```

We can easily copy data from the live domain to the local host.

```
antonio@antonio-HP-Laptop-15s-fq1xxx:~/QEMU_VMs$ sudo cp /mnt/mydata/home/antonio/documents/important_doc.txt .

antonio@antonio-HP-Laptop-15s-fq1xxx:~/QEMU_VMs$ ls important_doc.txt
important_doc.txt
```

virt-cat

Another tool included in the **libguestfs-tools** suite is **virt-cat**. We can use it to show the content of a file, as the name implies.

CHAPTER 5   VIRTUAL MACHINE DISK IMAGE MANAGEMENT

The available options are very similar to those of the **guestmount** tool. We'll see a couple of examples using a disk image and a libvirt domain.

```
antonio@antonio-Laptop:~/QEMU_VMs$ sudo virt-cat -a debian.
qcow2 /home/antonio/documents/important_doc.txt
This is a very important document
```

```
antonio@antonio-Laptop:~/QEMU_VMs$ sudo virt-cat -d debian12 /
home/antonio/documents/important_doc.txt
This is a very important document
```

An interesting option that we haven't seen so far is "-x". This parameter traces the **libguestfs** API calls, which can be useful when troubleshooting.

```
antonio@antonio-Laptop:~/QEMU_VMs$ sudo virt-cat -d debian12 -x
/home/antonio/documents/important_doc.txt
libguestfs: trace: add_domain "debian12" "readonly:true"
"allowuuid:true" "readonlydisk:read"
libguestfs: trace: add_libvirt_dom (virDomainPtr)0x63d4aafc5100
"readonly:true" "readonlydisk:read"
libguestfs: trace: clear_backend_setting "internal_libvirt_
norelabel_disks"
libguestfs: trace: clear_backend_setting = 0
libguestfs: trace: add_drive "/home/antonio/QEMU_VMs/debian.
qcow2" "readonly:true" "format:qcow2"
libguestfs: trace: get_tmpdir
libguestfs: trace: get_tmpdir = "/tmp"
libguestfs: trace: disk_create "/tmp/libguestfs4X1c3w/overlay1.
qcow2" "qcow2" -1 "backingfile:/home/antonio/QEMU_VMs/debian.
qcow2" "backingformat:qcow2"
libguestfs: trace: disk_create = 0
libguestfs: trace: add_drive = 0
libguestfs: trace: add_libvirt_dom = 1
```

CHAPTER 5 VIRTUAL MACHINE DISK IMAGE MANAGEMENT

```
libguestfs: trace: add_domain = 1
libguestfs: trace: launch
libguestfs: trace: max_disks
libguestfs: trace: max_disks = 255
libguestfs: trace: get_cachedir
libguestfs: trace: get_cachedir = "/var/tmp"
libguestfs: trace: get_cachedir
libguestfs: trace: get_cachedir = "/var/tmp"
libguestfs: trace: get_backend_setting "force_tcg"
libguestfs: trace: get_backend_setting = NULL (error)
libguestfs: trace: get_backend_setting "force_kvm"
libguestfs: trace: get_backend_setting = NULL (error)
libguestfs: trace: get_sockdir
libguestfs: trace: get_sockdir = "/tmp"
libguestfs: trace: get_backend_setting "gdb"
libguestfs: trace: get_backend_setting = NULL (error)
libguestfs: trace: launch = 0
libguestfs: trace: list_partitions
libguestfs: trace: list_partitions = ["/dev/sda1", "/dev/sda2", "/dev/sda5"]
libguestfs: trace: vfs_type "/dev/sda1"
libguestfs: trace: vfs_type = "ext2"
libguestfs: trace: vfs_type "/dev/sda2"
libguestfs: trace: vfs_type = ""
libguestfs: trace: vfs_type "/dev/sda5"
libguestfs: trace: vfs_type = "LVM2_member"
libguestfs: trace: inspect_os
libguestfs: trace: inspect_os = ["/dev/debian-vg/root"]
libguestfs: trace: inspect_get_mountpoints "/dev/debian-vg/root"
```

CHAPTER 5   VIRTUAL MACHINE DISK IMAGE MANAGEMENT

```
libguestfs: trace: inspect_get_mountpoints = ["/boot", "/dev/
sda1", "/", "/dev/debian-vg/root"]
libguestfs: trace: mount_ro "/dev/debian-vg/root" "/"
libguestfs: trace: mount_ro = 0
libguestfs: trace: mount_ro "/dev/sda1" "/boot"
libguestfs: trace: mount_ro = 0
libguestfs: trace: inspect_get_roots
libguestfs: trace: inspect_get_roots = ["/dev/debian-vg/root"]
libguestfs: trace: inspect_get_type "/dev/debian-vg/root"
libguestfs: trace: inspect_get_type = "linux"
libguestfs: trace: download "/home/antonio/documents/important_
doc.txt" "/dev/stdout"
This is a very important document
libguestfs: trace: download = 0
libguestfs: trace: close
libguestfs: trace: internal_autosync
libguestfs: trace: internal_autosync = 0
```

virt-copy-in

We can use virt-copy-in to copy files from the host to the disk image/libvirt domain.

We'll begin by creating a simple text file.

```
antonio@antonio-Laptop:~/QEMU_VMs$ echo "This is a very
simplistic text file" > newtextfile.txt
```

And we copy it to the disk image file.

```
antonio@antonio-Laptop:~/QEMU_VMs$ sudo virt-copy-in -a debian.
qcow2 ./newtextfile.txt /home/antonio/documents/
```

CHAPTER 5   VIRTUAL MACHINE DISK IMAGE MANAGEMENT

We can check that the file was copied by using the **virt-cat** command that we studied previously.

```
antonio@antonio-Laptop:~/QEMU_VMs$ sudo virt-cat -d debian12 /
home/antonio/documents/newtextfile.txt
This is a very simplistic text file
```

virt-copy-out

This tool complements **virt-copy-in**. While **virt-copy-in** allows to copy files from the host to the disk image/domain, **virt-copy-out** allows to copy files from the disk image/domain to the host.

We'll test this tool by copying any file from the disk image.

```
antonio@antonio-Laptop:~/QEMU_VMs$ sudo virt-copy-out -a
debian.qcow2 /etc/fstab .
```

After copying the file, we can see its contents as with any other local file.

```
antonio@antonio-Laptop:~/QEMU_VMs$ cat fstab
# /etc/fstab: static file system information.
#
# Use 'blkid' to print the universally unique identifier for a
# device; this may be used with UUID= as a more robust way to
  name devices
# that works even if disks are added and removed. See fstab(5).
#
# systemd generates mount units based on this file, see
  systemd.mount(5).
# Please run 'systemctl daemon-reload' after making
  changes here.
#
```

255

```
# <file system> <mount point>   <type>   <options>
<dump>  <pass>
/dev/mapper/debian--vg-root
/               ext4    errors=remount-ro 0      1
# /boot was on /dev/sda1 during installation
UUID=e5a28faa-6b7b-453e-95cc-e87cd9a13693 /
boot            ext2    defaults          0      2
/dev/mapper/debian--vg-swap_1 none         swap   sw
0       0
/dev/sr0        /media/cdrom0    udf,iso9660 user,noauto
0       0
```

virt-diff

Sometimes it might be useful to see the differences between two running instances, two image disk files, etc. For example, if we want to know what files have been created since we performed a snapshot. We can do this with **virt-diff**.

We'll begin by comparing the disk image file *debian.qcow2* and the libvirt domain "debian12".

```
antonio@antonio-Laptop:~/QEMU_VMs$ sudo virt-diff -a debian.qcow2 -D debian12
antonio@antonio-Laptop:~/QEMU_VMs$
```

As there are no differences, we don't see any output. Now we'll perform a simple test. We'll make a copy of the disk image file.

```
antonio@antonio-Laptop:~/QEMU_VMs$ cp debian.qcow2 debian_copy.qcow2
```

CHAPTER 5   VIRTUAL MACHINE DISK IMAGE MANAGEMENT

And we'll use **virt-copy-in** to copy any file to the new disk image file.

```
antonio@antonio-Laptop:~/QEMU_VMs$ sudo virt-copy-in -a debian_
copy.qcow2 test /home/antonio
```

If we compare now both disk images with **virt-diff**, we'll see this difference.

```
antonio@antonio-Laptop:~/QEMU_VMs$ sudo virt-diff -a debian.
qcow2 -A debian_copy.qcow2
+ - 0664           5 /home/antonio/test
```

virt-inspector

If we want to get information about the OS in a certain disk image file or libvirt domain, we can get it with **virt-inspector**. Let's see a simple example.

```
antonio@antonio-Laptop:~/QEMU_VMs$ sudo virt-inspector -a
debian.qcow2
<?xml version="1.0"?>
<operatingsystems>
  <operatingsystem>
    <root>/dev/debian-vg/root</root>
    <name>linux</name>
    <arch>x86_64</arch>
    <distro>debian</distro>
    <product_name>12.5</product_name>
    <major_version>12</major_version>
    <minor_version>5</minor_version>
    <package_format>deb</package_format>
    <package_management>apt</package_management>
    <hostname>debian</hostname>
```

257

```
      <osinfo>debian12</osinfo>
      <mountpoints>
        <mountpoint dev="/dev/debian-vg/root">/</mountpoint>
        <mountpoint dev="/dev/sda1">/boot</mountpoint>
      </mountpoints>
      <filesystems>
        <filesystem dev="/dev/debian-vg/root">
          <type>ext4</type>
          <uuid>c5eac4a7-3638-4207-bae3-23f02aaa4666</uuid>
        </filesystem>
        <filesystem dev="/dev/debian-vg/swap_1">
          <type>swap</type>
          <uuid>ba9163b0-13c8-4a4e-b640-ac059211c82c</uuid>
        </filesystem>
        <filesystem dev="/dev/sda1">
          <type>ext2</type>
          <uuid>e5a28faa-6b7b-453e-95cc-e87cd9a13693</uuid>
        </filesystem>
      </filesystems>
.
.
.
```

As the output is very lengthy, it is probably better to redirect it to a file. In the output, we can get a lot of information, like the root filesystem, the architecture, operating system version, software installed, and so on.

virt-filesystems

A disk image file or domain can contain many filesystems. When we studied the **libguestfs** interactive shell, we saw how to list the filesystems. We can do the same thing with the **virt-filesystems** command.

CHAPTER 5 VIRTUAL MACHINE DISK IMAGE MANAGEMENT

To test the tool, we'll list the filesystems of a couple of disk image files.

```
antonio@antonio-Laptop:~/QEMU_VMs$ sudo virt-filesystems -a
debian.qcow2
/dev/sda1
/dev/debian-vg/root
antonio@antonio-Laptop:~/QEMU_VMs$ sudo virt-filesystems -a
alpine_disk.qcow
/dev/sda1
/dev/sda3
```

If we want to get more details, like the type of filesystem or the size, we can use the "-l" option.

```
antonio@antonio-Laptop:~/QEMU_VMs$ sudo virt-filesystems -a
debian.qcow2 -l
Name                  Type        VFS   Label   Size        Parent
/dev/sda1             filesystem  ext2  -       476286976   -
/dev/debian-vg/root   filesystem  ext4  -       8923836416  -
```

virt-rescue

There could be certain circumstances that render a disk image unbootable. If that's the case, we can try to rescue the system with **virt-rescue**.

To start, we can use the "--suggest" option. As the name implies, this command suggests the commands that we must use once inside the rescue shell.

```
antonio@antonio-Laptop:~/QEMU_VMs$ sudo virt-rescue --suggest
-a debian.qcow2
Inspecting the virtual machine or disk image ...

This disk contains one or more operating systems.  You can use
these mount
```

CHAPTER 5 VIRTUAL MACHINE DISK IMAGE MANAGEMENT

commands in virt-rescue (at the ><rescue> prompt) to mount the filesystems.

```
# /dev/debian-vg/root is the root of a linux operating system
# type: linux, distro: debian, version: 12.5
# 12.5

mount /dev/debian-vg/root /sysroot/
mount /dev/sda1 /sysroot/boot
mount --rbind /dev /sysroot/dev
mount --rbind /proc /sysroot/proc
mount --rbind /sys /sysroot/sys

cd /sysroot
chroot /sysroot
```

The tool successfully recognized the filesystems contained in the disk image file, as well as the root filesystem and the boot partition. We're suggested to mount the root filesystem and the boot partition, as well as the special filesystems */dev*, */proc*, and */sys*.

We'll execute **virt-rescue** again and perform the suggested actions.

```
antonio@antonio-Laptop:~/QEMU_VMs$ sudo virt-rescue -a
debian.qcow2
supermin: mounting /proc
supermin: ext2 mini initrd starting up: 5.2.1
Starting /init script …
.
.
.
The virt-rescue escape key is '^]'.  Type '^] h' for help.
------------------------------------------------------------
Welcome to virt-rescue, the libguestfs rescue shell.
```

CHAPTER 5 VIRTUAL MACHINE DISK IMAGE MANAGEMENT

```
Note: The contents of / (root) are the rescue appliance.
You have to mount the guest's partitions under /sysroot
before you can examine them.

groups: cannot find name for group ID 0
><rescue>

><rescue> mount /dev/debian-vg/root /sysroot/
><rescue> mount /dev/sda1 /sysroot/boot
><rescue> mount --rbind /dev /sysroot/dev
><rescue> mount --rbind /proc /sysroot/proc
><rescue> mount --rbind /sys /sysroot/sys
><rescue>
```

Finally, we change to the */sysroot* folder and execute chroot to change the active root filesystem.

```
><rescue> cd /sysroot
><rescue> chroot /sysroot
```

Now we can perform the needed actions to repair the system. For instance, we can check the mount points, repair the filesystems, etc. For instance, let's suppose that we need to check the contents of the */etc/fstab* file. We can use cat from inside **virt-rescue** to do that.

```
><rescue> cat /etc/fstab
# /etc/fstab: static file system information.
#
# Use 'blkid' to print the universally unique identifier for a
# device; this may be used with UUID= as a more robust way to
  name devices
# that works even if disks are added and removed. See fstab(5).
#
```

CHAPTER 5   VIRTUAL MACHINE DISK IMAGE MANAGEMENT

```
# systemd generates mount units based on this file, see
  systemd.mount(5).
# Please run 'systemctl daemon-reload' after making
  changes here.
#
# <file system> <mount point>   <type>   <options>
<dump>  <pass>
/dev/mapper/debian--vg-root
/               ext4    errors=remount-ro 0       1
# /boot was on /dev/sda1 during installation
UUID=e5a28faa-6b7b-453e-95cc-e87cd9a13693 /
boot            ext2    defaults         0       2
/dev/mapper/debian--vg-swap_1 none               swap    sw
0       0
/dev/sr0        /media/cdrom0   udf,iso9660 user,noauto
0       0
><rescue>
```

If we need to edit the file, we can use **vi**. When we have performed the needed actions to repair the system, we can exit **virt-rescue** by pressing Ctrl+D.

virt-df

Linux administrators are familiar with the **df** command. There is also an equivalent command that performs the same operation on image disk file and/or libvirt domains.

CHAPTER 5   VIRTUAL MACHINE DISK IMAGE MANAGEMENT

The use of the **virt-df** command is very easy.

```
antonio@antonio-Laptop:~/QEMU_VMs$ sudo virt-df -a debian.qcow2 -h
Filesystem                          Size       Used   Available   Use%
debian.qcow2:/dev/sda1              454M       69M        361M    16%
debian.qcow2:/dev/debian-vg/root    8,3G       4,5G       3,4G    54%
```

virt-resize

All the libguestfs tools that we have seen so far are quite easy to use. That's not the case with virt-resize. Of course you don't need to learn rocket science to use it, but it is significantly more complicated to use than the other tools.

We'll begin by describing what the tool does. As the name implies, it resizes virtual machine disks; it can resize a single or multiple partitions. It is very advisable to check the man page of the tool. In that page, we can see many examples that will help us better understand how to use the tool. To avoid disk corruption, it is advisable to use it with powered-off virtual machines.

We'll resize one of the disk image files we worked with previously. We can get some basic information with **ls** and **qemu-img info** as we saw before.

```
antonio@antonio-Laptop:~/QEMU_VMs$ ls -lh debian.qcow2
-rw-r--r-- 1 antonio antonio 8,1G jul 10 22:21 debian.qcow2
```

```
antonio@antonio-Laptop:~/QEMU_VMs$ qemu-img info debian.qcow2
image: debian.qcow2
file format: qcow2
virtual size: 10 GiB (10737418240 bytes)
disk size: 7.98 GiB
cluster_size: 65536
```

CHAPTER 5   VIRTUAL MACHINE DISK IMAGE MANAGEMENT

```
Format specific information:
    compat: 1.1
    compression type: zlib
    lazy refcounts: false
    refcount bits: 16
    corrupt: false
    extended l2: false
```

In this example, we'll extend one of the partitions of the disk image file, so we'll need to list them with the **virt-filesystems** tool, which we already studied.

```
antonio@antonio-Laptop:~/QEMU_VMs$ sudo virt-filesystems --all
-h --long -a debian.qcow2
Name                    Type        VFS   Label MBR Size Parent
/dev/sda1               filesystem  ext2  -     -   454M -
/dev/debian-vg/root     filesystem  ext4  -     -   8,3G -
/dev/debian-vg/swap_1   filesystem  swap  -     -   976M -
/dev/debian-vg/root     lv          -     -     -   8,5G /dev/
                                                         debian-vg
/dev/debian-vg/swap_1   lv          -     -     -   976M /dev/
                                                         debian-vg
/dev/debian-vg          vg          -     -     -   9,5G /dev/sda5
/dev/sda5               pv          -     -     -   9,5G -
/dev/sda1               partition   -     -     83  487M /dev/sda
/dev/sda2               partition   -     -     05  1,0K /dev/sda
/dev/sda5               partition   -     -     8e  9,5G /dev/sda
/dev/sda                device      -     -     -   10G  -
```

Next, we need to create a new image disk file bigger in size. In this case, we create a 12 GB image disk file.

CHAPTER 5 VIRTUAL MACHINE DISK IMAGE MANAGEMENT

```
antonio@antonio-Laptop:~/QEMU_VMs$ qemu-img create -f qcow2 -o
preallocation=metadata NEW_debian.qcow2 12G
Formatting 'NEW_debian.qcow2', fmt=qcow2 cluster_size=65536
extended_l2=off preallocation=metadata compression_type=zlib
size=128846
```

We check that the new file was correctly created.

```
antonio@antonio-Laptop:~/QEMU_VMs$ ls -lh NEW_debian.qcow2
-rw-r--r-- 1 antonio antonio 13G jul 11 07:11 NEW_debian.qcow2
antonio@antonioLaptop:~/QEMU_VMs$ qemu-img info NEW_
debian.qcow2
image: NEW_debian.qcow2
file format: qcow2
virtual size: 12 GiB (12884901888 bytes)
disk size: 2.07 MiB
cluster_size: 65536
Format specific information:
    compat: 1.1
    compression type: zlib
    lazy refcounts: false
    refcount bits: 16
    corrupt: false
    extended l2: false
```

Now we can expand the disk by using the "old" file as the origin and the "new" file as the destination. As we can only resize partitions, we'll resize the */boot* partition as an example. We had identified this partition previously with **virt-filesystems**.

```
antonio@antonio-Laptop:~/QEMU_VMs$ sudo virt-resize --expand /
dev/sda1 debian.qcow2 NEW_debian.qcow2
[   0.0] Examining debian.qcow2
```

****

Summary of changes:

/dev/sda1: This partition will be resized from 487.0M to 2.5G. The
filesystem ext2 on /dev/sda1 will be expanded using the 'resize2fs'
method.

/dev/sda2: This partition will be left alone.

****
[3.0] Setting up initial partition table on NEW_debian.qcow2
[4.4] Copying /dev/sda1
[5.7] Copying /dev/sda2
 100%
⟦▒▒⟧ 00:00
[55.4] Expanding /dev/sda1 using the 'resize2fs' method

Resize operation completed with no errors. Before deleting the old disk, carefully check that the resized disk boots and works correctly.

As suggested by the command itself, we should check that the expanded disk actually works as expected. We can do that with QEMU for instance. We can also use virt-filesystems to see the size of the expanded partition.

```
antonio@antonio-Laptop:~/QEMU_VMs$ sudo virt-filesystems --all
-h --long -a NEW_debian.qcow2
Name                   Type            VFS   Label MBR Size Parent
/dev/sda1              filesystem ext2   -    -         2,3G  -
/dev/debian-vg/root    filesystem ext4   -    -         8,3G  -
/dev/debian-vg/swap_1  filesystem swap   -    -         976M  -
/dev/debian-vg/root    lv              -     -    -    8,5G /dev/
                                                              debian-vg
/dev/debian-vg/swap_1  lv              -     -    -    976M /dev/
                                                              debian-vg
/dev/debian-vg         vg              -     -    -    9,5G /dev/sda5
/dev/sda5              pv              -     -    -    9,5G  -
/dev/sda1              partition       -     -    83   2,5G /dev/sda
/dev/sda2              partition       -     -    05   1,0K /dev/sda
/dev/sda5              partition       -     -    8e   9,5G /dev/sda
/dev/sda                device         -     -    -    12G   -
```

We see that the size has increased from 487M to 2.5G. Now we launch **QEMU** to check that the new disk image file actually works as expected.

```
antonio@antonio-Laptop:~/QEMU_VMs$ sudo qemu-system-x86_64 -m
512 -accel kvm NEW_debian.qcow2
```

virt-sparsify

A tool that complements **virt-resizefs** is **virt-sparsify**; this latter tool reclaims unused disk space. Due to the risk of corrupting data, it is mandatory to use it when the associated virtual machine is powered off, thus minimizing the risk.

CHAPTER 5   VIRTUAL MACHINE DISK IMAGE MANAGEMENT

As an example, we'll reclaim the unused space in the disk we expanded previously. We'll begin by checking its size.

```
antonio@antonio-Laptop:~/QEMU_VMs$ ls -lh NEW_debian.qcow2
-rw-r--r-- 1 antonio antonio 13G jul 11 07:16 NEW_debian.qcow2
```

We now execute virt-sparsify; the syntax is very easy; we just need to specify the name of the disk we want to sparsify and the new disk. The new disk will be created by the tool (or overwritten if it already exists); as opposed to what we saw with **virt-resizefs,** we don't need to create the new image disk file explicitly.

```
antonio@antonio-Laptop~/QEMU_VMs$ sudo virt-sparsify NEW_
debian.qcow2 SPARSIFIEDdebian.qcow2
[sudo] password for antonio:
[   0.0] Create overlay file in /tmp to protect source disk
[   0.0] Examine source disk
[   2.5] Fill free space in /dev/debian-vg/root with zero
 100%
⟦▓▓▓▓▓▓▓▓▓▓▓▓▓▓▓▓▓▓▓▓▓▓▓▓▓▓▓▓▓▓▓▓▓▓▓▓▓▓▓▓▓▓▓▓▓▓▓▓▓▓⟧ 00:00
[  10.3] Clearing Linux swap on /dev/debian-vg/swap_1
[  12.0] Fill free space in /dev/sda1 with zero
 100%
⟦▓▓▓▓▓▓▓▓▓▓▓▓▓▓▓▓▓▓▓▓▓▓▓▓▓▓▓▓▓▓▓▓▓▓▓▓▓▓▓▓▓▓▓▓▓▓▓▓▓▓⟧ 00:00
[  42.8] Fill free space in volgroup debian-vg with zero
[  43.2] Copy to destination and make sparse
[ 111.2] Sparsify operation completed with no errors.
virt-sparsify: Before deleting the old disk, carefully check
that the target disk boots and works correctly.
```

CHAPTER 5   VIRTUAL MACHINE DISK IMAGE MANAGEMENT

If we check the size of the new file, we'll see that it is significantly smaller than the original file.

```
antonio@antonio-Laptop:~/QEMU_VMs$ ls -lh SPARSIFIEDdebian.qcow2
-rw-r--r-- 1 root root 5,0G jul 11 20:19 SPARSIFIEDdebian.qcow2
```

Finally, we launch QEMU with the new image disk file to make sure that it is working.

```
antonio@antonio-Laptop:~/QEMU_VMs$ sudo qemu-system-x86_64 -m 512 -accel kvm   SPARSIFIEDdebian.qcow2
```

virt-p2v

This tool converts a physical machine to a QEMU/KVM virtual machine managed by libvirt, OpenStack, RHV, or oVirt. We don't execute **virt-p2v** directly; instead, we must create a bootable image with **virt-p2v-make-disk**. Then we'll boot the physical machine we want to virtualize using that image, which will run automatically **virt-p2v**.

After that, we'll need to provide the IP address and the credentials needed to connect with SSH with the "conversion server." This "conversion server" is the QEMU/KVM hypervisor in which the converted virtual machine will run. This server also needs to have **virt-v2v** installed. Depending on the Linux distribution, **virt-v2v** can be included in the libguestfs suite or be independent. In Ubuntu 22, for instance, it is included in its own independent package.

```
antonio@antonio-Laptop:~/QEMU_VMs$ apt search virt-v2v
Sorting... Done
Full Text Search... Done
virt-v2v/jammy 1.44.2-1 amd64
  virtual-to-virtual machine converter
```

CHAPTER 5   VIRTUAL MACHINE DISK IMAGE MANAGEMENT

So we'll need to install it.

```
antonio@antonio-Laptop:~/QEMU_VMs$ sudo apt install virt-v2v
```

Next we need to create the bootable media. If we use the "--help" option, we can see the syntax of the **virt-p2v-make-disk** command.

```
antonio@antonio-Laptop:~/QEMU_VMs$ virt-p2v-make-disk --help
Usage:
  virt-p2v-make-disk [--options] -o /dev/sdX [os-version]
Read virt-p2v-make-disk(1) man page for more information.
```

We only need to specify the path of the device that we want to prepare to boot the target system. The OS version is usually not necessary as the tool will try to locate a suitable OS version for us. This OS version is related to the host in which we're creating the bootable image; it has no relation at all with the OS version of the target physical system that we want to virtualize.

So if we want to prepare a USB disk to boot a system and launch **virt-p2v**, we can do that easily with this command, assuming the USB disk in our system is at */dev/sda*.

```
antonio@antonio-Laptop:~/QEMU_VMs$ virt-p2v-make-disk -o
/dev/sda
virt-builder: error: cannot find os-version 'ubuntu-22.04' with
architecture 'x86_64'.
Use --list to list available guest types.

If reporting bugs, run virt-builder with debugging enabled and
include the
complete output:

  virt-builder -v -x [...]
```

CHAPTER 5   VIRTUAL MACHINE DISK IMAGE MANAGEMENT

Unfortunately in this occasion, the tool couldn't find a proper OS to build the image. As suggested, we'll list the available versions.

```
antonio@antonio-Laptop:~/QEMU_VMs$ virt-builder --list
opensuse-tumbleweed     x86_64      openSUSE Tumbleweed
alma-8.5                x86_64      AlmaLinux 8.5
centos-6                x86_64      CentOS 6.6
centos-7.0              x86_64      CentOS 7.0
centos-7.1              x86_64      CentOS 7.1
centos-7.2              aarch64     CentOS 7.2 (aarch64)
.
.
.
ubuntu-20.04            x86_64      Ubuntu 20.04 (focal)
.
.
.
```

As I'm working on an Ubuntu 22 system, I'll choose the ubuntu-20.04 OS version.

```
antonio@antonio-Laptop:~/QEMU_VMs$ virt-p2v-make-disk -o /dev/sda ubuntu-20.04
[   6.4] Downloading: http://builder.libguestfs.org/ubuntu-20.04.xz
########################################################## 100,0%
[  32.6] Planning how to build this image
[  32.6] Uncompressing
[  40.3] Opening the new disk
[  43.1] Setting a random seed
virt-builder: warning: random seed could not be set for this type of guest
```

271

CHAPTER 5 VIRTUAL MACHINE DISK IMAGE MANAGEMENT

```
[  43.1] Uploading: /tmp/tmp.IOqrkWErp8/policy-rc.d to /usr/sbin/policy-rc.d
[  43.2] Setting the hostname: p2v.local
[  44.1] Running: hostname p2v.local
[  44.2] Updating packages
[ 182.1] Installing packages: libpcre3 libxml2 libgtk-3-0 libdbus-1-3 openssh-client qemu-utils debianutils vim-tiny open-iscsi xorg xserves
[ 289.8] Uploading: /usr/share/virt-p2v/issue to /etc/issue
[ 289.9] Uploading: /usr/share/virt-p2v/issue to /etc/issue.net
[ 289.9] Making directory: /usr/bin
[ 289.9] Uploading: /tmp/tmp.IOqrkWErp8/virt-p2v to /usr/bin/virt-p2v
[ 290.0] Changing permissions of /usr/bin/virt-p2v to 0755
[ 290.0] Uploading: /usr/share/virt-p2v/launch-virt-p2v to /usr/bin/
[ 290.0] Changing permissions of /usr/bin/launch-virt-p2v to 0755
[ 290.0] Uploading: /usr/share/virt-p2v/p2v.service to /etc/systemd/system/
[ 290.1] Making directory: /etc/systemd/system/multi-user.target.wants
[ 290.1] Linking: /etc/systemd/system/multi-user.target.wants/p2v.service -> /etc/systemd/system/p2v.service
[ 290.1] Editing: /lib/systemd/system/getty@.service
[ 290.2] Editing: /etc/systemd/logind.conf
[ 290.3] Deleting: /usr/sbin/policy-rc.d
[ 290.3] Setting passwords
[ 291.3] Finishing off
                   Output file: image.iso
                   Output size: 6.0G
```

```
        Output format: raw
   Total usable space: 5.8G
         Free space: 2.4G (41%)
antonio@antonio-Laptop:~/QEMU_VMs$
```

In addition to the procedure of creating a bootable image to execute virt-p2v that we have just seen, some commercial distributions like Red Hat allow to download an already-created bootable image. This could be a better option if it is available, as the manual creation of the bootable image not always works as expected. In this case, we should write the ISO file to the USB device. This can be easily done; if we're working with Ubuntu 22, we can open the ISO file with the "Disk Image Writer" (Figure 5-8) and select the USB device in which we want to write the ISO file (Figure 5-9).

CHAPTER 5   VIRTUAL MACHINE DISK IMAGE MANAGEMENT

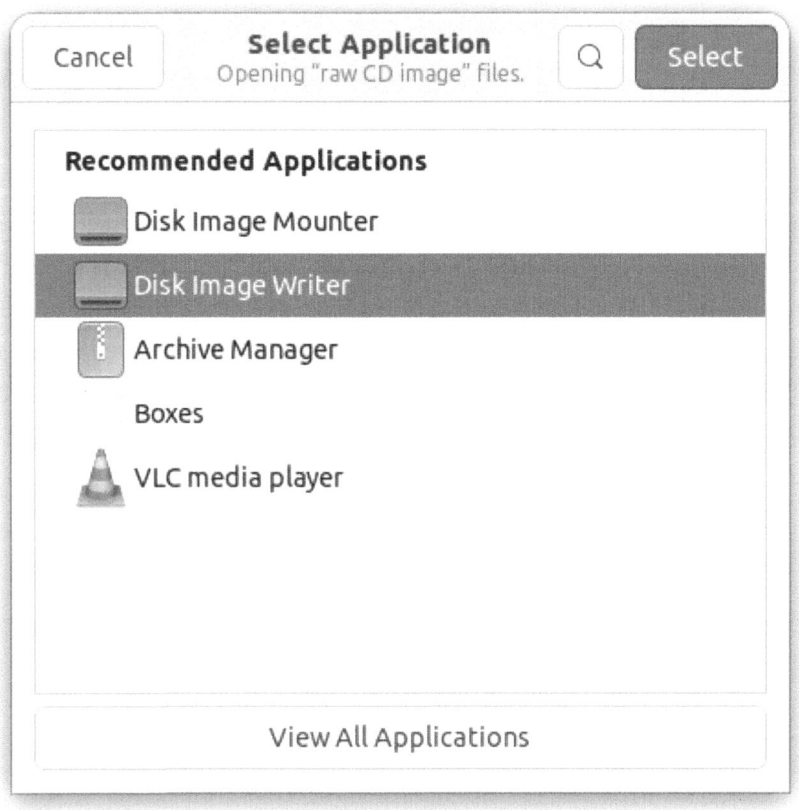

Figure 5-8. *Opening the ISO file with the Disk Image Writer*

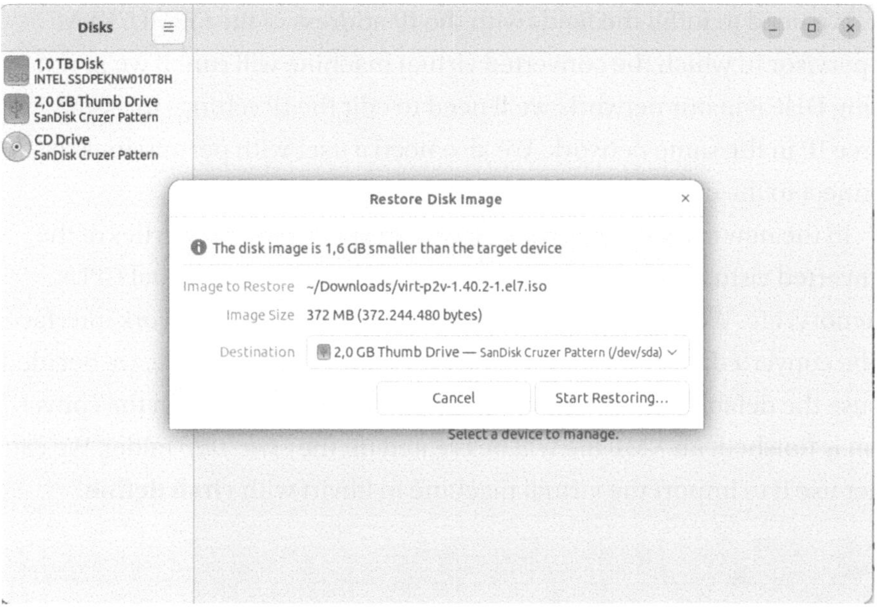

CHAPTER 5   VIRTUAL MACHINE DISK IMAGE MANAGEMENT

Figure 5-9. Writing the ISO file to the USB device

Whatever method we choose to create the USB bootable device, now we can take our USB disk and boot the target system. In a few seconds, the physical system will show us a screen similar to that of Figure 5-10.

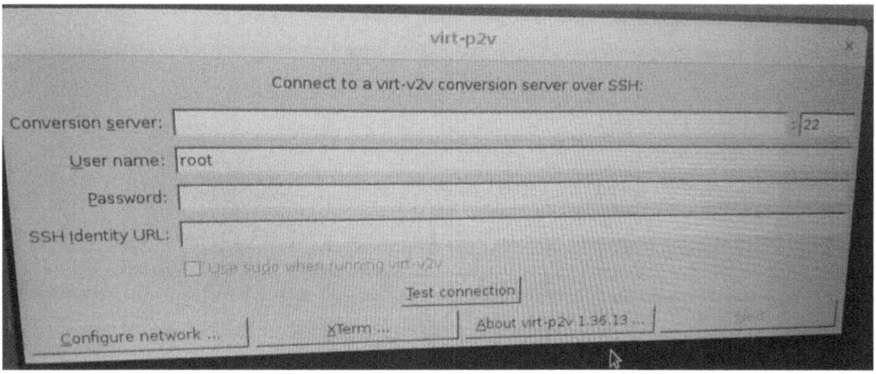

Figure 5-10. virt-p2v connecting to the conversion server

275

CHAPTER 5 VIRTUAL MACHINE DISK IMAGE MANAGEMENT

We need to fulfill the fields with the IP address of the QEMU/KVM hypervisor in which the converted virtual machine will run. If we're not using DHCP in our network, we'll need to edit the IP settings to assign a free IP in the same network. We also need a user with permissions to connect to the conversion server with SSH. We click "Next".

In the new screen (Figure 5-11), we can specify the properties of the converted virtual machine, such as the name, number of virtual CPUs, memory, etc. We can also choose the physical disks and network interfaces to be converted, the output format, and so on. In this example, we decided to use the default "local" output format; this means that when the conversion is finished, an XML file will be created on the */var/tmp* folder. We can later use it to import the virtual machine in libvirt with **virsh define**.

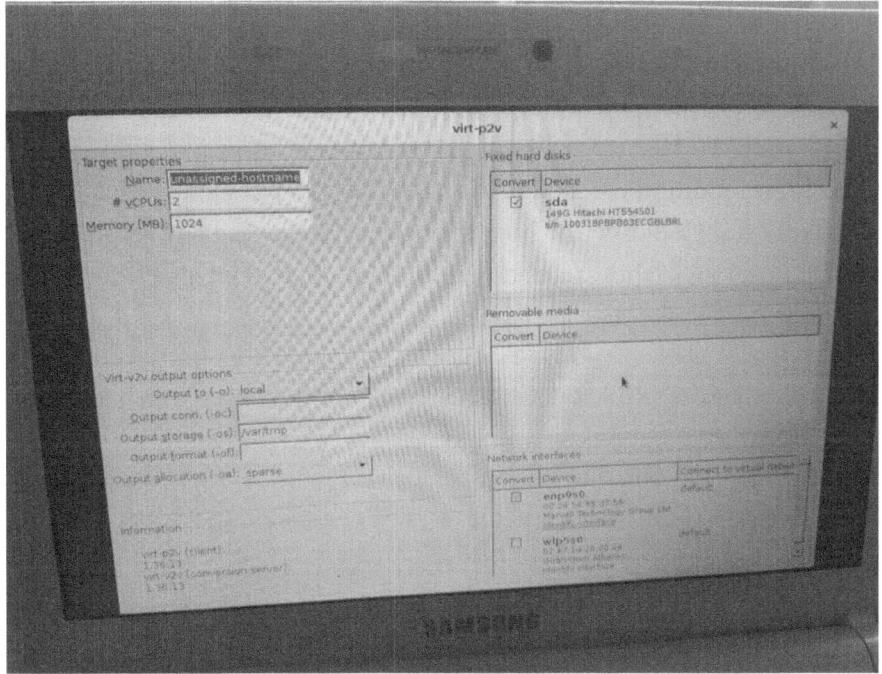

Figure 5-11. Conversion settings

CHAPTER 5   VIRTUAL MACHINE DISK IMAGE MANAGEMENT

We can now click "Start conversion". A new window will appear in which we can see the progress. When the procedure is finished, we'll see the corresponding message (Figure 5-12).

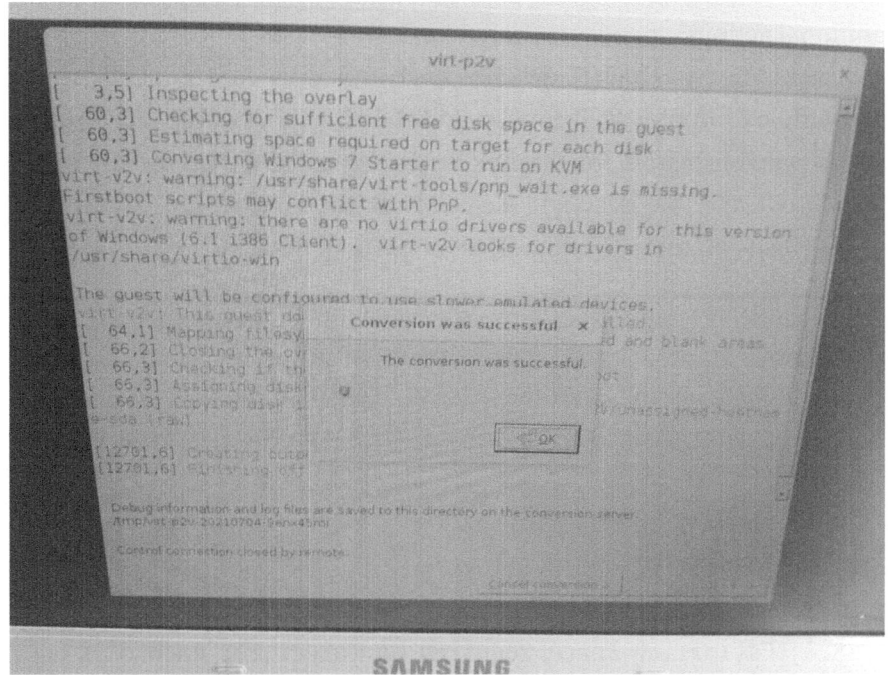

Figure 5-12. *The conversion was successful*

As we said, we can now import the newly created virtual machine in libvirt from the XML file created on */var/tmp*.

virt-v2v

We have seen already that we need **virt-v2v** installed when using **virt-p2v**. Besides using it to convert physical to virtual, it can also be used to convert between different virtual systems.

CHAPTER 5   VIRTUAL MACHINE DISK IMAGE MANAGEMENT

This is a very versatile and interesting tool, though it has some limitations. If we look at the man page of the tool, we can see that depending on the source guest and the destination format, there are specific versions supported; in some cases, we need to perform some additional actions.

It would take too long to describe each and every case so we'll just see a simple example. We'll convert a VMDK file, for example, the one we created previously from the original *debian.qcow2* file. We'll use the local output (-o local); that is, an xml file will be created in the *temp* folder (-os temp). The destination format will be qcow2 (-of qcow2).

```
antonio@antonio-Laptop:~/QEMU_VMs$ sudo virt-v2v -i disk
debian.vmdk -o local -of qcow2 -os temp
[   0.0] Opening the source -i disk debian.vmdk
[   0.0] Creating an overlay to protect the source from being
modified
[   0.1] Opening the overlay
[  13.5] Inspecting the overlay
[  15.8] Checking for sufficient free disk space in the guest
[  15.8] Estimating space required on target for each disk
[  15.8] Converting 12.5 to run on KVM
virt-v2v: warning: could not determine a way to update the
configuration of
Grub2
virt-v2v: This guest has virtio drivers installed.
[  52.6] Mapping filesystem data to avoid copying unused and
blank areas
[  69.8] Closing the overlay
[  70.1] Assigning disks to buses
[  70.1] Checking if the guest needs BIOS or UEFI to boot
[  70.1] Initializing the target -o local -os temp
```

CHAPTER 5 VIRTUAL MACHINE DISK IMAGE MANAGEMENT

```
[ 70.1] Copying disk 1/1 to temp/debian-sda (qcow2)
   (100.00/100%)
[ 107.2] Creating output metadata
[ 107.2] Finishing off
```

If we list the contents of the *temp* folder, we'll see the *debian.xml* file.

```
antonio@antonio-Laptop:~/QEMU_VMs$ ls -lh temp
total 5,5G
-rw-r--r-- 1 root root 5,5G jul 11 22:13 debian-sda
-rw-r--r-- 1 root root 1,5K jul 11 22:13 debian.xml
```

Now we can import the file into libvirt with **virsh**.

```
antonio@antonio-Laptop:~/QEMU_VMs$ virsh define temp/debian.xml
Domain 'debian' defined from temp/debian.xml

antonio@antonio-Laptop:~/QEMU_VMs$ virsh list --all
 Id   Name       State
---------------------------
 -    debian     shut off
 -    debian12   shut off
```

However, if we try to start the newly defined libvirt domain, we might get this error.

```
antonio@antonio-Laptop:~/QEMU_VMs$ virsh start debian
error: Failed to start domain 'debian'
error: internal error: qemu unexpectedly closed the monitor:
2024-07-14T12:54:18.899496Z qemu-system-x86_64: warning:
host doesn't support requested feature: CPUID.80000001H:ECX.
svm [bit 2]
Could not initialize SDL(x11 not available) - exiting
```

CHAPTER 5   VIRTUAL MACHINE DISK IMAGE MANAGEMENT

We can easily circumvent this error by editing the domain definition. We could use virsh edit debian to edit the xml file directly, but it is more friendly to use virt-manager instead. We'll open the virtual machine hardware settings; in the "CPUs" section, we'll check the "copy host CPU configuration" box (Figure 5-13).

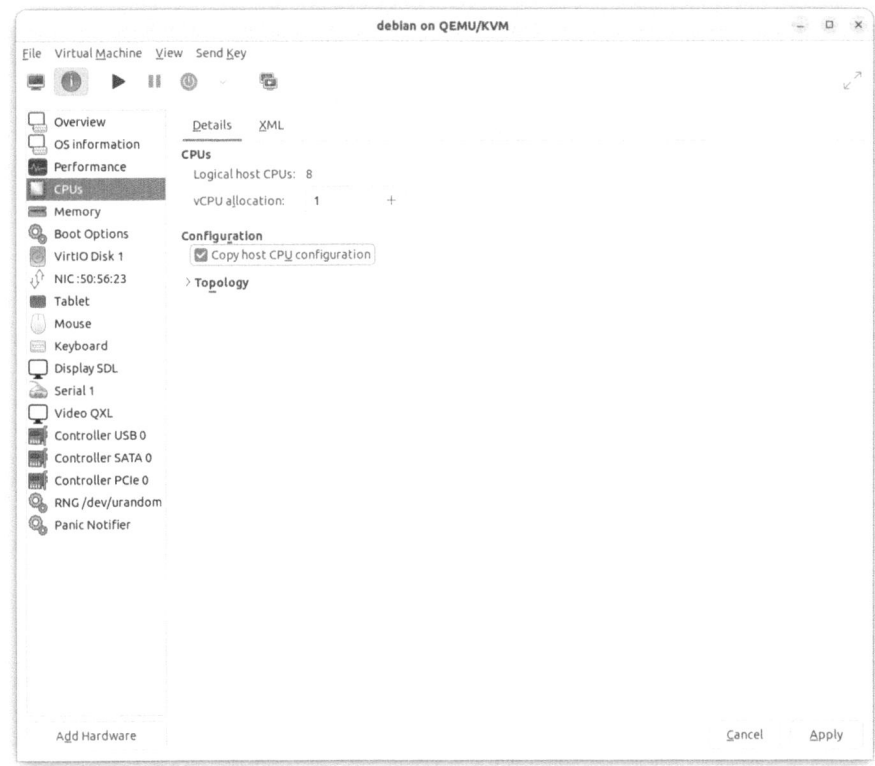

Figure 5-13. Editing the CPU settings

CHAPTER 5 VIRTUAL MACHINE DISK IMAGE MANAGEMENT

Next, we'll get to the "Display SDL" section, and we'll change the settings to use VNC server instead (Figure 5-14).

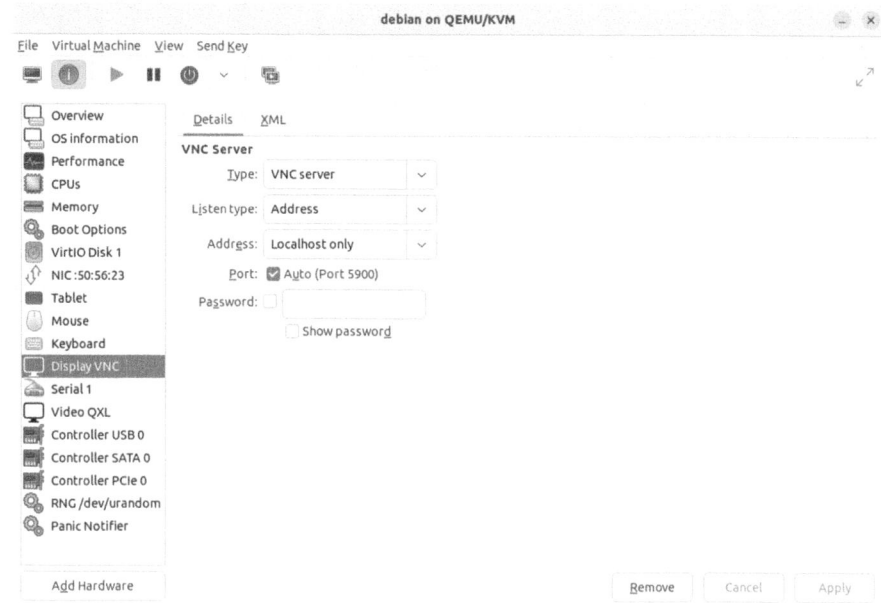

Figure 5-14. *Editing the display settings*

Now, we should be able to boot the debian domain (Figure 5-15).

281

CHAPTER 5 VIRTUAL MACHINE DISK IMAGE MANAGEMENT

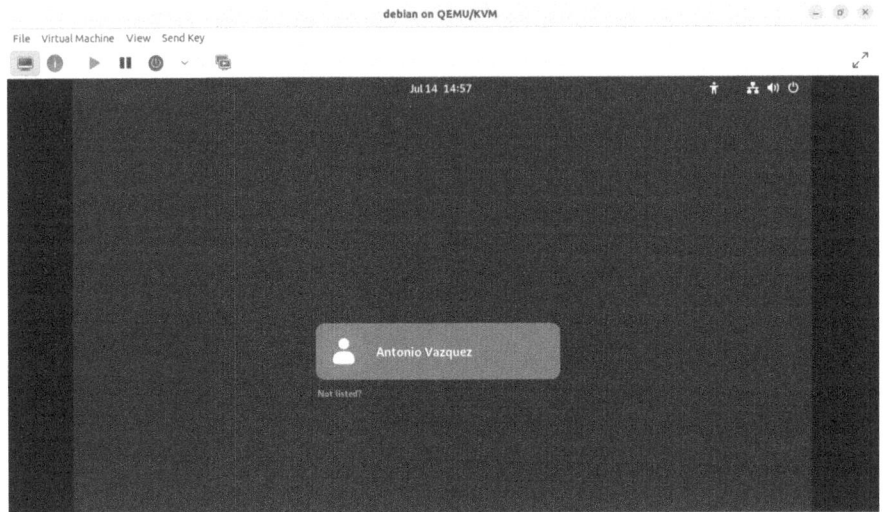

Figure 5-15. Debian domain running

virt-sysprep

We're almost finishing this review of the main libguestfs tools. This time we'll see **virt-sysprep**. This tool can be used to customize a virtual machine so that clones can be made. For instance, we can use it to remove ssh keys or network MAC persistent configuration. If we make a copy of a disk image file, the copy will have the same local user accounts, IP settings, and so on, so if we use it unmodified in the same network, it will get networking errors for having two identical IP addresses in the network. We could easily avoid this by using **virt-sysprep**.

The use of virt-sysprep is very easy. We'll see an easy example right now. First, we'll make a copy of a disk image file.

```
antonio@antonio-Laptop:~/QEMU_VMs$ cp alpine_disk.qcow COPY_
alpine_disk.qcow
```

CHAPTER 5 VIRTUAL MACHINE DISK IMAGE MANAGEMENT

Now we'll use virt-sysprep to delete the file with the command history (*.ash_history* in this Alpine Linux system) and to create a new */test* folder.

```
antonio@antonio-Laptop:~/QEMU_VMs$ sudo virt-sysprep --mkdir /
test --delete /root/.ash_history -a COPY_alpine_disk.qcow
[   0.0] Examining the guest ...
[   2.8] Performing "abrt-data" ...
[   2.8] Performing "backup-files" ...
[   2.9] Performing "bash-history" ...
[   2.9] Performing "blkid-tab" ...
[   3.0] Performing "crash-data" ...
[   3.0] Performing "cron-spool" ...
[   3.0] Performing "dhcp-client-state" ...
[   3.0] Performing "dhcp-server-state" ...
[   3.0] Performing "dovecot-data" ...
[   3.0] Performing "ipa-client" ...
[   3.0] Performing "kerberos-hostkeytab" ...
[   3.1] Performing "logfiles" ...
[   3.1] Performing "machine-id" ...
[   3.1] Performing "mail-spool" ...
[   3.1] Performing "net-hostname" ...
[   3.2] Performing "net-hwaddr" ...
[   3.2] Performing "pacct-log" ...
[   3.3] Performing "package-manager-cache" ...
[   3.3] Performing "pam-data" ...
[   3.3] Performing "passwd-backups" ...
[   3.3] Performing "puppet-data-log" ...
[   3.3] Performing "rh-subscription-manager" ...
[   3.4] Performing "rhn-systemid" ...
[   3.4] Performing "rpm-db" ...
[   3.4] Performing "samba-db-log" ...
[   3.5] Performing "script" ...
```

CHAPTER 5   VIRTUAL MACHINE DISK IMAGE MANAGEMENT

```
[   3.5] Performing "smolt-uuid" ...
[   3.5] Performing "ssh-hostkeys" ...
[   3.5] Performing "ssh-userdir" ...
[   3.5] Performing "sssd-db-log" ...
[   3.6] Performing "tmp-files" ...
[   3.6] Performing "udev-persistent-net" ...
[   3.6] Performing "utmp" ...
[   3.6] Performing "yum-uuid" ...
[   3.7] Performing "customize" ...
[   3.7] Setting a random seed
virt-sysprep: warning: random seed could not be set for this
type of guest
[   3.7] Making directory: /test
[   3.7] Deleting: /root/.ash_history
[   3.8] Performing "lvm-uuids" …
```

We'll launch now a QEMU instance to check the customized disk image file.

```
antonio@antonio-Laptop:~/QEMU_VMs$ sudo qemu-system-x86_64 -m
512 -accel kvm COPY_alpine_disk.qcow
```

If we log in the the system, we'll see that the history command has been reset.

```
alpine2:~# ls -a
.                    ..                    .ash_history
alpine2:~# history
    0 ls -a
    1 history
```

CHAPTER 5   VIRTUAL MACHINE DISK IMAGE MANAGEMENT

And we can also see that the new /*test* folder was created.

```
alpine2:~# ls /
bin        home         mnt     run      sys       var
boot       lib          opt     sbin     test
dev        lost+found   proc    srv      tmp
etc        media        root    swap     usr
alpine2:~#
```

Open Virtualization Format

Open Virtualization Format (OVF) is an open standard to distribute appliances (pre-configured virtual machines).

Nowadays most of the virtualization solutions provide a way to export virtual machines into OVF. For instance, if we're working with **VirtualBox**, which we already studied briefly in this chapter, we can click File ➤ Export Appliance and we'll see the window shown in Figure 5-16.

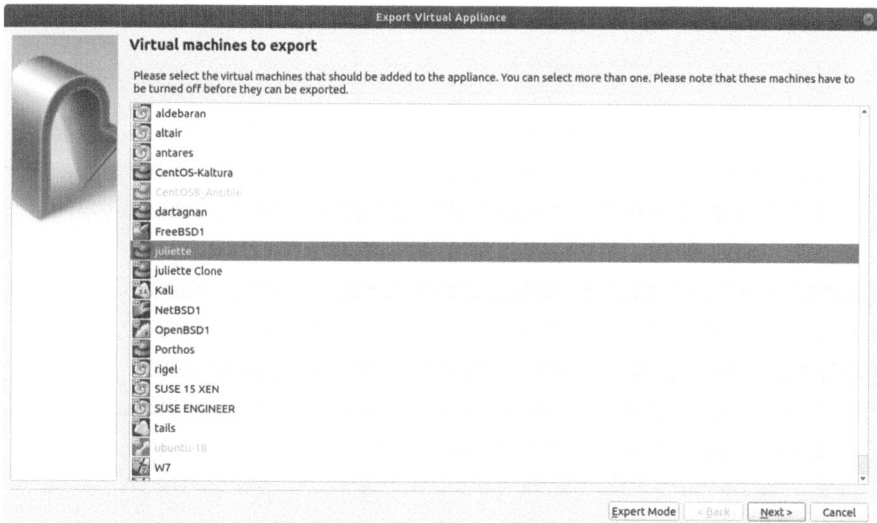

Figure 5-16. *Export Appliance*

CHAPTER 5   VIRTUAL MACHINE DISK IMAGE MANAGEMENT

We select the virtual machine we want to export, and we click "Next". In the next screen (Figure 5-17), we specify a few settings such as the OVF format or the location of the exported files. After clicking "Next", we can edit some descriptive information as well (Figure 5-18).

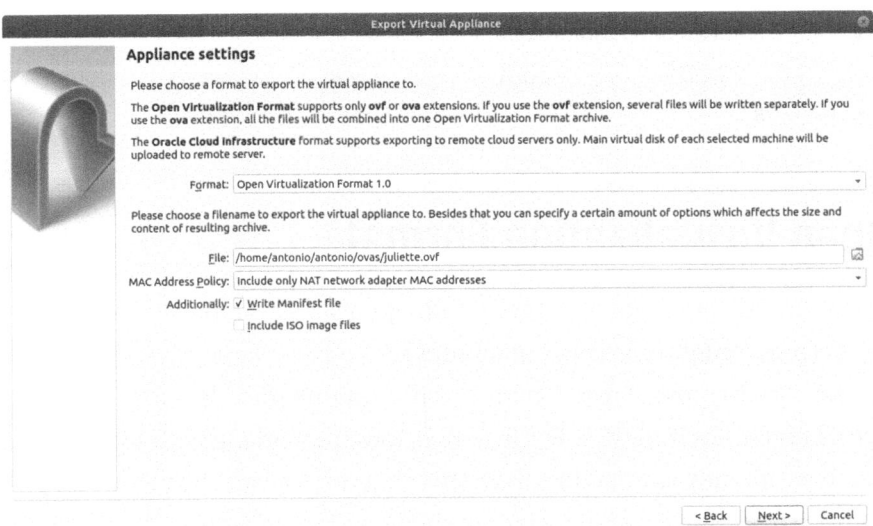

Figure 5-17. Appliance settings 1 of 2

CHAPTER 5   VIRTUAL MACHINE DISK IMAGE MANAGEMENT

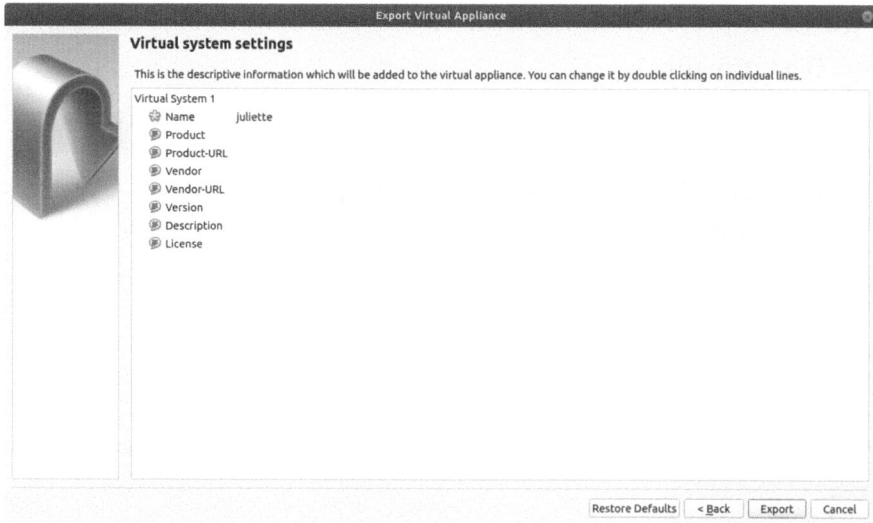

Figure 5-18. Appliance settings 2 of 2

Now that everything is ready, we click "Export", and the creation of the OVF begins (Figure 5-19).

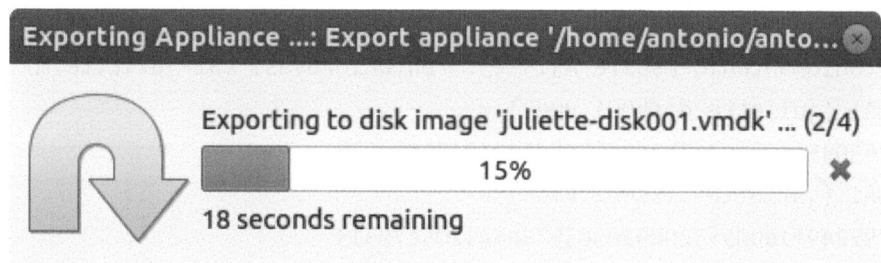

Figure 5-19. Exporting an OVF

CHAPTER 5   VIRTUAL MACHINE DISK IMAGE MANAGEMENT

When the process finishes, we'll have a series of files in the destination folder (Figure 5-20).

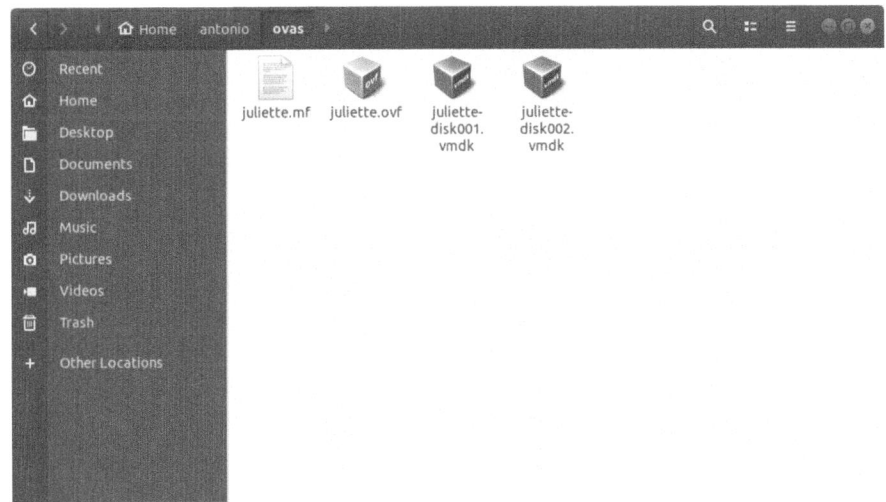

Figure 5-20. OVF files

In the mf file, we'll see the checksums of the other files.

```
antonio@antonio-Aspire-A315-23:~/antonio/ovas$ cat juliette.mf
SHA1 (juliette-disk001.vmdk) =
2463045ec06fc3f3b3d2c6346d14b40170f99078
SHA1 (juliette-disk002.vmdk) =
1c92249f1d0daf720b92e5e397ab841205c79313
SHA1 (juliette.ovf) = 57e497c886b17b28bd91243990bbf8cbbc5818cb
```

The VMDK files are the virtual disk files used by the virtual machine, and the ovf file is an xml file in which the hardware configuration of that same virtual machine is described.

CHAPTER 5 VIRTUAL MACHINE DISK IMAGE MANAGEMENT

```
antonio@antonio-Aspire-A315-23:~/antonio/ovas$ cat juliette.ovf
<?xml version="1.0"?>
<Envelope ovf:version="1.0" xml:lang="en-US" xmlns="http://
schemas.dmtf.org/ovf/envelope/1" xmlns:ovf="http://schemas.
dmtf.org/ovf/envelope/1" xmlns:rasd="http://schemas.dmtf.org/
wbem/wscim/1/cim-schema/2/CIM_ResourceAllocationSettingData"
xmlns:vssd="http://schemas.dmtf.org/wbem/wscim/1/cim-
schema/2/CIM_VirtualSystemSettingData" xmlns:xsi="http://
www.w3.org/2001/XMLSchema-instance" xmlns:vbox="http://www.
virtualbox.org/ovf/machine">
  <References>
    <File ovf:id="file1" ovf:href="juliette-disk001.vmdk"/>
    <File ovf:id="file2" ovf:href="juliette-disk002.vmdk"/>
  </References>
  <DiskSection>
    <Info>List of the virtual disks used in the package</Info>
    <Disk ovf:capacity="8589934592" ovf:diskId="vmdisk1"
ovf:fileRef="file1" ovf:format="http://www.vmware.com/
interfaces/specifications/vmdk.html#streamOptimized" vbox:uuid=
"dc47f76e-8461-4a65-88ad-f950b6e421e2"/>
    <Disk ovf:capacity="10737418240" ovf:diskId="vmdisk2"
ovf:fileRef="file2" ovf:format="http://www.vmware.com/
interfaces/specifications/vmdk.html#streamOptimized"
vbox:uuid="ffc82270-e015-43e1-870f-6b37129a0b58"/>
    .
    .
    .
```

Summary

In this chapter, we have learned a bit more about the different disk file formats. We've seen how to create disk files in different formats, getting information and converting between different formats.

We have also studied how we can mount filesystems contained inside disk files and how to copy files between the host and the disk file. We've also seen how we can expand or reduce the size of a virtual disk file and customize its content, adding or deleting settings as needed.

We also saw an example of converting a physical machine to a virtual one. And we used the OVF format to export a virtual machine.

CHAPTER 6

Proxmox and Open vSwitch

In this chapter, we'll cover the following concepts:

- Awareness of oVirt, Proxmox, and systemd-machined
- Awareness of Open vSwitch

Introduction to Proxmox

Proxmox is a virtualization platform, designed to easily manage virtual machines (and also containers).

When we studied QEMU/KVM and at the beginning of the book, we created the virtual machines launching the QEMU binary with the right parameters to set memory, network, storage, and so on. Later we learned about libvirt, and we saw how easier it was to manage virtual machines with tools like **virt-manager**. However, for big enterprise environments, even tools like virt-manager are not ideal. We need to go one step forward, and that's where **Proxmox** fits in.

We'll start by installing Proxmox. We can download the ISO installation file from the manufacturer web page: https://proxmox.com/en/ (Figure 6-1). Then we select "Downloads" and "Proxmox VE". And click the download button next to the ISO file.

CHAPTER 6   PROXMOX AND OPEN VSWITCH

We have to say that Proxmox offers several products, not only the Proxmox Virtual Environment or Proxmox VE for short that we're speaking about in this book. They also offer backup and mail-related software. When we speak about Proxmox in this book, we'll be speaking about Proxmox VE.

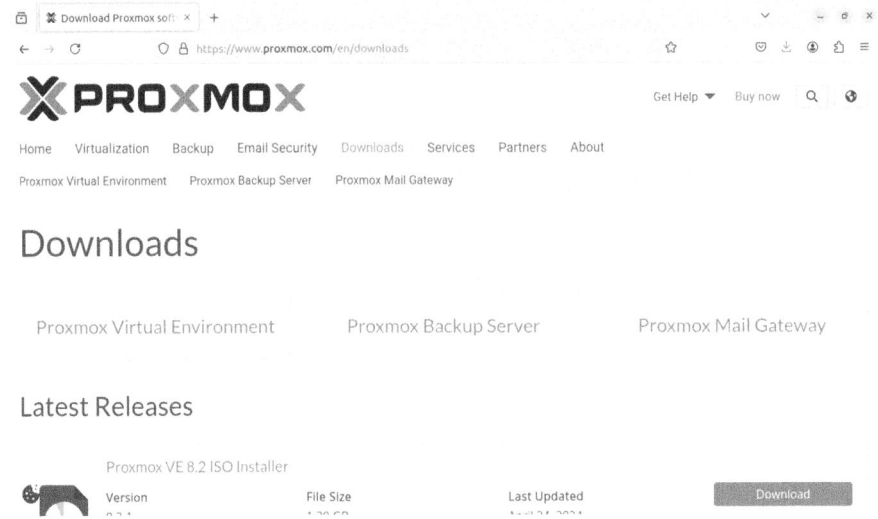

Figure 6-1. Downloading Proxmox

CHAPTER 6 PROXMOX AND OPEN VSWITCH

The way to install it is very easy. We just need to boot the server with the ISO file (Figure 6-2).

Figure 6-2. Booting from the Proxmox installer

CHAPTER 6   PROXMOX AND OPEN VSWITCH

We'll select the first option "Install Proxmox VE (Graphical)", as it is easier than the text installation. Then we select the disk device in which to install it (Figure 6-3).

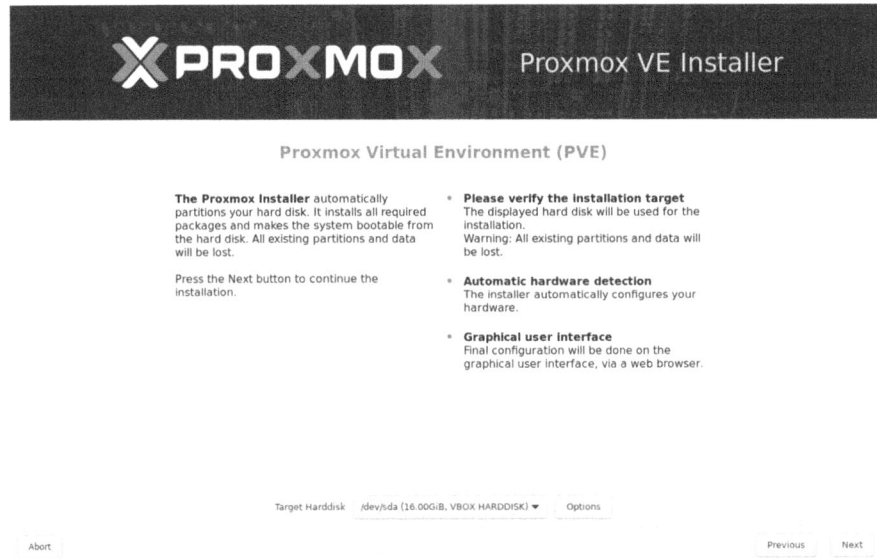

Figure 6-3. Installing Proxmox. Selecting the hard disk

We also select the country, time zone, and keyboard layout (Figure 6-4).

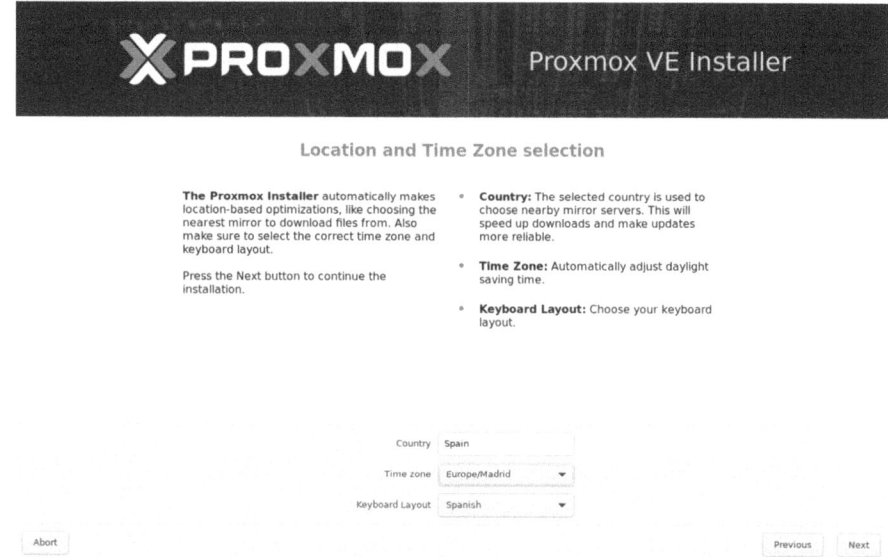

Figure 6-4. *Installing Proxmox. Setting the time zone and the keyboard layout*

CHAPTER 6   PROXMOX AND OPEN VSWITCH

We also need to set the root password (Figure 6-5).

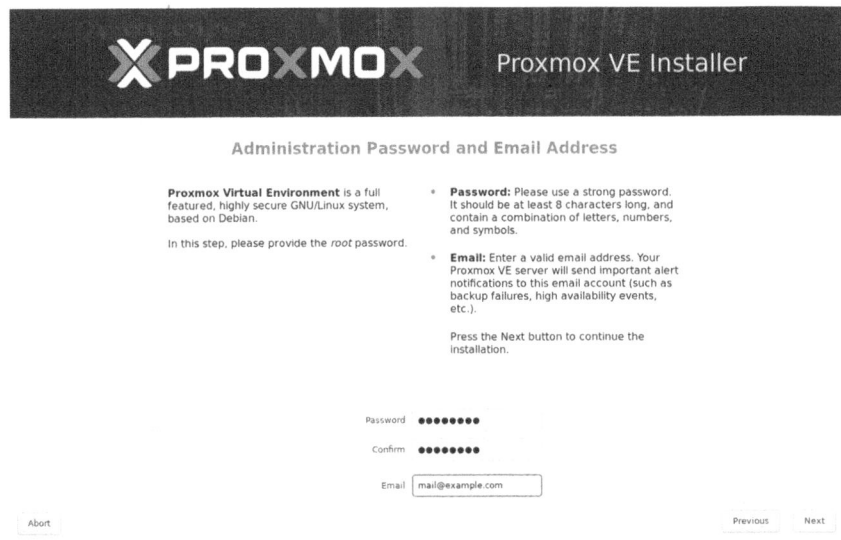

Figure 6-5. *Installing Proxmox. Setting the root password*

In the next screen, we specify the network settings (Figure 6-6).

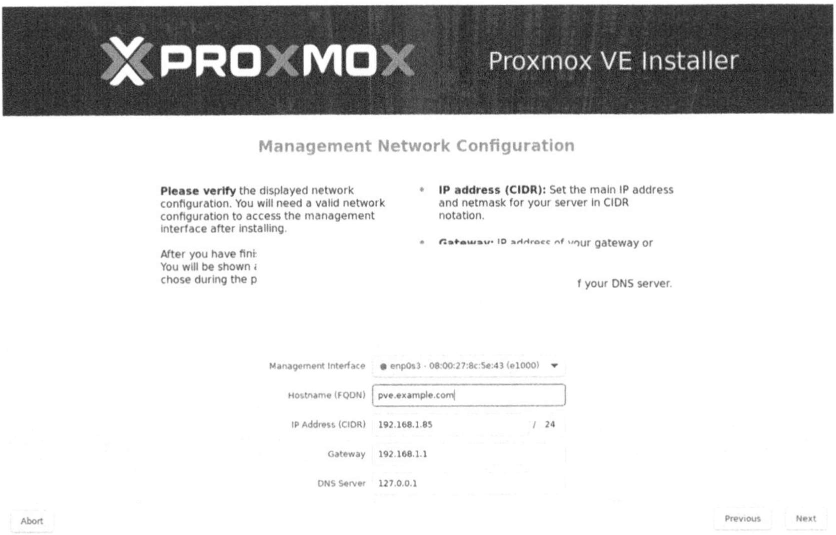

Figure 6-6. *Installing Proxmox. IP settings*

CHAPTER 6 PROXMOX AND OPEN VSWITCH

Finally, we can see a brief summary of the settings that will be used during the installation (Figure 6-7).

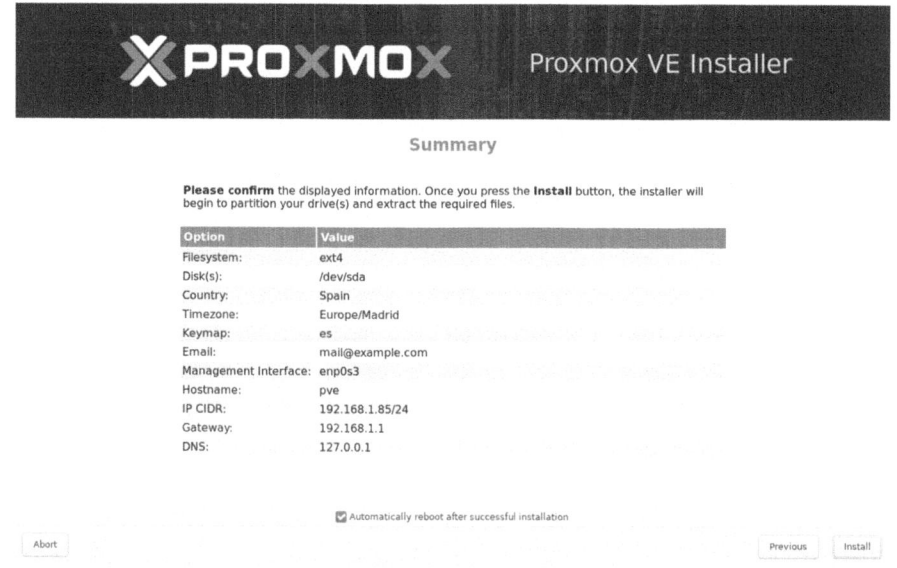

Figure 6-7. Installing Proxmox. Summary

The installation will take a few minutes to complete. After that, we can log in to the console (Figure 6-8).

CHAPTER 6   PROXMOX AND OPEN VSWITCH

Figure 6-8. Proxmox server console

From the server console, we can perform some basic actions like getting the Proxmox version or listing the Proxmox nodes. Currently we only have one Proxmox node, but Proxmox can be installed in cluster.

root@pve:~# pveversion
pve-manager/8.2.2/9355359cd7afbae4 (running kernel: 6.8.4-2-pve)

root@pve:~# pvesh get nodes

node	status	cpu	level	maxcpu	maxmem	mem
ssl_fingerprint						
pve	online	0.89%		2	3.83 GiB	1.12 GiB
F9:15:38:0F:74:1D:F6:01:ED:4C:1B:94:A4:95:AD:69:B4:AF:69:39:6B:03:1						

root@pve:~#

CHAPTER 6   PROXMOX AND OPEN VSWITCH

However, the preferred way to administer Proxmox is through the web console. We can see the exact URL on the server console banner. In our example, it is located at http://192.168.1.85:8006. We'll access using the credentials specified during the installation (Figure 6-9).

Figure 6-9. *Accessing Proxmox web interface*

Once authenticated, we can see the main page (Figure 6-10).

299

CHAPTER 6 PROXMOX AND OPEN VSWITCH

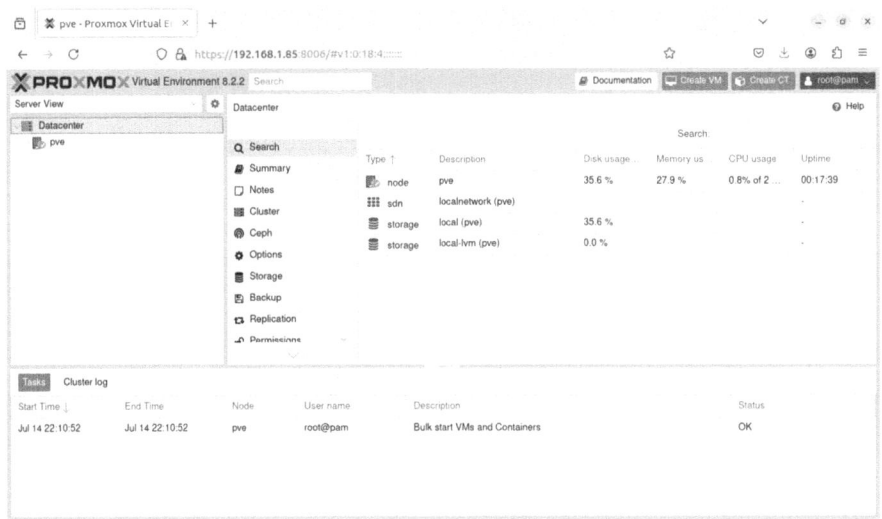

Figure 6-10. *Proxmox web interface*

A deep knowledge of Proxmox is not required for the LPIC-3 305 exam, so we'll just see a very simple example of how to create a virtual machine. We'll use the Alpine ISO file we downloaded when we studied Xen. We need to upload the ISO file to the local storage of Proxmox. We'll click on the Proxmox node, pve in our case, and then select "storage local (pve)" (Figure 6-11).

CHAPTER 6 PROXMOX AND OPEN VSWITCH

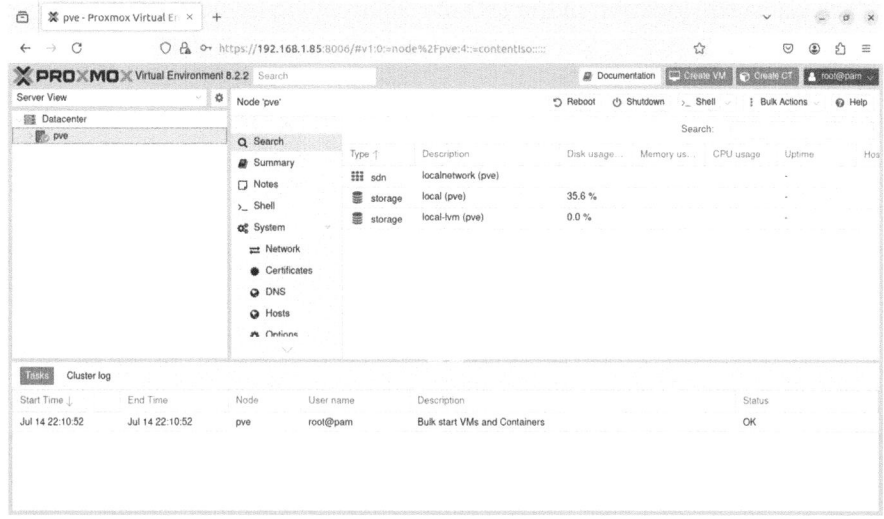

Figure 6-11. *Proxmox storage*

In the new window (Figure 6-12), we'll click "ISO Images" and then the "Upload" button.

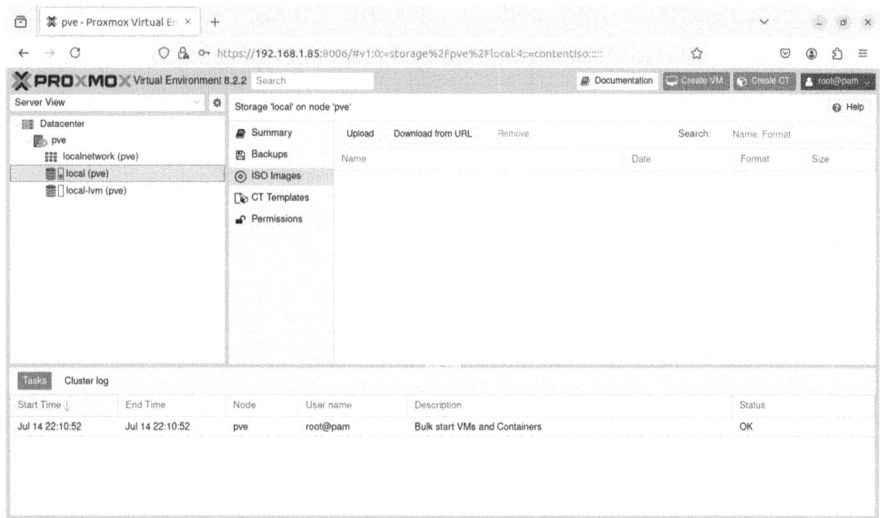

Figure 6-12. *Storing an ISO file*

CHAPTER 6   PROXMOX AND OPEN VSWITCH

We select the location of the ISO file (Figure 6-13). And click the "Upload" button.

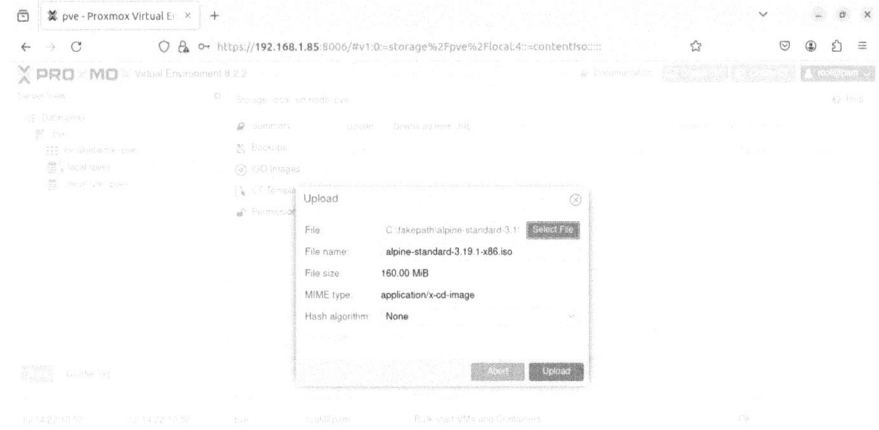

Figure 6-13. *Uploading an ISO file*

Once the ISO file is uploaded, we click the "Create VM" button, on the top of the window. Then we need to specify the needed parameters for the new VM. In the "General" tab (Figure 6-14), we select the node – in our case, we only have one node – and the VM ID; in this case, we accept the default values and click "Next".

CHAPTER 6　PROXMOX AND OPEN VSWITCH

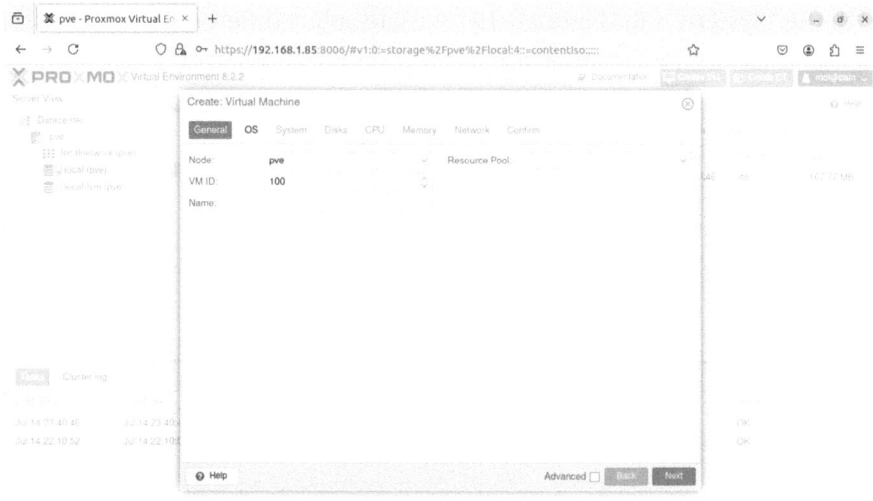

Figure 6-14. Creating a VM. General tab

In the "OS" tab (Figure 6-15), we'll select the ISO file we uploaded previously and click "Next".

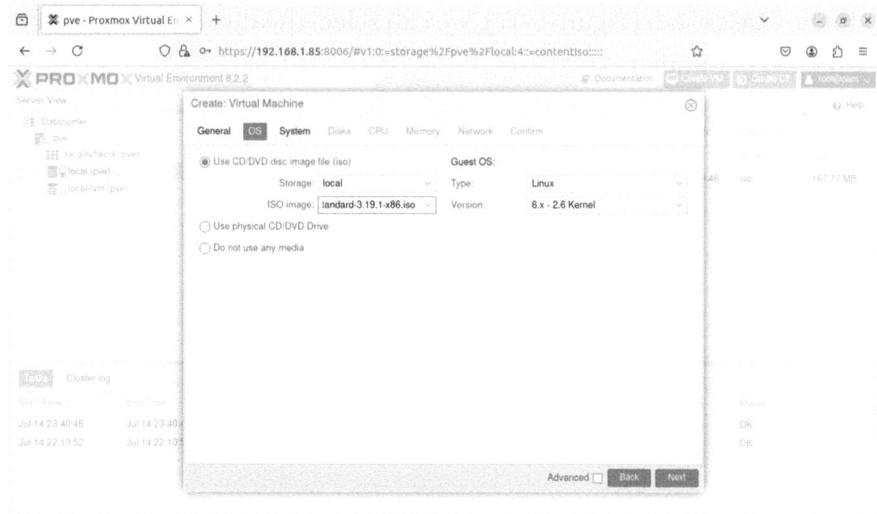

Figure 6-15. Creating a VM. OS tab

CHAPTER 6   PROXMOX AND OPEN VSWITCH

In the "System" tab (Figure 6-16), we can select different options for the Graphic card, SCSI Controller, etc.

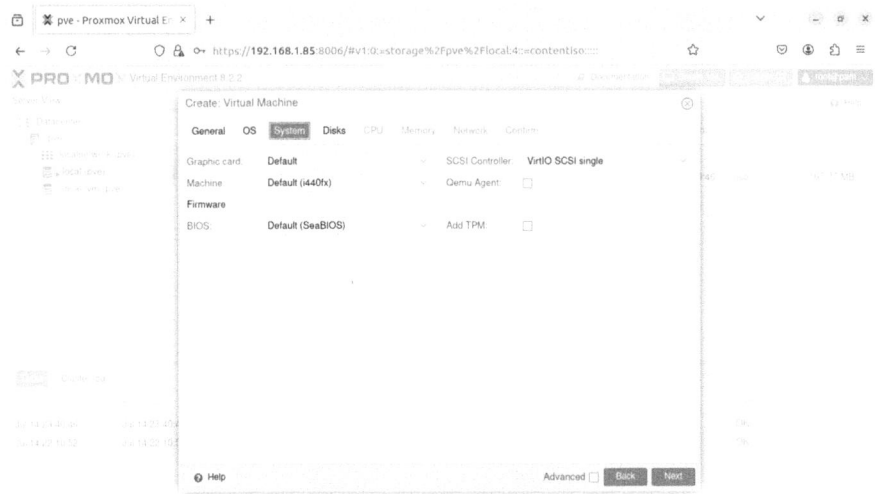

Figure 6-16. *Creating a VM. System tab*

In the "Disks" tab (Figure 6-17), we can select the disk size and other disk-related parameters.

CHAPTER 6   PROXMOX AND OPEN VSWITCH

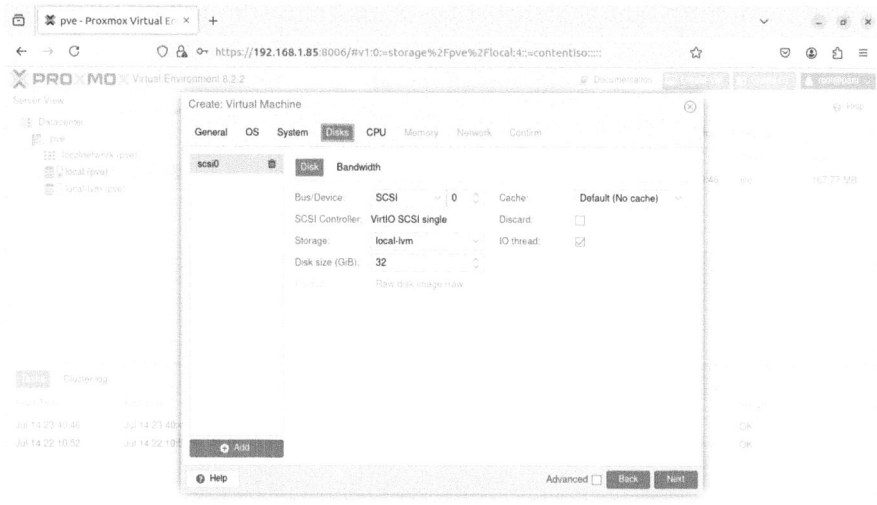

Figure 6-17. Creating a VM. Disks tab

In the "CPU" tab (Figure 6-18), we select the number of CPUs.

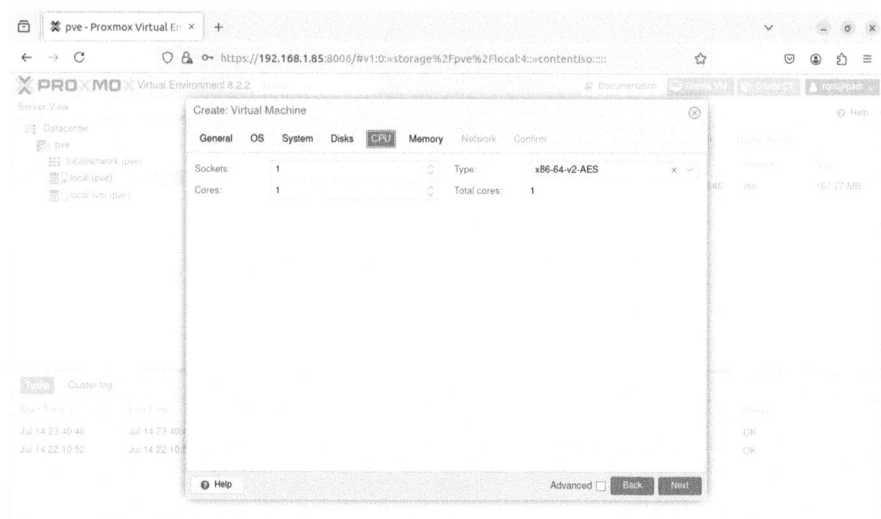

Figure 6-18. Creating a VM. CPU tab

305

CHAPTER 6   PROXMOX AND OPEN VSWITCH

In the "Memory" tab (Figure 6-19), we assign the desired amount of memory.

Figure 6-19. Creating a VM. Memory tab

Finally, in the "Network" tab (Figure 6-20), we can set some network-related settings, and in the "Confirm" tab (Figure 6-21), we can see a summary. We click "Finish".

CHAPTER 6   PROXMOX AND OPEN VSWITCH

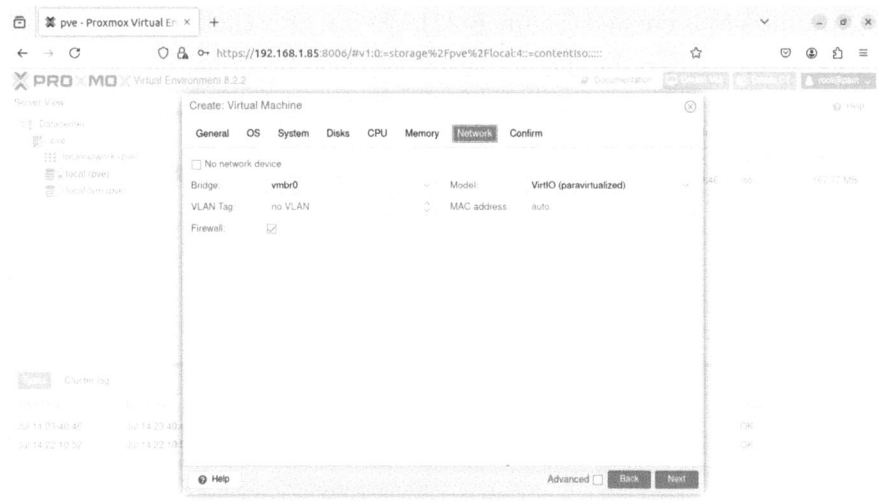

Figure 6-20.   *Creating a VM. Network tab*

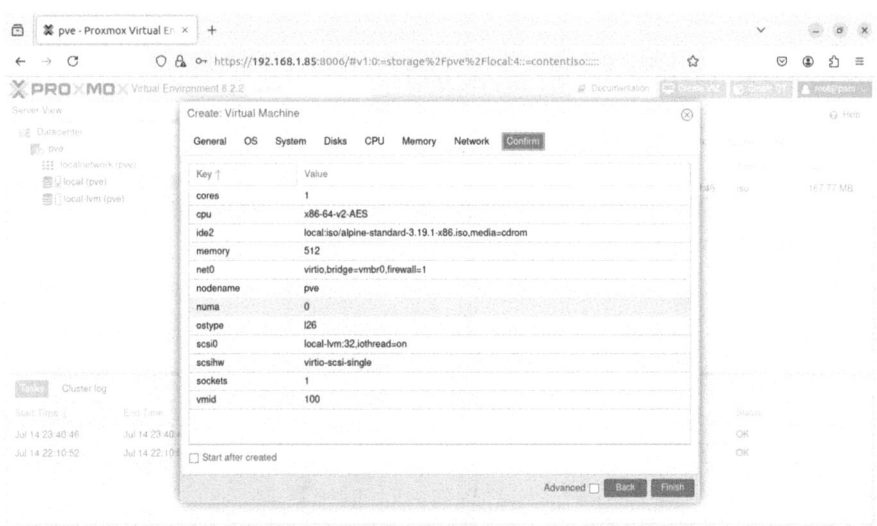

Figure 6-21.   *Creating a VM. Confirm tab*

307

CHAPTER 6   PROXMOX AND OPEN VSWITCH

Now the VM is created (Figure 6-22). We can now click the "Start" button. We can access the server console by clicking "Console" (Figure 6-23).

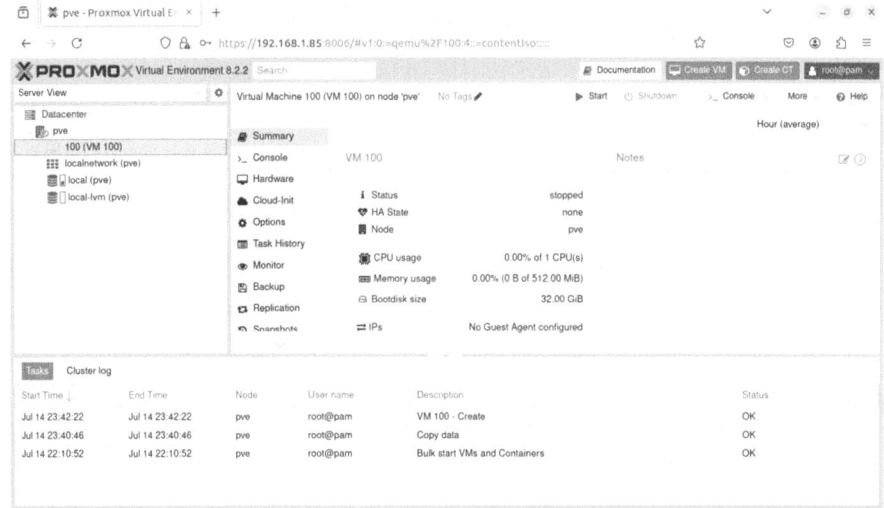

Figure 6-22.   Virtual machine created

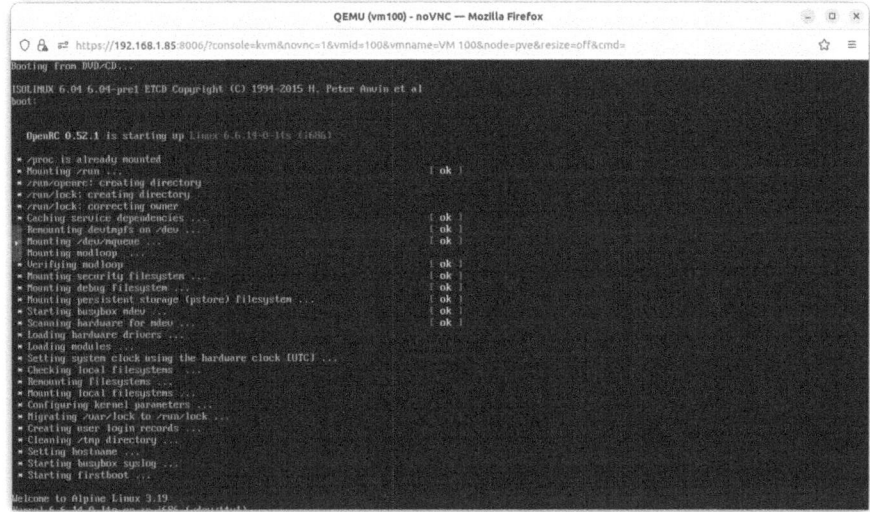

Figure 6-23.   Accessing the VM console

308

systemd-machined

According to the man page, "**systemd-machined** is a system service that keeps track of locally running virtual machines and containers." That is, it is a lightweight VM and container manager.

systemd-machined is actually a **systemd** service. We can check its status as we'd do with any other service.

```
antonio@antonio-Laptop:~$ systemctl status systemd-machined
• systemd-machined.service - Virtual Machine and Container
Registration Service
     Loaded: loaded (/lib/systemd/system/systemd-machined.
     service; static)
     Active: active (running) since Mon 2024-07-15 16:41:04
     CEST; 1h 37min ago
       Docs: man:systemd-machined.service(8)
             man:org.freedesktop.machine1(5)
   Main PID: 855 (systemd-machine)
     Status: "Processing requests..."
      Tasks: 1 (limit: 18712)
     Memory: 1.3M
        CPU: 278ms
     CGroup: /system.slice/systemd-machined.service
             └─855 /lib/systemd/systemd-machined
```

We can manage VMs and containers registered in **systemd-machined** using the **machinectl** command. Of course, right now we don't have any registered VM or container.

```
antonio@antonio-Laptop:~$ machinectl list
No machines.
```

Chapter 6   Proxmox and Open vSwitch

We need to create some machines. Similarly to what happened with Proxmox, we're only expected to have some basic knowledge of **systemd-machined**, so we won't get into much detail. We'll just see an easy example present in the man page of **machinectl**.

In this example, we'll download an Ubuntu image specifically crafted for being used in cloud environments. Then we'll use **systemd-nspawn** to open a shell in the image we just downloaded.

```
antonio@antonio-Laptop:~/VMs$ sudo machinectl pull-tar https://
cloud-images.ubuntu.com/trusty/current/trusty-server-cloudimg-
amd64-root.tar.gz
Enqueued transfer job 1. Press C-c to continue download in
background.
Pulling 'https://cloud-images.ubuntu.com/trusty/current/trusty-
server-
cloudimg-amd64-root.tar.gz', saving as 'trusty-server-
cloudimg-amd64-root'.
Downloading 186.4M for https://cloud-images.ubuntu.com/trusty/
current/trusty-server-cloudimg-amd64-root.tar.gz.
.
.
.
Created new local image 'trusty-server-cloudimg-amd64-root'.
Operation completed successfully.
Exiting.
```

Now we can launch a shell with **systemd-nspawn**.

```
antonio@antonio-Laptop:~/VMs$ sudo systemd-nspawn -M trusty-
server-cloudimg-amd64-root
[sudo] password for antonio:
Spawning container trusty-server-cloudimg-amd64-root on /var/
lib/machines/trusty-server-cloudimg-amd64-root.
```

```
Press ^] three times within 1s to kill container.
root@trusty-server-cloudimg-amd64-root:~#
```

In the host system, we can use **machinectl** again to list the machines; now we'll see one entry.

```
antonio@antonio-HP-Laptop-15s-fq1xxx:~/VMs$ machinectl list
MACHINE                          CLASS     SERVICE        OS
VERSION ADDRESSES
trusty-server-cloudimg-amd64-root container systemd-nspawn
ubuntu 14.04   -

1 machines listed.
```

As usual we can execute commands in the guest in the same way as if we were working in a physical machine.

```
root@trusty-server-cloudimg-amd64-root:~# hostname
trusty-server-cloudimg-amd64-root
```

We mentioned in the beginning of this section that systemd-machined can manage virtual machines as well as containers. The system we're working with now is not a full virtual machine, but a container.

We'll begin to study containers in the next chapter, but for now, we'll make a few remarks.

As opposed to a virtual machine, a container doesn't need to emulate hardware, as it relies on the characteristics of the kernel to provide isolation to the container. In fact, if we list the disks in our guest system, we'll see nothing.

```
root@trusty-server-cloudimg-amd64-root:~# fdisk -l
root@trusty-server-cloudimg-amd64-root:~#
```

CHAPTER 6 PROXMOX AND OPEN VSWITCH

All containers execute the same kernel as the host; we can check it by comparing the output of the uname command in guest and host.

```
root@trusty-server-cloudimg-amd64-root:~# uname -a
Linux trusty-server-cloudimg-amd64-root 6.5.0-44-generic
#44~22.04.1-Ubuntu SMP PREEMPT_DYNAMIC Tue Jun 18 14:36:16
UTC 2 x86_64 x86_64 x86_64 GNU/Linux
```

```
antonio@antonio-Laptop:~/VMs$ uname -a
Linux antonio-HP-Laptop-15s-fq1xxx 6.5.0-44-generic
#44~22.04.1-Ubuntu SMP PREEMPT_DYNAMIC Tue Jun 18 14:36:16
UTC 2 x86_64 x86_64 x86_64 GNU/Linux
```

The kernel feature used to isolate containers is the namespaces; we'll see this in detail in the upcoming chapter. We can use namespaces to isolate process IDs, mount points, networks, etc. We can use all these namespaces or just some of them. For instance, our current guest is not using an isolated network namespace; if we list the network interfaces from the guest, we'll see all the network interfaces defined in the host.

```
root@trusty-server-cloudimg-amd64-root:~# ip link
1: lo: <LOOPBACK,UP,LOWER_UP> mtu 65536 qdisc noqueue state UNKNOWN mode DEFAULT group default qlen 1000
    link/loopback 00:00:00:00:00:00 brd 00:00:00:00:00:00
2: wlo1: <BROADCAST,MULTICAST,UP,LOWER_UP> mtu 1500 qdisc noqueue state UP mode DORMANT group default qlen 1000
    link/ether b0:68:e6:14:aa:b3 brd ff:ff:ff:ff:ff:ff
```

.
.
.

After working with the guest, we can exit the command shell.

```
root@trusty-server-cloudimg-amd64-root:~# exit
logout
Container trusty-server-cloudimg-amd64-root exited
successfully.
```

Open vSwitch

Open vSwitch is an open source implementation of a distributed multilayer virtual switch. That means that it can work at different layers of the OSI model and supports distribution across several hosts.

Open vSwitch is an advanced tool that offers many possibilities. This advanced knowledge is well beyond the scope of this book and the LPIC-3 305 exam, which only requires a basic knowledge of the tool.

We'll begin by installing the software.

```
antonio@antonio-HP-Laptop-15s-fq1xxx:~$ sudo apt install
openvswitch-switch
```

After the installation is complete, we'll have two new related services installed.

```
antonio@antonio-HP-Laptop-15s-fq1xxx:~$ systemctl status ovs-vswitchd.service
• ovs-vswitchd.service - Open vSwitch Forwarding Unit
    Loaded: loaded (/lib/systemd/system/ovs-vswitchd.
    service; static)
    Active: active (running) since Mon 2024-07-15 21:43:47
    CEST; 59min ago
  Main PID: 28313 (ovs-vswitchd)
     Tasks: 1 (limit: 18712)
```

CHAPTER 6   PROXMOX AND OPEN VSWITCH

      Memory: 3.1M
         CPU: 77ms
      CGroup: /system.slice/ovs-vswitchd.service
              └─28313 ovs-vswitchd unix:/var/run/openvswitch/
db.sock -vconsole:emer -vsyslog:err -vfile:info --mlockall
--no-chdir ->

jul 15 21:43:47 antonio-HP-Laptop-15s-fq1xxx systemd[1]:
Starting Open vSwitch Forwarding Unit...

antonio@antonio-HP-Laptop-15s-fq1xxx:~$ systemctl status ovsdb-
server.service
• ovsdb-server.service - Open vSwitch Database Unit
     Loaded: loaded (/lib/systemd/system/ovsdb-server.
     service; static)
     Active: active (running) since Mon 2024-07-15 21:43:47
     CEST; 59min ago
   Main PID: 28249 (ovsdb-server)
      Tasks: 1 (limit: 18712)
     Memory: 2.2M
        CPU: 294ms
     CGroup: /system.slice/ovsdb-server.service
             └─28249 ovsdb-server /etc/openvswitch/
             conf.db -vconsole:emer -vsyslog:err
             -vfile:info --remote=punix:/var/run/openvswi>

jul 15 21:43:47 antonio-HP-Laptop-15s-fq1xxx systemd[1]:
Starting Open vSwitch Database Unit...

   The first one, **ovs-vswitchd**, implements the switch itself, while the second one, **ovsdb-server**, is a lightweight database that stores Open vSwitch configuration data.

CHAPTER 6   PROXMOX AND OPEN VSWITCH

Let's begin to interact with the switch. We can show some basic information with **ovs-vsctl** show.

```
antonio@antonio-Laptop:~$ sudo ovs-vsctl show
b060c9ea-8061-430c-82aa-b22968c68e95
    ovs_version: "2.17.9"
```

To start working, we need to define a new bridge inside Open vSwitch.

```
antonio@antonio-Laptop:~$ sudo ovs-vsctl add-br osbr0
```

If we execute **ovs-vsctl show** again, we'll see the newly created bridge.

```
antonio@antonio-HP-Laptop-15s-fq1xxx:~$ sudo ovs-vsctl show
b060c9ea-8061-430c-82aa-b22968c68e95
    Bridge osbr0
        Port osbr0
            Interface osbr0
                type: internal
    ovs_version: "2.17.9"
```

Now we'll associate a couple of local network interfaces to that bridge. For this, we can use TUN/TAP interfaces, which we already studied in Chapter 2.

```
antonio@antonio-Laptop:~$ sudo tunctl
Set 'tap0' persistent and owned by uid 0
antonio@antonio-Laptop:~$ sudo tunctl
Set 'tap1' persistent and owned by uid 0
antonio@antonio-Laptop:~$
```

And we add these two interfaces to the bridge.

```
antonio@antonio-Laptop:~$ sudo ovs-vsctl add-port osbr0 tap0
antonio@antonio-Laptop:~$ sudo ovs-vsctl add-port osbr0 tap1
```

CHAPTER 6 PROXMOX AND OPEN VSWITCH

We check that our switch now lists these two interfaces.

```
antonio@antonio-Laptop:~$ sudo ovs-vsctl show
b060c9ea-8061-430c-82aa-b22968c68e95
    Bridge osbr0
        Port tap0
            Interface tap0
        Port tap1
            Interface tap1
        Port osbr0
            Interface osbr0
                type: internal
    ovs_version: "2.17.9"
```

Another useful command is **ovs-appctl fdb/show**, which lists the devices connected to our switch.

```
antonio@antonio-Laptop:~$ sudo ovs-appctl fdb/show osbr0
 port  VLAN  MAC                 Age
```

Of course, in this present moment, we don't have any device attached. To do a simple test, we'll connect a couple of virtual machines. For convenience, we'll use two VirtualBox VMs. We'll edit the network settings of these two machines to use the interfaces tap0 and tap1 that we created previously (Figures 6-24 and 6-25).

CHAPTER 6   PROXMOX AND OPEN VSWITCH

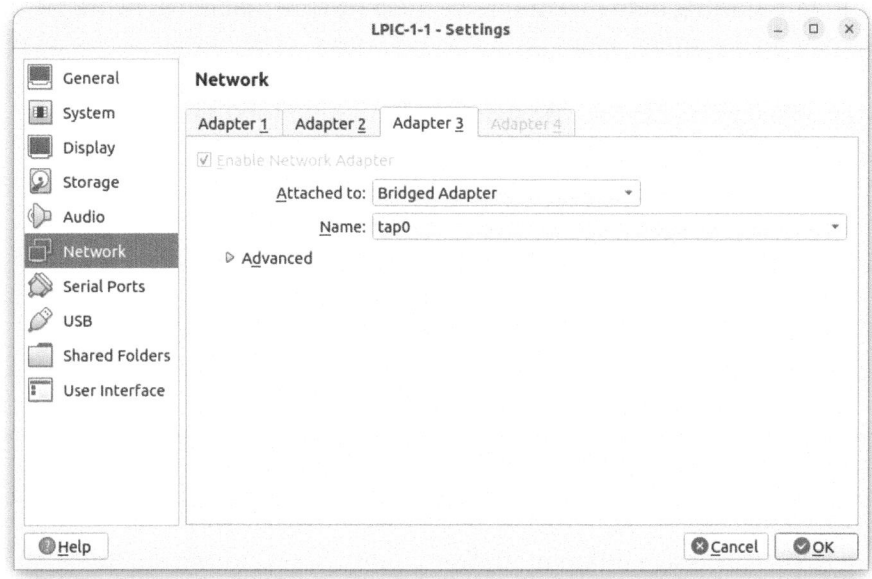

Figure 6-24. Connecting VM1 to Open vSwitch

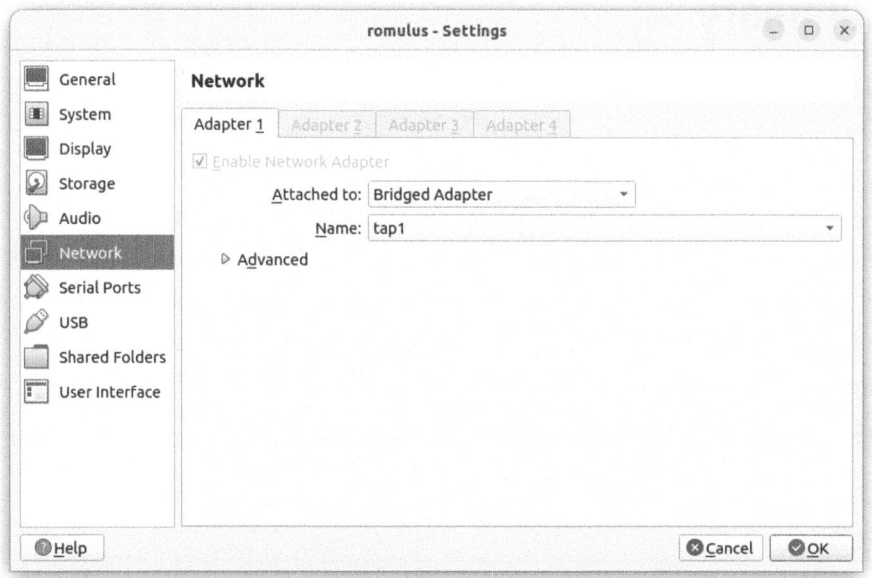

Figure 6-25. Connecting VM2 to Open vSwitch

Before starting both machines, we must be sure that the network interfaces tap0 and tap1 are up.

```
antonio@antonio-Laptop:~$ sudo ip link set tap0 up
antonio@antonio-Laptop:~$ sudo ip link set tap1 up
```

After starting the two machines, we'll see their MAC addresses connected to our switch.

```
antonio@antonio-Laptop:~$ sudo ovs-appctl fdb/show osbr0
 port  VLAN  MAC                Age
    1     0  08:00:27:ca:75:59   5
    2     0  08:00:27:bb:da:83   1
```

From this moment on, we can use Open vSwitch as any other normal switch. We can assign different VLANs, control flows, and so on. But all that is beyond the scope of this book.

Summary

In this brief chapter, we saw interesting tools that we hadn't seen so far. These tools are not the main focus of the 305 exam, but they can become very handy in many circumstances and it is good to know them.

The first tool we studied is **Proxmox**, which provides an enterprise-ready virtualization solution. The second one, **systemd-machined**, is quite the opposite as it is a lightweight virtual machine and container manager. This can be useful when we need to deploy VMs/containers locally. Finally, we touched briefly **Open vSwitch**; this virtual switch provides far better capabilities than the locally created bridges.

CHAPTER 7

Container Virtualization Concepts

In this chapter, we'll cover the following concepts:

- Understand the concepts of system and application container
- Understand and analyze kernel namespaces
- Understand and analyze control groups
- Understand and analyze capabilities
- Understand the role of seccomp, SELinux, and AppArmor for container virtualization

We will also be introduced to the following terms and utilities:
nsenter, **unshare**, **ip**, **capsh**, */sys/fs/cgroups*, */proc/[0-9]+/ns*, and */proc/[0-9]+/status*.

CHAPTER 7   CONTAINER VIRTUALIZATION CONCEPTS

System Containers and Application Containers

A container is basically a series of system processes isolated. It relies on a series of characteristics of the host operating system to provide this isolation, mainly namespaces and cgroups. In some documents, containerization is also known as OS-level virtualization.

A container that runs a full OS is a system container.

An application container, on the other hand, is a minimalistic stand-alone package that contains everything that is needed to run a certain application, and nothing more.

Kernel Namespaces

Linux namespaces are a feature of the Linux kernel that partitions kernel resources. That way a process or a group of processes sees a set of resources, while another process or group of processes sees a different set of resources. There are many kinds of namespaces, depending on the kind of resource isolated. And more are eventually added. Some of them are these:

- Mount
- Process ID (pid)
- Network (net)
- Inter-process communication (ipc)
- UTS (Unix time sharing)
- User ID (user)
- cgroup namespace
- Time space

CHAPTER 7   CONTAINER VIRTUALIZATION CONCEPTS

In order to list the namespaces currently in use in our system, we can use the **lsns** command.

```
antonio@antonio-Laptop:~$ sudo lsns
NS TYPE              NPROCS  PID USER  COMMAND
4026531834 time      303     1   root  /sbin/init splash
4026531835 cgroup    303     1   root  /sbin/init splash
4026531836 pid       304     1   root  /sbin/init splash
4026531837 user      274     1   root  /sbin/init splash
4026531838 uts       299     1   root  /sbin/init splash
4026531839 ipc       275     1   root  /sbin/init splash
4026531840 net       273     1   root  /sbin/init splash
4026531841 mnt       250     1   root  /sbin/init splash
4026531862 mnt       1       62  root  kdevtmpfs
4026532322 mnt       1       290 root  /lib/systemd/systemd-udevd
4026532323 uts       1       290 root  /lib/systemd/systemd-udevd
.
.
.
```

We can see a long listing with different types of namespaces: time, cgroup, pid, etc. If we want to be more specific, we can list the namespaces associated to a certain pid.

For instance, we can obtain the PID of the current shell session.

```
antonio@antonio-Laptop:~$ echo $$
33824
```

CHAPTER 7 CONTAINER VIRTUALIZATION CONCEPTS

After that, we can list the namespaces associated with this process.

```
antonio@antonio-Laptop:~$ lsns -p $$
    NS TYPE         NPROCS    PID USER    COMMAND
4026531834 time        129   3201 antonio /lib/systemd/systemd --user
4026531835 cgroup      129   3201 antonio /lib/systemd/systemd --user
4026531836 pid         130   3201 antonio /lib/systemd/systemd --user
4026531837 user        101   3201 antonio /lib/systemd/systemd --user
4026531838 uts         129   3201 antonio /lib/systemd/systemd --user
4026531839 ipc         101   3201 antonio /lib/systemd/systemd --user
4026531840 net         101   3201 antonio /lib/systemd/systemd --user
4026531841 mnt          92   3201 antonio /lib/systemd/systemd --user
```

We can also obtain the same information by listing the contents of the ns subfolder in the corresponding */proc* subtree.

```
antonio@antonio-Laptop:~$ ls -l /proc/$$/ns
total 0
lrwxrwxrwx 1 antonio antonio 0 sep 22 21:27 cgroup ->
'cgroup:[4026531835]'
lrwxrwxrwx 1 antonio antonio 0 sep 22 21:27 ipc ->
'ipc:[4026531839]'
lrwxrwxrwx 1 antonio antonio 0 sep 22 21:27 mnt ->
'mnt:[4026531841]'
lrwxrwxrwx 1 antonio antonio 0 sep 22 21:27 net ->
'net:[4026531840]'
lrwxrwxrwx 1 antonio antonio 0 sep 22 21:27 pid ->
'pid:[4026531836]'
lrwxrwxrwx 1 antonio antonio 0 sep 22 21:44 pid_for_children ->
'pid:[4026531836]'
lrwxrwxrwx 1 antonio antonio 0 sep 22 21:27 time ->
'time:[4026531834]'
lrwxrwxrwx 1 antonio antonio 0 sep 22 21:44 time_for_children
-> 'time:[4026531834]'
```

```
lrwxrwxrwx 1 antonio antonio 0 sep 22 21:27 user ->
'user:[4026531837]'
lrwxrwxrwx 1 antonio antonio 0 sep 22 21:27 uts ->
'uts:[4026531838]'
```

Mount Namespaces

Let's see now an example of mount namespaces. To work with namespaces, we'll use the **unshare** command. This command runs a program with some namespaces unshared from the parent. If we look at the contextual help, we'll see there are different options to work with different namespaces.

antonio@antonio-Laptop:~$ unshare --help

Usage:
 unshare [options] [<program> [<argument>...]]

Run a program with some namespaces unshared from the parent.

```
Options:
 -m, --mount[=<file>]      unshare mounts namespace
 -u, --uts[=<file>]        unshare UTS namespace (hostname etc)
 -i, --ipc[=<file>]        unshare System V IPC namespace
 -n, --net[=<file>]        unshare network namespace
 -p, --pid[=<file>]        unshare pid namespace
 -U, --user[=<file>]       unshare user namespace
 -C, --cgroup[=<file>]     unshare cgroup namespace
 -T, --time[=<file>]       unshare time namespace
 .
 .
 .
```

CHAPTER 7   CONTAINER VIRTUALIZATION CONCEPTS

In this example, we will execute a bash shell with the mount namespace unshared from the parent.

```
antonio@antonio-Laptop:~$ sudo unshare -m bash
root@antonio-Laptop:/home/antonio#
```

We can then list the namespaces associated to the newly created bash shell.

```
root@antonio-Laptop:/home/antonio# echo $$
57447
root@antonio-HP-Laptop-15s-fq1xxx:/home/antonio# lsns -p $$
        NS TYPE       NPROCS  PID   USER  COMMAND
4026531834 time         313    1    root  /sbin/init splash
4026531835 cgroup       313    1    root  /sbin/init splash
4026531836 pid          314    1    root  /sbin/init splash
4026531837 user         282    1    root  /sbin/init splash
4026531838 uts          309    1    root  /sbin/init splash
4026531839 ipc          283    1    root  /sbin/init splash
4026531840 net          281    1    root  /sbin/init splash
4026533562 mnt            2       57447  root  bash
root@antonio-HP-Laptop-15s-fq1xxx:/home/antonio#
```

As we can see, the mount namespace is associated to the bash shell itself, and it is not shared with the parent. We can see the difference by opening a new shell and executing **lsns** again.

```
antonio@antonio-Laptop:~$ lsns -p $$
        NS TYPE       NPROCS  PID   USER    COMMAND
4026531834 time         135   3201  antonio /lib/systemd/systemd --user
4026531835 cgroup       135   3201  antonio /lib/systemd/systemd --user
4026531836 pid          136   3201  antonio /lib/systemd/systemd --user
4026531837 user         105   3201  antonio /lib/systemd/systemd --user
4026531838 uts          135   3201  antonio /lib/systemd/systemd --user
```

CHAPTER 7   CONTAINER VIRTUALIZATION CONCEPTS

```
4026531839 ipc      105    3201 antonio /lib/systemd/systemd --user
4026531840 net      105    3201 antonio /lib/systemd/systemd --user
4026531841 mnt      96     3201 antonio /lib/systemd/systemd -user
```

If we execute **df -h** in our shell with unshared mount namespace, we see that we can see the information about the mounted filesystems in the host. This is because this information is propagated by default from the parent mount namespace.

```
root@antonio-Laptop:/home/antonio# df -h
Filesystem      Size  Used  Avail Use% Mounted on
/dev/nvme0n1p5  787G  407G  341G  55%  /
tmpfs           7,7G  0     7,7G  0%   /dev/shm
tmpfs           1,6G  2,2M  1,6G  1%   /run
tmpfs           5,0M  4,0K  5,0M  1%   /run/lock
tmpfs           7,7G  0     7,7G  0%   /run/qemu
tmpfs           1,6G  1,7M  1,6G  1%   /run/user/1000
/dev/nvme0n1p1  256M  84M   173M  33%  /boot/efi
```

However, if we create a new mount point in the shell with the isolated mount namespace, the result will be different. In this case, we can see the new mount point from the shell in which it was created.

```
root@antonio-Laptop:/home/antonio# mount -t tmpfs tmpfs /mnt/
root@antonio-Laptop:/home/antonio# df -h
Filesystem      Size  Used  Avail Use% Mounted on
/dev/nvme0n1p5  787G  407G  340G  55%  /
tmpfs           7,7G  0     7,7G  0%   /dev/shm
tmpfs           1,6G  2,2M  1,6G  1%   /run
tmpfs           5,0M  4,0K  5,0M  1%   /run/lock
tmpfs           7,7G  0     7,7G  0%   /run/qemu
tmpfs           1,6G  1,7M  1,6G  1%   /run/user/1000
```

CHAPTER 7 CONTAINER VIRTUALIZATION CONCEPTS

```
/dev/nvme0n1p1   256M   84M   173M  33%  /boot/efi
tmpfs            7,7G   0     7,7G  0%   /mnt
root@antonio-Laptop:/home/antonio#
```

However, if we execute **df** from a different shell, we won't see the mount point we just created.

```
antonio@antonio-Laptop:~$ df -h
Filesystem       Size   Used  Avail Use% Mounted on
tmpfs            1,6G   2,2M  1,6G  1%   /run
/dev/nvme0n1p5   787G   407G  340G  55%  /
tmpfs            7,7G   0     7,7G  0%   /dev/shm
tmpfs            5,0M   4,0K  5,0M  1%   /run/lock
tmpfs            7,7G   0     7,7G  0%   /run/qemu
/dev/nvme0n1p1   256M   84M   173M  33%  /boot/efi
tmpfs            1,6G   1,7M  1,6G  1%   /run/user/1000
```

We can work normally with the new mount point in the shell in which it was created.

```
root@antonio-Laptop:/home/antonio# echo hello > /mnt/my_file.txt
root@antonio-Laptop:/home/antonio# cat /mnt/my_file.txt
hello
root@antonio-Laptop:/home/antonio#
```

But this mount point is completely isolated from other shells.

```
antonio@antonio-Laptop:~$ cat /mnt/my_file.txt
cat: /mnt/my_file.txt: No such file or directory
```

When we're done, we can just unmount the mount point and exit the shell.

CHAPTER 7 CONTAINER VIRTUALIZATION CONCEPTS

Process Namespaces

Now we're going to see an example of process namespaces. We'll use the **unshare** command again.

This time we must use the "-p" parameter and also the "-f" to perform a fork.

```
antonio@antonio-Laptop:~$ sudo unshare -p -f bash
root@antonio-Laptop:/home/antonio#
```

If we list the processes with **ps**, we'll see all the processes in the system and not only those of its own process namespace. This is because it can access the */proc* tree.

```
root@antonio-Laptop:/home/antonio# ps -ef
UID        PID   PPID  C STIME TTY       TIME CMD
root         1      0  0 jul18 ?     00:00:06 /sbin/
                                              init splash
root         2      0  0 jul18 ?     00:00:00 [kthreadd]
root         3      2  0 jul18 ?     00:00:00 [rcu_gp]
root         4      2  0 jul18 ?     00:00:00 [rcu_par_gp]
root         5      2  0 jul18 ?     00:00:00 [slub_
                                              flushwq]
root         6      2  0 jul18 ?     00:00:00 [netns]
root         8      2  0 jul18 ?     00:00:00 [kworker/
                                              0:0H-events_
                                              highpri]
.
.
.
```

To avoid this, we can mount the */proc* filesystem in the new shell.

```
root@antonio-Laptop:/home/antonio# mount -t proc proc /proc
```

If we execute ps again, we'll only see the processes inside the isolated shell.

```
root@antonio-Laptop:/home/antonio# ps -ef
UID        PID   PPID  C STIME TTY      TIME CMD
root         1      0  0 14:38 pts/5    00:00:00 bash
root        10      1  0 14:39 pts/5    00:00:00 ps -ef
```

Of course, this additional step could be performed automatically when launching the shell. To see it, we'll exit the shell.

```
root@antonio-Laptop:/home/antonio# exit
```

Then we'll execute **unshare** again, but adding the –mount-proc option this time.

```
antonio@antonio-Laptop:~$ sudo unshare --mount-proc -p -f bash
```

Now, if we execute **ps -ef**, we'll only see the processes from the current shell.

```
root@antonio-Laptop:/home/antonio# ps -ef
UID        PID   PPID  C STIME TTY      TIME CMD
root         1      0  0 14:47 pts/5    00:00:00 bash
root         8      1  0 14:47 pts/5    00:00:00 ps -ef
```

User Namespaces

User namespaces isolate security-related identifiers, like UIDs and GIDs. If we look at the help of the **unshare** command, we'll see that we must use the -u option to unshare the user namespace.

There is also an interesting option (-r). This option unshares the user namespace and maps the root user to the current user. We'll see an easy example. In this case, we don't need root permissions.

```
antonio@antonio-Laptop:~$ unshare -r bash
root@antonio-Laptop:~#
```

We check that in the new bash shell, we are actually identified as the root user, and we'll launch a process; in this example, we executed **sleep**.

```
root@antonio-Laptop:~# whoami
root
root@antonio-Laptop:~# sleep 60
```

If we search for the executing sleep process from another shell in the host, we'll see that the "real" user that it is executing is "antonio", a normal user instead of root.

```
antonio@antonio-Laptop:~$ ps -ef | grep sleep
antonio    14091   14055  0 15:54 pts/0    00:00:00 sleep 60
```

Combining Several Namespaces to Craft Our First "Container"

We have seen already some examples on how to use unshare to launch a shell with some isolated namespace(s). Now we'll see an example that is little more complicated.

We'll unshare the mount, user, and pid namespaces. We'll also mount the proc filesystem and map the root user to the current user and perform a fork of the bash shell we're invoking.

```
antonio@antonio-Laptop:~$ unshare -m -u -p -f -r --mount-proc bash
root@antonio-Laptop:~#
```

We can see that we have a separated pid tree.

```
root@antonio-Laptop:~# echo $$
1
root@antonio-Laptop:~# ps -ef
UID         PID   PPID  C STIME TTY       TIME CMD
root          1      0  0 20:30 pts/1  00:00:00 bash
root          7      1  0 21:44 pts/1  00:00:00 ps -ef
```

We also have isolated UIDs.

```
root@antonio-Laptop:~# id
uid=0(root) gid=0(root) groups=0(root),65534(nogroup)
```

We are using an isolated mount namespace too. As we did before, we can create a mount point that will be only accessible from the current shell.

```
root@antonio-Laptop:~# mount -t tmpfs tmpfs /mnt/mydata/
root@antonio-Laptop:~# df -h
Filesystem      Size  Used Avail Use% Mounted on
/dev/nvme0n1p5  787G  717G   31G  96% /
tmpfs           7,7G     0  7,7G   0% /dev/shm
tmpfs           1,6G  2,5M  1,6G   1% /run
tmpfs           5,0M  4,0K  5,0M   1% /run/lock
tmpfs           7,7G     0  7,7G   0% /run/qemu
tmpfs           1,6G  124K  1,6G   1% /run/user/1000
efivarfs        192K   77K  111K  41% /sys/firmware/efi/efivars
/dev/nvme0n1p1  256M   84M  173M  33% /boot/efi
tmpfs           7,7G     0  7,7G   0% /mnt/mydata
```

As we did in a previous example, we can create a simple file in the mount point we just created.

```
root@antonio-Laptop:~# echo test > /mnt/mydata/file.txt
```

CHAPTER 7   CONTAINER VIRTUALIZATION CONCEPTS

We can also change locally the hostname of our isolated container.

root@antonio-Laptop:~# hostname mercury
root@antonio-Laptop:~# hostname
mercury

This shell is already similar in many ways to a standard container, as we'll see when we begin to study LXC and Docker. We have isolated UIDs, PIDs, and mount points. Though it is true that we're still sharing other namespaces with the host.

Executing Commands in Different Namespaces

As we have already built a rudimentary container, we're going to introduce a new tool, **nsenter**. This command is used to execute programs in different namespaces.

If we look at the help, we'll see it is very easy to use this tool.

antonio@antonio-Laptop:~$ nsenter --help

Usage:
 nsenter [options] [<program> [<argument>...]]

Run a program with namespaces of other processes.

Options:
 -a, --all   enter all namespaces
 -t, --target <pid>   target process to get namespaces from
 -m, --mount[=<file>]   enter mount namespace
 -u, --uts[=<file>]   enter UTS namespace (hostname etc)
 .
 .
 .

331

CHAPTER 7   CONTAINER VIRTUALIZATION CONCEPTS

To see an example, we need to locate the PID of the "isolated" bash shell we have created previously.

```
antonio@antonio-Laptop:~$ ps -ef | grep bash
antonio     6350    6327  0 14:56 pts/0    00:00:00 bash
antonio    14055    6350  0 15:53 pts/0    00:00:00 bash
antonio    14092    6327  0 15:54 pts/1    00:00:00 bash
antonio    24549   14092  0 20:30 pts/1    00:00:00 unshare
                                                    -m -u -p -f
                                                    -r --mount-
                                                    proc bash
antonio    24550   24549  0 20:30 pts/1    00:00:00 bash
antonio    29602    6327  0 22:08 pts/2    00:00:00 bash
```

In this case, that PID is 24549; we'll use nsenter to enter all namespaces associated with the process with PID 24549.

```
antonio@antonio-Laptop:~$ sudo nsenter -a -t 24549
-bash: /root/.bash_profile: Permission denied
root@mercury:/#
```

We have now access to the isolated shell. From now on, we can get the hostname of the container, which we previously changed. We can also retrieve the contents of the file we created in */mnt/mydata* and so on.

```
root@mercury:/# hostname
mercury
root@mercury:/# cat /mnt/mydata/file.txt
test
```

When we're done, we can exit the shell.

```
root@mercury:/# exit
logout
-bash: /root/.bash_logout: Permission denied
```

Network Namespaces

Namespaces can also isolate networks. As we did previously with the other namespaces, we'll see an easy example.

First of all, we need to list the network namespaces. We can do it with **ip netns**.

antonio@antonio-Laptop:~$ sudo ip netns ls

Currently we don't have any additional network namespaces. We'll create one.

antonio@antonio-Laptop:~$ sudo ip netns add isolated_network
antonio@antonio-Laptop:~$ sudo ip netns ls
isolated_network

To establish communication between different network namespaces, we need virtual Ethernet devices (veth). These virtual Ethernet devices are always created in pairs to create a bridge.

antonio@antonio-Laptop:~$ sudo ip link add dev veth0 type veth peer name veth1

We check that both interfaces have been created.

antonio@antonio-Laptop:~$ ip link show veth0
16: veth0@veth1: <BROADCAST,MULTICAST,M-DOWN> mtu 1500 qdisc noop state DOWN mode DEFAULT group default qlen 1000
    link/ether ae:00:1a:3e:6a:0d brd ff:ff:ff:ff:ff:ff
antonio@antonio-Laptop:~$ ip link show veth1
15: veth1@veth0: <BROADCAST,MULTICAST,M-DOWN> mtu 1500 qdisc noop state DOWN mode DEFAULT group default qlen 1000
    link/ether 5e:d3:e6:0f:77:64 brd ff:ff:ff:ff:ff:ff

CHAPTER 7   CONTAINER VIRTUALIZATION CONCEPTS

One of the virtual Ethernet devices must be assigned to the isolated_ network namespace so that we can establish the communication between both network namespaces.

```
antonio@antonio-Laptop:~$ sudo ip link set veth1 netns
isolated_network
```

To check that the interface is now assigned to the new network namespaces, we try to list it in the default namespace.

```
antonio@antonio-Laptop:~$ ip link show veth1
Device "veth1" does not exist.
```

As expected, we don't see it. Now let's list it on the new network namespace. The way to execute network-related commands in a different network namespace is by using "ip netns exec" + network namespace + "the network command," like this:

```
antonio@antonio-Laptop:~$ sudo ip netns exec isolated_network
ip link show veth1
15: veth1@if16: <BROADCAST,MULTICAST> mtu 1500 qdisc noop state
DOWN mode DEFAULT group default qlen 1000
    link/ether 5e:d3:e6:0f:77:64 brd ff:ff:ff:ff:ff:ff link-
    netnsid 0
```

Now that we have each veth interface placed in a different network namespace, we must assign the corresponding IPs.

```
antonio@antonio-Laptop:~$ sudo ip netns exec isolated_network
ip address add dev veth1 10.7.7.1/24
```

```
antonio@antonio-Laptop:~$ sudo ip netns exec isolated_network
ip address show veth1
```

CHAPTER 7 CONTAINER VIRTUALIZATION CONCEPTS

```
15: veth1@if16: <BROADCAST,MULTICAST> mtu 1500 qdisc noop state
DOWN group default qlen 1000
    link/ether 5e:d3:e6:0f:77:64 brd ff:ff:ff:ff:ff:ff link-
    netnsid 0
    inet 10.7.7.1/24 scope global veth1
       valid_lft forever preferred_lft forever
```

The IP has been set, but the interface is down; we must set it up.

```
antonio@antonio-Laptop:~$ sudo ip netns exec isolated_network
ip link set veth1 up
```

```
antonio@antonio-Laptop:~$ sudo ip netns exec isolated_network
ip link show veth1
15: veth1@if16: <NO-CARRIER,BROADCAST,MULTICAST,UP> mtu 1500
qdisc noqueue state LOWERLAYERDOWN mode DEFAULT group default
qlen 1000
    link/ether 5e:d3:e6:0f:77:64 brd ff:ff:ff:ff:ff:ff link-
    netnsid 0
```

The state of the veth is now LOWERLAYERDOWN, but this is normal because its peer is not ready yet. We'll set it up now.

```
antonio@antonio-Laptop:~$ sudo ip address add dev veth0
10.7.7.2/24
antonio@antonio-Laptop:~$ sudo ip link set veth0 up
antonio@antonio-Laptop:~$ sudo ip link show veth0
16: veth0@if15: <BROADCAST,MULTICAST,UP,LOWER_UP> mtu 1500
qdisc noqueue state UP mode DEFAULT group default qlen 1000
    link/ether ae:00:1a:3e:6a:0d brd ff:ff:ff:ff:ff:ff link-
    netns isolated_network
```

Now the link is finally up.

```
antonio@antonio-Laptop:~$ sudo ip netns exec isolated_network
ip link show veth1
15: veth1@if16: <BROADCAST,MULTICAST,UP,LOWER_UP> mtu 1500
qdisc noqueue state UP mode DEFAULT group default qlen 1000
    link/ether 5e:d3:e6:0f:77:64 brd ff:ff:ff:ff:ff:ff link-
    netnsid 0
```

And we can ping each veth.

```
antonio@antonio-Laptop:~$ ping 10.7.7.1
PING 10.7.7.1 (10.7.7.1) 56(84) bytes of data.
64 bytes from 10.7.7.1: icmp_seq=1 ttl=64 time=0.105 ms
64 bytes from 10.7.7.1: icmp_seq=2 ttl=64 time=0.057 ms
64 bytes from 10.7.7.1: icmp_seq=3 ttl=64 time=0.055 ms
^C
--- 10.7.7.1 ping statistics ---
3 packets transmitted, 3 received, 0% packet loss, time 2039ms
rtt min/avg/max/mdev = 0.055/0.072/0.105/0.023 ms
```

chroot

Before studying **cgroups**, I wanted to mention **chroot**. This is a system call that changes the apparent root directory for the running process and its children so that this process can't access files that reside below its working directory. This provides an isolation that is similar in some ways with the isolation provided by namespaces, but the approach is different. **chroot** is a system call and does not need namespaces to work. This is not part of the official curriculum for LPIC-3 305, but I think it might be useful to mention it briefly and see an example.

CHAPTER 7 CONTAINER VIRTUALIZATION CONCEPTS

We begin by creating the folder we'll use as the root for our chroot environment.

antonio@antonio-Laptop:~$ sudo mkdir /chrootenv

We could try to execute chroot right away, but we'll get this error:

antonio@antonio-Laptop:~$ sudo chroot /chrootenv
chroot: failed to run command '/bin/bash': No such file or directory

We need to have a */bin/bash* command interpreter inside of the chroot environment, so we'll copy it.

antonio@antonio-Laptop:~$ sudo mkdir /chrootenv/bin
antonio@antonio-Laptop:~$ sudo cp /bin/bash /chrootenv/bin
antonio@antonio-Laptop:~$

However, we're not done yet. If we try to run **chroot** again, we get the same error:

antonio@antonio-Laptop:~$ sudo chroot /chrootenv/
chroot: failed to run command '/bin/bash': No such file or directory

This is due to the fact that the bash executable file is dynamically linked and has to access a series of libraries. We can find out what libraries it needs by using the ldd command. **Note**: Libraries will vary, depending on the exact version of the operating system.

antonio@antonio-Laptop:~$ ldd /bin/bash
    linux-vdso.so.1 (0x00007ffccaff3000)
    libtinfo.so.6 => /lib/x86_64-linux-gnu/libtinfo.so.6
    (0x00007f5cb75f3000)
    libc.so.6 => /lib/x86_64-linux-gnu/libc.so.6
    (0x00007f5cb7200000)

337

CHAPTER 7 CONTAINER VIRTUALIZATION CONCEPTS

   /lib64/ld-linux-x86-64.so.2 (0x00007f5cb779e000)

So we create a new subfolder and copy the required files.

```
antonio@antonio-Laptop:~$ sudo mkdir -p /chrootenv/lib/x86_64-linux-gnu
antonio@antonio-Laptop:~$ sudo cp /lib/x86_64-linux-gnu/libtinfo.so.6 /chrootenv/lib/x86_64-linux-gnu/
antonio@antonio-Laptop:~$ sudo cp /lib/x86_64-linux-gnu/libc.so.6 /chrootenv/lib/x86_64-linux-gnu/
antonio@antonio-Laptop:~$ sudo mkdir -p /chrootenv/lib64
antonio@antonio-Laptop:~$ sudo cp /lib64/ld-linux-x86-64.so.2 /chrootenv/lib64
```

Now we can execute chroot successfully.

```
antonio@antonio-Laptop:~$ sudo chroot /chrootenv/
bash-5.1#
```

This chroot environment is still very limited and lacks many common Linux programs that we should copy manually as we did before with the command interpreter.

```
bash-5.1# pwd
/
bash-5.1# ls
bash: ls: command not found
bash-5.1#
```

An easier approach could be the use of a Linux minimal distribution to create our chroot environment. One Linux distribution that suits perfectly this description and is used commonly in containers is Alpine. We begin by downloading the corresponding tar file for our architecture.

```
bash-5.1# exit
exit
antonio@antonio-Laptop:~$ wget http://dl-cdn.alpinelinux.org/
alpine/v3.18/releases/x86_64/alpine-
minirootfs-3.18.3-x86_64.tar.gz
```

.

.

.

And we uncompress it in the folder we used for our chroot environment. Previously we'd delete the files we had copied.

```
antonio@antonio-Laptop:~$ sudo rm -rf /chrootenv/*
antonio@antonio-Laptop:~$ sudo tar -xzvf alpine-
minirootfs-3.18.3-x86_64.tar.gz -C /chrootenv/
```

We end up with the following structure:

```
antonio@antonio-Laptop:~$ ls /chrootenv/
bin   etc   lib     mnt   proc   run   srv   tmp   var
dev   home  media   opt   root   sbin  sys   usr
```

We can now execute **chroot** again.

```
antonio@antonio-Laptop:~$ sudo chroot /chrootenv/
chroot: failed to run command '/bin/bash': No such file or directory
```

We get an error because **chroot** can't locate */bin/bash*. When executing chroot, we must provide the command that will be executed in the chrooted environment. This command is usually a shell. If we don't specify a command, the default value is that of the shell used in the current session, which is */bin/bash* in our case.

```
antonio@antonio-Laptop:~$ echo $SHELL
/bin/bash
```

CHAPTER 7 CONTAINER VIRTUALIZATION CONCEPTS

And */bin/bash* doesn't exist in the minimalistic Alpine Linux distribution we just downloaded.

```
antonio@antonio-Laptop:~$ ls /chrootenv/bin/bash
ls: cannot access '/chrootenv/bin/bash': No such file or directory
```

We can easily fix this by specifying a different shell as the command for **chroot**. We check that */bin/sh* actually exists.

```
antonio@antonio-Laptop:~$ ls /chrootenv/bin/sh
/chrootenv/bin/sh
```

And we launch **chroot** again.

```
antonio@antonio-Laptop:~$ sudo chroot /chrootenv/ /bin/sh
/ #
```

We are working now in an isolated environment, where we're using the same kernel as the host, but we have an isolated root tree.

```
/ # uname -a
Linux antonio-Laptop 6.2.0-33-generic #33~22.04.1-Ubuntu SMP PREEMPT_DYNAMIC Thu Sep  7 10:33:52 UTC 2 x86_64 Linux
/ # cat /etc/issue
Welcome to Alpine Linux 3.18
Kernel \r on an \m (\l)
/ # pwd
/
/ #
```

CHAPTER 7   CONTAINER VIRTUALIZATION CONCEPTS

Control Groups

Control groups or **cgroups** for short are a Linux feature that limits, accounts, and isolates the resource usage of a process or a group of processes.

It was initially developed by Google around 2006. The version currently in use, version 2, was completely rewritten and is included in the kernel Linux. We can see cgroups as a subfolder inside of the */sys/fs* filesystem.

```
antonio@antonio-Laptop:~$ ls /sys/fs/cgroup/
cgroup.controllers       cgroup.threads            init.
scope      memory.numa_stat                sys-fs-fuse-
connections.mount
cgroup.max.depth         cpu.pressure              io.cost.
model   memory.pressure                  sys-kernel-config.mount
cgroup.max.descendants   cpuset.cpus.effective     io.cost.
qos     memory.reclaim                   sys-kernel-debug.mount
cgroup.pressure          cpuset.mems.effective     io.
pressure   memory.stat                   sys-kernel-
tracing.mount
cgroup.procs             cpu.stat                  io.prio.
class   misc.capacity                    system.slice
cgroup.stat              dev-hugepages.mount       io.
stat       misc.current                  user.slice
cgroup.subtree_control   dev-mqueue.mount          machine.
slice   proc-sys-fs-binfmt_misc.mount
```

In order to limit the resources a process can use, we need to create a new control group. We can do that by creating a subfolder inside of */sys/fs/cgroup*.

```
antonio@antonio-Laptop:~$ sudo mkdir /sys/fs/cgroup/example
```

Right after creating the new cgroup, we'll see it has inherited several parameters. We can see them by listing the cgroup.

```
antonio@antonio-Laptop:~$ ls /sys/fs/cgroup/example/
cgroup.controllers        cpu.max                 hugetlb.1GB.
current          hugetlb.2MB.rsvd.max   memory.numa_
stat        misc.current
cgroup.events             cpu.max.burst           hugetlb.1GB.
events        io.max                memory.oom.
group        misc.events
cgroup.freeze             cpu.pressure            hugetlb.1GB.
events.local    io.pressure           memory.
peak            misc.max
cgroup.kill               cpuset.cpus             hugetlb.1GB.
max             io.prio.class         memory.
pressure        pids.current
cgroup.max.depth          cpuset.cpus.effective   hugetlb.1GB.
numa_stat       io.stat               memory.
reclaim         pids.events
cgroup.max.descendants    cpuset.cpus.partition   hugetlb.1GB.
rsvd.current    io.weight             memory.stat
pids.max
cgroup.pressure           cpuset.mems             hugetlb.1GB.
rsvd.max        memory.current        memory.swap.
current         pids.peak
cgroup.procs              cpuset.mems.effective   hugetlb.2MB.
current         memory.events         memory.swap.
events          rdma.current
cgroup.stat               cpu.stat                hugetlb.2MB.
events          memory.events.local   memory.swap.
high            rdma.max
```

```
cgroup.subtree_control  cpu.uclamp.max       hugetlb.2MB.
events.local  memory.high              memory.swap.max
cgroup.threads          cpu.uclamp.min       hugetlb.2MB.max
memory.low              memory.swap.peak
cgroup.type             cpu.weight           hugetlb.2MB.
numa_stat     memory.max               memory.zswap.current
cpu.idle                cpu.weight.nice      hugetlb.2MB.
rsvd.current  memory.min               memory.zswap.max
```

We're going to test this cgroup by establishing a limit on the max amount of memory. For that, we must edit the */sys/fs/cgroup/example/memory.max* file.

```
antonio@antonio-Laptop:~$ sudo vi /sys/fs/cgroup/example/memory.max
antonio@antonio-Laptop:~$ sudo cat /sys/fs/cgroup/example/memory.max
8192
```

Now, we'll create a simple script and execute in the background.

```
antonio@antonio-Laptop:~$ cat takemem.sh
#!/bin/bash

sleep 100
mount -t tmpfs tmpfs /mnt/mydata
sleep 100
antonio@antonio-Laptop:~$ chmod a+x takemem.sh
antonio@antonio-Laptop:~$ ./takemem.sh &
[1] 53075
```

To put this process under the control of the cgroup "example", we need to edit the */sys/fs/cgroup/example/cgroup.procs* file to include the PID of the script in execution.

CHAPTER 7   CONTAINER VIRTUALIZATION CONCEPTS

```
antonio@antonio-Laptop:~$ sudo vi /sys/fs/cgroup/example/
cgroup.procs
antonio@antonio-Laptop:~$ cat /sys/fs/cgroup/example/
cgroup.procs
53075
```

If we review the cgroup assigned to the process, we'll see this:

```
antonio@antonio-Laptop:~$ ps -o cgroup 53362
CGROUP
0::/example
```

We just confirmed that the cgroup assigned is actually "example", the one we created and customized. If we check the cgroup assigned to another process like the current shell, we'll see that the cgroup assigned is completely different.

```
antonio@antonio-Laptop:~$ ps -o cgroup $$
CGROUP
0::/user.slice/user-1000.slice/user@1000.service/app.slice/
app-org.gnome.Terminal.slice/vte-spawn-36c24765-2726-4ef0-
a6b2-60c4c32150
```

Now we'll wait a few seconds. We'll see the script has been killed due to the memory restriction we set. In the journalctl, we'll see a message similar to this one:

```
jul 21 17:12:22 antonio-Laptop kernel: oom-
kill:constraint=CONSTRAINT_MEMCG,nodemask=(null),cpuset=example
,mems_allowed=0,oom_memcg=/example,task_memcg=/example,task=sud
o,pid=53841,uid=1000
jul 21 17:12:22 antonio-Laptop kernel: Memory cgroup out
of memory: Killed process 53841 (sudo) total-vm:17064kB,
anon-rss:896kB, file-rss:5376kB, shmem-rss:0kB, UID:1000
pgtables:76kB oom_score_adj:0
```

CHAPTER 7　CONTAINER VIRTUALIZATION CONCEPTS

Linux Capabilities

Traditionally we have two sorts of processes in Linux/UNIX: those whose effective UID is 0, also called privileged, and those whose effective UID is nonzero, also called unprivileged. Privileged processes can bypass permissions checks, while unprivileged cannot. Since kernel version 2.2, the privileges usually associated with processes whose effective UID is 0 are divided into distinct units called capabilities.

There are three "categories" of capabilities: inherited(i), permitted(p), and effective(e).

The full list of capabilities can be obtained by executing "man capabilities" in any Linux terminal; as an example, we can mention just a few of them:

- CAP_AUDIT. Enable and disable kernel auditing.

- CAP_CHOWN. Make arbitrary changes to file UIDs and GIDs.

- CAP_KILL. Bypass permissions checks to send signals.

- CAP_MKNOD. Create special files using **mknod**.

- CAP_NET_BIND_SERVICE. Bind a socket to Internet domain privileged ports.

To better understand capabilities, we can use the **capsh** command. If we execute it in a command shell with the --print option, we'll see the capabilities that we have currently associated.

```
antonio@antonio-Laptop:~$ capsh --print
Current: =
Bounding set =cap_chown,cap_dac_override,cap_dac_read_search,
cap_fowner,cap_fsetid,cap_kill,cap_setgid,cap_setuid,
cap_setpcap,cap_linux_immutable,cap_net_bind_service,
cap_net_broadcast,cap_net_admin,cap_net_raw,cap_ipc_lock,
```

cap_ipc_owner,cap_sys_module,cap_sys_rawio,cap_sys_chroot,
cap_sys_ptrace,cap_sys_pacct,cap_sys_admin,cap_sys_boot,
cap_sys_nice,cap_sys_resource,cap_sys_time,cap_sys_tty_config,
cap_mknod,cap_lease,cap_audit_write,cap_audit_control,
cap_setfcap,cap_mac_override,cap_mac_admin,cap_syslog,cap_wake_
alarm,cap_block_suspend,cap_audit_read,cap_perfmon,cap_bpf,cap_
checkpoint_restore
Ambient set =
Current IAB:
Securebits: 00/0x0/1'b0
 secure-noroot: no (unlocked)
 secure-no-suid-fixup: no (unlocked)
 secure-keep-caps: no (unlocked)
 secure-no-ambient-raise: no (unlocked)
uid=1000(antonio) euid=1000(antonio)
gid=1000(antonio)
groups=4(adm),24(cdrom),27(sudo),30(dip),46(plugdev),122(lpadmin),135(lxd),136(sambashare),140(libvirt),1000(antonio)
Guessed mode: UNCERTAIN (0)
```

As we can see, the current capabilities field appears empty. This is normal, as we're logged in as a regular user and regular users by default have no privileges. Let's execute the command again as the root user to see the differences.

```
antonio@antonio-Laptop:~$ sudo su - root
root@antonio-Laptop:~# capsh --print
Current: =ep
Bounding set =cap_chown,cap_dac_override,cap_dac_read_
search,cap_fowner,cap_fsetid,cap_kill,cap_setgid,cap_
setuid,cap_setpcap,cap_linux_immutable,cap_net_bind_
service,cap_net_broadcast,cap_net_admin,cap_net_raw,cap_

ipc_lock,cap_ipc_owner,cap_sys_module,cap_sys_rawio,cap_
sys_chroot,cap_sys_ptrace,cap_sys_pacct,cap_sys_admin,cap_
sys_boot,cap_sys_nice,cap_sys_resource,cap_sys_time,cap_sys_
tty_config,cap_mknod,cap_lease,cap_audit_write,cap_audit_
control,cap_setfcap,cap_mac_override,cap_mac_admin,cap_
syslog,cap_wake_alarm,cap_block_suspend,cap_audit_read,cap_
perfmon,cap_bpf,cap_checkpoint_restore
Ambient set =
Current IAB:
Securebits: 00/0x0/1'b0
 secure-noroot: no (unlocked)
 secure-no-suid-fixup: no (unlocked)
 secure-keep-caps: no (unlocked)
 secure-no-ambient-raise: no (unlocked)
uid=0(root) euid=0(root)
gid=0(root)
groups=0(root)
Guessed mode: UNCERTAIN (0)
```

We see now the following line:

```
Current: =ep
```

This means that the root user has all capabilities effective and permitted assigned. Again, this is normal as the root user has all privileges.

We can also obtain the same information about capabilities by checking the */proc* filesystem. We need to get the PID of the process, in this case the current shell.

```
antonio@antonio-Laptop:~$ echo $$
25112
```
```

CHAPTER 7 CONTAINER VIRTUALIZATION CONCEPTS

And then we read the *status* file.

```
antonio@antonio-Laptop:~$ cat /proc/25112/status
Name:           bash
Umask:          0002
State:          S (sleeping)
Tgid:           25112
Ngid:           0
Pid:            25112
PPid:           4669
TracerPid:      0
Uid:            1000    1000    1000    1000
Gid:            1000    1000    1000    1000
FDSize:         256
Groups:         4 24 27 30 46 122 135 136 140 1000
.
.
.
CapInh:         0000000000000000
CapPrm:         0000000000000000
CapEff:         0000000000000000
CapBnd:         000001ffffffffff
CapAmb:         0000000000000000
.
.
.
```

We can see that the shell currently has no inherited, permitted, or effective capabilities assigned. The entry CapBnd shows the capabilities that the system recognizes and can be assigned. The value appears in hexadecimal format, but we can easily decode it with **capsh**.

CHAPTER 7 CONTAINER VIRTUALIZATION CONCEPTS

```
antonio@antonio-Laptop:~$ capsh --decode=000001ffffffffff
0x000001ffffffffff=cap_chown,cap_dac_override,cap_dac_
read_search,cap_fowner,cap_fsetid,cap_kill,cap_setgid,cap_
setuid,cap_setpcap,cap_linux_immutable,cap_net_bind_
service,cap_net_broadcast,cap_net_admin,cap_net_raw,cap_
ipc_lock,cap_ipc_owner,cap_sys_module,cap_sys_rawio,cap_sys_
chroot,cap_sys_ptrace,cap_sys_pacct,cap_sys_admin,cap_sys_
boot,cap_sys_nice,cap_sys_resource,cap_sys_time,cap_sys_
tty_config,cap_mknod,cap_lease,cap_audit_write,cap_audit_
control,cap_setfcap,cap_mac_override,cap_mac_admin,cap_
syslog,cap_wake_alarm,cap_block_suspend,cap_audit_read,cap_
perfmon,cap_bpf,cap_checkpoint_restore
```

We can repeat this test with a root shell, and we'll see that it has all the capabilities assigned.

```
antonio@antonio-Laptop:~$ sudo su - root
root@antonio-Laptop:~# cat /proc/$$/status
.
.
.
CapInh:      0000000000000000
CapPrm:      000001ffffffffff
CapEff:      000001ffffffffff
CapBnd:      000001ffffffffff
.
.
.
root@antonio-Laptop:~# capsh --decode=000001ffffffffff
0x000001ffffffffff=cap_chown,cap_dac_override,cap_dac_
read_search,cap_fowner,cap_fsetid,cap_kill,cap_setgid,cap_
setuid,cap_setpcap,cap_linux_immutable,cap_net_bind_service,
```

cap_net_broadcast,cap_net_admin,cap_net_raw,cap_ipc_lock,cap_ipc_owner,cap_sys_module,cap_sys_rawio,cap_sys_chroot,cap_sys_ptrace,cap_sys_pacct,cap_sys_admin,cap_sys_boot,cap_sys_nice,cap_sys_resource,cap_sys_time,cap_sys_tty_config,cap_mknod,cap_lease,cap_audit_write,cap_audit_control,cap_setfcap,cap_mac_override,cap_mac_admin,cap_syslog,cap_wake_alarm,cap_block_suspend,cap_audit_read,cap_perfmon,cap_bpf,cap_checkpoint_restore

Let's see now a practical example about how to use capabilities to grant a specific privilege to a process.

We're going to use Python to create a basic web server. If we execute Python as a regular user, we can get the server to listen on any nonprivileged port, such as port 8888.

```
antonio@antonio-Laptop:~$ python3 -m http.server 8888
Serving HTTP on 0.0.0.0 port 8888 (http://0.0.0.0:8888/) ...
```

However, if we try the server to listen on any of the privileged ports, such as 80, we get an error.

```
antonio@antonio-Laptop:~$ python3 -m http.server 80
Traceback (most recent call last):
  File "/usr/lib/python3.10/runpy.py", line 196, in _run_module_as_main
.
.
.
    self.socket.bind(self.server_address)
PermissionError: [Errno 13] Permission denied
```

CHAPTER 7   CONTAINER VIRTUALIZATION CONCEPTS

To remediate this, we'll use the capabilities. First of all, we identify the path of the Python executable file. We'll need it later to add the desired capabilities.

```
antonio@antonio-Laptop:~$ which python3
/usr/bin/python3
antonio@antonio-Laptop:~$ file /usr/bin/python3
/usr/bin/python3: symbolic link to python3.10
antonio@antonio-Laptop:~$ ls -l /usr/bin/python3
lrwxrwxrwx 1 root root 10 ago  4  2023 /usr/bin/python3 ->
python3.10
```

We'll take a look at the man page of the capabilities to identify the capability that we need to use.

```
antonio@antonio-Laptop:~$ man capabilities
```

In the page, we'll see this entry:

```
CAP_NET_BIND_SERVICE
        Bind a socket to Internet domain privileged ports
        (port numbers less than 1024).
```

We're ready now to add the capability to the Python executable.

```
antonio@antonio-Laptop:~$ sudo setcap CAP_NET_BIND_SERVICE+ep /usr/bin/python3.10
```

We confirm that the assignment was made.

```
antonio@antonio-Laptop:~$ getcap /usr/bin/python3.10
/usr/bin/python3.10 cap_net_bind_service=ep
   Now our Python based web server can listen on a
   privileged port.
antonio@antonio-Laptop:~$ python3 -m http.server 80
Serving HTTP on 0.0.0.0 port 80 (http://0.0.0.0:80/) ...
```

351

CHAPTER 7   CONTAINER VIRTUALIZATION CONCEPTS

Another way to check that the process has the CAP_NET_BIND_SERVICE capability assigned is by consulting the */proc* filesystem, as we saw earlier.

```
antonio@antonio-Laptop:~$ ps -ef | grep python | grep http
antonio    35151   25112  0 13:02 pts/1    00:00:00 python3 -m http.server 80
```

```
antonio@antonio-Laptop:~$ cat /proc/35151/status
Name:           python3
Umask:          0002
State:          S (sleeping)
Tgid:           35151
Ngid:           0
.
.
.
CapInh:         0000000000000000
CapPrm:         0000000000000400
CapEff:         0000000000000400
.
.
.
```

```
antonio@antonio-Laptop:~$ capsh --decode=0000000000000400
0x0000000000000400=cap_net_bind_service
```

After this easy test, we can remove the capability from the Python executable again.

```
antonio@antonio-Laptop:~$ sudo setcap CAP_NET_BIND_SERVICE-ep /usr/bin/python3.10
antonio@antonio-Laptop:~$ python3 -m http.server 80
```

-
-
-

```
PermissionError: [Errno 13] Permission denied
```

Security and Containers

We have seen so far how important it is to properly secure and isolate containers. We have already seen how Linux namespaces help us to isolate processes running in the same host. Now we'll see how a series of security facilities are also used by Linux containers to secure the system.

SELinux

SELinux (Security-Enhanced Linux) is a set of kernel modifications and user space tools that provide mandatory access control (MAC). It was initially developed by the NSA, and it is now included in many of the main Linux distributions. Mandatory access controls are established by the system administrator and can't be edited by regular users.

As SELinux is mainly a subject from LPIC-3 303 Security, we'll just highlight its main points here.

SELinux uses a set of security policies; these are rules that tell what can and can't be accessed. The security policies apply to applications, processes, and files. For example, when a process or application tries to access a file, SELinux checks if that access is allowed. Each application, process, and file have an SELinux context associated.

As SELinux is applied to all applications, processes, and files in the host system, that also applies to container-related processes and files. This is something that must be taken into account.

CHAPTER 7 CONTAINER VIRTUALIZATION CONCEPTS

We'll see a short demonstration. By default, Ubuntu 22 does not use SELinux, so we'll use a Red Hat 8 system for this. First, we check the status of SELinux.

```
[root@RH8 ~]# sestatus
SELinux status:                 enabled
SELinuxfs mount:                /sys/fs/selinux
SELinux root directory:         /etc/selinux
Loaded policy name:             targeted
Current mode:                   enforcing
Mode from config file:          enforcing
Policy MLS status:              enabled
Policy deny_unknown status:     allowed
Memory protection checking:     actual (secure)
Max kernel policy version:      33
```

In this case, SELinux is enabled, and it is in "enforcing" mode. SELinux can be in permissive mode or in enforcing mode. When in enforcing mode, it will block those actions that are not allowed by the SELinux policies. On the other hand, permissive mode will not block any action that is not allowed, but it will log them. We can change between these two modes with the **setenforce** command.

We can check the SELinux context of any given file or folder with the -Z option of the **ls** command.

```
[root@RH8 ~]# ls -lZd /var/lib/containers/
drwxr-xr-x. 5 root root system_u:object_r:container_var_
lib_t:s0 4096 sep 23  2023 /var/lib/containers/

[root@RH8 ~]# ls -lZd /tmp/
drwxrwxrwt. 6 root root system_u:object_r:tmp_t:s0 4096 may 25
04:38 /tmp/
```

CHAPTER 7 CONTAINER VIRTUALIZATION CONCEPTS

There are many SELinux file context available in a system; we can list them with **semanage**.

```
[root@RH8 ~]# semanage fcontext -l
SELinux fcontext          type                Context

/                         directory           system_u:object_r:root_t:s0
/.*                       all files           system_u:object_r:default_t:s0
/[^/]+                    regular file        system_u:object_r:etc_runtime_t:s0
/\.autofsck               regular file        system_u:object_r:etc_runtime_t:s0
/\.autorelabel            regular file        system_u:object_r:etc_runtime_t:s0
/\.ismount-test-file      regular file        system_u:object_r:sosreport_tmp_t:s0
.
.
.
```

As we said before, processes also have SELinux context associated; we can see them with the -Z option of the **ps** command.

```
[root@RH8 ~]# ps -efZ | grep podman
unconfined_u:unconfined_r:container_runtime_t:s0-s0:c0.c1023
root 190890 190570  0 04:36 pts/0 00:00:00 podman run -it ubi8
unconfined_u:unconfined_r:container_runtime_t:s0 root 190942
1  0 04:36 ?        00:00:00 /usr/bin/conmon --api-version 1 -c
9ddbab3dc608d913346e55fd44fa45a87b51e9f1d11ee64fcdeb0fe422b-
ba178 -u 9ddbab3dc608d913346e55fd44fa45a87b51e9f1d11ee64
fcdeb0fe422bba178 -r /usr/bin/runc -b /var/lib/containers/stor-
age/overlay-containers/9ddbab3dc608d913346e55fd44fa45a87b51e9f1
```

d11ee64fcdeb0fe422bba178/userdata -p /run/containers/storage/
overlay-containers/9ddbab3dc608d913346e55fd44fa45a87b51e9f1
d11ee64fcdeb0fe422bba178/userdata/pidfile -n suspicious_mayer
--exit-dir /run/libpod/exits --full-attach -s -l k8s-file:/
var/lib/containers/storage/overlay-containers/9ddbab3dc608d9
13346e55fd44fa45a87b51e9f1d11ee64fcdeb0fe422bba178/userdata/
ctr.log --log-level warning --syslog --runtime-arg --log-
format=json --runtime-arg --log --runtime-arg=/run/containers/
storage/overlay-containers/9ddbab3dc608d913346e55fd44fa45a87
b51e9f1d11ee64fcdeb0fe422bba178/userdata/oci-log -t --conmon-
pidfile /run/containers/storage/overlay-containers/9ddbab3dc60
8d913346e55fd44fa45a87b51e9f1d11ee64fcdeb0fe422bba178/userdata/
conmon.pid --exit-command /usr/bin/podman --exit-command-arg
--root --exit-command-arg /var/lib/containers/storage --exit-
command-arg --runroot --exit-command-arg /run/containers/stor-
age --exit-command-arg --log-level --exit-command-arg warning --exit-command-arg --cgroup-manager --exit-command-arg
systemd --exit-command-arg --tmpdir --exit-command-arg /run/
libpod --exit-command-arg --network-config-dir --exit-command-
arg --exit-command-arg --network-backend --exit-command-arg
cni --exit-command-arg --volumepath --exit-command-arg /var/
lib/containers/storage/volumes --exit-command-arg --db-backend
--exit-command-arg boltdb --exit-command-arg --transient-
store=false --exit-command-arg --runtime --exit-command-arg
runc --exit-command-arg --storage-driver --exit-command-arg
overlay --exit-command-arg --storage-opt --exit-command-arg
overlay.mountopt=nodev,metacopy=on --exit-command-arg --events-
backend --exit-command-arg file --exit-command-arg container
--exit-command-arg cleanup --exit-command-arg 9ddbab3dc608d91
3346e55fd44fa45a87b51e9f1d11ee64fcdeb0fe422bba178

CHAPTER 7 CONTAINER VIRTUALIZATION CONCEPTS

```
[root@RH8 ~]# ps -efZ | grep bash
unconfined_u:unconfined_r:unconfined_t:s0-s0:c0.c1023 root
75460 672   0 may22 tty1 00:00:00 -bash
unconfined_u:unconfined_r:unconfined_t:s0-s0:c0.c1023 root
190570 190569  0 04:30 pts/0 00:00:00 -bash
system_u:system_r:container_t:s0:c917,c999 root 190950
190942  0 04:36 pts/0 00:00:00 /bin/bash
```

SELinux also can control the network ports a given program can use. We can list these ports with **semanage**.

```
[root@RH8 ~]# semanage port -l
SELinux Port Type            Proto    Port Number

afs3_callback_port_t         tcp      7001
afs3_callback_port_t         udp      7001
afs_bos_port_t               udp      7007
afs_fs_port_t                tcp      2040
.
.
.
```

Let's see now a simple example about SELinux. We'll assume we have a web server running locally on port 80. We check that the server is working.

```
[root@RH8 ~]# curl http://localhost
Hello
```

We'll edit the properties so that the web server listens on port 85 instead of port 80.

```
[root@RH8 ~]# vi /etc/httpd/conf/httpd.conf
```

We'll replace this line

```
Listen 80
```

357

CHAPTER 7 CONTAINER VIRTUALIZATION CONCEPTS

with this one

```
Listen 85
```

If we restart now the httpd service, we'll get an error.

```
[root@RH8 ~]# systemctl restart httpd
Job for httpd.service failed because the control process exited
with error code.
See "systemctl status httpd.service" and "journalctl -xe" for
details.
```

And looking at the journal, we'll see a line similar to the following:

```
jul 21 14:00:07 RH8.example.com setroubleshoot[192565]: SELinux
is preventing /usr/sbin/httpd from name_bind access on the tcp_
socket port 85. For complete SELinux messages run: sealert -l
fbf5bdc4-3747-47de-88a8-099872380ea5
```

As we can see, the log says clearly that SELinux is preventing httpd to use TCP port 85. And it suggests to execute a **sealert** command.

```
[root@RH8 ~]# sealert -l fbf5bdc4-3747-47de-88a8-099872380ea5
SELinux is preventing /usr/sbin/httpd from name_bind access on
the tcp_socket port 85.

*******  Plugin bind_ports (99.5 confidence) suggests    *******

If you want to allow /usr/sbin/httpd to bind to network port 85
Then you need to modify the port type.
Do
# semanage port -a -t PORT_TYPE -p tcp 85
    where PORT_TYPE is one of the following: http_cache_port_t,
    http_port_t, jboss_management_port_t, jboss_messaging_
    port_t, ntop_port_t, puppet_port_t.
```

CHAPTER 7　CONTAINER VIRTUALIZATION CONCEPTS

-
-
-

The output of the command tells us what the problem is and also how to fix it. To do it, we just need to add TCP port 85 as one of the ports that httpd can use. We'll use semanage to add the port.

```
[root@RH8 ~]# semanage port --add -t http_port_t -p tcp 85
```

Now, we restart the service again and check that the web server now works perfectly on port 85.

```
[root@RH8 ~]# systemctl restart httpd
[root@RH8 ~]# curl http://localhost:85
Hello
```

AppArmor

AppArmor is a Linux kernel security module that also provides mandatory access control (MAC). It works by using profiles associated with the programs.

As we did before with SELinux, we'll see a simple example of the use of AppArmor. Again, I must insist this is only a very brief description of AppArmor, as it is a subject for LPIC-3 303 instead.

In this example, we're going to use an AppArmor profile to control what a certain program can and can't do. We'll use for the test the text-based web browser w3m. We'll begin by installing it.

```
antonio@antonio-Laptop:~$ sudo apt install w3m
```

Now we need to create a profile for that program. To generate the profile, we need to install the AppArmor utils as well.

```
antonio@antonio-Laptop:~$ sudo apt install apparmor-utils
```

We need the full path of the **w3m** program to generate the profile.

```
antonio@antonio-Laptop:~$ which w3m
/usr/bin/w3m
```

We can now proceed to create the profile with **aa-genprof**.

```
antonio@antonio-Laptop:~$ sudo aa-genprof /usr/bin/w3m
```

It is possible that we get this error, or one similar:

```
ERROR: Include file /etc/apparmor.d/libvirt/
libvirt-84e6987c-5f67-443d-ad67-ff6c29a428c4.files not found
```

This seems to be a bug regarding AppArmor and libvirt; to remediate it, we can just create an empty file with the same name.

```
antonio@antonio-Laptop:~$ touch /etc/apparmor.d/libvirt/
libvirt-84e6987c-5f67-443d-ad67-ff6c29a428c4.files
```

After that, we can generate the profile; we'll see this information:

```
antonio@antonio-Laptop:~$ sudo aa-genprof /usr/bin/w3m
Updating AppArmor profiles in /etc/apparmor.d.
Writing updated profile for /usr/bin/w3m.
Setting /usr/bin/w3m to complain mode.

Before you begin, you may wish to check if a
profile already exists for the application you
wish to confine. See the following wiki page for
more information:
https://gitlab.com/apparmor/apparmor/wikis/Profiles

Profiling: /usr/bin/w3m

Please start the application to be profiled in
another window and exercise its functionality now.
```

CHAPTER 7   CONTAINER VIRTUALIZATION CONCEPTS

```
Once completed, select the "Scan" option below in
order to scan the system logs for AppArmor events.

For each AppArmor event, you will be given the
opportunity to choose whether the access should be
allowed or denied.

[(S)can system log for AppArmor events] / (F)inish
```

We must open another shell and launch w3m on it to perform the normal actions that the program does.

```
antonio@antonio-Laptop:~$ w3m http://www.apress.com
```

In the first shell, we'll press "S" to scan for the AppArmor events.

```
[(S)can system log for AppArmor events] / (F)inish
Reading log entries from /var/log/audit/audit.log.

Profile:  /usr/bin/w3m
Execute:  /usr/bin/dash
Severity: unknown

(I)nherit / (C)hild / (N)amed / (U)nconfined / (X) ix On / (D)
eny / Abo(r)t / (F)inish
```

We'll have to repeat this procedure for some time. Using the application in a terminal shell and scanning the AppArmor events on the other terminal shell. In the end, we'll save the profile.

This profile will be located on */etc/apparmor.d/usr.bin.w3m*.

```
antonio@antonio-Laptop:~$ ls /etc/apparmor.d/usr.bin.w3m
/etc/apparmor.d/usr.bin.w3m

antonio@antonio-Laptop:~$ sudo cat /etc/apparmor.d/usr.bin.w3m
# Last Modified: Sun Jul 21 14:39:52 2024
abi <abi/3.0>,
```

```
include <tunables/global>

/usr/bin/w3m {
  include <abstractions/base>
  include <abstractions/bash>

  /usr/bin/dash mrix,
  /usr/bin/gunzip mrix,
  /usr/bin/w3m mr,

}
```

seccomp

seccomp (security component) allows a Linux process to enter into a state in which it can only work with a small subset of system calls: exit(), sigreturn(), read(), and write() to already open file descriptors.

We'll see this in an example when we study how it can be implemented in LXC and Docker.

Summary

In this introductory chapter to containers, we have seen what a container is and also the kernel features needed to provide containers with their functionality.

Hopefully, after reading this chapter, you'll have a better understanding about what namespaces and control groups are and how they work. Apart from these two kernel features, we've also seen other technologies that can influence how containers work, such as capabilities, SELinux, and AppArmor. And we also crafted a small container by using the aforementioned kernel features.

CHAPTER 8

Linux Containers (LXC)

In this chapter, we'll cover the following concepts:

- Understand the architecture of LXC and LXD
- Manage LXC containers based on existing images using LXD, including networking and storage
- Configure LXC container properties
- Limit LXC container resource usage
- Use LXD profiles
- Understand LXC images
- Awareness of traditional LXC tools
- Understand how LXC leverages namespaces, cgroups, capabilities, seccomp, and MAC

LXC

LXC (Linux containers) is a virtualization method for running several Linux systems, called containers, in a single host. Instead of creating a virtual machine, LXC relies on the technologies we've studied in the

CHAPTER 8 LINUX CONTAINERS (LXC)

previous chapter, mainly cgroups and kernel namespaces. This way they limit and isolate the resource usage (CPU, memory, etc.) of a series of processes.

Installing LXC

The official repositories of the main Linux distributions already include the package needed to manage and run LXC in the computer. So the installation is very simple.

```
antonio@antonio-Laptop:~$ sudo apt install lxc
```

Actually if we review the information about the lxc package, we'll see that this is a transitional package. And when we install it, we're installing the lxc-utils package.

```
antonio@antonio-Laptop:~$ apt show lxc
Package: lxc
Version: 1:5.0.0~git2209-g5a7b9ce67-0ubuntu1
.
.
.
Description: Transitional package - lxc -> lxc-utils
 This is a transitional dummy package. It can safely be
 removed.
.
 lxc is now replaced by lxc-utils.
```

If we take a look now at the description of the lxc-utils package, we'll see the following paragraph, which should be already familiar as it is a summary of the theorical concepts we've seen in the previous chapter.

CHAPTER 8 LINUX CONTAINERS (LXC)

```
antonio@antonio-Laptop:~$ apt show lxc-utils
Package: lxc-utils
.
.
.
Description: Linux Containers userspace tools
 Containers are insulated areas inside a system, which have
 their own namespace for filesystem, network, PID, IPC, CPU and
 memory allocation and which can be created using the Control
 Group and Namespace features included in the Linux kernel.
 .
 This package provides the lxc-* tools, which can be used
 to start a single daemon in a container, or to boot an
 entire "containerized" system, and to manage and debug your
 containers.
```

Configuring LXC

Now that we've installed the needed utils, we can start creating our containers. To check whether everything is ready before using LXC, we can execute the **lxc-checkconfig** command.

```
antonio@antonio-Laptop:~$ lxc-checkconfig
LXC version 5.0.0~git2209-g5a7b9ce67
Kernel configuration not found at /proc/config.gz; searching...
Kernel configuration found at /boot/config-6.2.0-36-generic
--- Namespaces ---
Namespaces: enabled
Utsname namespace: enabled
Ipc namespace: enabled
Pid namespace: enabled
User namespace: enabled
Network namespace: enabled
```

CHAPTER 8   LINUX CONTAINERS (LXC)

```
--- Control groups ---
Cgroups: enabled
Cgroup namespace: enabled

Cgroup v1 mount points:

Cgroup v2 mount points:
/sys/fs/cgroup

Cgroup v1 systemd controller: missing
Cgroup v1 freezer controller: missing
Cgroup ns_cgroup: required
Cgroup device: enabled
Cgroup sched: enabled
Cgroup cpu account: enabled
Cgroup memory controller: enabled
Cgroup cpuset: enabled

--- Misc ---
Veth pair device: enabled, not loaded
Macvlan: enabled, not loaded
Vlan: enabled, not loaded
Bridges: enabled, loaded
Advanced netfilter: enabled, loaded
CONFIG_IP_NF_TARGET_MASQUERADE: enabled, not loaded
CONFIG_IP6_NF_TARGET_MASQUERADE: enabled, not loaded
CONFIG_NETFILTER_XT_TARGET_CHECKSUM: enabled, loaded
CONFIG_NETFILTER_XT_MATCH_COMMENT: enabled, not loaded
FUSE (for use with lxcfs): enabled, not loaded

--- Checkpoint/Restore ---
checkpoint restore: enabled
CONFIG_FHANDLE: enabled
CONFIG_EVENTFD: enabled
```

CHAPTER 8 LINUX CONTAINERS (LXC)

```
CONFIG_EPOLL: enabled
CONFIG_UNIX_DIAG: enabled
CONFIG_INET_DIAG: enabled
CONFIG_PACKET_DIAG: enabled
CONFIG_NETLINK_DIAG: enabled
File capabilities:

Note : Before booting a new kernel, you can check its
       configuration
usage : CONFIG=/path/to/config /usr/bin/lxc-checkconfig
```

In the output, we can see clearly these two lines:

```
Namespaces: enabled
Cgroups: enabled
```

As we studied in the previous chapter, these two technologies provide the isolation and resource limitation needed to create containers.

In order to create a new container, we use the **lxc-create** command. We assign a name for the new container with the "-n" parameter, and we execute the command as root.

```
antonio@antonio-Laptop:~$ sudo lxc-create -n my_container
lxc-create: my_container: tools/lxc_create.c: main: 214 A
template must be specified
lxc-create: my_container: tools/lxc_create.c: main: 215 Use
"none" if you really want a container without a rootfs
```

As we see, we need to specify a template. We should install the **lxc-templates** package in order to obtain a series of predefined templates.

```
antonio@antonio-Laptop:~$ sudo apt install lxc-templates
```

CHAPTER 8   LINUX CONTAINERS (LXC)

We can see that there is a list of predefined templates in the */usr/share/lxc/templates/* folder.

```
antonio@antonio-Laptop:~/antonio/LXC$ ls /usr/share/lxc/templates/
lxc-alpine       lxc-download        lxc-opensuse     lxc-sshd
lxc-altlinux     lxc-fedora          lxc-oracle       lxc-ubuntu
lxc-archlinux    lxc-fedora-legacy   lxc-plamo        lxc-ubuntu-
                                                        cloud
lxc-busybox      lxc-gentoo          lxc-pld          lxc-voidlinux
lxc-centos       lxc-local           lxc-sabayon
lxc-cirros       lxc-oci             lxc-slackware
lxc-debian       lxc-openmandriva    lxc-sparclinux
```

In our example, we'll use the ubuntu template.

```
antonio@antonio-Laptop:~/antonio/LXC$ sudo lxc-create -t ubuntu -n my_container
Checking cache download in /var/cache/lxc/jammy/rootfs-amd64 ...
Installing packages in template: apt-transport-https,ssh,vim,language-pack-en
Downloading ubuntu jammy minimal ...
I: Target architecture can be executed
I: Retrieving InRelease
I: Checking Release signature
I: Valid Release signature (key id
   F6ECB3762474EDA9D21B7022871920D1991BC93C)
I: Retrieving Packages
I: Validating Packages
I: Retrieving Packages
I: Validating Packages
I: Resolving dependencies of required packages...
```

```
I: Resolving dependencies of base packages...
I: Checking component main on http://archive.ubuntu.com/
   ubuntu...
I: Checking component universe on http://archive.ubuntu.com/
   ubuntu...
I: Retrieving adduser 3.118ubuntu5
I: Validating adduser 3.118ubuntu5
I: Retrieving apt 2.4.5
I: Validating apt 2.4.5
.
.
.
Installing updates
Get:1 http://security.ubuntu.com/ubuntu jammy-security
      InRelease [110 kB]
Hit:2 http://archive.ubuntu.com/ubuntu jammy InRelease
Get:3 http://archive.ubuntu.com/ubuntu jammy-updates InRelease
      [119 kB]
Get:4 http://security.ubuntu.com/ubuntu jammy-security/main
      amd64 Packages [953 kB]
.
.
.
Copy /var/cache/lxc/jammy/rootfs-amd64 to /var/lib/lxc/my_
container/rootfs ...
Copying rootfs to /var/lib/lxc/my_container/rootfs ...
Generating locales (this might take a while)...
  en_US.UTF-8... done
Generation complete.
```

CHAPTER 8   LINUX CONTAINERS (LXC)

.
.
.
```
##
# The default user is 'ubuntu' with password 'ubuntu'!
# Use the 'sudo' command to run tasks as root in the container.
##
```

The container has been successfully created. We can list it with **lxc-ls**.

```
antonio@antonio-Laptop:~/antonio/LXC$ sudo lxc-ls
my_container
```

We can get a bit more information with the --fancy option.

```
antonio@antonio-Laptop:~$ sudo lxc-ls --fancy
NAME          STATE    AUTOSTART GROUPS IPV4 IPV6 UNPRIVILEGED
my_container  STOPPED  0                -    -    false
```

When creating a new container with the default options, a new folder will appear in the */var/lib/lxc* folder.

```
antonio@antonio-Laptop:~/antonio/LXC$ ls /var/lib/lxc
ls: cannot open directory '/var/lib/lxc': Permission denied
antonio@antonio-Laptop:~/antonio/LXC$ sudo ls /var/lib/lxc
my_container
```

Inside the my_container folder, we see a config file and a rootfs subfolder.

```
antonio@antonio-Laptop:~/antonio/LXC$ sudo ls -l /var/lib/lxc/my_container
total 8
-rw-r-----  1 root root  687 nov 18 13:10 config
drwxr-xr-x 17 root root 4096 nov 18 13:09 rootfs
```

In the config file, we can see parameters regarding the network settings and the root filesystem used. We can also see that the settings included in the */usr/share/lxc/config/ubuntu.common.conf* file are included.

```
antonio@antonio-Laptop:~/antonio/LXC$ sudo cat /var/lib/lxc/
my_container/config
# Template used to create this container: /usr/share/lxc/
templates/lxc-ubuntu
# Parameters passed to the template:
# For additional config options, please look at lxc.
container.conf(5)

# Uncomment the following line to support nesting containers:
#lxc.include = /usr/share/lxc/config/nesting.conf
# (Be aware this has security implications)

# Common configuration
lxc.include = /usr/share/lxc/config/ubuntu.common.conf

# Container specific configuration
lxc.rootfs.path = dir:/var/lib/lxc/my_container/rootfs
lxc.uts.name = my_container
lxc.arch = amd64

# Network configuration
lxc.net.0.type = veth
lxc.net.0.link = lxcbr0
lxc.net.0.flags = up
lxc.net.0.hwaddr = 00:16:3e:fb:1d:36
```

CHAPTER 8 LINUX CONTAINERS (LXC)

The root filesystem used is precisely the */var/lib/lxc/my_container/rootfs* folder we talked about earlier. If we list its contents, we'll see that it contains the usual directories that can be found in a Linux computer.

```
antonio@antonio-Laptop:~/antonio/LXC$ sudo ls /var/lib/lxc/my_container/rootfs
bin   dev  home  lib32  libx32  mnt  proc  run   srv   tmp  var
boot  etc  lib   lib64  media   opt  root  sbin  sys   usr
```

The template named ubuntu usually includes a user named "ubuntu" with a password "ubuntu". However, we'll see how to customize it, resetting the root password and creating a new user.

To do this, we'll change the root path to that of the container.

```
antonio@antonio-Laptop:~/antonio/LXC$ sudo chroot /var/lib/lxc/my_container/rootfs
root@antonio-Laptop:/#
```

We proceed now to change the root password and create a new user.

```
root@antonio-Laptop:/# passwd root
New password:
Retype new password:
passwd: password updated successfully
root@antonio-Laptop:/# useradd -m lxc-user
root@antonio-Laptop:/# passwd lxc-user
New password:
Retype new password:
passwd: password updated successfully
root@antonio-Laptop:/#
```

Finally, we leave the chroot environment.

```
root@antonio-Laptop:/# exit
exit
```

CHAPTER 8 LINUX CONTAINERS (LXC)

We are ready to start the container with the **lxc-start** command.

antonio@antonio-Laptop:~/antonio/LXC$ sudo lxc-start -n my_container

And we check that the container is actually running.

```
antonio@antonio-Laptop:~/antonio/LXC$ sudo lxc-ls --fancy
NAME          STATE    AUTOSTART  GROUPS  IPV4        IPV6  UNPRIVILEGED
my_container  RUNNING  0          -       10.0.3.48   -     false
```

In the output, we can see the IP of the container. Of course we can ping this IP address.

```
antonio@antonio-Laptop:~/antonio/LXC$ ping -c 3 10.0.3.48
PING 10.0.3.48 (10.0.3.48) 56(84) bytes of data.
64 bytes from 10.0.3.48: icmp_seq=1 ttl=64 time=0.070 ms
64 bytes from 10.0.3.48: icmp_seq=2 ttl=64 time=0.067 ms
64 bytes from 10.0.3.48: icmp_seq=3 ttl=64 time=0.067 ms

--- 10.0.3.48 ping statistics ---
3 packets transmitted, 3 received, 0% packet loss, time 2047ms
rtt min/avg/max/mdev = 0.067/0.068/0.070/0.001 ms
```

Once the container is started, we can connect to it with **linux-console**.

```
antonio@antonio-Laptop:~/antonio/LXC$ sudo lxc-console -n my_container

Connected to tty 1
Type <Ctrl+a q> to exit the console, <Ctrl+a Ctrl+a> to enter Ctrl+a itself

Ubuntu 22.04.3 LTS mycontainer pts/1

mycontainer login:
```

CHAPTER 8   LINUX CONTAINERS (LXC)

We log in as the user we created before.

```
mycontainer login: lxc-user
Password:
Welcome to Ubuntu 22.04.3 LTS (GNU/Linux 6.5.0-44-generic x86_64)

 * Documentation:  https://help.ubuntu.com
 * Management:     https://landscape.canonical.com
 * Support:        https://ubuntu.com/advantage

The programs included with the Ubuntu system are free software;
the exact distribution terms for each program are described
in the individual files in /usr/share/doc/*/copyright.

Ubuntu comes with ABSOLUTELY NO WARRANTY, to the extent
permitted by applicable law.

$
```

And we can execute any command as we'd do in any other Ubuntu computer.

```
$ su - root
Password:
root@mycontainer:~# ip address show
1: lo: <LOOPBACK,UP,LOWER_UP> mtu 65536 qdisc noqueue state
UNKNOWN group default qlen 1000
    link/loopback 00:00:00:00:00:00 brd 00:00:00:00:00:00
    inet 127.0.0.1/8 scope host lo
       valid_lft forever preferred_lft forever
    inet6 ::1/128 scope host
       valid_lft forever preferred_lft forever
2: eth0@if11: <BROADCAST,MULTICAST,UP,LOWER_UP> mtu 1500 qdisc
noqueue state UP group default qlen 1000
```

```
    link/ether 00:16:3e:fb:1d:36 brd ff:ff:ff:ff:ff:ff link-
    netnsid 0
    inet 10.0.3.48/24 metric 100 brd 10.0.3.255 scope global
    dynamic eth0
       valid_lft 3097sec preferred_lft 3097sec
       inet6 fe80::216:3eff:fefb:1d36/64 scope link
       valid_lft forever preferred_lft forever
root@mycontainer:~# ip route
default via 10.0.3.1 dev eth0 proto dhcp src 10.0.3.48
metric 100
10.0.3.0/24 dev eth0 proto kernel scope link src 10.0.3.48
metric 100
10.0.3.1 dev eth0 proto dhcp scope link src 10.0.3.48
metric 100
root@mycontainer:~#
```

When we're done, we exit the container console by pressing Ctrl+a and q; this way, the container we'll remain executing, and we can reconnect again at any moment. We can connect to the console as we just did or we can connect with ssh. By default, the ssh port is open and accessible.

```
antonio@antonio-Laptop:~/antonio/LXC$ nmap 10.0.3.48
Starting Nmap 7.80 ( https://nmap.org ) at 2024-07-22
21:37 CEST
Nmap scan report for 10.0.3.48
Host is up (0.00012s latency).
Not shown: 999 closed ports
PORT   STATE SERVICE
22/tcp open  ssh
```

CHAPTER 8 LINUX CONTAINERS (LXC)

```
Nmap done: 1 IP address (1 host up) scanned in 0.06 seconds
antonio@antonio-Laptop:~/antonio/LXC$ ssh ubuntu@10.0.3.48
ubuntu@10.0.3.48's password:
Welcome to Ubuntu 22.04.3 LTS (GNU/Linux
6.5.0-44-generic x86_64)

 * Documentation:  https://help.ubuntu.com
 * Management:     https://landscape.canonical.com
 * Support:        https://ubuntu.com/advantage
Last login: Mon Jul 22 19:56:12 2024 from 10.0.3.1
```

You probably remember that when we introduced the concept of container, we said there were two types of containers: system containers and application containers. This Ubuntu container we just created is a system container as it includes most (if not all) of the tools we expect to see in a real Ubuntu server.

When we decide that we don't need the container to be executed anymore, we can stop the container with the **lxc-stop** command.

```
antonio@antonio-Laptop:~/antonio/LXC$ sudo lxc-stop -n my_
container
antonio@antonio-Laptop:~/antonio/LXC$ sudo lxc-ls --fancy
NAME         STATE    AUTOSTART GROUPS IPV4 IPV6 UNPRIVILEGED
my_container STOPPED  0         -      -    -    false
```

After installing LXC, we can see that a new bridge interface has been created on the host.

```
antonio@antonio-Laptop:~/antonio/LXC$ ip address show
```

•
•
•

```
8: lxcbr0: <NO-CARRIER,BROADCAST,MULTICAST,UP> mtu 1500 qdisc
noqueue state DOWN group default qlen 1000
    link/ether 00:16:3e:00:00:00 brd ff:ff:ff:ff:ff:ff
    inet 10.0.3.1/24 brd 10.0.3.255 scope global lxcbr0
       valid_lft forever preferred_lft forever
    inet6 fe80::216:3eff:fe00:0/64 scope link
       valid_lft forever preferred_lft forever
.
.
.
```

If we remember, we already mentioned the */var/lib/lxc/my_container/config* file, where the container configuration is stored. At the bottom of the file, we have the network configuration.

```
# Network configuration
lxc.net.0.type = veth
lxc.net.0.link = lxcbr0
lxc.net.0.flags = up
lxc.net.0.hwaddr = 00:16:3e:fb:1d:36
```

This configuration is generated using the */etc/lxc/default.conf* file as a template.

```
antonio@antonio-Laptop:~/antonio/LXC$ cat /etc/lxc/default.conf
lxc.net.0.type = veth
lxc.net.0.link = lxcbr0
lxc.net.0.flags = up
lxc.net.0.hwaddr = 00:16:3e:xx:xx:xx
```

When we studied network namespaces in the previous chapter, we could establish a connection between two network namespaces using a pair of virtual Ethernet devices. This is exactly how Linux containers (LXC) communicate with the host. The only difference is that LXC does

CHAPTER 8   LINUX CONTAINERS (LXC)

it automatically. When a container is running, we can see that the bridge interface lxcbr0 is assigned to a veth interface.

```
antonio@antonio-Laptop:~$ sudo lxc-start -n my_container
antonio@antonio-Laptop:~/antonio/LXC$ brctl show
bridge name     bridge id           STP enabled     interfaces
br-4d7a80d63283 8000.02422b187d46   no
docker0         8000.0242ecdd0b5f   no
lxcbr0          8000.00163e000000   no              vethnXYPDf
virbr0          8000.52540035f114   yes
virbr1          8000.5254009a49a6   yes
virbr2          8000.52540052acbc   yes
```

And we'll see the corresponding veth interface in the host.

```
antonio@antonio-Laptop:~/antonio/LXC$ ip link
.
.
.
12: vethnXYPDf@if2: <BROADCAST,MULTICAST,UP,LOWER_UP> mtu 1500 qdisc noqueue master lxcbr0 state UP mode DEFAULT group default qlen 1000
    link/ether fe:7a:2b:b3:a0:34 brd ff:ff:ff:ff:ff:ff link-netnsid 0
```

Of course in the container, we can see the other veth interface, as they're always created in pairs.

```
antonio@antonio-Laptop:~/antonio/LXC$ sudo lxc-attach -n my_container -- ip link
1: lo: <LOOPBACK,UP,LOWER_UP> mtu 65536 qdisc noqueue state UNKNOWN mode DEFAULT group default qlen 1000
    link/loopback 00:00:00:00:00:00 brd 00:00:00:00:00:00
```

2: eth0@if12: <BROADCAST,MULTICAST,UP,LOWER_UP> mtu 1500 qdisc noqueue state UP mode DEFAULT group default qlen 1000
    link/ether 00:16:3e:fb:1d:36 brd ff:ff:ff:ff:ff:ff link-netnsid 0

The interface lxcbr0 is created automatically in Ubuntu when installing LXC. However, this is not always the case with other Linux distributions. If the interface is not created, we should create and configure a bridge interface for the container to be accessible through the network.

LXC Storage

When we created our first container, we used the default storage option, which is local storage. The local storage is a local folder in the host, */var/lib/lxc* to be exact. However, we can choose different storage options. If we look at the help of the **lxc-create** command, we'll see these options:

antonio@antonio-Laptop:~$ lxc-create -help
.
.
.
  -B, --bdev=BDEV   Backing store type to use
.
.
.
  BDEV options for LVM (with -B/--bdev lvm):
      --lvname=LVNAME   Use LVM lv name LVNAME
                                (Default: container name)
      --vgname=VG   Use LVM vg called VG
                                (Default: lxc)
      --thinpool=TP   Use LVM thin pool called TP
                                (Default: lxc)

CHAPTER 8   LINUX CONTAINERS (LXC)

```
BDEV options for Ceph RBD (with -B/--bdev rbd) :
    --rbdname=RBDNAME          Use Ceph RBD name RBDNAME
                               (Default: container name)
    --rbdpool=POOL             Use Ceph RBD pool name POOL
                               (Default: lxc)

BDEV option for ZFS (with -B/--bdev zfs) :
    --zfsroot=PATH             Create zfs under given zfsroot
                               (Default: tank/lxc)
```

-
-
-

As we can see, we can store the container in a logical volume, Ceph, or ZFS.

You're probably familiar with logical volumes, as they have been widely used for many years and are studied in the LPIC-2 certification.

Ceph is a distributed data storage solution that provides object, block, and file storage. It's fault tolerant and very scalable, making it a great platform to work with big data.

Finally, ZFS is a filesystem originally used in Sun Solaris systems that has been ported to other operating systems like Linux. Usually, in storage systems, we have two different parts: the volume management and the management of the data. For example, we can use LVM as the volume manager, and then we can format the volumes with different filesystems like xfs, btrfs, ext4, etc. Or maybe we could use RAID as the volume manager. ZFS is an all-in-one storage system, as it unifies both parts: the volume management and the filesystem. Due to this characteristic, ZFS has complete knowledge of the storage system and provides a very good protection against data corruption. Besides that, it also provides other interesting features like snapshots, compression, and quotas.

CHAPTER 8 LINUX CONTAINERS (LXC)

We're going to see an example in which we'll store a container in a logical volume. For that, we'll create a volume group, and then **lxc-create** will create the corresponding logical volume. To create a volume group, we need to have a disk or partition available to create the physical volume that will be used by the volume group. In my case, I don't have any physical volume available, but we can use a loop device to emulate a disk. We'll begin by creating a file that will be used as a virtual disk.

```
antonio@antonio-Laptop:~/antonio/LXC$ dd if=/dev/zero of=disk.dsk bs=1M count=2048
2048+0 records in
2048+0 records out
2147483648 bytes (2,1 GB, 2,0 GiB) copied, 0,938241 s, 2,3 GB/s
```

Then, we associate the disk to a loop device.

```
antonio@antonio-Laptop:~/antonio/LXC$ sudo losetup -fP disk.dsk
```

And we identify the exact loop device.

```
antonio@antonio-Laptop:~/antonio/LXC$ losetup -a | grep disk.dsk
/dev/loop45: []: (/home/antonio/antonio/LXC/disk.dsk)
```

From now on, we can use */dev/loop45* as if it were a "normal" disk. We'll use **fdisk** to create an LVM-type partition that we'll use later to create a physical volume.

```
antonio@antonio-Laptop:~/antonio/LXC$ sudo fdisk /dev/loop45

Welcome to fdisk (util-linux 2.37.2).
Changes will remain in memory only, until you decide to write them.
Be careful before using the write command.

Device does not contain a recognized partition table.
Created a new DOS disklabel with disk identifier 0xd9bcd143.
```

```
Command (m for help): n
Partition type
   p   primary (0 primary, 0 extended, 4 free)
   e   extended (container for logical partitions)
Select (default p):

Using default response p.
Partition number (1-4, default 1):
First sector (2048-4194303, default 2048):
Last sector, +/-sectors or +/-size{K,M,G,T,P} (2048-4194303,
default 4194303):

Created a new partition 1 of type 'Linux' and of size 2 GiB.

Command (m for help): t
Selected partition 1
Hex code or alias (type L to list all): 8e
Changed type of partition 'Linux' to 'Linux LVM'.

Command (m for help): p
Disk /dev/loop45: 2 GiB, 2147483648 bytes, 4194304 sectors
Units: sectors of 1 * 512 = 512 bytes
Sector size (logical/physical): 512 bytes / 512 bytes
I/O size (minimum/optimal): 512 bytes / 512 bytes
Disklabel type: dos
Disk identifier: 0xd9bcd143

Device         Boot Start      End Sectors Size Id Type
/dev/loop45p1       2048  4194303 4192256   2G 8e Linux LVM

Command (m for help): w
The partition table has been altered.
Calling ioctl() to re-read partition table.
Syncing disks.
```

CHAPTER 8 LINUX CONTAINERS (LXC)

Now we'll create a physical volume (PV) from the partition just created in the loopback device.

```
antonio@antonio-Laptop:~/antonio/LXC$ sudo pvcreate /dev/loop45p1
  Physical volume "/dev/loop45p1" successfully created.
antonio@antonio-Laptop:~/antonio/LXC$ sudo pvs
  PV             VG Fmt  Attr PSize  PFree
  /dev/loop45p1     lvm2 ---  <2,00g <2,00g
```

And finally, we'll create a new VG using that PV.

```
antonio@antonio-Laptop:~/antonio/LXC$ sudo vgcreate VG_LXC /dev/loop45p1
  Volume group "VG_LXC" successfully created
```

We're now ready to create a new container that will be stored inside the volume group.

```
antonio@antonio-Laptop:~/antonio/LXC$ sudo lxc-create -n my_containerLV -t ubuntu -B lvm --vgname=VG_LXC
Checking cache download in /var/cache/lxc/jammy/rootfs-amd64 ...
Copy /var/cache/lxc/jammy/rootfs-amd64 to /usr/lib/x86_64-linux-gnu/lxc ...
Copying rootfs to /usr/lib/x86_64-linux-gnu/lxc ...
Generating locales (this might take a while)...
  en_US.UTF-8... done
Generation complete.

Current default time zone: 'Etc/UTC'
Local time is now:      Wed Jul 24 16:45:13 UTC 2024.
Universal Time is now:  Wed Jul 24 16:45:13 UTC 2024.
```

383

CHAPTER 8   LINUX CONTAINERS (LXC)

```
##
# The default user is 'ubuntu' with password 'ubuntu'!
# Use the 'sudo' command to run tasks as root in the container.
##
```

We have created our new container. We can start it the usual way.

```
antonio@antonio-Laptop:~/antonio/LXC$ sudo lxc-start my_containerLV
antonio@antonio-Laptop:~/antonio/LXC$ sudo lxc-ls --fancy
NAME             STATE    AUTOSTART GROUPS IPV4        IPV6 UNPRIVILEGED
my_container     STOPPED  0         -      -           -    false
my_containerLV   RUNNING  0         -      10.0.3.172  -    false
```

We can connect with ssh just to prove that the container is working as expected.

```
antonio@antonio-HP-Laptop-15s-fq1xxx:~/antonio/LXC$ ssh ubuntu@10.0.3.172
ubuntu@10.0.3.172's password:
Welcome to Ubuntu 22.04.3 LTS (GNU/Linux 6.5.0-44-generic x86_64)
.
.
.
```

Now we'll take a look at the */var/lib/lxc* folder.

```
antonio@antonio-Laptop:~/antonio/LXC$ sudo ls /var/lib/lxc
my_container   my_containerLV
```

CHAPTER 8 LINUX CONTAINERS (LXC)

We see that there is a *my_containerLV* folder; let's look into it.

```
antonio@antonio-Laptop:~/antonio/LXC$ sudo ls /var/lib/lxc/
my_containerLV
config     rootfs
```

There is a rootfs folder and a config file. However, the rootfs folder is empty, and in the config file, we can see that the location of the root filesystem is the logical volume we had created.

```
antonio@antonio-Laptop:~/antonio/LXC$ sudo ls /var/lib/lxc/
my_containerLV/rootfs
antonio@antonio-Laptop:~/antonio/LXC$
antonio@antonio-Laptop:~/antonio/LXC$ sudo cat /var/lib/lxc/
my_containerLV/config
.
.
.
# Container specific configuration
lxc.rootfs.path = lvm:/dev/VG_LXC/my_containerLV
.
.
.
```

If we want to, we can mount the logical volume in a local path to access its content.

```
antonio@antonio-Laptop:~/antonio/LXC$ sudo mount /dev/VG_LXC/
my_containerLV /mnt/mydata/
antonio@antonio-Laptop:~/antonio/LXC$ ls /mnt/mydata/
bin   boot  dev   etc   home   lib    lib32  lib64  libx32
lost+found  media  mnt   opt   proc   root   run    sbin   srv   sys
tmp   usr   var
```

385

When we're done, we can delete the container with **lxc-destroy**.

```
antonio@antonio-Laptop:~/antonio/LXC$ sudo umount /mnt/mydata
antonio@antonio-Laptop:~/antonio/LXC$ sudo lxc-stop -n
my_containerLV
antonio@antonio-Laptop:~/antonio/LXC$ sudo lxc-destroy -n
my_containerLV
```

We will also remove the volume group, the loopback device, and so on.

```
antonio@antonio-Laptop:~/antonio/LXC$ sudo vgremove VG_LXC
  Volume group "VG_LXC" successfully removed
antonio@antonio-Laptop:~/antonio/LXC$ sudo vgremove VG_LXC
  Volume group "VG_LXC" successfully removed
antonio@antonio-Laptop:~/antonio/LXC$ sudo pvremove
/dev/loop45p1
  Labels on physical volume "/dev/loop45p1" successfully wiped.
antonio@antonio-Laptop:~/antonio/LXC$ sudo losetup -d /
dev/loop45
antonio@antonio-Laptop:~/antonio/LXC$ rm disk.dsk
```

LXC in RedHat/Rocky/CentOS

We've already seen how to install and configure LXC on Ubuntu. Now we're gonna do the same in Rocky Linux. We're not going to describe in detail every step because I don't want to repeat the same information once and again. We'll just see the commands used, and we'll focus on the differences.

We'll install the needed packages.

```
[root@pc-1196 ~]# dnf install -y lxc
[root@pc-1196 ~]# dnf install -y lxc-templates
```

CHAPTER 8   LINUX CONTAINERS (LXC)

When we check the templates available, we'll see the first differences.

```
[root@pc-1196 ~]# ls /usr/share/lxc/templates/
lxc-busybox   lxc-download   lxc-local   lxc-oci
```

If we try to create a busybox container, we'll get an error because we need to have the busybox binary.

```
[root@pc-1196 ~]# lxc-create -n my_rockycont -t busybox
/usr/bin/which: no busybox in (/usr/local/sbin:/usr/local/bin:/usr/sbin:/usr/bin:/opt/puppetlabs/bin:/root/bin)
ERROR: Please pass a pathname for busybox binary
lxc-create: my_rockycont: lxccontainer.c: create_run_template: 1625 Failed to create container from template
lxc-create: my_rockycont: tools/lxc_create.c: main: 331 Failed to create container my_rockycont
```

We'll try to use the "download" template.

```
[root@pc-1196 ~]# lxc-create -n my_rockycont -t download
Setting up the GPG keyring
ERROR: Unable to fetch GPG key from keyserver
lxc-create: my_rockycont: lxccontainer.c: create_run_template: 1625 Failed to create container from template
lxc-create: my_rockycont: tools/lxc_create.c: main: 331 Failed to create container my_rockycont
```

We get an error because the system tries to fetch a GPG key from the key server and fails. If we execute the template with the "--help" parameter, we'll see this at the bottom of the page:

```
[root@pc-1196 ~]# /usr/share/lxc/templates/lxc-download --help
LXC container image downloader
```

CHAPTER 8 LINUX CONTAINERS (LXC)

```
Special arguments:
[ -h | --help ]: Print this help message and exit
[ -l | --list ]: List all available images and exit

Required arguments:
[ -d | --dist <distribution> ]: The name of the distribution
[ -r | --release <release> ]: Release name/version
[ -a | --arch <architecture> ]: Architecture of the container
.
.
.
Environment Variables:
DOWNLOAD_KEYSERVER : The URL of the key server to use, instead
of the default.
                    Can be further overridden by using
                    optional argument --keyserver
```

As the default key server doesn't seem to work, we'll use the ubuntu key server instead. We can also see another interesting option, -l, which shows a list of the available images.

```
[root@pc-1196 ~]# DOWNLOAD_KEYSERVER="hkp://keyserver.ubuntu.com" /usr/share/lxc/templates/lxc-download --list
Setting up the GPG keyring
Downloading the image index

---
DIST          RELEASE      ARCH       VARIANT        BUILD
---
almalinux     8            amd64      default        20240723_23:08
almalinux     8            arm64      default        20240723_23:08
almalinux     9            amd64      default        20240723_23:08
almalinux     9            arm64      default        20240723_23:08
```

CHAPTER 8   LINUX CONTAINERS (LXC)

-
-
-

Now we'll try to create a new container based on the Ubuntu image. We have seen the options we need for the "download" template, and we'll take a look at the options needed for **lxc-create** in this distribution.

```
[root@pc-1196 ~]# lxc-create --help
Usage: lxc-create --name=NAME --template=TEMPLATE [OPTION...]
[-- template-options]
```

We launch the creation of the container.

```
[root@pc-1196 ~]# DOWNLOAD_KEYSERVER="hkp://keyserver.ubuntu.com" lxc-create -t download -n my_rockycont -- -d ubuntu -a amd64 -r bionic
Setting up the GPG keyring
Downloading the image index
Downloading the rootfs
Downloading the metadata
The image cache is now ready
Unpacking the rootfs

---
You just created an Ubuntu bionic amd64 (20240724_07:42) container.

To enable SSH, run: apt install openssh-server
No default root or user password are set by LXC.
```

In this case, we have no default user and password. We can reset the root password executing **chroot** on the container root filesystem. We did this in a previous example. Another possibility is to use **lxc-attach** to execute commands in the container. We also saw an example of this command previously.

CHAPTER 8 LINUX CONTAINERS (LXC)

If we try to start the container, we'll get this error:

```
[root@pc-1196 ~]# lxc-start -n my_rockycont
lxc-start: my_rockycont: lxccontainer.c: wait_on_daemonized_
start: 851 Received container state "ABORTING" instead of
"RUNNING"
lxc-start: my_rockycont: tools/lxc_start.c: main: 329 The
container failed to start
lxc-start: my_rockycont: tools/lxc_start.c: main: 332 To get
more details, run the container in foreground mode
lxc-start: my_rockycont: tools/lxc_start.c: main: 335
Additional information can be obtained by setting the --logfile
and --logpriority options
```

As suggested by the output text, we'll try to start the container on the foreground to get some more information.

```
[root@pc-1196 ~]# lxc-start -F -n my_rockycont
lxc-start: my_rockycont: network.c: lxc_ovs_attach_bridge: 2008
Failed to attach "lxcbr0" to openvswitch bridge "veth6MMLUB":
lxc-start: my_rockycont: utils.c: run_command_internal: 1648
Failed to exec command
lxc-start: my_rockycont: network.c: instantiate_veth: 173
Operation not permitted - Failed to attach "veth6MMLUB" to
bridge "lxcbr0"
lxc-start: my_rockycont: network.c: lxc_create_network_priv:
2577 Failed to create network device
lxc-start: my_rockycont: start.c: lxc_spawn: 1682 Failed to
create the network
lxc-start: my_rockycont: start.c: __lxc_start: 2019 Failed to
spawn container "my_rockycont"
lxc-start: my_rockycont: tools/lxc_start.c: main: 329 The
container failed to start
```

CHAPTER 8 LINUX CONTAINERS (LXC)

```
lxc-start: my_rockycont: tools/lxc_start.c: main: 335
Additional information can be obtained by setting the --logfile
and --logpriority options
```

We can see that when starting the containers, it tries to use the lxcbr0 interface, which currently doesn't exist. We'll install the **bridge-utils** package to create it.

```
[root@pc-1196 ~]# dnf install bridge-utils

[root@pc-1196 ~]# brctl addbr lxcbr0
[root@pc-1196 ~]# brctl show lxcbr0
bridge name     bridge id              STP enabled     interfaces
lxcbr0          8000.000000000000      no
```

Now that we have created the bridge interface, we can start the container.

```
[root@pc-1196 ~]# lxc-start -n my_rockycont
[root@pc-1196 ~]# brctl show lxcbr0
bridge name     bridge id              STP enabled     interfaces
lxcbr0          8000.febb5e5f4ad2      no              vethLCTPSW

[root@pc-1196 ~]# lxc-ls --fancy
NAME          STATE    AUTOSTART  GROUPS  IPV4  IPV6  UNPRIVILEGED
my_rockycont  RUNNING  0          -       -     -     false
```

We can see that the container was started, but obviously it has no IP address because we didn't configure any IP settings; we just created the lxcbr0 interface.

Now we can do a couple of things; we can manually configure the IP settings in both the host and the container and edit the firewall rules accordingly to be able to connect or we can use the lxc-net service instead. If we choose the second, and easier, option, we need to start the service.

```
[root@pc-1196 ~]# systemctl start lxc-net
```

However, if we restart the container right now, we'll see that it still has no IP address assigned. To find out more, we'll take a look at the definition of the service.

```
[root@pc-1196 ~]# systemctl cat lxc-net.service
# /usr/lib/systemd/system/lxc-net.service
[Unit]
Description=LXC network bridge setup
After=network-online.target
Wants=network-online.target
Before=lxc.service

[Service]
Type=oneshot
RemainAfterExit=yes
ExecStart=/usr/libexec/lxc/lxc-net start
ExecStop=/usr/libexec/lxc/lxc-net stop

[Install]
WantedBy=multi-user.target
```

We see that the service executes the */usr/libexec/lxc/lxc-net* script when it starts; we'll execute manually with the "-x" option to see more details of the execution.

```
[root@pc-1196 ~]# sh -x /usr/libexec/lxc/lxc-net start
+ distrosysconfdir=/etc/sysconfig
+ varrun=/run/lxc
+ varlib=/var/lib
+ USE_LXC_BRIDGE=true
+ LXC_BRIDGE=lxcbr0
+ LXC_BRIDGE_MAC=00:16:3e:00:00:00
+ LXC_ADDR=10.0.3.1
+ LXC_NETMASK=255.255.255.0
```

CHAPTER 8 LINUX CONTAINERS (LXC)

```
+ LXC_NETWORK=10.0.3.0/24
+ LXC_DHCP_RANGE=10.0.3.2,10.0.3.254
+ LXC_DHCP_MAX=253
+ LXC_DHCP_CONFILE=
+ LXC_DHCP_PING=true
+ LXC_DOMAIN=
+ LXC_IPV6_ADDR=
+ LXC_IPV6_MASK=
+ LXC_IPV6_NETWORK=
+ LXC_IPV6_NAT=false
+ '[' '!' -f /etc/sysconfig/lxc ']'
+ . /etc/sysconfig/lxc
++ LXC_AUTO=true
++ BOOTGROUPS=onboot,
++ SHUTDOWNDELAY=5
++ OPTIONS=
++ STOPOPTS='-a -A -s'
++ USE_LXC_BRIDGE=false
++ '[' '!' -f /etc/sysconfig/lxc-net ']'
+ use_iptables_lock=-w
+ iptables -w -L -n
+ case "$1" in
+ start
+ '[' xfalse = xtrue ']'
+ exit 0
```

In the first lines of execution, we see this line:

```
+ USE_LXC_BRIDGE=true
```

But later we see this other line:

```
++ USE_LXC_BRIDGE=false
```

CHAPTER 8 LINUX CONTAINERS (LXC)

This last value seems to be taken from the */etc/sysconfig/lxc* file. In fact, that's the case. In the file, we can see the following line:

```
USE_LXC_BRIDGE="false"   # overridden in lxc-net
```

And we change the value from "false" to "true".

```
USE_LXC_BRIDGE="true"    # overridden in lxc-net
```

If we run the script again, we'll see that now it seems to execute successfully.

```
[root@pc-1196 ~]# sh -x /usr/libexec/lxc/lxc-net start
+ distrosysconfdir=/etc/sysconfig
+ varrun=/run/lxc
+ varlib=/var/lib
+ USE_LXC_BRIDGE=true
+ LXC_BRIDGE=lxcbr0
+ LXC_BRIDGE_MAC=00:16:3e:00:00:00
+ LXC_ADDR=10.0.3.1
+ LXC_NETMASK=255.255.255.0
+ LXC_NETWORK=10.0.3.0/24
+ LXC_DHCP_RANGE=10.0.3.2,10.0.3.254
+ LXC_DHCP_MAX=253
+ LXC_DHCP_CONFILE=
+ LXC_DHCP_PING=true
+ LXC_DOMAIN=
+ LXC_IPV6_ADDR=
+ LXC_IPV6_MASK=
+ LXC_IPV6_NETWORK=
+ LXC_IPV6_NAT=false
+ '[' '!' -f /etc/sysconfig/lxc ']'
+ . /etc/sysconfig/lxc
++ LXC_AUTO=true
```

```
++ BOOTGROUPS=onboot,
++ SHUTDOWNDELAY=5
++ OPTIONS=
++ STOPOPTS='-a -A -s'
++ USE_LXC_BRIDGE=true
++ '[' '!' -f /etc/sysconfig/lxc-net ']'
+ use_iptables_lock=-w
+ iptables -w -L -n
+ case "$1" in
+ start
+ '[' xtrue = xtrue ']'
+ '[' '!' -f /run/lxc/network_up ']'
+ echo 'lxc-net is already running'
lxc-net is already running
+ exit 1
[root@pc-1196 ~]#
```

In fact, if we restart the service and the container, we will see now an associated IP address.

```
[root@pc-1196 ~]# systemctl restart lxc-net.service
[root@pc-1196 ~]# lxc-stop -n my_rockycont
[root@pc-1196 ~]# lxc-start -n my_rockycont
[root@pc-1196 ~]# lxc-ls --fancy
NAME          STATE    AUTOSTART GROUPS IPV4       IPV6 UNPRIVILEGED
my_rockycont RUNNING 0           -      10.0.3.96 -    false
```

And of course we can ping the container from the host and vice versa.

```
[root@pc-1196 ~]# ping -c 3 10.0.3.96
PING 10.0.3.96 (10.0.3.96) 56(84) bytes of data.
64 bytes from 10.0.3.96: icmp_seq=1 ttl=64 time=0.037 ms
64 bytes from 10.0.3.96: icmp_seq=2 ttl=64 time=0.086 ms
64 bytes from 10.0.3.96: icmp_seq=3 ttl=64 time=0.072 ms
```

CHAPTER 8　LINUX CONTAINERS (LXC)

```
--- 10.0.3.96 ping statistics ---
3 packets transmitted, 3 received, 0% packet loss, time 2053ms
rtt min/avg/max/mdev = 0.037/0.065/0.086/0.020 ms
```

As part of the setup, the lxc-net service has modified the iptables chains.

```
[root@pc-1196 ~]# iptables -L -t nat
Chain PREROUTING (policy ACCEPT)
target     prot opt source               destination

Chain INPUT (policy ACCEPT)
target     prot opt source               destination

Chain POSTROUTING (policy ACCEPT)
target     prot opt source               destination
MASQUERADE all  --  10.0.3.0/24          !10.0.3.0/24

Chain OUTPUT (policy ACCEPT)
target     prot opt source               destination
```

The service lxc-net has its parameters (IP addresses, DHCP ranges, etc.) hard-coded in the */usr/libexec/lxc/lxc-net* file. These are some of the relevant lines:

-
-
-

```
USE_LXC_BRIDGE="true"
LXC_BRIDGE="lxcbr0"
LXC_BRIDGE_MAC="00:16:3e:00:00:00"
LXC_ADDR="10.0.3.1"
LXC_NETMASK="255.255.255.0"
LXC_NETWORK="10.0.3.0/24"
LXC_DHCP_RANGE="10.0.3.2,10.0.3.254"
```

LXC_DHCP_MAX="253"

·
·
·

DHCP services are provided by dnsmasq, which we already saw briefly when we studied QEMU.

·
·
·

```
dnsmasq $LXC_DHCP_CONFILE_ARG $LXC_DOMAIN_ARG $LXC_DHCP_
PING_ARG -u ${DNSMASQ_USER} \
        --strict-order --bind-interfaces --pid-
          file="${varrun}"/dnsmasq.pid \
        --listen-address ${LXC_ADDR} --dhcp-range ${LXC_
          DHCP_RANGE} \
        --dhcp-lease-max=${LXC_DHCP_MAX} --dhcp-no-
          override \
        --except-interface=lo --interface=${LXC_BRIDGE} \
        --dhcp-leasefile="${varlib}"/misc/dnsmasq.${LXC_
          BRIDGE}.leases \
        --dhcp-authoritative $LXC_IPV6_ARG || cleanup
```

·
·
·

We can see the dnsmasq program in execution in the host.

```
[root@pc-1196 ~]# ps -ef | grep dnsmasq
dnsmasq    161019       1  0 23:20 ?        00:00:00 dnsmasq
-u dnsmasq --strict-order --bind-interfaces --pid-file=/
run/lxc/dnsmasq.pid --listen-address 10.0.3.1 --dhcp-range
```

CHAPTER 8 LINUX CONTAINERS (LXC)

```
10.0.3.2,10.0.3.254 --dhcp-lease-max=253 --dhcp-no-override
--except-interface=lo --interface=lxcbr0 --dhcp-leasefile=/var/
lib/misc/dnsmasq.lxcbr0.leases –dhcp-authoritative
```

This is also true if we work in Ubuntu. But in that case, it was all transparent for us because we didn't need to create the bridge interface and the lxc-net service was automatically started before lxc. But it is present.

```
antonio@antonio-Laptop:~$ systemctl status lxc-net
● lxc-net.service - LXC network bridge setup
    Loaded: loaded (/lib/systemd/system/lxc-net.service;
    enabled; vendor preset: enabled)
    Active: active (exited) since Tue 2024-07-23 19:15:11
    CEST; 2 days ago
●
●
●
```

And the **dnsmasq** is running too.

```
antonio@antonio-Laptop:~$ ps -ef | grep dnsmasq
lxc-dns+    3080       1  0 jul23 ?        00:00:00 dnsmasq
--conf-file=/dev/null -u lxc-dnsmasq --strict-order --bind-
interfaces --pid-file=/run/lxc/dnsmasq.pid --listen-address
10.0.3.1 --dhcp-range 10.0.3.2,10.0.3.254 --dhcp-lease-max=253
--dhcp-no-override --except-interface=lo --interface=lxcbr0
--dhcp-leasefile=/var/lib/misc/dnsmasq.lxcbr0.leases --dhcp-
authoritative
antonio   159839   41440  0 19:19 pts/1    00:00:00 grep
--color=auto dnsmasq
```

Security in LXC

We have seen a few commands and characteristics related to LXC, though there are many more available and it is not possible to cover all of them in this book. And it is also outside the scope of the 305 exam. But we'll see some additional options we have available.

Let's get back to our Ubuntu system and look again at the *config* file.

```
antonio@antonio-Laptop:~/antonio/LXC$ sudo cat /var/lib/lxc/my_container/config
# Template used to create this container: /usr/share/lxc/templates/lxc-ubuntu
# Parameters passed to the template:
# For additional config options, please look at lxc.container.conf(5)
.
.
.
```

In the file, we have a few options set, and we're told that we can check the man page of lxc.container.conf for a full list. We'll open this man page, and we'll see a lot of different config options.

We'll focus this time in the security-related options. We'll see a wide section about cgroups.

```
CONTROL GROUPS ("CGROUPS")
    The  control  group section contains the configuration
    for the different subsystem.
.
.
.
```

CHAPTER 8 LINUX CONTAINERS (LXC)

> lxc.cgroup.dir
> > specify a directory or path in which the container's cgroup will be created.

-
-
-

We also have a capabilities section. As you probably remember, because we studied them in the previous chapter, these capabilities are subsets of privileges usually associated to the root user. We can grant (or deny) a container any of these capabilities.

-
-

> CAPABILITIES
> > The capabilities can be dropped in the container if this one is run as root.
>
> lxc.cap.drop
> > Specify the capability to be dropped in the container.

-
-

> lxc.cap.keep
> > Specify the capability to be kept in the container.

-
-

We also have a section for namespaces:

-
-

> NAMESPACES

400

CHAPTER 8 LINUX CONTAINERS (LXC)

```
A namespace can be cloned (lxc.namespace.clone),
kept (lxc.namespace.keep) or shared (lxc.namespace.
share.[namespace
identifier]).
```

-
-

Another section for AppArmor:

-
-

```
APPARMOR PROFILE
    If lxc was compiled and installed with apparmor support,
    and the host system has apparmor enabled, then the
    apparmor pro- file under which the container should be
    run can be specified in the container configuration.
```

-
-

...and for SELinux...

-
-

```
SELINUX CONTEXT
    If lxc was compiled and installed with SELinux support
```

-
-

```
lxc.selinux.context
        Specify the SELinux context under which the
        container should be run or unconfined_t.
        For example
```

401

CHAPTER 8   LINUX CONTAINERS (LXC)

```
            lxc.selinux.context = system_u:system_r:lxc_t:s0:c22
```

-
-
-

And finally, seccomp:

-
-

SECCOMP CONFIGURATION

A container can be started with a reduced set of available system calls by loading a seccomp profile at startup.

-
-

We're gonna see a small example changing the AppArmor profile. The first thing we need to do is to list the profiles with **aa-status**.

```
antonio@antonio-Laptop:~/antonio/LXC$ sudo aa-status
apparmor module is loaded.
99 profiles are loaded.
97 profiles are in enforce mode.
```

-
-
-

  lxc-container-default
  lxc-container-default-cgns
  lxc-container-default-with-mounting
  lxc-container-default-with-nesting

-
-
-

We can see there are four different AppArmor profiles for LXC. If the host kernel is cgroup namespace aware – most of the kernels in use today are – then the default AppArmor profile will be lxc-container-default.

We're going to change this default profile. To make a very simplistic test, we edit the *config* file of the container and add this line to select an unexisting profile:

`lxc.apparmor.profile = lxc-container-default-blablabla`

If we start the container, we get an error.

```
antonio@antonio-Laptop:~$ sudo lxc-start -n my_container
lxc-start: my_container: lxccontainer.c: wait_on_daemonized_start: 877 Received container state "ABORTING" instead of "RUNNING"
lxc-start: my_container: tools/lxc_start.c: main: 306 The container failed to start
lxc-start: my_container: tools/lxc_start.c: main: 309 To get more details, run the container in foreground mode
lxc-start: my_container: tools/lxc_start.c: main: 311 Additional information can be obtained by setting the --logfile and --logpriority options
```

We'll use the --logfile option to obtain more information.

```
antonio@antonio-Laptop:~$ sudo lxc-start -n my_container --logfile /tmp/lxclog.txt
```

We'll open the log file, and we'll see clearly that AppArmor couldn't locate the AppArmor profile.

```
antonio@antonio-Laptop:~$ sudo cat /tmp/lxclog.txt
lxc-start my_container 20240725194051.671 ERROR    apparmor - lsm/apparmor.c:apparmor_process_label_set_at:1183 - No such
```

file or directory - Failed to write AppArmor profile "lxc-container-default-blablabla" to 13
.
.
.

The AppArmor profiles for LXC are located in */etc/apparmor.d/lxc*.

```
antonio@antonio-Laptop:~$ ls /etc/apparmor.d/lxc
lxc-default   lxc-default-cgns   lxc-default-with-mounting   lxc-default-with-nesting
```

We can simply copy the default profile and rename it.

```
antonio@antonio-Laptop:~$ sudo cp /etc/apparmor.d/lxc/lxc-default /etc/apparmor.d/lxc/lxc-default-blablabla
```

We also need to edit the copied file to change the name of the profile.

```
profile lxc-container-default-blablabla
```

And we restart the AppArmor service.

```
antonio@antonio-Laptop:~$ sudo systemctl restart apparmor.service
```

Now we can start the container.

```
antonio@antonio-Laptop:~$ sudo lxc-start -n my_container
```

Other LXC Commands

There are many more LXC-related commands. We'll see a couple of them here that might be interesting.

lxc-monitor

This tool monitors the state of the container(s). To see an example, we'll launch it in a terminal shell.

antonio@antonio-Laptop:~$ sudo lxc-monitor

In another shell, we'll perform several operations in a container. We'll start it.

antonio@antonio-Laptop:~$ sudo lxc-start -n my_container

Then we'll freeze it.

antonio@antonio-Laptop:~$ sudo lxc-freeze -n my_container

After a while, we'll unfreeze it again.

antonio@antonio-Laptop:~$ sudo lxc-unfreeze -n my_container

And finally we'll stop the container.

antonio@antonio-Laptop:~$ sudo lxc-stop -n my_container

In the first terminal shell (the one in which we executed **lxc-monitor**), we'll see this:

```
antonio@antonio-Laptop:~$ sudo lxc-monitor
'my_container' changed state to [STARTING]
'my_container' changed state to [RUNNING]
'my_container' changed state to [FREEZING]
'my_container' changed state to [FROZEN]
'my_container' changed state to [THAWED]
'my_container' changed state to [RUNNING]
'my_container' exited with status [0]
'my_container' changed state to [STOPPING]
'my_container' changed state to [STOPPED]
```

lxc-cgroups

We have studied in the previous chapter how control groups, cgroups for short, can limit the use of resources by certain processes. This is one of the core technologies used by containers because it allows to account and limit the resources used by each container.

We already saw how to use cgroup to limit the use of resources by manually editing files in the */sys/fs/cgroup* tree. We can do the same thing for a certain container with the **lxc-cgroup** command.

The way to use it is very simple; we pass the name of the container and the cgroup object to get the actual value of that cgroup.

```
antonio@antonio-Laptop:~$ sudo lxc-cgroup -n my_container memory.max
max
```

If we want to set a new value, we repeat the command adding the desired value at the end.

```
antonio@antonio-Laptop:~$ sudo lxc-cgroup -n my_container memory.max 10240000
antonio@antonio-Laptop:~$ sudo lxc-cgroup -n my_container memory.max
10240000
```

Of course, at any point, we can restore it to its default value.

```
antonio@antonio-Laptop:~$ sudo lxc-cgroup -n my_container memory.max max
antonio@antonio-Laptop:~$ sudo lxc-cgroup -n my_container memory.max
max
```

CHAPTER 8 LINUX CONTAINERS (LXC)

LXD

LXD is a container management tool developed by Canonical. It is built on top of LXC, and it offers several advantages, like a REST API to remotely manage containers over the network. It also supports live migration. As it was developed by the creators of Ubuntu, it is available for installation in the official Ubuntu repositories.

In older versions of Ubuntu, it can be installed as any other application from the official repositories. In newer versions, it is installed as a snap.

```
antonio@antonio-Laptop:~$ lxd
Command 'lxd' not found, but can be installed with:
sudo snap install lxd          # version 6.1-c14927a, or
sudo apt  install lxd-installer # version 1
See 'snap info lxd' for additional versions.

antonio@antonio-Laptop:~$ sudo snap install lxd
[sudo] password for antonio:
lxd (5.21/stable) 5.21.2-34459c8 from Canonical✓ installed
```

When we install LXD, we're basically installing a server (**lxd**) and a client (**lxc**). We'll perform most of the work on the client, using the many subcommands available. For instance, if we want to list the remote repositories currently available, we'd do it like this:

```
antonio@antonio-Laptop:~$ lxc remote list
If this is your first time running LXD on this machine, you
should also run: lxd init
To start your first container, try: lxc launch ubuntu:24.04
Or for a virtual machine: lxc launch ubuntu:24.04 --vm
```

NAME	URL	PROTOCOL	AUTH TYPE	PUBLIC	STATIC	GLOBAL
images	https://images.lxd.canonical.com	simplestreams	none	YES	NO	NO
local (current)	unix://	lxd	file access	NO	YES	NO
ubuntu	https://cloud-images.ubuntu.com/releases	simplestreams	none	YES	YES	NO
ubuntu-daily	https://cloud-images.ubuntu.com/daily	simplestreams	none	YES	YES	NO

```
| ubuntu-minimal        | https://cloud-images.ubuntu.com/
minimal/releases/ | simplestreams | none           | YES    |
YES    | NO     |
+--------------------+------------------------------
-----------------+-------------+-------------+-------+
-------+-------+
| ubuntu-minimal-daily | https://cloud-images.ubuntu.com/
minimal/daily/    | simplestreams | none           | YES    |
YES    | NO     |
+--------------------+------------------------------
-----------------+-------------+-------------+-------+
-------+-------+
```

We won't interact very often with **lxd**, but there are some cases in which we need to. When we listed the remote repositories, the output suggested to run "**lxd init**". This is usually the first command to execute to set up LXD. We'll execute it in a moment, but for now, let's take a look at the different options available for the **lxd** command.

```
antonio@antonio-Laptop:~$ lxd --help
Description:
  The LXD container manager (daemon)
.
.
.
Available Commands:
  activateifneeded   Check if LXD should be started
  cluster            Low-level cluster administration commands
  help               Help about any command
  import             Command has been replaced with "lxd
                     recover"
```

CHAPTER 8 LINUX CONTAINERS (LXC)

```
    init                Configure the LXD daemon
    recover             Recover missing instances and volumes from
                        existing and unknown storage pools
    shutdown            Tell LXD to shutdown all containers
                        and exit
    version             Show the server version
    waitready           Wait for LXD to be ready to process
                        requests
```

We see there are various options available; we can use "init" to configure it properly, "version" to get the version, "shutdown" to gracefully shut down all the containers and exit, etc. We're gonna check our LXD version and use "init" to configure our LXD server. We'll review the configuration step by step.

```
antonio@antonio-Laptop:~$ lxd --version
5.21.2 LTS
antonio@antonio-Laptop:~$ sudo lxd init
Would you like to use LXD clustering? (yes/no) [default=no]:
```

LXD can be installed in cluster. For our purpose, this is not necessary.

```
Do you want to configure a new storage pool? (yes/no)
[default=yes]:
Name of the new storage pool [default=default]:
Name of the storage backend to use (powerflex, zfs, btrfs,
ceph, dir, lvm) [default=zfs]: dir
```

In LXD, we can use different types of storage pools: simple directories and logical volumes. You can also choose Ceph or ZFS, which we already mentioned in the "LXC" section. It is also possible to use PowerFlex, a software-based SAN. In our case, we chose to use a simple directory.

```
Would you like to connect to a MAAS server? (yes/no)
[default=no]:
```

CHAPTER 8   LINUX CONTAINERS (LXC)

We don't want to connect to a MAAS server. MAAS (Metal as a Service) is a new service developed by Canonical, the creator of Ubuntu, that allows the provisioning of bare-metal servers.

```
Would you like to create a new local network bridge? (yes/no)
[default=yes]:
```

We could use an existing bridge, but we prefer to create a new bridge interface for its use on LXD.

```
What should the new bridge be called? [default=lxdbr0]:
What IPv4 address should be used? (CIDR subnet notation, "auto"
or "none") [default=auto]:
What IPv6 address should be used? (CIDR subnet notation, "auto"
or "none") [default=auto]:
```

We use the default values for the new bridge.

```
Would you like the LXD server to be available over the network?
(yes/no) [default=no]:
```

We don't need the LXD server to be available over the network, as we'll only use it locally.

```
Would you like stale cached images to be updated automatically?
(yes/no) [default=yes]:
Would you like a YAML "lxd init" preseed to be printed? (yes/
no) [default=no]:
```

When we download images to create a container, these images are cached. We can choose whether to update these images or not. It's not really important for our purposes, so we choose the default value. We could also see all the parameters selected during the setup in YAML, but we declined this possibility.

CHAPTER 8   LINUX CONTAINERS (LXC)

Creating Our First Container on LXD

To create our first container on LXD, we need to select an image first. We can search for the images available for a certain Linux distribution, like Ubuntu.

antonio@antonio-Laptop:~$ lxc image list ubuntu:

.

.

.

```
---------+-----------------------------------------------+
|                    | ffae848ee5a0 | yes    | ubuntu 20.04 LTS
amd64 (release) (20200529.1)    | x86_64       | CONTAINER       |
303.76MiB   | May 29, 2020 at 12:00am (UTC) |
+------------------+--------------+-------+------------------
----------------------------+-------------+---------------+
----------+----------------------------+
|                    | ffb876ca48fb | yes    | ubuntu 18.04 LTS
i386 (release) (20200107)       | i686         | VIRTUAL-MACHINE |
318.13MiB   | Jan 7, 2020 at 12:00am (UTC)  |
+------------------+--------------+-------+------------------
----------------------------+-------------+---------------+
----------+----------------------------+
```

We can see that the list is really long. We'll launch an Ubuntu 24 container.

antonio@antonio-Laptop:~$ lxc launch ubuntu:24.04
Creating the instance
Instance name is: harmless-monarch
Starting harmless-monarch

CHAPTER 8 LINUX CONTAINERS (LXC)

After a few seconds, we can list this new instance:

```
antonio@antonio-Laptop:~$ lxc list
+----------------+---------+------------------------+-----------------------------------------------+-----------+-----------+
|      NAME      |  STATE  |          IPV4          |                     IPV6                      |   TYPE    | SNAPSHOTS |
+----------------+---------+------------------------+-----------------------------------------------+-----------+-----------+
| harmless-monarch | RUNNING | 10.216.182.156 (eth0) | fd42:45f7:c283:6d95:216:3eff:fe35:96d9 (eth0) | CONTAINER | 0         |
+----------------+---------+------------------------+-----------------------------------------------+-----------+-----------+
```

We can connect to the container console in a similar way to what we have seen with the classical LXC-related tools.

```
antonio@antonio-Laptop:~$ lxc console harmless-monarch
To detach from the console, press: <ctrl>+a q

harmless-monarch login: ubuntu
Password:

Login incorrect
harmless-monarch login:
```

However, in this container, we don't have a default user and password that we can use to log in. So we'll use **lxc exec** to execute commands. For instance, we can list the IP addresses in the container.

```
antonio@antonio-Laptop:~$ lxc exec harmless-monarch -- ip a
1: lo: <LOOPBACK,UP,LOWER_UP> mtu 65536 qdisc noqueue state UNKNOWN group default qlen 1000
    link/loopback 00:00:00:00:00:00 brd 00:00:00:00:00:00
```

```
    inet 127.0.0.1/8 scope host lo
       valid_lft forever preferred_lft forever
    inet6 ::1/128 scope host
       valid_lft forever preferred_lft forever
23: eth0@if24: <BROADCAST,MULTICAST,UP,LOWER_UP> mtu 1500 qdisc
noqueue state UP group default qlen 1000
    link/ether 00:16:3e:35:96:d9 brd ff:ff:ff:ff:ff:ff link-
    netnsid 0
    inet 10.216.182.156/24 metric 100 brd 10.216.182.255 scope
    global dynamic eth0
       valid_lft 3047sec preferred_lft 3047sec
    inet6 fd42:45f7:c283:6d95:216:3eff:fe35:96d9/64 scope
    global mngtmpaddr noprefixroute
       valid_lft forever preferred_lft forever
    inet6 fe80::216:3eff:fe35:96d9/64 scope link
       valid_lft forever preferred_lft forever
```

We'll use this option to create a new user.

```
antonio@antonio-Laptop:~$ lxc exec harmless-monarch -- useradd
-m antonio
```

And now we'll open a shell to change the password for the user we just created.

```
antonio@antonio-Laptop:~$ lxc exec harmless-monarch -- /
bin/bash
root@harmless-monarch:~# passwd antonio
New password:
Retype new password:
passwd: password updated successfully
root@harmless-monarch:~# exit
exit
```

CHAPTER 8 LINUX CONTAINERS (LXC)

Now that we have a valid username and a valid password, we can connect to the console.

```
antonio@antonio-Laptop:~$ lxc console harmless-monarch
To detach from the console, press: <ctrl>+a q

harmless-monarch login: antonio
Password:
run-parts: /etc/update-motd.d/98-fsck-at-reboot exited with
return code 2

The programs included with the Ubuntu system are free software;
the exact distribution terms for each program are
described in the
individual files in /usr/share/doc/*/copyright.

Ubuntu comes with ABSOLUTELY NO WARRANTY, to the extent
permitted by
applicable law.

$
```

Unfortunately, we didn't include our user in the *sudoers* file.

```
$ sudo su - root
[sudo] password for antonio:
antonio is not in the sudoers file.
```

To execute commands as root, we could do several things; we could reset the root password as we did with the password of this user. We could also include the user "antonio" in the sudoers file or we could try to log in as the "ubuntu" user, which is usually included in the Ubuntu containers and can execute sudo commands. We check if this user exists.

```
$ id ubuntu
uid=1000(ubuntu) gid=1000(ubuntu) groups=1000(ubuntu),4(adm),24
(cdrom),27(sudo),30(dip),105(lxd)$ exit
```

As the user "ubuntu" exists, we'll execute a shell to reset the password.

```
antonio@antonio-Laptop:~$ lxc exec harmless-monarch -- /bin/bash
root@harmless-monarch:~# passwd ubuntu
New password:
Retype new password:
passwd: password updated successfully
root@harmless-monarch:~# exit
exit
```

Now we can connect to the console with the ubuntu user.

```
antonio@antonio-Laptop:~$ lxc console harmless-monarch
To detach from the console, press: <ctrl>+a q
.
.
.
To run a command as administrator (user "root"), use "sudo <command>".
See "man sudo_root" for details.

ubuntu@harmless-monarch:~$
```

From now on, we can fully manage our container with the "ubuntu" user. Apart from that, we can stop the container with "**lxc stop**" or start it again with "**lxc start**".

Managing Server and Container Configuration

We can show and manage server and container configuration options with "**lxc config**". For instance, we can check the configuration options of our container.

```
antonio@antonio-Laptop:~$ lxc config show harmless-monarch
architecture: x86_64
config:
  image.architecture: amd64
  image.description: ubuntu 24.04 LTS amd64 (release)
(20240725)
  image.label: release
  image.os: ubuntu
  image.release: noble
  image.serial: "20240725"
.
.
.
```

We can also get some information about the LXD server with **lxc info**.

```
antonio@antonio-Laptop:~$ lxc info
config: {}
api_extensions:
- storage_zfs_remove_snapshots
- container_host_shutdown_timeout
- container_stop_priority
- container_syscall_filtering
- auth_pki
- container_last_used_at
- etag
- patch
- usb_devices
.
.
.
```

```
storage: dir
storage_version: "1"
storage_supported_drivers:
- name: cephobject
  version: 17.2.7
  remote: true
- name: dir
  version: "1"
  remote: false
- name: lvm
  version: 2.03.11(2) (2021-01-08) / 1.02.175 (2021-01-08)
  / 4.48.0
  remote: false
- name: powerflex
  version: 1.16 (nvme-cli)
  remote: true
- name: zfs
  version: 2.2.0-0ubuntu1~23.10.3
  remote: false
- name: btrfs
  version: 5.16.2
  remote: false
- name: ceph
  version: 17.2.7
  remote: true
- name: cephfs
  version: 17.2.7
  remote: true
```

We can also use **lxc info** to get information about a container by appending the name of the container to the command.

```
antonio@antonio-Laptop:~$ lxc info harmless-monarch
Name: harmless-monarch
Status: RUNNING
Type: container
Architecture: x86_64
PID: 39785
Created: 2024/07/27 03:01 CEST
Last Used: 2024/07/27 03:01 CEST

Resources:
  Processes: 27
  CPU usage:
    CPU usage (in seconds): 11
  Memory usage:
    Memory (current): 59.41MiB
    Swap (current): 4.00KiB
  Network usage:
    eth0:
      Type: broadcast
      State: UP
```

·
·
·

Networking in LXD

When we executed **lxd init**, we chose to create a new bridge interface to use with LXD with the default configuration.

CHAPTER 8 LINUX CONTAINERS (LXC)

At any moment, we can list the networks available to LXD, which are all the networks the host is connected to.

```
antonio@antonio-Laptop:~$ lxc network list
+----------------+----------+--------+----------------+
+--------------------------+-------------+---------+--------+
|      NAME      |   TYPE   | MANAGED |      IPV4      |
          IPV6               | DESCRIPTION | USED BY | STATE |
+----------------+----------+--------+----------------+
+--------------------------+-------------+---------+-------+
| br-4d7a80d63283 | bridge  | NO     |                |
                            |             | 0       |        |
+----------------+----------+--------+----------------+
+--------------------------+-------------+---------+-------+
| docker0        | bridge   | NO     |                |
                            |             | 0       |        |
+----------------+----------+--------+----------------+
+--------------------------+-------------+---------+-------+
| lxcbr0         | bridge   | NO     |                |
                            |             | 0       |        |
+----------------+----------+--------+---------+--------+
+--------------------------+----------------------+--------+
| lxdbr0         | bridge   | YES    | 10.216.182.1/24 |
 fd42:45f7:c283:6d95::1/64  |             | 2       | CREATED |
+----------------+----------+--------+---------+-------+
+--------------------------+-------------+--------+--------+
```

-
-
-

We can get more information about a certain network with **lxc network show**.

```
antonio@antonio-Laptop:~$ lxc network show lxdbr0
name: lxdbr0
description: ""
type: bridge
managed: true
status: Created
config:
  ipv4.address: 10.216.182.1/24
  ipv4.nat: "true"
  ipv6.address: fd42:45f7:c283:6d95::1/64
  ipv6.nat: "true"
used_by:
- /1.0/instances/harmless-monarch
- /1.0/profiles/default
locations:
- none
```

We can see here that the container "harmless-monarch" is attached to the lxdbr0 network. And we can also see the network settings. We can obtain similar information with **lxc network info**, but with the latter command, we can also get information about the VLAN and the statistics of usage.

```
antonio@antonio-Laptop:~$ lxc network info lxdbr0
Name: lxdbr0
MAC address: 00:16:3e:55:1d:e3
MTU: 1500
State: up
```

CHAPTER 8   LINUX CONTAINERS (LXC)

Type: broadcast

IP addresses:
  inet   10.216.182.1/24 (global)
  inet6   fd42:45f7:c283:6d95::1/64 (global)
  inet6   fe80::216:3eff:fe55:1de3/64 (link)

Network usage:
  Bytes received: 414.76kB
  Bytes sent: 30.66MB
  Packets received: 5196
  Packets sent: 7179

Bridge:
  ID: 8000.00163e551de3
  STP: false
  Forward delay: 1500
  Default VLAN ID: 1
  VLAN filtering: true
  Upper devices: veth4e29f2a6

It is also possible to list the DHCP leases.

```
antonio@antonio-Laptop:~$ lxc network list-leases lxdbr0
+------------------+-------------------+----------------------------------------+---------+
|     HOSTNAME     |    MAC ADDRESS    |                IP ADDRESS              |   TYPE  |
+------------------+-------------------+----------------------------------------+---------+
| harmless-monarch | 00:16:3e:35:96:d9 | 10.216.182.156                         | DYNAMIC |
+------------------+-------------------+----------------------------------------+---------+
| harmless-monarch | 00:16:3e:35:96:d9 | fd42:45f7:c283:6d95:216:3eff:fe35:96d9 | DYNAMIC |
+------------------+-------------------+----------------------------------------+---------+
| lxdbr0.gw        |                   | 10.216.182.1                           | GATEWAY |
+------------------+-------------------+----------------------------------------+---------+
| lxdbr0.gw        |                   | fd42:45f7:c283:6d95::1                 | GATEWAY |
+------------------+-------------------+----------------------------------------+---------+
```

CHAPTER 8 LINUX CONTAINERS (LXC)

If we want to or we need to, it is very easy to create a new network.

```
antonio@antonio-Laptop:~$ lxc network create new_lxd_net
Network new_lxd_net created
```

We can see immediately the new network listed.

```
antonio@antonio-Laptop:~$ lxc network list | grep new_lxd_net
| new_lxd_net      | bridge  | YES    | 10.181.16.1/24   |
fd42:6c3f:1f2f:fd9d::1/64 |           | 0        | CREATED |
```

And we can see the default configuration of the newly created network.

```
antonio@antonio-Laptop:~$ lxc network show new_lxd_net
name: new_lxd_net
description: ""
type: bridge
managed: true
status: Created
config:
  ipv4.address: 10.181.16.1/24
  ipv4.nat: "true"
  ipv6.address: fd42:6c3f:1f2f:fd9d::1/64
  ipv6.nat: "true"
used_by: []
locations:
- none
```

If we want to edit the network settings, we can use lxc network edit. An editor will appear with the default configuration, and we can edit this configuration according to our needs.

```
antonio@antonio-Laptop:~$ lxc network edit new_lxd_net
```

CHAPTER 8 LINUX CONTAINERS (LXC)

Storage in LXD

When we initialized LXD, we saw briefly the options when choosing what storage to use in LXD. Similarly to what we did with the networks, we can list the storage currently in use.

```
antonio@antonio-Laptop:~$ lxc storage list
+---------+--------+-----------------------------------------+-------------+---------+---------+
| NAME    | DRIVER |                 SOURCE                  | DESCRIPTION | USED BY |  STATE  |
+---------+--------+-----------------------------------------+-------------+---------+---------+
| default | dir    | /var/snap/lxd/common/lxd/storage-pools/default |      |    2    | CREATED |
+---------+--------+-----------------------------------------+-------------+---------+---------+
```

Remember that we created a storage of the type "dir", a simple directory in the host. Let's review its configuration.

```
antonio@antonio-Laptop:~$ lxc storage info default
info:
  description: ""
  driver: dir
  name: default
  space used: 719.75GiB
  total space: 786.75GiB
used by:
  instances:
  - harmless-monarch
  profiles:
  - default
```

Now, we'll create a new storage. This time we'll choose btrfs.

```
antonio@antonio-Laptop:~$ lxc storage create mynewstorage btrfs
Storage pool mynewstorage created
```

When we list the available storage pools, we'll see the default and the new one.

424

```
antonio@antonio-Laptop:~$ lxc storage list
+--------------+--------+-------------------------------------
-----------+-------------+---------+---------+
|    NAME      | DRIVER |
SOURCE                        | DESCRIPTION | USED BY |  STATE  |
+--------------+--------+-------------------------------------
-----------+-------------+---------+---------+
| default      | dir    | /var/snap/lxd/common/lxd/storage-pools/
default   |                  | 2       | CREATED |
+--------------+--------+-------------------------------------
-----------+-------------+---------+---------+
| mynewstorage | btrfs  | /var/snap/lxd/common/lxd/disks/
mynewstorage.img |                 | 0       | CREATED |
+--------------+--------+-------------------------------------
-----------+-------------+---------+---------+
```

And this new storage pool is an image file formatted with the btrfs filesystem.

```
antonio@antonio-Laptop:~$ sudo file /var/snap/lxd/common/lxd/
disks/mynewstorage.img
/var/snap/lxd/common/lxd/disks/mynewstorage.img: BTRFS
Filesystem label "mynewstorage", sectorsize 4096,
nodesize 16384, leafsize 16384, UUID=911f4a1f-1f5b-4042-
a8b1-778c3eda580f, 147456/5368709120 bytes used, 1 devices
```

In fact, we can mount this disk image file, and we'll see all the folders included.

```
antonio@antonio-Laptop:~$ ls /mnt/mydata/
buckets   containers   containers-snapshots   custom   custom-
snapshots   images   virtual-machines   virtual-machines-snapshots
```

```
antonio@antonio-Laptop:~$ sudo mount | grep -i btrfs
/var/snap/lxd/common/lxd/disks/mynewstorage.img on /mnt/mydata
type btrfs (rw,relatime,ssd,discard=async,space_cache=v2,user_
subvol_rm_allowed,subvolid=5,subvol=/)
```

As we don't need to mount the disk file, we'll unmount it.

```
antonio@antonio-Laptop:~$ sudo umount /mnt/mydata
```

At any moment, we can obtain information about this storage pool with the commands lxc storage show and lxc storage info.

```
antonio@antonio-Laptop:~$ lxc storage show mynewstorage
name: mynewstorage
description: ""
driver: btrfs
status: Created
config:
  size: 4GiB
  source: /var/snap/lxd/common/lxd/disks/mynewstorage.img
used_by: []
locations:
- none
antonio@antonio-Laptop:~$ lxc storage info mynewstorage
info:
  description: ""
  driver: btrfs
  name: mynewstorage
  space used: 5.78MiB
  total space: 4.00GiB
used by: {}
```

CHAPTER 8   LINUX CONTAINERS (LXC)

LXD Profiles

Profiles are sets of configuration options that can be applied to a container instance. Initially, we only have one profile defined.

```
antonio@antonio-Laptop:~$ lxc profile list
+---------+----------------------+---------+
|  NAME   |     DESCRIPTION      | USED BY |
+---------+----------------------+---------+
| default | Default LXD profile  | 1       |
+---------+----------------------+---------+
```

If we check the characteristics of this default profile, we'll see that it uses the lxdbr0 network, the default storage pool, etc. We'll also see that the only container instance we have right now is associated to this profile.

```
antonio@antonio-Laptop:~$ lxc profile show default
name: default
description: Default LXD profile
config: {}
devices:
  eth0:
    name: eth0
    network: lxdbr0
    type: nic
  root:
    path: /
    pool: default
    type: disk
used_by:
- /1.0/instances/harmless-monarch
```

CHAPTER 8   LINUX CONTAINERS (LXC)

To see an easy example, we're going to create a new profile.

```
antonio@antonio-Laptop:~$ lxc profile create my_new_profile
Profile my_new_profile created
```

This new profile will appear now in the profile listing.

```
antonio@antonio-HP-Laptop-15s-fq1xxx:~$ lxc profile list
+----------------+----------------------+---------+
|      NAME      |     DESCRIPTION      | USED BY |
+----------------+----------------------+---------+
| default        | Default LXD profile  | 1       |
+----------------+----------------------+---------+
| my_new_profile |                      | 0       |
+----------------+----------------------+---------+
```

We'll edit the new profile to add a description and associate it with the network we created previously.

```
antonio@antonio-Laptop:~$ lxc profile edit my_new_profile
.
.
.
name: my_new_profile
description: A new profile
config: {}
devices:
  eth0:
    name: eth0
    network: new_lxd_net
    type: nic
  root:
    path: /
    pool: default
```

CHAPTER 8 LINUX CONTAINERS (LXC)

```
    type: disk
used_by: []
```

And we'll launch a new instance using the new profile (-p) and the new storage (-s).

```
antonio@antonio-Laptop:~$ lxc launch ubuntu:24.04 -p my_new_
profile -s mynewstorage
Creating the instance
Instance name is: shining-flounder
Starting shining-flounder
```

If we list the instances now, we'll see two running instances: the old one and the new one.

```
antonio@antonio-Laptop:~$ lxc list
+------------------+---------+-----------------------+---------
------------------------------------+-----------+-----------+
|       NAME       |  STATE  |         IPV4
|                     IPV6                       |   TYPE    |
SNAPSHOTS |
+------------------+---------+-----------------------+---------
------------------------------------+-----------+-----------+
| harmless-monarch | RUNNING | 10.216.182.156 (eth0) | fd42:45f7
:c283:6d95:216:3eff:fe35:96d9 (eth0) | CONTAINER | 0         |
+------------------+---------+-----------------------+---------
------------------------------------+-----------+-----------+
| shining-flounder | RUNNING | 10.136.213.51 (eth0)  | fd42:76c
3:13a4:c5a:216:3eff:fee5:6630 (eth0) | CONTAINER | 0         |
+------------------+---------+-----------------------+---------
------------------------------------+-----------+-----------+
```

CHAPTER 8　LINUX CONTAINERS (LXC)

And if we check the new_lxd_net network and the mynewstorage storage pool, we'll see that this new instance is associated with them.

```
antonio@antonio-Laptop:~$ lxc network show new_lxd_net
name: new_lxd_net
description: ""
type: bridge
managed: true
status: Created
config:
  ipv4.address: 10.136.213.1/24
  ipv4.nat: "true"
  ipv6.address: fd42:76c3:13a4:c5a::1/64
  ipv6.nat: "true"
used_by:
- /1.0/instances/shining-flounder
- /1.0/profiles/my_new_profile
locations:
- none

antonio@antonio-Laptop:~$ lxc storage info mynewstorage
info:
  description: ""
  driver: btrfs
  name: mynewstorage
  space used: 950.24MiB
  total space: 4.00GiB
used by:
  images:
  - 258c6e58b22623f0af151315541452ddd74ee120e1ade4a6
1e546f9f3b63e911
  instances:
  - shining-flounder
```

CHAPTER 8 LINUX CONTAINERS (LXC)

Now that we've seen this example, we can stop and delete the new instance.

```
antonio@antonio-Laptop:~$ lxc stop shining-flounder
antonio@antonio-Laptop:~$ lxc list
+------------------+---------+----------------------+---------
--------------------------------------+----------+----------+
|      NAME        |  STATE  |         IPV4
|                  IPV6                           |   TYPE   |
SNAPSHOTS |
+------------------+---------+----------------------+---------
--------------------------------------+----------+----------+
| harmless-monarch | RUNNING | 10.216.182.156 (eth0) | fd42:45f7
:c283:6d95:216:3eff:fe35:96d9 (eth0) | CONTAINER | 0         |
+------------------+---------+----------------------+---------
--------------------------------------+----------+----------+
| shining-flounder | STOPPED |                      |
| CONTAINER | 0              |
+------------------+---------+----------------------+---------
--------------------------------------+----------+----------+
antonio@antonio-Laptop:~$ lxc delete shining-flounder
antonio@antonio-Laptop:~$ lxc list
+------------------+---------+----------------------+---------
--------------------------------------+----------+----------+
|      NAME        |  STATE  |         IPV4
|                  IPV6                           |   TYPE   |
SNAPSHOTS |
+------------------+---------+----------------------+---------
--------------------------------------+----------+----------+
| harmless-monarch | RUNNING | 10.216.182.156 (eth0) | fd42:45f7
:c283:6d95:216:3eff:fe35:96d9 (eth0) | CONTAINER | 0         |
+------------------+---------+----------------------+---------
--------------------------------------+----------+----------+
```

We'll delete the network and the storage pool we had created as well.

```
antonio@antonio-Laptop:~$ lxc storage delete mynewstorage
Storage pool mynewstorage deleted
antonio@antonio-Laptop:~$ lxc network delete new_lxd_net
Error: The network is currently in use
```

When we try to delete the network, we get an error because the customized profile we created is using it. We need to delete the profile first.

```
antonio@antonio-Laptop:~$ lxc profile delete my_new_profile
Profile my_new_profile deleted
antonio@antonio-Laptop:~$ lxc network delete new_lxd_net
Network new_lxd_net deleted
```

Limiting the Use of Resources on LXD

When we studied in the previous chapter how containers work, we could see that control groups could be used to limit resource usage for a certain process. And we even saw some practical examples.

In this same chapter we've studied LXC, we saw how to use **lxc-cgroups** to limit resource utilization, without needing to edit manually the files from the *ptip/fs/cgroups* tree. Now we'll do the same thing but using the specific tools provided by LXD.

We'll begin by connecting to the console of our running instance and checking the memory in use.

```
antonio@antonio-Laptop:~$ lxc console harmless-monarch
To detach from the console, press: <ctrl>+a q

harmless-monarch login: ubuntu
Password:
•
•
•
```

```
ubuntu@harmless-monarch:~$ free -m
        total   used    free    shared  buff/cache  available
Mem:    15674   49      15524   0       101         15625
Swap:   0       0       0
ubuntu@harmless-monarch:~$
```

We can see we're using about 16 GB of memory. Now let's open a new shell and use **lxc config** to limit the amount of memory used.

```
antonio@antonio-Laptop:~/QEMU_VMs$ lxc config set harmless-monarch limits.memory 100MB
```

If we return to the container console and execute free again, we'll see the amount of memory has been limited to a maximum below 100 MB.

```
ubuntu@harmless-monarch:~$ free -m
        total   used    free    shared  buff/cache  available
Mem:    95      46      4       0       44          48
Swap:   0       0       0
```

Summary

In this chapter, we have seen an example of a container technology widely used in Linux servers, the Linux containers or LXC for short. LXC uses the technologies we studied in the previous chapter to create the containers, but in a more friendly way that makes creating and managing containers much easier.

We've also seen LXD, which can be considered an add-on to the classical LXC implementation that makes working with remote repositories much easier.

CHAPTER 9

Docker

In this chapter, we'll cover the following concepts:

- Understand the architecture and components of Docker
- Manage Docker containers by using images from a Docker registry
- Understand and manage images and volumes for Docker containers
- Understand and manage logging for Docker containers
- Understand and manage networking for Docker
- Use Dockerfiles to create container images
- Run a Docker registry using the registry Docker image
- Understand the principle of runc
- Understand the principle of containerd

Introduction to Docker

Docker uses a client-server architecture. The **docker** command used to download images, start containers, etc., is the client, which, in turn, connects to the **dockerd** service. And it is the dockerd service that's responsible for executing the needed tasks to complete the requested actions.

CHAPTER 9 DOCKER

The client (**docker**) and the server (**dockerd**) can reside in the same or in different machines.

Installing Docker

The binaries for Docker are usually included in the repositories of the main Linux distributions. For instance, in Ubuntu 22, we can install it by selecting the **docker.io** package.

```
antonio@antonio-Laptop:~$ apt search docker.io
Sorting... Done
Full Text Search... Done
docker.io/jammy-updates,now 24.0.7-0ubuntu2~22.04.1 amd64 [installed]
  Linux container runtime
antonio@antonio-Laptop:~$ sudo apt install docker.io
```

It is also possible to install Docker from the official site. In this case, we can install it as part of the Docker desktop product, or install only the Docker Engine by adding the official repositories to our host machine (Figure 9-1).

CHAPTER 9   DOCKER

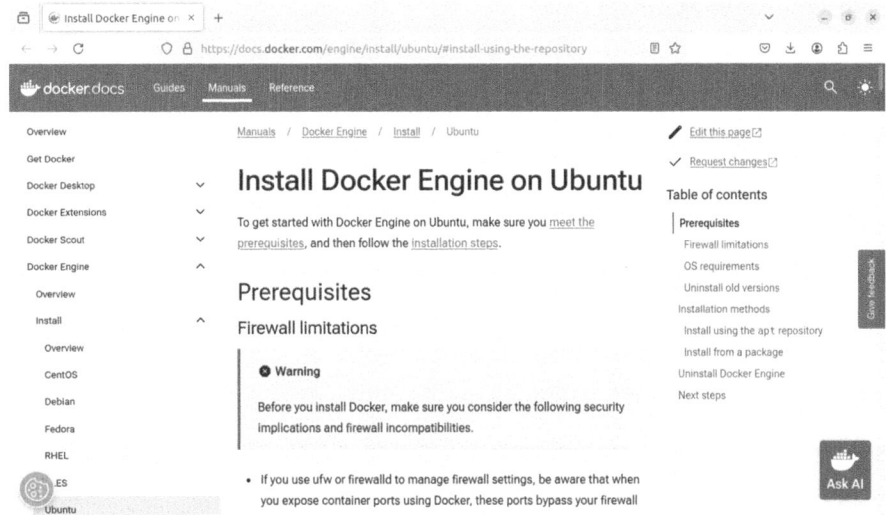

***Figure 9-1.** Installing from the official repositories*

Once the binaries have been installed, we can check that the installation was successful by executing the **docker info** command.

```
antonio@antonio-Laptop:~$ sudo docker info
Client:
 Version:    24.0.7
 Context:    default
 Debug Mode: false

Server:
 ·
 ·
 ·
 Storage Driver: overlay2
 ·
 ·
 Default Runtime: runc
 Init Binary: docker-init
```

CHAPTER 9   DOCKER

```
 containerd version:
 runc version:
 init version:
 Security Options:
  apparmor
  seccomp
   Profile: builtin
  cgroupns
·
·
```

We need to ensure that the Docker service starts automatically when the system boots.

`antonio@antonio-Laptop:~$ sudo systemctl enable docker`

Docker Images

To create a Docker container, we first need a Docker image. There are many ways to get an image; the easiest one is probably to download it from Docker's official registry. We can search for the available debian Docker images with the **docker search** command.

```
antonio@antonio-Laptop:~$ sudo docker search debian
NAME    DESCRIPTION                                     STARS
   OFFICIAL    AUTOMATED
debian  Debian is a Linux distribution that's compos…   5046
   [OK]
ubuntu  Ubuntu is a Debian-based Linux operating sys…   17178
   [OK]
·
·
·
```

CHAPTER 9   DOCKER

In addition, we could use a web browser and navigate to the docker hub to search for debian Docker images (Figures 9-2 and 9-3).

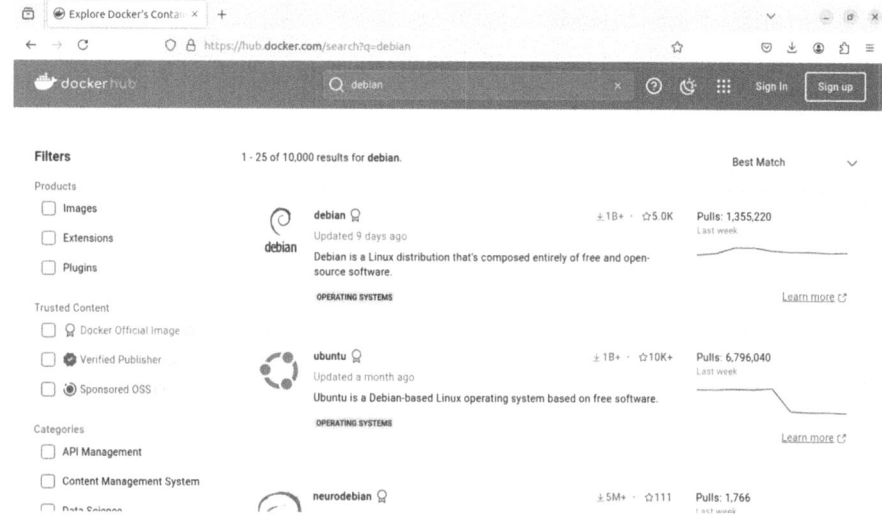

Figure 9-2.   Docker hub

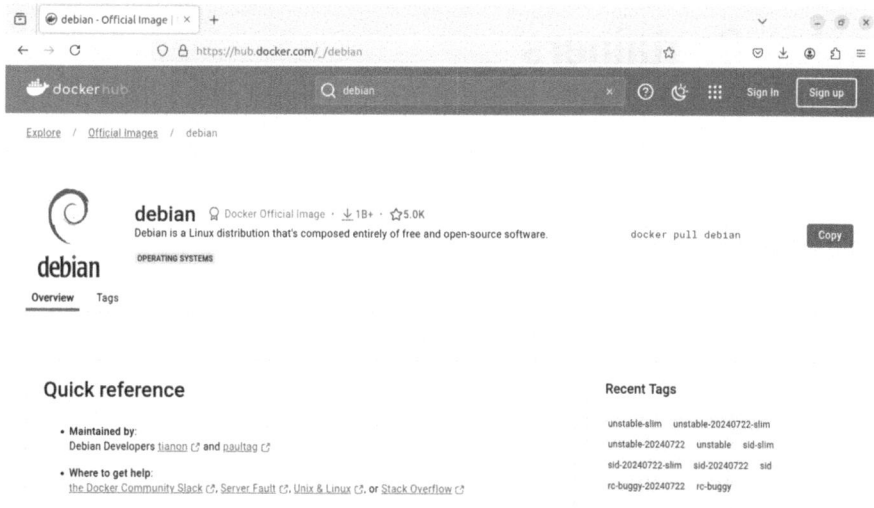

Figure 9-3.   Debian official Docker image

CHAPTER 9　DOCKER

From the command line, we can download images with **docker pull**.

```
antonio@antonio-Laptop:~$ sudo docker pull debian
Using default tag: latest
latest: Pulling from library/debian
ca4e5d672725: Pull complete
Digest: sha256:45f2e735295654f13e3be10da2a6892c708f71a71be84581
8f6058982761a6d3
Status: Downloaded newer image for debian:latest
docker.io/library/debian:latest
```

Once the image has been downloaded, it can be listed with **Docker image list**.

```
antonio@antonio-Laptop:~$ sudo docker image ls
REPOSITORY   TAG       IMAGE ID        CREATED       SIZE
debian       latest    2e5b8d3ef33e    9 days ago    117MB
```

Docker Containers

Previously we downloaded a Docker image; now we can use that image to create a container. To create a container, we use the **docker create** command. The only mandatory parameter is the name of the image used by the container.

If we take a look at the contextual help, we'll see that we can use a lot of options. We can add or drop capabilities, choose the cgroup namespace to use, connect an interactive pseudo-terminal, or attach a volume, to mention just a few.

```
antonio@antonio-Laptop:~$ sudo docker create --help

Usage:  docker create [OPTIONS] IMAGE [COMMAND] [ARG...]

Create a new container
```

CHAPTER 9 DOCKER

Aliases:
  docker container create, docker create

Options:

-
-
-
        --cap-add list   Add Linux capabilities
        --cap-drop list   Drop Linux capabilities
-
-
        --cgroupns string   Cgroup namespace to use (host|private)
-
-
  -i, --interactive   Keep STDIN open even if not attached
-
-
  -t, --tty   Allocate a pseudo-TTY
-
-
  -v, --volume list   Bind mount a volume

We'll begin with something simple, and we'll use the default values to create a container based on the debian image we just downloaded.

antonio@antonio-Laptop:~$ sudo docker create debian
5c29acf554a283d16b1125bd378d49f4acd5851b219618d62b1b4ed317
023562

This command creates a container, but it doesn't start it. If we check the status of the running containers in the host, we'll see just an empty list.

441

CHAPTER 9   DOCKER

```
antonio@antonio-Laptop:~$ sudo docker container ls
CONTAINER ID    IMAGE       COMMAND    CREATED     STATUS
PORTS        NAMES
antonio@antonio-Laptop:~$
```

To check the stopped containers as well as the running containers, we'll use the **docker container ls -a** command. Or we could also get the same result by typing **docker ps -a**.

```
CONTAINER ID    IMAGE       COMMAND    CREATED     STATUS    PORTS
NAMES
antonio@antonio-Laptop:~$ sudo docker container ls -a
CONTAINER ID    IMAGE           COMMAND         CREATED
STATUS                  PORTS       NAMES
5c29acf554a2    debian          "bash"          3 minutes ago
Created                                         heuristic_turing
```

In the list of containers, we can see the ID of the container we just created; this is the value returned by the **docker create** command. We also see the base image of the container, debian in this case. We can also see when the container was created and its status. When creating a container, we can specify a name; if we don't do it, the system will assign a name automatically. Later in this book we'll speak about the "command" and the "ports" columns.

To start the container, we use the **start** subcommand.

```
antonio@antonio-Laptop:~$ sudo docker container start
heuristic_turing
heuristic_turing
```

However, if we list the running containers, we won't see anything.

```
antonio@antonio-Laptop:~$ sudo docker container ls
CONTAINER ID    IMAGE    COMMAND    CREATED    STATUS    ORTS    NAMES
antonio@antonio-Laptop:~$
```

And if we list all the containers, we'll see that this container exited almost immediately after it was launched.

```
antonio@antonio-Laptop:~$ sudo docker container ls -a
CONTAINER ID    IMAGE           COMMAND         CREATED
STATUS                          PORTS       NAMES
5c29acf554a2    debian          "bash"          43 minutes ago
Exited (0) 15 seconds ago                   heuristic_turing
```

Let's see why this happened. When the container runs, it executes an associated command; in the case of the default debian container we created, this command is bash, so the container runs bash and immediately exits. To avoid this behavior and interact with the container, we'll see a few options we can choose.

In this first example, we created the container and then we started it. It is also possible to create and start a container in a single step by using **docker container run**. We can use many options with this command; for instance, we can use (-i) so that the container is interactive, and we can specify the command that the container will run; by default, this image will execute */bin/bash,* so we don't really need to specify the same value, but we'll do it anyway as an example.

```
antonio@antonio-Laptop:~$ sudo docker container run -i debian /bin/bash
pwd
/
cat /etc/issue
Debian GNU/Linux 12 \n \l

exit
```

As we can see, we can type shell commands as if we were working in a physical Ubuntu Linux console. After exiting the container, the container will be stopped because the execution of bash will be over.

CHAPTER 9 DOCKER

```
antonio@antonio-Laptop:~$ sudo docker container ls
CONTAINER ID   IMAGE   COMMAND   CREATED   STATUS   PORTS   NAMES
antonio@antonio-Laptop:~$
```

In this second example, we could type commands to interact to the container, but the experience was not very friendly as we didn't get a prompt. We can improve this experience by allocating a pseudo-terminal with the -t parameter.

```
antonio@antonio-Laptop:~$ sudo docker container run -it debian /bin/bash
root@143ae578eb3a:/# pwd
/
root@143ae578eb3a:/# cat /etc/debian_version
12.6
root@143ae578eb3a:/# exit
exit
```

This is definitely better! Another possibility is to run the container in the background with "-d".

```
antonio@antonio-Laptop:~$ sudo docker container run -d -it debian /bin/bash
e051edecf7206a46ad931f2bff8b9cee606af1760936df32826cb501b765bdeb
```

After entering the docker command, we'll be given the ID of the container and get the prompt back.

If we list the running containers, however, we'll see a new container is running. It will remain in this state until we connect to it, and thus, the bash shell completes its execution.

```
antonio@antonio-Laptop:~$ sudo docker container ls
CONTAINER ID   IMAGE     COMMAND       CREATED
STATUS              PORTS      NAMES
e051edecf720   debian    "/bin/bash"   About a minute ago
Up About a minute              sleepy_hodgkin
```

And we can connect to it with **docker container attach**.

```
antonio@antonio-Laptop:~$ sudo docker container attach
sleepy_hodgkin
root@e051edecf720:/# ls
bin   boot  dev   etc   home  lib   lib64  media  mnt  opt
proc  root  run   sbin  srv   sys   tmp    usr    var
root@e051edecf720:/# exit
exit
antonio@antonio-Laptop:~$ sudo docker container ls
CONTAINER ID   IMAGE    COMMAND    CREATED    STATUS   PORTS    NAMES
antonio@antonio-Laptop:~$
```

Docker Architecture

After seeing a couple of simple examples, let's study a bit about Docker architecture. We already saw a very brief description in the introduction, and now we're going to study it more in depth.

We have worked with the **docker** command. This command is used to manage images, containers, and other container-related objects. It works by interacting with the **dockerd** service.

The **dockerd** service is the program that really manages containers and the related objects. The **docker** command is just a frontend used to interact with **dockerd**.

CHAPTER 9   DOCKER

The **containerd** service is the container runtime used by dockerd. If we list the **dockerd** process running, we'll see this:

```
antonio@antonio-Laptop:~$ ps -ef | grep dockerd
root        2968       1  0 jul26 ?        00:01:31 /usr/bin/dockerd -H fd:// --containerd=/run/containerd/containerd.sock
```

dockerd communicates with the **containerd** service, which must be also running on the host.

```
antonio@antonio-Laptop:~$ ps -ef | grep containerd
root        1107       1  0 jul26 ?        00:43:34 /usr/bin/containerd
```

Finally, **runc** is the lower-level container runtime. Let's see it in an example. First, we'll launch a container.

```
antonio@antonio-Laptop:~$ sudo docker container ls
CONTAINER ID   IMAGE     COMMAND    CREATED    STATUS
PORTS          NAMES
antonio@antonio-Laptop:~$ sudo docker container ls -a
CONTAINER ID   IMAGE            COMMAND           CREATED
STATUS                          PORTS       NAMES
e051edecf720   debian           "/bin/bash"       22 hours
ago   Exited (137) 36 minutes ago                 sleepy_hodgkin
antonio@antonio-Laptop:~$ sudo docker container start sleepy_hodgkin
sleepy_hodgkin
```

If we check the processes again, we'll see a new **runc** process that is executing the container with the ID e051edecf720....

```
antonio@antonio-Laptop:~$ ps -ef | grep containerd
root        1107       1  0 jul26 ?        00:43:35 /usr/bin/containerd
```

```
root        2968       1  0 jul26 ?        00:01:32 /usr/bin/
dockerd -H fd:// --containerd=/run/containerd/containerd.sock
root      750120       1  0 22:28 ?        00:00:00 /usr/bin/
containerd-shim-runc-v2 -namespace moby -id e051edecf7206a46a
d931f2bff8b9cee606af1760936df32826cb501b765bdeb -address /run/
containerd/containerd.sock
```

It's important to remember that the architecture of Docker is very modular and some components can be replaced for others with a similar functionality.

We can customize the **dockerd** service by using a */etc/docker/daemon.json* file. After installing Docker, the **dockerd** service will be created and enabled with the default settings. However, it is also possible to execute it manually with a different set of parameters. If we type **dockerd --help**, we'll see the different options available.

```
antonio@antonio-Laptop:~$ dockerd --help

Usage:      dockerd [OPTIONS]

A self-sufficient runtime for containers.

Options:
      --add-runtime runtime
Register an additional OCI compatible runtime (default [])
      --allow-nondistributable-artifacts list
Allow push of nondistributable artifacts to registry
      --api-cors-header string
Set CORS headers in the Engine API
```

-
-
-

If we want to use any of these options, we can specify them in the command line when executing dockerd. But it is also possible to specify them in a json file, the */etc/docker/daemon.json* file we talked about a bit earlier.

To see this with an example we'll focus on this **dockerd** option:

```
-D, --debug                             Enable debug mode
```

This option enables/disables debug mode. Let's see the default value of this option by using the **docker info** command.

```
antonio@antonio-Laptop:~$ sudo docker info
.
.
Server:
.
.
 Debug Mode: false
.
.
```

Now, we'll create a */etc/docker/daemon.json* file with this content.

```
{
"debug": true
}
```

We stop the Docker service currently running in the host.

```
antonio@antonio-Laptop:~$ sudo systemctl stop docker
Warning: Stopping docker.service, but it can still be activated by:
  docker.socket
antonio@antonio-Laptop:~$ sudo systemctl stop docker.socket
```

And we execute manually **dockerd** without parameters so that it takes those specified in the json file.

```
antonio@antonio-Laptop:~$ sudo dockerd
INFO[2024-08-05T00:49:56.410689420+02:00] Starting up
DEBU[2024-08-05T00:49:56.411227288+02:00] Listener created for HTTP on unix (/var/run/docker.sock)
INFO[2024-08-05T00:49:56.411355931+02:00] detected 127.0.0.53 nameserver, assuming systemd-resolved, so using resolv.conf: /run/systemd/resolve/resolv.conf
DEBU[2024-08-05T00:49:56.411578101+02:00] Golang's threads limit set to 112230
```

.
.
.

When **dockerd** has initialized completely, we'll run **docker info** again to check the active settings.

```
antonio@antonio-Laptop:~$ sudo docker info
.
.
Server:
.
.
 Debug Mode: true
.
.
```

We can see that the debug mode is enabled. In fact, when we launched manually **dockerd**, we could see many debug messages.

After this simple test, we can stop the **dockerd** instance we launched manually and delete the json file. Then we restart the Docker service to restore the default settings.

```
antonio@antonio-Laptop:~$ sudo rm /etc/docker/daemon.json
antonio@antonio-Laptop:~$ sudo systemctl start docker
```

Docker Volumes

Docker containers are based on images, as we've already seen. And they add a writable layer over that image layer. The truth is that this is a bit more complicated, and we'll see it later in more detail. But for now, you can get that idea. Let's try to explain this with an example.

We need a running Docker container.

```
antonio@antonio-Laptop:~$ sudo docker container ls
CONTAINER ID    IMAGE       COMMAND         CREATED
STATUS          PORTS       NAMES
e051edecf720    debian      "/bin/bash"     39 hours ago
Up 16 hours                 sleepy_hodgkin
```

We'll connect to the running container with **docker container attach**, as we saw previously.

```
antonio@antonio-Laptop:~$ sudo docker container attach sleepy_hodgkin
root@e051edecf720:/#
```

And we'll create a new file.

```
root@e051edecf720:/# touch test_file_1.txt
root@e051edecf720:/# exit
exit
```

CHAPTER 9　DOCKER

Now we'll search for the file in the host. By default, Docker containers store information in folders inside the */var/lib/docker* directory. So we'll search for the file in this path.

```
antonio@antonio-Laptop:~$ sudo find /var/lib/docker/ -iname test_file_1.txt
/var/lib/docker/overlay2/cdd6342b6f3d55239cbc30edd414c3e9e47c27e841feb0620ec5505a0bfe4c12/diff/test_file_1.txt
```

We can see the location of the file in the host. We'll get back to it in a moment. But now, we're going to see another useful command, **docker container inspect**, which provides useful information about a container. We'll use it to inspect the container in which we created the test file.

```
antonio@antonio-Laptop:~$ sudo docker container inspect sleepy_hodgkin
.
.
.
        "GraphDriver": {
            "Data": {
                "LowerDir": "/var/lib/docker/overlay2/cdd6342b6f3d55239cbc30edd414c3e9e47c27e841feb0620ec5505a0bfe4c12-init/diff:/var/lib/docker/overlay2/f2e4afe19fc3c1f3d65f0030705e4881f9577e2a95d4f120f62d7e99b12ccd59/diff",
                "MergedDir": "/var/lib/docker/overlay2/cdd6342b6f3d55239cbc30edd414c3e9e47c27e841feb0620ec5505a0bfe4c12/merged",
                "UpperDir": "/var/lib/docker/overlay2/cdd6342b6f3d55239cbc30edd414c3e9e47c27e841feb0620ec5505a0bfe4c12/diff",
```

CHAPTER 9 DOCKER

```
            "WorkDir": "/var/lib/docker/overlay2/cdd6342b
            6f3d55239cbc30edd414c3e9e47c27e841feb0
            620ec5505a0bfe4c12/work"
        },
        "Name": "overlay2"
    },
```

•
•
•

Let's review what we have seen so far. Docker containers need a writable layer to store the modified information. For that, a storage driver is needed. The storage driver controls how information is stored and how to properly manage the read-only image layer and the writable container layer.

There are several storage drivers available for Docker. According to the official documentation, these are

- overlay2
- fuse-overlayfs
- btrfs and zfs
- vfs

The preferred one is "overlay2". If we execute **docker info** on the host, we'll see the following line. The backing filesystem can be other than extfs, for example, xfs. That depends on the filesystem we're using in our system.

```
 Storage Driver: overlay2
  Backing Filesystem: extfs
```

And if we remember, when we located the test file in the host and reviewed the container with **docker inspect**, the word "overlay" appeared very often. The file *test_file_1.txt* was located on */var/lib/docker/overlay2/ cdd6342b6f3d55239cbc30edd414c3e9e47c27e841feb0620ec5505a0bfe4c12/ diff/test_file_1.txt*. According to what we saw on the output of the docker inspect command, that path is named "UpperDir".

In the Docker version we're using right now, the one installed from Ubuntu repositories, the overlay storage driver uses a plug-in named graphdriver. This plug-in uses a "LowerDir", which is the base image read-only layer; an "UpperDir", which is the writable container layer; and a "MergeDir" and a "WorkDir" needed internally to work properly. As expected, the file we created was located in the writable layer, the UpperDir.

Bind Mounts

We just saw that we can access a file either from the container itself or from the host. Because the storage driver stores the information in the filesystem, and of course that filesystem is accessible to the host.

Nevertheless, this is probably not a very friendly way to share files because the paths are very long and have hash-like names. It would be better to use an easier-to-remember path to share information between the host and the container.

To do this, we must use the **-v** or **--mount** parameter and specify the location of the path in the host and the container. This is known as a bind mount. We'll start by creating a local folder in the host computer.

antonio@antonio-Laptop:~$ mkdir VOLUMES

Next, we launch a container in the background (-d) and in interactive (-i) mode. We'll also connect a pseudo-terminal (-t) to it and will assign it explicitly a name instead of letting the system to assign one. This container will use the path */home/antonio/VOLUMES/* in the host computer as a volume mapped as */VOLUMES/*.

Chapter 9   Docker

```
antonio@antonio-Laptop:~$ sudo docker run -v /home/antonio/
VOLUMES/:/VOLUMES/ --name another_container -itd debian /
bin/bash
fe0a743619448be099821fde7b0995d596795b73a934fdb658cf474
09682e920
```

If we list the containers currently running, we'll see this new container named "another_container".

```
antonio@antonio-Laptop:~$ sudo docker container ls
CONTAINER ID    IMAGE      COMMAND        CREATED
STATUS                PORTS       NAMES
fe0a74361944    debian     "/bin/bash"    About a minute ago    Up
About a minute                another_container
```

If we inspect the container, we'll see clearly the bind mount we just created.

```
antonio@antonio-Laptop:~$ sudo docker inspect another_container
.
.
.
        "Mounts": [
            {
                "Type": "bind",
                "Source": "/home/antonio/VOLUMES",
                "Destination": "/VOLUMES",
                "Mode": "",
                "RW": true,
                "Propagation": "rprivate"
            }
        ],
.
```

CHAPTER 9 DOCKER

-
-

Now, we connect to the container we just launched, and we create a text file inside the volume.

```
antonio@antonio-Laptop:~$ sudo docker container attach another_container
root@fe0a74361944:/# echo Hello > /VOLUMES/hello.txt
root@fe0a74361944:/# exit
exit
```

This time it is much easier to access the file from the host.

```
antonio@antonio-Laptop:~$ cat /home/antonio/VOLUMES/hello.txt
Hello
```

Instead of the (-v) parameter, we could also use the (--mount) parameter, which is indeed the recommended way to work with containers. It supports more options. Let's see an example.

```
antonio@antonio-Laptop:~$ sudo docker run --mount type=bind,source=/home/antonio/VOLUMES/,target=/VOLUMES/ --name yet_another_container -itd debian /bin/bash
c6e04e97accc7b3f14a49291120ea4b3850adcce77ccaa48651c57f5239113f1
```

Named Volumes

Using bind mounts has some advantages over using the default storage. However, the preferred way to store data is to use docker volumes. Docker volumes allow to share data between containers, and the data contained in those volumes is persistent.

455

CHAPTER 9   DOCKER

We'll start by creating a volume.

antonio@antonio-Laptop:~$ sudo docker volume create volume_one
volume_one

We can list the volumes in the host, similarly as we did with the containers.

```
antonio@antonio-Laptop:~$ sudo docker volume ls
DRIVER     VOLUME NAME
.
.
.
local      volume_one
```

And we can inspect the volume as well.

```
antonio@antonio-Laptop:~$ sudo docker volume inspect volume_one
[
    {
        "CreatedAt": "2024-08-04T21:48:25+02:00",
        "Driver": "local",
        "Labels": null,
        "Mountpoint": "/var/lib/docker/volumes/volume_
        one/_data",
        "Name": "volume_one",
        "Options": null,
        "Scope": "local"
    }
]
```

The way to work with volumes in containers is very easy; the syntax is very similar to what we did when working with bind mounts. Let's see an example.

CHAPTER 9 DOCKER

```
antonio@antonio-Laptop:~$ sudo docker run -d -it --name
container_vol --mount source=volume_one,target=/vol_1 ubuntu
bedb5e6a87ebd08a3716a61e78313e5b96a76322beb831491dda94
b260afb77c
```

By inspecting the container, we'll see that the volume was mounted.

```
antonio@antonio-Laptop:~$ sudo docker container inspect
container_vol
```

.
.
.

```
        "Mounts": [
            {
                "Type": "volume",
                "Name": "volume_one",
                "Source": "/var/lib/docker/volumes/volume_
                one/_data",
                "Destination": "/vol_1",
                "Driver": "local",
                "Mode": "z",
                "RW": true,
                "Propagation": ""
            }
        ],
```

.
.
.

457

CHAPTER 9   DOCKER

tmpfs Volumes

There is another type of volumes, the tmpfs volumes. These volumes are temporary, and the volume and its content are removed when the container stops.

```
antonio@antonio-Laptop:~/docker$ sudo docker container run -it --tmpfs /temp_dir debian
root@618d6312f4cf:/# touch /temp_dir/file1.txt
root@618d6312f4cf:/# ls /temp_dir/
file1.txt
root@618d6312f4cf:/#
```

Sharing Volumes Between Containers

It is very easy to share volumes between containers; we can do it with the --volumes-from option.

First, we launch the first container that will use the volume. We can reuse the container_vol container that we used previously in this book, or we can use a new one.

```
antonio@antonio-Laptop:~/docker$ sudo docker container start container_vol
container_vol
```

This container used a volume named volume_one that was mounted on */vol_1*. If we don't remember these details, we can check them with **docker container inspect**.

```
antonio@antonio-Laptop:~$ sudo docker container inspect container_vol
```
•
•

```
        "Mounts": [
            {
                "Type": "volume",
                "Name": "volume_one",
                "Source": "/var/lib/docker/volumes/volume_
                one/_data",
                "Destination": "/vol_1",
```
-
-
-

We'll connect to the container and add some content to the folder.

```
antonio@antonio-Laptop:~$ sudo docker container attach
container_vol
root@bedb5e6a87eb:/# ls /vol_1/
root@bedb5e6a87eb:/# echo hello > /vol_1/aa
```

Then, we'll launch a second container with the --from-volumes option. This way we're instructing the container to mount the same volumes that the container_vol container.

```
antonio@antonio-Laptop:~/docker$ sudo docker container run
--rm -it --volumes-from=container_vol debian /bin/bash
root@e070dbac48a3:/#
```

We'll be able to access the volume and see its content.

```
root@e070dbac48a3:/# ls /vol_1/
aa
root@e070dbac48a3:/# cat /vol_1/aa
hello
```

CHAPTER 9   DOCKER

Using Remote Volumes

When creating a volume, we can specify which driver to use. If we don't specify any driver, the "local" driver is used. This is what we did previously. But there are some drivers that let us store volume on remote hosts.

Let's see an example using a volume accessed through ssh. For that, we need to install a plug-in. Docker plug-ins add extra functionality to Docker. We can list the plug-ins currently installed with **docker plugin list**.

```
antonio@antonio-Laptop:~$ sudo docker plugin list
ID        NAME       DESCRIPTION     ENABLED
```

Currently, we don't have any plug-in installed. We need to install a plug-in named vieux/sshfs.

```
antonio@antonio-Laptop:~$ sudo docker plugin install vieux/sshfs
Plugin "vieux/sshfs" is requesting the following privileges:
 - network: [host]
 - mount: [/var/lib/docker/plugins/]
 - mount: []
 - device: [/dev/fuse]
 - capabilities: [CAP_SYS_ADMIN]
Do you grant the above permissions? [y/N] y
latest: Pulling from vieux/sshfs
Digest: sha256:1d3c3e42c12138da5ef7873b97f7f32cf99fb6edde75fa4f0bcf9ed277855811
52d435ada6a4: Complete
Installed plugin vieux/sshfs
```

The plug-in requests a series of permissions. After granting those permissions, the plug-in is installed and we can list it.

```
antonio@antonio-Laptop:~$ sudo docker plugin list
ID               NAME                    DESCRIPTION           ENABLED
822e70f45289     vieux/sshfs:latest      sshFS plugin for
Docker      true
```

We can also use the subcommand inspect to obtain more information about the plug-in.

```
antonio@antonio-Laptop:~$ sudo docker plugin inspect
vieux/sshfs
```

-
-

```
            "Description": "sshFS plugin for Docker",
            "DockerVersion": "18.05.0-ce-rc1",
            "Documentation": "https://docs.docker.com/engine/
            extend/plugins/",
```

-
-

When using this plug-in, we're going to use as a volume a folder inside a remote host. And we're connected to the remote host through ssh. Now we're going to create a folder and some files on the remote server.

```
[root@rocky ~]# mkdir /EXT_VOLUME
[root@rocky ~]# touch /EXT_VOLUME/one /EXT_VOLUME/two /EXT_
VOLUME/three
```

We're ready to create the volume now. We need to pass the driver type and the needed options, the path to the folder that will be used as a volume, and the password.

```
antonio@antonio-Laptop:~$ sudo docker volume create --driver
vieux/sshfs -o sshcmd=root@192.168.56.104:/EXT_VOLUME -o
password=root SSH_volume
SSH_volume
```

CHAPTER 9 DOCKER

The volume has been created and can be listed.

```
antonio@antonio-Laptop:~$ sudo docker volume ls
DRIVER               VOLUME NAME
.
.
vieux/sshfs:latest   SSH_volume
local                volume_one
```

We can inspect this new volume to see its characteristics.

```
antonio@antonio-Laptop:~$ sudo docker volume inspect SSH_volume
[
    {
        "CreatedAt": "0001-01-01T00:00:00Z",
        "Driver": "vieux/sshfs:latest",
        "Labels": null,
        "Mountpoint": "/mnt/volumes/2fc3798a413c12383d36829f
        ac8bef49",
        "Name": "SSH_volume",
        "Options": {
            "password": "root",
            "sshcmd": "root@192.168.56.104:/EXT_VOLUME"
        },
        "Scope": "local"
    }
]
```

And we start a container using this volume; the syntax is similar to the one we saw before.

```
antonio@antonio-Laptop:~$ sudo docker container run --rm
-it --name cont_ssh --mount source=SSH_volume,target=/vol_
ssh busybox
```

```
/ # ls /
bin     dev     etc     home    lib     lib64   proc
root    sys     tmp     usr     var     vol_ssh
/ # ls /vol_ssh/
one     three   two
/ #
```

Deleting and Pruning Volumes

Volumes have a life cycle independent of that of the container they belong to. We could easily end up with many volumes that are no longer needed. If that's the case, we can use docker volume prune to remove those unused volumes.

```
antonio@antonio-Laptop:~$ sudo docker volume prune
WARNING! This will remove anonymous local volumes not used by
at least one container.
Are you sure you want to continue? [y/N] y
Deleted Volumes:
0b537d7a4b3ad06bf0d9290b2be285e8ff1e45d0917f2258139ef3cd9ca8c57a
2bb41e2aef80faedff990b6aaccea47436e9896923a216dac32bfcb5c92e1b92
046cac64459c7b52346ca61d721b0c42671a457d48ed4ed704cf841f81b53941
5490aa3aa0a7adef26c348de022824cfba026b257a36de643e78042e14c4e1fd
8d262581063febe45348d0f960af666994dc503b4f131ac41d4b4c9556343498

Total reclaimed space: 5B
```

If we want to remove a single volume, we can do it with docker volume rm.

```
antonio@antonio-Laptop:~$ sudo docker volume create
other_volume
other_volume
antonio@antonio-Laptop:~$ sudo docker volume rm other_volume
```

CHAPTER 9   DOCKER

Docker Networking

After installing Docker in our host computer, we'll see that a new network interface is created.

```
antonio@antonio-Laptop:~$ ip address show docker0
10: docker0: <BROADCAST,MULTICAST,UP,LOWER_UP> mtu 1500 qdisc noqueue state UP group default
    link/ether 02:42:da:bf:35:7c brd ff:ff:ff:ff:ff:ff
    inet 172.17.0.1/16 brd 172.17.255.255 scope global docker0
       valid_lft forever preferred_lft forever
    inet6 fe80::42:daff:febf:357c/64 scope link
       valid_lft forever preferred_lft forever
```

If we still have a docker container running, we can inspect the container to see the network settings. We will see that the defined gateway is precisely the IP address of this docker0 interface.

```
antonio@antonio-Laptop:~$ sudo docker container inspect container_vol
```
·
·
·
```
                "Gateway": "172.17.0.1",
                "IPAddress": "172.17.0.3",
```
·
·
·

Of course, we can ping the container from the host. It should be also possible to ping the host from the container, but given the compact nature of containers, sometimes commands like "ping" are not even installed.

```
antonio@antonio-Laptop:~$ ping -c 1 172.17.0.3
PING 172.17.0.3 (172.17.0.3) 56(84) bytes of data.
64 bytes from 172.17.0.3: icmp_seq=1 ttl=64 time=0.114 ms

--- 172.17.0.3 ping statistics ---
1 packets transmitted, 1 received, 0% packet loss, time 0ms
rtt min/avg/max/mdev = 0.114/0.114/0.114/0.000 ms
```

Communication between the host and the container is possible because docker automatically creates a network object that associates the docker0 interface with the containers.

We can list the existing networks in docker with **docker network ls**.

```
antonio@antonio-Laptop:~$ sudo docker network ls
NETWORK ID      NAME      DRIVER    SCOPE
23024a0a6b04    bridge    bridge    local
12d6ec81db06    host      host      local
d2a2d2adacba    none      null      local
```

By default, we see three different networks. The default bridge network is the one used by default by the containers if we don't explicitly set a different one. A bridge network allows for communication between the container and the host, as well as with the external network. The host network driver allows the container to see all the network interfaces in the host. Finally, the none network driver isolates the container. This last driver can be useful if, for example, we need our containers to perform some computing operations but prefer not to be accessible in the network.

There are also other network drivers like the MacVLAN driver. This assigns a virtual MAC address to the container interface.

In the next chapter, when we study orchestration and docker swarm, we'll see new network driver types like overlay.

CHAPTER 9   DOCKER

For now, let's inspect the default network.

```
antonio@antonio-Laptop:~$ sudo docker network inspect bridge
[
    {
        "Name": "bridge",
        "Id": "23024a0a6b041d792365e54046e410dd9
        4161cad50b7e9391468d856f0d0e5cd",
        "Created": "2024-08-06T11:32:22.354338844+02:00",
        "Scope": "local",
        "Driver": "bridge",
```
·
·
```
                    "Subnet": "172.17.0.0/16",
                    "Gateway": "172.17.0.1"
```
·
·
```
            "com.docker.network.bridge.name": "docker0",
```
·
·

We see clearly the network driver (bridge), the network settings, and the host network interface used. We can also see that the scope is "local". This means that the network is local to the host. When we study docker swarm in the next chapter, we'll create docker networks that span across all the nodes in the docker swarm cluster.

Now, we'll see an example of the host network. We'll create a container connected to the host network.

```
antonio@antonio-Laptop:~$ sudo docker container run --rm -it
--network=host busybox sh
/ #
```

CHAPTER 9 DOCKER

If we list the network interfaces, we'll see all those interfaces existing in the host.

```
/ # ip link
1: lo: <LOOPBACK,UP,LOWER_UP> mtu 65536 qdisc noqueue qlen 1000
    link/loopback 00:00:00:00:00:00 brd 00:00:00:00:00:00
2: wlo1: <NO-CARRIER,BROADCAST,MULTICAST,UP> mtu 1500 qdisc
    noqueue qlen 1000
    link/ether b0:68:e6:14:aa:b3 brd ff:ff:ff:ff:ff:ff
3: ovs-system: <BROADCAST,MULTICAST> mtu 1500 qdisc noop
    qlen 1000
    link/ether ce:f7:54:0a:c9:92 brd ff:ff:ff:ff:ff:ff
.
.
.
```

And if we use the "none" network, which uses the null driver, we'll only see the loopback network interface in the container.

```
antonio@antonio-Laptop:~$ sudo docker container run --rm -it
--network=none busybox sh
/ # ip link
1: lo: <LOOPBACK,UP,LOWER_UP> mtu 65536 qdisc noqueue qlen 1000
    link/loopback 00:00:00:00:00:00 brd 00:00:00:00:00:00
/ #
```

Creating a New Network

We're going to create a new docker network and connect some containers to it.

```
antonio@antonio-Laptop:~$ sudo docker network create --driver
bridge new_docker_nw
9374a4b6163f93a3cd85d37a456b7ee901e1c59142e1feba3cea67de55887e22
```

CHAPTER 9 DOCKER

If we inspect the new network, we'll see the new IP settings that were automatically assigned.

```
antonio@antonio-Laptop:~$ sudo docker network inspect new_docker_nw
[
    {
        "Name": "new_docker_nw",
        "Id": "9374a4b6163f93a3cd85d37a456b7ee901e1c59142e1f
        eba3cea67de55887e22",
.
.
                "Subnet": "172.18.0.0/16",
                "Gateway": "172.18.0.1"
```

Now we'll create two new containers that will be connected to this new network. To be able to use tools like **ping** and **ip**, we'll use the busybox image.

```
antonio@antonio-Laptop:~$ sudo docker container run -it
--network=new_docker_nw --name=cont1 busybox sh

antonio@antonio-Laptop:~$ sudo docker container run -it
--network=new_docker_nw --name=cont2 busybox sh
```

We'll check the IP address assigned to each container.

```
/ # ip a
.
.
23: eth0@if24: <BROADCAST,MULTICAST,UP,LOWER_UP,M-DOWN> mtu
1500 qdisc noqueue
```

```
    link/ether 02:42:ac:12:00:03 brd ff:ff:ff:ff:ff:ff
    inet 172.18.0.3/16 brd 172.18.255.255 scope global eth0
       valid_lft forever preferred_lft forever
/ #
```

And we can ping one container from the other one.

```
/ # ping -c 2 172.18.0.2
PING 172.18.0.2 (172.18.0.2): 56 data bytes
64 bytes from 172.18.0.2: seq=0 ttl=64 time=0.162 ms
64 bytes from 172.18.0.2: seq=1 ttl=64 time=0.119 ms

--- 172.18.0.2 ping statistics ---
2 packets transmitted, 2 packets received, 0% packet loss
round-trip min/avg/max = 0.119/0.140/0.162 ms
/ #
```

We can inspect the new network, and we'll see the two containers attached to it.

```
antonio@antonio-Laptop:~$ sudo docker network inspect new_
docker_nw
.
.
        "Containers": {
            "15f393f52e6643db50e9afd1799c3516fef839fa500d77b
            5dbec87114e34a7fc": {
                "Name": "cont1",
                "EndpointID": "764bb5463cb6c2efd8d917f0d236b38
                0019b0b89262f0c025853f13e9c32dee8",
                "MacAddress": "02:42:ac:12:00:02",
                "IPv4Address": "172.18.0.2/16",
                "IPv6Address": ""
            },
```

CHAPTER 9   DOCKER

```
            "53edeaa4bfd855cd04cf183b48529e9b9c04249504baed71
            81a24cd84634ac20": {
                "Name": "cont2",
                "EndpointID": "ce384eab30d999d4e750a22f9b80da
                b94a58fcae44f236a3ba2e84e4e2870042",
                "MacAddress": "02:42:ac:12:00:03",
                "IPv4Address": "172.18.0.3/16",
                "IPv6Address": ""
            }
```

Mapping Ports

We can map a certain port in the host to a certain port in the container so that every request addressed to that specific port on the host computer is handled by the container. For instance, we can execute a container based on an nginx image and map port 8000 in the host to port 80 in the container. We do that using the -p option.

```
antonio@antonio-Laptop:~$ sudo docker container run -d -p 8000:80 nginx
f47b70f1930208742952ab9f562a6d33e9b927aadc0c246b
1b483b5da4e26a39
```

We can check on the host that a docker process is listening on port 8000.

```
antonio@antonio-Laptop:~$ sudo lsof -i :8000
COMMAND     PID USER   FD   TYPE DEVICE SIZE/OFF NODE NAME
docker-pr 20985 root    4u  IPv4 438978      0t0  TCP *:8000
(LISTEN)
docker-pr 20991 root    4u  IPv6 441411      0t0  TCP *:8000
(LISTEN)
```

And if we open a web browser and point to TCP port 8000 on the localhost, we'll see the nginx welcome page (Figure 9-4).

Figure 9-4. *Redirecting ports from the host to the container*

Customizing Our Own Containers

When working with containers, we can install additional software as if we were working with a standard machine; we can edit configuration files and customize in many ways our containers.

After the customization is complete, we might want to save this container.

Exporting a Container to an Image

One way to save the changes made to a container is to create an image from the customized container.

CHAPTER 9 DOCKER

We'll launch a new container based on the Ubuntu image, and we'll connect to it.

```
antonio@antonio-Laptop:~$ sudo docker run -d -it --name
container_v1 ubuntu /bin/bash
348e78cb098f5607966e9840d495b97fb7dc1486500f13713d998db8b
15870c5
antonio@antonio-Laptop:~$ sudo docker attach container_v1
root@348e78cb098f:/#
```

Once connected, we can install software or perform other operations. In our case, we'll perform an update.

```
root@348e78cb098f:/# apt update
```

When the update is complete, we'll execute docker container commit to generate a new image from the container. This new image will be named image_container_v2.

```
antonio@antonio-Laptop:~$ sudo docker container commit
container_v1 image_container_v2
sha256:83dcb9837c499649c13d4b54a11faeba3f684219b48c26780bb6341
a146e2cdc
```

We can list now the new image.

```
antonio@antonio-Laptop:~$ sudo docker image ls
REPOSITORY           TAG         IMAGE
ID        CREATED            SIZE
image_container_v2   latest      83dcb9837c49     28 seconds
ago     117MB
```

And we can use this new image as a base image to create a container, exactly in the same way as we did with the official debian and ubuntu images. We'll create a temporary container using the --rm option. This option automatically deletes the container after its execution.

CHAPTER 9   DOCKER

```
antonio@antonio-Laptop:~$ sudo docker container run --rm -it
image_container_v2 /bin/bash
root@dea4de3536b0:/#
```

The container will have all the changes performed previously. In our example, it will be updated. While the container is executing, we can see it listed.

```
antonio@antonio-Laptop:~$ sudo docker container ls
CONTAINER ID    IMAGE                COMMAND
CREATED         STATUS         PORTS        NAMES
dea4de3536b0    image_container_v2   "/bin/bash"
29 seconds ago  Up 28 seconds               relaxed_jepsen
```

When we exit the container, it will be automatically deleted.

```
antonio@antonio-Laptop:~$ sudo docker container ls
CONTAINER ID    IMAGE                COMMAND           CREATED
        STATUS         PORTS        NAMES
antonio@antonio-Laptop:~$
```

Let's get back to the concept of layers we mentioned briefly before. When we create a container, we use a base image. That image will be a read-only layer, and over this layer a new writable layer will be created to store the changes.

We'll inspect the ubuntu base image and pay attention to a few parameters.

```
antonio@antonio-Laptop:~$ sudo docker image inspect ubuntu
[
    {
        "Id": "sha256:35a88802559dd2077e584394471ddaa1a2c5bfd1
        6893b829ea57619301eb3908",
    .
    .
```

CHAPTER 9 DOCKER

```
        "Parent": "",
.
.
        "RootFS": {
            "Type": "layers",
            "Layers": [
                "sha256:a30a5965a4f7d9d5ff76a46eb8939f58e95be
                844de1ac4a4b452d5d31158fdea"
            ]
        },
```

This image is given an ID, it has no parent, and it only contains one layer.

Let's compare it to our newly created image_container_v2 image.

```
antonio@antonio-Laptop:~$ sudo docker image inspect image_
container_v2
[
    {
        "Id": "sha256:83dcb9837c499649c13d4b54a11faeba3f684219
        b48c26780bb6341a146e2cdc",
.
.
        "Parent": "sha256:35a88802559dd2077e584394471ddaa1a2c5b
        fd16893b829ea57619301eb3908",
.
.
        "RootFS": {
            "Type": "layers",
            "Layers": [
                "sha256:a30a5965a4f7d9d5ff76a46eb8939f58e95b
                e844de1ac4a4b452d5d31158fdea",
```

```
            "sha256:ac4beaab0ee851efd70299f648f9db72984c6d
            e42d27df80a48c3826a60a677"
        ]
    },
```
-
-

If you remember, we created this image from a container based on the Ubuntu image. And we performed a series of changes in the container, an update to be exact. So in this case, the image has a parent, the Ubuntu image. Besides, the changes were stored in the writable layer of the container, which was later exported to a new image. For that reason, this image has two layers.

Using a Dockerfile to Create a Container

Another way to customize a container is by using a Dockerfile to explicitly define a new image. Then we can use this image to create new containers.

We'll begin with a very easy example. In this example, we're repeating basically what we had done in the previous section, but using a Dockerfile this time and Debian as the parent image. A Dockerfile is simply a text file with a series of instructions that Docker will interpret to create the image.

This is the first version of our Dockerfile:

```
antonio@antonio-Laptop:~/docker$ cat Dockerfile
FROM debian:latest

RUN apt update

antonio@antonio-Laptop:~/docker$
```

We can create an image with **Docker image build**. This way docker will create an image according to the instructions from the file specified in the (-f) option. If no file name is specified, docker will search a file named *Dockerfile*.

```
antonio@antonio-Laptop:~/docker$ sudo docker image build -f
Dockerfile .
DEPRECATED: The legacy builder is deprecated and will be
            removed in a future release.
            Install the buildx component to build images with
            BuildKit:
            https://docs.docker.com/go/buildx/

Sending build context to Docker daemon  2.048kB
Step 1/2 : FROM debian:latest
 ---> 2e5b8d3ef33e
Step 2/2 : RUN apt update
 ---> Running in aa560ff2c33d

WARNING: apt does not have a stable CLI interface. Use with
caution in scripts.

Get:1 http://deb.debian.org/debian bookworm InRelease [151 kB]
Get:2 http://deb.debian.org/debian bookworm-updates InRelease
[55.4 kB]
Get:3 http://deb.debian.org/debian-security bookworm-security
InRelease [48.0 kB]
Get:4 http://deb.debian.org/debian bookworm/main amd64 Packages
[8788 kB]
Get:5 http://deb.debian.org/debian bookworm-updates/main amd64
Packages [13.8 kB]
Get:6 http://deb.debian.org/debian-security bookworm-security/
main amd64 Packages [169 kB]
Fetched 9225 kB in 2min 35s (59.4 kB/s)
Reading package lists...
Building dependency tree...
Reading state information...
All packages are up to date.
```

CHAPTER 9 DOCKER

```
Removing intermediate container aa560ff2c33d
 ---> 1284259d5ade
Successfully built 1284259d5ade
```

We have our new image created. We can list it as usual.

```
antonio@antonio-Laptop:~/docker$ sudo docker image list
REPOSITORY              TAG         IMAGE
ID          CREATED                 SIZE
<none>                  <none>      1284259d5ade   About a minute
ago     136MB
image_container_v2      latest      83dcb9837c49   3 hours
ago             117MB
```

And we can use it to create containers.

```
antonio@antonio-Laptop:~$ sudo docker run --rm -it 1284259d5ade
/bin/bash
root@8fec261cb909:/#
```

Now we'll review the two Dockerfile instructions we used in our Dockerfile:

- FROM: It's used to set the base image (ubuntu, debian, etc.). We could also use the special name "scratch" to create a new image from zero.

- RUN: It executes the command specified and commits the result to a new layer. That is, every RUN sentence will create a new layer.

The image we created had one RUN sentence and used ubuntu as the base image. So the resulting image has two layers. We can check with Docker image inspect that this is actually the case.

477

```
antonio@antonio-Laptop:~$ sudo docker image inspect
1284259d5ade
.
.
        "RootFS": {
            "Type": "layers",
            "Layers": [
                "sha256:f6faf32734e0870d82ea890737958fe33ce9ddf
                ed27b3b157576d2aadbab3322",
                "sha256:a5060b2c6a69409f084db46dff247c998854fb
                d5f07342d443651207cbe6c888"
            ]
        },
.
.
```

Besides the FROM and RUN instructions, there are many more than we can use in our Dockerfile. We'll enumerate some of the most used here:

- WORKDIR: Sets the working directory for the next sentences.
- LABEL: It is used to add metadata to an image, like version, maintainer, and so on.
- ARG: It defines a variable that can be used later in the Dockerfile.
- COPY: Copies new files and directories from the host to the container.
- ADD: Similar to COPY, but it also can copy content directly from URLs and tar files.
- VOLUME: It defines a volume.

- EXPOSE: Informs docker on what ports the container is listening on.
- CMD: It sets the command to be executed when running a container from an image. It includes all the default arguments for the command. Sometimes it omits the command itself; in these cases, the command must be specified in the ENTRYPOINT instruction.
- ENTRYPOINT: As explained before, it sets the command the container will run as an executable.

Let's see these additional instructions with another Dockerfile example file. We'll list here the file and explain later each sentence.

```
antonio@antonio-Laptop:~/docker$ cat Dockerfile2
FROM busybox

WORKDIR /etc
COPY test_file.txt .
ENTRYPOINT ["/bin/sleep", "60"]
```

We set the working directory to the */etc* directory. We copy the *test_file.txt* file, and we'll execute the sleep command for 60 seconds when the container is launched. We'll create the *test_file.txt* and build the image.

```
antonio@antonio-Laptop:~/docker$ echo test > test_file.txt
antonio@antonio-Laptop:~/docker$ sudo docker image build -f
Dockerfile2 .
DEPRECATED: The legacy builder is deprecated and will be
removed in a future release.
            Install the buildx component to build images with
BuildKit:
            https://docs.docker.com/go/buildx/

Sending build context to Docker daemon  4.096kB
```

CHAPTER 9 DOCKER

```
Step 1/4 : FROM busybox
 ---> 65ad0d468eb1
Step 2/4 : WORKDIR /etc
 ---> Running in 6d8afc97005d
Removing intermediate container 6d8afc97005d
 ---> 25fc806ab094
Step 3/4 : COPY test_file.txt .
 ---> bb415647959c
Step 4/4 : ENTRYPOINT ["/bin/sleep", "60"]
 ---> Running in c0cb7d19f91f
Removing intermediate container c0cb7d19f91f
 ---> b9cbf2b918b4
Successfully built b9cbf2b918b4
```

The image was successfully created and now we can create a container based on this image.

```
antonio@antonio-Laptop:~/docker$ sudo docker container run --rm -d b9cbf2b918b4
2acc023edbe8e95364ea9ec02c4a395e062cffd989bde5a404d5aedc35976de8
```

We can check that the container is executing.

```
antonio@antonio-Laptop:~/docker$ sudo docker container ls
CONTAINER ID    IMAGE           COMMAND
CREATED         STATUS          PORTS       NAMES
2acc023edbe8    b9cbf2b918b4    "/bin/sleep 60"    4 seconds
ago    Up 4 seconds             serene_bartik
```

In the listing, we see the command executing, which is "sleep 60". So far we have used **docker container attach** to connect to the standard input and the standard output of the container when the executing command

CHAPTER 9 DOCKER

is a shell. But if we do that with this container, we'll connect to the sleep process and won't be able to execute commands.

To execute commands in a Docker container, we can use **docker container exec**. We'll use this option to see the content of the *test_file.txt* file we copied during the building process.

```
antonio@antonio-Laptop:~/docker$ sudo docker container exec
serene_bartik cat /etc/test_file.txt
test
```

Another image-related option that can be useful to know is Docker image history, which will show the steps to create the image.

```
antonio@antonio-Laptop:~/docker$ sudo docker image history
b9cbf2b918b4
IMAGE           CREATED          CREATED BY
                                 SIZE         COMMENT
b9cbf2b918b4    23 minutes ago   /bin/sh -c
#(nop)  ENTRYPOINT ["/bin/sleep" …   0B
bb415647959c    23 minutes ago   /bin/sh -c
#(nop)  COPY file:2539c4b17295c856…   5B
25fc806ab094    23 minutes ago   /bin/sh -c
#(nop)  WORKDIR /etc                  0B
65ad0d468eb1    14 months ago    BusyBox
1.36.1 (glibc), Debian 12             4.26MB
```

We can compare this output to that of the Ubuntu image.

```
antonio@antonio-HP-Laptop-15s-fq1xxx:~/docker$ sudo docker
image history ubuntu
IMAGE           CREATED          CREATED BY
                                 SIZE         COMMENT
35a88802559d    2 months ago     /bin/sh -c
#(nop)  CMD ["/bin/bash"]             0B
```

CHAPTER 9   DOCKER

```
<missing>      2 months ago    /bin/sh -c
#(nop) ADD file:5601f441718b0d192…    78.1MB
<missing>      2 months ago    /bin/sh -c
#(nop)  LABEL org.opencontainers.…    0B
<missing>      2 months ago    /bin/sh -c
#(nop)  LABEL org.opencontainers.…    0B
<missing>      2 months ago    /bin/sh -c
#(nop)  ARG LAUNCHPAD_BUILD_ARCH       0B
<missing>      2 months ago    /bin/sh -c
#(nop)  ARG RELEASE                    0B
```

Logging in Docker

We can obtain the logs of a certain container with **docker container logs**. Let's see an example.

We start any given container, and then we check the logs. We'll execute a temporary container based on the nginx image. We'll use port mapping to make the nginx application accessible.

```
antonio@antonio-Laptop:~$ sudo docker container run --rm -d -it -p 8000:80 nginx
3426d53c3082decda7e88e9cfc8108b9a24d316b53bab267d75650b261b23db4
```

We check that the container is actually running.

```
antonio@antonio-Laptop:~$ sudo docker container ls
CONTAINER ID   IMAGE    COMMAND                  CREATED         STATUS         PORTS                                   NAMES
3426d53c3082   nginx    "/docker-entrypoint.…"   5 seconds ago   Up 5 seconds   0.0.0.0:8000->80/tcp, :::8000->80/tcp   friendly_mahavira
```

CHAPTER 9 DOCKER

And we review the logs.

```
antonio@antonio-Laptop:~$ sudo docker logs friendly_mahavira
/docker-entrypoint.sh: /docker-entrypoint.d/ is not empty, will
attempt to perform configuration
/docker-entrypoint.sh: Looking for shell scripts in /docker-
entrypoint.d/
/docker-entrypoint.sh: Launching /docker-entrypoint.d/10-
listen-on-ipv6-by-default.sh
10-listen-on-ipv6-by-default.sh: info: Getting the checksum of
/etc/nginx/conf.d/default.conf
10-listen-on-ipv6-by-default.sh: info: Enabled listen on
IPv6 in /etc/nginx/conf.d/default.conf
/docker-entrypoint.sh: Sourcing /docker-entrypoint.d/15-local-
resolvers.envsh
/docker-entrypoint.sh: Launching /docker-entrypoint.d/20-
envsubst-on-templates.sh
/docker-entrypoint.sh: Launching /docker-entrypoint.d/30-tune-
worker-processes.sh
/docker-entrypoint.sh: Configuration complete; ready for
start up
2024/08/07 12:16:25 [notice] 1#1: using the "epoll"
event method
2024/08/07 12:16:25 [notice] 1#1: nginx/1.27.0
2024/08/07 12:16:25 [notice] 1#1: built by gcc 12.2.0 (Debian
12.2.0-14)
2024/08/07 12:16:25 [notice] 1#1: OS: Linux 6.5.0-45-generic
2024/08/07 12:16:25 [notice] 1#1: getrlimit(RLIMIT_NOFILE):
1048576:1048576
2024/08/07 12:16:25 [notice] 1#1: start worker processes
2024/08/07 12:16:25 [notice] 1#1: start worker process 29
2024/08/07 12:16:25 [notice] 1#1: start worker process 30
```

CHAPTER 9   DOCKER

```
2024/08/07 12:16:25 [notice] 1#1: start worker process 31
2024/08/07 12:16:25 [notice] 1#1: start worker process 32
2024/08/07 12:16:25 [notice] 1#1: start worker process 33
2024/08/07 12:16:25 [notice] 1#1: start worker process 34
2024/08/07 12:16:25 [notice] 1#1: start worker process 35
2024/08/07 12:16:25 [notice] 1#1: start worker process 36
```

We can access the nginx welcome page using any web browser. In this example, we'll use curl.

```
antonio@antonio-Laptop:~$ curl -i http://localhost:8000
HTTP/1.1 200 OK
Server: nginx/1.27.0
.
.
<body>
<h1>Welcome to nginx!</h1>
<p>If you see this page, the nginx web server is successfully installed and
working. Further configuration is required.</p>
.
.
.
```

In the container logs, we can see immediately this access.

```
antonio@antonio-Laptop:~$ sudo docker logs friendly_mahavira
.
.
172.17.0.1 - - [07/Aug/2024:12:19:12 +0000] "GET / HTTP/1.1" 200 615 "-" "curl/7.81.0" "-"
```

CHAPTER 9 DOCKER

To log information, Docker used a logging driver, which is json-file by default. We can get this information with **docker info**.

```
antonio@antonio-Laptop:~$ sudo docker info | grep Logging
 Logging Driver: json-file
```

If we want to change the driver, we can pass the --log-driver option to dockerd or use a /etc/docker/daemon.json file with this option set. These are the options we have available from the man page of **dockerd**.

```
--log-driver="json-file|syslog|journald|gelf|fluentd|awslog
s|splunk|etwlogs|gcplogs|none"
  Default driver for container logs. Default is
  json-file.
  Warning: docker logs command works only for json-file
  logging driver.
```

We'll see this in an example. First, we stop any running containers.

```
antonio@antonio-Laptop:~$ sudo docker stop friendly_mahavira
friendly_mahavira
```

Then we'll create a /etc/docker/daemon.json file.

```
antonio@antonio-Laptop:~$ cat /etc/docker/daemon.json
{
"log-driver": "journald"
}
```

To apply the change, we need to stop and start the **dockerd** service.

```
antonio@antonio-Laptop:~$ sudo systemctl stop docker
Warning: Stopping docker.service, but it can still be
activated by:
  docker.socket
antonio@antonio-Laptop:~$ sudo systemctl stop docker.socket
antonio@antonio-Laptop:~$ sudo systemctl start docker
```

485

CHAPTER 9   DOCKER

We can execute **docker info** again to see that the logging driver actually changed.

```
antonio@antonio-Laptop:~$ sudo docker info | grep Logging
 Logging Driver: journald
```

We'll start another nginx container and access it with **curl** or other web browser.

```
antonio@antonio-Laptop:~$ sudo docker container run --rm -d -it -p 8000:80 nginx
0eed0a0c6f260684e27985780692fe9cfbec05644541d7ed32db4bec65494ada
```

After accessing the container with curl, we'll see this entry on the journal file.

```
antonio@antonio-Laptop:~$ journalctl -f
.
.
ago 07 15:29:58 antonio-Laptop 0eed0a0c6f26[20989]: 172.17.0.1 - - [07/Aug/2024:13:29:58 +0000] "GET / HTTP/1.1" 200 615 "-" "curl/7.81.0" "-"
```

This is how we changed the default logging driver, but we can also run a container and tell it to use a logging driver different from the default. We'll stop the running container, remove the *ABC/etc/docker/daemon.json* file, and restart docker again.

```
antonio@antonio-Laptop:~$ sudo docker container stop 0eed0a0c6f26
antonio@antonio-Laptop:~$ sudo rm /etc/docker/daemon.json
antonio@antonio-Laptop:~$ sudo systemctl restart docker
```

We confirm with **docker info** the default logging driver.

```
antonio@antonio-Laptop:~$ sudo docker info | grep Logging
 Logging Driver: json-file
```

And we launch a new container with a different logging driver, "none" in this case.

```
antonio@antonio-Laptop:~$ sudo docker run --rm -d -it --log-driver=none -p 8000:80 nginx
6ef76fcf302f6cda4eea4604fa6a147ffadf4e9448244f3be3996b70a80354f2
```

We list the running containers and try to see the container logs.

```
antonio@antonio-Laptop:~$ sudo docker container ls
CONTAINER ID   IMAGE     COMMAND                  CREATED
STATUS         PORTS                                      NAMES
6ef76fcf302f   nginx     "/docker-entrypoint.…"   30 seconds
ago     Up 29 seconds   0.0.0.0:8000->80/tcp, :::8000->80/tcp   sleepy_cray
antonio@antonio-Laptop:~$ sudo docker container logs sleepy_cray
Error response from daemon: configured logging driver does not support reading
```

As expected, we can't see any logs because we explicitly used the "none" logging driver option.

Saving and Restoring Containers

Containers have the advantage of being very light and easy to create, start, stop, etc. We can easily save containers and restore them, either in the same node or a different one.

CHAPTER 9 DOCKER

In the "Customizing Our Own Containers" section, we already saw how to make changes to a running container and commit that container to a new image. But we didn't export that image to import it later in a different node.

We're going to repeat the procedure, very quickly because we're already familiar with it. But this time, we'll export the image.

We'll begin by launching a new container based on nginx.

```
antonio@antonio-Laptop:~$ sudo docker container run -d -p 8000:80 nginx
d559e553ab24af71ec35690e9d05ff5527355ba53a155270243e51e7e33aa638
```

We get the container name.

```
antonio@antonio-Laptop:~$ sudo docker container ls
CONTAINER ID   IMAGE    COMMAND                  CREATED
STATUS           PORTS                                   NAMES
d559e553ab24   nginx    "/docker-entrypoint...."  44 seconds
ago     Up 43 seconds   0.0.0.0:8000->80/tcp, :::8000->80/
tcp     vigilant_hoover
```

We're going to customize the container by substituting the default web page, which is currently located at */usr/share/nginx/html/index.html*. We'll change it for this html file.

```
antonio@antonio-Laptop:~$ cat index.html
<html>
<head>
<title>My Web Page</title>
</head>
<body>
<h1>Welcome to my Page</h1>
</body>
</html>
```

CHAPTER 9 DOCKER

To copy files between the host and the container, or vice versa, we can use the **docker container cp** command.

antonio@antonio-Laptop:~$ sudo docker container cp index.html vigilant_hoover:/usr/share/nginx/html/index.html
Successfully copied 2.05kB to vigilant_hoover:/usr/share/nginx/html/index.html

We can check with a browser that the new default web page has been changed (Figure 9-5).

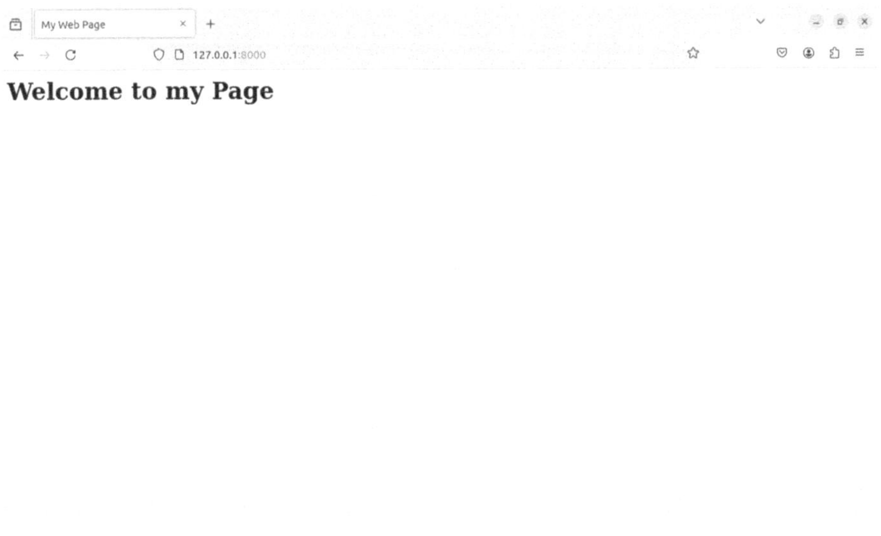

Figure 9-5. Customized default web page

We stop the container and commit it to a new image; this is something we already know how to do.

antonio@antonio-Laptop:~$ sudo docker container stop vigilant_hoover
vigilant_hoover

CHAPTER 9 DOCKER

```
antonio@antonio-Laptop:~$ sudo docker container commit
vigilant_hoover customized_nginx
sha256:4317003e3c61e9512d50b4a95ee7c90522aac50cb27e3352cd6c979
bab0efed2
```

And we save the image to a tar file (-o option) with the **Docker image save** command.

```
antonio@antonio-Laptop:~$ sudo docker image save customized_
nginx -o customized_nginx.tar
antonio@antonio-Laptop:~$ ls -lh customized_nginx.tar
-rw------- 1 root root 183M ago  8 01:51 customized_nginx.tar
```

This tar file can already be copied to a different host with tools like **scp**. Once they're copied, they can be imported with **Docker image load**. As currently I don't have another host with docker installed, I'll simulate this procedure in the same node.

First, we delete the image customized_nginx.

```
antonio@antonio-Laptop:~$ sudo docker image rm customized_nginx
Untagged: customized_nginx:latest
Deleted: sha256:4317003e3c61e9512d50b4a95ee7c90522aac50cb27e335
2cd6c979bab0efed2
Deleted: sha256:194a1d8d46bbca24736e8e4740a2ea5a7ce30b54ce9950
5b0b769894bbafc162
```

And we load the image again from the tar file.

```
antonio@antonio-Laptop:~$ sudo docker image load -i customized_
nginx.tar
d3e15dbef7c9: Loading layer
[==================================================>]
12.29kB/12.29kB
Loaded image: customized_nginx:latest
```

CHAPTER 9　DOCKER

We list the images to check that they were successfully imported.

```
antonio@antonio-Laptop:~$ sudo docker image list
REPOSITORY            TAG        IMAGE
ID          CREATED         SIZE
customized_nginx      latest     4317003e3c61    12 hours
ago      188MB
```

We'll create a new container. This time we'll use another option that can be useful sometimes, the --label option. As the name implies, this assigns a label to the container, and later we can use this label to better identify each container. For example, we can assign the label "development" to this new container.

```
antonio@antonio-Laptop:~$ sudo docker container run -d -it -p
8000:80 --label=development customized_nginx:latest
11e1bf5c80d745ec4ff8bf498adcfe417756f0baa25f2e4659764f01b0
a2daf6
```

From now on, it is possible to list the containers that have the label "development". This can be very interesting to identify the containers that belong to different life cycles.

```
antonio@antonio-Laptop:~$ sudo docker container ls -a --filter
label=development
CONTAINER
ID    IMAGE                     COMMAND                  CREATED
STATUS          PORTS                            NAMES
11e1bf5c80d7   customized_nginx:latest   "/
docker-entrypoint.…"   About a minute ago   Up 59
seconds    0.0.0.0:8000->80/tcp, :::8000->80/tcp   unruffled_
chandrasekhar
```

491

CHAPTER 9   DOCKER

Creating a Local Registry

In this chapter, we have used the **docker search** command to search for images. When doing this, we were contacting a remote registry, the default Docker hub registry.

It is also possible to use a different registry and even use our own local registry. To use a local registry, we need to execute locally a specific container that can be downloaded from the Docker hub registry.

```
antonio@antonio-Laptop:~$ sudo docker search registry
NAME                    DESCRIPTION
     STARS     OFFICIAL    AUTOMATED
registry                Distribution implementation for storing and
...    4027      [OK]
docker/dtr-registry                                                   0
```

We just need to download this registry image to our host to start working with it.

```
antonio@antonio-Laptop:~$ sudo docker image pull
registry:latest
latest: Pulling from library/registry
930bdd4d222e: Pull complete
a15309931e05: Pull complete
6263fb9c821f: Pull complete
86c1d3af3872: Pull complete
a37b1bf6a96f: Pull complete
Digest: sha256:12120425f07de11a1b899e418d4b0ea174c8d4d572d45
bdb640f93bc7ca06a3d
Status: Downloaded newer image for registry:latest
docker.io/library/registry:latest
```

This registry listens for connections on port 5000/tcp. We can see this information with the "inspect" subcommand.

```
antonio@antonio-Laptop:~$ sudo docker image inspect registry
.
.
        "ExposedPorts": {
            "5000/tcp": {}
        },
.
.
```

So we'll run a container mapping port 5000 in the host to port 5000 in the container. We'll also use an option that we hadn't seen so far, the restart option, to tell the container to restart every time the Docker service restarts.

```
antonio@antonio-Laptop:~$ sudo docker container run -d -p
5000:5000 --restart=always --name=local_registry registry
c262e80b9b70659b753819b3081d1987adc9cb70c3c7d1a2209c02cb
6a64d1de
```

If we list the running containers, we'll see our local registry.

```
antonio@antonio-Laptop:~$ sudo docker container ls
CONTAINER ID   IMAGE      COMMAND                  CREATED
STATUS            POR
TS                                NAMES
c262e80b9b70   registry   "/entrypoint.sh /etc..."   37 seconds
ago    Up 37 seconds   0.0.0.0:5000->5000/tcp, :::5000->5000/
tcp    local_registry
```

CHAPTER 9 DOCKER

Now, let's see how to upload and download images to and from our local registry. For that purpose, we could use any of the images that we have downloaded previously, but for convenience, we'll download an alpine image, which is very light. We start by downloading this image the usual way.

```
antonio@antonio-Laptop:~$ sudo docker pull alpine
Using default tag: latest
latest: Pulling from library/alpine
c6a83fedfae6: Pull complete
Digest: sha256:0a4eaa0eecf5f8c050e5bba433f58c052be7587ee8af3e
8b3910ef9ab5fbe9f5
Status: Downloaded newer image for alpine:latest
docker.io/library/alpine:latest
```

To upload an image to our local registry, the first thing we need to do is tag the image.

```
antonio@antonio-Laptop:~$ sudo docker tag alpine:latest
localhost:5000/alpine_local
```

Then, if we list the images, we'll see two tags associated to the same alpine image: the original "alpine" tag and the new "localhost:5000/alpine_local" tag.

```
antonio@antonio-Laptop:~$ sudo docker image ls
REPOSITORY                    TAG         IMAGE
ID         CREATED        SIZE
customized_nginx              latest      4317003e3c61    15 hours
ago     188MB
.
.
```

```
localhost:5000/alpine_local   latest    324bc02ae123    2 weeks
ago        7.8MB
alpine                        latest    324bc02ae123    2 weeks
ago        7.8MB
```

To upload the image to our local registry, we'll use the "push" subcommand.

```
antonio@antonio-Laptop:~$ sudo docker image push
localhost:5000/alpine_local
Using default tag: latest
The push refers to repository [localhost:5000/alpine_local]
78561cef0761: Pushed
latest: digest: sha256:eddacbc7e24bf8799a4ed3cdcfa50d4b88a32369
5ad80f317b6629883b2c2a78 size: 528
```

We already have our first image uploaded to our local registry. Now we'll see how to use this image to create new containers. For that, we'll start by deleting the local alpine image. As we have two different tags associated to the same image, we'll need to remove both tags.

```
antonio@antonio-Laptop:~$ sudo docker image rm alpine
Untagged: alpine:latest
Untagged: alpine@sha256:0a4eaa0eecf5f8c050e5bba433f58c052be7587
ee8af3e8b3910ef9ab5fbe9f5
antonio@antonio-Laptop:~$ sudo docker image rm localhost:5000/
alpine_local
Untagged: localhost:5000/alpine_local:latest
Untagged: localhost:5000/alpine_local@sha256:eddacbc7e24bf8799a
4ed3cdcfa50d4b88a323695ad80f317b6629883b2c2a78
Deleted: sha256:324bc02ae1231fd9255658c128086395d3fa0aedd5a41ab
6b034fd649d1a9260
Deleted: sha256:78561cef0761903dd2f7d09856150a6d4fb48967a8f113f
3e33d79effbf59a07
```

Finally, we create a container using explicitly the alpine image located in our local registry.

```
antonio@antonio-Laptop:~$ sudo docker container run -it localhost:5000/alpine_local
Unable to find image 'localhost:5000/alpine_local:latest' locally
latest: Pulling from alpine_local
c6a83fedfae6: Pull complete
Digest: sha256:eddacbc7e24bf8799a4ed3cdcfa50d4b88a323695ad80f317b6629883b2c2a78
Status: Downloaded newer image for localhost:5000/alpine_local:latest
/ #
```

Customizing Security Options

In Chapter 7, we studied the technologies used when working with containers, such as namespaces, cgroups, seccomp, capabilities, etc.

Then we studied Linux containers (LXC) and Docker containers, and we saw that these solutions automatically make use of these technologies to isolate the containers and limit the amount of resources they can use. This way working with containers becomes much more convenient.

Usually, we don't need to customize the way a certain Docker container uses cgroups, capabilities, and so on. But in some specific cases that might be necessary. We'll see an easy example about capabilities.

We'll begin by executing a temporary container, without any particular customization.

```
antonio@antonio-Laptop:~$ sudo docker container run --rm -it busybox
[sudo] password for antonio:
/ #
```

CHAPTER 9 DOCKER

We'll change the owner of the */home* folder.

```
/ # ls -ld /home
drwxr-xr-x    2 nobody    nobody          4096 May 18  2023 /home
/ # chown root /home
/ # ls -ld /home
drwxr-xr-x    1 root      nobody          4096 May 18  2023 /home
/ # exit
```

As expected, the owner of the folder was successfully changed. Let's repeat this test with a new container, but this time we'll drop all the capabilities from the container.

```
antonio@antonio-Laptop:~$ sudo docker container run --rm --cap-drop=ALL -it busybox
/ # ls -ld /home
drwxr-xr-x    2 nobody    nobody          4096 May 18  2023 /home
/ # chown root /home
chown: /home: Operation not permitted
/ # exit
```

This time, when we try to change the owner, we get an error because the operation is not permitted.

Finally, we're going to repeat the test by adding the needed capability to change the owner of a file/folder. If we look at the man page for capabilities, we'll see this line:

> CAP_CHOWN
>
> Make arbitrary changes to file UIDs and GIDs (see chown(2)).

So the capability we need to add is CAP_CHOWN. We'll launch a new temporary container.

```
antonio@antonio-Laptop:~$ sudo docker container run --rm --cap-drop=ALL --cap-add=CAP_CHOWN -it busybox
/ # ls -ld /home
drwxr-xr-x    2 nobody   nobody        4096 May 18  2023 /home
/ # chown root /home
/ # exit
```

As expected, we could change the owner successfully again.

Summary

We've reached the end of this chapter, which has a heavy weight in the LPIC-3 305 exam. We began by getting a glimpse of the Docker architecture and installing it. Then we started searching for images and running our first Docker containers.

After that, we saw a bit more of detail about the Docker architecture, and we learned how to work with docker volumes and docker networks. We created our own images either from a customized container or from a Dockerfile.

We also studied how logging in dockerd works and how to save and restore images. Finally, we created our own local Docker registry and reviewed how to use some advanced features like capabilities.

CHAPTER 10

Container Orchestration Platforms

In this chapter, we'll cover the following concepts:

- Understand the relevance of container orchestration
- Understand the key concepts of docker compose and docker swarm
- Understand the key concepts of Kubernetes and Helm
- Awareness of OpenShift and Rancher

Container Orchestration

In previous chapters, we studied containers individually. A container can be useful by itself, but when having several containers working in a coordinated manner, we can achieve things that wouldn't be possible with containers completely independent from each other. We can easily make an analogy with an orchestra in which a conductor directs the performance of all the musicians.

When executing applications in containers, we can have several scenarios:

- The application is executed in a single container and therefore in a single host.
- The application, or parts of the application, is executed in several containers, but always in the same host. To define these multi-container applications, we can use **docker compose**, as we'll see in a while.
- The application is executed in many containers distributed across several hosts. In this case, we need to coordinate all the hosts and containers so that the application works as expected. This is accomplished thanks to the orchestration platforms.

docker compose

This is a tool for defining and running multi-container applications; these applications that work on containers are usually called microservices. It uses a YAML configuration file to define the needed containers, networks, volumes, etc.

Installing docker compose

We have different options to install docker compose. We can install it from the Ubuntu repositories.

antonio@antonio-Laptop:~$ sudo apt install docker-compose

This tool is very easy to use, as we'll see later. We can take a look at the contextual help to get a hint about the way to work with it.

```
antonio@antonio-Laptop:~$ docker-compose --help
Define and run multi-container applications with Docker.

Usage:
  docker-compose [-f <arg>...] [--profile <name>...] [options]
[--] [COMMAND] [ARGS...]
  docker-compose -h|--help
.
.
.
```

When installing **docker compose** in this way, we're installing a stand-alone executable file. And the version will be older than the current version available from the Docker repositories.

```
antonio@antonio-Laptop:~$ docker-compose --version
docker-compose version 1.29.2, build unknown
```

If we compare this with the version of a CentOS server using the Docker repositories, we'll see that the versions are significantly different. Besides, in the case of the CentOS server, **docker compose** is no longer a stand-alone executable file, but a Docker plug-in.

```
[root@rocky ~]# docker compose version
Docker Compose version v2.17.3
```

To install docker compose from the Docker repositories, we need to add the official Docker repository to our CentOS server.

```
[root@rocky ~]# yum-config-manager --add-repo
https://download.docker.com/linux/centos/docker-ce.repo
```

For the purposes of the LPIC-3 305 exam, we can use any of the two versions: the older from the Ubuntu repositories or the newer from the CentOS server. During the course of the book, we'll favor the use of the newer version.

CHAPTER 10   CONTAINER ORCHESTRATION PLATFORMS

Creating a Service with docker compose

Let's see an easy example of how to use **docker compose** to deploy an application. To keep things as simple as possible, we'll use a single container. Obviously, it doesn't make much sense to use **docker compose** to deploy a single container, as it would be easier to deploy it directly from the command line. But it will make us understand better how docker compose works when we use it for more advanced deployments.

This is the first YAML file that we'll use for the first deployment.

```
[root@rocky docker-compose]# cat docker-compose.yml
version: "3"
services:
  web:
    image: httpd
    ports:
      - 8080:80
```

First, we specify the version; the current version is "3". Then we enumerate the services that we're deploying. For naming convention, when we use **docker compose** to deploy applications, we are deploying "services".

In this case, we're deploying a single service named "web". The "web" service uses the image "httpd"(Apache Web Server) and will map port 8000 in the host to port 80 in the container.

To create the service, we need to execute "**docker compose up**". This command will create and start the needed containers.

```
[root@rocky docker-compose]# docker compose up
[+] Running 2/1
 ✔ Network docker-compose_default   Created 0.3s
 ✔ Container docker-compose-web-1   Created 0.1s
Attaching to docker-compose-web-1
docker-compose-web-1  | AH00558: httpd: Could not reliably
```

determine the server's fully qualified domain name, using
172.19.0.2. Set the 'ServerName' directive globally to suppress
this message
docker-compose-web-1 | AH00558: httpd: Could not reliably
determine the server's fully qualified domain name, using
172.19.0.2. Set the 'ServerName' directive globally to suppress
this message
docker-compose-web-1 | [Fri Jul 05 22:21:30.385934 2024]
[mpm_event:notice] [pid 1:tid 139697548614976] AH00489:
Apache/2.4.56 (Unix) configured -- resuming normal operations
docker-compose-web-1 | [Fri Jul 05 22:21:30.386123 2024]
[core:notice] [pid 1:tid 139697548614976] AH00094: Command
line: 'httpd -D FOREGROUND'

After a few seconds, the service will be ready to listen for connections. So we can connect to port 8080 in the host.

antonio@antonio-Laptop:~$ curl http://192.168.1.51:8080
<html><body><h1>It works!</h1></body></html>

In the shell window where we launched **docker compose**, we can see this successful connection attempt.

docker-compose-web-1 | 192.168.1.20 - - [05/Jul/2024:22:22:48
+0000] "GET / HTTP/1.1" 200 45

In addition to deploying the services, there are many more subcommands available. As the command shell we used to build and start the containers ran in the foreground, we can't use that same command shell, and we'll need to open a new one. Later, we'll see how to build and start the containers and detach automatically.

We can list the containers with **docker compose ps**.

```
[root@rocky docker-compose]# docker compose ps
NAME                    IMAGE               COMMAND
SERVICE                 CREATED             STATUS
PORTS
docker-compose-web-1    httpd               "httpd-foreground"
web                     4 minutes ago       Up 4 minutes
0.0.0.0:8080->80/tcp, :::8080->80/tcp
```

As this first deployment uses a single container, we only see a container in the listing. We can also list the services with **docker compose ls**.

```
[root@rocky docker-compose]# docker compose ls
NAME                STATUS              CONFIG FILES
docker-compose      running(1)          /root/docker-compose/
                                        docker-compose.yml
```

It is also possible to see the logs of the containers in the service with the "logs" subcommand.

```
[root@rocky docker-compose]# docker compose logs
docker-compose-web-1  | AH00558: httpd: Could not reliably
determine the server's fully qualified domain name, using
172.19.0.2. Set the 'ServerName' directive globally to suppress
this message
docker-compose-web-1  | AH00558: httpd: Could not reliably
determine the server's fully qualified domain name, using
172.19.0.2. Set the 'ServerName' directive globally to suppress
this message
docker-compose-web-1  | [Fri Jul 05 22:21:30.385934 2024]
[mpm_event:notice] [pid 1:tid 139697548614976] AH00489:
Apache/2.4.56 (Unix) configured -- resuming normal operations
docker-compose-web-1  | [Fri Jul 05 22:21:30.386123 2024]
[core:notice] [pid 1:tid 139697548614976] AH00094: Command
line: 'httpd -D FOREGROUND'
```

CHAPTER 10   CONTAINER ORCHESTRATION PLATFORMS

```
docker-compose-web-1  | 192.168.1.20 - - [05/Jul/2024:22:22:48
+0000] "GET / HTTP/1.1" 200 45
docker-compose-web-1  | 192.168.1.20 - - [05/Jul/2024:22:23:29
+0000] "GET / HTTP/1.1" 200 45
docker-compose-web-1  | 192.168.1.20 - - [05/Jul/2024:22:23:56
+0000] "GET / HTTP/1.1" 200 45
```

Another useful command is docker compose top, which lists the processes currently running in the containers.

```
[root@rocky docker-compose]# docker compose top
docker-compose-web-1
UID     PID     PPID    C    STIME   TTY    TIME       CMD
root    47251   47229   0    00:21   ?      00:00:00   httpd
-DFOREGROUND
33      47282   47251   0    00:21   ?      00:00:00   httpd
-DFOREGROUND
33      47283   47251   0    00:21   ?      00:00:00   httpd
-DFOREGROUND
33      47284   47251   0    00:21   ?      00:00:00   httpd
-DFOREGROUND
```

When we create a service, if we don't specify otherwise, a new network will be created to be used by **docker compose**. We can list this network, and the rest, with **docker network ls**.

```
[root@rocky docker-compose]# docker network ls
NETWORK ID       NAME                      DRIVER    SCOPE
46947c7695b7     bridge                    bridge    local
9f1b3a9a759f     docker-compose_default    bridge    local
219b2e97e8e8     docker_gwbridge           bridge    local
900f9f3284e0     host                      host      local
1111c925d0de     none                      null      local
07f217159cd4     root_default              bridge    local
```

505

We can see clearly a network named docker-compose_default, which is the network that was automatically created for the service deployed.

Now that we checked our service, we can shut it down, stopping and removing the containers.

```
[root@rocky docker-compose]# docker compose down
[+] Running 2/2
 ✔ Container docker-compose-web-1   Removed 1.3s
 ✔ Network docker-compose_default   Removed
```

Creating a Multi-container Service

Now that we're a bit more familiar with docker compose, let's see a second example.

This time we'll use several containers so the YAML file will be a bit more complicated. This is the file that we'll use.

```
[root@rocky docker-compose]# cat docker-compose-example2.yaml
version: "3"
services:
  postgresql:
    image: postgres
    restart: always
    environment:
      - POSTGRES_PASSWORD="password"
    volumes:
      - pgdata:/var/lib/postgresql/data
  adminer:
    image: adminer
    restart: always
```

```
    ports:
      - 8080:8080
volumes:
  pgdata:
```

We keep using version 3. We define two services. For the postgresql service, we use the postgres image; we include the restart option to make sure that the service restarts automatically every time the Docker service restarts. For a postgres container to work, we need to define an environment variable with the name POSTGRES_PASSWORD and the password for the Postgres database. We also specify that we'll use a volume named pgdata mounted at /var/lib/postgresql/data.

For the adminer service, we use the adminer image. If you're not familiar with it, adminer is a PHP application used to manage databases. We also tell Docker to restart this container automatically, and we map port 8080 in the host to port 8080 in the container.

Finally, we define the local volume pgdata.

We're ready to deploy these services; this time we'll use the --detach option so that the services keep running in the background after the execution. We also need to use -f to specify the name of the file because in this occasion, we're not using the default *docker-compose.yml* name.

```
[root@rocky docker-compose]# docker compose -f docker-compose-ejemplo.yaml up --detach
[+] Running 3/3
 ✔ Network docker-compose_default            Created 0.4s
 ✔ Container docker-compose-adminer-1        Started 0.7s
 ✔ Container docker-compose-postgresql-1     Started 0.7s
```

CHAPTER 10   CONTAINER ORCHESTRATION PLATFORMS

When we list the containers, we'll see now two different containers.

```
[root@rocky docker-compose]# docker compose ps
NAME                               IMAGE
   COMMAND                         SERVICE                 CREATED
STATUS                 PORTS
docker-compose-adminer-1      adminer
   "entrypoint.sh php -…"    adminer                 2 minutes ago
Up 2 minutes            0.0.0.0:8080->8080/tcp, :::8080->8080/tcp
docker-compose-postgresql-1   postgres
   "docker-entrypoint.s…"    postgresql              2 minutes ago
Up 2 minutes            5432/tcp
```

The services are up and running, so we can use a browser and point it to port 8080 in the host (Figure 10-1).

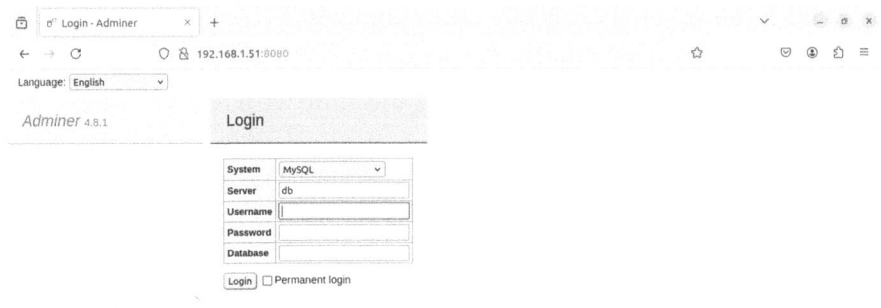

Figure 10-1. Accessing adminer

CHAPTER 10 CONTAINER ORCHESTRATION PLATFORMS

To connect to the PostgreSQL instance running in the second container, we need to know the IP address of the second container. We can obtain this information with **docker container inspect**, as we saw in the previous chapter.

```
[root@rocky docker-compose]# docker container inspect docker-compose-postgresql-1
            "IPAddress": "172.22.0.3",
```

With this information and using the default user and database (postgres in both cases) and the password specified in the file, we can establish the connection with the PostgreSQL instance (Figure 10-2).

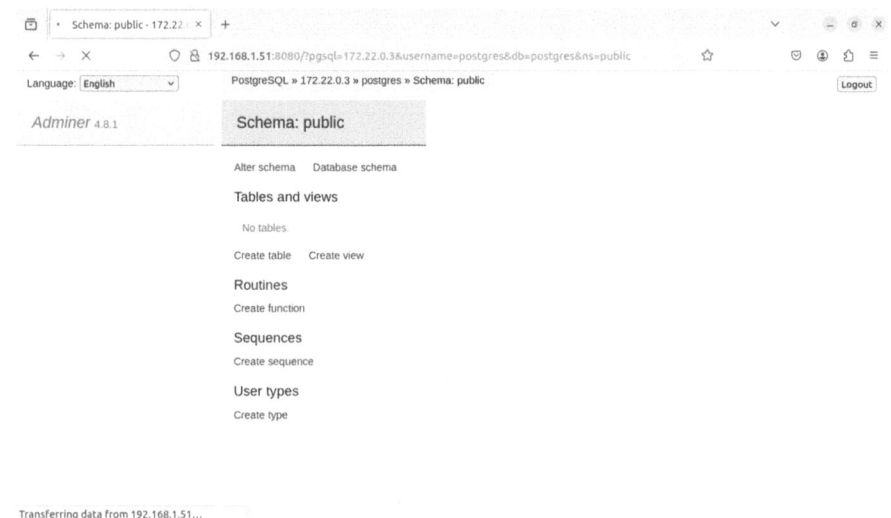

Figure 10-2. *Connection to the PostgreSQL instance established*

When we finish this second test, we can shut the services down as well.

```
[root@rocky docker-compose]# docker compose -f docker-compose-ejemplo.yaml down
[+] Running 3/3
```

```
✔ Container docker-compose-postgresql-1   Removed
                                                       0.4s
✔ Container docker-compose-adminer-1      Removed
                                                       0.4s
✔ Network docker-compose_default          Removed
```

In both of our examples, we used images from the Docker hub registry to deploy our services, but it is possible to use the option "build" in our docker-compose file. In that case, we need to type the path of a Dockerfile with the instructions to build a container.

We also said before that docker compose will create automatically a network to be used by the services we are deploying. But if we want to, we can use the "network" option and set the network that will be used.

docker swarm

The original orchestration solution developed by Docker is still included with the Docker engine packages, so we don't need to install any additional software.

docker swarm Architecture

In docker swarm, we have two types of nodes:

- Managers: These nodes manage where applications are deployed. Besides that, they can also execute workloads like the worker nodes.
- Workers: These nodes execute workloads.

CHAPTER 10 CONTAINER ORCHESTRATION PLATFORMS

Initializing a docker swarm Cluster

To start working with docker swarm, we don't need to install any additional software. We just need to use the docker swarm commands. To create a docker swarm cluster, we'll execute **docker swarm init**.

```
[root@rocky ~]# docker swarm init
Swarm initialized: current node (11g3pu6qhi0btehudzt0ut9sz) is
now a manager.

To add a worker to this swarm, run the following command:

    docker swarm join --token SWMTKN-1-137120iv6byj47mtmfwoz
    1h5p54gog8eb2vjjpx40l84bsbiyr-7hi1bbdgw6bvgayzz6e0oghyu
    192.168.1.51:2377

To add a manager to this swarm, run 'docker swarm join-token
manager' and follow the instructions.
```

The command exited successfully, and it shows the command we need to use to add worker nodes to the docker swarm cluster. As the cluster is already initialized, we can list its nodes.

```
[root@rocky ~]# docker node ls
ID                          HOSTNAME           STATUS
AVAILABILITY   MANAGER STATUS    ENGINE VERSION
11g3pu6qhi0btehudzt0ut9sz * rocky.example.com  Ready
Active         Leader            26.1.3
```

Obviously, right now we only have one node. This node is a manager; it is ready and it is the leader. Being the leader means that when there is an even number of manager nodes, the leader has the last word about any decision.

Another interesting command is docker node inspect, which shows data like the status of the node.

```
[root@rocky ~]# docker node inspect 11g3pu6qhi0btehudzt0ut9sz
```

511

CHAPTER 10 CONTAINER ORCHESTRATION PLATFORMS

We're already familiar with the docker info command. When having a docker swarm cluster, this command will also show some information about that cluster.

```
[root@rocky ~]# docker info
·
·
·
 Swarm: active
  NodeID: llg3pu6qhi0btehudzt0ut9sz
  Is Manager: true
  ClusterID: w3kqss3zllzjefuw5bkwz4109
  Managers: 1
  Nodes: 1
  Default Address Pool: 10.0.0.0/8
  SubnetSize: 24
  Data Path Port: 4789
  Orchestration:
   Task History Retention Limit: 5
  Raft:
   Snapshot Interval: 10000
   Number of Old Snapshots to Retain: 0
   Heartbeat Tick: 1
   Election Tick: 10
  Dispatcher:
   Heartbeat Period: 5 seconds
  CA Configuration:
·
·
·
```

CHAPTER 10   CONTAINER ORCHESTRATION PLATFORMS

Adding Additional Nodes to the Swarm Cluster

When working with a docker swarm cluster, the nodes need to communicate between them. We can check the ports **dockerd** is listening on by identifying the PID and using **lsof** to see the open ports. Usually this should be done automatically when installing the cluster, but we'll check it manually to be sure and to better understand how the swarm cluster works.

```
[root@rocky ~]# ps -ef | grep dockerd
root        40274       1  0 jul05 ?        00:00:04 /usr/bin/
dockerd -H fd:// --containerd=/run/containerd/containerd.sock
root        63943   50107  0 03:31 pts/0    00:00:00 grep
--color=auto dockerd
[root@rocky ~]# lsof -p 40274 | grep -i ipv
dockerd 40274 root    41u     IPv6            200460
    0t0         TCP *:swarm (LISTEN)
dockerd 40274 root    52u     IPv6            200488
    0t0         TCP *:7946 (LISTEN)
dockerd 40274 root    54u     IPv6            200489
    0t0         UDP *:7946
```

We can see that our only manager node is listening on port 7946/tcp and on swarm port (2377/tcp).

```
[root@rocky ~]# grep swarm /etc/services
swarm           2377/tcp                # RPC interface for
                                        Docker Swarm
```

We need to make sure that the local firewall allows for traffic in these ports.

CHAPTER 10   CONTAINER ORCHESTRATION PLATFORMS

```
[root@rocky ~]# firewall-cmd --add-port=2377/tcp
success
[root@rocky ~]# firewall-cmd --add-port=2377/tcp --permanent
success
[root@rocky ~]# firewall-cmd --add-port=7946/tcp --permanent
success
[root@rocky ~]# firewall-cmd --add-port=7946/tcp
success
[root@rocky ~]# firewall-cmd --add-port=7946/udp
success
[root@rocky ~]# firewall-cmd --add-port=7946/udp --permanent
success
```

Now we're ready to add a second node to the cluster. The token needed to join a new worker node was displayed when we executed **docker swarm init**, but we can check it at any time with **docker swarm join-token worker**.

```
[root@rocky ~]# docker swarm join-token worker
To add a worker to this swarm, run the following command:

    docker swarm join --token SWMTKN-1-137120iv6byj47mtmfwoz
    1h5p54gog8eb2vjjpx40l84bsbiyr-7hi1bbdgw6bvgayzz6e0oghyu
    192.168.1.51:2377
```

We get to the second node and type the command.

```
[root@apollo ~]# docker swarm join --token SWMTKN-
1-137120iv6byj47mtmfwoz1h5p54gog8eb2vjjpx40l84bsbi
yr-7hi1bbdgw6bvgayzz6e0oghyu 192.168.1.51:2377
This node joined a swarm as a worker.
```

The output of the command shows that the node joined the swarm. We can now list both nodes of the cluster.

```
[root@rocky ~]# docker node ls
ID                          HOSTNAME            STATUS
    AVAILABILITY   MANAGER STATUS   ENGINE VERSION
so8rbhx9dav9k7j8ezgopine5   apollo.example.com  Ready
    Active                           20.10.17
llg3pu6qhi0btehudzt0ut9sz * rocky.example.com   Ready
    Active         Leader            26.1.3
```

It is important to note that management commands like **docker node** can only be executed on manager nodes. We have many subcommands available when working with nodes; we can see them in the contextual help. For instance, if we wanted to promote a worker node (apollo) to a manager node, we'd execute the following command (from a manager):

```
[root@rocky ~]# docker node promote so8rbhx9dav9k7j8ezgopine5
```

If later we want to demote the node back to worker, we can use **docker node demote**. For now, we'll keep working with a single manager and a single worker.

Deploying Services in docker swarm

Similarly to what we have seen with docker compose, in docker swarm, we also deploy services. If we list the current services, we'll see there is none.

```
[root@rocky ~]# docker service ls
ID        NAME        MODE        REPLICAS    IMAGE      PORTS
```

We're going to deploy our first service. We'll deploy a service based on the httpd image(Apache Web Server).

```
[root@rocky ~]# docker service create
--name my_web_service httpd
j6e1857uaqatxrcr5i8rdu6wd
```

```
overall progress: 1 out of 1 tasks
1/1: running   [==============================================>]
verify: Service converged
```

The service converged successfully. This means that it was deployed in all the nodes in which it should be deployed. When deploying a service, we can explicitly set in which nodes it will be deployed. In this example, we didn't so the service was deployed in the only worker node currently running.

We can now list the service we just deployed.

```
[root@rocky ~]# docker service ls
ID              NAME             MODE         REPLICAS
IMAGE           PORTS
j6e1857uaqat    my_web_service   replicated   1/1
httpd:latest
```

We can see the ID and the name of the service, the image it is based on, and the number of replicas. In this case, we have one running replica of a maximum of one.

When deploying the service, we can choose between two modes:

- Global: When in this mode, a service will execute in all nodes of the cluster.

- Replicated: In this case, the service will run in one or more nodes of the cluster, depending on the number of replicas set and the possible constraints.

We have just mentioned constraints. We can set constraints to better control on which nodes a service will run on.

At any point, we can get information from the service with **docker service inspect**.

```
[root@rocky ~]# docker service inspect my_web_service
```

CHAPTER 10   CONTAINER ORCHESTRATION PLATFORMS

We can also list the processes in a service with **docker service ps**.

```
[root@rocky ~]# docker service ps my_web_service
ID               NAME                  IMAGE
NODE                    DESIRED STATE   CURRENT STATE
ERROR        PORTS
ttrt7az26dyb     my_web_service.1      httpd:latest
rocky.example.com       Running         Running 3 minutes ago
```

We can change some settings on the service while it is running. We can do that with **docker service update**. For instance, if we want to update the number of replicas to 2, we'll execute this command:

```
[root@rocky ~]# docker service update --replicas 2 my_web_service
my_web_service
overall progress: 2 out of 2 tasks
1/2: running   [==============================================>]
2/2: running   [==============================================>]
verify: Service converged
```

Let's list the processes in the service again. This time we see there are two processes running, one on each node.

```
[root@rocky ~]# docker service ps my_web_service
ID               NAME                  IMAGE
NODE                    DESIRED STATE   CURRENT STATE
ERROR        PORTS
ttrt7az26dyb     my_web_service.1      httpd:latest
rocky.example.com       Running         Running 5 minutes ago
ki7hv1zbd8f2     my_web_service.2      httpd:latest     apollo.
example.com     Running         Running about a minute ago
```

517

The service we have deployed is an Apache Web Server. However, we don't see any published port in the output of the **docker service ps** command. We could also check this with **docker service ls**. The container is listening internally on port 80. But we can't access it from outside the host because the port is not published.

To publish the port, we'll use the **docker service update** command again.

```
[root@rocky ~]# docker service update --publish-add 80 my_web_service
my_web_service
overall progress: 2 out of 2 tasks
1/2: running   [==================================================>]
2/2: running   [==================================================>]
verify: Service converged
```

This time, when listing the service, we can clearly see the port mapping.

```
[root@rocky ~]# docker service ls
ID             NAME             MODE          REPLICAS
IMAGE          PORTS
j6e1857uaqat   my_web_service   replicated    2/2
httpd:latest   *:30000→80/tcp
```

When we published the port, we didn't say which port to map on the host, so the system chose port 30000/tcp. We'll open this port on the nodes.

```
[root@rocky ~]# firewall-cmd --add-port=30000/tcp
success
[root@apollo ~]# firewall-cmd --add-port=30000/tcp
success
```

If we launch a web browser now and point it to any of the nodes, we'll see the Apache default web page (Figure 10-3).

It works!

Figure 10-3. Accessing our httpd docker swarm service

If for any reason any of the replicas fails, the node shuts down, etc. A new replica will be immediately launched.

Overlay Networks

In the previous chapter, we studied Docker and the different types of network that we could use. We already mentioned that there was a network type, named overlay, that appeared when working with a docker swarm.

```
[root@rocky ~]# docker network ls
NETWORK ID     NAME                     DRIVER    SCOPE
46947c7695b7   bridge                   bridge    local
1ab169c903b8   docker-compose_default   bridge    local
219b2e97e8e8   docker_gwbridge          bridge    local
900f9f3284e0   host                     host      local
jtbsiwshur7g   ingress                  overlay   swarm
1111c925d0de   none                     null      local
07f217159cd4   root_default             bridge    local
```

An overlay network spans across all the nodes in the docker swarm cluster. It sits on top of the host network to allow containers to communicate securely independently of the node they're running on.

Constraints

Let's take a look again at our service.

```
[root@rocky ~]# docker service ls
ID              NAME              MODE          REPLICAS
IMAGE           PORTS
j6e1857uaqat    my_web_service    replicated    2/2
httpd:latest    *:30000→80/tcp
```

Remember that we have a replicated service, running currently two replicas. Let's see the location of those replicas with **docker service ps**.

```
[root@rocky ~]# docker service ps my_web_service
ID              NAME              IMAGE
NODE                   DESIRED STATE   CURRENT STATE
ERROR      PORTS
g68hokno0u5e    my_web_service.1         httpd:latest
rocky.example.com      Running         Running 10 minutes ago
ttrt7az26dyb     \_ my_web_service.1     httpd:latest
rocky.example.com      Shutdown        Shutdown 10 minutes ago
inbm1zk8rfwz    my_web_service.2         httpd:latest
apollo.example.com     Running         Running 12 minutes ago
ki7hv1zbd8f2     \_ my_web_service.2     httpd:latest
apollo.example.com     Shutdown        Shutdown 12 minutes ago
```

We see that one replica is running on rocky and the other one is running on apollo. We can also see that a couple of instances were previously running and were shut down.

CHAPTER 10   CONTAINER ORCHESTRATION PLATFORMS

We're going to use a constraint. A constraint makes sure that a service runs only on the nodes that comply with the constraint. As an example, we'll use a constraint that forces the execution of the service only on nodes with the role worker.

```
[root@rocky ~]# docker service update --constraint-add node.role==worker my_web_service
my_web_service
overall progress: 2 out of 2 tasks
1/2: running   [==================================================>]
2/2: running   [==================================================>]
verify: Service converged
```

Once the service has converged, we can execute again **docker service ps**.

```
[root@rocky ~]# docker service ps my_web_service
ID                NAME                IMAGE           NODE
DESIRED STATE     CURRENT STATE             ERROR     PORTS
r547bz1r6xeb      my_web_service.1    httpd:latest    apollo.example.com     Running             Running 3 minutes ago
g68hokno0u5e      \_ my_web_service.1 httpd:latest    rocky.example.com      Shutdown            Shutdown 49 seconds ago
ttrt7az26dyb      \_ my_web_service.1 httpd:latest    rocky.example.com      Shutdown            Shutdown 13 minutes ago
inbm1zk8rfwz      my_web_service.2    httpd:latest    apollo.example.com     Running             Running 14 minutes ago
ki7hv1zbd8f2      \_ my_web_service.2 httpd:latest    apollo.example.com     Shutdown            Shutdown 14 minutes ago
```

We can see that we still have two running instances, but this time both instances are running on apollo, the worker node.

CHAPTER 10   CONTAINER ORCHESTRATION PLATFORMS

Creating a Global Service

We already said that a global service is a service that runs on every node in the cluster, unless any constraint prevents its execution in certain nodes.

The way to create a global service is basically the same as the one we saw when we created a replicated service. The only difference is that we need to specify the --global option. Otherwise, we'll create a replicated service, because that's the default value.

```
[root@rocky ~]#  docker service create --mode global --publish 8000:80 nginx:latest
w0fdqm3u7mib7u6maw4bra6rn
overall progress: 2 out of 2 tasks
llg3pu6qhi0b: running   [====================================>]
so8rbhx9dav9: running   [====================================>]
verify: Service converged
```

After the service converged, we can list the services and see a replicated service and a new global service.

```
[root@rocky ~]# docker service ls
ID              NAME             MODE
REPLICAS    IMAGE          PORTS
j6e1857uaqat    my_web_service   replicated
2/2         httpd:latest   *:30000->80/tcp
w0fdqm3u7mib    trusting_bouman  global
2/2         nginx:latest   *:8000→80/tcp
```

If we check on which nodes the service is running, we'll see that it is running on the two nodes of our docker swarm cluster.

```
[root@rocky ~]# docker service ps trusting_bouman
ID                  NAME
IMAGE               NODE                   DESIRED STATE     CURRENT
STATE               ERROR       PORTS
7mzlpbxf8dlf        trusting_bouman.
1lg3pu6qhi0btehudzt0ut9sz    nginx:latest      rocky.example.com
Running             Running 46 seconds ago
pi3g75s9pkym        trusting_bouman.
so8rbhx9dav9k7j8ezgopine5    nginx:latest      apollo.example.
com      Running             Running 3 minutes ago
```

Docker Secrets

This is a very useful object. Previously, when we studied docker compose, we deployed a service with a PostgreSQL container. For the container to work properly, we had to create an environmental variable to store the PostgreSQL password in plain text.

Storing a password in plain text can be OK for a test, but it's definitely unacceptable in a production environment. To avoid that, we use Docker secrets.

We're going to use a secret to store the password of the PostgreSQL database.

```
[root@rocky ~]# echo password | docker secret create postgres_password -
1zfr9pou9u7f5geaevg1j3ds9
```

Once the secret is created, we can list it. And we can also inspect it, but we'll see that the value we assigned to it, "password" in this example, does not appear anywhere in plain text.

```
[root@rocky ~]# docker secret ls
ID                          NAME                DRIVER
  CREATED             UPDATED
1zfr9pou9u7f5geaevg1j3ds9   postgres_password
  40 seconds ago      40 seconds ago
[root@rocky ~]# docker secret inspect postgres_password
[
    {
        "ID": "1zfr9pou9u7f5geaevg1j3ds9",
        "Version": {
            "Index": 194
        },
        "CreatedAt": "2024-07-06T02:15:42.86045616Z",
        "UpdatedAt": "2024-07-06T02:15:42.86045616Z",
        "Spec": {
            "Name": "postgres_password",
            "Labels": {}
        }
    }
]
```

We'll see how to use Docker secrets in a moment.

Stacks

So far, we've been defining the services in a very simple way, directly from the command line. This is OK for simple services, but when the service becomes more complicated and we need to specify many different options, it is much more convenient to use a file.

We'll see an example of one of these files here, and later we'll review the options used.

```
[root@rocky ~]# cat stackPG.yml
version: "3.5"
services:
  postgresql:
    image: postgres:latest
    deploy:
      placement:
        constraints:
          - node.role == worker
    environment:
      - POSTGRES_PASSWORD_FILE=/run/secrets/postgres_password
    secrets:
      - source: postgres_password
        target: "/run/secrets/postgres_password"
    volumes:
      - type: volume
        source: POSTGREDATA
        target: /var/lib/postgresql/data
    ports:
      - target: 5432
        published: 5432
        protocol: tcp
secrets:
  postgres_password:
    external: true
volumes:
  POSTGREDATA:
```

The syntax is pretty much the same as the one we used in docker compose files. We begin by telling the version used. Then we begin defining the services to deploy. In this example, we're deploying a single service.

CHAPTER 10   CONTAINER ORCHESTRATION PLATFORMS

In our only service, we'll use a postgres image, and we'll apply a constraint so that the service only runs on worker nodes. We know that for the postgres container to work, we need to pass it somehow the PostgreSQL password. We'll do it by defining an environment variable named POSTGRES_PASSWORD_FILE, but this variable will point to a location generated by the Docker secret we had created before.

In the service definition, we need to specify that we'll be using a volume and mapping port 5432/TCP, and of course the Docker secret we just talked about.

After the service definition, we have additional sections to define the secret and the volume that will be used by the postgres service.

This file, in which we defined a service and also a secret and a volume that the service uses, is called a **stack**.

We'll deploy this stack with docker stack deploy and assign it the name stackPG.

```
[root@rocky ~]# docker stack deploy -c stackPG.yml stackPG
Creating network stackPG_default
Creating service stackPG_postgresql
```

After the deployment is complete, we can list the stacks. And we'll see the stackPG stack.

```
[root@rocky ~]# docker stack ls
NAME        SERVICES
stackPG     1
```

We can list the running tasks in the stack with **docker stack ps**.

```
[root@rocky ~]# docker stack ps stackPG
ID                 NAME
IMAGE              NODE                        DESIRED STATE    CURRENT
STATE              ERROR                       PORTS
1fcmcbrjhqar       stackPG_postgresql.1
postgres:latest    apollo.example.com          Ready            Ready 3
minutes ago
```

We see that the stack has been deployed in the only worker node that we have available right now. To check the port mapping, we can execute **docker stack services**.

```
[root@rocky ~]# docker stack services stackPG
ID              NAME                    MODE          REPLICAS
   IMAGE                PORTS
oe9ljx145lsq    stackPG_postgresql      replicated    0/1
   postgres:latest    *:5432->5432/tcp
```

Kubernetes

Kubernetes is probably the most used container orchestration platform. We'll begin by looking at Kubernetes architecture and then install it and work with it.

Kubernetes Architecture

The architecture of Kubernetes is a bit more complicated than that of docker swarm. We'll begin by taking a look at Figure 10-4.

CHAPTER 10 CONTAINER ORCHESTRATION PLATFORMS

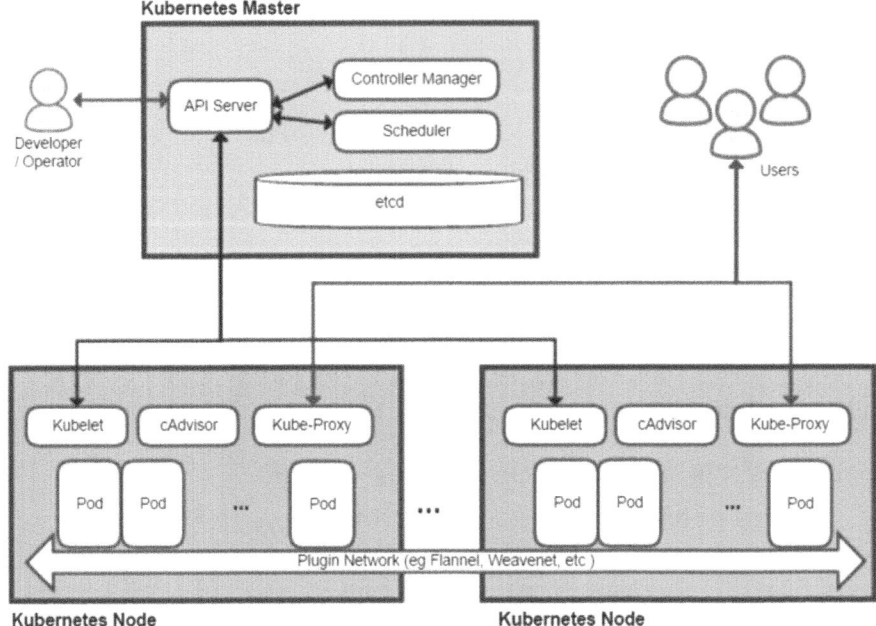

Figure 10-4. *Kubernetes architecture. Image taken from Wikipedia used under Creative Commons License*

In a Kubernetes cluster, we have two different parts:

- The Kubernetes Control Plane or the Kubernetes Master
- The worker nodes

The Control Plane manages the whole cluster, deciding how to distribute the workload. Inside the Control Plane we have these components:

- The etcd database: The database that stores the cluster configuration.
- The API server: It offers the API that can be queried to manage Kubernetes.

CHAPTER 10 CONTAINER ORCHESTRATION PLATFORMS

- The scheduler: This component is in charge of deciding on which node a pod must run. We'll see what a pod is very soon.

- The control manager: It is in charge of replicating components, handling failures of nodes, checking the health of the nodes, etc.

On the other hand, the worker node runs the needed container. It has these components:

- Kubelet: This agent is the component that makes sure that the pods that should run in this node actually run. To do it, it is continually communicating with the API server to know which pods are scheduled to run in the node.

- Kube-proxy: It performs load-balancing operations.

- Container runtime: This is the component that actually runs the containers inside the pods. It can be Docker, rkt, or others.

Installing minikube

To study Kubernetes, we'll install minikube; this is an all-in-one solution intended to provide everything that is needed to better understand Kubernetes, installing all the components in a single desktop/laptop computer. Of course this is not the optimal way to deploy Kubernetes in a production environment, in which case you should install different components in different nodes, but for didactical purposes, it is fine.

CHAPTER 10   CONTAINER ORCHESTRATION PLATFORMS

According to the minikube official web page (Figure 10-5), all we need to install Kubernetes is a computer with the following requirements:

- Two CPUs
- 2 GB of free RAM
- 20 GB of free disk space
- An Internet connection
- A container or virtual machine manager, such as Docker, Hyper-V, and VirtualBox

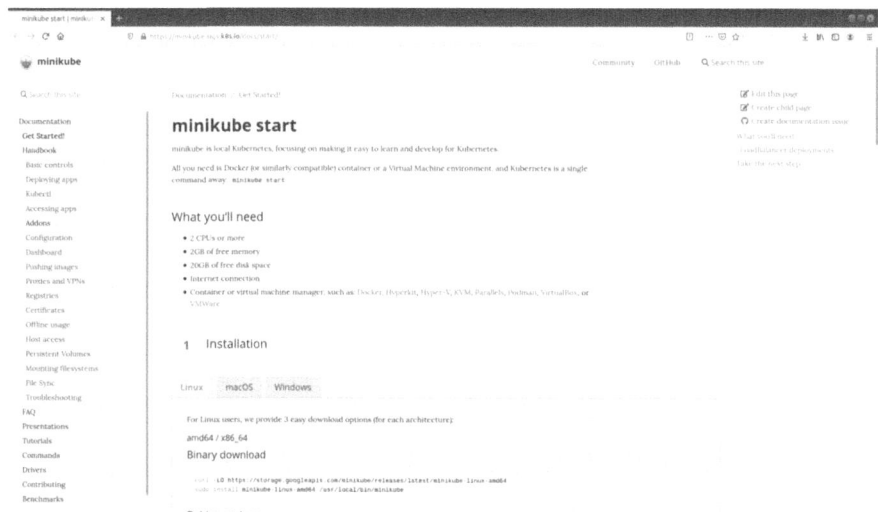

Figure 10-5. minikube web page

Depending on our OS, we have many options available for installing Kubernetes; in our case, we'll install it in an Ubuntu 22 computer, and we'll use the binary installation, though we could have decided to install the deb package as well.

We begin by downloading the binary file.

antonio@antonio-Laptop:~$ curl -LO https://storage.googleapis.com/minikube/releases/latest/minikube-linux-amd64

CHAPTER 10 CONTAINER ORCHESTRATION PLATFORMS

And then we install it.

```
antonio@antonio-Laptop:~$ sudo install minikube-linux-amd64 /usr/local/bin/minikube
```

We also need the **kubectl** command to manage our Kubernetes environment. According to the Kubernetes official page, we can install it with these two commands:

```
antonio@antonio-Laptop:~$ curl -LO "https://dl.k8s.io/release/$(curl -L -s https://dl.k8s.io/release/stable.txt)/bin/linux/amd64/kubectl"
antonio@antonio-Laptop:~$ sudo install -o root -g root -m 0755 kubectl /usr/local/bin/kubectl
```

After the installation, we can check the version to make sure that it is running properly.

```
antonio@antonio-Laptop:~$ kubectl version --client
Client Version: version.Info{Major:"1", Minor:"20", GitVersion:"v1.20.4", GitCommit:"e87da0bd6e03ec3fea7933c4b5263d151aafd07c", GitTreeState:"clean", BuildDate:"2021-02-18T16:12:00Z", GoVersion:"go1.15.8", Compiler:"gc", Platform:"linux/amd64"}
```

Pods

Before we start working with Kubernetes, we must define the concept of pod.

A pod is the smallest management unit in Kubernetes. It can contain one or more containers. If there are more than one container in the pod, they'll share the same IP address.

CHAPTER 10   CONTAINER ORCHESTRATION PLATFORMS

First Steps with minikube

We can check the status of our minikube installation at any point in time with the **minikube status** command.

```
antonio@antonio-Laptop:~$ minikube status
minikube
minikube
type: Control Plane
host: Stopped
kubelet: Stopped
apiserver: Stopped
kubeconfig: Stopped
```

Obviously, the first thing to do to work with minikube is to start it.

```
antonio@antonio-Laptop:~$ minikube start
😄  minikube v1.32.0 on Ubuntu 22.04
✨  Using the virtualbox driver based on existing profile
👍  Starting control plane node minikube in cluster minikube
🔄  Restarting existing virtualbox VM for "minikube" ...
🐳  Preparing Kubernetes v1.28.3 on Docker 24.0.7 ...
🔗  Configuring bridge CNI (Container Networking Interface) ...
    ▪ Using image docker.io/kubernetesui/dashboard:v2.7.0
    ▪ Using image docker.io/kubernetesui/metrics-scraper:v1.0.8
    ▪ Using image gcr.io/k8s-minikube/storage-provisioner:v5
```

```
|                                                           |
|   You have selected "virtualbox" driver, but there        |
|   are better options !                                    |
|   For better performance and support consider             |
|   using a different driver:                               |
|           - qemu2                                         |
|                                                           |
```

CHAPTER 10   CONTAINER ORCHESTRATION PLATFORMS

```
    To turn off this warning run:

            $ minikube config set WantVirtual
            BoxDriverWarning false


    To learn more about on minikube drivers
    checkout https://minikube.sigs.k8s.io/docs/drivers/
    To see benchmarks checkout
    https://minikube.sigs.k8s.io/docs/benchmarks/cpuusage/
```

🔍 Verifying Kubernetes components...
💡 Some dashboard features require the metrics-server addon. To enable all features please run:

   minikube addons enable metrics-server

🌟 Enabled addons: storage-provisioner, default-storageclass, dashboard
🏃 Done! kubectl is now configured to use "minikube" cluster and "default" namespace by default

As we can see in one of the last messages, **kubectl** is configured to use minikube cluster. We can use it to list the existing pods in all namespaces (option -A).

```
antonio@antonio-Laptop:~$ kubectl get pods -A
NAMESPACE               NAME
   READY    STATUS     RESTARTS        AGE
kube-system                     coredns-5dd5756b68-whfzc
```

CHAPTER 10 CONTAINER ORCHESTRATION PLATFORMS

```
     1/1     Running   5 (14m ago)   6d1h
kube-system              etcd-minikube
     1/1     Running   5 (14m ago)   6d1h
kube-system              kube-apiserver-minikube
     1/1     Running   5 (13m ago)   6d1h
kube-system              kube-controller-manager-minikube
     1/1     Running   5 (14m ago)   6d1h
kube-system              kube-proxy-ktzh4
     1/1     Running   5 (14m ago)   6d1h
kube-system              kube-scheduler-minikube
     1/1     Running   5 (14m ago)   6d1h
kube-system              storage-provisioner
     1/1     Running   10 (12m ago)  6d1h
kubernetes-dashboard     dashboard-metrics-scraper-7fd5cb4ddc-nbs2v
     1/1     Running   2 (14m ago)   6d1h
kubernetes-dashboard     kubernetes-dashboard-8694d4445c-klkd9
     1/1     Running   3 (14m ago)   6d1h
```

We can also start the dashboard to manage our Kubernetes environment from a web browser.

```
antonio@antonio-Laptop:~$ minikube dashboard
🤔  Verifying dashboard health ...
🚀  Launching proxy ...
🤔  Verifying proxy health ...
🎉  Opening http://127.0.0.1:46379/api/v1/namespaces/
kubernetes-dashboard/services/http:kubernetes-dashboard:/proxy/
in your default browser...
```

The system will automatically launch our default web browser (Figure 10-6).

CHAPTER 10   CONTAINER ORCHESTRATION PLATFORMS

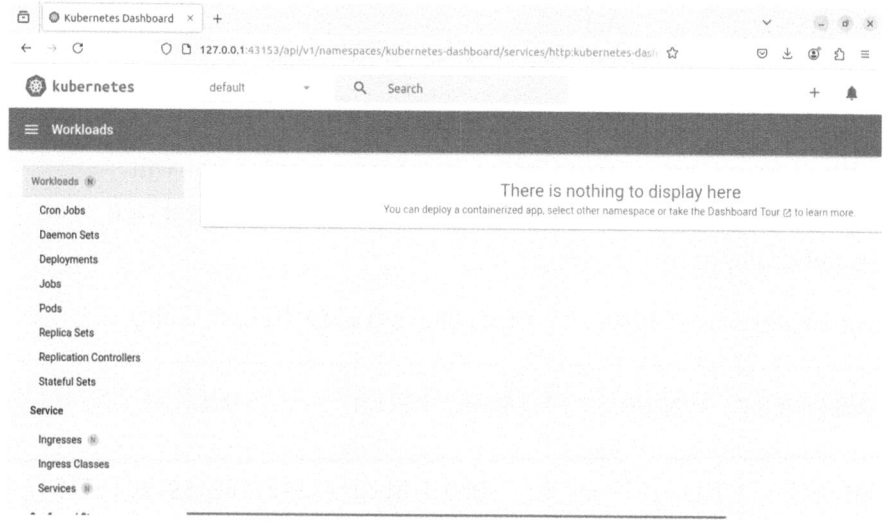

Figure 10-6. Kubernetes dashboard

In the dashboard, we can see that the default namespace appears empty. When we deploy new apps, we'll see them here. We can start by deploying the sample hello-minikube application.

antonio@antonio-Laptop:~$ kubectl create deployment hi-minikube
--image=k8s.gcr.io/echoserver:1.4
deployment.apps/hi-minikube created

Besides deploying the application, we'll expose it to the outer world.

antonio@antonio-Laptop:~$ kubectl expose deployment hi-minikube
--type=NodePort --port=8080
service/hi-minikube exposed

Once exposed, we can list the associated service(s) to the corresponding application.

antonio@antonio-Laptop:~$ kubectl get services hi-minikube
NAME   TYPE   CLUSTER-IP   EXTERNAL-IP

535

CHAPTER 10   CONTAINER ORCHESTRATION PLATFORMS

```
   PORT(S)            AGE
hi-minikube   NodePort    10.104.42.3   <none>
   8080:31557/TCP    2m
```

We can access the service with a web browser. minikube will automatically launch it for us after invoking the **minikube service** command (Figure 10-7).

```
antonio@antonio-Laptop:~$ minikube service hi-minikube
|-----------|--------------|-------------|------------------------|
| NAMESPACE |     NAME     | TARGET PORT |          URL           |
|-----------|--------------|-------------|------------------------|
|  default  |  hi-minikube |     8080    | http://192.168.59.101:31557 |
|-----------|--------------|-------------|------------------------|
🎉  Opening service default/hi-minikube in default browser...
```

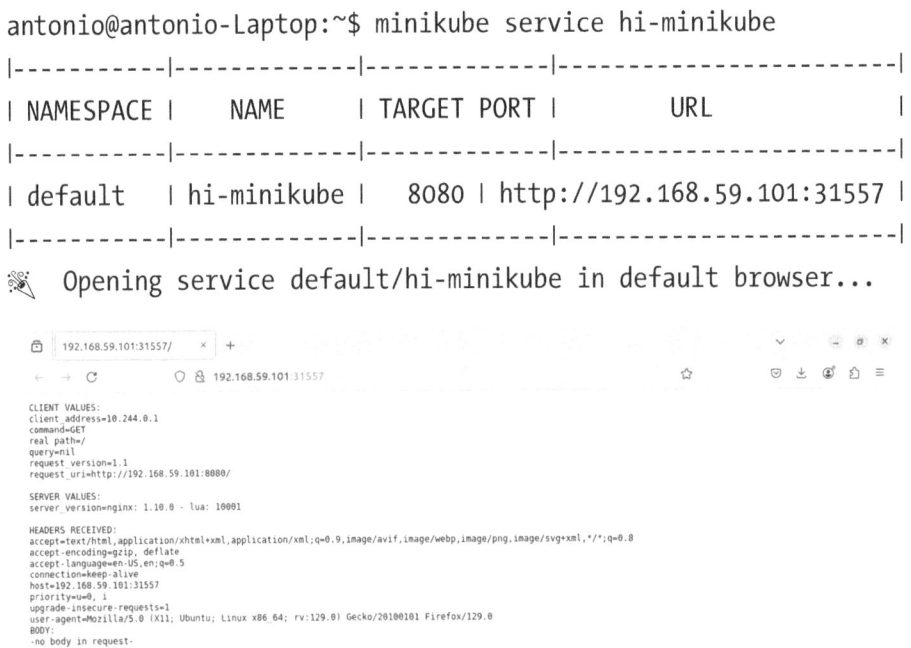

Figure 10-7. hi-minikube service

CHAPTER 10   CONTAINER ORCHESTRATION PLATFORMS

In the dashboard, we can now see the deployment in the default namespace (Figure 10-8).

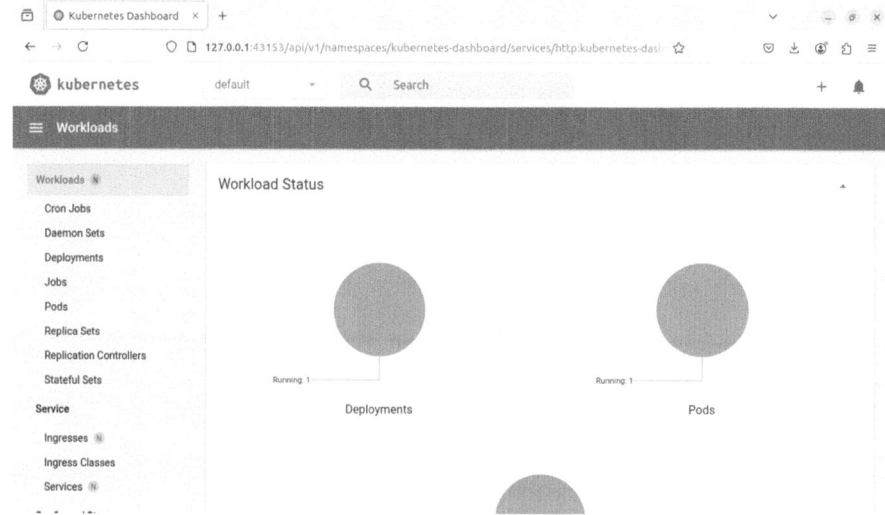

Figure 10-8. *Dashboard with one deployment in the default namespace*

We can get the list of the add-ons in our cluster. For the purposes of the exam, we don't need to understand each and every item from the list. We'll see the helm add-on listed. In the next section, we'll see how to use Helm.

```
antonio@antonio-Laptop:~$ minikube addons list
|-----------------------------|----------|----------|-------------------------------|
|          ADDON NAME         | PROFILE  |  STATUS  |          MAINTAINER           |
|-----------------------------|----------|----------|-------------------------------|
| ambassador                  | minikube | disabled | 3rd party (Ambassador)        |
| auto-pause                  | minikube | disabled | minikube                      |
| cloud-spanner               | minikube | disabled | Google                        |
| csi-hostpath-driver         | minikube | disabled | Kubernetes                    |
| dashboard                   | minikube | enabled ✓| Kubernetes                    |
| default-storageclass        | minikube | enabled ✓| Kubernetes                    |
| efk                         | minikube | disabled | 3rd party (Elastic)           |
| freshpod                    | minikube | disabled | Google                        |
```

537

CHAPTER 10   CONTAINER ORCHESTRATION PLATFORMS

gcp-auth	minikube	disabled	Google
gvisor	minikube	disabled	minikube
headlamp	minikube	disabled	3rd party (kinvolk.io)
helm-tiller	minikube	disabled	3rd party (Helm)
inaccel	minikube	disabled	3rd party (InAccel
			[info@inaccel.com])
ingress	minikube	disabled	Kubernetes
ingress-dns	minikube	disabled	minikube
inspektor-gadget	minikube	disabled	3rd party
			(inspektor-gadget.io)
istio	minikube	disabled	3rd party (Istio)
istio-provisioner	minikube	disabled	3rd party (Istio)
kong	minikube	disabled	3rd party (Kong HQ)
kubeflow	minikube	disabled	3rd party
kubevirt	minikube	disabled	3rd party (KubeVirt)
logviewer	minikube	disabled	3rd party (unknown)
metallb	minikube	disabled	3rd party (MetalLB)
metrics-server	minikube	disabled	Kubernetes
nvidia-device-plugin	minikube	disabled	3rd party (NVIDIA)
nvidia-driver-installer	minikube	disabled	3rd party (Nvidia)
nvidia-gpu-device-plugin	minikube	disabled	3rd party (Nvidia)
olm	minikube	disabled	3rd party (Operator Framework)
pod-security-policy	minikube	disabled	3rd party (unknown)
portainer	minikube	disabled	3rd party (Portainer.io)
registry	minikube	disabled	minikube
registry-aliases	minikube	disabled	3rd party (unknown)
registry-creds	minikube	disabled	3rd party (UPMC Enterprises)
storage-provisioner	minikube	enabled ✅	minikube
storage-provisioner-gluster	minikube	disabled	3rd party (Gluster)
storage-provisioner-rancher	minikube	disabled	3rd party (Rancher)
volumesnapshots	minikube	disabled	Kubernetes

CHAPTER 10 CONTAINER ORCHESTRATION PLATFORMS

Deploying a Pod in Kubernetes

Let's see a more practical example and create a pod. As we said, a pod is the smallest management unit in Kubernetes and can contain one or more containers. We'll create the following file in YAML format:

```
antonio@antonio-Laptop:~/kubernetes$ cat firstpod.yaml
apiVersion: v1
kind: Pod
metadata:
  name: firstpod
  labels:
    example: firstpod
spec:
  containers:
    - name: containerfirstpod
      image: nginx
```

The syntax is quite simple. First, we specify the version (v1 in this case). Then, we enumerate the metadata; here we set the name of the pod, and we can also add labels. Finally, in "specs", we define the container or containers in the pod. In this example, we use an nginx container.

We deploy the pod with **kubectl apply**.

```
antonio@antonio-Laptop:~/kubernetes$ kubectl apply -f firstpod.yaml
pod/firstpod created
```

We can list the pod and see the new pod.

```
antonio@antonio-Laptop:~/kubernetes$ kubectl get pods
NAME                          READY   STATUS    RESTARTS   AGE
firstpod                      1/1     Running   0          11s
hi-minikube-7fdf9777bc-x75zn  1/1     Running   0          7h34m
```

Another interesting command is **kubectl logs**, which allows us to see the logs of the pod.

```
antonio@antonio-Laptop:~/kubernetes$ kubectl logs firstpod
/docker-entrypoint.sh: /docker-entrypoint.d/ is not empty, will attempt to perform configuration
/docker-entrypoint.sh: Looking for shell scripts in /docker-entrypoint.d/
.
.
.
2024/08/18 15:02:48 [notice] 1#1: OS: Linux 5.10.57
2024/08/18 15:02:48 [notice] 1#1: getrlimit(RLIMIT_NOFILE): 1048576:1048576
2024/08/18 15:02:48 [notice] 1#1: start worker processes
2024/08/18 15:02:48 [notice] 1#1: start worker process 29
2024/08/18 15:02:48 [notice] 1#1: start worker process 30
```

When we finish working with the pod, we can safely delete it.

```
antonio@antonio-Laptop:~/kubernetes$ kubectl delete pod firstpod
pod "firstpod" deleted
```

Replicasets

When we deploy a single pod in Kubernetes, we can't scale the number of pods if the demand increases, which defeats the very purpose of container orchestration. To be able to scale the number of pods depending on the increase or decrease of the demand, we can deploy a replicaset.

We'll create a new YAML file with this content. The syntax is similar to what we saw in the previous example of the pod. Now we use version apps/v1 and use the kind Replicaset instead of Pod; we also specify the base image for the container and the selector that will be used to identify the members of the replicaset, the label example: firstreplica in this case.

CHAPTER 10 CONTAINER ORCHESTRATION PLATFORMS

```
antonio@antonio-Laptop:~/kubernetes$ cat firstreplicaset.yaml
apiVersion: apps/v1
kind: ReplicaSet
metadata:
  name: firstreplica
  labels:
    example: firstreplica
spec:
  replicas: 3
  selector:
    matchLabels:
      example: firstreplica
  template:
    metadata:
      name: containerfirstreplica
      labels:
        example: firstreplica
    spec:
      containers:
        - name: containerfirstreplica
          image: nginx
```

Again, we use **kubectl apply** to deploy the replicaset.

```
antonio@antonio-Laptop:~/kubernetes$ kubectl apply -f firstreplicaset.yaml
replicaset.apps/firstreplica created
```

We can list the replicas and check if it was correctly deployed.

```
antonio@antonio-Laptop:~/kubernetes$ kubectl get replicaset
NAME                    DESIRED   CURRENT   READY   AGE
firstreplica            3         3         3       53s
hi-minikube-7fdf9777bc  1         1         1       34h
```

From the output, we know that three pods were deployed. We can list those pods as well.

```
antonio@antonio-Laptop:~$ kubectl get pods
NAME                          READY   STATUS    RESTARTS      AGE
firstreplica-4649k            1/1     Running   0             144m
firstreplica-8pn8d            1/1     Running   0             144m
firstreplica-dps8z            1/1     Running   0             144m
hi-minikube-7fdf9777bc-x75zn  1/1     Running   1 (28h ago)   36h
```

When we're done, we can delete our replicaset.

```
antonio@antonio-Laptop:~$ kubectl delete replicaset firstreplica
replicaset.apps "firstreplica" deleted
```

Deployments

Deployments are similar to replicasets, but they have some advantages. For instance, when using deployments instead of replicasets, we can update the base image in use, keeping the service available. This is possible because the image is updated in the containers sequentially instead of all at the same time. In fact, deployments are the preferred way to deploy applications.

Let's see an example by creating this new YAML file. The only new parameter we specify here is containerPort so that we can later access this application.

```
antonio@antonio-Laptop:~$ cat firstdeployment.yaml
apiVersion: apps/v1
kind: Deployment
metadata:
```

```
  name: firstdeployment
  labels:
    example: firstdeployment
spec:
  replicas: 4
  selector:
    matchLabels:
      example: firstdeployment
  template:
    metadata:
      name: firstdeployment
      labels:
        example: firstdeployment
    spec:
      containers:
        - name: containerfirstdeployment
          image: nginx
          ports:
          - containerPort: 80
```

And we deploy it in our Kubernetes cluster.

```
antonio@antonio-Laptop:~$ kubectl apply -f firstdeployment.yaml
deployment.apps/firstdeployment created
```

We can check the status of the deployment.

```
antonio@antonio-Laptop:~$ kubectl get deployments
NAME                READY   UP-TO-DATE   AVAILABLE   AGE
firstdeployment     4/4     4            4           5m50s
hi-minikube         1/1     1            1           37h
```

We should notice that the deployment automatically creates a replicaset that we can also list with **kubectl**.

```
antonio@antonio-Laptop:~$ kubectl get replicaset
NAME                          DESIRED   CURRENT   READY   AGE
firstdeployment-5fb89d6857    4         4         4       21h
hi-minikube-7fdf9777bc        1         1         1       2d10h
```

When creating the deployment, we declared a port to access nginx; however, we're not done yet to make the application available from the outside. We have created the deployment, but we need to create a service. A service in Kubernetes defines how to access the pods included in a deployment. Let's see an example.

```
antonio@antonio-Laptop:~$ kubectl expose deployment firstdeployment --type=NodePort --port=80
service/firstdeployment exposed
```

We declare that we want to access the pods from the deployment named "firstdeployment" using port 80. The "Nodeport" option sets that we can access the application externally pointing to any node of the Kubernetes cluster.

If we list the services now, we'll see the new service.

```
antonio@antonio-Laptop:~$ kubectl get services
NAME              TYPE        CLUSTER-IP
   EXTERNAL-IP    PORT(S)         AGE
firstdeployment   NodePort    10.102.167.50
   <none>         80:32614/TCP    15s
hi-minikube       NodePort    10.104.42.3
   <none>         8080:31557/TCP  37h
kubernetes        ClusterIP   10.96.0.1
   <none>         443/TCP         7d22h
```

CHAPTER 10 CONTAINER ORCHESTRATION PLATFORMS

We'll use **kubectl port-forward** to forward a local port to the port used by the pods in the deployment.

```
antonio@antonio-Laptop:~$ kubectl port-forward service/
firstdeployment 9999:80
Forwarding from 127.0.0.1:9999 -> 80
Forwarding from [::1]:9999 -> 80
```

In a different shell, we can check that **kubectl** is listening locally on port 9999.

```
antonio@antonio-Laptop:~$ lsof -i :9999
COMMAND     PID    USER   FD   TYPE DEVICE SIZE/OFF NODE NAME
kubectl 142339 antonio    8u   IPv4 2710146      0t0  TCP localhost:9999 (LISTEN)
kubectl 142339 antonio    9u   IPv6 2710147      0t0  TCP ip6-localhost:9999 (LISTEN)
```

And we can open a web browser and point it to port 9999 on the localhost (Figure 10-9).

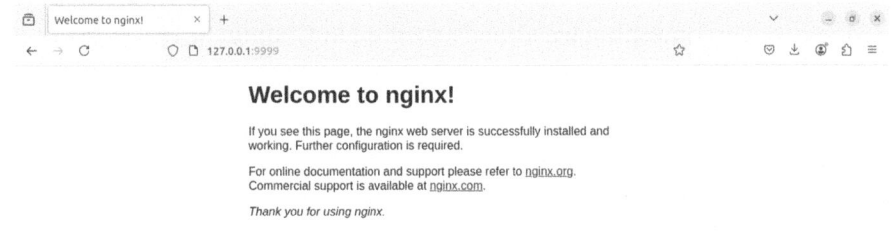

***Figure 10-9.** Accessing our nginx application on Kubernetes*

We'll delete now the deployment so that it doesn't affect the next operations.

```
antonio@antonio-Laptop:~$ kubectl delete service firstdeployment
service "firstdeployment" deleted

antonio@antonio-Laptop:~$ kubectl delete deployment firstdeployment
deployment.apps "firstdeployment" deleted
```

Other Kubernetes-Related Items

In this brief introduction to Kubernetes, we have worked with pods, replicasets, deployments, and services. There are, however, many more items that we'll define briefly here.

A configmap is an object used to store data unencrypted. They are similar to the Docker secrets we saw when we studied docker swarm.

A secret is like a configmap, but it stores the information encrypted. It is the equivalent on Kubernetes to the docker swarm secrets we studied before.

A volume is something we already studied in Chapter 9. The concept is the same, but in this case, the volume is defined in the Kubernetes cluster.

Helm

Helm is a tool designed to help you to manage Kubernetes applications. We could define Helm as some sort of a package manager for Kubernetes.

To understand Helm's architecture, we must introduce the concept of "chart." A chart is a group of files that represent a set of Kubernetes resources.

Installing Helm is very easy; we just need to go to the official page (Figure 10-10), search for the right binary for our OS and architecture (Figure 10-11), and download it.

CHAPTER 10   CONTAINER ORCHESTRATION PLATFORMS

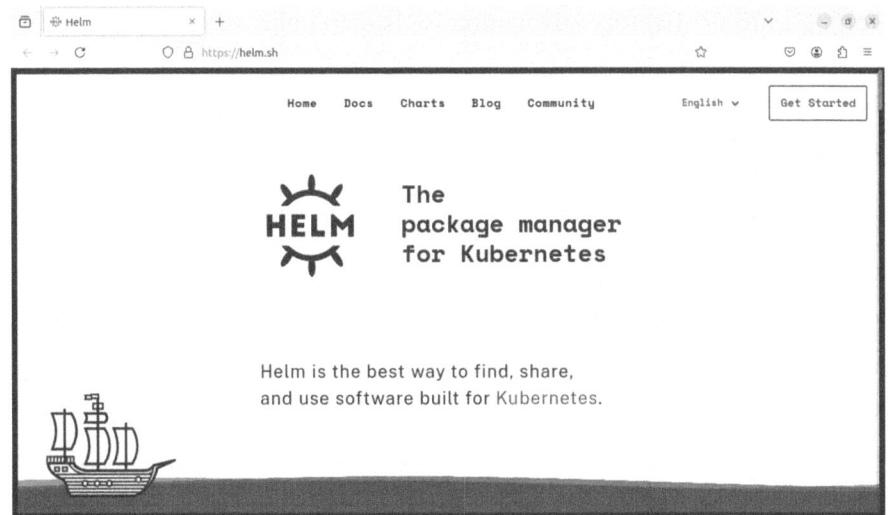

Figure 10-10. *Helm official web page*

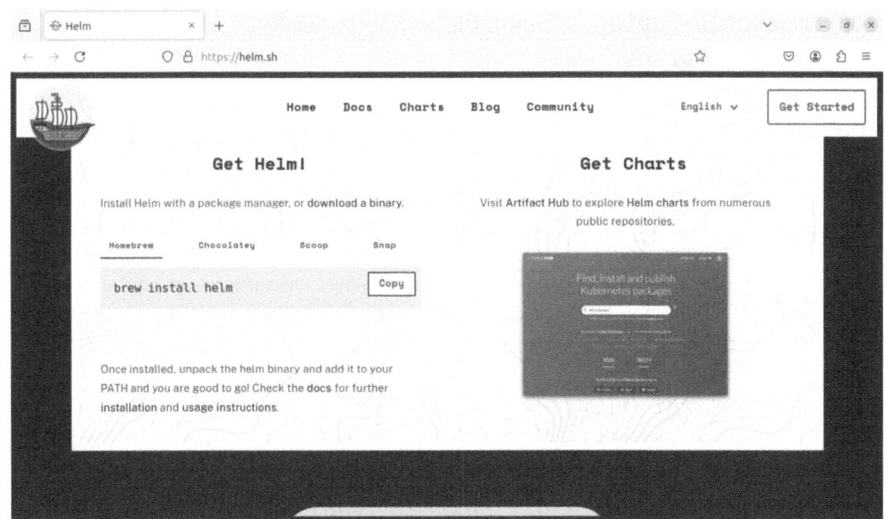

Figure 10-11. *Downloading Helm binary*

CHAPTER 10 CONTAINER ORCHESTRATION PLATFORMS

```
antonio@antonio-Laptop:~/Downloads$ ls -lrth helm-v3.15.3-linux-amd64.tar.gz
-rw-rw-r-- 1 antonio antonio 16M ago 13 00:10 helm-v3.15.3-linux-amd64.tar.gz
```

We uncompress the file.

```
antonio@antonio-Laptop:~/Downloads$ tar -xzvf helm-v3.15.3-linux-amd64.tar.gz
linux-amd64/
linux-amd64/helm
linux-amd64/README.md
linux-amd64/LICENSE
```

And we copy the binary file to a location included in our PATH.

```
antonio@antonio-Laptop:~/Downloads$ cd linux-amd64/
antonio@antonio-Laptop:~/Downloads/linux-amd64$ ls
helm   LICENSE   README.md

antonio@antonio-Laptop:~/Downloads/linux-amd64$ sudo cp helm /usr/local/bin/
```

If we execute **helm** without any arguments, we'll see the main options.

```
antonio@antonio-Laptop:~$ helm
The Kubernetes package manager

Common actions for Helm:

- helm search:     search for charts
- helm pull:       download a chart to your local
                   directory to view
```

```
- helm install:   upload the chart to Kubernetes
- helm list:      list releases of charts
```
-
-
-

We said before that Helm works with charts. These charts can be downloaded from Helm repositories. Initially, we won't have any configured repository.

```
antonio@antonio-Laptop:~$ helm repo list
Error: no repositories to show
```

We can add, for example, the bitnami repository. Bitnami is a library of software applications ready to be deployed.

```
antonio@antonio-Laptop:~$ helm repo add bitnami https://charts.bitnami.com/bitnami
"bitnami" has been added to your repositories
```

The new repository was added, and we can list it.

```
antonio@antonio-Laptop:~$ helm repo list
NAME        URL
bitnami     https://charts.bitnami.com/bitnami
```

It is advised to update the repositories periodically.

```
antonio@antonio-Laptop:~$ helm repo update
Hang tight while we grab the latest from your chart repositories...
...Successfully got an update from the "bitnami" chart repository
Update Complete. ⎈Happy Helming!⎈
```

CHAPTER 10   CONTAINER ORCHESTRATION PLATFORMS

The use of Helm is very easy; we can start by searching the available charts in the bitnami repo.

```
antonio@antonio-Laptop:~$ helm search repo bitnami
NAME                                        CHART VERSION
   APP VERSION      DESCRIPTION
bitnami/airflow                                 19.0.1
   2.10.0           Apache Airflow is a tool to express and
execute...
bitnami/apache                                  11.2.14
   2.4.62           Apache HTTP Server is an open-source HTTP
serve...
bitnami/apisix                                  3.3.10
   3.10.0           Apache APISIX is high-performance, real-
time AP...
bitnami/appsmith                                4.0.1
   1.36.0           Appsmith is an open source platform for
buildin...
bitnami/argo-cd
   7.0.3            2.12.1            Argo CD is a continuous
delivery tool for Kuber…
.
.
.
```

When we have located the chart that we want, we can easily install it.

```
antonio@antonio-Laptop:~$ helm install bitnami/apache
--generate-name
NAME: apache-1724188480
LAST DEPLOYED: Tue Aug 20 22:56:16 2024
NAMESPACE: default
STATUS: deployed
```

CHAPTER 10   CONTAINER ORCHESTRATION PLATFORMS

```
REVISION: 1
TEST SUITE: None
NOTES:
CHART NAME: apache
CHART VERSION: 11.2.14
APP VERSION: 2.4.62

** Please be patient while the chart is being deployed **

1. Get the Apache URL by running:

** Please ensure an external IP is associated to the
apache-1724188480 service before proceeding **
** Watch the status using: kubectl get svc --namespace default
-w apache-1724188480 **

 ·
 ·
 ·
```

And that's all. Apache has been deployed. We can check its status using the command suggested by the output of Helm.

```
antonio@antonio-Laptop:~$ kubectl get svc --namespace default
-w apache-1724188480
NAME                    TYPE            CLUSTER-IP     EXTERNAL-
IP    PORT(S)                           AGE
apache-1724188480    LoadBalancer    10.96.19.8    <pending>
80:32176/TCP,443:31831/TCP      56s
```

We can access the Apache web page using kubectl to forward a local port, similarly to what we did when we created our first deployment (Figure 10-12).

CHAPTER 10 CONTAINER ORCHESTRATION PLATFORMS

```
antonio@antonio-Laptop:~$ kubectl port-forward service/
apache-1724188480 9999:80
```

Figure 10-12. Apache installed with Helm

And there is also another possibility to access Apache using the minikube service command.

```
antonio@antonio-Laptop:~$ minikube service apache-1724188480
|-----------|-------------------|-------------|-----------------|
| NAMESPACE |        NAME       | TARGET PORT |      URL        |
|-----------|-------------------|-------------|-----------------|
| default   | apache-1724188480 | http/80     |
http://192.168.59.101:32176 |
|           |                   | https/443   |
http://192.168.59.101:31831 |
|-----------|-------------------|-------------|-----------------|
[default apache-1724188480 http/80
https/443 http://192.168.59.101:32176
http://192.168.59.101:31831]
```

Here we can see two different URLs to access Apache using http or https (Figure 10-13).

Figure 10-13. *Accessing Apache from minikube*

Finally, we can uninstall the service using **helm** as well.

```
antonio@antonio-Laptop:~helm uninstall apache-1724188480
release "apache-1724188480" uninstalled
```

OpenShift

OpenShift is another container orchestration platform. Developed by Red Hat, it includes components of Kubernetes, but it also adds new productivity and security features.

Installing an OpenShift cluster is not a trivial task. There is an interesting project named minishift that allows to run an OpenShift cluster locally. Unfortunately, this project is currently inactive and hasn't been updated in years.

CHAPTER 10 CONTAINER ORCHESTRATION PLATFORMS

At the time of writing this book, probably the easiest option to get a grasp of OpenShift is to use the free developer sandbox offered by Red Hat (Figure 10-14). This is free to use, though we need to register in the Red Hat developer site.

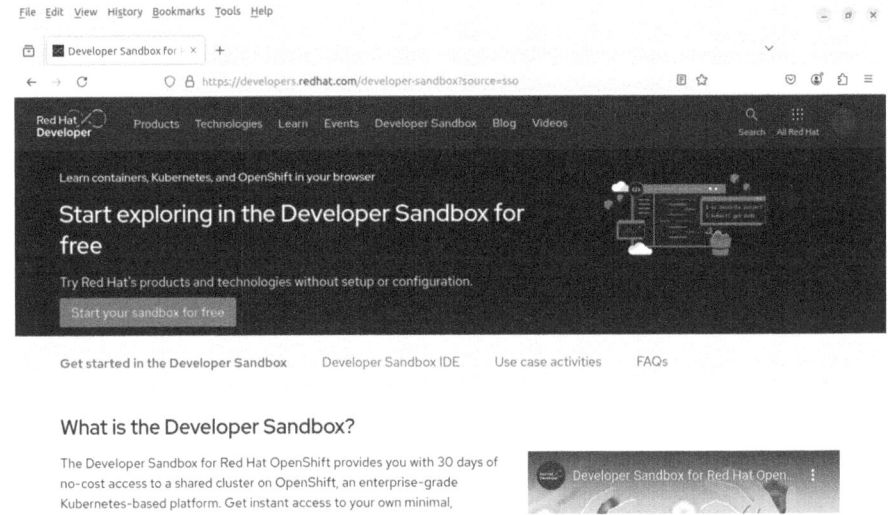

***Figure 10-14.** Red Hat developer sandbox*

After launching the sandbox, we can open the OpenShift console. To manage an OpenShift cluster, we use the **oc** command, though we could also use **kubectl**. Many commands are identical to those that we've seen when we studied Kubernetes. Of course there are also advanced commands exclusively used on OpenShift, but we won't see them here, as it is outside the scope of the LPIC-3 305 exam.

We can list all the items in the OpenShift cluster with "**oc get all**" (Figure 10-15).

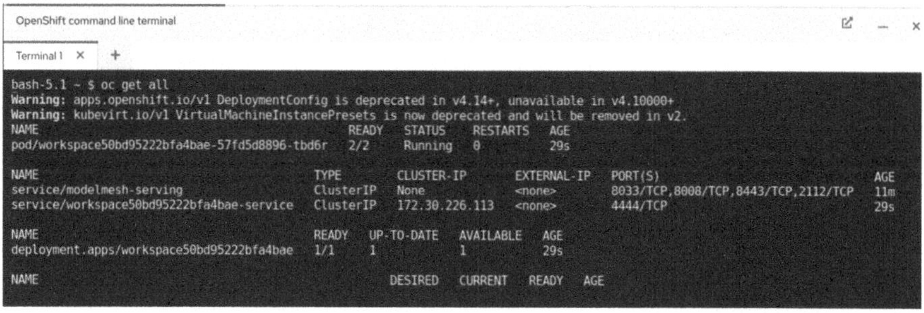

CHAPTER 10   CONTAINER ORCHESTRATION PLATFORMS

Figure 10-15. Getting all objects in an OpenShift cluster

We can use the same commands we learned in Kubernetes to create deployments (Figure 10-16).

Figure 10-16. Creating a deployment in OpenShift

If we prefer to work visually instead of using the command line, we can browse the sample applications available (Figure 10-17).

CHAPTER 10 CONTAINER ORCHESTRATION PLATFORMS

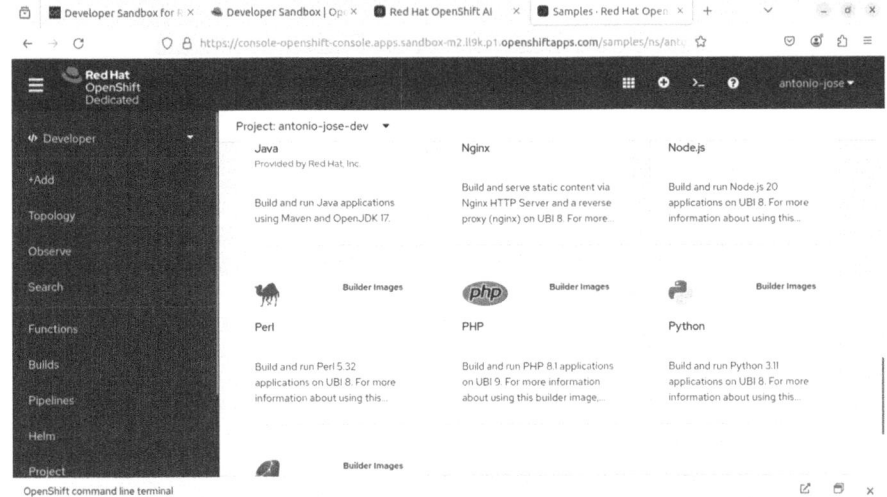

Figure 10-17. OpenShift samples

To install any of these sample applications, we just need to select it and click "Create" (Figure 10-18).

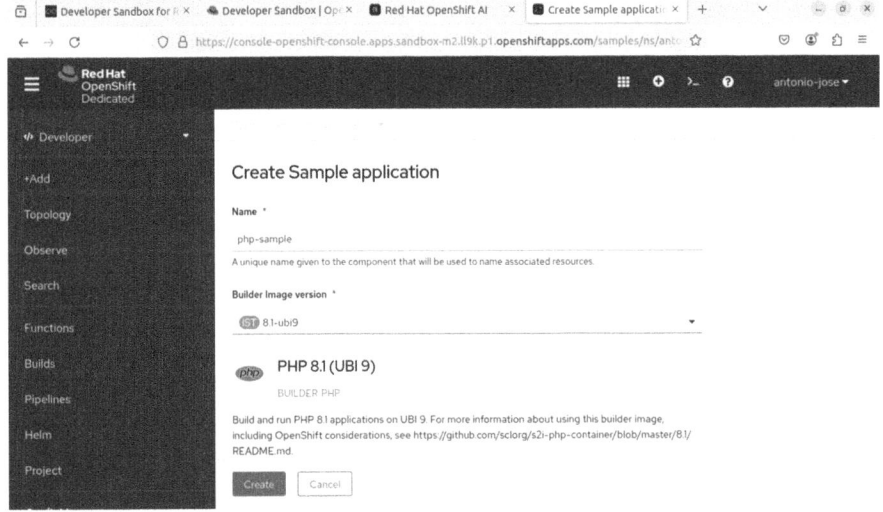

Figure 10-18. Installing PHP on OpenShift

CHAPTER 10 CONTAINER ORCHESTRATION PLATFORMS

Rancher

Another popular enterprise-level orchestration platform is Rancher, developed by the enterprise with the same name, which was later acquired by SUSE.

To install it, we need to go to the official web page (Figure 10-19) and then click the "Get started" button.

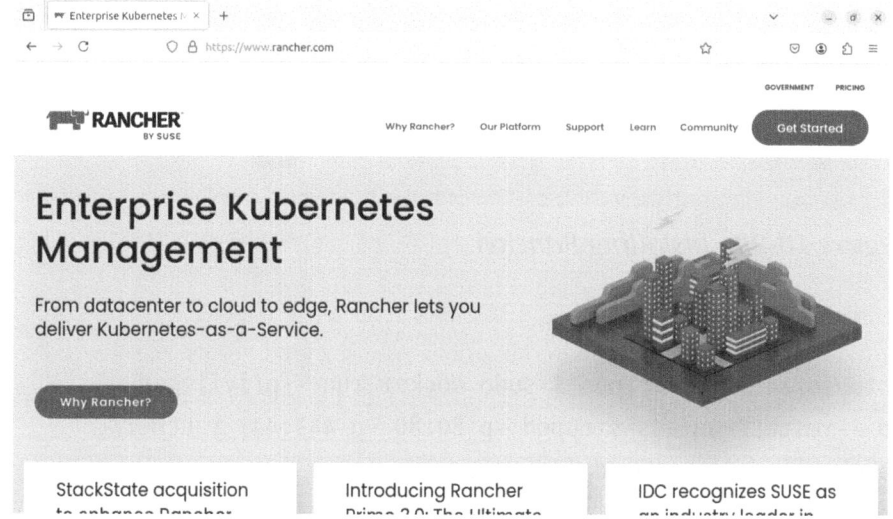

Figure 10-19. *Rancher web page*

In the new page, we scroll down a bit and see the instructions to deploy Rancher (Figure 10-20). It is a containerized application, and we only need a host with Docker installed. As we're already familiar with Docker, the command should be familiar to us, but we'll summarize it here. We'll run a container based on the Rancher image; the container will run in the background and in privileged mode; if the container accidentally stops, it will restart automatically, and we'll be able to access it through a port redirection of ports 80/tcp and 443/tcp.

CHAPTER 10 CONTAINER ORCHESTRATION PLATFORMS

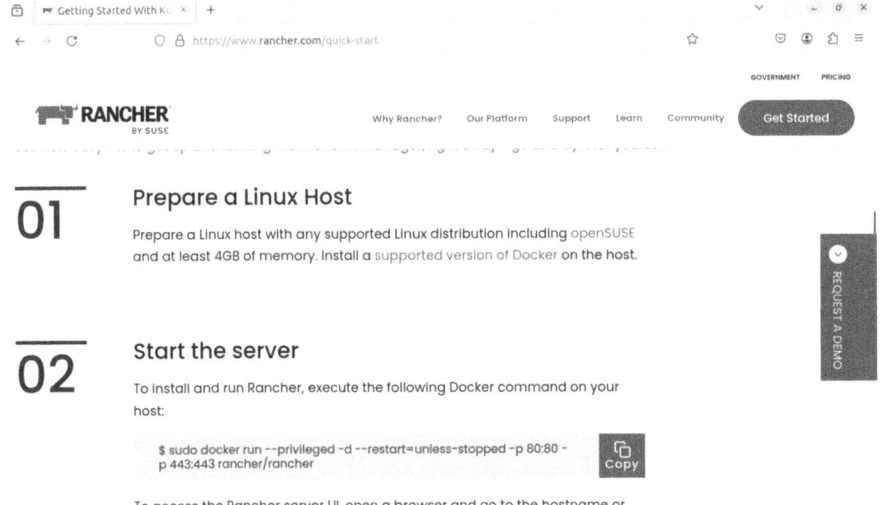

Figure 10-20. Installing Rancher

We execute the command:

```
antonio@antonio-Laptop:~$ sudo docker run --privileged
-d --restart=unless-stopped -p 80:80 -p 443:443 rancher/
rancher[sudo] password for antonio:
Unable to find image 'rancher/rancher:latest' locally
latest: Pulling from rancher/rancher
2e9baa440d53: Pull complete
359c3a62b959: Pull complete
.
.
.
Digest: sha256:e57b0720fdfc6051c6d811b2f62e7a403eb09fcace142f89
1bb9cc0d59ed53f9
Status: Downloaded newer image for rancher/rancher:latest
3ba0ede6224d757d135baa006207936f3ee521fa65fcb9d0ad4ccd36191f6ec1
```

CHAPTER 10   CONTAINER ORCHESTRATION PLATFORMS

We can check that the container is actually running.

```
antonio@antonio-Laptop:~$ sudo docker container ls
CONTAINER ID   IMAGE              COMMAND
   CREATED              STATUS
   PORTS
                        NAMES
3ba0ede6224d   rancher/rancher    "entrypoint.sh"
   About a minute ago   Up About a minute
   0.0.0.0:80->80/tcp, :::80->80/tcp, 0.0.0.0:443->443/tcp,
   :::443->443/tcp      suspicious_snyder
```

We can access Rancher by opening a web browser and pointing it to the localhost (Figure 10-21).

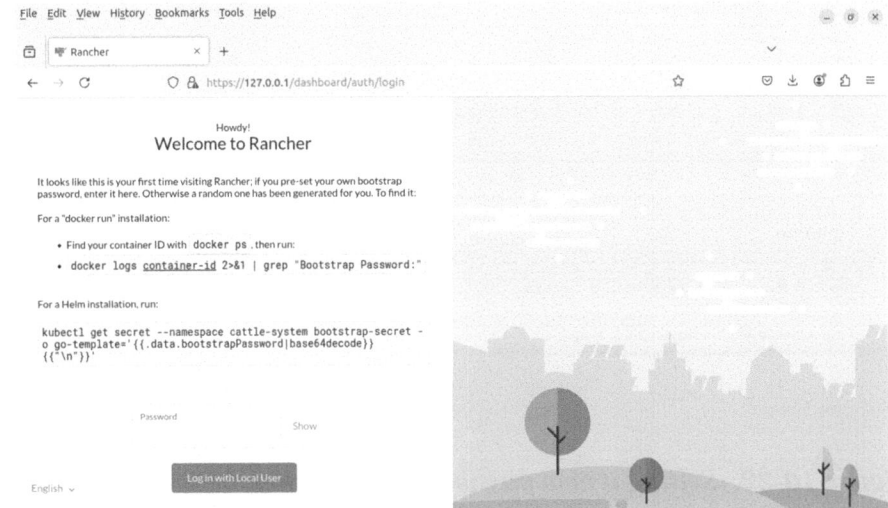

Figure 10-21. *Rancher welcome page*

CHAPTER 10 CONTAINER ORCHESTRATION PLATFORMS

To access, we need a password that was randomly generated during the installation. In the welcome page, we can see the docker command we need to run to obtain it.

```
antonio@antonio-Laptop:~$ sudo docker logs 3ba0ede6224d 2>&1 |
grep "Bootstrap Password:"
2024/08/21 20:52:18 [INFO] Bootstrap Password:
5zxgwvhx77rpz9nrmsn4jzjhgx2smzx8t9blf9ttvl49gn7xkx2hzp
```

We enter the password, and immediately Rancher requests us to create a new password (Figure 10-22). We set the new password and can start to manage Rancher (Figure 10-23).

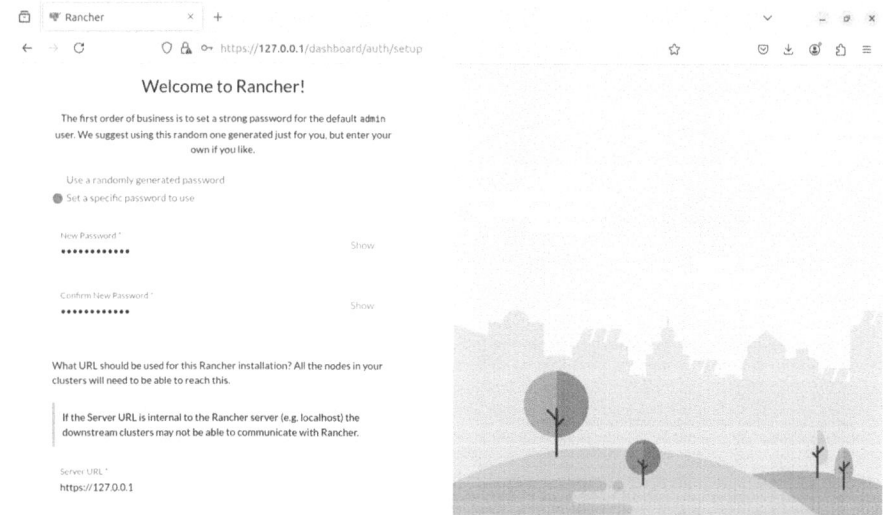

Figure 10-22. *Setting a new password for Rancher*

CHAPTER 10   CONTAINER ORCHESTRATION PLATFORMS

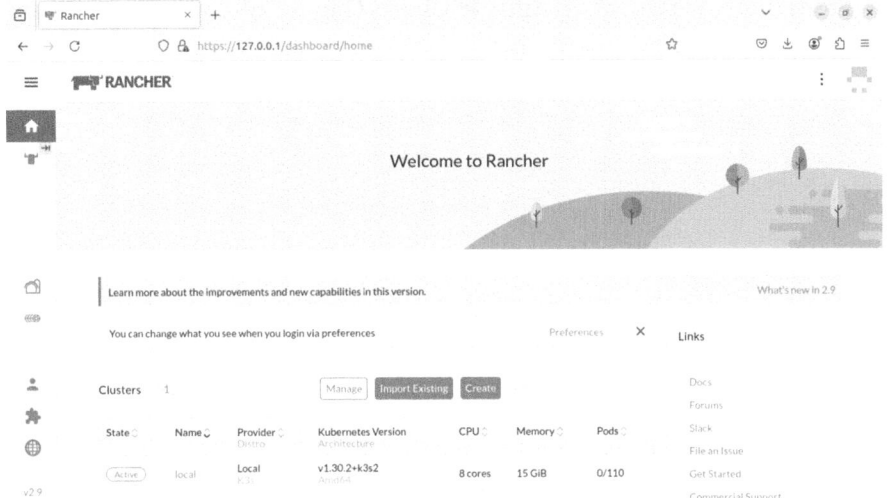

Figure 10-23.   Welcome to Rancher

Rancher works on top of a Kubernetes cluster, but it makes much easier working with Kubernetes. If we go to clusters, we'll see the local Kubernetes cluster created (Figure 10-24).

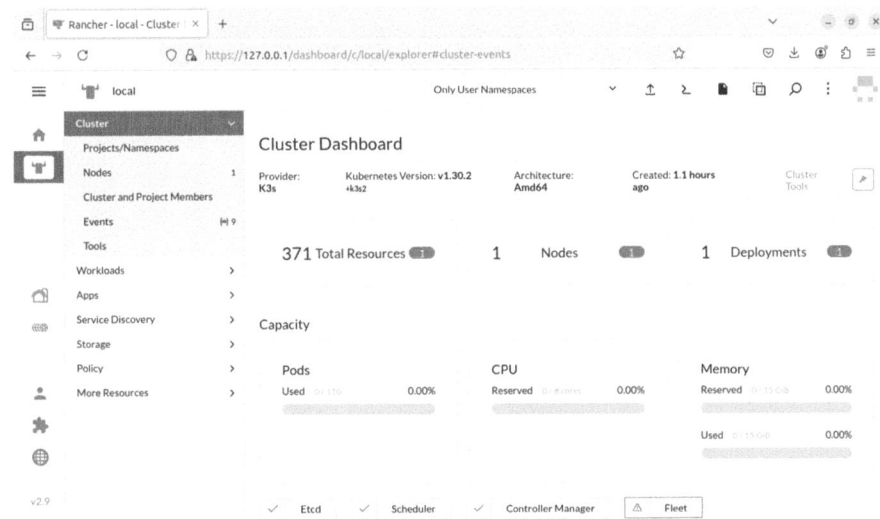

Figure 10-24.   Kubernetes cluster in Rancher

CHAPTER 10   CONTAINER ORCHESTRATION PLATFORMS

From there, we can go to Apps ➤ Charts (Figure 10-25) and install any of the listed charts (Figure 10-26).

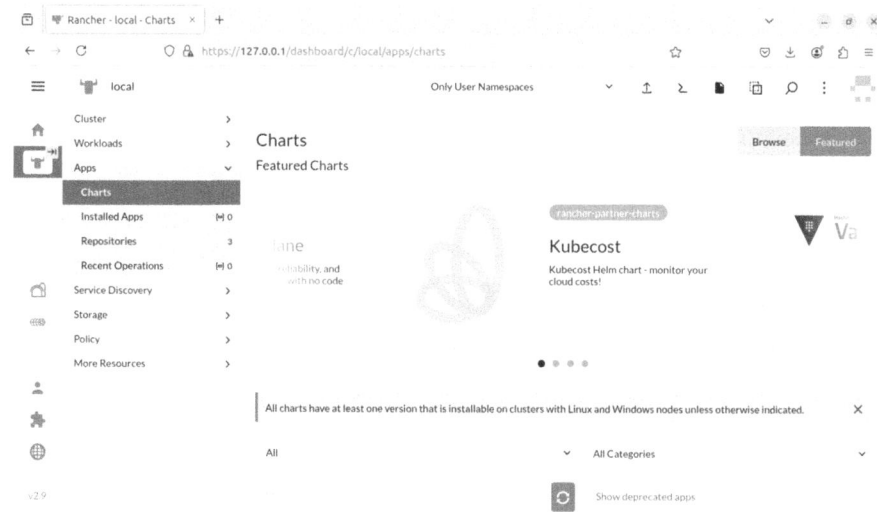

Figure 10-25. Available charts in Rancher

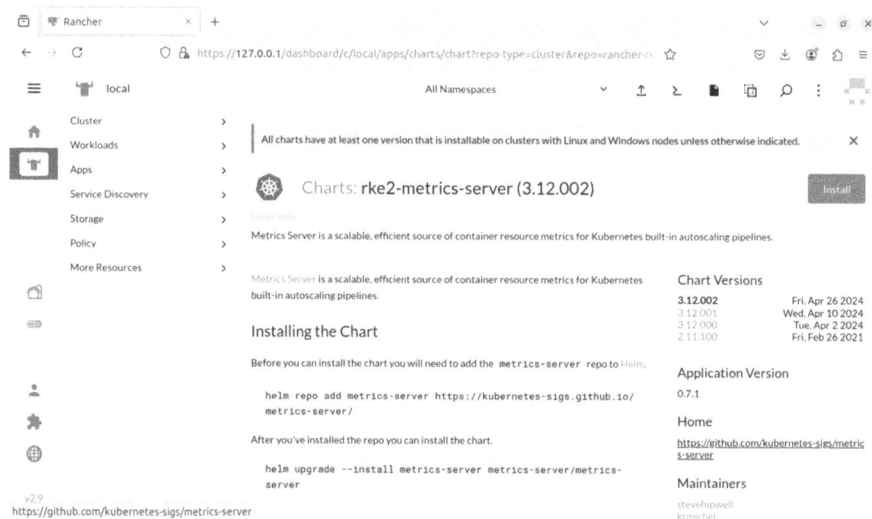

Figure 10-26. Installing a chart in Rancher

Summary

In this chapter, we studied container orchestration. This subject is a subject with a lot of relevance in today's world so it is important to know it.

We began by defining orchestration to better understand the underlying concepts. Then we studied docker compose, which is not technically an orchestration platform but a tool that deploys multi-container apps. And then we started to see the main orchestration solutions available: docker swarm and, of course, Kubernetes.

CHAPTER 11

podman and Other Container-Related Tools

In this chapter, we'll cover the following concepts:

- Awareness of podman, buildah, and skopeo
- Awareness of OCI runtime and image specifications
- Awareness of OpenVZ, rkt, and BSD jails

Introduction

In this last chapter about containers, we'll see a series of concepts and tools that are included in the LPIC-3 305 exam but hadn't been covered yet in the previous chapters.

As the exam only requires a very basic knowledge about these tools, we'll see a very brief explanation of how they work. Of course you're more than welcome to further investigate them, as they can be very useful depending on your needs.

CHAPTER 11   PODMAN AND OTHER CONTAINER-RELATED TOOLS

Open Container Initiative

We have seen in previous chapters what is a container and how it is created using several features of the Linux kernel (mainly kernel namespaces and control groups). We have seen two different implementations of these technologies: Linux containers (LXC) and Docker.

To try and establish a series of standards about the creation and management of containers, in 2015, the Open Container Initiative (OCI) was created.

Currently, there are three OCI specifications:

- Runtime-spec
- Image-spec
- Distribution-spec

As the names imply, these specifications set the standards about container runtimes, container images, and container distribution.

podman

podman is a container runtime that complies with OCI specifications. As opposed to Docker, it doesn't require a running service like **dockerd** to work.

Installing podman

podman was developed by Red Hat, and it is the recommended container runtime in Red Hat servers from version 8 onward. In this case, we're going to use a Red Hat clone, Rocky Linux, to install podman.

```
[root@rocky ~]# cat /etc/rocky-release
Rocky Linux release 8.9 (Green Obsidian)

[root@rocky ~]# dnf search podman
Last metadata expiration check: -77 days, 15:45:18 ago on lun
22 jul 2024 07:54:51 CEST.
============== Name Exactly Matched: podman ==================
podman.x86_64 : Manage Pods, Containers and Container Images

[root@rocky ~]# dnf install -y podman
```

Note In case we installed Docker previously, we'll have to uninstall it. Some packages installed with podman conflict with those installed with Docker.

The way to work with podman is basically similar to what we observed when we studied Docker. We can download images, create containers from those images, mount volumes, etc.

podman Images

As we've seen when we studied **Docker**, to work with **podman**, we also need images. The images used by **podman** are the same we used for Docker. In fact, we can use the same registry we used with **Docker**, the Docker hub, or those registries freely provided by Red Hat for **podman**. The use of **podman** is almost identical to the use of **Docker** as we'll see.

We can, for example, search for an nginx image:

```
[root@rocky ~]# podman image search nginx
NAME                                       DESCRIPTION
registry.access.redhat.com/ubi8/nginx-120  Platform for
running nginx 1.20 or building...
```

registry.access.redhat.com/rhel9/nginx-124   rhcc_registry.
access.redhat.com_rhel9/nginx-...
.
.
docker.io/library/nginx   Official build of Nginx.
.
.
.

and download that image:

```
[root@rocky ~]# podman image pull docker.io/library/nginx
Trying to pull docker.io/library/nginx:latest...
Getting image source signatures
Copying blob 14b7e5e8f394 done
.
.
.
Writing manifest to image destination
5ef79149e0ec84a7a9f9284c3f91aa3c20608f8391f5445eabe92ef07d
bda03c
```

We can repeat the procedure and download as many images as we want. In this example, we have an nginx image and a busybox image.

```
[root@rocky ~]# podman image ls
REPOSITORY                 TAG     IMAGE ID
CREATED           SIZE
docker.io/library/nginx    latest  5ef79149e0ec
7 days ago        192 MB
docker.io/library/busybox  latest  ba5dc23f65d4
11 months ago     4.5 MB
```

Now that we have some images available, it is time to create a container using any of those images.

podman Containers

Similarly to what happened when we worked with images, we can work with containers in pretty much the same way as we did when we studied **Docker**.

We can list the containers currently running at any point. Of course right now we don't have any.

```
[root@rocky ~]# podman container ls
CONTAINER ID  IMAGE  COMMAND  CREATED  STATUS  PORTS  NAMES
```

Let's run a container from the nginx image we downloaded previously.

```
[root@rocky ~]# podman container run -d -p 8080:80 docker.io/library/nginx
3d5176718cae3b220b60a0a92007e939c59ba7c1bfc9e96dc221caf4ee0f6d54
```

The syntax is very easy, and you're already familiar with it. We execute a container based on the nginx image in the background (-d), and we redirect port 8080 in the host to port 80 in the container.

```
[root@rocky ~]# podman container run -d nginx
4e602e82464a945052c59f7844a54d981ee33e8bba9a53e7602cdce864aeadc3
```

Now we can list this new container.

```
[root@rocky ~]# podman container ls
CONTAINER ID  IMAGE
COMMAND           CREATED       STATUS
PORTS             NAMES
```

```
3d5176718cae   docker.io/library/nginx:latest
nginx -g daemon o...   3 minutes ago   Up 3 minutes
0.0.0.0:8080->80/tcp   busy_grothendieck
```

We can access the nginx welcome page with a web browser pointed at port 8080 in the host (Figure 11-1).

Figure 11-1. *nginx running on a podman container*

Of course, we can inspect the container to see its characteristics.

```
[root@rocky ~]# podman container inspect busy_grothendieck
.
.
.
[
    {
        "Id": "3d5176718cae3b220b60a0a92007e939c59ba7c1bf
        c9e96dc221caf4ee0f6d54",
        "Created": "2024-08-22T21:23:07.268497515+02:00",
        "Path": "/docker-entrypoint.sh",
```

```
            "Args": [
                "nginx",
```
-
-
```
            "NetworkSettings": {
                "EndpointID": "",
                "Gateway": "10.88.0.1",
                "IPAddress": "10.88.0.10",
```
-
-

When we're done, we can stop the container.

```
[root@rocky ~]# podman container stop busy_grothendieck
busy_grothendieck
```

There are many more options available, but this is enough for a quick introduction to podman containers. You're more than welcome to repeat what we saw about Docker containers using podman instead.

buildah

buildah is a tool to create OCI images; it works like the **Docker image build** command.

It is an independent tool, so we need to install it.

```
[root@rocky ~]# dnf search buildah
Last metadata expiration check: -77 days, 21:07:52 ago on lun 22 jul 2024 07:54:51 CEST.
=================== Name Exactly Matched: buildah ==============
buildah.x86_64 : A command line tool used for creating
OCI Images

[root@rocky ~]# dnf -y install buildah
```

To create an image, we need to define a *Containerfile* file. As a simple example, we'll use this one:

```
[root@rocky ~]# cat Containerfile
FROM docker.io/library/nginx
COPY hello.txt /usr/share/nginx/html
```

In this simple example, we just create a new image using the nginx image as the base. Then, we copy a text file to the default website directory. In the text file, we'll type any short text.

```
[root@rocky ~]# cat hello.txt
Hello
```

We launch **buildah** and assign the tag (-t) customized_image to the new image. We can specify the location of the Containerfile with -f. By default, **buildah** will search for a file named Containerfile in the current directory, so in this case, we could omit this parameter; we included it for clarity.

```
[root@rocky ~]# buildah build -t customized_image -f Containerfile
STEP 1/2: FROM docker.io/library/nginx
STEP 2/2: COPY hello.txt /usr/share/nginx/html
COMMIT customized_image
Getting image source signatures
Copying blob 9853575bc4f9 skipped: already exists
.
.
Writing manifest to image destination
--> a67bd3c10231
Successfully tagged localhost/customized_image:latest
a67bd3c102310ef1bfbce8e683e03d86091ed8fbc34a1552cd40af504453e3f7
```

Now it is possible to list the image:

```
[root@rocky ~]# podman image ls
REPOSITORY                     TAG       IMAGE ID
CREATED            SIZE
localhost/customized_image     latest    a67bd3c10231
38 seconds ago     192 MB
docker.io/library/nginx        latest    5ef79149e0ec
8 days ago         192 MB
docker.io/library/busybox      latest    ba5dc23f65d4
15 months ago      4.5 MB
```

and create a new container from that image:

```
[root@rocky ~]# podman container run --rm -d -p 8000:80
localhost/customized_image
1d1230ef8589daf9e32b76134db2911900534fa06c7c97f2006070e9dea7f102
```

We can use any web browser, curl in this case, to access the text file we copied when creating the customized image.

```
[root@rocky ~]# curl http://localhost:8000/hello.txt
Hello
```

skopeo

skopeo is a tool used to manage and analyze images in a registry without having to download them.

As we did before with **podman** and **buildah**, we need to install it first.

```
[root@rocky ~]# dnf search skopeo
Last metadata expiration check: 0:28:41 ago on vie 23 ago 2024
00:32:55 CEST.
```

CHAPTER 11 PODMAN AND OTHER CONTAINER-RELATED TOOLS

```
=============== Name Exactly Matched: skopeo ================
skopeo.x86_64 : Inspect container images and repositories on
registries
```

[root@rocky ~]# dnf install -y skopeo

Let's see skopeo in action. First, we'll search for any image, for example, Fedora.

```
[root@rocky ~]# podman search fedora
NAME                        DESCRIPTION
docker.io/library/fedora    Official Docker builds of Fedora
docker.io/ustclug/fedora    Official Fedora Image with
                            USTC Mirror
docker.io/srcml/fedora      Build, package, and test srcml
                            on Fedora
```
•
•
•

With **skopeo**, it is possible to inspect the image before downloading it.

```
[root@rocky ~]# skopeo inspect docker://docker.io/
library/fedora
{
    "Name": "docker.io/library/fedora",
    "Digest": "sha256:5ce8497aeea599bf6b54ab3979133923d82aaa4f6
    ca5ced1812611b197c79eb0",
    "RepoTags": [
```
•
•
•
```
    "Created": "2024-04-22T18:26:21.555217891Z",
    "DockerVersion": "20.10.23",
```

```
    "Labels": {
        "maintainer": "Clement Verna \u003ccverna@
        fedoraproject.org\u003e"
    },
    "Architecture": "amd64",
    "Os": "linux",
    "Layers": [
        "sha256:d4df0db66c89d7e6225ce9d3597a045fb95c020f3174a
        f1830df88a37a871db8"
    ],
```
·
·
·

FreeBSD Jails

This is an OS-level virtualization solution provided on FreeBSD systems. When we studied "container virtualization concepts" in Chapter 7, we saw how to use the system call "chroot" to get an isolated system. FreeBSD jails work in a similar way, but this is a more powerful solution.

Like chroot, jail works by using a system call also named "jail". And it has a userland command, which also has the name "jail".

Let's suppose we already have a running FreeBSD system, and we want to install another jailed instance of the OS. To do it, we use the **bsdinstall jail** command and pass the path where we'll install the new jailed instance.

root@freebsd1:~ # bsdinstall jail /alcatraz

Then we'll select the close mirror to install the new instance (Figure 11-2).

CHAPTER 11   PODMAN AND OTHER CONTAINER-RELATED TOOLS

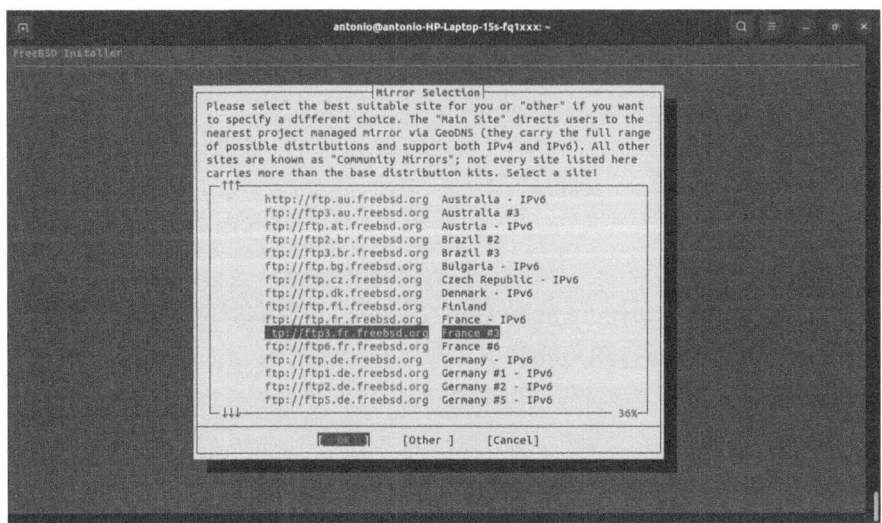

Figure 11-2. Installing a jailed instance of FreeBSD (1)

After selecting the mirror, choosing the components to install, and so on, the installation will begin (Figure 11-3).

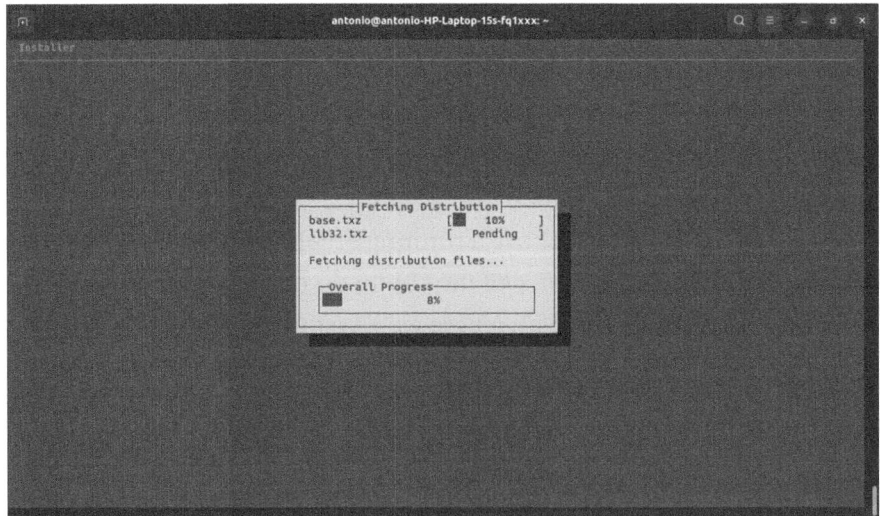

Figure 11-3. Installing a jailed instance of FreeBSD (2)

After setting the root password, adding new users if needed, etc., the installation will be complete. We can list the path where we installed the jailed instance, and we'll see the typical folder tree present in a FreeBSD system.

```
root@freebsd1:~ # ls /alcatraz/
.cshrc      bin     entropy   lib       mnt    rescue   sys    var
.profile    boot    etc       libexec   net    root     tmp
COPYRIGHT   dev     home      media     proc   sbin     usr
```

Now it's time to launch the jail. We do it by executing the jail command; we specify the path and we set the hostname; we tell it to mount the device pseudo filesystem and finally the name of the command that will be jailed, a shell in this case.

```
root@freebsd1:~ # jail -c path=/alcatraz/ mount.devfs host.hostname=testjail command=/bin/sh
```

As expected, we get a shell that will be isolated from the main system.

```
root@testjail:/ #
```

In the main system, we can list the running jails with **jls**.

```
root@freebsd1:~ # jls
   JID  IP Address      Hostname                      Path
     1                  testjail                      /alcatraz
```

rkt

rkt, also known as "Rocket," is a container runtime engine designed to run application containers in Linux. Unfortunately, the project seems to have been discontinued, as we can see on its GitHub page (Figure 11-4), but we can still download it and try to see it in action.

CHAPTER 11   PODMAN AND OTHER CONTAINER-RELATED TOOLS

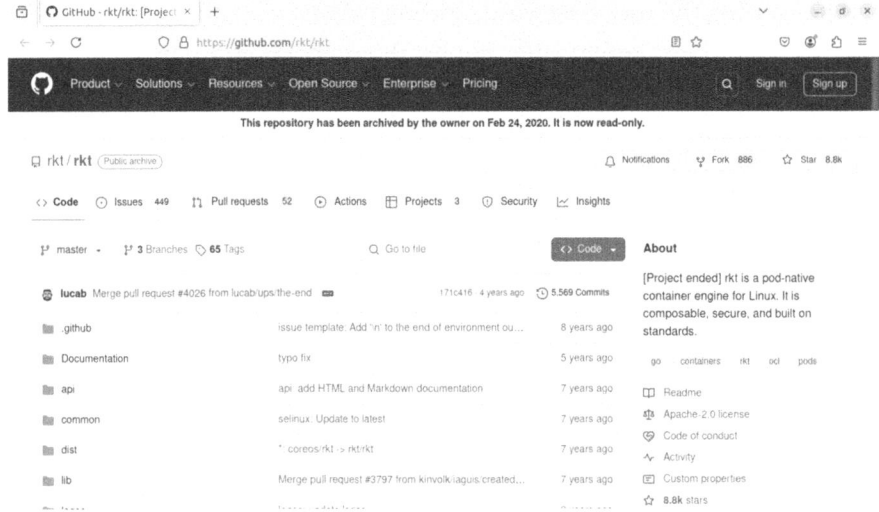

Figure 11-4. *rkt GitHub page*

If we scroll down a bit, we'll see the last release (v.1.30.0). By clicking there and scrolling down in the new page, we'll see the links to download it in different formats: tar, rpm, deb, etc. (Figure 11-5).

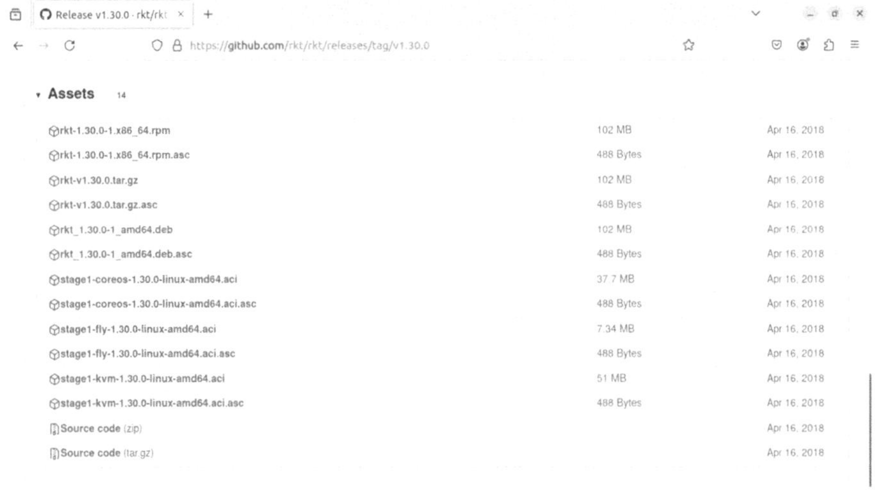

Figure 11-5. *Downloading the last release of rkt*

CHAPTER 11   PODMAN AND OTHER CONTAINER-RELATED TOOLS

We'll download the tar compressed file in a new folder.

```
[root@rocky ~]# mkdir rocket
[root@rocky ~]# cd rocket/
[root@rocky rocket]# wget https://github.com/rkt/rkt/releases/download/v1.30.0/rkt-v1.30.0.tar.gz
--2024-08-24 01:44:50--  https://github.com/rkt/rkt/releases/download/v1.30.0/rkt-v1.30.0.tar.gz
Resolving github.com (github.com)... 140.82.121.3
Connecting to github.com (github.com)|140.82.121.3|:443...
connected.
.
.
.
2024-08-24 01:44:55 (24,7 MB/s) - 'rkt-v1.30.0.tar.gz' saved [106761266/106761266]
```

And we extract it.

```
[root@rocky rocket]# tar -xzvf rkt-v1.30.0.tar.gz
```

If we list the folder now, we'll see the rkt binary, as well as other files like man pages.

```
[root@rocky rkt-v1.30.0]# ls
bash_completion  init  manpages  rkt  scripts  stage1-coreos.aci  stage1-fly.aci  stage1-kvm.aci
```

The syntax is quite easy; it's not the same syntax that we saw on Docker or podman, but it doesn't differ that much. To run a container, we need the option run and the image.

```
[root@rocky rkt-v1.30.0]# ./rkt run docker://nginx
run: signature verification for docker images is not supported (try -insecure-options=image)
```

579

CHAPTER 11 PODMAN AND OTHER CONTAINER-RELATED TOOLS

After this first execution, we get an error about the signature, but we also get a suggestion about how to circumvent this error using an option. We repeat the command adding that option.

```
[root@rocky rkt-v1.30.0]# ./rkt run --insecure-options=image docker://nginx
run: name doesn't match what was requested, expected: library/nginx, downloaded:
```

Now we get a more cryptic error message; well use the "debug" option to try to obtain more information.

```
[root@rocky rkt-v1.30.0]# ./rkt run --insecure-options=image --debug docker://nginx
.
.
.
image: remote fetching from URL "docker://nginx"
image: fetching image from docker://nginx
run:
  └─error converting docker image to ACI
     └─name doesn't match what was requested, expected: library/nginx, downloaded:
```

There seems to be a problem with the conversion of the image. rkt uses its own image format named ACI, and it seems to have difficulty converting the image from the Docker registry (with another format) into ACI. Unfortunately, as we said before, **rkt** is no longer an active project. The error we see here is quite likely to be due to small changes in the Docker image format specifications that this old version of **rkt** can no longer process.

In case you're curious, I have an older system in which I installed rkt and could download the nginx image some time ago. The nginx image in that system is already locally installed and can be listed.

```
[root@rocky rkt-v1.29.0]# ./rkt image list
ID                     NAME
    SIZE       IMPORT TIME     LAST USED
sha512-e50b77423452    coreos.com/rkt/stage1-coreos:1.29.0
    211MiB     1 year ago      1 year ago
sha512-e30149195c55    registry-1.docker.io/library/nginx:latest
    272MiB     1 year ago      1 year ago
```

So when we execute run, rkt will use the locally installed image without downloading it again from the Docker registry.

```
[root@rocky rkt-v1.29.0]# ./rkt run --insecure-options=image
docker://nginx
/usr/lib/systemd/systemd: error while loading shared libraries:
/lib64/libc.so.6: cannot apply additional memory protection
after relocation: Permission denied
```

The system we're working in right now is a Rocky Linux with SELinux. By default, SELinux might interfere with the execution of **rkt**. We should modify the SELinux policies to allow the execution of **rkt**, but for a quick test, we'll just set SELinux to the permissive mode.

```
[root@rocky rkt-v1.29.0]# sestatus
SELinux status:                 enabled
SELinuxfs mount:                /sys/fs/selinux
SELinux root directory:         /etc/selinux
Loaded policy name:             targeted
Current mode:                   enforcing
Mode from config file:          enforcing
Policy MLS status:              enabled
Policy deny_unknown status:     allowed
Memory protection checking:     actual (secure)
Max kernel policy version:      33
[root@rocky rkt-v1.29.0]# setenforce permissive
```

Now, at last, we can execute the container successfully.

```
[root@rocky rkt-v1.29.0]# ./rkt run --insecure-options=image docker://nginx
[27232.520014] nginx[6]: /docker-entrypoint.sh: /docker-entrypoint.d/ is not empty, will attempt to perform configuration
.
.
.
2024/07/06 03:08:25 [notice] 6#6: start worker processes
2024/07/06 03:08:25 [notice] 6#6: start worker process 34
```

The container executes in the foreground. If we open a new command shell, we can list the containers.

```
[root@rocky rkt-v1.29.0]# ./rkt list
UUID        APP      IMAGE NAME
STATE       CREATED          STARTED           NETWORKS
c7104ffc    nginx    registry-1.docker.io/library/
nginx:latest    running    1 minute ago    1 minute
ago     default:ip4=172.16.28.3
```

And if we try to access port 80/tcp on the container IP, we'll see nginx welcome page.

```
[root@rocky rkt-v1.29.0]# curl http://172.16.28.3
<!DOCTYPE html>
<html>
<head>
<title>Welcome to nginx!</title>
```

CHAPTER 11   PODMAN AND OTHER CONTAINER-RELATED TOOLS

In the command shell in which the container is running in the foreground, we'll see the HTTP request.

```
172.16.28.1 - - [06/Jul/2024:03:11:11 +0000] "GET / HTTP/1.1"
200 615 "-" "curl/7.61.1" "-"
```

Finally, we can stop the container.

```
[root@rocky rkt-v1.29.0]# ./rkt stop c7104ffc
"c7104ffc-48a2-452e-904c-02ffbcfc8b03"
[root@rocky rkt-v1.29.0]#
```

OpenVZ

OpenVZ is another container-based virtualization solution for Linux. It's been developed by Virtuozzo and released as open source. We can install it from its official web page (Figure 11-6).

Figure 11-6. *OpenVZ official web page*

583

CHAPTER 11   PODMAN AND OTHER CONTAINER-RELATED TOOLS

OpenVZ is a customized Red Hat family server that includes the software developed by Virtuozzo to create and manage the OpenVZ containers. The main client tool to manage these containers is **prlctl**. We can use it, for instance, to list the existing containers. Obviously we don't have any running container right now.

```
[root@pc-3625 ~]# prlctl list
UUID                      STATUS          IP_ADDR          T  NAME
```

Let's create our new container (vmtype ct).

```
[root@pc-3625 ~]# prlctl create myopenvzcont --vmtype ct
WARNING: You are using a deprecated CLI component that won't be installed by default in the next major release. Please use virsh instead
Creating the Container...
Creating cache
Processing metadata for almalinux-8-x86_64
Creating temporary Container
Creating virtual disk
Running the script pre-cache
Package manager: installing
Running the script post-cache
Running the script post-install
Resizing virtual disk
Packing cache
The Container has been successfully created.
```

If we list the containers again, we'll see the new container listed. Currently it is stopped.

CHAPTER 11   PODMAN AND OTHER CONTAINER-RELATED TOOLS

```
[root@pc-3625 ~]# prlctl list --all
UUID                                    STATUS
IP_ADDR          T   NAME
{2232099e-5ade-41ab-83cc-1eb713d75238}  stopped
-                    CT  myopenvzcont
```

We start the container.

```
[root@pc-3625 ~]# prlctl start myopenvzcont
WARNING: You are using a deprecated CLI component that won't
be installed by default in the next major release. Please use
virsh instead
Starting the CT...
The CT has been successfully started.
```

If we list it again, we'll see the container running.

```
[root@pc-3625 ~]# prlctl list
UUID                                    STATUS
IP_ADDR          T   NAME
{2232099e-5ade-41ab-83cc-1eb713d75238}  running
-                    CT  myopenvzcont
```

When we first executed prlctl, we saw that **prlctl** is deprecated, and we were advised to use **virsh** instead. We already studied **virsh** in Chapter 4. So you're probably familiar with it. We'll see briefly how we should proceed to use **virsh**. The first thing we need to do is connect to the OpenVZ system.

```
[root@pc-3625 ~]# virsh connect vz:///system
error: failed to connect to the hypervisor
error: no connection driver available for vz:///system
```

Initially, we get an error because we don't have the needed driver to integrate OpenVZ with libvirt. We'll search for the driver, and we'll install it.

```
[root@pc-3625 ~]# yum search libvirt
.
.
.
libvirt-daemon-driver-vz.x86_64 : Virtuozzo driver plugin for the libvirtd daemon
libvirt-daemon-driver-vzct.x86_64 : Virtuozzo Containers driver plugin for the libvirtd daemon
[root@pc-3625 ~]# yum install -y libvirt-daemon-driver-vz libvirt-daemon-driver-vzct
```

Now we can use virsh to connect to the OpenVZ system.

```
[root@pc-3625 ~]# virsh connect vz:///system
[root@pc-3625 ~]#
```

Of course we can't list here the container we installed previously because libvirt is not aware of it, but if we use **virsh** to install a new container, we'll be able to manage it with virsh or any other libvirt-based tool.

```
[root@pc-3625 ~]# virsh list
 Id    Name                           State
--------------------------------------------
```

Another interesting option that we can use is **prlctl list -i** to get more information about the running containers.

```
root@pc-3625 ~]# prlctl list -i
INFO
ID: {2232099e-5ade-41ab-83cc-1eb713d75238}
```

CHAPTER 11   PODMAN AND OTHER CONTAINER-RELATED TOOLS

```
EnvID: 2232099e-5ade-41ab-83cc-1eb713d75238
Name: myopenvzcont
Description:
Type: CT
State: running
OS: linux
Template: no
Uptime: 00:00:00 (since 2024-08-18 23:52:20)
Home: /vz/private/2232099e-5ade-41ab-83cc-1eb713d75238
Backup path:
Owner: root
GuestTools: state=possibly_installed
GuestTools autoupdate: on
Autostart: on
Autostop: suspend
Autocompact: on
Boot order:
EFI boot: off
Allow select boot device: off
External boot device:
Remote display: mode=off address=0.0.0.0
Remote display state: stopped
Hardware:
  cpu sockets=1 cpus=unlimited cores=unlimited VT-x hotplug
  accl=high mode=64 cpuunits=1000 ioprio=4
  memory 512Mb hotplug
  video 0Mb 3d acceleration=off vertical sync=yes
  memory_guarantee auto
  hdd0 (+) scsi:0 image='/vz/private/2232099e-5ade-41ab-83
  cc-1eb713d75238/root.hdd' type='expanded' 10240Mb mnt=/
  state=connected subtype=virtio-scsi
  veneto (+) type='routed'
```

CHAPTER 11   PODMAN AND OTHER CONTAINER-RELATED TOOLS

```
Features:
Disabled Windows logo: on
Nested virtualization: off
Offline management: (-)
```

Summary

In this brief chapter, we studied a series of concepts and tools that are included in the LPIC-3 305 exam. Although they're not given a lot of weight in the official curriculum, I think it is interesting to know them.

Tools like podman, buildah, and skopeo are heavily backed by Red Hat, which makes these tools very relevant nowadays. Other tools may not be as widely used as the former ones, but they all have something interesting to offer.

CHAPTER 12

Cloud Management Tools

In this chapter, we'll cover the following concepts:

- Understand common offerings in public clouds
- Basic feature knowledge of OpenStack
- Basic feature knowledge of Terraform
- Awareness of CloudStack, Eucalyptus, and OpenNebula

We will also be introduced to the following terms and utilities: IaaS, PaaS, SaaS, OpenStack, and Terraform.

Introduction to Cloud Computing

We could define briefly cloud computing as a model that provides on-demand access to computer system resources. A more detailed description, which we summarize below, was provided by the US National Institute of Standards and Technology. This later definition stated that a cloud computing model should have five essential characteristics:

- On-demand self-service: A consumer can provision computer resources automatically, without human intervention.

CHAPTER 12 CLOUD MANAGEMENT TOOLS

- Broad network access: Capabilities are available over the network and accessed through standard protocols.

- Resource pooling: The provider's computing resources are pooled to serve multiple consumers using a multi-tenant model.

- Rapid elasticity: Capabilities can be elastically provisioned and released.

- Measured service: Cloud systems control, monitor, and report resource use.

Besides, a cloud computing model can provide different service models. The three main models are

- Infrastructure as a Service (IaaS): The consumer is given control to deploy new computing instances, manage storage, etc. We could think of it similarly to what we did when we created virtual machines in QEMU/KVM and Xen, we decided the amount of RAM, number of CPUs, storage, IP settings, etc.

- Platform as a Service (PaaS): The consumer can create and deploy applications onto the cloud using programming languages and libraries provided by the Cloud Services provider. The consumer has no control over the underlying server infrastructure.

- Software as a Service (SaaS): The consumer can use the software applications running on the cloud. The control of the application, regarding updates, adding of new features, etc., belongs to the Cloud Services provider.

CHAPTER 12   CLOUD MANAGEMENT TOOLS

We can see a clearer distinction between the different service models in Figure 12-1.

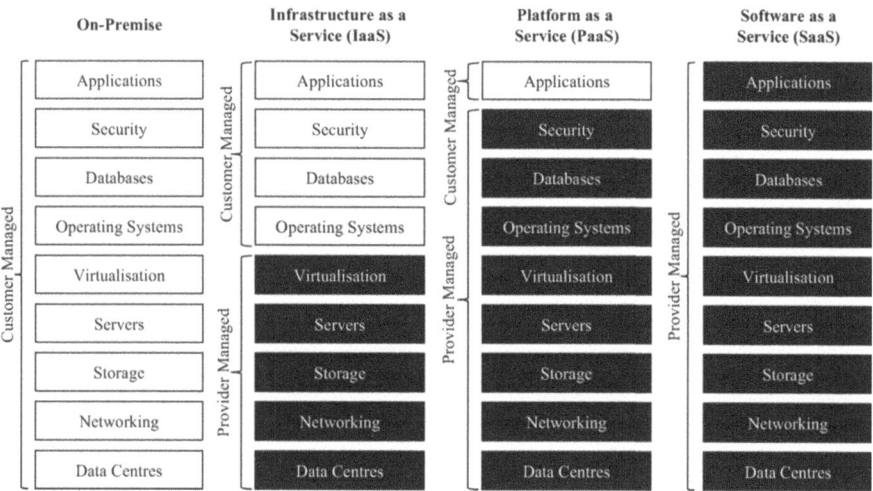

Figure 12-1. *Comparison of on-premises, IaaS, PaaS, and SaaS. Credits to Rosati, Pierangelo; Lynn, Theo*

Before finishing this brief introduction to cloud computing, we must also mention the deployment model of the cloud infrastructure. Depending on whether the cloud infrastructure resides entirely in an external cloud provider, in our own organization, and so on, we can differentiate many types of cloud:

- Private cloud: The infrastructure is operated exclusively by a single organization.

- Community cloud: The infrastructure is shared by different organizations that share common concerns.

- Public cloud: The infrastructure is made publicly available by the Cloud Services provider to anybody.

- Hybrid cloud: In this case, we have a mixture of some of the previous deployment models.

CHAPTER 12   CLOUD MANAGEMENT TOOLS

OpenStack

OpenStack is an open source cloud computing platform. It is used mainly as an IaaS service model. It was created in 2010 in a project developed by Rackspace Hosting and NASA.

OpenStack is composed of many modules; each one of these modules provides different functionality, like computing, storage, networking, etc. We'll see some of the main components, also called services, here:

- Compute (Nova): It provides computing; that is, it is used to provision virtual machines. This component supports the use of many different hypervisors.

- Block storage (Cinder): It provides persistent storage in the form of block devices, like the disks we expect to see in any server. The data in this case is stored as blocks within sectors and tracks.

- Object storage (Swift): In addition to storing data in a block device like a hard disk, OpenStack can store data as a big amount of unstructured data associated to some metadata. This is called object storage or blob storage.

- Image (Glance): It deals with discovery, registering, and retrieval of images to be used by other services.

- Dashboard (Horizon): It provides the user web interface to manage OpenStack.

- Identity (Keystone): This is the API that provides client authentication.

- Networking (Neutron): It provides network connectivity.

CHAPTER 12   CLOUD MANAGEMENT TOOLS

- Orchestration (Heat): It does precisely what the name suggests.

- Telemetry (Ceilometer): It measures the use of resources for billing purposes.

First Steps with OpenStack

As you have noticed, along the book, when we study a new tool, we begin by installing it. I would like to do the same in the case of OpenStack, but due to the fast evolution of OpenStack, it is quite difficult to provide an easy installation method that is fully operational for more than a short time.

There used to be a project named openstack training-labs at opendev. org. This was perfect to know and practice the basics of OpenStack that we need for the LPIC-3 305 exam. Unfortunately, this project is no longer maintained (Figure 12-2).

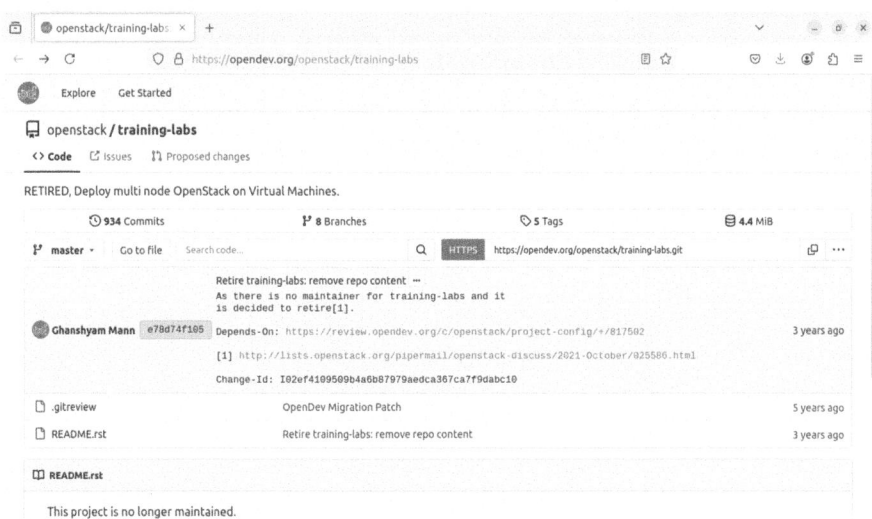

Figure 12-2. *OpenStack training-labs (retired)*

CHAPTER 12 CLOUD MANAGEMENT TOOLS

Some vendors provide their own installers to get a running OpenStack environment. For example, we can install the OpenStack customized by Canonical, the creator of Ubuntu, by visiting this link (Figure 12-3). To meet the hardware requirements, you'll need a computer with a good performance.

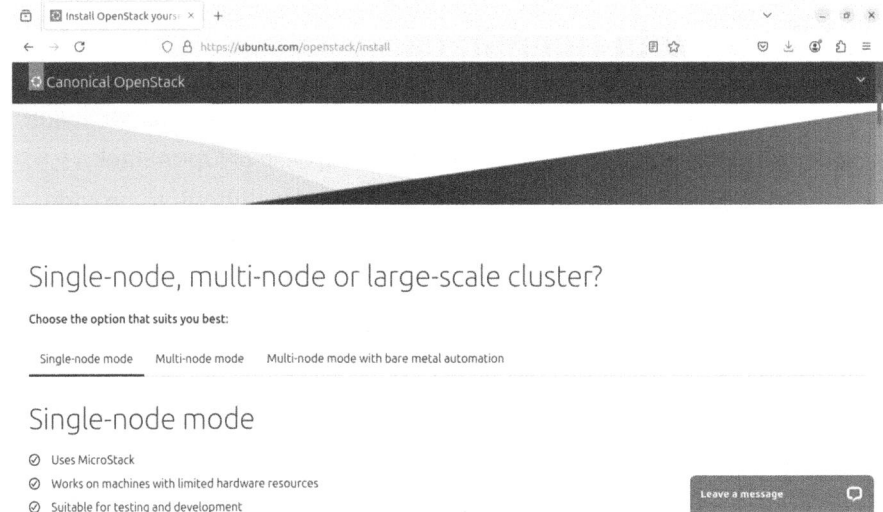

Figure 12-3. Canonical OpenStack

Using the OpenStack Dashboard (Horizon)

Once we have OpenStack installed, we'll access our Dashboard (Horizon) (Figure 12-4).

CHAPTER 12 CLOUD MANAGEMENT TOOLS

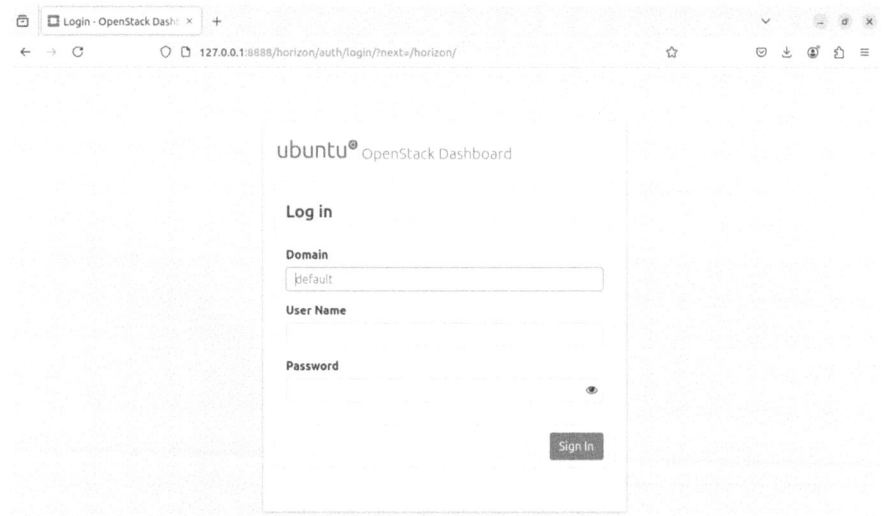

Figure 12-4. OpenStack Dashboard (Horizon)

We enter our admin credentials, and we'll see a summary of the status of OpenStack (Figure 12-5).

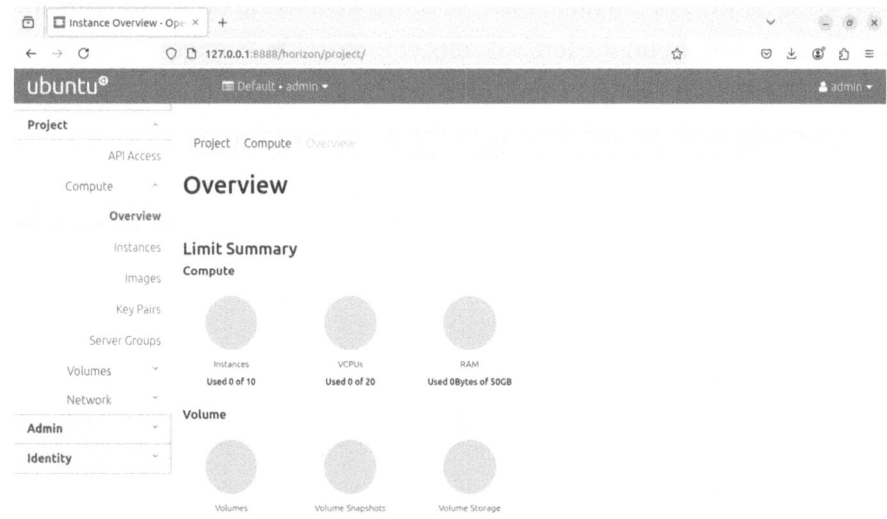

Figure 12-5. OpenStack summary

CHAPTER 12 CLOUD MANAGEMENT TOOLS

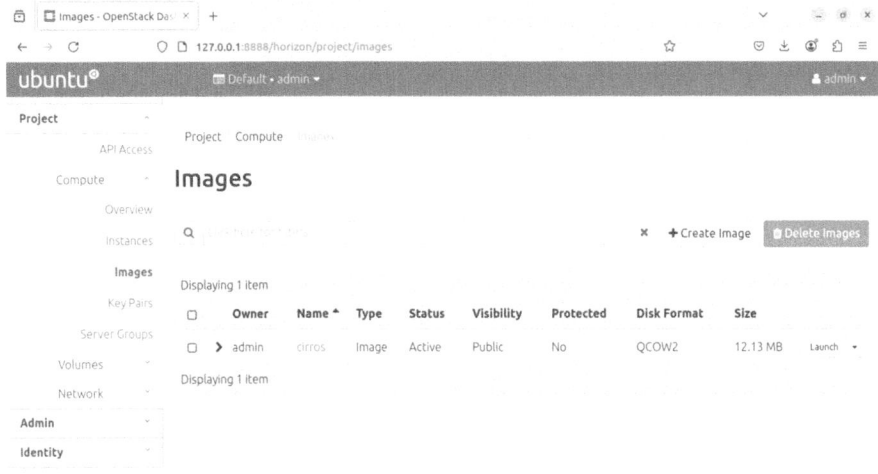

Figure 12-6. *OpenStack images*

Right now we haven't defined any VM in OpenStack, so the summary doesn't show much information. We'll make a quick demo of OpenStack by creating a new VM. To do it, the first thing we need to do is to create an image. On the menu on the left, we select "Project" ➤ "Images". In the new window (Figure 2-6), we click the "Create Image" button.

In the new window, we can use the "Browse" button to select an image file. That file should have been downloaded previously. In cloud environment, it is very common to use cirros images. Cirros is a light Linux distribution optimized for being used in the cloud. We can download it from their website.

```
antonio@antonio-Laptop:~/openstack$ wget https://download.
cirros-cloud.net/0.6.2/cirros-0.6.2-x86_64-disk.img
```

-
-
-

```
cirros-0.6.2-x86_64-disk.img
100%[=========================>]   20,44M  12,0MB/s   in 1,7s

2024-08-27 20:22:36 (12,0 MB/s) - 'cirros-0.6.2-x86_64-disk.
img' saved [21430272/21430272]
```

Now we can select the downloaded image (Figure 12-7). We assign a name and select the format, qcow in this case. If we're not sure about the format, we can use the "file" command to check it.

```
antonio@antonio-Laptop:~/openstack$ file cirros-0.6.2-
x86_64-disk.img
cirros-0.6.2-x86_64-disk.img: QEMU QCOW2 Image (v3),
117440512 bytes
```

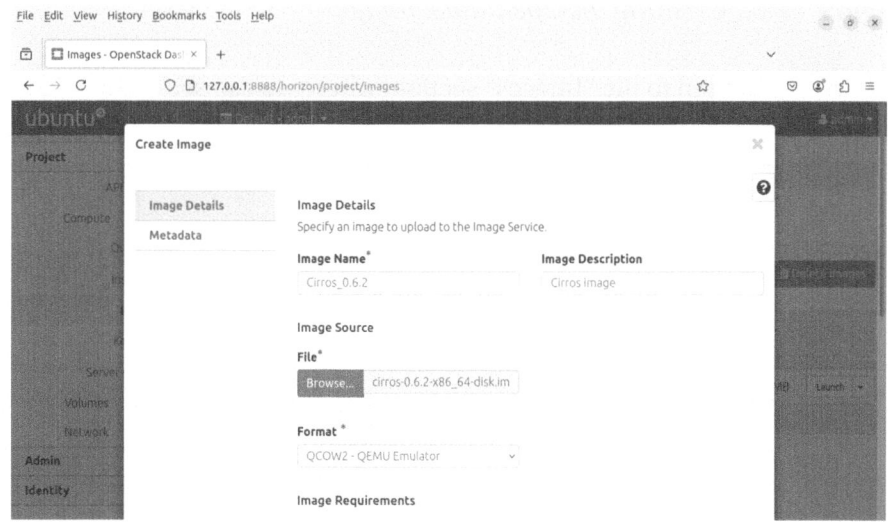

Figure 12-7. *Creating an image*

We scroll down the window and click the "Create Image" button (Figure 12-8).

CHAPTER 12 CLOUD MANAGEMENT TOOLS

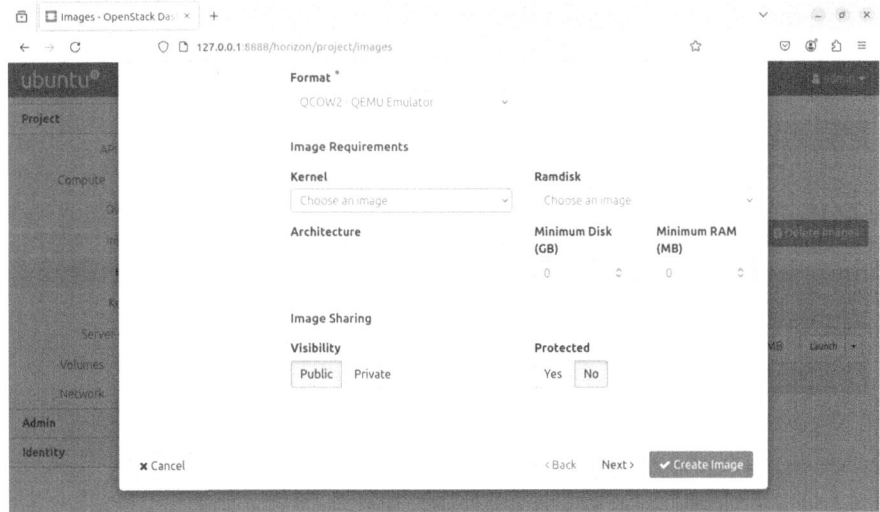

Figure 12-8. Creating an OpenStack image

We return then to the "Images" section, where we can see the new image listed (Figure 12-9).

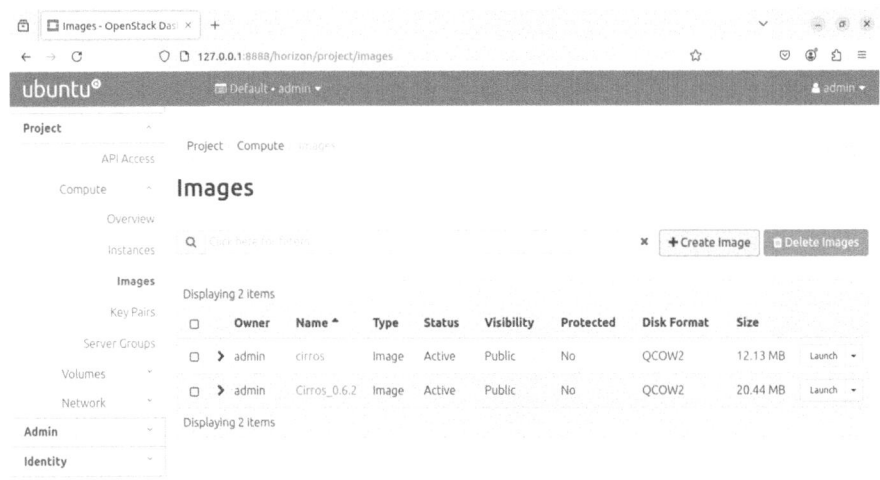

Figure 12-9. OpenStack images

CHAPTER 12   CLOUD MANAGEMENT TOOLS

To launch a new instance based on the new image, we click the "Launch" button on the right. A new window appears (Figure 12-10).

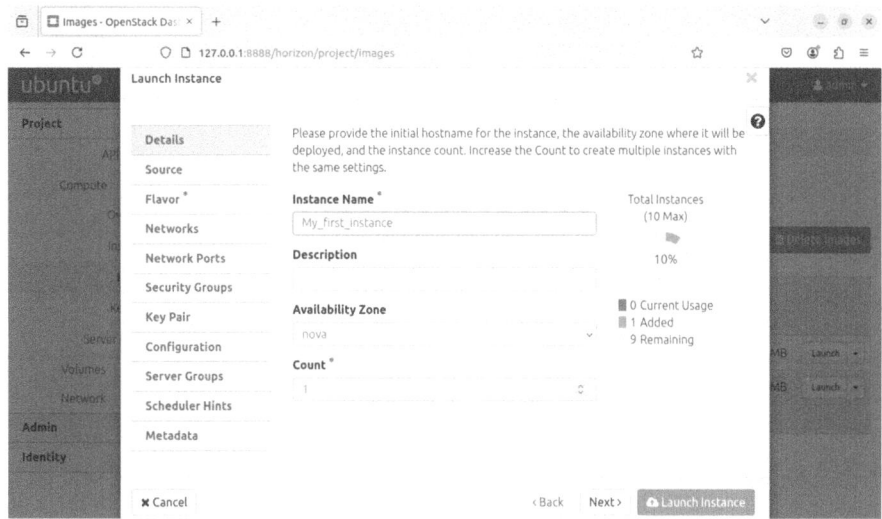

Figure 12-10. *Naming an OpenStack instance*

We assign a name to our instance and click "Next". In the next screen (Figure 12-11), we see the image source of the instance; we click "Next" again.

599

CHAPTER 12 CLOUD MANAGEMENT TOOLS

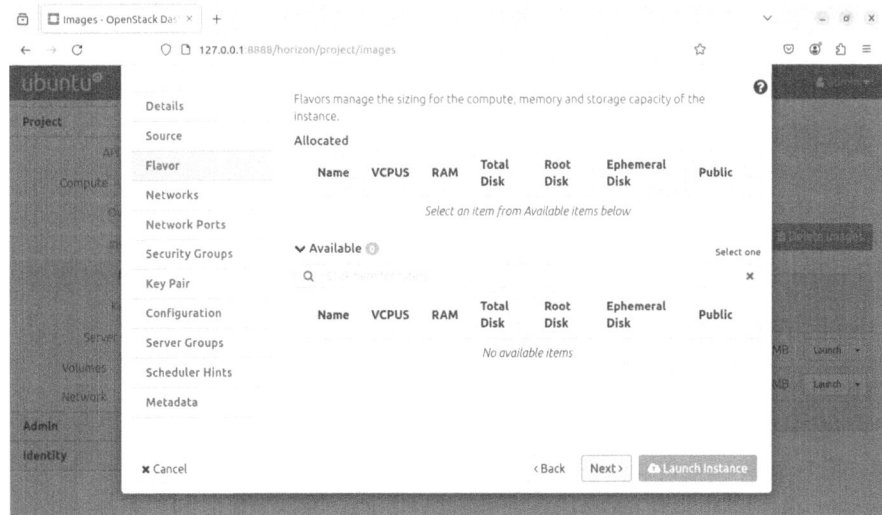

Figure 12-11. Source image

In the next screen (Figure 12-12), we must select a "flavor" for the VM. A "flavor" is basically a template in which we set the computing resources (CPU, RAM) used by the instance. Currently we don't have any "flavor" defined. We'll cancel the wizard and create a flavor.

CHAPTER 12   CLOUD MANAGEMENT TOOLS

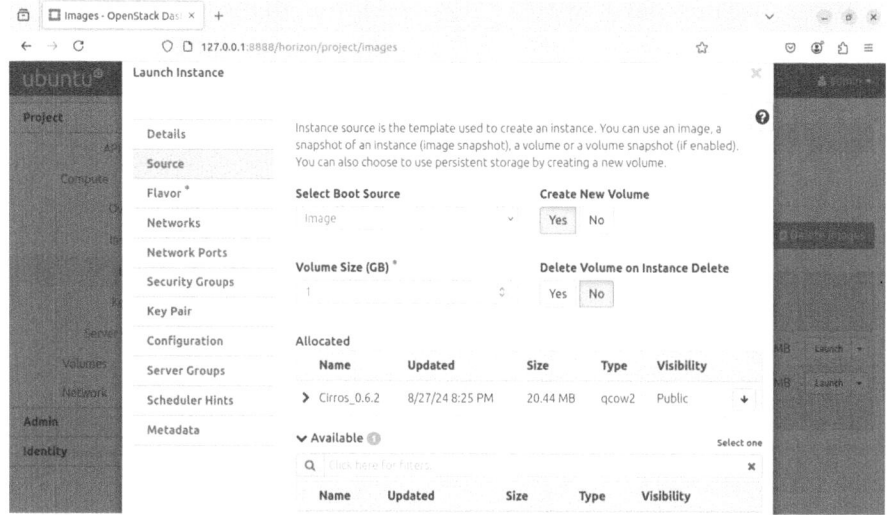

Figure 12-12.   Selecting a flavor

To create a "flavor," we'll use the left menu and select "Admin" ➤ "Compute" ➤ "Flavors" (Figure 12-13).

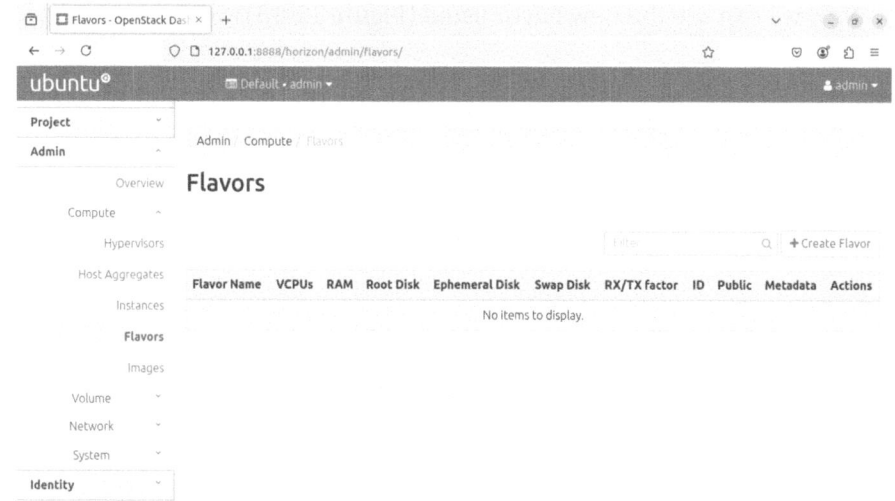

Figure 12-13.   OpenStack Flavors

601

CHAPTER 12   CLOUD MANAGEMENT TOOLS

To create a new flavor, we click "Create Flavor". In the new screen (Figure 12-14), we assign a name and set the amount of CPU and RAM. Then, we click "Create Flavor".

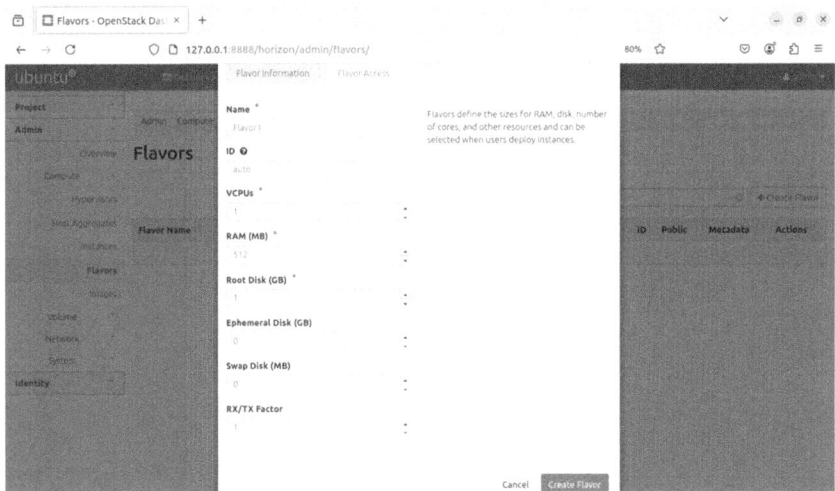

Figure 12-14.   Creating a new OpenStack flavor

Now we can see the new flavor listed (Figure 12-15).

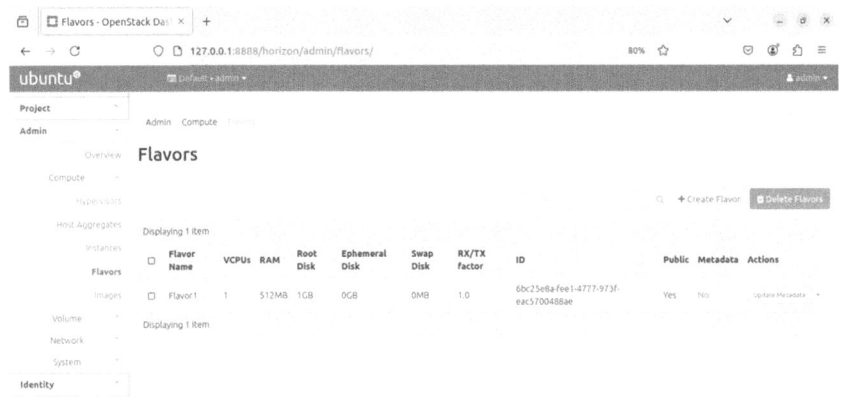

Figure 12-15.   OpenStack Flavors

602

CHAPTER 12   CLOUD MANAGEMENT TOOLS

With the flavor created, we can resume the creation of an instance. We pass through the initial steps from Figures 12-10 and 12-11; in the "Flavor" window, we select the flavor we just created (Figure 12-16) and click "Next".

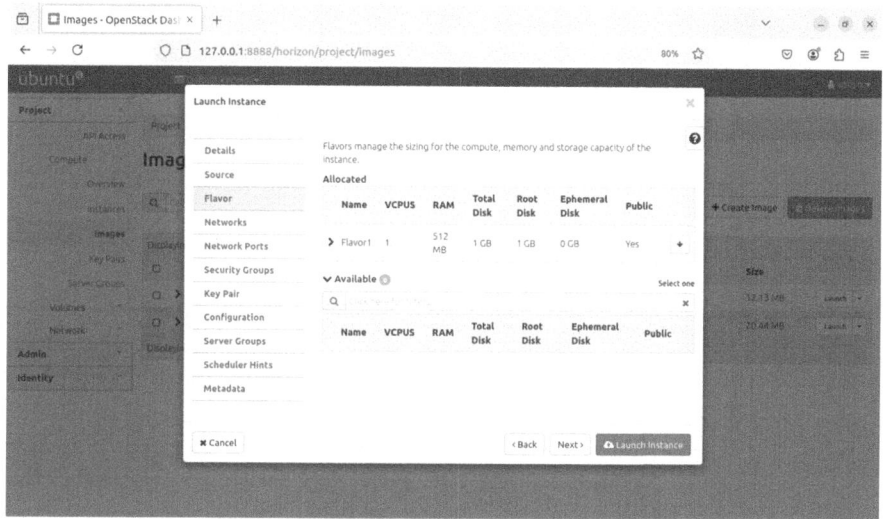

Figure 12-16. *Choosing a flavor for the instances*

In the next screen, we'll leave the default network selected (Figure 12-17).

CHAPTER 12   CLOUD MANAGEMENT TOOLS

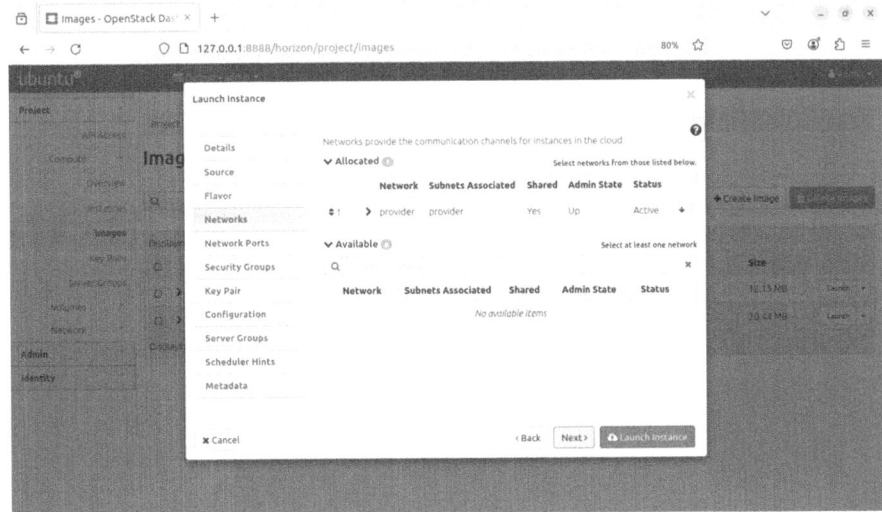

Figure 12-17. *OpenStack networks*

The rest of the options can be left unchanged; then we click "Launch Instance", and we go to "Project" ➤ "Compute" ➤ "Instances" (Figure 12-18).

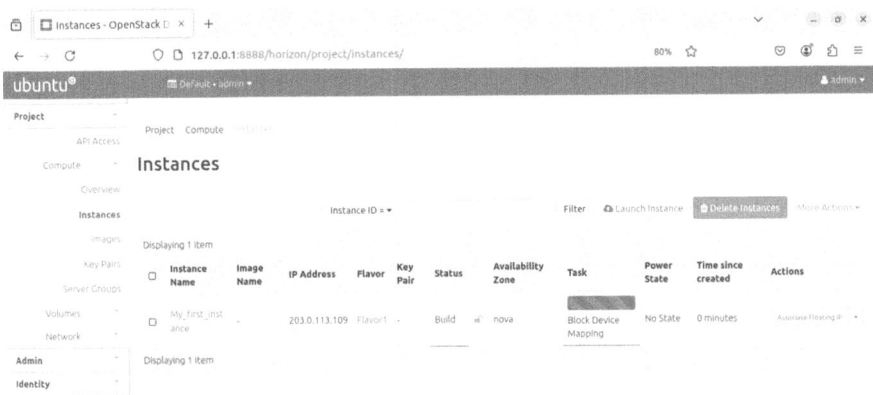

Figure 12-18. *OpenStack instances*

CHAPTER 12 CLOUD MANAGEMENT TOOLS

We'll wait for a few seconds till the instance finishes the build process (Figure 12-19).

Figure 12-19. *OpenStack instance running*

By clicking on the instance name, we can see an overview of its characteristics (Figure 12-20), its interfaces (Figure 12-21), the console log (Figure 12-22), and finally the server console (Figure 12-23).

605

CHAPTER 12   CLOUD MANAGEMENT TOOLS

Figure 12-20.   OpenStack instance overview

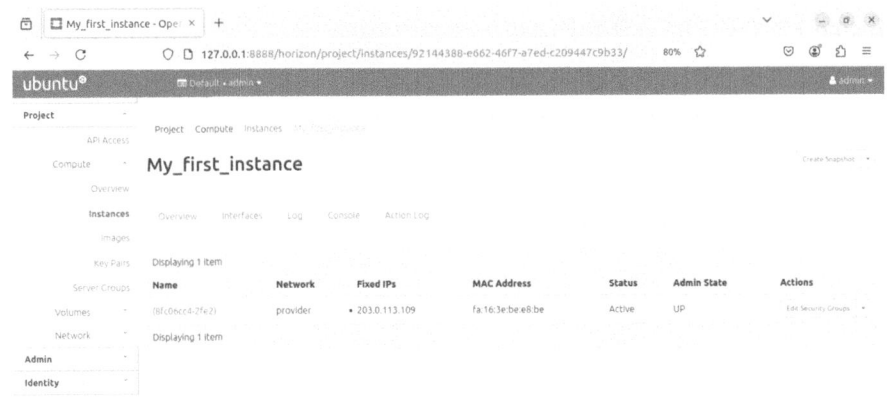

Figure 12-21.   OpenStack instance interfaces

CHAPTER 12 CLOUD MANAGEMENT TOOLS

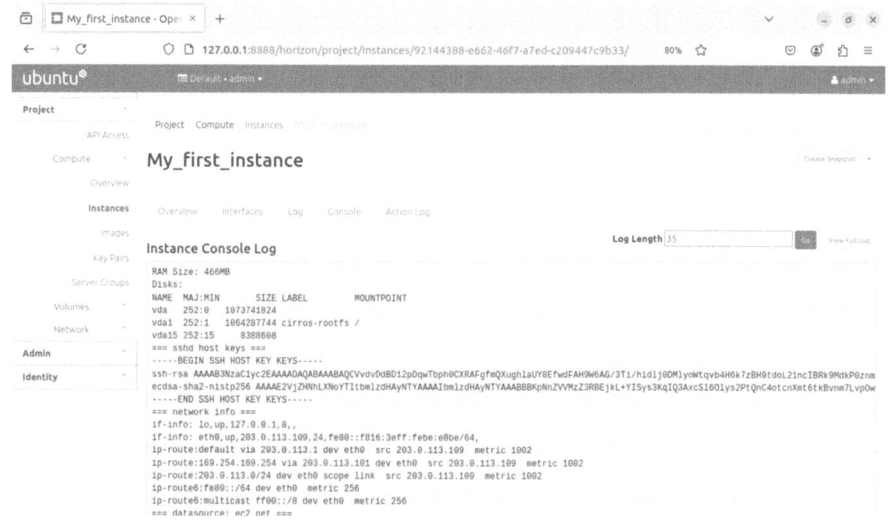

Figure 12-22. *OpenStack instance console log*

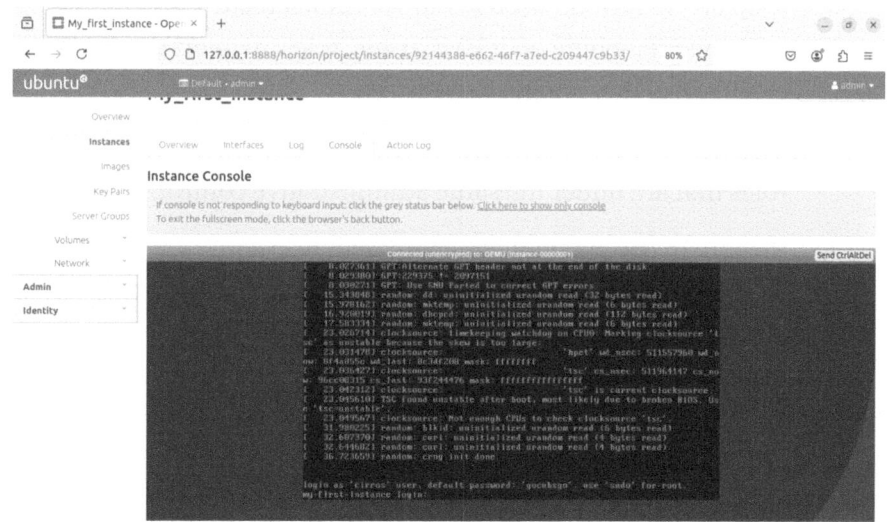

Figure 12-23. *OpenStack server console*

607

Of course, from the console, we can execute any command; we can see the credentials in the login page.

OpenStack Concepts

We have seen how to manage OpenStack from the dashboard. Before we move to the CLI, I'd like to introduce you to some important concepts used in OpenStack as well as in public cloud environments.

These concepts are

- Service: These are the components of OpenStack that we saw in the introduction, Nova, Glance, Neutron, etc.

- Endpoint: This is the URL to access any service. The easiest example is the URL we used to access Horizon, the dashboard.

- Project: We haven't used it, but we could create a project and include on it VMs, users, roles, networks, etc. It's useful to organize resources.

- Domain: They can be used to group projects, users, and roles that are under the same administrative control.

- Region: In certain deployments, it can be useful to have endpoints and other resources in a certain geographical area.

- User: This is self-explanatory.

- Role: This is a set of permissions associated with a user.

Using the CLI

So far, we have launched an OpenStack instance using the dashboard. But it is also possible to manage OpenStack using the command-line interface. We'll see some easy examples.

CHAPTER 12   CLOUD MANAGEMENT TOOLS

We already studied that OpenStack is composed of many components that provide different resources to end users. These components are called services, and we can get a list of them with **openstack service list**. This command must be executed as an OpenStack administrator. Usually, we log in the compute node as a normal user and then execute a bash file that contains the environmental variables needed to run commands in OpenStack as an administrator.

```
osbash@compute1:~$ ls -a
.               .cache        .ssh
config          log
..              .gnupg        .sudo_as_admin_successful
demo-openrc.sh  scripts
.bash_logout    .novaclient   .wget-hsts                  img
.bashrc         .profile      admin-openrc.sh             lib
osbash@compute1:~$ cat admin-openrc.sh
export OS_USERNAME=admin
export OS_PASSWORD=admin_user_secret
export OS_PROJECT_NAME=admin
export OS_USER_DOMAIN_NAME=Default
export OS_PROJECT_DOMAIN_NAME=Default
export OS_AUTH_URL=http://10.0.0.11:5000/v3
export OS_IDENTITY_API_VERSION=3
export OS_IMAGE_API_VERSION=2
osbash@compute1:~$
```

After loading this bash file in the current terminal session, we can execute the **openstack service list** command.

CHAPTER 12   CLOUD MANAGEMENT TOOLS

```
osbash@compute1:~$ source admin-openrc.sh
osbash@compute1:~$ openstack service list
+----------------------------------+-----------+---------------+
| ID                               | Name      | Type          |
+----------------------------------+-----------+---------------+
| 126bbd85513c492b91b49f4d35623ce5 | keystone  | identity      |
| 23f28d225f5c457c8257cf78ae20cad1 | glance    | image         |
| 278e59c0595e4fdda8e43b6fdfd0c126 | heat      | orchestration |
| 3032588ab8b1443f99e1ea90635a0ad7 | cinderv2  | volumev2      |
| 60a222d4fbff41ebaf9307ffcfbc1e94 | cinderv3  | volumev3      |
| 9041b237ff0a4245a5b6ab8d101b3dd7 | nova      | compute       |
| ed74e8d789004f098bcb7ae4621021d7 | placement | placement     |
| eda42ba1a7984357af9b3b50795a2c0f | neutron   | network       |
+----------------------------------+-----------+---------------+
```

We can also list the endpoints.

```
osbash@compute1:~$ openstack endpoint list
+----------------------------------+-----------+--------------
---------------+---------+----------+-----------------------------+
| ID                               | Region    | Service Name
| Service Type  | Enabled | Interface | URL                    |
+----------------------------------+-----------+--------------
---------------+---------+----------+-----------------------------+
| 10e12d4122db45c184974c13d370595d | RegionOne | glance
| image         | True    | internal  | http://controller:9292 |
| 247845229bc64bf8abdeff043229c965 | RegionOne | placement
| placement     | True    | internal  | http://controller:8778 |
| 2c49b2118b96403db98f29abb6ebecd8 | RegionOne | neutron
| network       | True    | internal  | http://controller:9696 |
| 2d128542789247999a16af7266e1bceb | RegionOne | keystone
| identity      | True    | public    | http://controller:5000/v3/ |
```

CHAPTER 12 CLOUD MANAGEMENT TOOLS

```
| 37de1cc8ab6b4288813b781da36a47e9 | RegionOne | nova
| compute        | True    | public    | http://controller:8774/v2.1 |
| 391fdce9c7c74066a8e0816a6d1d1bf2 | RegionOne | heat
| orchestration  | True    | admin     |
    .
    .
    .
```

It is also possible to list the users and the roles.

```
osbash@compute1:~$ openstack user list
+----------------------------------+------------------+
| ID                               | Name             |
+----------------------------------+------------------+
| 2d609f62ce35430cba06c1cf7ba5b494 | admin            |
    .
    .
    .

osbash@compute1:~$ openstack role list
+----------------------------------+------------------+
| ID                               | Name             |
+----------------------------------+------------------+
| 32d7a172d30d45a1b74ac1d934c338ba | reader           |
| 621734c9633e40389b1a36971b8d0957 | heat_stack_user  |
| c92d768fba804fbcb1f810713af703a4 | member           |
    .
    .
    .
```

611

CHAPTER 12   CLOUD MANAGEMENT TOOLS

We can list networks and images too.

```
osbash@compute1:~$ openstack network list
+--------------------------------------+-------------
+-----------------------------------+
| ID                                   | Name
| Subnets                           |
+--------------------------------------+-------------
+-----------------------------------+
| c1c3b68c-e173-4b22-94b0-c1d2abe76910 | provider
| 57d8116a-840e-49b6-92ec-96012153b2c3 |
| cfa15ed1-7316-4ae4-a281-f5a152bebf48 | selfservice
| f3b9f7de-1486-4459-8c6f-2897765c61e1 |
+--------------------------------------+-------------
+-----------------------------------+

osbash@compute1:~$ openstack image list
+--------------------------------------+--------------+-------+
| ID                                   | Name         | Status |
+--------------------------------------+--------------+-------+
| 066418a5-c297-46f4-a9f8-cfbd7db23434 | Cirros_0.6.2 | active |
| eb95752a-7cd9-45a3-8bfc-b20129e4028e | cirros       | active |
+--------------------------------------+--------------+-------+
```

It is also possible to list the instances on OpenStack:

```
osbash@compute1:~$ openstack server list
+--------------------------------------+------------------
+-------+----------------------+-------+---------+
| ID                                   | Name
| Status | Networks            | Image | Flavor  |
+--------------------------------------+------------------
+-------+----------------------+-------+---------+
```

```
| 92144388-e662-46f7-a7ed-c209447c9b33 | My_first_instance
| ACTIVE | provider=203.0.113.109 |          | Flavor1 |
+--------------------------------------+-------------------
+-------+-----------------------+-------+--------+
```

and show the characteristics of the instance:

```
osbash@compute1:~$ openstack server show My_first_instance
+-------------------------------------+--------------------+
| Field                               | Value              |
+-------------------------------------+--------------------+
| OS-DCF:diskConfig                   | AUTO               |
| OS-EXT-AZ:availability_zone         | nova               |
| OS-EXT-SRV-ATTR:host                | compute1           |
| OS-EXT-SRV-ATTR:hypervisor_hostname | compute1           |
| OS-EXT-SRV-ATTR:instance_name       | instance-00000001  |
| OS-EXT-STS:power_state              | Running            |
```

.

.

.

Terraform

Terraform is an Infrastructure as Code (IaC) software developed by the company HashiCorp. But what's exactly IaC? According to many, IaC consists of managing and provisioning computer data centers through definition files. These definition files are easily readable by both humans and machines alike.

Installing Terraform

We can download Terraform from its official website (Figure 12-24).

CHAPTER 12   CLOUD MANAGEMENT TOOLS

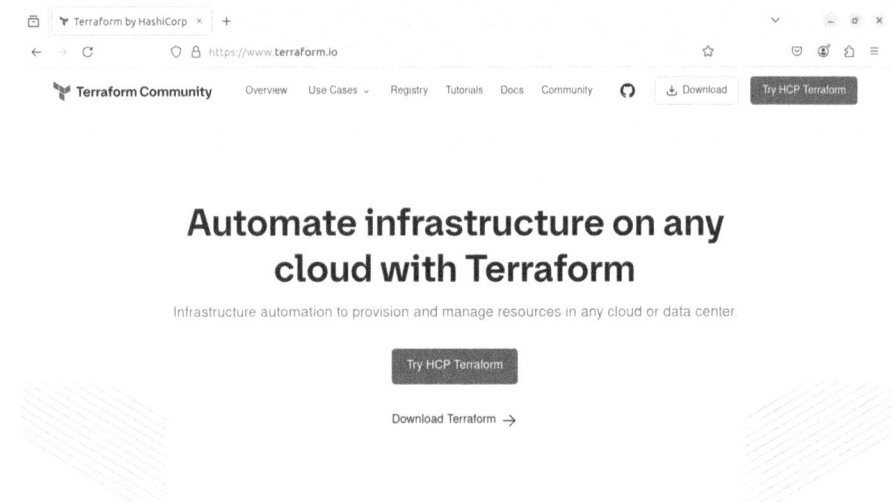

Figure 12-24. Terraform website

We click "Download Terraform" and select our OS (Figure 12-25).

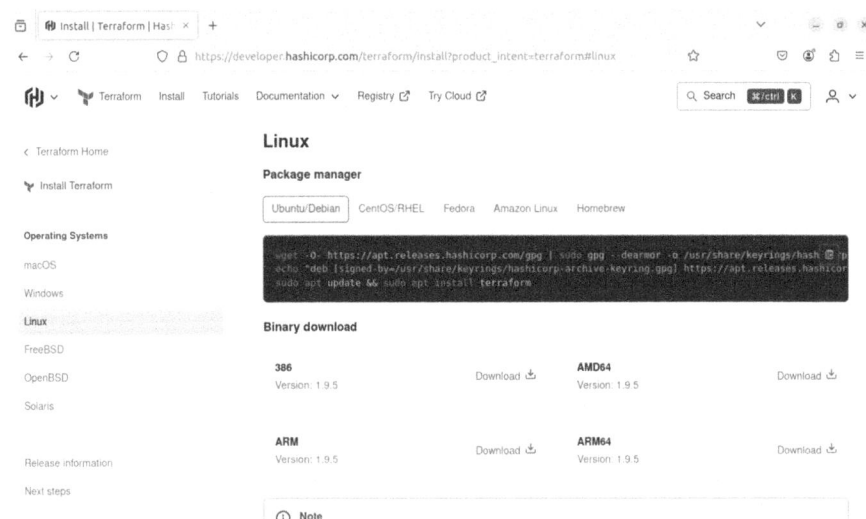

Figure 12-25. Downloading Terraform for Linux

CHAPTER 12   CLOUD MANAGEMENT TOOLS

We'll see that we have many options to install Terraform in our computer. At the time of writing this book, there are available versions for Windows, macOS, Linux, Solaris, FreeBSD, and OpenBSD. The instructions for installing it are very clear, so we won't go into much detail here.

If we're installing it in a Linux machine, we can define a new software repository from which to install Terraform. This is usually the preferred approach, as the binary and all of its associated libraries will be updated.

We can also install a stand-alone binary downloaded directly from the Terraform website. In that case, we'll need to unzip the package file and copy the binary extracted to a folder included in our PATH.

```
antonio@antonio-Laptop:~/terraform$ unzip terraform_1.9.5_linux_amd64.zip
Archive:  terraform_1.9.5_linux_amd64.zip
  inflating: LICENSE.txt
  inflating: terraform
antonio@antonio-Laptop:~/terraform$ cp terraform /usr/local/bin/
cp: cannot create regular file '/usr/local/bin/terraform': Permission denied
antonio@antonio-Laptop:~/terraform$ sudo cp terraform /usr/local/bin/
antonio@antonio-Laptop:~/terraform$
```

Whatever method we choose to install Terraform, we can easily check whether it is correctly installed by executing the following command:

```
antonio@antonio-Laptop:~/terraform$ terraform -version
Terraform v1.9.5
on linux_amd64
```

Chapter 12   Cloud Management Tools

Terraform Providers

Terraform is a tool that can help us to automate the deployment of new infrastructures; with Terraform, we can deploy new infrastructures in AWS, Azure, and many other different providers.

We can see the providers supported by Terraform on the Terraform registry (Figure 12-26). We can access this page by clicking "Registry" in the upper menu of the window from which we downloaded the Terraform software.

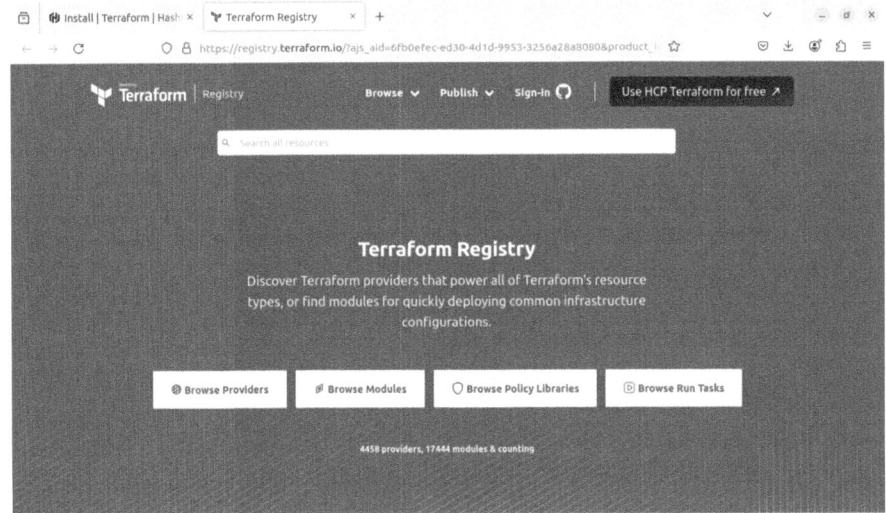

Figure 12-26. Terraform registry

By clicking "Browse Providers", we can search for the provider that we're interested in (Figure 12-27).

CHAPTER 12   CLOUD MANAGEMENT TOOLS

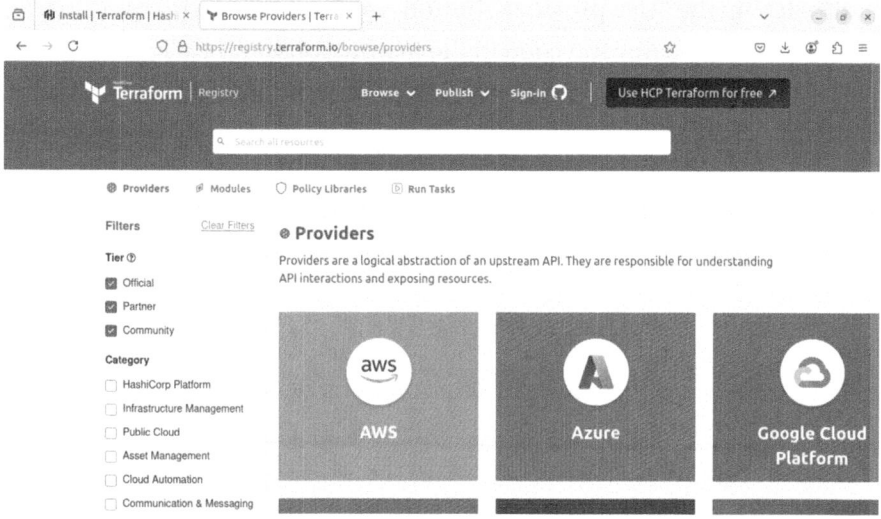

Figure 12-27. *Terraform providers*

In our example, we'll search for a Docker provider (Figure 12-28).

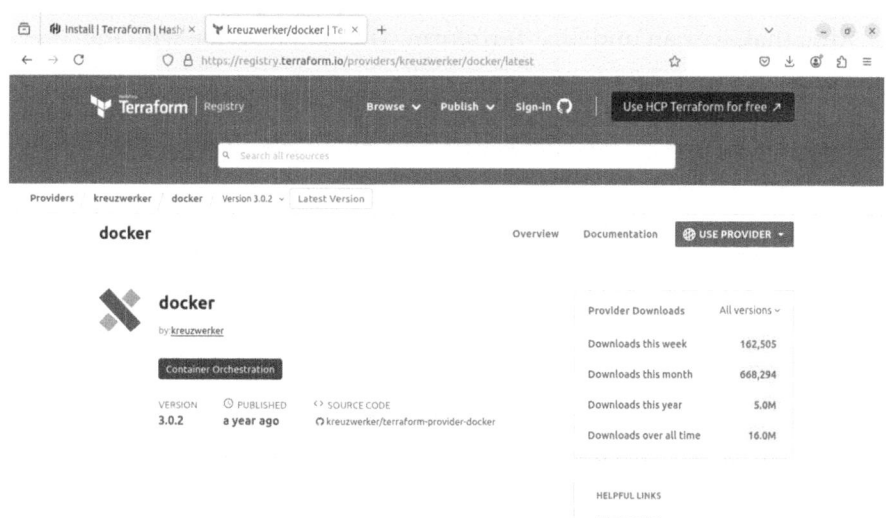

Figure 12-28. *Docker provider for Terraform*

By clicking the "Use provider" button, we'll see the instructions to use the provider. We'll copy the code in the instructions, and we'll paste it in a new Terraform file with tf extension named *"docker_example.tf"*.

```
antonio@antonio-Laptop:~/terraform$ cat docker_example.tf
terraform {
  required_providers {
    docker = {
      source = "kreuzwerker/docker"
      version = "3.0.2"
    }
  }
}

provider "docker" {
  # Configuration options
}
```

After that, we can initialize Terraform. This can be done with the **terraform init** command.

```
antonio@antonio-Laptop:~/terraform$ terraform init
Initializing the backend...
Initializing provider plugins...
- Finding kreuzwerker/docker versions matching "3.0.2"...
- Installing kreuzwerker/docker v3.0.2...
- Installed kreuzwerker/docker v3.0.2 (self-signed, key ID BD080C4571C6104C)
```

.
.
.

CHAPTER 12 CLOUD MANAGEMENT TOOLS

```
Terraform has been successfully initialized!
```
-
-
-

We are informed that Terraform initialized successfully. In the same page in which we saw the instructions to use the provider, we can click the "Documentation" link, and we'll see an example of how to use it (Figure 12-29).

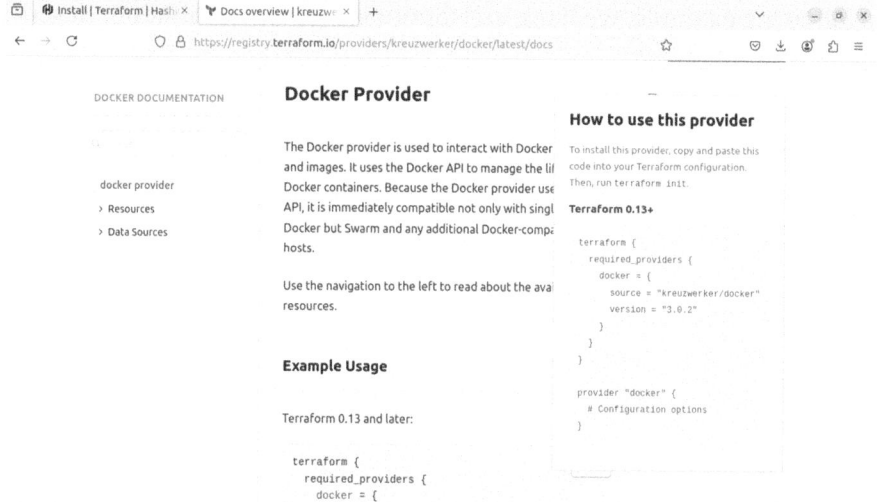

Figure 12-29. *Docker provider example usage*

First, we must specify the provider to use.

```
terraform {
  required_providers {
    docker = {
      source  = "kreuzwerker/docker"
      version = "3.0.2"
    }
  }
}
```

CHAPTER 12 CLOUD MANAGEMENT TOOLS

Second, we set the method we'll use to connect to docker, a unix socket in this case.

```
provider "docker" {
  host = "unix:///var/run/docker.sock"
}
```

Then we include the Docker resources we'll use in our deployment, for example, a Docker image that will be used to create a Docker container. In the following example, we'll use an Ubuntu image and a container based on that Ubuntu image.

```
# Pulls the image
resource "docker_image" "ubuntu" {
  name = "ubuntu:latest"
}

# Create a container
resource "docker_container" "foo" {
  image = docker_image.ubuntu.image_id
  name  = "foo"
}
```

If we need additional information about the parameters that we can use in Terraform with this provider, we can check for additional information in the left menu (Figure 12-30).

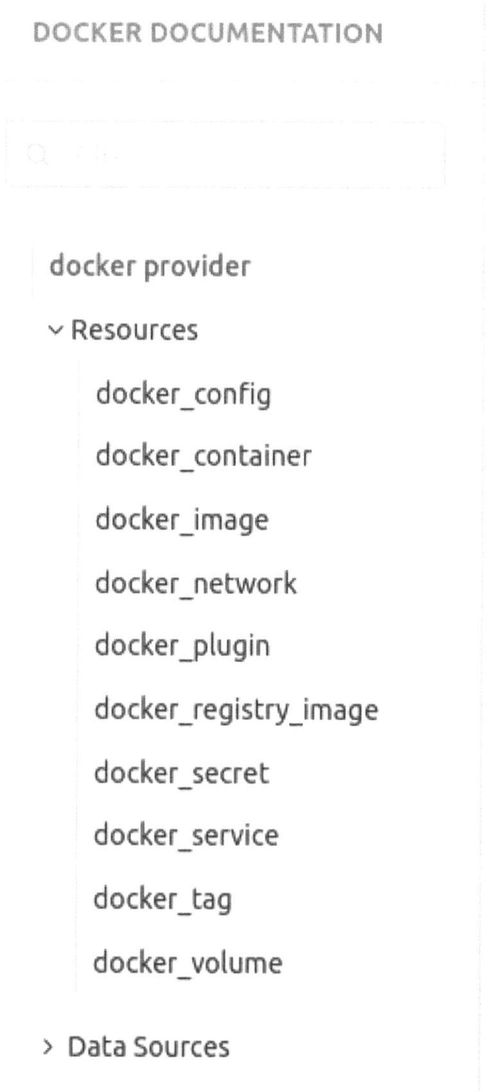

CHAPTER 12   CLOUD MANAGEMENT TOOLS

DOCKER DOCUMENTATION

docker provider

∨ Resources

docker_config

docker_container

docker_image

docker_network

docker_plugin

docker_registry_image

docker_secret

docker_service

docker_tag

docker_volume

> Data Sources

Figure 12-30. *Docker Terraform provider help*

CHAPTER 12   CLOUD MANAGEMENT TOOLS

Deploying Our Docker Infrastructure with Terraform

We are ready now to deploy Docker resources using Terraform; we'll see a few simple examples to better understand how Terraform works.

Deploying a Simple Ubuntu Docker Container

Let's get back to our *docker_example.tf* file and add the sections we just saw to have a complete example. This will be the full content of the file.

```
antonio@antonio-Laptop:~/terraform$ cat docker_example.tf
terraform {
  required_providers {
    docker = {
      source = "kreuzwerker/docker"
      version = "3.0.2"
    }
  }
}
provider "docker" {
  host = "unix:///var/run/docker.sock"
}

# Pulls the image
resource "docker_image" "ubuntu" {
  name = "ubuntu:latest"
}

# Create a container
resource "docker_container" "foo" {
  image = docker_image.ubuntu.image_id
  name  = "foo"
}
```

CHAPTER 12   CLOUD MANAGEMENT TOOLS

We'll initialize Terraform.

```
antonio@antonio-Laptop:~/terraform$ terraform init
Initializing the backend...
Initializing provider plugins...
- Reusing previous version of kreuzwerker/docker from the
dependency lock file
- Using previously-installed kreuzwerker/docker v3.0.2

Terraform has been successfully initialized!
.
.
```

Then we can validate the Terraform file. Validating a file checks whether the file is a valid Terraform file.

```
antonio@antonio-Laptop:~/terraform$ terraform validate
Success! The configuration is valid.
```

The next step will be to generate a plan; this way we enumerate all the actions that Terraform will perform while executing the file, but without actually performing them.

```
antonio@antonio-Laptop:~/terraform$ terraform plan

Planning failed. Terraform encountered an error while
generating this plan.

Error: Error pinging Docker server: Got permission denied
while trying to connect to the Docker daemon socket at
unix:///var/run/docker.sock: Get "http://%2Fvar%2Frun
.
.
.
```

623

CHAPTER 12 CLOUD MANAGEMENT TOOLS

We get an error because we need **sudo** permissions to connect to docker. We'll execute the command again using **sudo**.

antonio@antonio-Laptop:~/terraform$ sudo terraform plan

Terraform used the selected providers to generate the following execution plan. Resource actions are indicated with the following symbols:
  + create

Terraform will perform the following actions:

```
  # docker_container.foo will be created
  + resource "docker_container" "foo" {
      + attach                      = false
      + bridge                      = (known after apply)
      + command                     = (known after apply)
```
·
·
·
```
  # docker_image.ubuntu will be created
  + resource "docker_image" "ubuntu" {
      + id          = (known after apply)
      + image_id    = (known after apply)
      + name        = "ubuntu:latest"
      + repo_digest = (known after apply)
    }
```
·
·

CHAPTER 12　CLOUD MANAGEMENT TOOLS

Finally, we use terraform apply to actually execute all the actions.

antonio@antonio-Laptop:~/terraform$ sudo terraform apply

Terraform used the selected providers to generate the following execution plan. Resource actions are indicated with the following symbols:
  + create

Terraform will perform the following actions:

```
  # docker_container.foo will be created
  + resource "docker_container" "foo" {
      + attach                      = false
      + bridge                      = (known after apply)
      + command                     = (known after apply)
      + container_logs              = (known after apply)
.
.
.
Plan: 2 to add, 0 to change, 0 to destroy.

Do you want to perform these actions?
  Terraform will perform the actions described above.
  Only 'yes' will be accepted to approve.

  Enter a value: yes

docker_image.ubuntu: Creating...
docker_image.ubuntu: Creation complete after 0s [id=sha256:35
a88802559dd2077e584394471ddaa1a2c5bfd16893b829ea57619301eb3908u
buntu:latest]
docker_container.foo: Creating...
```

```
Error: container exited immediately
  with docker_container.foo,
  on docker_example.tf line 20, in resource "docker_
  container" "foo":
  20: resource "docker_container" "foo" {
```

We can see that the container was created, but then we immediately get an error. We can clearly see the message "container exited immediately". This is normal behavior; if we remember, when we studied containers, we saw that containers have a main process associated that they're supposed to execute. When the execution is completed, the container exits. A system container, like the Ubuntu container we used in our first deployment with Terraform, usually executes a shell as the main process. So the shell executes and, as there is no interaction with that shell, immediately exits.

We also saw that we could execute application containers, like Apache or nginx containers. In these cases, the main process is a server process, httpd or nginx, respectively. These processes keep running until they're explicitly shut down or an error arises.

When we use Terraform to deploy Docker containers, we're just automating what we'd do by hand. So as we said before, the behavior with the deployed Ubuntu container is normal.

Deploying an Apache httpd Docker Container

To better understand this, let's create another Terraform file. This time we'll use an Apache web container.

```
antonio@antonio-Laptop:~/terraform$ cat docker_example2.tf
terraform {
  required_providers {
```

CHAPTER 12 CLOUD MANAGEMENT TOOLS

```
    docker = {
      source = "kreuzwerker/docker"
      version = "3.0.2"
    }
  }
}
provider "docker" {
  host = "unix:///var/run/docker.sock"
}
# Pulls the image
resource "docker_image" "httpd" {
  name = "httpd:latest"
}
# Create a container
resource "docker_container" "apache" {
  image = docker_image.httpd.image_id
  name  = "apache"
}
```

This file is very similar to the first example; in this case, we replaced the Ubuntu image with an Apache httpd image, and we create a container based on that Apache httpd container.

We should keep every Terraform example in its own folder, so we'll create a new folder and copy our new *docker_example2.tf* file to that folder.

```
antonio@antonio-Laptop:~/terraform$ mkdir ../terraform2
antonio@antonio-Laptop:~/terraform$ mv docker_example2.tf ../
terraform2/
antonio@antonio-Laptop:~/terraform$ cd ../terraform2/
```

CHAPTER 12   CLOUD MANAGEMENT TOOLS

We initialize Terraform as we did in the first example.

```
antonio@antonio-Laptop:~/terraform2$ terraform init
Initializing the backend...
Initializing provider plugins...
- Finding kreuzwerker/docker versions matching "3.0.2"...
- Installing kreuzwerker/docker v3.0.2...
- Installed kreuzwerker/docker v3.0.2 (self-signed, key ID BD080C4571C6104C)
.
.
.
Terraform has been successfully initialized!
```

We can also validate the file to make sure it is valid.

```
antonio@antonio-Laptop:~/terraform2$ terraform validate
Success! The configuration is valid.
```

Finally, we apply the configuration.

```
antonio@antonio-Laptop:~/terraform2$ sudo terraform apply
.
.
.
Terraform will perform the following actions:
  # docker_container.apache will be created
  + resource "docker_container" "apache" {
      + attach                                      = false
      + bridge                                      = (known after apply)
      + command                                     = (known after apply)
.
.
```

CHAPTER 12   CLOUD MANAGEMENT TOOLS

Plan: 2 to add, 0 to change, 0 to destroy.

Do you want to perform these actions?

·
·

  Enter a value: yes

·
·

Apply complete! Resources: 2 added, 0 changed, 0 destroyed.

This time we didn't get any error, and we can check with **docker ps** that a new container has been created.

```
antonio@antonio-Laptop:~/terraform2$ sudo docker ps
CONTAINER ID     IMAGE           COMMAND                 CREATED
   STATUS            PORTS       NAMES
13b34fc50ea9     a49fd2c04c02    "httpd-foreground"      33 seconds ago
   Up 33 seconds     80/tcp      apache
```

We can work normally with our deployed infrastructure; when we no longer need it, we delete it with **terraform destroy**.

```
antonio@antonio-Laptop:~/terraform2$ sudo terraform destroy
```
·
·
·

Terraform will perform the following actions:

  # docker_container.apache will be destroyed
  - resource "docker_container" "apache" {
    - attach   = false -> null
·
·
·

629

CHAPTER 12 CLOUD MANAGEMENT TOOLS

```
Do you really want to destroy all resources?
•
•
Destroy complete! Resources: 2 destroyed.
```

Deploying a Customized Ubuntu Docker Container

Now that we could successfully deploy a Docker Apache container, we'll see how to customize the deployment from the first example.

We already saw on the Docker Terraform provider page that we could get help about the different parameters we can use in our Terraform file (Figure 12-30).

We are interested in changing the command used to start the container so that the container doesn't exit immediately. If we review again the help, we'll see this option (Figure 12-31).

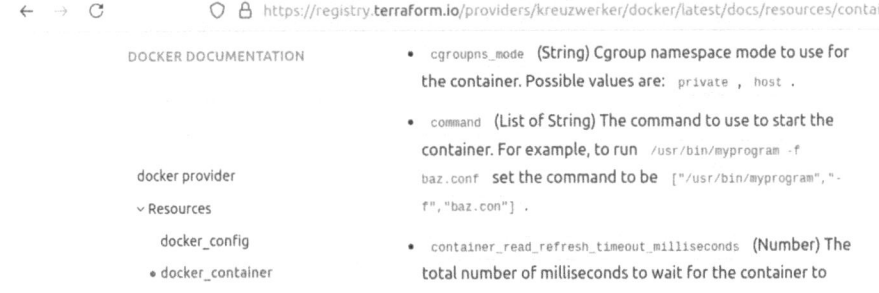

Figure 12-31. The command option

We'll edit our *docker_example.tf* file to include this new parameter. We'll define as the new command a **tail -f** of the */dev/null* special device. This command doesn't do anything; it's just a way to keep the command executing so that the container doesn't exit immediately.

CHAPTER 12 CLOUD MANAGEMENT TOOLS

```
antonio@antonio-Laptop:~/terraform$ cat docker_example.tf
terraform {
  required_providers {
    docker = {
      source = "kreuzwerker/docker"
      version = "3.0.2"
    }
  }
}

provider "docker" {
  host = "unix:///var/run/docker.sock"
}

# Pulls the image
resource "docker_image" "ubuntu" {
  name = "ubuntu:latest"
}

# Create a container
resource "docker_container" "foo" {
  image = docker_image.ubuntu.image_id
  name  = "foo"
  command = ["tail", "-f", "/dev/null"]
}
```

And we'll repeat the procedure to deploy it.

```
antonio@antonio-Laptop:~/terraform$ terraform init
  .
  .
antonio@antonio-Laptop:~/terraform$ terraform validate
Success! The configuration is valid.
```

```
antonio@antonio-HP-Laptop-15s-fq1xxx:~/terraform$ sudo
terraform apply
docker_image.ubuntu: Refreshing state...
.
.
Apply complete! Resources: 1 added, 0 changed, 0 destroyed.
```

This time we don't get any error. And if we list the containers with docker ps, we'll see a new Ubuntu container.

```
antonio@antonio-Laptop:~/terraform$ sudo docker ps
CONTAINER ID    IMAGE           COMMAND
CREATED              STATUS          PORTS     NAMES
8f12ab780ff8    35a88802559d    "tail -f /dev/null"
10 seconds ago    Up 9 seconds              foo
```

When we finish, we can destroy our Terraform infrastructure.

```
antonio@antonio-Laptop:~/terraform$ sudo terraform destroy
```

Deploying a Customized Apache httpd Docker Container

Now we'll make a small customization to our Apache container to map a port. We'll look at the help in the Docker provider web page, and we'll see the ports option (Figure 12-32).

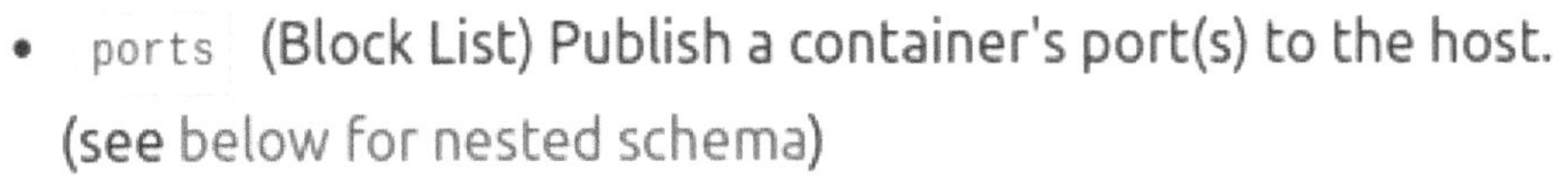

- `ports` (Block List) Publish a container's port(s) to the host. (see below for nested schema)

Figure 12-32. *The ports option*

So we'll edit the *docker_example2.tf* file to map port 8080 in the host to port 80 in the container. Now it should look more or less like this:

```
antonio@antonio-Laptop:~/terraform2$ cat docker_example2.tf
terraform {
  required_providers {
    docker = {
      source  = "kreuzwerker/docker"
      version = "3.0.2"
    }
  }
}
provider "docker" {
  host = "unix:///var/run/docker.sock"
}

# Pulls the image
resource "docker_image" "httpd" {
  name = "httpd:latest"
}

# Create a container
resource "docker_container" "apache" {
  image = docker_image.httpd.image_id
  name  = "apache"
  ports {
    internal = 80
    external = 8080
  }
}
```

CHAPTER 12   CLOUD MANAGEMENT TOOLS

We'll repeat the usual procedure to apply the Terraform configuration.

```
antonio@antonio-Laptop:~/terraform2$ terraform init
antonio@antonio-Laptop:~/terraform2$ terraform validate
antonio@antonio-Laptop:~/terraform2$ sudo terraform apply
.
.
    + ports {
        + external = 8080
        + internal = 80
        + ip       = "0.0.0.0"
        + protocol = "tcp"
      }
.
.
```

If we list the containers, we'll see the port redirection.

```
antonio@antonio-Laptop:~/terraform2$ sudo docker container ls
CONTAINER ID    IMAGE              COMMAND
CREATED                 STATUS             PORTS                    NAMES
1e76ffd7cc74    a49fd2c04c02    "httpd-foreground"
 About a minute ago  Up About a minute  0.0.0.0:8080->80/tcp   apache
```

Of course, if we open a web browser and point it to port 8080 on the localhost in which we applied the Terraform file, we'll see the Apache welcome page (Figure 12-33).

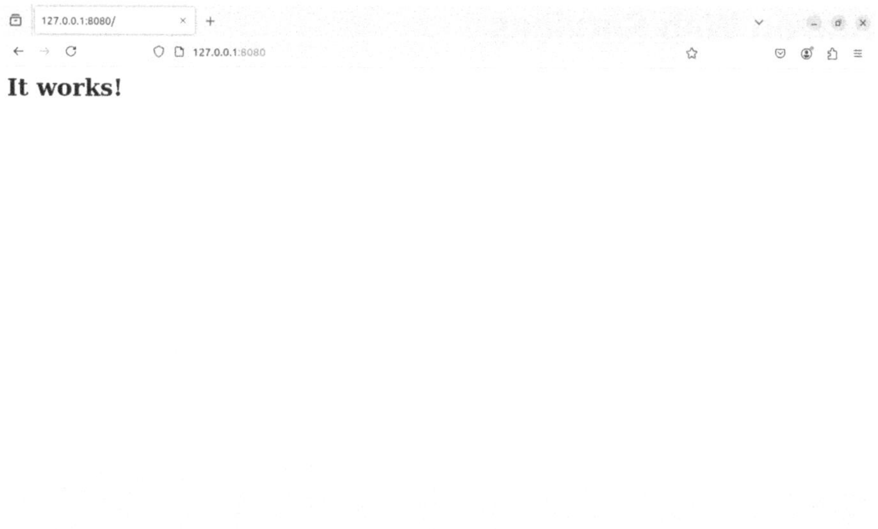

CHAPTER 12   CLOUD MANAGEMENT TOOLS

Figure 12-33.   Apache welcome page

Public Clouds

We've already studied the main characteristics of cloud computing. We saw that we can have different types of clouds, such as public clouds, private clouds, or hybrid clouds. When the cloud services are made available to the general public, either freely or by a paid subscription, we consider the cloud to be public.

Some of the best-known public cloud offerings are

- Amazon Web Services
- Microsoft Azure
- Google Cloud

But there are also many more.

CHAPTER 12   CLOUD MANAGEMENT TOOLS

Amazon Web Services

Amazon Web Services, AWS for short, is the on-demand cloud computing platform offered by Amazon to individuals and companies. From the main page (Figure 12-34), we can access the different offerings, documentation, etc.

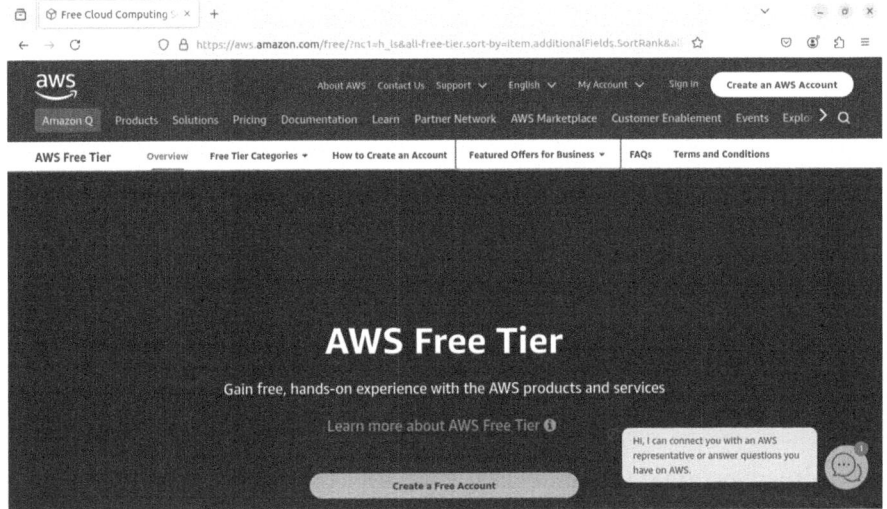

Figure 12-34.   Amazon Web Services main page

The public cloud offering changes very often, and it is quite likely that when you read this book, the services offered by AWS, and the other providers, will have changed. For that reason, we won't go into detail about the services provided. However, we can always assume that we'll be given several solutions of the type IaaS, PaaS, and SaaS. To better understand which one is the right one for us, we'll need to review the official documentation or talk to a sales representative. If we browse through the site, we'll see that currently a lot of products are available on the cloud either for free or for a fee.

CHAPTER 12   CLOUD MANAGEMENT TOOLS

Microsoft Azure

Microsoft also has its own public cloud computing offering, which is called Microsoft Azure. From the main page (Figure 12-35), we can access the Azure-related products and resources.

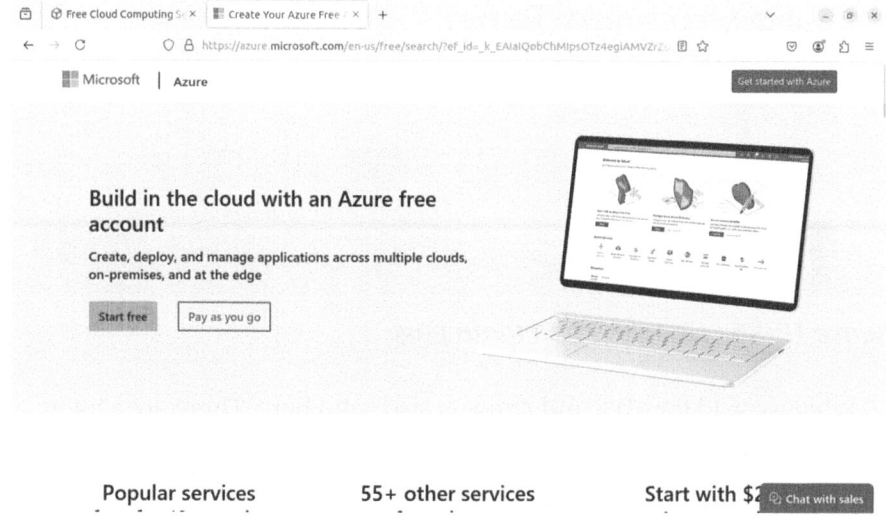

Figure 12-35. Azure main page

What we explained for AWS is also valid for Azure. The offering is so large, and it changes so fast that it is not very useful to memorize it. It is definitely more important to understand the concepts of IaaS, PaaS, and SaaS that we studied before. This way, we'll be capable to determine which solution provided by Azure, or other provider, suits better to our needs.

Google Cloud

Another major player in the public cloud field is, of course, Google (Figure 12-36).

Chapter 12 Cloud Management Tools

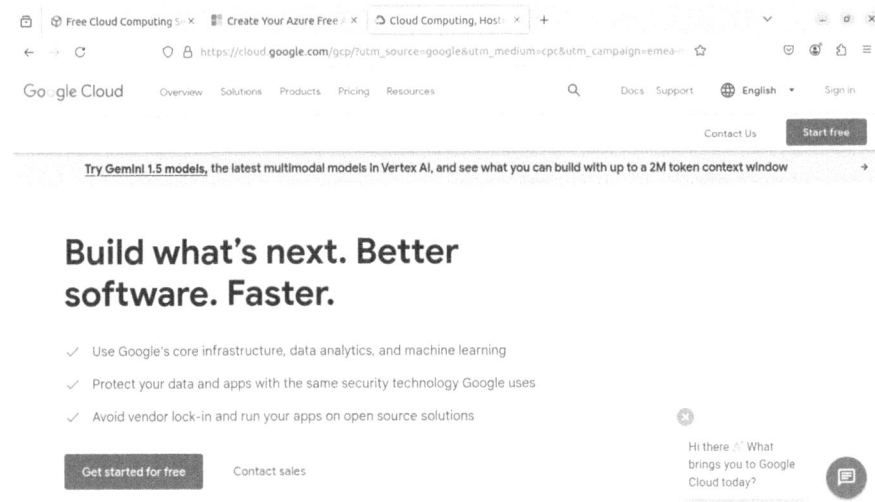

Figure 12-36. Google Cloud main page

What we said for AWS and Azure is also valid here. There are a lot of products available, but if we understand the cloud computing concepts that we studied, we'll know which one fits our needs.

Summary

In this brief chapter, we studied cloud computing, understanding its main concepts. We learned the basics of managing a private cloud using OpenStack. We also introduced Terraform, a very powerful for automating provisioning. We saw a couple of examples in which we used Terraform to provision Docker containers, but Terraform can be used with a lot of different providers and supports deployments much more complex than the ones we've seen in our examples.

CHAPTER 12　CLOUD MANAGEMENT TOOLS

We also took a look at some of the most important public cloud providers. Though we didn't go in depth investigating their offerings because they change frequently, the most important thing is to understand the key concepts.

In addition to OpenStack, there are also other similar cloud computing platforms like Apache CloudStack, Eucalyptus, and OpenNebula. We haven't studied these platforms here, but it is important that you're aware of their existence. They're great tools that, in certain cases, could be more appropriate than OpenStack itself.

CHAPTER 13

Packer

In this chapter, we'll cover the following concepts:

- Understand the functionality and features of Packer
- Create and maintain template files
- Build images from template files using different builders

Introduction to Packer

Packer is an open source tool to create golden images for different platforms from a single source file. It standardizes and automates the process of building system and container images. It can generate images for VirtualBox, AWS, VMware, and many others.

Installing Packer

Packer can be installed from the official website (Figure 13-1), but it can also be installed from the official repositories of the main distributions. The preferred way to install it is by adding the official repositories so that the software is always up to date. But we could also install a stand-alone binary or use the repositories of our favorite Linux distribution.

CHAPTER 13   PACKER

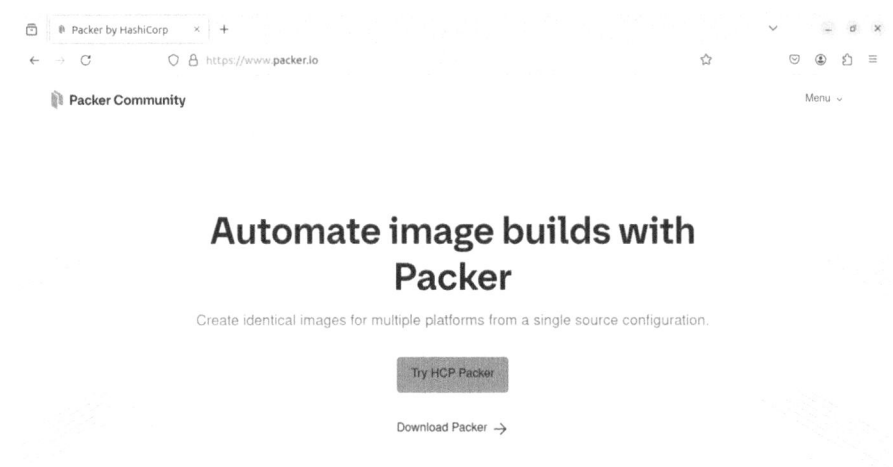

Figure 13-1. Packer website

Even though it is not the preferred way to install it, for the purposes of this book, we'll install it by downloading the binary version (Figure 13-2).

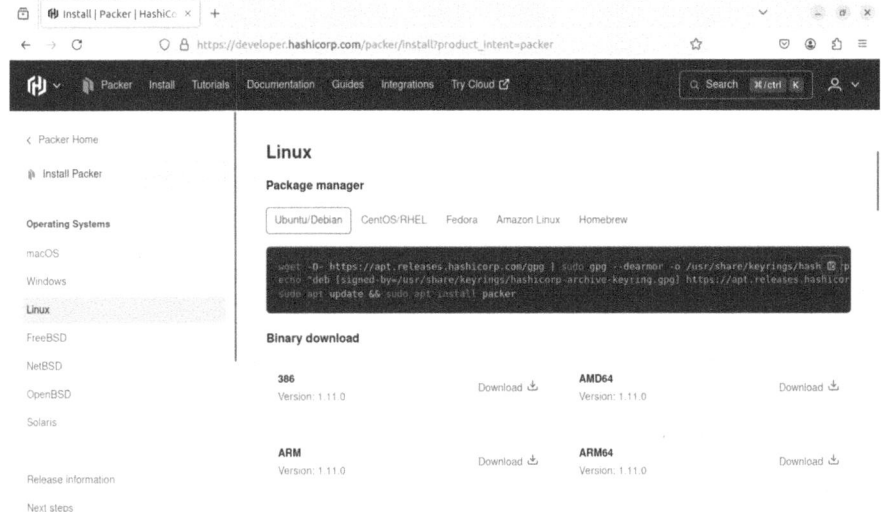

Figure 13-2. Downloading the Packer binary

After downloading the zip package with the binary file, we uncompress it.

```
antonio@antonio-Laptop:~/packer$ wget https://releases.
hashicorp.com/packer/1.11.0/packer_1.11.0_linux_amd64.zip
antonio@antonio-Laptop:~/packer$ unzip packer_1.11.0_linux_
amd64.zip
Archive:  packer_1.11.0_linux_amd64.zip
  inflating: LICENSE.txt
  inflating: packer
```

We can now start to work with **packer,** for our convenience, we can copy the binary file to a destination included in our path so that it can be launched from anywhere.

```
antonio@antonio-Laptop:~/packer$ cp packer /usr/local/bin/
antonio@antonio-Laptop:~/packer$ packer
Usage: packer [--version] [--help] <command> [<args>]

Available commands are:
    build           build image(s) from template
    console         creates a console for testing variable
                    interpolation
    fix             fixes templates from old versions of packer
    fmt             Rewrites HCL2 config files to
                    canonical format
    hcl2_upgrade    transform a JSON template into an HCL2
                    configuration
    init            Install missing plugins or upgrade plugins
    inspect         see components of a template
    plugins         Interact with Packer plugins and catalog
    validate        check that a template is valid
    version         Prints the Packer version
```

CHAPTER 13   PACKER

Packer Integrations (Plug-ins)

Packer uses plug-ins to create the images. We can have an overview of the Packer Integrations available by selecting "Integrations" in the upper menu (Figure 13-3).

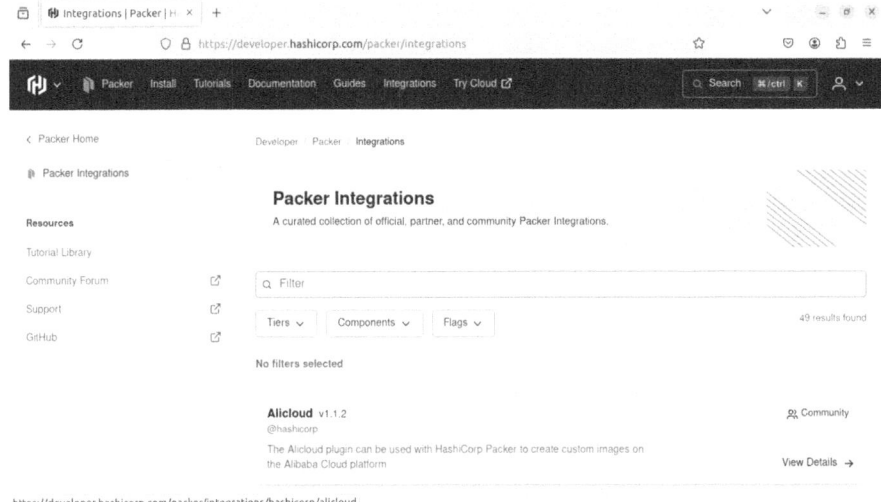

Figure 13-3.   Packer Integrations

There are many plug-ins available; we can select the VirtualBox, for example (Figure 13-4).

CHAPTER 13 PACKER

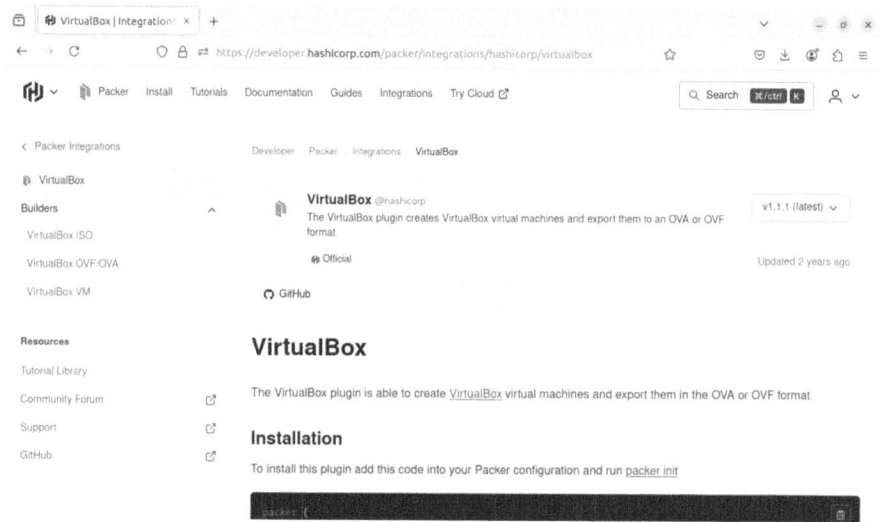

Figure 13-4. *VirtualBox Packer Integration*

We can see the instructions to install this plug-in. This plug-in comes with three different builders that we can use to build the image. Depending on the builder we use, we can start from an ISO file, an ova/ovf file, or a running virtual machine.

Installing a Packer Plug-In

To work with the plug-in, we need to install it. As we can see in the documentation, there are two ways to do it. We can create a file with the following content:

```
antonio@antonio-Laptop:~/packer$ cat vboxplugin.pkr.hcl
packer {
    required_plugins {
        virtualbox = {
            version = "~> 1"
```

645

```
            source  = "github.com/hashicorp/virtualbox"
        }
    }
}
```

And then we execute **packer init**.

```
antonio@antonio-Laptop:~/packer$ packer init vboxplugin.pkr.hcl
Installed plugin github.com/hashicorp/virtualbox v1.1.1 in "/
home/antonio/.config/packer/plugins/github.com/hashicorp/
virtualbox/packer-plugin-virtualbox_v1.1.1_x5.0_linux_amd64"
```

Or we can execute **packer plugins install**.

```
antonio@antonio-Laptop:~/packer$ packer plugins install github.
com/hashicorp/virtualbox
```

Whatever method we choose, the plug-in will be installed.

```
antonio@antonio-Laptop:~/packer$ packer plugins installed
/home/antonio/.config/packer/plugins/github.com/hashicorp/
virtualbox/packer-plugin-virtualbox_v1.1.1_x5.0_linux_amd64
```

Building an Image

Once we have the needed plug-in installed, we can create the corresponding image. We can use different plug-ins to create different images. We'll see a couple of examples.

Building a VirtualBox Image

We'll use an ISO file to generate an image; to do it, we can follow the instructions in the page from HashiCorp (Figure 13-5).

CHAPTER 13   PACKER

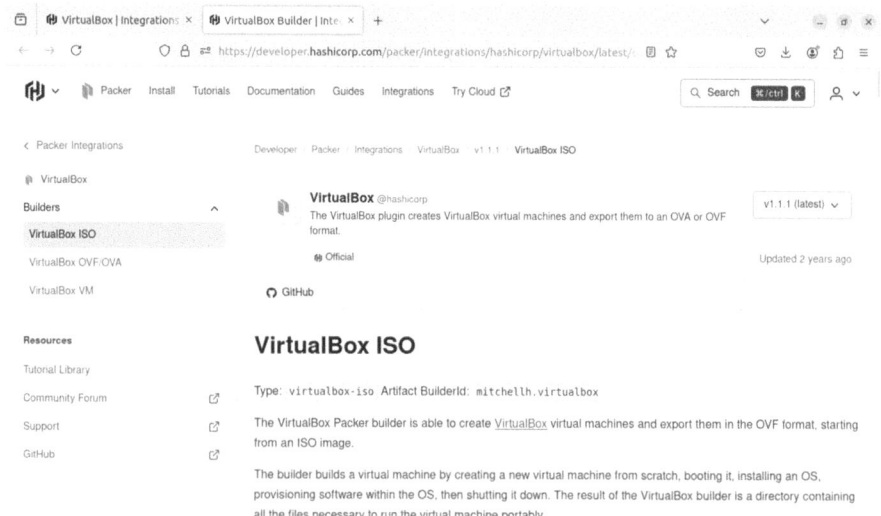

Figure 13-5. *VirtualBox Packer builder*

In the same page, we can see a code sample to generate the image. We just need to create a new file and paste that code into it. The code is written in HashiCorp Configuration Language (HCL); sometimes we can find code in JSON, but the HCL format is preferred. This file will be our source file.

```
antonio@antonio-Laptop:~/packer$ cat virtualboxiso.pkr.hcl
source "virtualbox-iso" "basic-example" {
  guest_os_type = "Ubuntu_64"
  iso_url = "http://releases.ubuntu.com/12.04/ubuntu-12.04.5-
  server-amd64.iso"
  iso_checksum = "md5:769474248a3897f4865817446f9a4a53"
  ssh_username = "packer"
  ssh_password = "packer"
  shutdown_command = "echo 'packer' | sudo -S shutdown -P now"
}
```

647

```
build {
  sources = ["sources.virtualbox-iso.basic-example"]
}
```

To generate the image, we use **packer build**.

```
antonio@antonio-Laptop:~/packer$ packer build
virtualboxiso.pkr.hcl
virtualbox-iso.basic-example: output will be in this color.

==> virtualbox-iso.basic-example: Retrieving Guest additions
==> virtualbox-iso.basic-example: Trying /usr/share/virtualbox/
VBoxGuestAdditions.iso
==> virtualbox-iso.basic-example: Trying /usr/share/virtualbox/
VBoxGuestAdditions.iso
==> virtualbox-iso.basic-example: /usr/share/virtualbox/
VBoxGuestAdditions.iso => /usr/share/virtualbox/
VBoxGuestAdditions.iso
==> virtualbox-iso.basic-example: Retrieving ISO
==> virtualbox-iso.basic-example: Trying http://releases.
ubuntu.com/12.04/ubuntu-12.04.5-server-amd64.iso
==> virtualbox-iso.basic-example: Trying http://releases.
ubuntu.com/12.04/ubuntu-12.04.5-server-amd64.iso?checksum=md5%
3A769474248a3897f4865817446f9a4a53
```

.
.
.

In a few seconds, we'll see a VirtualBox console popping up (Figure 13-6).

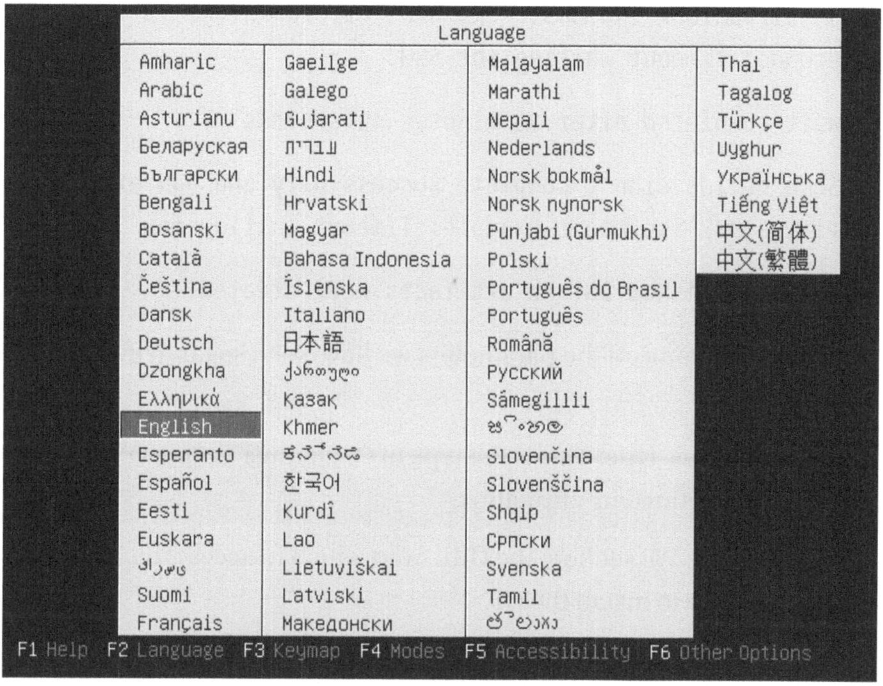

Figure 13-6. Ubuntu server installation

As the documentation said, this example is not completely functional because we haven't provided a way to automate the installation of the server. We can either cancel the build of the server or wait for the standard timeout to trigger; in any case, the VM created to generate the final image will be deleted.

```
==> virtualbox-iso.basic-example: Waiting for SSH to become
available...
==> virtualbox-iso.basic-example: Timeout waiting for SSH.
==> virtualbox-iso.basic-example: Cleaning up floppy disk...
==> virtualbox-iso.basic-example: Deregistering and
deleting VM...
==> virtualbox-iso.basic-example: Deleting output directory...
```

CHAPTER 13   PACKER

```
Build 'virtualbox-iso.basic-example' errored after 12 minutes
49 seconds: Timeout waiting for SSH.

==> Wait completed after 12 minutes 49 seconds

==> Some builds didn't complete successfully and had errors:
--> virtualbox-iso.basic-example: Timeout waiting for SSH.

==> Builds finished but no artifacts were created.
```

Let's review some of the parameters we have seen so far in the source file:

- guest_os_type: This is the type of OS; it must be one OS type defined in VirtualBox.
- iso_url: We set here the URL from which to access the ISO file to install the OS.
- iso_checksum: This is the checksum of the ISO file.
- ssh_username and ssh_password: These are the credentials used to access the VM through ssh.
- shutdown_command: This is the command that will be used to gracefully shut down the VM. Otherwise, some changes might not be saved to the image.

The file has two main sections: a source section and a build section that references precisely the source section.

We can get a list of the OS types defined in VirtualBox with **VboxManage**.

```
antonio@antonio-Laptop:~/packer$ VBoxManage list ostypes
 ·
 ·
ID:          Ubuntu_64
Description: Ubuntu (64-bit)
```

CHAPTER 13 PACKER

```
Family ID:    Linux
Family Desc:  Linux
64 bit:       true
```
·
·
```
ID:           Ubuntu21_64
Description:  Ubuntu 21.04 (Hirsute Hippo) / 21.10 (Impish
Indri) (64-bit)
Family ID:    Linux
Family Desc:  Linux
64 bit:       true

ID:           Ubuntu22_LTS_64
Description:  Ubuntu 22.04 LTS (Jammy Jellyfish) (64-bit)
Family ID:    Linux
Family Desc:  Linux
64 bit:       true
```
·
·

Building an LXC Image

Now, we're going to create an LXC image. In the Packer web page, we can also find an LXC plug-in (Figure 13-7).

CHAPTER 13   PACKER

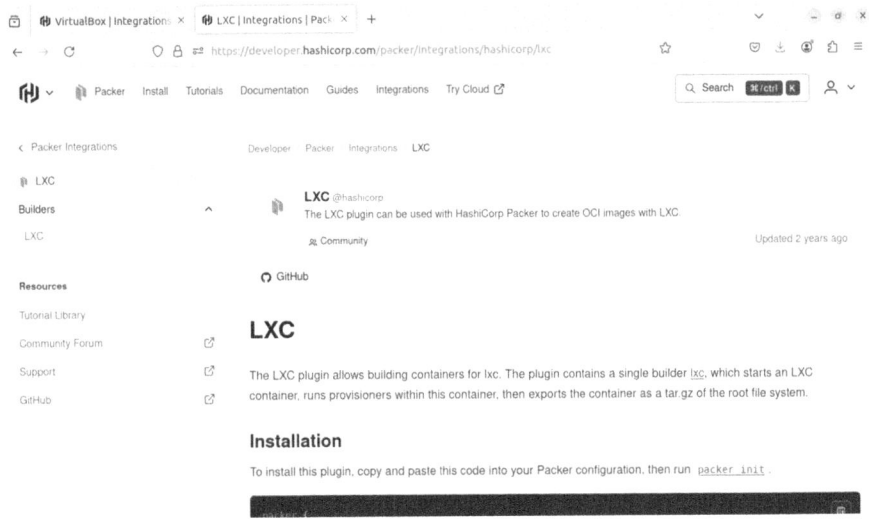

Figure 13-7. *LXC Packer Integration*

We follow the instructions to install the plug-in, as we did before.

antonio@antonio-Laptop:~/packer$ packer plugins install github.com/hashicorp/lxc
Installed plugin github.com/hashicorp/lxc v1.0.2 in "/home/antonio/.config/packer/plugins/github.com/hashicorp/lxc/packer-plugin-lxc_v1.0.2_x5.0_linux_amd64"

If we list the installed plug-ins again, we'll see that we have both: the VirtualBox plug-in and the LXC plug-in.

antonio@antonio-Laptop:~/packer$ packer plugins installed
/home/antonio/.config/packer/plugins/github.com/hashicorp/lxc/packer-plugin-lxc_v1.0.2_x5.0_linux_amd64
/home/antonio/.config/packer/plugins/github.com/hashicorp/virtualbox/packer-plugin-virtualbox_v1.1.1_x5.0_linux_amd64

CHAPTER 13 PACKER

The VirtualBox Packer Integration/plug-in had three different builders. This plug-in instead has only one, and in the documentation, we can see a sample file that we can use as a basic example with some modifications. Below we can see the sample file.

```
antonio@antonio-Laptop:~/packer/lxc$ cat lxc.json
{
  "builders": [
    {
      "type": "lxc",
      "name": "lxc-trusty",
      "config_file": "/tmp/lxc/config",
      "template_name": "ubuntu",
      "template_environment_vars": ["SUITE=trusty"]
    },
    {
      "type": "lxc",
      "name": "lxc-xenial",
      "config_file": "/tmp/lxc/config",
      "template_name": "ubuntu",
      "template_environment_vars": ["SUITE=xenial"]
    },
    {
      "type": "lxc",
      "name": "lxc-jessie",
      "config_file": "/tmp/lxc/config",
      "template_name": "debian",
      "template_environment_vars": ["SUITE=jessie"]
    },
```

```
    {
      "type": "lxc",
      "name": "lxc-centos-7-x64",
      "config_file": "/tmp/lxc/config",
      "template_name": "centos",
      "template_parameters": ["-R", "7", "-a", "x86_64"]
    }
  ]
}
```

This file is in JSON format, and the preferred format is the HCL format, so the first thing we need to do is to convert it to hcl.

```
antonio@antonio-Laptop:~/packer/lxc$ packer hcl2_upgrade lxc.json
Ignoring following sources.Parse error: unknown builder type(s): [lxc lxc lxc lxc]

Successfully created lxc.json.pkr.hcl. Exit 1
```

We get an error message; we'll get back to it later, but the conversion seems to have created a new file in HCL format.

```
antonio@antonio-Laptop:~/packer/lxc$ cat lxc.json.pkr.hcl
source "lxc" "lxc-centos-7-x64" {
  config_file         = "/tmp/lxc/config"
  template_name       = "centos"
  template_parameters = ["-R", "7", "-a", "x86_64"]
}

source "lxc" "lxc-jessie" {
  config_file              = "/tmp/lxc/config"
  template_environment_vars = ["SUITE=jessie"]
  template_name            = "debian"
}
```

```
source "lxc" "lxc-trusty" {
  config_file               = "/tmp/lxc/config"
  template_environment_vars = ["SUITE=trusty"]
  template_name             = "ubuntu"
}
source "lxc" "lxc-xenial" {
  config_file               = "/tmp/lxc/config"
  template_environment_vars = ["SUITE=xenial"]
  template_name             = "ubuntu"
}
build {
  sources = ["source.lxc.lxc-centos-7-x64", "source.lxc.lxc-jessie", "source.lxc.lxc-trusty", "source.lxc.lxc-xenial"]
}
```

Now we'll edit this file; we just need a single LXC container, so we'll remove the rest and edit the build section accordingly. The final file will look like this:

```
antonio@antonio-Laptop:~/packer/lxc$ cat lxc.json.pkr.hcl
source "lxc" "lxc-trusty" {
  config_file               = "/tmp/lxc/config"
  template_environment_vars = ["SUITE=trusty"]
  template_name             = "ubuntu"
}
build {
  sources = ["source.lxc.lxc-trusty"]
}
```

CHAPTER 13   PACKER

We still need to make some more modifications; in the parameter config file, we need to specify the path of the configuration file for LXC. As we know from Chapter 8, this file is */etc/lxc/default.conf*, so we'll use this value.

```
antonio@antonio-Laptop:~/packer/lxc$ ls /etc/lxc/
default.conf   lxc-usernet
```

The modified line will look like this:

```
  config_file                = "/etc/lxc/default.conf"
```

We also need to check if we have an LXC template named ubuntu.

```
antonio@antonio-Laptop:~/packer/lxc$ ls /usr/share/lxc/templates/
lxc-alpine       lxc-centos        lxc-fedora         lxc-oci
lxc-plamo        lxc-sparclinux    lxc-voidlinux
lxc-altlinux     lxc-cirros        lxc-fedora-legacy  lxc-openmandriva
lxc-pld          lxc-sshd
lxc-archlinux    lxc-debian        lxc-gentoo         lxc-opensuse
lxc-sabayon      lxc-ubuntu
lxc-busybox      lxc-download      lxc-local          lxc-oracle
lxc-slackware    lxc-ubuntu-cloud
```

Finally, the modified file will be something like this:

```
antonio@antonio-Laptop:~/packer/lxc$ cat lxc.json.pkr.hcl
source "lxc" "lxc-trusty" {
  config_file                = "/etc/lxc/default.conf"
  template_environment_vars  = ["SUITE=trusty"]
  template_name              = "ubuntu"
}
build {
  sources = ["source.lxc.lxc-trusty"]
}
```

We try now to build the image with **packer build**.

```
antonio@antonio-Laptop:~/packer/lxc$ packer build lxc.json.pkr.hcl
lxc.lxc-trusty: output will be in this color.

==> lxc.lxc-trusty: Creating container...
==> lxc.lxc-trusty: Error creating container: Command error:
lxc-create: packer-lxc-trusty: parse.c: lxc_file_for_each_line_
mmap: 78 No such file or directory - Failed to open file "/
home/antonio/.config/lxc/default.conf"
==> lxc.lxc-trusty: lxc-create: packer-lxc-trusty: conf.c:
userns_exec_mapped_root: 5409 No uid mapping for container root
.
.
.
==> Builds finished but no artifacts were created.
```

We get an error. As some operations performed with Linux containers need to be executed with root permissions by default, we repeat the command using **sudo**.

```
antonio@antonio-Laptop:~/packer/lxc$ sudo packer build lxc.
json.pkr.hcl
Error: Unknown source type lxc

  on lxc.json.pkr.hcl line 7:
  (source code not available)

The source lxc is unknown by Packer, and is likely part of a
plugin that is not
installed.
You may find the needed plugin along with installation
instructions documented
on the Packer integrations page.

https://developer.hashicorp.com/packer/integrations?filter=lxc
```

CHAPTER 13   PACKER

We get a different error this time. A message that says that we might need a plug-in installed. This is the same error we got during the conversion from JSON format to HCL format. If we validate the file, we see that the file is valid.

```
antonio@antonio-Laptop:~/packer/lxc$ packer validate lxc.json.pkr.hcl
The configuration is valid.
```

This seems to be a bug, because the plug-in is installed and the name of the builder according to the documentation is lxc as well. I also found out that using an older Packer version, it was possible to generate the image.

Currently we're using Packer v1.11.

```
antonio@antonio-Laptop:~/packer/lxc$ packer --version
Packer v1.11.0
```

Manually I downloaded Packer v1.8.6.

```
antonio@antonio-Laptop:~/packer/lxc$ ../Downloads/packer --version 1.8.6
```

Using the older version, I could generate the image.

```
antonio@antonio-Laptop:~/packer/lxc$ sudo ../../Downloads/packer build lxc.json.pkr.hcl
lxc.lxc-trusty: output will be in this color.

==> lxc.lxc-trusty: Creating container...
==> lxc.lxc-trusty: Waiting for container to finish init...
==> lxc.lxc-trusty: Container finished init!
==> lxc.lxc-trusty: Exporting container...
==> lxc.lxc-trusty: Unregistering and deleting virtual machine...
```

```
Build 'lxc.lxc-trusty' finished after 25 seconds 758
milliseconds.

==> Wait completed after 25 seconds 758 milliseconds

==> Builds finished. The artifacts of successful builds are:
--> lxc.lxc-trusty: VM files in directory: output-lxc-trusty
antonio@antonio-Laptop:~/packer/lxc$
```

We can check that the image was actually created.

```
antonio@antonio-Laptop:~/packer/lxc$ ls output-lxc-trusty/
lxc-config   rootfs.tar.gz
```

Automating the Installation of Ubuntu to Generate an Image with Packer

In the first example, we tried to create a VirtualBox image; we couldn't complete the creation of the image because we hadn't provided a method to autoinstall the VM used to generate the image.

We can check the Ubuntu installation documentation (Figure 13-8) to better understand how to automate the installation of the Ubuntu system.

CHAPTER 13   PACKER

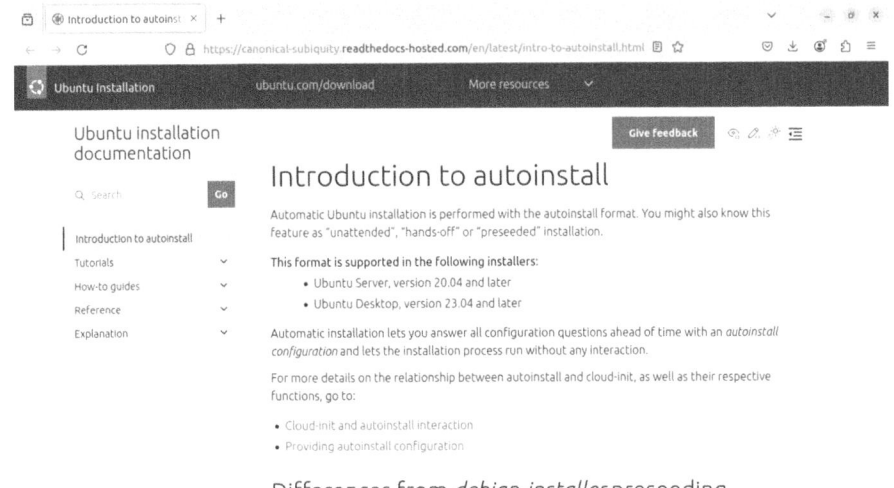

Figure 13-8.   Ubuntu autoinstall documentation

In newer Ubuntu systems, from Ubuntu Server 20.04 onward and Ubuntu Desktop 23.04 onward, autoinstall is installed. Older versions still used the debian-installer. Autoinstall configuration can be provided by **cloud-init** or directly on the installation media. Let's see a simple example based on the official documentation.

We need to download a supported Ubuntu server ISO file. We'll use in this example Ubuntu Server 20.04.

```
antonio@antonio-Laptop:~/packer$ ls iso/ubuntu-20.04.6-live-
server-amd64.iso
iso/ubuntu-20.04.6-live-server-amd64.iso
```

We'll use the file from our first example, which we need to modify accordingly.

```
antonio@antonio-Laptop:~/packer$ cat virtualboxiso.pkr.hcl
source "virtualbox-iso" "basic-example" {
  guest_os_type = "Ubuntu_64"
```

```
    iso_url = "http://releases.ubuntu.com/12.04/ubuntu-12.04.5-
    server-amd64.iso"
    iso_checksum = "md5:769474248a3897f4865817446f9a4a53"
    ssh_username = "packer"
    ssh_password = "packer"
    shutdown_command = "echo 'packer' | sudo -S shutdown -P now"
}
build {
    sources = ["sources.virtualbox-iso.basic-example"]
}
```

We need to make a few changes. First, we edit the parameter iso_url and use the location of the new downloaded ISO.

```
    iso_url = "./iso/ubuntu-20.04.6-live-server-amd64.iso"
```

Then we calculate the md5 sum.

```
antonio@antonio-Laptop:~/packer$ md5sum iso/ubuntu-20.04.6-
live-server-amd64.iso
5a4fcbde8b0585d78b3de3cb33bcd874  iso/ubuntu-20.04.6-live-
server-amd64.iso
```

And we edit the iso_checksum parameter.

```
    iso_checksum = "md5:5a4fcbde8b0585d78b3de3cb33bcd874"
```

We also need to add a few parameters.

```
boot_wait = "5s"
boot_command = ["<enter><enter><f6><esc><wait>", "autoinstall
ds=nocloud-net;s=http://{{ .HTTPIP }}:{{ .HTTPPort }}/",
"<enter>"]
```

The "boot_wait" parameter sets a delay, giving the virtual machine some time to load. The "boot_command" is very important; it provides an array of strings that are typed in sequence; in this example, we press enter twice, then "f6" and then "esc".

Then we specify that we're using autoinstall; the autoinstall configuration will be provided by **cloud-init**. We'll study cloud-init in the next chapter; for now, it is enough to know that we'll use a special datasource named nocloud-net. This datasource allows to provide the configuration locally using an http server.

If we check the documentation of the VirtualBox ISO Packer builder, we can read the following:

> *"Packer will create an http server serving* `http_directory` *when it is set, a random free port will be selected and the architecture of the directory referenced will be available in your builder."*

We can use this http server created by Packer to provide the cloud-init configuration. We can access this http server internally from Packer using the special variables {{ .HTTPIP }} and {{ .HTTPPORT }}. This is what we did in the boot_command parameter.

Besides, we need to add the http_directory parameter. This specifies the location of a folder whose content will be served by the http server created by Packer. We'll create a subfolder named *http*, and we'll create the needed files.

```
antonio@antonio-Laptop:~/packer$ mkdir http
antonio@antonio-Laptop:~/packer$ cd http
antonio@antonio-Laptop:~/packer/http$
```

cloud-init needs a couple of files at least to work properly. The first one is *meta-data*. For our purposes, we don't need to include any information in it, but we need it to exist. We create an empty file with that name.

```
antonio@antonio-Laptop:~/packer/http$ touch meta-data
```

Next we create the second file, user-data. Contrary to the first one, we need to include some information in it.

```
antonio@antonio-Laptop:~/packer/http$ cat user-data
#cloud-config
autoinstall:
  version: 1
  early-commands:
  - systemctl stop ssh
  locale: en_US
  keyboard:
    layout: en
  identity:
    hostname: vagrant
    password: $6$UFt2frQzGcqUEN47$zqBeWAgkrfV4QmLg9CjAhvcppC6
    Kf3BZTlsXWQK4JGj4xVotyCv6y0YPzE3TScGP.QhBmTDT2o0QlYk1AiOf41
    username: vagrant
  ssh:
    install-server: yes
    allow-pw: yes
```

We'll summarize the content of the file here. At the beginning, we specify that we're providing information to autoinstall. Then we stop the ssh service and set the locale and keyboard layout. And we add a user named "vagrant" with the password "vagrant". The password is encrypted; we obtain the encrypted value using the **mkpasswd** command.

```
antonio@antonio-Laptop:~/packer/http$ mkpasswd -m sha-512
Password:
$6$UFt2frQzGcqUEN47$zqBeWAgkrfV4QmLg9CjAhvcppC6Kf3BZTlsXWQK4J
Gj4xVotyCv6y0YPzE3TScGP.QhBmTDT2o0QlYk1AiOf41
```

CHAPTER 13   PACKER

I know all this can be confusing at first, and it is probably a good idea to review the documentation about VirtualBox ISO Packer and Autoinstall, which were already mentioned earlier in this chapter. It would be also good to review the cloud-init documentation, even though we'll study a bit more about this tool in the next chapter.

Another change we need to do is replacing in the packer hcl file the ssh credentials for the packer user, and we'll use the vagrant user instead.

```
ssh_username = "vagrant"
ssh_password = "vagrant"
```

And we'll also need to edit the shutdown_command entry.

```
shutdown_command = "echo 'vagrant' | sudo -S shutdown -P now"
```

We're almost there; we just need to add three more options.

```
format = "ova"
ssh_timeout = "10000s"
vm_name = "Ubuntu_packer"
vboxmanage = [["modifyvm", "{{ .Name }}", "--memory", "1024"], ["modifyvm", "{{ .Name }}", "--vram", "36"], ["modifyvm", "{{ .Name }}", "--cpus", "2"]]
```

With the format option, we tell Packer that we want the image to be created in ova format, which is a single file; the default output format is ovf (several files). We also add a timeout big enough to give time to the VM creation to complete. We assign a customized name to the virtual machine, and we also specify some options to pass to VboxManage to customize the virtual machine; this last parameter is needed because the default settings for the Ubuntu_64 OS type are too low for a modern Ubuntu distribution.

This is the final content of the file:

```
antonio@antonio-Laptop:~/packer$ cat virtualboxiso.pkr.hcl
source "virtualbox-iso" "basic-example" {
  boot_wait = "5s"
  boot_command = ["<enter><enter><f6><esc><wait>", "autoinstall
  ds=nocloud-net;s=http://{{ .HTTPIP }}:{{ .HTTPPort }}/",
  "<enter>"]
  http_directory = "http"
  guest_os_type = "Ubuntu_64"
  iso_url = "./iso/ubuntu-20.04.6-live-server-amd64.iso"
  iso_checksum = "md5:5a4fcbde8b0585d78b3de3cb33bcd874"
  ssh_username = "vagrant"
  ssh_password = "vagrant"
  shutdown_command = "echo 'vagrant' | sudo -S shutdown -P now"
  format = "ova"
  ssh_timeout = "10000s"
  vm_name = "Ubuntu_packer"
  vboxmanage = [["modifyvm", "{{ .Name }}", "--memory",
  "1024"], ["modifyvm", "{{ .Name }}", "--vram", "36"],
  ["modifyvm", "{{ .Name }}", "--cpus", "2"]]
}
build {
  sources = ["sources.virtualbox-iso.basic-example"]
}
```

Finally, we're ready to build the image.

```
antonio@antonio-HP-Laptop-15s-fq1xxx:~/packer$ packer build
virtualboxiso.pkr.hcl
virtualbox-iso.basic-example: output will be in this color.
```

CHAPTER 13   PACKER

```
==> virtualbox-iso.basic-example: Retrieving Guest additions
•
•
•
```

Packer accesses the ISO file.

```
•
==> virtualbox-iso.basic-example: Trying ./iso/ubuntu-20.04.6-
live-server-amd64.iso?checksum=md5%3A5a4fcbde8b0585d78b3de3
cb33bcd874
```

And Packer starts the http server that will be used later to provide the autoinstall configuration using cloud-init.

```
•
==> virtualbox-iso.basic-example: Starting HTTP server on
port 8391
•
```

And then it waits for the virtual machine to boot.

```
•
•
==> virtualbox-iso.basic-example: Waiting 5s for boot...
•
```

At the same time, a VirtualBox console will pop up; as instructed in the boot_command parameter, the virtual machine is instructed to get the autoinstall configuration using cloud-init (Figure 13-9).

CHAPTER 13 PACKER

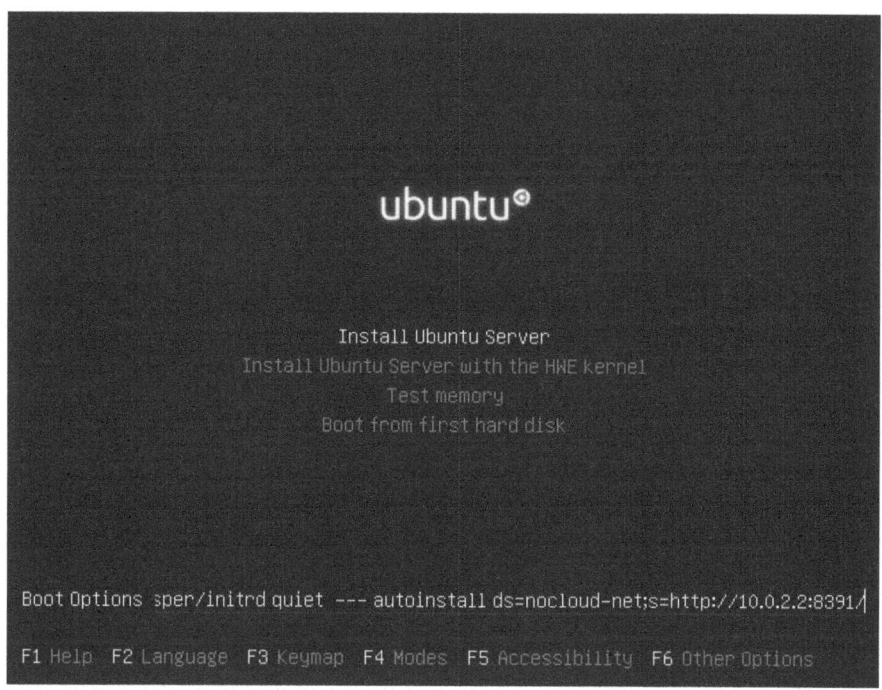

Figure 13-9. *Launching the automated installation*

And after a few seconds, we'll see how cloud-init is used to configure the virtual machine (Figure 13-10).

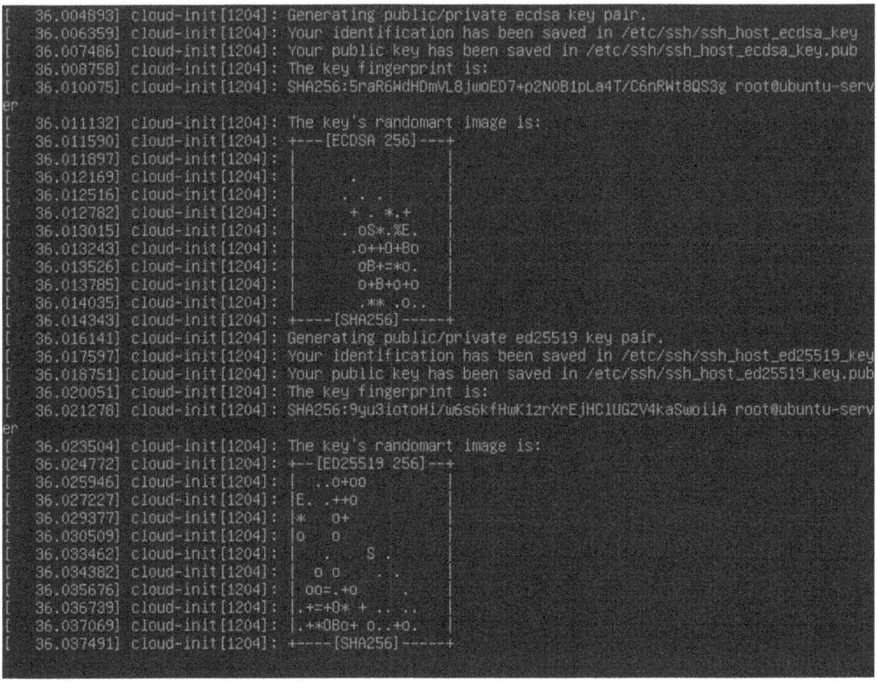

Figure 13-10. Using cloud-init during the virtual machine installation

In the command shell in which we launched packer install, we'll see a few more lines.

==> virtualbox-iso.basic-example: Typing the boot command...
==> virtualbox-iso.basic-example: Using SSH communicator to connect: 127.0.0.1
==> virtualbox-iso.basic-example: Waiting for SSH to become available...

At some point, the installation will be finished, and we can log in normally to it if we want to with the user "vagrant" and the password "vagrant" (Figure 13-11).

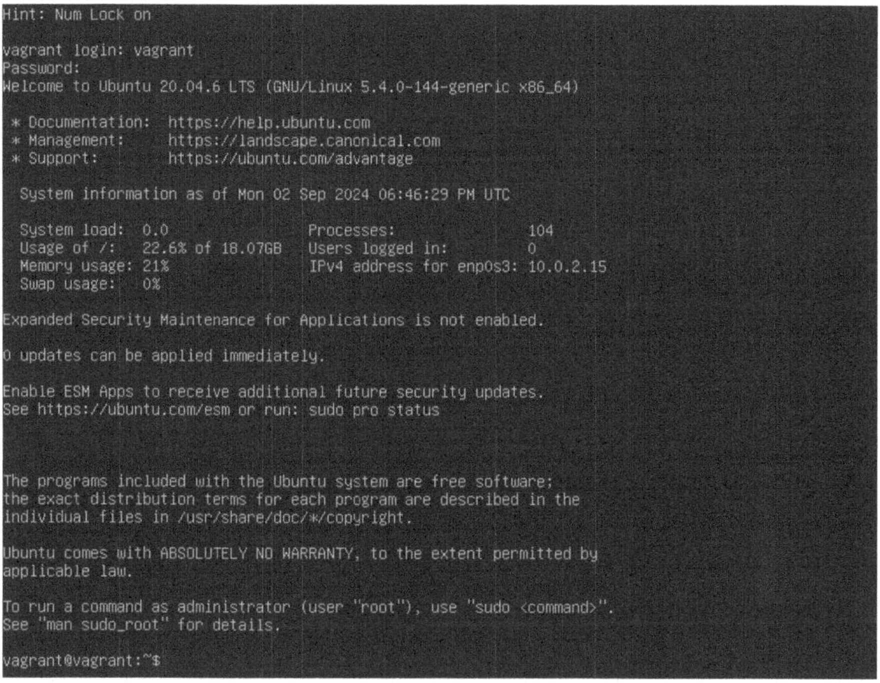

Figure 13-11. Logged in as the vagrant user

After a while, the automated process will connect to the VM as the vagrant user as well; it will perform the last actions and shut down and delete the VM.

==> virtualbox-iso.basic-example: Waiting for SSH to become available...
==> virtualbox-iso.basic-example: Connected to SSH!
==> virtualbox-iso.basic-example: Uploading VirtualBox version info (7.0.20)
==> virtualbox-iso.basic-example: Uploading VirtualBox guest additions ISO...
==> virtualbox-iso.basic-example: Gracefully halting virtual machine...

```
==> virtualbox-iso.basic-example: [sudo] password for vagrant:
==> virtualbox-iso.basic-example: Preparing to export
machine...
    virtualbox-iso.basic-example: Deleting forwarded port
mapping for the communicator (SSH, WinRM, etc) (host port 3603)
==> virtualbox-iso.basic-example: Exporting virtual machine...
    virtualbox-iso.basic-example: Executing: export Ubuntu_
packer --output output-basic-example/Ubuntu_packer.ova
==> virtualbox-iso.basic-example: Cleaning up floppy disk...
==> virtualbox-iso.basic-example: Deregistering and
deleting VM...
Build 'virtualbox-iso.basic-example' finished after 5 minutes
19 seconds.

==> Wait completed after 5 minutes 19 seconds

==> Builds finished. The artifacts of successful builds are:
--> virtualbox-iso.basic-example: VM files in directory:
output-basic-example
```

The image file has been successfully created inside the *output-basic-example* folder.

```
antonio@antonio-Laptop:~/packer$ ls output-basic-example
Ubuntu_packer.ova
```

Of course this could be done with more recent distributions like Ubuntu 23.10 Mantic Minotaur. But this last version has different menus, and we'll need to use different sequences of keys to access the boot options and specify the location of the autoinstall configuration.

Provisioning with Packer and Integration with vagrant

We have successfully built a Packer image, but we can also use Packer to provision a virtual machine. Provisioning a virtual machine consists in making the needed changes for the virtual machine to be in the desired state. These changes can be installing additional software, server hardening, etc.

To provision virtual machines, Packer uses different provisioners like PowerShell, shell, file, etc. You can see the full list in the documentation. In this example, we'll use the shell provider, which consists in using shell scripts to perform the required actions. This is the code we'll need to add:

```
provisioner "shell" {
  environment_vars   = ["HOME_DIR=/home/vagrant"]
  execute_command    = "echo 'vagrant' | {{ .Vars }} sudo -S -E sh -eux '{{ .Path }}'"
  expect_disconnect  = true
  scripts            = ["scripts/update.sh"]
}
```

The code is basically self-explanatory. We execute the script as the vagrant user, with sudo permissions, and we define the HOME_DIR environment variable. The script will be located in the *scripts* folder and will have this content:

```
antonio@antonio-Laptop:~/packer$ cat scripts/update.sh
#!/bin/bash -eux

sudo apt-get update -y
sudo apt-get upgrade -y
```

As a proof of concept, this simple provisioning example just updates and upgrades the system. Of course we could also perform additional actions like assigning sudo permissions, installing specific software, and so on.

In addition to provisioners, in Packer, we can also use post-processors . These post-processors are run after provisioners, and they can be used to perform actions like repackaging files. As an example, we'll use the vagrant post-processor to generate a vagrant box from the provisioned image. This way, we can later execute it in vagrant. Both **packer** and **vagrant** have been developed by the same company, HashiCorp, so they integrate easily.

This is the additional code that we need.

```
post-processor "vagrant" {
  compression_level = "8"
  output = "output/ubuntu-20.04-{{ .Provider }}.box"
}
```

To clarify, we'll see the full content of the file here.

```
antonio@antonio-Laptop:~/packer$ cat virtualboxiso.pkr.hcl
source "virtualbox-iso" "basic-example" {
  boot_wait = "5s"
  boot_command = ["<enter><enter><f6><esc><wait>", "autoinstall ds=nocloud-net;s=http://{{ .HTTPIP }}:{{ .HTTPPort }}/", "<enter>"]
  http_directory = "http"
  guest_os_type = "Ubuntu_64"
  iso_url = "./iso/ubuntu-20.04.6-live-server-amd64.iso"
  iso_checksum = "md5:5a4fcbde8b0585d78b3de3cb33bcd874"
  ssh_username = "vagrant"
  ssh_password = "vagrant"
  shutdown_command = "echo 'vagrant' | sudo -S shutdown -P now"
  format = "ova"
```

```
    ssh_timeout = "10000s"
    vm_name = "Ubuntu_packer"
    vboxmanage = [["modifyvm", "{{ .Name }}", "--memory",
    "1024"], ["modifyvm", "{{ .Name }}", "--vram", "36"],
    ["modifyvm", "{{ .Name }}", "--cpus", "2"]]
}
build {
  sources = ["sources.virtualbox-iso.basic-example"]

  provisioner "shell" {
    environment_vars  = ["HOME_DIR=/home/vagrant"]
    execute_command   = "echo 'vagrant' | {{ .Vars }} sudo -S -E
    sh -eux '{{ .Path }}'"
    expect_disconnect = true
    scripts           = ["scripts/update.sh", "scripts/
                        sudoers.sh"]
  }

  post-processor "vagrant" {
    compression_level = "8"
    output = "output/ubuntu-20.04-{{ .Provider }}.box"
  }

}
```

We execute **packer build** again.

```
antonio@antonio-Laptop:~/packer$ packer build
virtualboxiso.pkr.hcl
Error: Unknown post-processor type "vagrant"

  on virtualboxiso.pkr.hcl line 27:
  (source code not available)
```

673

CHAPTER 13   PACKER

```
The post-processor vagrant is unknown by Packer, and is likely
part of a plugin
that is not installed.
You may find the needed plugin along with installation
instructions documented
on the Packer integrations page.

https://developer.hashicorp.com/packer/
integrations?filter=vagrant
```

We get an error because we need to install a new plug-in to use the vagrant post-processor. We install it.

```
antonio@antonio-Laptop:~/packer$ packer plugins install github.
com/hashicorp/vagrant
Installed plugin github.com/hashicorp/vagrant v1.1.4 in "/home/
antonio/.config/packer/plugins/github.com/hashicorp/vagrant/
packer-plugin-vagrant_v1.1.4_x5.0_linux_amd64"
antonio@antonio-HP-Laptop-15s-fq1xxx:~/packer$ packer build
virtualboxiso.pkr.hcl
```

We try to execute **packer build** once more.

```
antonio@antonio-Laptop:~/packer$ packer build
virtualboxiso.pkr.hcl
.
.
```

This time, it will execute successfully. In the command shell, we'll see the same lines of information that we saw when we created the VirtualBox ova. However, in this occasion, we'll also see many lines like these below because the virtual machine is updating its software.

-
-
  virtualbox-iso.basic-example: Unpacking libldap-common
  (2.4.49+dfsg-2ubuntu1.10) over (2.4.49+dfsg-2ubuntu1.9) ...
   virtualbox-iso.basic-example: Preparing to unpack .../38-li
   bldap-2.4-2_2.4.49+dfsg-2ubuntu1.10_amd64.deb ...
  virtualbox-iso.basic-example: Unpacking libldap-2.4-2:amd64
  (2.4.49+dfsg-2ubuntu1.10) over (2.4.49+dfsg-2ubuntu1.9) ...
  virtualbox-iso.basic-example: Preparing to unpack .../39-li
  bssh-4_0.9.3-2ubuntu2.5_amd64.deb ...
  virtualbox-iso.basic-example: Unpacking libssh-4:amd64
  (0.9.3-2ubuntu2.5) over (0.9.3-2ubuntu2.2) ...
  virtualbox-iso.basic-example: Preparing to unpack
  .../40-libcurl3-gnutls_7.68.0-1ubuntu2.23_amd64.deb ...
-
-
-

In the end, we get this message:

-
Build 'virtualbox-iso.basic-example' finished after 10 minutes
3 seconds.

==> Wait completed after 10 minutes 3 seconds

==> Builds finished. The artifacts of successful builds are:
--> virtualbox-iso.basic-example: 'virtualbox' provider box:
output/ubuntu-20.04-virtualbox.box

We see clearly that a **vagrant** box has been created. We'll study vagrant in the last chapter of the book so if you don't fully understand the next commands, don't worry we'll study them later.

We can add the new vagrant box with **vagrant box add**.

```
antonio@antonio-Laptop:~/packer$ vagrant box add output/
ubuntu-20.04-virtualbox.box --name packer_made_ubuntu20server
==> box: Box file was not detected as metadata. Adding it
directly...
==> box: Adding box 'packer_made_ubuntu20server' (v0) for
provider:
    box: Unpacking necessary files from: file:///home/antonio/
packer/output/ubuntu-20.04-virtualbox.box
==> box: Successfully added box 'packer_made_ubuntu20server'
(v0) for 'virtualbox'!
```

And now we can list it in vagrant with **vagrant box list**.

```
antonio@antonio-Laptop:~/packer$ vagrant box list
packer_made_ubuntu20server (virtualbox, 0)
```

Summary

In this chapter, we studied Packer, a tool that we can use to automate the creation of images from many different providers like AWS, Azure, LXC, VirtualBox, QEMU, etc.

Reviewing each and every Packer Integration would be completely impossible, but after the examples that we have seen in the chapter, you should have a good grasp of how Packer works and the different options we can use to generate the images.

Finally, we saw an easy example of provisioning a virtual machine and exporting it as a vagrant box to use it later in vagrant.

CHAPTER 14

cloud-init

In this chapter, we'll cover the following concepts:

- Understand the features and concepts of cloud-init, including user-data, initializing and configuring cloud-init

- Use cloud-init to create and mount file systems, configure user accounts, including login credentials, and install software packages from the distribution's repository

- Integrate cloud-init into system images

- Use config drive datasource for testing

Introduction to cloud-init

cloud-init is the standard for customizing cloud instances. It was developed initially by Canonical for the ubuntu images used in AWS. In the official web page (Figure 14-1), we can see some basic information about cloud-init.

CHAPTER 14   CLOUD-INIT

Figure 14-1. cloud-init website

It is used to configure instances, mainly cloud instances, install software, customize permissions, etc. In the official website, we can see a lot of documentation as well as practical examples.

Configuring a Local QEMU Instance

Let's begin with a very easy example. We'll begin by creating a temporary folder.

```
antonio@antonio-Laptop:~/cloud-init$ mkdir temp
antonio@antonio-Laptop:~/cloud-init$ cd temp/
antonio@antonio-Laptop:~/cloud-init/temp$
```

Then, we'll download a very light Ubuntu image specially crafted for cloud environments.

CHAPTER 14 CLOUD-INIT

```
antonio@antonio-Laptop:~/cloud-init/temp$ wget https://cloud-
images.ubuntu.com/jammy/current/jammy-server-cloudimg-amd64.img
.
.
.
2024-09-03 15:06:48 (21,9 MB/s) - 'jammy-server-cloudimg-amd64.
img' saved [652869632/652869632]
```

If we inspect the file, we'll see it is a qcow2 file.

```
antonio@antonio-Laptop:~/cloud-init/temp$ file jammy-server-
cloudimg-amd64.img
jammy-server-cloudimg-amd64.img: QEMU QCOW2 Image (v2),
2361393152 bytes
```

If you remember, in Chapter 13, we used **cloud-init** to provide the autoinstall configuration to the VirtualBox virtual machine that we used to generate the final image.

In that example, we used a *user-data* file and an empty *meta-data* file. In this new example, we'll do something similar. We begin by creating the following *user-data* file:

```
antonio@antonio-Laptop:~$ cat user-data
#cloud-config
password: password
chpasswd:
  expire: false
```

The header "#cloud-config" tells cloud-init that this file will be used to configure the virtual machine instance. With the option password, we set the password of the default user. With the options "chpasswd" and "expire", we tell that the user password won't expire.

Next, we'll create a *meta-data* file. This time, we'll use this file to specify the instance id and customize the hostname of the instance.

```
antonio@antonio-Laptop:~/cloud-init/temp$ cat meta-data
instance-id: 001/cloudqemu
local-hostname: charlie
```

Finally, we create an empty *vendor-data* file. This file usually contains specifications about the cloud provider, AWS, Azure, Google Cloud, etc. In our example, it is not necessary to include any information on it.

```
antonio@antonio-Laptop:~/cloud-init/temp$ touch vendor-data
```

When the instance to be configured boots, the client component of cloud-init executes and needs to access the files we've just created. In cloud environments, the instance contacts the instance metadata service through http. We'll see more about the instance metadata service later; meanwhile, we can provide the same functionality by using any web server to serve the needed files. If you remember from the last chapter, when we used Packer to create an image and used cloud-init to configure the virtual machine, we used the internal web server created by Packer. In this case, however, we need to use our own web server,

An easy approach would be to use Python to create a temporary web server using the http.server module like this:

```
antonio@antonio-Laptop:~/cloud-init/temp$ python3 -m http.server 8888
Serving HTTP on 0.0.0.0 port 8888 (http://0.0.0.0:8888/) ...
```

We're now ready to launch a QEMU instance that will be configured with cloud-init. We already studied QEMU, so you're probably familiar with the syntax. Anyway, we'll review very briefly the options used here.

We launch an instance with 1024 MB of RAM (option -m), using hardware virtualization (option --accel kvm), with user mode networking (options -netdev and -device). The instance will use the same CPU

CHAPTER 14 CLOUD-INIT

specifications as the host's CPU; we won't open a new graphical console but use the command shell window as the server console. The disk will be the file we downloaded previously, the one with the ubuntu cloud image. We also use a new option, smbios; this option defines some specific settings for the system we're emulating. In the example below, we use it to get the cloud-init data through http.

```
antonio@antonio-Laptop:~/cloud-init/temp$ qemu-system-x86_64
-m 1024 --accel kvm -netdev user,id=myusernet -device
e1000,netdev=myusernet -cpu host -nographic -hda jammy-
server-cloudimg-amd64.img -smbios type=1,serial=ds='nocloud-
net;s=http://10.0.2.2:8888/'
```

We'll see the system booting.

```
SeaBIOS (version 1.15.0-1)

iPXE (https://ipxe.org) 00:03.0 CA00 PCI2.10 PnP
PMM+3FF8B3A0+3FECB3A0 CA00
.
.
```

After a few seconds, we'll see the cloud-init-related lines.

```
.
.
.
[    9.175354] cloud-init[543]: Cloud-init v.
   24.1.3-0ubuntu1~22.04.5 running 'init' at Wed, 04 Sep 2024
   15:31:07 +0000. Up 9.15 se.
```

681

CHAPTER 14   CLOUD-INIT

```
[    9.184233] cloud-init[543]: ci-info: ++++++++++++++++++++++++
++++++Net device info++++++++++++++++++++++++++++
[    9.185717] cloud-init[543]: ci-info:
[    9.190214] cloud-init[543]: ci-info:
| Device |  Up  |   Address    |     Mask    |  Scope  |   Hw-Address     |
[    9.191676] cloud-init[543]: ci-info:
[    9.194366] cloud-init[543]: ci-info: |  ens3  | True
|  10.0.2.15 | 255.255.255.0 | global | 52:54:00:12:34:56  |
.
.
.
[  OK  ] Finished Initial cloud-ini…ob (metadata service crawler).
.
.
.
```

And we'll get to the login screen. We can see that the hostname has been changed to charlie, as we had specified in the *meta-data* file.

```
Ubuntu 22.04.4 LTS charlie ttyS0

charlie login:
```

In the command shell window in which we launched the Python web server, we'll see that the three files were accessed through HTTP requests.

```
antonio@antonio-Laptop:~/cloud-init/temp$ python3 -m http.server 8888
Serving HTTP on 0.0.0.0 port 8888 (http://0.0.0.0:8888/) ...
127.0.0.1 - - [04/Sep/2024 17:31:07] "GET /meta-data HTTP/1.1" 200 -
127.0.0.1 - - [04/Sep/2024 17:31:07] "GET /user-data HTTP/1.1" 200 -
```

CHAPTER 14   CLOUD-INIT

```
127.0.0.1 - - [04/Sep/2024 17:31:07] "GET /vendor-data
HTTP/1.1" 200 -
```

In the server console, we can log in with the user ubuntu and the password set by **cloud-init**. Once logged in, we can see the status of the cloud-init configuration with the cloud-init status command.

```
ubuntu@charlie:~$ cloud-init status
status: done
```

If we want to get more detailed information, we can use the --long option.

```
ubuntu@charlie:~$ cloud-init status --long
status: done
extended_status: degraded done
boot_status_code: enabled-by-generator
last_update: Wed, 04 Sep 2024 15:31:09 +0000
detail: DataSourceNoCloudNet [seed=dmi,http://10.0.2.2:8888/]
[dsmode=net]
errors: []
recoverable_errors:
DEPRECATED:
     - The 'nocloud-net' datasource name is deprecated in 24.1
       and scheduled to be removed in 29.1. Use 'nocloud'
       instead, which.
ubuntu@charlie:~$ cloud-init status --wait

status: done
```

CHAPTER 14   CLOUD-INIT

We can see that the cloud-init configuration was applied, but we see a warning because the datasource name "nocloud-net" is deprecated and it will be removed in a future version. For that reason, we're advised to use the datasource name no-cloud instead.

It is also possible to check cloud-init log files if we suspect that something went wrong.

```
ubuntu@charlie:~$ tail /var/log/cloud-init.log
2024-09-04 15:31:09,811 - util.py[DEBUG]: Writing to /var/lib/cloud/instance/boot-finished - wb: [644] 69 bytes
2024-09-04 15:31:09,812 - handlers.py[DEBUG]: finish: modules-final/config-final_message: SUCCESS: config-final_message ran successy
2024-09-04 15:31:09,812 - main.py[DEBUG]: Ran 10 modules with 0 failures
.
.
.
ubuntu@charlie:~$ tail /var/log/cloud-init-output.log
ci-info: | Route | Destination | Gateway | Interface | Flags |
ci-info: +------+-------------+---------+-----------+-------+
ci-info: |   1  |  fe80::/64  |    ::   |    ens3   |   U   |
ci-info: |   3  |    local    |    ::   |    ens3   |   U   |
ci-info: |   4  |  multicast  |    ::   |    ens3   |   U   |
ci-info: +------+-------------+---------+-----------+-------+
2024-09-04 15:31:07,274 - util.py[DEPRECATED]: The 'nocloud-net' datasource name is deprecated in 24.1 and scheduled to be removed .
.
.
.
ubuntu@charlie:~$
```

When an instance is using cloud-init, we can see that a */var/lib/cloud/* folder exists.

```
ubuntu@charlie:~$ ls -l /var/lib/cloud/
total 24
drwxr-xr-x 2 root root 4096 Sep  5 20:56 data
drwxr-xr-x 2 root root 4096 Sep  3 20:58 handlers
lrwxrwxrwx 1 root root   38 Sep  5 20:56 instance -> /var/lib/cloud/instances/001_cloudqemu
drwxr-xr-x 4 root root 4096 Sep  3 21:16 instances
drwxr-xr-x 6 root root 4096 Sep  3 20:58 scripts
drwxr-xr-x 2 root root 4096 Sep  3 20:58 seed
drwxr-xr-x 2 root root 4096 Sep  3 21:12 sem
ubuntu@charlie:~$
```

Inside this folder, we can get some information. For instance, we can access the content of the *user-data* file that was provided to cloud-init.

```
ubuntu@charlie:~$ sudo cat /var/lib/cloud/instances/001_cloudqemu/user-data.txt
#cloud-config
password: password
chpasswd:
  expire: false
package_reboot_if_required: true
package_update: true
packages:
  - gcc
ubuntu@charlie:~$
```

Or we can obtain information about the datasource used by **cloud-init**.

```
ubuntu@charlie:~$ sudo cat /var/lib/cloud/instances/001_
cloudqemu/datasource
DataSourceNoCloudNet: DataSourceNoCloudNet
[seed=dmi,http://10.0.2.2:8888/][dsmode=net]
```

Instance Metadata Services (IMDS)

We already mentioned that cloud environments usually have instance metadata services to configure and manage virtual machines. The actual implementation of the service differs a bit between the different providers, but they usually support REST APIs and can be accessed and managed using simple HTTP requests. For more details, you should check the specifications related to a particular vendor.

Datasources

Datasources are sources of configuration data for cloud-init. In the documentation page, we can see many supported datasources: AWS, Azure, no-cloud, etc.

If we check the documentation about the no-cloud datasource, the one we used before, we see we have different options to provide the configuration. In our case, we used a custom web server and the smbios option passed to the QEMU instance. But we could also have used a local filesystem and a kernel command line for instance.

Config Drive

A special type of datasource is an OpenStack configuration drive. This drive attaches to the OpenStack instance when it boots, and it is used to store metadata.

CHAPTER 14 CLOUD-INIT

Configuring a LXD Container Instance

Let's see another example now about configuring a LXD container. We'll begin by creating a *user-data* file.

```
antonio@antonio-Laptop:~/cloud-init$ cat /tmp/user-data
#cloud-config
runcmd:
  - echo "Hi" > /var/tmp/hi.txt
```

In the *user-data* file, we just tell cloud-init to run an echo command and redirect the output to a file.

Now we'll create and run a new LXD container named mytest and use the config option to pass the location of the *user-data* file.

```
antonio@antonio-Laptop:~/cloud-init$ lxc launch ubuntu:24.04 mytest --config=user.user-data="$(cat /tmp/user-data)"
Creating mytest
Starting mytest
```

After a few seconds, the new instance will be running.

```
antonio@antonio-Laptop:~/cloud-init$ lxc list
+----------------+---------+----------------------+----------------------------------------------+-----------+----------+
|      NAME      |  STATE  |         IPV4         |                     IPV6                     |   TYPE    | SNAPSHOTS |
+----------------+---------+----------------------+----------------------------------------------+-----------+----------+
| harmless-monarch | STOPPED |                      |                                              | CONTAINER | 0        |
|
```

687

CHAPTER 14   CLOUD-INIT

```
+-----------------+---------+---------------------+
--------------------------------------------+----------+
----------+
| mytest           | RUNNING | 10.216.182.123 (eth0) |
 fd42:45f7:c283:6d95:216:3eff:fe68:ae4 (eth0) | CONTAINER |
 0               |
+-----------------+---------+---------------------+
--------------------------------------------+----------+
----------+
```

We'll connect to it.

```
antonio@antonio-Laptop:~/cloud-init$ lxc shell mytest
root@mytest:~#
```

And we'll check the status of **cloud-init**.

```
root@mytest:~# cloud-init status --wait

status: done
root@mytest:~#
```

We'll see now some useful commands to check and troubleshoot cloud-init. We can query cloud-init about the user-data settings that were provided.

```
root@mytest:~# cloud-init query userdata
#cloud-config
runcmd:
  - echo "Hi" > /var/tmp/hi.txt
```

As expected, we get the exact same content that was included in the *user-data* file. We can also check that the syntax is correct according to the schema.

```
root@mytest:~# cloud-init schema --system --annotate
Found cloud-config data types: user-data, network-config
```

1. user-data at /var/lib/cloud/instances/56167d1f-a6f1-45ff-813e-1d5590de43a9/cloud-config.txt:
   Valid schema user-data

2. network-config at /var/lib/cloud/instances/56167d1f-a6f1-45ff-813e-1d5590de43a9/network-config.json:
   Valid schema network-config

In this case, the data is valid. We can also check if the file that was supposed to be created with the runcmd option actually exists.

```
root@mytest:~# cat /var/tmp/hi.txt
Hi
```

We see that the file was actually created. We can log out now:

```
root@mytest:~# logout
```

and stop and remove the container.

```
antonio@antonio-Laptop:~/cloud-init$ lxc stop mytest

antonio@antonio-Laptop:~/cloud-init$ lxc rm mytest
```

Managing Filesystems with cloud-init

cloud-init can also be used to create, resize, and mount filesystems. We're going to see an example in which we'll mount a new filesystem with cloud-init. We'll begin by creating a new 1 GB disk image file.

CHAPTER 14   CLOUD-INIT

antonio@antonio-Laptop:~/cloud-init/temp$ qemu-img create -f qcow2 NEWDISK.qcow 1G
Formatting 'NEWDISK.qcow', fmt=qcow2 cluster_size=65536 extended_l2=off compression_type=zlib size=1073741824 lazy_refcounts=off refcount_bits=16

We'll launch a new QEMU instance. We'll use the same command line that was used in our first example, but this time we'll add this new second disk.

antonio@antonio-Laptop:~/cloud-init/temp$ qemu-system-x86_64 -m 1024 --accel kvm -netdev user,id=myusernet -device e1000,netdev=myusernet -cpu host -nographic -hda jammy-server-cloudimg-amd64.img -hdb NEWDISK.qcow -smbios type=1,serial=ds='nocloud-net;s=http://10.0.2.2:8888/'

We could use cloud-init to create the new filesystem, but to simplify things, we'll do it from the instance itself.

ubuntu@charlie:~$ sudo fdisk -l

.

.

Disk /dev/sdb: 1 GiB, 1073741824 bytes, 2097152 sectors
Disk model: QEMU HARDDISK

.

.

ubuntu@charlie:~$ sudo fdisk /dev/sdb

.

.

Command (m for help): n

.

.

Select (default p):
·
·
Created a new partition 1 of type 'Linux' and of size 1023 MiB.

Now we'll edit our *user-data* file that we used in the first example to format and mount the newly created partition. cloud-init has specific modules to do that, like **fs_setup** and **mounts** to create a filesystem and mount a partition, respectively. In fact, theoretically we could even use the **disk_setup** module to partition a disk instead of doing it manually. Unfortunately, these modules can be tricky, and they do not always work as expected depending on the provider we use. For that reason, we'll use a different approach.

We'll use the **bootcmd** module to execute commands early in the boot process. We'll format the partition we created before and mount it on the */mnt* folder.

This is the new modified *user-data* file.

```
antonio@antonio-Laptop:~/cloud-init/temp$ cat user-data
#cloud-config
bootcmd:
 - mkfs -t ext4 /dev/sdb1
 - mount /dev/sdb1 /mnt
password: password
chpasswd:
  expire: false
```

Next, we launch the QEMU instance again.

```
antonio@antonio-Laptop:~/cloud-init/temp$ qemu-system-x86_64
-m 1024 --accel kvm -netdev user,id=myusernet -device
e1000,netdev=myusernet -cpu host -nographic -hda jammy-
server-cloudimg-amd64.img -hdb NEWDISK.qcow -smbios
type=1,serial=ds='nocloud-net;s=http://10.0.2.2:8888/'
```

CHAPTER 14 CLOUD-INIT

After a moment, we log in and we check that the new filesystem was mounted.

```
ubuntu@charlie:~$ df -h
Filesystem      Size  Used Avail Use% Mounted on
tmpfs            96M  956K   95M   1% /run
/dev/sda1       2.0G  1.5G  456M  78% /
tmpfs           479M     0  479M   0% /dev/shm
tmpfs           5.0M     0  5.0M   0% /run/lock
/dev/sda15      105M  6.1M   99M   6% /boot/efi
/dev/sdb1       989M   24K  922M   1% /mnt
tmpfs            96M  4.0K   96M   1% /run/user/1000
```

We saw that the result was exactly what we expected.

Installing Software Packages

As part of the provisioning process, we might need to install or update software packages. This can be easily done with cloud-init. Again, we edit our user-data file to tell cloud-init to update the software packages, rebooting the machine if necessary, and install an additional software package.

```
antonio@antonio-Laptop:~/cloud-init/temp$ cat user-data
#cloud-config
password: password
chpasswd:
  expire: false
package_reboot_if_required: true
package_update: true
packages:
  - gcc
```

692

Once we have modified the file, we make sure that our Python web server is still running, and we launch the QEMU instance again.

antonio@antonio-Laptop:~/cloud-init/temp$ qemu-system-x86_64 -m 1024 --accel kvm -netdev user,id=myusernet -device e1000,netdev=myusernet -cpu host -nographic -hda jammy-server-cloudimg-amd64.img -hdb NEWDISK.qcow -smbios type=1,serial=ds='nocloud-net;s=http://10.0.2.2:8888/'

When the system boots up and we log in, we'll see information messages about the installation of software. So we can assume that the software upgrade is working as expected.

.
.
.
```
[   24.551432] cloud-init[766]: Reading package lists...
[   24.897866] cloud-init[766]: Reading package lists...
[   25.067252] cloud-init[766]: Building dependency tree...
[   25.068557] cloud-init[766]: Reading state information...
[   25.251023] cloud-init[766]: The following additional
   packages will be installed:
[   25.252360] cloud-init[766]:   cpp cpp-11 fontconfig-config
   fonts-dejavu-core gcc-11 gcc-11-base libasan6
[   25.253526] cloud-init[766]:   libatomic1 libc-dev-bin libc-
   devtools libc6-dev libcc1-0 libcrypt-dev
[   25.256233] cloud-init[766]:   libdeflate0 libfontconfig1
   libgcc-11-dev libgd3 libgomp1 libisl23 libitm1
```
.
.

When the software installation finishes, we can try to execute **gcc** to see if it was properly installed.

```
ubuntu@charlie:~$ gcc
gcc: fatal error: no input files
compilation terminated.
ubuntu@charlie:~$
```

As we can see, **gcc** was correctly installed.

Summary

In this chapter, we studied more in depth a tool that we saw briefly in the previous chapter, **cloud-init**.

We saw several examples in which we applied different configurations to the instances using **cloud-init**. We also saw some useful commands that can be of great help when troubleshooting.

We've seen that we can manage disks and filesystems from cloud-init. It is possible to use specific modules to partition disk, managing, resizing, and mounting filesystems. Besides using these specific modules, we can also take different approaches like using bootcmd to execute the needed commands.

Of course, **cloud-init** can also be helpful when managing users; we used it to explicitly set a password for the default user, but we could also have done many more things, like creating additional users. We saw an example about this when we used Packer and cloud-init to create a system image.

Finally, we also updated the software in our instance and installed additional packages on it.

I hope that after reading this chapter and Chapter 13, you have a good grasp of what cloud-init is and how it can be used to simplify the provisioning of new instances.

CHAPTER 15

vagrant

In this chapter, we'll cover the following concepts:

- Understand vagrant architecture and concepts, including storage and networking
- Retrieve and use boxes from Atlas
- Create and run Vagrantfiles
- Access vagrant virtual machines
- Share and synchronize a folder between a vagrant virtual machine and the host system
- Understand vagrant provisioning
- Understand multi-machine setup

vagrant Architecture

vagrant is a software solution developed by HashiCorp. It is used to create portable development environments. When created, it used VirtualBox as the only provider, but now it supports many other options like KVM, VMware, and many others.

It is a solution that makes it possible to define an Infrastructure as Code (IaC) so that it is very easy to share that infrastructure with other computers.

CHAPTER 15 VAGRANT

Installing vagrant

Installing vagrant is very easy. We just need to access the official web page (Figure 15-1).

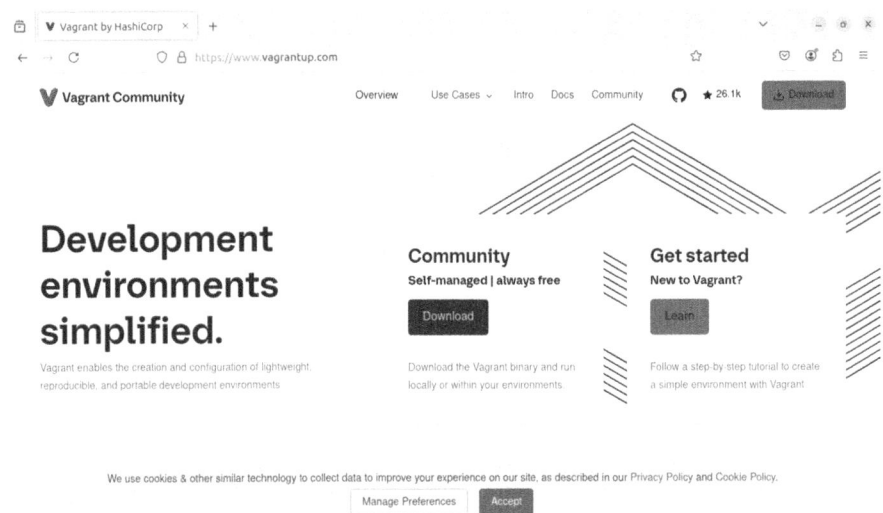

Figure 15-1. *vagrant official page*

We click the "Download" button and get to the page "Install vagrant" (Figure 15-2).

CHAPTER 15 VAGRANT

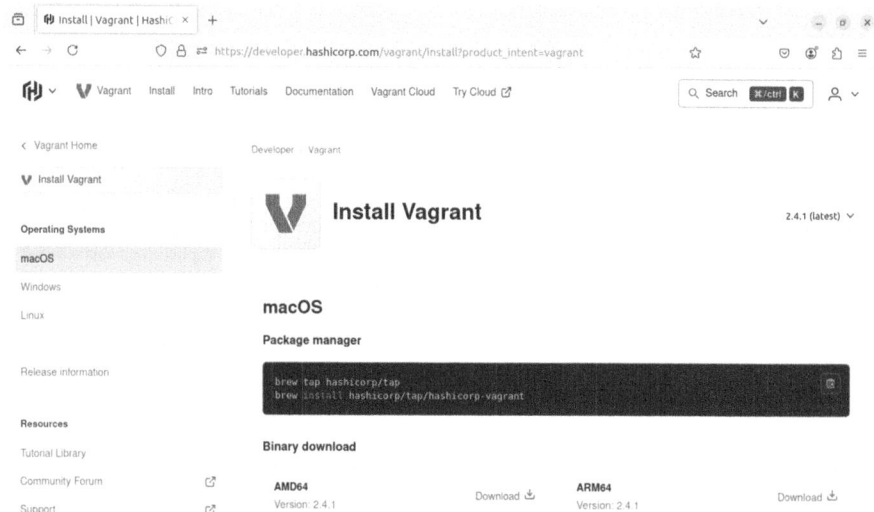

Figure 15-2. Install vagrant

As we can see, vagrant can be installed on Windows, macOS, and Linux. We select our OS, Linux in this example. Once we select Linux (Figure 15-3), we can either configure a new repository to install vagrant or download a precompiled binary version. In this case, we'll choose to download the precompiled binary for AMD64.

CHAPTER 15   VAGRANT

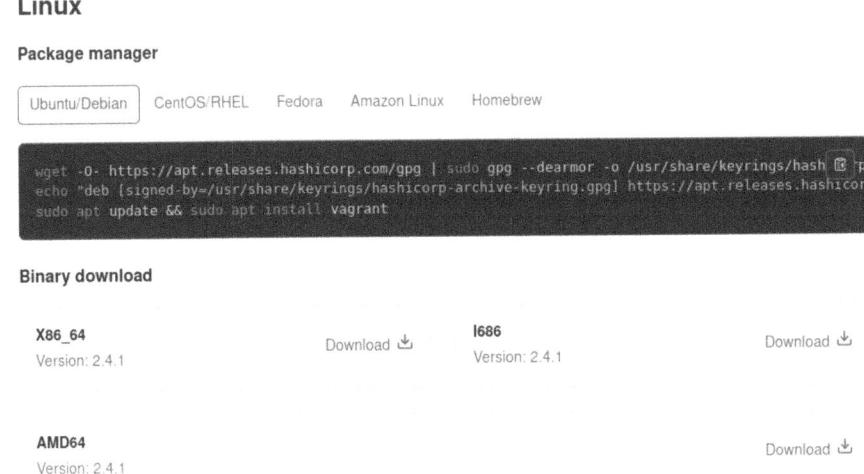

Figure 15-3. Choosing the appropiate version for our OS

We copy the downloaded file to a folder named "vagrant" and unzip it.

```
antonio@antonio-Laptop:~/vagrant$ ls
vagrant_2.3.7_linux_amd64.zip
antonio@antonio-Laptop:~/vagrant$ unzip vagrant_2.3.7_linux_
amd64.zip
Archive:  vagrant_2.3.7_linux_amd64.zip
  inflating: vagrant
```

After that, we have a new binary called "vagrant" in our folder. We'll copy that file to a folder included in the $PATH variable, for instance, to */usr/local/bin/*.

```
antonio@antonio-Laptop:~/vagrant$ sudo cp vagrant /usr/
local/bin/
```

Now we can execute **vagrant** from any location. However, we might get this error:

```
antonio@antonio-Laptop:~/vagrant$ vagrant
dlopen(): error loading libfuse.so.2

AppImages require FUSE to run.
You might still be able to extract the contents of this AppImage
if you run it with the --appimage-extract option.
See https://github.com/AppImage/AppImageKit/wiki/FUSE
for more information
```

We need to install the libfuse package; we search for it in the local repositories.

```
antonio@antonio-Laptop:~/vagrant$ apt search libfuse
Sorting... Done
Full Text Search... Done
.
.
.
libfuse2/jammy 2.9.9-5ubuntu3 amd64
  Filesystem in Userspace (library)
.
.
.
```

And we install the package.

```
antonio@antonio-Laptop:~/vagrant$ sudo apt install libfuse2
Reading package lists... Done
Building dependency tree... Done
Reading state information... Done
```

CHAPTER 15 VAGRANT

-
-
-

```
The following NEW packages will be installed:
  libfuse2
0 upgraded, 1 newly installed, 0 to remove and 22 not upgraded.
Need to get 90,3 kB of archives.
After this operation, 330 kB of additional disk space will
be used.
Get:1 http://es.archive.ubuntu.com/ubuntu jammy/universe amd64
libfuse2 amd64 2.9.9-5ubuntu3 [90,3 kB]
Fetched 90,3 kB in 0s (379 kB/s)
Selecting previously unselected package libfuse2:amd64.
(Reading database ... 249805 files and directories currently
installed.)
Preparing to unpack .../libfuse2_2.9.9-5ubuntu3_amd64.deb ...
Unpacking libfuse2:amd64 (2.9.9-5ubuntu3) ...
Setting up libfuse2:amd64 (2.9.9-5ubuntu3) ...
Processing triggers for libc-bin (2.35-0ubuntu3.1) ...
```

From now on, we can execute vagrant successfully. If we launch it without parameters, we'll get this help:

```
antonio@antonio-Laptop:~/vagrant$ vagrant
Usage: vagrant [options] <command> [<args>]

    -h, --help                       Print this help.

Common commands:
     autocomplete    manages autocomplete installation on host
     box             manages boxes: installation, removal, etc.
```

-
-
-

CHAPTER 15 VAGRANT

Deploying Our First Virtual Environment with vagrant

Now that we have installed vagrant, we'll see how easy it is to provision a test environment. We'll begin with a very simple example. There are many vagrant boxes that we can download directly from vagrant. We point our favorite web browser to vagrant cloud, formerly known as Atlas (Figure 15-4).

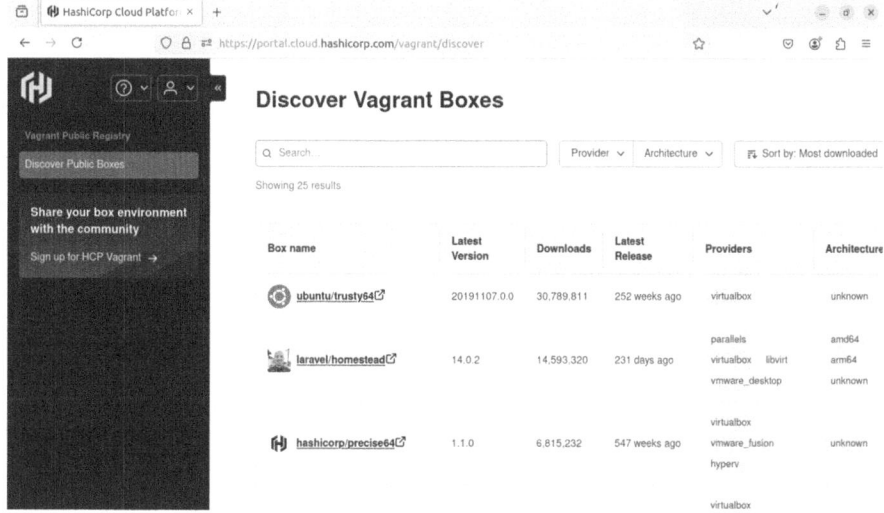

Figure 15-4. *Publicly available vagrant boxes*

We can use the search field to search for certain images, such as AlmaLinux (Figure 15-5).

CHAPTER 15 VAGRANT

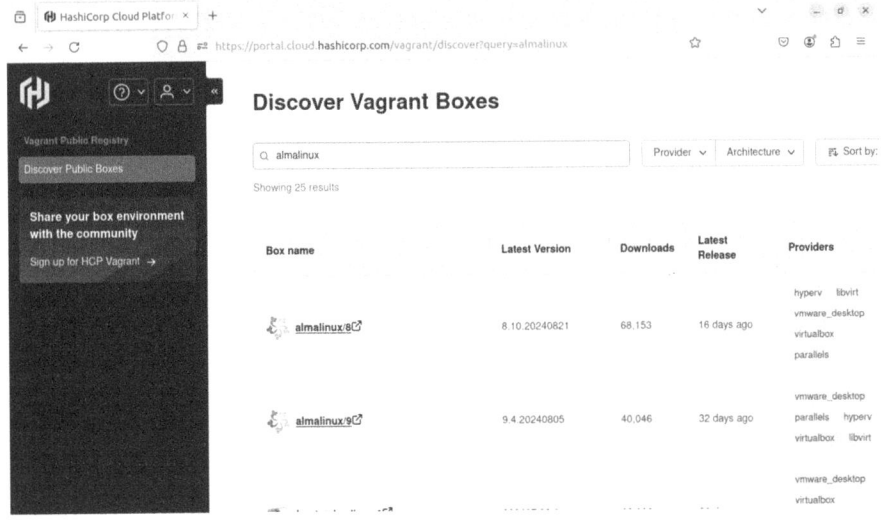

Figure 15-5. AlmaLinux vagrant boxes

Initializing vagrant

Once we have located the box that fits our needs, the first step is to initialize vagrant with the **vagrant init** command. If we want to use the almalinux/8 vagrant box that we spoke about, we need to specify the name of that box.

```
antonio@antonio-Laptop:~/vagrant$ vagrant init almalinux/8
A `Vagrantfile` has been placed in this directory. You are now
ready to `vagrant up` your first virtual environment!
Please read
the comments in the Vagrantfile as well as documentation on
`vagrantup.com` for more information on using Vagrant.
```

After executing **vagrant init**, a file named *Vagrantfile* will be created; we'll see more details of this file in the next section.

CHAPTER 15   VAGRANT

vagrant Files

The Vagrantfile we just created will contain several lines, most of which are commented. We'll take a look at the first lines.

```
antonio@antonio-Laptop:~/vagrant$ cat Vagrantfile
# -*- mode: ruby -*-
# vi: set ft=ruby :

# All Vagrant configuration is done below. The "2" in Vagrant.
configure
# configures the configuration version (we support older
styles for
# backwards compatibility). Please don't change it unless you
know what
# you're doing.
Vagrant.configure("2") do |config|
  # The most common configuration options are documented and
  commented below.
  # For a complete reference, please see the online
  documentation at
  # https://docs.vagrantup.com.

  # Every Vagrant development environment requires a box. You
  can search for
  # boxes at https://vagrantcloud.com/search.
  config.vm.box = "almalinux/8"
.
.
.
```

The configuration begins with the following line:

```
Vagrant.configure("2") do |config|
```

703

In this line, we specify the version we are using, 2 in this case. In the next lines, we set the different options. In this simple example, there is only this line:

config.vm.box = "almalinux/8"

We tell vagrant that we want to use the box named almalinux/8, which will be downloaded from the URL we mentioned in the previous section.

Running a Vagrantfile

To launch this simple environment, we just need to execute **vagrant up**.

```
antonio@antonio-Laptop:~/vagrant$ vagrant up
Bringing machine 'default' up with 'virtualbox' provider…
```

As the almalinux/8 box is not locally installed, **vagrant** will try to find it and download it from vagrant cloud.

.
.
```
==> default: Box 'almalinux/8' could not be found. Attempting to find and install...
    default: Box Provider: virtualbox
    default: Box Version: >= 0
==> default: Loading metadata for box 'almalinux/8'
    default: URL: https://vagrantcloud.com/almalinux/8
==> default: Adding box 'almalinux/8' (v8.8.20230606) for
            provider: virtualbox
    default: Downloading: https://vagrantcloud.com/almalinux/
             boxes/8/versions/8.8.20230606/providers/
             virtualbox.box
```
.
.

vagrant will assign a name to the virtual machine. As we're using the default provider, this VM will be created in VirtualBox.

```
==> default: Setting the name of the VM: vagrant_
default_1725636733750_50290
```

One of the last steps is setting the network and creating the port redirection to access the box.

```
==> default: Clearing any previously set network interfaces...
==> default: Preparing network interfaces based on
             configuration...
    default: Adapter 1: nat
==> default: Forwarding ports...
    default: 22 (guest) => 2222 (host) (adapter 1)
==> default: Booting VM...
==> default: Waiting for machine to boot. This may take a few
             minutes...
    default: SSH address: 127.0.0.1:2222
    default: SSH username: vagrant
    default: SSH auth method: private key
    default:
==> default: Machine booted and ready!
==> default: Checking for guest additions in VM...
==> default: Mounting shared folders...
    default: /vagrant => /home/antonio/vagrant
```

CHAPTER 15   VAGRANT

Finally, the box is ready. We can see it directly in VirtualBox itself (Figure 15-6).

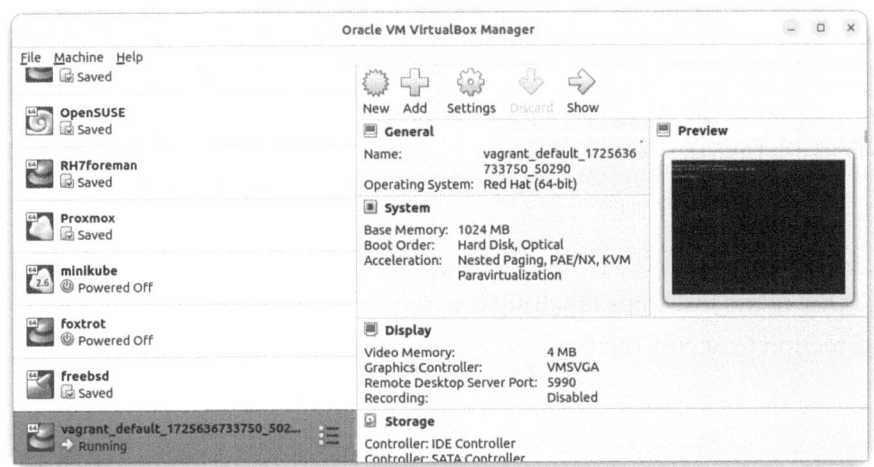

Figure 15-6.   The VirtualBox instance launched by vagrant

We can access the VM through ssh. When starting the vagrant environment, we could see these two lines:

```
default: SSH address: 127.0.0.1:2222
default: SSH username: vagrant
```

So we just need to execute this command (the default password is also "vagrant"):

```
antonio@antonio-Laptop:~/vagrant$ ssh -p 2222 vagrant@127.0.0.1
The authenticity of host '[127.0.0.1]:2222 ([127.0.0.1]:2222)' can't be established.
ED25519 key fingerprint is SHA256:DKiGWJAH9+17SA5urR5PE5g0vDYlD MM7128+ZnIH43k.
This key is not known by any other names
Are you sure you want to continue connecting (yes/no/ [fingerprint])? yes
```

```
Warning: Permanently added '[127.0.0.1]:2222' (ED25519) to the
list of known hosts.
vagrant@127.0.0.1's password:
[vagrant@localhost ~]$
```

However, it is also possible to connect to the VM by typing only **vagrant ssh**.

```
[vagrant@localhost ~]$ exit
logout
Connection to 127.0.0.1 closed.
antonio@antonio-Laptop:~/vagrant$ vagrant ssh
Last login: Sat Sep 16 07:38:55 2023 from 10.0.2.2
[vagrant@localhost ~]$
[vagrant@localhost ~]$ cat /etc/redhat-release
AlmaLinux release 8.8 (Sapphire Caracal)
```

When we're done working with the virtual environment, we can execute **vagrant destroy** to release all the resources used by the environment and delete the VM associated.

```
antonio@antonio-Laptop:~/vagrant$ vagrant destroy
    default: Are you sure you want to destroy the 'default'
          VM? [y/N] y
==> default: Forcing shutdown of VM...
==> default: Destroying VM and associated drives…
```

Working with Different vagrant Environments

After creating our first deployment, let's see a few more advanced examples. When working with different vagrant environments in the same host, it is a good practice to have every environment in its own folder.

CHAPTER 15 VAGRANT

```
antonio@antonio-Laptop:~/vagrant$ mkdir project1
antonio@antonio-Laptop:~$ cd project1/
antonio@antonio-Laptop:~/project1$
```

We know that the first step to deploy a vagrant environment is to create a *Vagrantfile* with **vagrant init**. In the first example, we pass the name of the box we wanted for the environment. This time we'll execute it without specifying any box name.

```
antonio@antonio-Laptop:~/vagrant/project1$ vagrant init
A `Vagrantfile` has been placed in this directory. You are now
ready to `vagrant up` your first virtual environment!
Please read
the comments in the Vagrantfile as well as documentation on
`vagrantup.com` for more information on using Vagrant.
```

If we look at the *Vagrantfile*, we'll see it is basically similar to what was created in the first example, with a single difference. This line:

```
  config.vm.box = "base"
```

This time, we ran **vagrant init** without arguments; for that reason, vagrant uses the generic name "base" for this parameter. If we try to create a vagrant environment with this configuration, we'll see this:

```
antonio@antonio-Laptop:~/vagrant/project1$ vagrant up
Bringing machine 'default' up with 'virtualbox' provider...
.
.
.
==> default: Adding box 'base' (v0) for provider: virtualbox
    default: Downloading: base
```

An error occurred while downloading the remote file. The error message, if any, is reproduced below. Please fix this error and try again.

Couldn't open file /home/antonio/vagrant/project1/base

We get an error because "base" is not the name of any valid vagrant box. When creating a virtual environment, vagrant searches for the used box locally, and if it can't find it, it tries to download and install that box from vagrant cloud.

Installing Additional vagrant Boxes

It is also possible to install additional boxes using the **vagrant box** command. For instance, we can install the ubuntu/xenial64 box with this command:

```
antonio@antonio-Laptop:~/vagrant/project1$ vagrant box add
ubuntu/xenial64
==> box: Loading metadata for box 'ubuntu/xenial64'
    box: URL: https://vagrantcloud.com/ubuntu/xenial64
==> box: Adding box 'ubuntu/xenial64' (v20211001.0.1) for
          provider: virtualbox
    box: Downloading: https://vagrantcloud.com/ubuntu/boxes/
          xenial64/versions/20211001.0.1/providers/virtualbox/
          unknown/vagrant.box
Download redirected to host: cloud-images.ubuntu.com
==> box: Successfully added box 'ubuntu/xenial64'
          (v20211001.0.1) for 'virtualbox'!
```

Now we're going to edit the Vagrantfile previously created with vagrant init, and we'll replace "base" with "ubuntu/xenial64" in the config.vm.box option.

CHAPTER 15 VAGRANT

```
antonio@antonio-Laptop:~/vagrant/project1$ cat Vagrantfile
.
.
  config.vm.box = "ubuntu/xenial64"
.
.
```

After editing the file, we execute **vagrant up** again to create the environment.

```
antonio@antonio-Laptop:~/vagrant/project1$ vagrant up
Bringing machine 'default' up with 'virtualbox' provider...
==> default: Importing base box 'ubuntu/xenial64'...
==> default: Matching MAC address for NAT networking...
==> default: Checking if box 'ubuntu/xenial64' version
             '20211001.0.1' is up to date...
==> default: Setting the name of the VM: project1_
             default_1724504690080_79454
.
.
.
==> default: Machine booted and ready!
.
.
.
==> default: Mounting shared folders...
    default: /vagrant => /home/antonio/vagrant/project1
antonio@antonio-Laptop:~/vagrant/project1$
```

The environment is now up and running.

Checking the Status of the vagrant Deployments

We can check the status of our deployments with the **vagrant status** command.

antonio@antonio-Laptop:~/vagrant/project1$ vagrant status
Current machine states:

default   running (virtualbox)

.
.
.

antonio@antonio-Laptop:~/vagrant/project1$

We can also use the **vagrant global status** command, which returns some additional information.

antonio@antonio-Laptop:~/vagrant/project1$ vagrant global-status
id   name   provider   state   directory

17e8b29   default virtualbox running   /home/antonio/vagrant/project1

.
.
.

antonio@antonio-Laptop:~/vagrant/project1$

In the output of the command, we can see that we have a running VirtualBox VM, and this environment is defined inside the */home/antonio/vagrant/project1* folder.

We can also list the locally installed boxes with **vagrant box list**.

```
antonio@antonio-Laptop:~/vagrant/project1$ vagrant box list
almalinux/8              (virtualbox, 8.8.20230606)
ubuntu/xenial64          (virtualbox, 20211001.0.0)
ubuntu/xenial64          (virtualbox, 20211001.0.1)
packer_made_ubuntu20server (virtualbox, 0)
```

Searching for vagrant Boxes

In our first example, we used the web interface to search for vagrant boxes. This method is very friendly and easy, but it is also possible to search for available boxes from the command line.

Let's suppose we want to search for available ubuntu boxes. We'd need to execute this command:

```
antonio@antonio-Laptop:~/vagrant/project1$ vagrant cloud search ubuntu
| NAME                    | VERSION       | DOWNLOADS  |
  PROVIDERS                                                           |
+------------------------+---------------+-----------+
-------------------------------------------------------------+
| ubuntu/trusty64         | 20191107.0.0  | 30,789,336 |
  virtualbox                                                          |
| hashicorp/precise64     | 1.1.0         | 6,815,055  |
  virtualbox, vmware_fusion, hyperv                                   |
| ubuntu/xenial64         | 20211001.0.1  | 3,627,771  |
  virtualbox                                                          |
| puphpet/ubuntu1404-x64  | 20161102      | 2,522,864  |
  vmware_desktop, virtualbox, parallels                               |
| hashicorp/precise32     | 1.0.0         | 2,301,428  |
  virtualbox                                                          |
```

```
| bento/ubuntu-16.04     | 202212.11.0 | 1,886,760 |
 virtualbox                                         |
| ubuntu/trusty32        | 20191107.0.0 | 1,854,678 |
 virtualbox                                         |
| bento/ubuntu-14.04     | 201808.24.0 |   989,815 |
 hyperv, parallels, vmware_desktop, virtualbox      |
| generic/ubuntu1804     | 4.3.12      |   981,839 |
 qemu, parallels, libvirt, vmware_desktop, hyperv, virtualbox |
| generic/ubuntu1604     | 4.3.12      |   968,883 |
 qemu, libvirt, vmware_desktop, parallels, hyperv, virtualbox |
+-----------------------+--------------+-----------+
----------------------------------------------------------------+
.
.
.
```

Provisioning with vagrant

So far, we have created "default" vagrant environments. That is, we created virtual machines based on AlmaLinux, Ubuntu, etc., but without any additional configuration.

However, we might be interested in provisioning these environments, installing additional software, creating additional users, etc. This can also be done with vagrant.

In the *Vagrantfile* previously created, we can see the following section:

.
.
.

```
# Enable provisioning with a shell script. Additional
  provisioners such as
```

CHAPTER 15 VAGRANT

```
  # Ansible, Chef, Docker, Puppet and Salt are also available. Please see the
  # documentation for more information about their specific syntax and use.
  # config.vm.provision "shell", inline: <<-SHELL
  #   apt-get update
  #   apt-get install -y apache2
  # SHELL
.
.
.
```

As we can read in the file itself, it is possible to configure provisioning using shell scripts, ansible, puppet, salt, etc. In our case, we'll use the shell option.

As a proof of concept, we only need to uncomment the entries we mentioned above. The section should look more or less like this:

```
.
.
  config.vm.provision "shell", inline: <<-SHELL
    apt-get update
    apt-get install -y apache2
  SHELL
.
.
```

To apply the changes, we need to reload vagrant.

antonio@antonio-Laptop:~/vagrant/project1$ vagrant reload

CHAPTER 15   VAGRANT

vagrant will try to gracefully shut down the virtual machine.

```
==> default: Attempting graceful shutdown of VM...
```

After a few seconds, the machine will be back and ready.

```
==> default: Machine booted and ready!
```

We get a final message saying that the machine is provisioned.

```
==> default: Machine already provisioned. Run `vagrant provision` or use the `--provision`
==> default: flag to force provisioning. Provisioners marked to run always will still run.
antonio@antonio-Laptop:~/vagrant/project1$
```

Anyway, if we want to, we can force the provisioning.

```
antonio@antonio-Laptop:~/vagrant/project1$ vagrant provision
==> default: Running provisioner: shell...
    default: Running: inline script
```

CHAPTER 15   VAGRANT

After a few seconds, we'll see that the VM is contacting the repositories to perform the update if needed.

-
-
    ```
    default: Get:1 http://security.ubuntu.com/ubuntu xenial-security InRelease [106 kB]
    default: Hit:2 http://archive.ubuntu.com/ubuntu xenial InRelease
    default: Get:3 http://archive.ubuntu.com/ubuntu xenial-updates InRelease [106 kB]
    ```
-
-
    ```
    default: Fetched 18.7 MB in 5s (3,294 kB/s)
    default: Reading package lists...
    default: Reading package lists...
    default: Building dependency tree...
    default: Reading state information…
    ```
-
-

And Apache will be installed.

-
-
    ```
    default: The following additional packages will be installed:
    default:   apache2-bin apache2-data apache2-utils libapr1 libaprutil1
    ```
-
-
    ```
    antonio@antonio-Laptop:~/vagrant/project1$
    ```

To check that everything is OK, we'll connect to the virtual machine.

antonio@antonio-Laptop:~/vagrant/project1$ vagrant ssh

And we'll check if the Apache web server was installed.

vagrant@ubuntu-xenial:~$ systemctl status apache2
* apache2.service - LSB: Apache2 web server
  Loaded: loaded (/etc/init.d/apache2; bad; vendor preset: enabled)
  Drop-In: /lib/systemd/system/apache2.service.d
           └─apache2-systemd.conf
  Active: active (running) since Sat 2024-08-24 13:13:51 UTC; 1min 44s ago
    Docs: man:systemd-sysv-generator(8)
  CGroup: /system.slice/apache2.service
          ├─2766 /usr/sbin/apache2 -k start
          ├─2769 /usr/sbin/apache2 -k start
          └─2770 /usr/sbin/apache2 -k start

We just confirmed that it was actually installed, and everything seems to be working fine. We can also use a web browser to check that we can access the welcome page.

vagrant@ubuntu-xenial:~$ curl http://localhost

After performing all the tests, we log out.

vagrant@ubuntu-xenial:~$ logout

Port Redirection

As we already have a vagrant environment with a web server, we're gonna review how to edit the network setting to access the web server externally.

CHAPTER 15   VAGRANT

By checking the *Vagrantfile* again, we'll see the following lines:

-
-
  ```
  # Create a forwarded port mapping which allows access to a specific port
  # within the machine from a port on the host machine. In the example below,
  # accessing "localhost:8080" will access port 80 on the guest machine.
  # NOTE: This will enable public access to the opened port
  # config.vm.network "forwarded_port", guest: 80, host: 8080
  ```
-
-

The comments in the file are quite clear, so I don't think any further explanation is needed. In fact, the example provided is just what we need. We only need to uncomment the config.vm.network.

-
-
  ```
  config.vm.network "forwarded_port", guest: 80, host: 8080
  ```
-
-

To apply the new configuration, we need to reload vagrant. But before doing it, we'll examine the port redirections known to vagrant with **vagrant port**.

```
antonio@antonio-Laptop:~/vagrant/project1$ vagrant port
The forwarded ports for the machine are listed below. Please note that
```

CHAPTER 15   VAGRANT

these values may differ from values configured in the Vagrantfile if the
provider supports automatic port collision detection and resolution.

```
    22 (guest) => 2222 (host)
```

When creating a vagrant environment, vagrant automatically creates a port redirection to port 22 (ssh) in the guest virtual machine. To be more precise, we should say that vagrant tells VirtualBox to create this redirection. This is the only active port redirection right now.

If we check port 2222 in the host, we'll see that the process currently listening on it is VirtualBox.

```
antonio@antonio-Laptop:~/vagrant/project1$ sudo lsof -i :2222
COMMAND      PID    USER    FD   TYPE DEVICE SIZE/OFF NODE NAME
VBoxHeadl  16312 antonio    21u  IPv4 152711       0t0  TCP
localhost:2222 (LISTEN)
```

After this small pause, we reload vagrant.

```
antonio@antonio-Laptop:~/vagrant/project1$ vagrant reload
==> default: Attempting graceful shutdown of VM...
·
·
```

We can see now that two ports are being redirected.

·
·
```
==> default: Forwarding ports...
    default: 80 (guest) => 8080 (host) (adapter 1)
    default: 22 (guest) => 2222 (host) (adapter 1)
```
·
·

719

We'll wait for the reload to finish.

.
.
==> default: Machine booted and ready!
.
.
.

We'll use **vagrant port** again to list the new port redirection.

antonio@antonio-Laptop:~/vagrant/project1$ vagrant port
The forwarded ports for the machine are listed below. Please note that
these values may differ from values configured in the Vagrantfile if the
provider supports automatic port collision detection and resolution.

    22 (guest) => 2222 (host)
    80 (guest) => 8080 (host)

From now on, we can use a web browser to open the host address and port 8080, and we'll see the Apache web page (Figure 15-7).

CHAPTER 15 VAGRANT

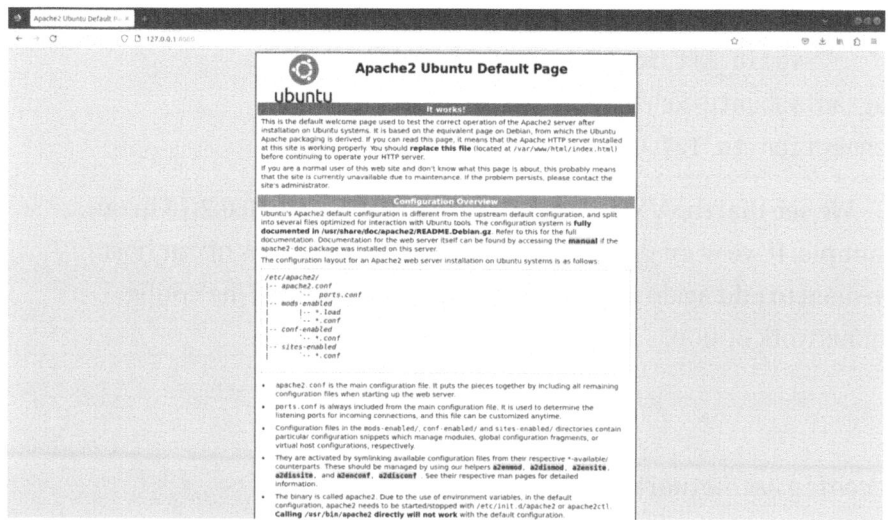

Figure 15-7. Apache welcome page

Customizing Network Settings

In all the vagrant environments created so far, we used the default network configuration. This default configuration uses NAT, which is the default network configuration in VirtualBox.

We'll connect to our current vagrant instance to check the IP settings.

```
antonio@antonio-Laptop:~/vagrant/project1$ vagrant ssh
.
.
vagrant@ubuntu-xenial:~$ ip address show
.
.
2: enp0s3: <BROADCAST,MULTICAST,UP,LOWER_UP> mtu 1500 qdisc
pfifo_fast state UP group default qlen 1000
    link/ether 02:be:82:6b:cc:1d brd ff:ff:ff:ff:ff:ff
    inet 10.0.2.15/24 brd 10.0.2.255 scope global enp0s3
       valid_lft forever preferred_lft forever
```

721

CHAPTER 15   VAGRANT

```
     inet6 fe80::be:82ff:fe6b:cc1d/64 scope link
        valid_lft forever preferred_lft forever
vagrant@ubuntu-xenial:~$ logout
Connection to 127.0.0.1 closed.
```

We see that the VM is using a private IP address, 10.0.2.15 in our example. If we want the VM to access the local network of our host, we need to edit again the *Vagrantfile* and uncomment the config.vm.network option.

-
-
  config.vm.network "public_network"
-
-

Again, we reload vagrant.

```
antonio@antonio-Laptop:~/vagrant/project1$ vagrant reload
==> default: Attempting graceful shutdown of VM...
```
-
-

vagrant will detect the network interfaces present in the host and request which one we want to use as a network bridge.

```
==> default: Clearing any previously set network interfaces...
==> default: Available bridged network interfaces:
1) wlp2s0
2) veth0a8a00c
3) enp3s0
4) docker0
5) br-5d100a76afaf
6) br-58df75541e61
```

722

7) vmnet1
8) vmnet8
9) virbr0
10) lxcbr0
11) virbr1
==> default: When choosing an interface, it is usually the one that is
==> default: being used to connect to the internet.
==> default:
    default: Which interface should the network bridge to?

We'll select the main network interface in the host, that is, the one used to access the Internet.

.
.
==> default:
    default: Which interface should the network bridge to? 1
==> default: Preparing network interfaces based on configuration...
    default: Adapter 1: nat
    default: Adapter 2: bridged
.
.
antonio@antonio-Laptop:~/vagrant/project1$

After the environment is reloaded, we connect to the instance again.

antonio@antonio-Laptop:~/vagrant/project1$ vagrant ssh
.
.

And we check the IP settings again.

```
vagrant@ubuntu-xenial:~$ ip address show
.
.
2: enp0s3: <BROADCAST,MULTICAST,UP,LOWER_UP> mtu 1500 qdisc
pfifo_fast state UP group default qlen 1000
    link/ether 02:be:82:6b:cc:1d brd ff:ff:ff:ff:ff:ff
    inet 10.0.2.15/24 brd 10.0.2.255 scope global enp0s3
       valid_lft forever preferred_lft forever
    inet6 fe80::be:82ff:fe6b:cc1d/64 scope link
       valid_lft forever preferred_lft forever
3: enp0s8: <BROADCAST,MULTICAST,UP,LOWER_UP> mtu 1500 qdisc
pfifo_fast state UP group default qlen 1000
    link/ether 08:00:27:d9:f0:8e brd ff:ff:ff:ff:ff:ff
    inet 192.168.1.73/24 brd 192.168.1.255 scope global enp0s8
       valid_lft forever preferred_lft forever
    inet6 fe80::a00:27ff:fed9:f08e/64 scope link
       valid_lft forever preferred_lft forever
vagrant@ubuntu-xenial:~$
```

We can see that a new network interface was created, and it was assigned an IP in the host network address space. That's exactly what we expected. Now any computer device can communicate with this VM and vice versa.

Shared Folders in vagrant

We might need to share files between our host and our vagrant VM. We can do this in different ways, but probably the most convenient way is to use a shared folder.

CHAPTER 15 VAGRANT

By default, vagrant shares the folder in which the Vagrantfile is located. For instance, we can list the content of the *project1* folder.

```
antonio@antonio-Laptop:~/vagrant/project1$ ls -lrth
total 48K
-rw-rw-r-- 1 antonio antonio 3,0K ago 24 15:31 Vagrantfile
-rw------- 1 antonio antonio  42K ago 24 15:33 ubuntu-
xenial-16.04-cloudimg-console.log
antonio@antonio-Laptop:~/vagrant/project1$
```

Next, we connect to our running instance. If we list the contents of the root folder, we'll see a *vagrant* subfolder.

```
vagrant@ubuntu-xenial:~$ ls /
bin   boot  dev   etc   home   initrd.img  initrd.img.old  lib
lib64 lost+found  media mnt   opt   proc   root   run   sbin
snap  srv   sys   tmp   usr   vagrant  var   vmlinuz  vmlinuz.old
```

And inside this folder, we can list the exact same content that we listed previously from the host.

```
vagrant@ubuntu-xenial:~$ ls /vagrant/
Vagrantfile   ubuntu-xenial-16.04-cloudimg-console.log
vagrant@ubuntu-xenial:~$
```

If we want to share a different folder, we can easily do it by editing the Vagrantfile again. This time, we need to modify the config.vm.synced_folder parameter. As an example, we'll share the */home/antonio/QEMU* folder in the host as the */qemu* folder in the guest. The line should look like this:

.
.

  config.vm.synced_folder "/home/antonio/QEMU", "/qemu"

.
.

725

We'll reload vagrant to apply these changes.

```
antonio@antonio-Laptop:~/vagrant/project1$ vagrant reload
==> default: Attempting graceful shutdown of VM...
.
.
.
.
.
.
==> default: Mounting shared folders...
    default: /qemu => /home/antonio/QEMU
    default: /vagrant => /home/antonio/vagrant/project1
.
.
```

We can clearly see in the output that the new shared folder was created. To check it, we'll access the instance and list the contents of the */qemu* folder.

```
vagrant@ubuntu-xenial:~$ ls /qemu/
README.txt        alpine-virt-3.17.0-x86_64.iso
ch2-p2v1.jpg   .
.
.
```

Managing the State of the VM from vagrant

By now, we are already familiar with some vagrant commands related to the management of the underlying virtual machine(s).

We have used **vagrant up** to create a new vagrant environment, which includes creating a new virtual machine and starting it.

We have also used **vagrant destroy** to delete the associated virtual machine and release its resources.

And we have checked the status of the virtual machines with **vagrant status** too.

In addition to these commands, we have many other available to manage virtual machines. We can use **vagrant suspend**, which suspends the VM instead of shutting it down or destroying it.

```
antonio@antonio-Laptop:~/vagrant/project1$ vagrant suspend
==> default: Saving VM state and suspending execution…
```

After that, we can check the new status of the VM.

```
antonio@antonio-Laptop:~/vagrant/project1$ vagrant status
Current machine states:

default                   saved (virtualbox)
```

To return the VM to the running state, we can use **vagrant up**.

```
antonio@antonio-Laptop:~/vagrant/project1$ vagrant up
Bringing machine 'default' up with 'virtualbox' provider…
.
.
antonio@antonio-Laptop:~/vagrant/project1$ vagrant status
Current machine states:

default                   running (virtualbox)
```

If we prefer to shut down the VM, we'll use **vagrant halt**.

```
antonio@antonio-Laptop:~/vagrant/project1$ vagrant halt
==> default: Attempting graceful shutdown of VM...
```

Again, we can check the new status with **vagrant status**.

```
antonio@antonio-Laptop:~/vagrant/project1$ vagrant status
Current machine states:

default                   poweroff (virtualbox)
```

Deploying Multiple Virtual Machines from a Single Vagrantfile

In all the previous examples, we edited many options in the *Vagrantfile*. However, we always have deployed a single VM in every vagrant deployment. This is not something mandatory, and we can actually deploy several VMs using a single *Vagrantfile*.

To see a simple example of this kind of deployment, we'll create a new folder for this new project and execute **vagrant init** to generate a default *Vagrantfile*.

```
antonio@antonio-Laptop:~/vagrant/multi$ vagrant init
A `Vagrantfile` has been placed in this directory. You are now
ready to `vagrant up` your first virtual environment! Please read
the comments in the Vagrantfile as well as documentation on
`vagrantup.com` for more information on using Vagrant.
```

We need to edit the default Vagrantfile to declare as many virtual machines as we want. We'll use two in this example.

This time, the changes we need to do in the file are a bit more complicated, so we need to pay close attention. Near the top of the file we'll see this line:

```
Vagrant.configure("2") do |config|
```

CHAPTER 15 VAGRANT

Just below it, we'll create two new blocks of code, one for each VM. We'll name the two virtual machines server1 and server2.

```
config.vm.define :server1 do |server1|

end

config.vm.define :server2 do |server2|

end
```

In the previous examples, we have seen the option config.vm.box, which was used to specify the name of the box to use in the single machine deployment. For our multiple machine deployment, we need to use a similar parameter in the form name_of_the_vm.vm.box. We'll add this information inside the two new blocks we created previously. We'll use an ubuntu box. The modified part of the Vagrantfile should be something like this:

```
Vagrant.configure("2") do |config|
  config.vm.define :server1 do |server1|
    server1.vm.box="ubuntu/xenial64"
  end

  config.vm.define :server2 do |server2|
    server2.vm.box="ubuntu/xenial64"
  end
```

And we'll also comment out the default config.vm.box option in the file.

```
#    config.vm.box = "base"
```

We're ready to create this new environment with **vagrant up**.

```
antonio@antonio-Aspire-A315-23:~/vagrant/multi$ vagrant up
```

Right after executing the command, we see that vagrant realizes it needs to start two virtual machines.

```
Bringing machine 'server1' up with 'virtualbox' provider...
Bringing machine 'server2' up with 'virtualbox' provider...
```

And it will create two different port redirections.

```
==> server1: Preparing network interfaces based on configuration...
    server1: Adapter 1: nat
==> server1: Forwarding ports...
    server1: 22 (guest) => 2222 (host) (adapter 1)


    server2: Adapter 1: nat
==> server2: Forwarding ports...
    server2: 22 (guest) => 2200 (host) (adapter 1)
```

After the deployment is complete, we can use vagrant status to check that there are actually two virtual machines deployed.

```
antonio@antonio-Laptop:~/vagrant/multi$ vagrant status
Current machine states:

server1                   running (virtualbox)
server2                   running (virtualbox)
```

We can connect perfectly to any of the two instances.

antonio@antonio-Laptop:~/vagrant/multi$ vagrant ssh server1
.
.
vagrant@ubuntu-xenial:~$

antonio@antonio-Laptop:~/vagrant/multi$ vagrant ssh server2
.
.
vagrant@ubuntu-xenial:~$

We already have two virtual machines deployed, but if we check the IP settings in any of these two machines, we'll see we're using the same IP address and both are using NAT.

```
vagrant@ubuntu-xenial:~$ ip address show
1: lo: <LOOPBACK,UP,LOWER_UP> mtu 65536 qdisc noqueue state
.
.
2: enp0s3: <BROADCAST,MULTICAST,UP,LOWER_UP> mtu 1500 qdisc
pfifo_fast state UP group default qlen 1000
    link/ether 02:be:82:6b:cc:1d brd ff:ff:ff:ff:ff:ff
    inet 10.0.2.15/24 brd 10.0.2.255 scope global enp0s3
       valid_lft forever preferred_lft forever
    inet6 fe80::be:82ff:fe6b:cc1d/64 scope link
       valid_lft forever preferred_lft forever
vagrant@ubuntu-xenial:~$
```

This can be confusing, so we're going to use a bridged network for both instances and we'll make sure they receive different IP addresses and can communicate with each other.

CHAPTER 15 VAGRANT

We need to edit again the *Vagrantfile*. We'll include a new vm.network parameter to set a new network for each one of the virtual machines. We'll use the 192.168.56.0/24 network address as this is one of the default private addresses used on VirtualBox. The relevant part of the *Vagrantfile* is this:

```
Vagrant.configure("2") do |config|
  config.vm.define :server1 do |server1|
    server1.vm.box="ubuntu/xenial64"
    server1.vm.network "private_network", ip: "192.168.56.1"
  end

  config.vm.define :server2 do |server2|
    server2.vm.box="ubuntu/xenial64"
    server2.vm.network "private_network", ip: "192.168.56.2"
  end
```

And we execute **vagrant reload**.

```
antonio@antonio-Laptop:~/vagrant/multi$ vagrant reload
.
.
```

After the deployment is complete, we can connect to both instances and check that we have the same IP that was assigned in the *Vagrantfile*.

```
antonio@antonio-Laptop:~/vagrant/multi$ vagrant ssh server1
.
.
vagrant@ubuntu-xenial:~$ ip address show
.
.
3: enp0s8: <BROADCAST,MULTICAST,UP,LOWER_UP> mtu 1500 qdisc pfifo_fast state UP group default qlen 1000
    link/ether 08:00:27:1c:85:ed brd ff:ff:ff:ff:ff:ff
```

        inet 192.168.56.1/24 brd 192.168.56.255 scope global enp0s8
           valid_lft forever preferred_lft forever
        inet6 fe80::a00:27ff:fe1c:85ed/64 scope link
           valid_lft forever preferred_lft forever

antonio@antonio-Laptop:~/vagrant/multi$ vagrant ssh server2
.
.
vagrant@ubuntu-xenial:~$ ip address show
.
.
3: enp0s8: <BROADCAST,MULTICAST,UP,LOWER_UP> mtu 1500 qdisc pfifo_fast state UP group default qlen 1000
    link/ether 08:00:27:1c:85:ed brd ff:ff:ff:ff:ff:ff
    inet 192.168.56.2/24 brd 192.168.56.255 scope global enp0s8
       valid_lft forever preferred_lft forever
    inet6 fe80::a00:27ff:fe1c:85ed/64 scope link
       valid_lft forever preferred_lft forever

Of course we can ping server2 from server1 and vice versa.

```
vagrant@ubuntu-xenial:~$ ping 192.168.56.2
PING 192.168.56.2 (192.168.56.2) 56(84) bytes of data.
64 bytes from 192.168.56.2: icmp_seq=1 ttl=64 time=0.755 ms
64 bytes from 192.168.56.2: icmp_seq=2 ttl=64 time=0.566 ms
64 bytes from 192.168.56.2: icmp_seq=3 ttl=64 time=0.683 ms
^C
```

CHAPTER 15   VAGRANT

Summary

In this final chapter of the book, we studied **vagrant**. We began by installing vagrant and creating a simple environment. We saw that we can download many preinstalled vagrant boxes from vagrant cloud. It is also possible to create our own vagrant box by using Packer, as we did in Chapter 13.

By now, we have become familiar with the *Vagrantfile* and how easy it is to edit it to customize options like the IP settings or the provisioning.

We used vagrant to manage the status of the associated virtual machine and created our own customized shared folders.

Finally, we saw an example about how to deploy several virtual machines using a single *Vagrantfile*.

Index

A

Alpine Linux
 alpine.pvlinux file, 109
 bridge creation, 112, 113
 CDROM drive, 114–117
 configuration file, 107–113
 Ethernet interface, 118
 installation procedure, 117
 interfaces, 117
 ISO files, 105, 106
 kernel/ramdisk files, 124
 logical volume/hard disk, 120–127
 network configuration, 118–120
 paravirtualization, 114
 setup-alpine installation, 121
 website, 104
Amazon Web Services (AWS), 616, 635–638, 641, 680
AppArmor, 359–362, 402–404
API, *see* Application programming interface (API)
Application container, 320, 376, 577, 626
Application programming interface (API)
 libvirt, 148
AWS, *see* Amazon Web Services (AWS)

B

buildah, 571–573, 588

C

CLI, *see* Command-line interface (CLI)
Cloud computing model
 AWS, 636
 characteristics, 589
 comparison, 591
 concepts, 589
 deployment model, 591
 Google cloud, 637, 638
 Microsoft Azure, 637
 OpenStack, 592–613
 public cloud offerings, 635
 service models, 590
 terms/utilities, 589
 Terraform, 613–635
 types, 591
cloud-init
 concepts, 677
 datasources, 686
 filesystems, 689–692
 instance metadata services, 686
 LXD container, 687–689

cloud-init (*cont.*)
   OpenStack configuration
      drive, 686
   QEMU instance
     datasource, 686
     hardware virtualization, 680
     HTTP requests, 682
     http.server module, 680
     information, 683
     log files, 684
     meta-data file, 680, 682
     qcow2 file, 679
     status command, 683
     system booting, 681
     temporary folder, 678
     user-data file, 679, 685
     vendor-data file, 680
   software package, 692–694
   web page, 677
   website, 678
Command-line interface (CLI)
   characteristics, 613
   components, 608
   endpoints, 610
   networks/images, 612
   openstack service list
     command, 609, 612
   run commands, 609
   services, 609
   users/roles, 611
Container orchestration, *see*
   Orchestration solution
Container virtualization
   AppArmor, 359–362

concepts, 319
control groups, 341–344
Linux/UNIX, 345–353
LXC (Linux containers), 363
namespaces (*see* Namespaces)
seccomp, 362
security, 353
SELinux, 353–359
system processes/
   application, 320
unprivileged processes, 345
Control groups (cgroups), 341–344

D

Disk image management
   access/modify files
     command line, 242
     conversion server, 275, 277
     CPU configuration, 280
     Debian domain, 282
     debian.xml file, 279
     destination format, 278
     df command, 262
     disk image writer, 274
     filesystems, 258, 264, 265
     guestfish, 242, 243
     guestmount/
       guestunmount, 248–251
     inspector, 257
     p2v, 269–277
     rescue, 262–265
     resizes, 263–267
     sparsify, 267–269

INDEX

sysprep, 282–285
troubleshooting
  libguestfs, 244–248
USB device, 275
versatile/interesting
  tool, 278
virt-cat, 251–254
virt-copy-in, 254
virt-copy-out, 255
virt-diff, 256
VirtualBox instance, 246
virtual disks, 241
v2v, 277–282
computer forensic tools, 228
concepts, 227
formats, 228
qcow/qcow2, 229
qemu-img
  creation, 232, 233
  disk file conversion, 235, 236
  hardware specifications, 239
  information, 230–232
  overlay images, 233–235
  qemu-utils package, 230
  snapshots, 231
  VirtualBox, 236–241
  VMDK disk file, 237
raw images, 228, 229
terms/utilities, 227
virtualization solutions, 285–289
VMDK disk image, 230
Docker
  architecture, 445–450
  client-server architecture, 435

concepts, 435
containers, 440–445
  customization, 471
  Dockerfile, 475–482
  export images, 475–479
  FROM/RUN
    instructions, 478
  security options, 496–498
  test_file.txt file, 479
containers mapping port, 493
dockerd service, 445
docker info command, 437
docker.io package, 436
images, 438–440
installation, 436–438
local/hub registry, 492–496
logging map, 482–487
networking
  communication, 465
  creation, 467–470
  interfaces, 464, 467
  IP address, 464
  loopback interface, 467
  mapping ports, 470, 471
  orchestration, 465
  ping, 464
official repositories, 436
save/restore
  containers, 487–491
search command, 438
security options, 496–498
swarm cluster, 510–527
volumes
  attach file, 450

INDEX

Docker (cont.)
  bind mounts, 453–455
  container, 450
  delete/prune volumes, 463
  named volumes, 455–457
  overlay, 452, 453
  plug-ins, 460
  remote, 460–463
  shares, 458, 459
  storage drivers, 452
  test file, 451
  tmpfs, 458
 web page, 489

E

Emulation
  definition, 2, 3
  DOSBox, 2
  game console, 3, 4
  network (GNS3), 6
  printer, 5
  PuTTY, 4, 5
  QEMU (see Quick
    Emulator (QEMU))
  retro VM, 4
  systems, 6
  terminals, 4, 5

F

FreeBSD systems, 575–577
Full system emulation
  ARM system

  architecture, 29
  disk image, 31
  initrd file, 30, 32–34
  kernel loading option, 30
  parameters, 32
 qemu-system-xxx
    commands, 17, 18
 SPARC system, 34–41
 x86 system
    BOOT device, 19
    command prompts, 19, 20
    contextual option, 24
    distributions, 18
    graphical installation, 25, 28
    initramfs file, 22
    installation menu, 20, 21
    installation program, 25
    login screen, 28
    no disk drive, 26
    official documentation, 28
    operating system, 28
    QEMU monitor, 22, 23
    qemu-system
      command, 26, 27
    RAM memory, 24

G

Google Cloud, 635, 637, 638, 680

H

Hardware virtualized machine
  (HVM), 127–130, 145

INDEX

Helm
    Apache installation, 552
    architecture, 546
    arguments, 548
    binary file, 547
    bitnami repository, 549, 550
    chart information, 550
    kubectl command, 551
    minikube service command, 552, 553
    official web page, 547
    repositories, 549
HVM, *see* Hardware virtualized machine (HVM)

I, J

IaaS, *see* Infrastructure as a Service (IaaS)
IaC, *see* Infrastructure as Code (IaC)
IMDS, *see* Instance metadata services (IMDS)
Infrastructure as a Service (IaaS), 590–592, 636, 637
Infrastructure as Code (IaC), 613–635, 695
Instance metadata services (IMDS), 680, 686

K

Kernel-based virtual machine (KVM), 12, 45, 46, 87, 94, 139, 246

Kubernetes, 527–546
    architecture, 527–529
    components, 529
    configmap, 546
    control plane, 528
    deployments, 542–546
    items, 546
    minikube
        binary file, 530
        dashboard, 535
        deployment, 537
        helm, 537, 538
        hi-minikube service, 536
        installation, 529–531
        kubectl, 531, 533
        requirements, 530
        service command, 536
        status command, 532
        web browser, 534, 535
        web page, 530
        working process, 532, 533
    nginx application, 545
    pod deployment, 539, 540
    pods, 531
    replicasets, 540–542
KVM, *see* Kernel-based virtual machine (KVM)

L

Libvirt virtual machine management
    concepts, 147
    C program, 177–180
    dnsmasq, 223, 225

INDEX

Libvirt virtual machine
    management (*cont.*)
  installation, 148
  libvirt.conf, 219, 220
  libvirtd.conf file, 220–222
  migration
    add connection, 182
    error message, 186, 187, 190
    execution process, 191
    remote hypervisor, 183
    server console, 191–193
    source/destination host, 184
    storage file, 190
    storage pool, 187
    summary, 186
    unsafe migration, 187–189
  monitoring process, 212–214
  networking
    communication, 201
    connection settings, 208
    dnsmasq, 205
    firewall configuration, 205
    hardware details option, 202
    installation, 204
    interfaces, 202, 204, 208
    isolated mode, 210, 211
    NAT details, 203
    network settings, 204
    open/routed modes, 212
    routed mode, 206, 207
    web server, 209
    web server logs, 205
  Python program, 180–182
  qemu.conf, 222

radvd service, 225
snapshots, 193–196
storage pools/volumes
  creation, 197
  local directory, 197
  logical type, 199, 200
  netfs, 198
  network exports, 199
  storage volume, 200, 201
virsh
  code configuration, 216, 217
  command line, 214
  listing process, 215
  network details, 217
  parameters, 215
  snapshots, 217
  storage pool/volumes, 218
  XML file, 216
virtlockd, 223
virtlogd.conf, 223
virt-manager
  add connection, 151, 152
  browse button, 171
  CPU/memory settings, 174
  disk space, 175
  error message, 151–154, 158
  graphical application, 149
  import existing disk
    image, 161–169
  installation/management,
    159, 160
  installation process, 175–177
  ISO file, 172
  Libvirt-LXC, 157

INDEX

   LXC, 158, 159
   media installation, 171, 173
   network installation, 160
   operating system, 173
   QEMU/KVM hypervisor,
      155, 156
   several options, 160
   ssh-askpass package, 153
   storage path, 161–164
   VM creation, 170
   Xen hypervisor, 149, 150, 155
Linux
   configuration file, 100–104
Linux Containers (LXC)
   bare-metal servers, 411
   commands, 404
      cgroups, 406
      monitors, 405
   concepts, 363
   configuration
      bridge interfaces, 376
      chroot environment, 372
      IP address, 373
      linux-console, 373
      logical volume, 385
      lxc-checkconfig
         command, 365–379
      lxc-create command, 367
      lxc-templates packages, 367
      network configuration, 377
      network namespaces, 377
      network settings, 371
      root filesystem, 372
      root password, 372

   storage option, 379–386
   system/application
      containers, 376
   Ubuntu computer, 374
   ubuntu template, 368
   veth interfaces, 378
   volume group, 383
containers, 363
Docker security options, 496
installation, 364, 365
LXD (see Linux Containers
   Daemon (LXD))
OCI technologies, 566
Packer system
   configuration file, 655
   documentation, 653, 658
   error message, 654
   integration, 652
   JSON format, 654
   modification, 656
   operations, 657
   template, 656
   VirtualBox/LXC plug-in, 652
   web page, 651
RedHat/Rocky/
      CentOS, 386–398
   bridge-utils package, 391
   busybox binary, 387
   creation, 389
   DHCP services, 397
   dnsmasq program, 397
   download template, 387
   error message, 387, 390
   IP settings, 391

741

INDEX

Linux Containers (LXC) (*cont.*)
    lxc-net service, 396, 397
    packages, 386
    restart option, 395
    root password, 389
    script running, 394
    service execution, 392, 393
    Ubuntu image, 389
  security, 399–404
    aa-status, 402
    AppArmor, 401, 403, 404
    capabilities, 400
    cgroups, 399
    commands/
      characteristics, 399
    logfile option, 403
    seccomp, 402
    unexisting profile, 403
Linux Containers Daemon (LXD)
  advantages, 407
  cloud-init
    configuration, 687–689
  configuration, 410
  container, 412–416
  installation, 407
  networking process, 420–424
  profiles, 427–432
  resource utilization, 432, 433
  server/container
    configuration, 416–419
  server (lxd)/client (lxc), 407, 409
  storage, 424–426
  storage pools, 410
Linux system, 7

Alpine website, 104–127
capabilities, 345–353
chroot, 338
emulation, 42
LXC (*see* Linux
    Containers (LXC))
OpenVZ, 583–588
Packer, 641
SELinux, 353–359
Terraform, 614–636
virt-df, 262
x86 system, 18
LXC, *see* Linux Containers (LXC)
LXD, *see* Linux Containers
    Daemon (LXD)

M

MAC, *see* Mandatory access
    control (MAC)
MAME, *see* Multiple Arcade
    Machine Emulator (MAME)
Mandatory access control (MAC)
  AppArmor, 359–362
  SELinux, 353–359
Microsoft Azure, 635, 637
Multiple Arcade Machine
    Emulator (MAME), 2

N

Namespaces
  chroot
    error message, 337, 339

INDEX

libraries, 337
Linux distribution, 338
root directory, 336–340
structure, 339
subfolder, 338
execute programs, 331
interfaces, 333
isolated namespace, 329–332
kernel resources, 320–323
mount, 323–326
network, 333–336
process namespace, 327, 328
user identifiers (UIDs/ GIDs), 328
virtual Ethernet devices (veth), 333
NAT, *see* Network Address Translation (NAT)
Network Address Translation (NAT), 203, 205, 209, 721, 731
Networking process
bridge-utils package, 68
external access, 68–70
libvirt virtual machine management, 201–212
operational network, 47
TUN/TAP devices, 62
communication, 68
connection failed message, 64
information, 64
interfaces, 67, 68
IP settings, 66
netdev/dev parameters, 62
tap interfaces, 63, 66
tunctl command, 62
user networking, 48–52

O

OCI, *see* Open Container Initiative (OCI)
Open Container Initiative (OCI), 566, 571
OpenShift cluster
deployments, 555
objects, 555
PHP installation, 556
productivity/security features, 553
Red Hat sandbox, 554
sample applications, 555, 556
OpenStack
configuration drive, 686
OpenStack system
Canonical, 594
command-line interface, 608–613
components, 592
concepts, 608
console log, 607
dashboard, 595, 596
flavor selection, 600–602
image creation, 596–598
installation method, 593
instances, 604, 605

743

INDEX

OpenStack system (cont.)
  interfaces, 606
  modules, 592
  naming instance, 599
  networks, 604
  overview, 606
  server console, 605, 607
  services, 592
  source image, 599, 600
  summary, 595
  training-labs, 593
  website, 596
Open Virtualization Format (OVF), 227, 285–289
  appliance settings, 286, 287
  destination folder, 288
  export appliance, 285
  files, 288
  VMDK files, 288
Open vSwitch, 313–318
OpenVZ system
  containers, 584
  error message, 586
  libvirt-based tool, 586
  prlctl, 585, 586, 588
  virtualization solution, 583
  Virtuozzo, 584
  vmtype ct, 584
  web page, 583
Orchestration solution
  concepts, 499
  docker compose
    accessing adminer, 508
    installation, 500–506

  microservices, 500
  multi-container
    service, 506–510
  PostgreSQL instance, 509
  repositories, 501
  service creation, 502–506
Helm, 546–553
Kubernetes, 527–546
OpenShift cluster, 553–556
Rancher, 557–562
scenarios, 500
swarm cluster
  accessing services, 519
  architecture, 510
  constraints, 520, 521
  global service, 522, 523
  initialization, 511, 512
  modes, 516
  nodes, 510, 513–515
  overlay network, 520, 521
  replicated service, 522
  secrets, 523, 524
  services
    deployment, 515–519
  stacks, 524–527
OVF, *see* Open Virtualization Format (OVF)

P

PaaS, *see* Platform as a Service (PaaS)
Packer
  building images, 646

INDEX

HashiCorp code language
(HCL), 647
LXC image, 651–659
source file, 650
Ubuntu server
installation, 649
VboxManage, 650
VirtualBox builder, 647–652
building system/container
images, 641
concepts, 641
installation
binary file, 642, 643
website, 641, 642
zip package, 643
integration, 671–676
integrations (plug-ins)
installation, 645
upper menu, 644
VirtualBox, 644
provision virtual machines
documentation, 671
message, 675
packer/vagrant, 672
post-processors, 672
scripts folder, 671
source file, 672, 673
vagrant, 675
vagrant post-processor, 674
Ubuntu system
access file, 666
autoinstall documentation,
660, 666
automated installation, 667

automated process, 669
cloud-init, 662
content file, 665
documentation, 662
format option, 664
http server, 662
image file, 670
installation
documentation, 659
parameters, 661
server ISO file, 660
shutdown_command, 664
vagrant, 663, 664, 668
VM installation, 668
Page Description Language
(PDL), 5
Paravirtualization, 10, 11, 90,
114, 128
PCL, *see* Printer Command
Language (PCL)
PDL, *see* Page Description
Language (PDL)
Platform as a Service (PaaS), 590,
591, 636, 637
podman
bsdinstall jail command, 575
buildah, 571–573
characteristics, 570
concepts/tools, 565
containers, 569–571
FreeBSD systems, 575–577
installation, 566, 567
nginx image, 567–569
OCI technologies, 566

745

INDEX

podman (*cont.*)
  OpenVZ, 583–588
  rkt, 577–583
  skopeo, 573–575
Printer Command
    Language (PCL), 5
Proxmox, 291
  confirm tab, 307
  console option, 308
  CPU tab, 305
  disks tab, 304, 305
  downloading app, 292
  general tab, 302, 303
  hard disk selection, 294
  installation, 291, 293
  IP settings, 296
  ISO images, 301
  memory tab, 306
  network settings, 296
  network tab, 306, 307
  OS tab, 303
  root password, 296
  server console, 297–299
  storage, 300, 301
  summarisation, 297
  systemd-machined (*see*
      Systemd-machined)
  system tab, 304
  time zone/keyboard
      layout, 295
  upload button, 302
  virtualization platform, 291
  web interface, 299, 300

Q

QEMP, *see* Quick Emulator (QEMU)
QEMU machine
    protocol (QMP), 74, 75
QMP, *see* QEMU machine
    protocol (QMP)
Quick Emulator (QEMU), 16
  cloud-init configuration,
      678–686
  concepts, 15
  device information, 89
  full system (*see* Full system
      emulation)
  graphical window, 89, 90
  guest agent package, 70–76
  Kernel-based virtual
      machine (KVM), 45, 46
  monitor
    aspects, 76
    CD/DVD insertion, 79
    disk devices information, 78
    file manager, 80
    info commands, 77
    screendump command, 81
    screenshots, 81, 82
    shutting down, 88
    snapshot, 82–86
    system information, 87
  networking (*see* Networking
      process)
  paravirtualization, 90
  server console, 91

INDEX

Ubuntu installation, 16, 17
user mode emulation, 41–45

R

Rancher
   charts, 562
   command execution, 558, 559
   installation, 558, 562
   instructions, 557
   Kubernetes cluster, 561
   password setting, 560
   web page, 557
   welcome page, 559–561
Rocket (rkt)
   containers, 582
   cryptic error message, 580
   Docker registry, 581
   download process, 578
   execution, 580
   formats, 578
   GitHub page, 577
   HTTP request, 583
   installation, 580
   nginx welcome page, 582
   SELinux, 581
   tar file, 579

S

Scalable Processor
   ARChitecture (SPARC)
   -boot option, 36
   commands, 35
   error message, 38
   firmware implementations, 38
   nographic/device option, 40
   OpenBIOS, 38, 39
   package installation, 34
   SeaBIOS, 38
   Solaris box, 36, 37
   source code, 40, 41
   tar archive, 39
   UltraSPARC, 37
   wiki page, 35
Security component
   (seccomp), 362
Security-Enhanced Linux
   (SELinux), 353–359, 581
skopeo, 573–575
Socket networking, 47
Software as a Service (SaaS), 590,
   591, 636, 637
SPARC, *see* Scalable Processor
   ARChitecture (SPARC)
System container, 320, 376
Systemd-machined
   containers, 309, 311
   kernel feature, 312
   machinectl command, 309
   nspawn, 310

T

Terraform
   binary installation, 615
   command, 615
   definition, 613

INDEX

Terraform (cont.)
    Docker resources, 622
        Apache container, 632–635
        Apache web
          container, 626–630
        application containers, 626
        command option, 630
        configuration, 634
        deployment, 622–626
        destroy, 629
        error message, 624
        httpd container, 627
        port redirection, 634
        ports option, 632
        Ubuntu container, 632–634
    download process, 614, 615
    official website, 613
    providers
        additional information, 620
        browse mode, 616
        docker_example.tf, 618
        Docker provider, 617
        documentation link, 619
        help menu, 620, 621
        registry, 616
        terraform init command, 618
        Ubuntu image, 620

U

Ubuntu 20, 95–97
User networking
    automatic configuration, 51, 52
    customized settings, 57, 58

device models, 54
DNS server/default gateway, 50
gateway, 50
info network, 56
IP address, 58, 59
IP configuration, 49
monitor settings, 57
netdev option, 53
netdev parameters, 57
port forwarding, 59–61
qemu-system-x86, 54–56
representation, 48
SLIRP, 48
web server, 51

V, W

vagrant system
    architecture, 695
    concepts, 695
    environments
        Apache welcome page, 721
        deployment, 707–709
        installation, 709, 710
        network
          configuration, 721–724
        port redirection, 717–721
        provisioning
          process, 713–717
        search option, 712, 713
        status command, 711, 712
    installation
        appropiate version, 697, 698
        binary file, 698

INDEX

    download button, 696, 697
    downloaded file, 698
    error message, 699
    execution, 700
    libfuse package, 699
    web page, 696
  shared folder, 725–727
  state management, 726–728
  virtual environment
    AlmaLinux, 701, 702
    execution, 704
    initialization, 702
    network interfaces, 705
    public boxes, 701
    resources, 707
    Vagrantfile, 703
    VirtualBox instance, 706
    web browser, 701
  VMs
    blocks, 729
    config.vm.box option, 729
    init format, 728
    instances, 731
    IP settings, 731
    machine deployment, 729
    network address, 732
    port redirections, 730
    server code, 733
    Vagrantfile, 728–730
Virtual Distributed
    Ethernet (VDE), 47
Virtualization
  advantages, 11
  characteristics, 7
  concepts, 1
  containers, 11
  disadvantages, 12
  emulation, 2–6
  hypervisors, 9
  Intel VT-x/AMD-V, 7–10
  Oracle VirtualBox, 10
  OS-level virtualization, 11
  paravirtualization, 10
  physical machine
    Clonezilla, 13
    migration, 12
    openQRM, 13
    virt-p2v converts, 12
    VMware converter, 12
    V2V, 14
  pros/cons, 11
  simulation, 7
  terms/utilities, 1
  types of, 10, 11
Virtual Machine Disk (VMDK), 228, 230, 232
Virtual machines (VMs)
  configuration file, 100
  disk image (*see* Disk image management)
  libvirt (*see* Libvirt virtual machine management)
  Linux
    Alpine Linux
      website, 104–127
    configuration file, 100–104
    HVM configuration file, 127–130

INDEX

Virtual machines (VMs) (*cont.*)
    server console, 129, 130
    VNC viewer, 129
    paravirtualization, 128
VMDK, *see* Virtual Machine
    Disk (VMDK)

X, Y, Z

Xen
    architecture, 93, 94
    concepts, 93
    configuration, 97, 98
    GRUB start options, 132–134
    installation, 94
        grub menu, 97
    project web page, 95
    Ubuntu 20, 95–97
    logical volume, 98–100
    troubleshooting, 144, 145
    VMs (*see* Virtual machines)
    XenStore, 130–132
    xl/xm/XAPI, 135
        default values, 136
        hypervisors, 139
        OpenXenManager, 143
        restoration, 137
        subcommands,
            136, 137, 140
        toolstacks, 135
        VMs, 141, 143
        Xenserver, 139, 140

SPRINGER NATURE

GPSR Compliance

The European Union's (EU) General Product Safety Regulation (GPSR) is a set of rules that requires consumer products to be safe and our obligations to ensure this.

If you have any concerns about our products, you can contact us on ProductSafety@springernature.com

In case Publisher is established outside the EU, the EU authorized representative is:

Springer Nature Customer Service Center GmbH
Europaplatz 3
69115 Heidelberg, Germany

The manufacturer's authorised representative in the EU is Springer Nature Customer Service Centre GmbH, Europaplatz 3, 69115 Heidelberg, Germany. If you have any concerns regarding our products, please contact ProductSafety@springernature.com

Printed and bound by CPI Group (UK) Ltd, Croydon, CR0 4YY

26/03/2026

02078952-0014